TuffMap™

The Map that LASTS

Patent applied for.

GW01219687

Contents

ii Drivers Web-Sites

iii Key to Maps

iv-v Country Factfile

vi-vii Distance Map and Chart

viii Map Legend

1-76 Map Pages

77-136 Index

DRIVERS WEB-SITES

MOTORING INFORMATION

ROUTE PLANNING

Continental route-planning services offered through

The AA
www.theaa.com

The RAC
www.rac.co.uk

ShellGeoStar
www.shellgeostar.com

Map Blast
www.mapblast.com

CAR FERRIES

Car ferry information can be accessed through

Ferry Centre
(for Nordic countries)
www.ferrycenter.se/index.htm

ferrybooker.com
(for UK)
www.ferrybooker.com

Northern Europe ferries
www.ferrytravel.de/N__Europe/n__europe.html

Southern Europe ferries
www.ferrytravel.de/S__Europe_/s__europe_.html

UK Public Transport Information
www.pti.org.uk

moto·europa ferries of Scandinavia
www.ideamerge.com/motoeuropa/scandferries/links

Viamare Travel
(for the the Mediterranean)
www.viamare.com

moto·europa ferries of the Mediterranean
www.ideamerge.com/motoeuropa/medferries/links

Paleologos Shipping and Travel Agency
(for Greece)
www.greekislands.gr

Kavi Club Ferries
(for Greece)
www.greekferries.gr

TOLL ROADS

ASECAP the European Association of Toll Motorway Concessionaires and Agencies
www.asecap.com

MOTORAIL

For rail and car travel in Europe

Rail Europe Rail'n drive
www.raileurope.com/us/rail/rail_drive

Railsavers
www.railsavers.com

ROAD SIGNS

For information on international road signs, access

moto·europa roadsigns and signals
www.ideamerge.com/motoeuropa/roadsigns

European road signs point and read
www.bitb-hs.eu.odedodca.edu/signs/signs.html

Informative, regulative and warning signs
www.rothery.org

Travlang European international road signs and conventions
www.travlang.com/signs

TRAVEL INFORMATION

For information on European countries, access

moto·europa
www.ideamerge.com/motoeuropa

European road travel information
Budget Travel
www.budgettravel.com/euroroad.htm

Information by destination and topic
MyTravelGuide
www.mytravelguide.com

Detailed information by country
Columbus World Travel Guide
www.worldtravelguide.net/navigate/region/eur.asp

WEATHER

European Weather reports are available from

The Weather Underground, Inc
www.wunderground.com/global/EU_ST_Index.html

The Met. Office
www.met-office.gov.uk/weather/europe/europeforecast.html

CNN
www.cnn.com

Produced for Tuffmap by Collins Bartholomew

Key to Maps

IS
S
FIN
N
EST
LV
LT
1
DK
København
2 - 3
Edinburgh
Dublin
IRL
GB
Birmingham
London
Hamburg
4 - 5
6 - 7
NL
PL
Rotterdam
Amsterdam
D
Berlin
8 - 9
10 - 11
12 - 13
Bruxelles
Köln
B
14 - 15
16 - 17
Frankfurt am Main
Praha
CZ
20 - 21
18 - 19
Paris
SK
22 - 23
24 - 25
Strasbourg
26 - 27
München
28 - 29
Wien
30 - 31
Zürich
H
CH
A
32 - 33
F
Lyon
34 - 35
36 - 37
38 - 39
SLO
HR
Torino
Milano
Venezia
40 - 41
BIH
YU
53
54 - 55
Toulouse
42 - 43
44 - 45
46 - 47
56 - 57
Marseille
I
58 - 59
60 - 61
62 - 63
Roma
Madrid
64 - 65
Barcelona
48 - 49
50 - 51
AL
P
E
Lisboa
66 - 67
Napoli
68 - 69
Valencia
70 - 71
52
72 - 73
Sevilla
74 - 75
76

Country Factfile

COUNTRY IDENTIFICATION CAPITAL CITY NATIONAL FLAG		OFFICIAL LANGUAGE	CURRENCY	ELECTRICAL POWER	PETROL AVAILABLE
A **Austria** Wien		German	Euro = 100 cents	220 v	Unleaded. Unleaded with additive.
AND **Andorra** Andorra la Vella		Catalan	Euro = 100 cents	220 v	Unleaded. Unleaded with additive.
B **Belgium** Bruxelles		French Dutch Flemish	Euro = 100 cents	220 v	Unleaded. Unleaded with additive.
CH **Switzerland** Bern		German French Italian	Swiss Franc = 100 rappen/ centimes	220 v	Unleaded. Unleaded with additive.
D **Germany** Berlin		German	Euro = 100 cents	220 v	Unleaded. Unleaded with additive.
DK **Denmark** København		Danish	Krone = 100 øre	220 v	Unleaded. Unleaded with additive.
E **Spain** Madrid		Spanish Catalan Galician, Basque	Euro = 100 cents	220 v	Unleaded. Unleaded with additive.
F **France** Paris		French	Euro = 100 cents	220 v	Unleaded. Unleaded with additive.
FL **Liechtenstein** Vaduz		German	Swiss Franc = 100 rappen	220 v	Unleaded. Unleaded with additive.
I **Italy** Roma		Italian	Euro = 100 cents	220 v	Unleaded. Unleaded with additive.
L **Luxembourg** Luxembourg		French	Euro = 100 cents	220 v	Unleaded. Unleaded with additive.
MC **Monaco** Monaco-ville		French	Euro = 100 cents	220 v	Unleaded. Unleaded with additive.
NL **The Netherlands** Amsterdam		Dutch	Euro = 100 cents	220 v	Unleaded. Unleaded with additive.
P **Portugal** Lisbon		Portuguese	Euro = 100 cents	220 v	Unleaded. Unleaded with additive.
RSM **San Marino** San Marino		Italian	Euro = 100 cents	220 v	Unleaded. Unleaded with additive.

EMERGENCY NUMBERS	SPEED LIMITS	BLOOD ALCOHOL LEGAL LIMIT mg/100ml	COUNTRY IDENTIFICATION CAPITAL CITY NATIONAL FLAG
Police ....133 Fire ....122 Ambulance 144	Motorway ....130 km/h Rural ....100 km/h Town ....50 km/h	50 mg	A **Austria** Wien
Police ....17 Fire ....18 Ambulance 19	Rural ....70 km/h Town ....40 km/h	80 mg	AND **Andorra** Andorra la Vella
Police ....101 Fire ....100 Ambulance 100	Motorway ....120 km/h Dual carriageway ....120 km/h Rural ....90 km/h Town ....50 km/h	50 mg	B **Belgium** Bruxelles
Police ....117 Fire ....118 Ambulance 114/117	Motorway ....120 km/h Rural ....80 km/h Town ....50 km/h	80 mg	CH **Switzerland** Bern
Police ....110 Fire ....112 Ambulance 110	Motorway ....130 km/h Rural ....100 km/h Town ....50 km/h	50 mg	D **Germany** Berlin
Police ....112 Fire ....112 Ambulance 112	Motorway ....110 km/h Rural ....80 km/h Town ....50 km/h	50 mg	DK **Denmark** København
Police ....091/112 Fire ....080/112 Ambulance 092/112	Motorway ....120 km/h Rural ....90/100 km/h Town ....50 km/h	50 mg	E **Spain** Madrid
Police ....112 Fire ....112 SAMU/Ambulance 112	Motorway ....130 km/h Dual carriageway ....110 km/h Rural ....90 km/h Town ....50 km/h	50 mg	F **France** Paris
Police ....117 Fire ....118 Ambulance 144	Motorway ....120 km/h Rural ....80 km/h Town ....50 km/h	50 mg	FL **Liechtenstein** Vaduz
Police ....113 Fire ....115 Ambulance 118	Motorway ....130 km/h Dual carriageway ....110 km/h Rural ....90 km/h Town ....50 km/h	80 mg	I **Italy** Roma
Police ....113 Fire ....112 Ambulance 112	Motorway ....120 km/h Dual carriageway ....120 km/h Rural ....90 km/h Town ....50 km/h	80 mg	L **Luxembourg** Luxembourg
Police ....17 Fire ....18 SAMU 15	Toll motorway ....130 km/h Motorway ....110 km/h Rural ....90 km/h Town ....50 km/h	50 mg	MC **Monaco** Monaco-ville
Police ....112 Fire ....112 Ambulance 112	Motorway ....120 km/h Dual carriageway ....100 km/h Rural ....80 km/h Town ....50 km/h	50 mg	NL **The Netherlands** Amsterdam
Police ....115 Fire ....115 Ambulance 115	Motorway ....120 km/h Rural ....90/100 km/h Town ....50 km/h	50 mg	P **Portugal** Lisbon
Police ....113 Fire ....115 Ambulance 118	Motorway ....130 km/h Dual carriageway ....100 km/h Rural ....90 km/h Town ....50 km/h	80 mg	RSM **San Marino** San Marino

Distance Map and Chart

Kilometres

Amsterdam	880	1160	1220	1677	2274	1390	1730	1967	910	510	2690	1370	840	2520	1140	1280	1760	390	550	2300	260	760	2780	440	880	460	1190	1100	1410	210	1070	660	1620	2970	3230
Ankara	2600	2050	2360	2807	3404	3780	2430	3097	2310	3380	3570	3700	2400	2930	2490	3030	4180	2950	3550	4830	2930	3100	420	2990	2750	2740	4200	4100	1740	3190	3500	2700	3560	1690	
Athina	2530	1810	2250	2847	3444	3470	2450	3137	2130	2940	3340	3460	2210	2970	2210	2750	3880	2600	3200	4530	2740	2880	1130	2770	2530	2530	3840	3750	1570	2810	3400	2470	3250		
Barcelona	1090	1760	2450	2927	3524	2740	1410	3217	1690	1110	2370	2720	1430	3770	1040	500	630	750	1560	1280	1350	2110	3060	1790	770	1340	2200	2110	2020	1410	660	1840			
Berlin	850	660	560	1007	1604	1020	1490	1297	340	1090	2450	1000	590	1850	1010	1520	2350	1160	1170	3000	570	390	2290	290	1080	530	1810	1720	910	780	1660				
Bordeaux	970	1720	2300	2877	3424	2430	1540	3156	1540	560	2500	2410	1300	3670	1000	630	690	880	980	1230	1020	1800	3020	1480	710	1030	1620	1530	1990	860					
Bruxelles	660	1120	1340	1867	2494	1550	1520	2157	910	300	2480	1530	790	2710	930	1070	1550	220	390	2090	220	920	2650	600	680	410	1030	940	1370						
Budapest	1010	250	680	1127	1724	1920	1250	1417	570	1460	2210	1900	690	1970	1010	1530	2620	1200	1760	3240	1160	1290	1320	1200	1280	970	2400	2310							
Dublin	1500	2060	2280	2807	3324	2490	2360	3097	1860	1000	3320	2470	1690	3092	1770	1760	2220	1150	550	2870	1130	1860	3560	1540	1480	1350	500								
Edinburgh	1620	2150	2370	2817	3414	2580	2450	3107	1950	1090	3410	2560	1800	3660	1860	1850	2310	1240	640	2960	1250	1950	3650	1630	1570	1440									
Frankfurt a.M.	430	720	1100	1647	2244	1440	1280	1937	500	570	2240	1420	380	2490	720	1000	1820	230	800	2470	200	810	2320	490	570										
Genève	280	1010	1550	2077	2674	2010	910	2367	930	510	1870	1990	570	2920	330	430	1400	490	930	2050	710	1380	2330	1060											
Hamburg	820	950	850	1297	1894	950	1680	1587	630	920	2640	930	780	2140	1200	1450	2170	630	990	2710	430	320	2560												
Istanbul	2230	1570	1940	2387	2984	3300	2260	2677	1890	2750	3150	3280	1980	2510	2020	2560	3690	2420	3010	4340	2510	2680													
København	1240	1040	970	2347	2364	630	2000	2057	740	1240	2960	610	1090	2610	1520	1770	2490	950	1310	3050	750														
Köln	500	910	1130	1597	2194	1380	1470	1887	700	490	2430	1360	570	2440	880	1000	1740	200	610	2360															
Lisboa	2230	3000	3530	4247	4844	3660	2690	4537	2910	1790	3650	3640	2700	5040	2300	1780	650	2130	2320																
London	1030	1510	1730	2177	2774	1940	1810	2467	1310	450	2770	1920	1160	3022	1220	1210	1670	600																	
Luxembourg	420	930	1350	1877	2474	1580	1300	2167	730	340	2260	1560	530	2720	710	820	1590																		
Madrid	1690	2380	2930	3697	4204	3120	2040	3987	2310	1250	3000	3100	2050	4320	1670	1130																			
Marseille	710	1370	1980	2597	3194	2400	910	2887	1360	770	1870	2380	1010	3440	540																				
Milano	300	820	1510	2087	2684	2150	590	2377	870	820	1550	2130	530	2930																					
Moskva	2640	1978	1290	930	1045	1560	3780	1220	1910	3060	4740	2086	2280																						
München	300	440	990	1437	2034	1720	950	1727	370	860	1870	1700																							
Oslo	1830	1660	1490	3732	3135	540	2610	3442	1350	1850	3570																								
Palermo	1840	2030	2720	3617	4214	3590	960	3907	2250	2360																									
Paris	580	1200	1620	2217	2814	1870	1400	2507	1000																										
Praha	670	320	620	1067	1664	1370	1290	1357																											
Rīga	2087	1425	737	290	307	2902	2947																												
Roma	890	1140	1830	2315	3064	2630																													
Stockholm	1860	1680	1470	3192	2595																														
Tallinn	2394	1732	1044	597																															
Vilnius	1797	1135	447																																
Warszawa	1350	690																																	
Wien	748																																		
Zürich																																			

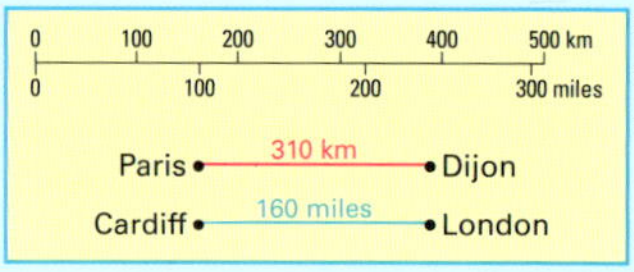

0 100 200 300 400 500 km
0 100 200 300 miles
Paris 310 km Dijon
Cardiff 160 miles London

Belfast
IRL
Dublin
Holyhead
Cork
Rosslare
Fishguard
Exeter
Penzance
Brest

GB	Country Identification	Désignation des Pays	Länderkennzeichen
A	Austria	Autriche	Österreich
AL	Albania	Albanie	Albanien
AND	Andorra	Andorre	Andorra
B	Belgium	Belgique	Belgien
BG	Bulgaria	Bulgarie	Bulgarien
BIH	Bosnia - Herzegovina	Bosnie Herzégovine	Bosnien-Herzegowina
BY	Belarus	Bélarus	Belarus
CH	Switzerland	Suisse	Schweiz
CZ	Czech Republic	République tchèque	Tschechische Republik
D	Germany	Allemagne	Deutschland
DK	Denmark	Danemark	Dänemark
E	Spain	Espagne	Spanien
EST	Estonia	Estonie	Estland
F	France	France	Frankreich
FIN	Finland	Finlande	Finnland
FL	Liechtenstein	Liechtenstein	Liechtenstein
GB	United Kingdom	Grande-Bretagne	Grossbritannien
GR	Greece	Grèce	Griechenland
H	Hungary	Hongrie	Ungarn
HR	Croatia	Croatie	Kroatien
I	Italy	Italie	Italien
IRL	Ireland	Irlande	Irland
IS	Iceland	Islande	Island
L	Luxembourg	Luxembourg	Luxemburg
LT	Lithuania	Lituanie	Litauen
LV	Latvia	Lettonie	Lettland
MC	Monaco	Monaco	Monaco
MK	Macedonia (F.Y.R.O.M.)	Ancienne République yougoslave de Macédoine	Ehemalige jugoslawische Republik Mazedonien
N	Norway	Norvège	Norwegen
NL	Netherlands	Pays-Bas	Niederlande
P	Portugal	Portugal	Portugal
PL	Poland	Pologne	Polen
RO	Romania	Roumanie	Rumänien
RSM	San Marino	Saint-Marin	San Marino
RUS	Russian Federation	Russie	Russische Föderation
S	Sweden	Suède	Schweden
SK	Slovakia	République slovaque	Slowakei
SLO	Slovenia	Slovénie	Slowenien
UA	Ukraine	Ukraine	Ukraine
YU	Yugoslavia	Yougoslavie	Jugoslawien

A Coruña
Santander
Bilbao
Porto
Salamanca
Coimbra
P
Madrid
Lisboa
E
Badajoz
Córdoba
Bailén
Alicante
Murcia
Faro
Sevilla
Granada
Málaga
Almería
Gibraltar

Trondheim
Vaasa
FIN
N
S
Bergen
Oslo
Gävle
Helsinki
Sankt-Peterburg
Stockholm
Stavanger
Tallinn
EST
RUS
Kristiansand
Göteborg
Rīga
LV
Inverness
Aberdeen
Ålborg
Århus
Glasgow
Edinburgh
DK
København
Malmö
LT
Vilnius
Minsk
Esbjerg
Odense
Newcastle upon Tyne
Carlisle
York
Manchester
Liverpool
Gdańsk
BY
Nottingham
Hamburg
Groningen
Bremen
Norwich
Birmingham
GB
Amsterdam
Berlin
Warszawa
Den Haag
NL
Hannover
PL
Cardiff
London
Rotterdam
Dortmund
D
Southampton
Dover
Calais
Bruxelles
Köln
Lille
B
Liège
Bonn
UA
Cherbourg
Frankfurt am Main
Praha
CZ
Le Havre
Luxembourg
Caen
Paris
Nürnberg
SK
Rennes
Le Mans
Nancy
Stuttgart
Strasbourg
Linz
Wien
Bratislava
Nantes
Orléans
München
A
Budapest
Tours
Basel
Zürich
Salzburg
F
Dijon
Bern
CH
Innsbruck
Graz
H
Moulins
RO
Limoges
Genève
Ljubljana
SLO
Zagreb
Clermont-Ferrand
Lyon
Milano
Trieste
Beograd
Bordeaux
Torino
Venezia
HR
BIH
Genova
Bologna
YU
BG
Biarritz
Toulouse
Nîmes
Avignon
Sarajevo
Sofiya
Nice
Ancona
Narbonne
Marseille
Livorno
Dubrovnik
Perpignan
I
Andorra la Vella
Pescara
Skopje
Zaragoza
MK
Barcelona
Roma
Bari
AL
Thessaloniki
Napoli
Taranto
Ioannina
Larisa
Valencia
GR
Cosenza
Patra
Athina
Messina
Palermo
Reggio di Calabria
Catania

	Legend	Légende	Zeichenerklärung
	Road Information	**Classification des routes**	**Strassenklassifizierung**
	Motorway	Autoroute	Autobahn
	Motorway - Toll	Autoroute à péage	Gebührenpflichtige Autobahn
	Motorway junction - full access	Echangeur d'autoroute avec accès libre	Autobahnauffahrt mit vollem Zugang
	Motorway junction - restricted access	Echangeur d'autoroute avec accès limité	Autobahnauffahrt mit beschränktem Zugang
	Motorway services	Aire de service sur autoroute	Autobahnservicestelle
	Main road - dual carriageway	Route principale à chaussées séparées	Hauptstrasse - Zweispurig
	Main road - single carriageway	Route principale à une seule chaussée	Hauptstrasse - Einspurig
	Secondary road - dual carriageway	Route secondaire à chaussées séparées	Zweispurige Nebenstrasse
	Secondary road - single carriageway	Route secondaire à seule chaussée	Einspurige Nebenstrasse
	Other road	Autre route	Andere Strasse
	Motorway / road under construction	Autoroute/route en construction	Autobahn/Strasse im Bau
	Road Numbering	**Numérotation des routes**	**Strassennumerierung**
E27	Euro route number	Route européenne	Europastrasse
N9	Motorway number	Autoroute	Autobahn
12	Main road number	Route principale	Hauptstrasse
406	Secondary road number	Route secondaire	Nebenstrasse
	Other Road Information	**Renseignements supplémentaires sur les routes**	**Zusätzliche Strassen Informationen**
	Road toll	Route à péage	Gebührenpflichtige Strasse
10	Distance marker	Marquage des distances	Distanz-Markierung
	Distances in kilometres	Distances en km.	Distanzen in Kilometern
	Steep hill	Colline abrupte	Steile Strasse
	Mountain pass (Height in metres)	Col (Altitude en mètres)	Pass (Höhe in Metern)
	Other Transport Information	**Autres moyens de transport**	**Sonstige Transportmöglichkeiten**
	International airport	Aéroport international	Internationaler Flughafen
	Car transport by rail	Transport des autos par voie ferrée	Autotransport per Bahn
	Railway	Chemin de fer	Eisenbahn
	Tunnel	Tunnel	Tunnel
	Funicular railway	Funiculaire	Seilbahn
	Car ferry	Bac pour autos	Autofähre
Rotterdam	Car ferry destination	Destination du bac pour autos	Autofähre-Bestimmungsort
	Other Information	**Renseignements supplémentaires**	**Zusätzliche Informationen**
	Summit (Height in metres)	Sommet (Altitude en mètres)	Berg (Höhe in Metern)
	Volcano	Volcan	Vulkan
	Canal	Canal	Kanal
	Dam	Digue	Damm
	Waterfall	Chute d'eau	Wasserfall
	International boundary	Frontière d'Etat	Landesgrenze
GB	Country abbreviation	Abréviation du pays	Regionsgrenze
	Urban area	Zone urbaine	Stadtgebiet
18	Adjoining page indicator	Indication de la page contigüe	Randhinweis auf Folgekarte

Scale 1:1 200 000

0 10 20 30 40 50 km

0 10 20 30 miles

A
B
C
1
2
3
4
S K A G E R R A K
Kristiansand
Larvik, Mos Oslo
Egersund, Bergen
Tórshavn, Lerwick Seyðisfjörður
Grenen
Skagen
Tannis Bugt
Ålbæk Bugt
Hirtshals
Hjørring
Frederikshavn
Hirsholmene
Jammerbugten
Brønderslev
VENDSYSSEL
Læsø Rende
Sæby
Vigsø Bugt
Hanstholm
THY
Thisted
Limfjorden
Løgstør Bredning
Nibe Bredning
Nørresundby
Ålborg
Ålborg Bugt
MORS
Nykøbing Mors
Fur
Livø
HIMMERLAND
Hals
Hobro
Mariager Fjord
Randers Fjord
SALLING
Skive
Thyholm
Thyborøn
Nissum Bredning
Struer
Viborg
Randers
DJURSLAND
Grenå
Holstebro
Lemvig
Ferring Sø
HARSYSSEL
JYLLAND
Herning
Ikast
Silkeborg
Århus
Helgenæs
Mols Bjerge
Ebeltoft
Hjelm
Århus Bugt
Ringkøbing
Ringkøbing Fjord
Holmsland Klit
Skanderborg
Horsens
Horsens Fjord
Samsø
Samsø Bælt
Endelave
Vejle
Juelsminde
Trelde Næs
Æbelø
Skjern
Stadil Fjord
DK
E39
E45

A
B
C
1
2
3
4
5
6
DK
D
HARSYSSEL
JYLLAND
DJURSLAND
Holstebro
Struer
Skive
Viborg
Hobro
Randers
Herning
Ikast
Silkeborg
Århus
Skanderborg
Horsens
Vejle
Fredericia
Kolding
Middelfart
Odense
Fyn
Svendborg
Fåborg
Haderslev
Åbenrå
Sønderborg
Flensburg
Schleswig
Husum
Eckernförde
Kappeln
Esbjerg
Varde
Ribe
Fanø
Rømø
Sylt
Föhr
Amrum
Pellworm
Nordstrand
Halligen
Nordfriesische Inseln
SCHWANSEN
Samsø
Tåsinge
Ærø
Als
Lille Bælt
Helgenæs
Århus Bugt
Ringkøbing Fjord
Nissum Fjord
Stadil Fjord
Horsens Fjord
Flensborg Fjord
Kieler Bucht
Eckernförder Bucht
Fanø Bugt
Harwich
Törshavn
E20
E45

D
E
F
3
1
2
3
4
7
S
D
Anholt
Halmstad
Gullbrandstorp
Villshärad
Frösakull
Tylösand
Laxvik
Eldsberga
Gullbranna
Genevad
Laholmsbukten
Veinge
Knäred
Mellbystrand
Lilla Tjärby
Laholm
Vallberga
Hallands Väderö
Torekov
Rännesló
Våxtorp
Hishult
Västra Karup
Båstad
Hasslöv
Hallandsåsen
Grevie
Skånes-Fagerhult
Skälderviken
Förslöv
Åsljunga
Kullen
Vejbystrand
Hjärnarp
Munka-Ljungby
Eket
Örkelljunga
Mölle
Arild
Barkåkra
Ängelholm
Göinge
Höganäs
Jonstorp
Stidsvig
Östra Ljungby
Lerberget
Strövelstorp
Tyringe
Viken
Kvidinge
Klippan
Ödåkra
Perstorp
Åstorp
Hyllinge
Bjuv
Söderåsen
Ljungbyhed
Helsingborg
Billesholm
Röstånga
Ekeby
Kågeröd
Vallåkra
Stockamöllan
Svalöv
Stehag
Ven
Landskrona
Marieholm
Eslöv
Häljarp
Hofterup
Kävlinge
Gårdstånga
Löddeköpinge
Flyinge
Södra Sandby
Bjärred
Lund
Dalby
Lommabukten
Lomma
Åkarp
Staffanstorp
Malmö
Veberöd
Saltholm
Genarp
Dragør
Bunkeflostrand
Klågerup
Norra Klagshamn
Bara
Tygelsjö
Oxie
Svedala
Vellinge
Östra Grevie
Alstad
Anderslöv
Skurup
Skivarp
Skanör med Falsterbo
Skegrie
Måkläppen
Trelleborg
Simremarken
Beddinges
Smygehamn
Sassnitz
Sankt-Peterburg
Kap Arkona
Wittow
Altenkirchen
Dranske
Wiek
Tromper Wiek
Hiddensee
Neuenkirchen
Glowe
Trent
Ploggshagen
Schaprode
Ummanz
Gingst
Darßer Ort
Ostseebad Prerow am Darß
Ostseebad Zingst am Darß
Bock
Rostock
Bønnerup Strand
Gjerrild
Glesborg
Voldby
Fornæs
Kolindsund
Grenå
Lyngby
Trustrup
Ålsrode
Balle
Hesselø
Hassensør
Hjelm
Gilbjerg Hoved
Gilleleje
Smidstrup
Blistrup
Hornbæk
Hittarp
Vejby
Græsted
Esbønderup
Hellebæk
Tisvilde
Helsingør
Liseleje
Helsinge
Tikøb
Espergærde
Frederiksværk
Ramløse
Humlebæk
Nødebo
Fredensborg
Hundested
Tulstrup
Hillerød
Rørvig
Nivå
Nykøbing Sjælland
Ølsted
Skævinge
Rungsted
Gniben
Sjællands Odde
Havnebyen
Sejerø
Sejerø Bugt
Sejerby
Ordrup Næs
Højby
Svinninge
Isefjord
Egebjerg
Jægerspris
Frederikssund
Gørløse
Slangerup
Hørsholm
Birkerød
Holte
Kongens Lyngby
Vig
Fårevejle
Asnæs
Grevinge
Orø
Kyndby Huse
Gerlev
Ølstykke
Ganløse
Værløse
Stenløse
Fårevejle Stationsby
Bybjerg
Skuldelev
Jyllinge
Nekselø
Havnsø
Hørve
Udby
Røsnaes
Ulstrup
Føllenslev
Svinninge
Gislinge
Holbæk
Skibby
Ballerup
Snertinge
Tuse
Sønderby
Gundsømagle
Herlev
Gladsakse
Kalundborg
Regstrup
Kirke Hyllinge
Ågerup
Frederiksberg
Asnæs
Rørby
Ejby
Vipperød
Veddelev
Tåstrup
Rødovre
KØBENHAVN
Arby
Svebølle
Jyderup
Mørkøv
Roskilde
Hvidovre
Ubby
Jerslev
Kirke Såby
Svogerslev
Vindinge
Svallerup
Undløse
Tølløse
Hvalsø
Snoldelev
Amager
Jammerland Bugt
Bjerge
Ugerløse
Store Merløse
Gadstrup
Tissø
Osted
Gyldenløveshøj
Romsø
Gørlev
Sæby
Ruds Vedby
Vedde
Stenlille
Jystrup
Viby
Borup
Ejby
Lille Skensved
Dianalund
Kirke Helsinge
Høng
Løve
Kværkeby
Køge Bugt
Musholm
Store Bælt
Kirke Stillinge
Havrebjerg
Gyrstinge
Sorø
Fjenneslev
Slimminge
Bjæverskov
Køge
Strøby Egede
Slagelse
Frederiksberg
Ringsted
Valløby
Musholm Bugt
Vetterslev
Høm
Terslev
Strøby
Sprogø
Svenstrup
Forlev
SJÆLLAND
Algestrup
Klippinge
Nyborg
Halsskov
Korsør
Sørbymagle
Glumsø
Førslev
Hårlev
Stevns Klint
Knudshoved
Flakkebjerg
Skelby
Hasley
Store Heddinge
Boeslunde
Fuglebjerg
Herlufmagle
Hellested
Dalby
Karise
Lyderslev
Dalmose
Gelsted
Fensmark
Agersø
Skælsør
Sandved
Hyllinge
Næstved
Holme-Olstrup
Rønnede
Fakse
Rødvig
Vresen
Tornemark
Rønnebæk
Fakse Ladeplads
Omø
Karrebæksminde
Mogenstrup
Fakse Bugt
Everdrup
Lundeborg
Lohals
Karrebæksminde Bugt
Dybsø Fjord
Tappernøje
Præstø Fjord
Lov
Bårse
Præstø
Smålandsfarvandet
Snøde
Avnø Fjord
Kong
Lundby
Skibinge
Allerslev
Nyord
Langeland
Vejrø
Søhundehavn
Ørslev
Mern
Neder Vindinge
Vordingborg
Langebæk
Møn
Stege
Borre
Møns Klint
Tullebølle
Langelands Bælt
Nyråd
Stensved
Storstrøm
Orehoved
Bogø
Utterslev
Vesterby
Fejø
Femø
Stege Nor
Spodsbjerg
Birket
Guldborg Sund
Vålse
Damsholte
Horslunde
Askø
Store Damme
Tårs
Sandby
Hjelm Bugt
Guldborg
Nørre Alslev
Stubbekøbing
Nakskov Fjord
Tårs Vig
Eskilstrup
Albuen
Grønsund
Stokkemarke
Bandholm
Nakskov
Sakskøbing
Østerlev
Langø
Søllested
Nørreballe
Falster
Hestehoved
Maribo
Horreby
Dannemare
Lolland
Nykøbing
Søndersø
Idestrup
Toreby
Olstrup
Rødby
Væggerløse
Fehmarn Bælt
Holeby
Øster Ulslev
Kettinge
Rødbyhavn
Errindlev
Nysted
Guldborg Sund
Rødsand
Markelsdorfer Huk
Hyllekrog
Gedser
Gedser Odde
Fehmarn
Puttgarden
Landkirchen auf Fehmarn
Burg auf Fehmarn
OSTSEE
E20
E47/55
E20/E47
E55
E47
E4
E6/E20
E6/E22
E65
E22/251

4
A
B
C
1
2
3
4
9
Ostfriesis
Norderney
Juist
Borkum
Norddeich
Norden
Rottumerplaat
Rottumeroog
Eemshaven
Wirdum
Pewsum
Hinte
Rysum
Emden
Woldendorp
Wagenborgen
Nieuwolda
Midwolda
Finsterwolde
Beerta
Winschoten
Bellingwolde
Wadden eilanden
Schiermonnikoog
Ameland
Nes
Hollum
Ballum
Terschelling
West-Terschelling
Vlieland
Oost-Vlieland
Richel
Harwich
Engelschmangat
Texel
De Cocksdorp
De Koog
Den Burg
Oosterend
Oudeschild
Waddenzee
Afsluitdijk
Den Helder
Den Oever
Hippolytushoef
De Kooy
Anna Paulowna
Callantsoog
Slootdorp
Wieringerwerf
Petten
Schagen
Nieuwe Niedorp
Middenmeer
Medemblik
Dirkshorn
Langedijk
Bergen
Wervershoof
Andijk
Enkhuizen
Hoogkarspel
Opmeer
Alkmaar
Heerhugowaard
Berkhout
Avenhorn
Hoorn
Venhuizen
Egmond aan Zee
Heiloo
Scharwoude
Schermerhorn
Oosthuizen
Limmen
De Rijp
Uitgeest
Middenbeemster
Purmerend
Krommenie
Wormerveer
Edam
Volendam
Marken
Assendelft
Zaandam
Koog aan de Zaan
AMSTERDAM
Markermeer
IJsselmeer
Lelystad
Noordoost Polder
Urk
Emmeloord
Creil
Bant
Espel
Rutten
Ens
Nagele
Marknesse
Swifterbant
Ketelmeer
Dronten
Biddinghuizen
Oostendorp
Harlingen
Franeker
Tzummarum
Minnertsga
St Annaparochie
Menaldum
Winsum
Witmarsum
Bolsward
Makkum
Workum
IJlst
Heeg
Woudsend
Koudum
Stavoren
Balk
Lemmer
Oudemirdum
Sneek
Joure
St Nicolaasga
Leeuwarden
Dronrijp
Stiens
Roordahuizum
Wommels
Grouw
Irnsum
Akkrum
Drachten
Pikmeer
Sneekermeer
Tijnje
Heerenveen
Oudehaske
Wolvega
Oldemarkt
Kuinre
Steenwijk
Havelte
Blokzijl
Vollenhove
Zwartsluis
Meppel
Genemuiden
IJsselmuiden
Kampen
Zwolle
Hattem
Wapenveld
Heerde
Harde
Hasselt
Staphorst
Ternaard
Holwerd
Ferwerd
Dokkum
Metslawier
Anjum
Marrum
Damwoude
Oenkerk
Buitenpost
Kootstertille
Bergum
Garijp
Opeinde
Surhuisterveen
Grootegast
Grijpskerk
Ureterp
Beetsterzwaag
Gorredijk
Donkerbroek
Appelscha
Hooghersmilde
Noordwolde
Vledder
Diever
Dwingeloo
Ruinen
Ruinerwold
De Wijk
Zuidwolde
Hoogeveen
Pesse
Beilen
Westerbork
Oosterhesselen
HUNSINGO
Zoutkamp
Oldehove
Zuidhorn
Leek
Marum
Roden
Norg
Haulerwijk
Uithuizermeeden
Uithuizen
Warffum
Baflo
Winsum
Middelstum
Bedum
Ten Boer
Loppersum
Spijk
Delfzijl
Siddeburen
Slochteren
Groningen
Haren
Hoogkerk
Hoogezand-Sappemeer
Zuidlaren
Vries
Veendam
Muntendam
Scheemda
Oude Pekela
Nieuwe Pekela
Annen
Gieten
Assen
Rolde
Smilde
Gasselternijveen
Gasselte
Onstwedde
Wedde
Bourtange
Stadskanaal
Sellingen
Musselkanaal
Borger
Exloo
Odoorn
Ter Apel
Emmen
Emmer-Compascuum
Emmer-Erfscheidenveen
Sleen
Klazienaveen
Erica
Dalen
Schoonebeek
Coevorden
Emlichheim
Twist
Hoogstede
Gramsbergen
Dedemsvaart
Hardenberg
Georgsdorf
Wilsum
Ommen
Den Ham
Kloosterhaar
Uelsen
Itterbeck
Neuenhaus
Wietmarschen
Nordhorn
Vroomshoop
Lemele
Dalfsen
Vriezenveen
Balkbrug
NL
EMS
A31
A32
A7
A6
A9
A28
A37
E22
E232
E233
N31
N354
N355
N360
N46
N33
N34
N372
N371
N381
N48
N50
N302
N242
N99
N250
N247
N202
N36
N348
N340
N35
N366
N364
N374
N377
N375
N353
N351
N333
N334
N352
N331
N307
N309
N305
N359
N357
N356
N361
N363
N362
N380
N248
N249
N347
N349
403
366
213
Vechte

D
E
F
2
5
1
6
3
4
10
11
Amrum
Nebel
Langeness
Wittdün
Gröde-Appelland
Bordelum
Breklum
Bredstedt
Hallig en
Tammensiel
Nordstrand
Pellworm
Süden
Süderoog
Südfall
Norder Hever
Simonsberg
Witzwort
Husum
Mildstedt
Schwabstedt
Friedrichstadt
Osterhever
Oldenswort
Garding
Tating
Tönning
St Peter-Ording
Helgoländer Bucht
Helgoland
Blauort
Tertius
Büsum
Trischen
Heide
Wesselburen
Wöhrden
Meldorf
Elpersbüttel
Friedrichskoog
Kronprinzenkoog
Marne
Eddelak
St Michaelisdonn
St Margarethen
Brunsbüttel
Neufeld
Schleswig
Eckernförde
Rendsburg
Büdelsdorf
Itzehoe
Glückstadt
Elmshorn
Uetersen
Pinneberg
Halstenbek
Schenefeld
Rellingen
Wedel
Hamburg
Stade
Buxtehude
Jork
Bad Bramstedt
Kaltenkirchen
Quickborn
Tornesch
Kellinghusen
Wrist
Hohenlockstedt
Nord-Ostsee-Kanal
Eider
Scharhörn
Neuwerk
Cuxhaven
Altenbruch-Westerende
Otterndorf
Nordholz
LAND HADELN
LAND WURSTEN
LAND KEHDINGEN
Drochtersen
Bremervörde
Mellum
Wangerooge
Spiekeroog
Langeoog
Baltrum
Neuharlingersiel
Dornumersiel
Esens
Jever
Wittmund
Schortens
Wilhelmshaven
HARLINGERLAND
Aurich
Wiesmoor
Jadebusen
Sande
Varel
Zetel
OSTFRIESLAND
AMMERLAND
Westerstede
Leer
Weener
Papenburg
Bad Zwischenahn
Edewecht
Oldenburg
Rastede
Wiefelstede
Bremerhaven
Langen
Nordenham
BUTJADINGEN
Brake
Elsfleth
Schwanewede
Loxstedt
Schiffdorf
Bremen
Delmenhorst
Ganderkesee
Hude
Lilienthal
Osterholz-Scharmbeck
Ritterhude
Worpswede
TEUFELS MOOR
Zeven
Rotenburg
Scheeßel
Tostedt
Buchholz in der Nordheide
Schneverdingen
Soltau
Ottersberg
Oyten
Achim
Stuhr
Weyhe
Syke
Verden
Langwedel
Visselhövede
Walsrode
Fallingbostel
Wildeshausen
Großenkneten
Cloppenburg
Friesoythe
Garrel
Wardenburg
Bassum
Twistringen
Sulingen
Vechta
Lohne
Dinklage
Diepholz
Damme
Quakenbrück
Löningen
Haselünne
Meppen
Haren
Lingen
Fürstenau
Nienburg
Hoya
Neustadt am Rübenberge
Langenhagen
Garbsen
Seelze
Hannover
Steinhuder Meer
Dümmer
Rahden
Petershagen
Bramsche
Uchte
Loccum
E45
E22
E37
E233
E234
27
28
29

6
A
2
B
C
SCHWANSEN
Schleswig
Eckernförde
Eckernförder Bucht
Kieler Förde
Kieler Bucht
Fehmarn
Puttgarden
Burg auf Fehmarn
Staberhuk
Fehmarnbelt
Rødbyhavn
Guldborg Sund
Rødsand
Gedser Odde
Hyllekrog
Markelsdorfer Huk
Petersdorf auf Fehmarn
Landkirchen auf Fehmarn
Bannesdorf auf Fehmarn
Heiligenhafen
Großenbrode
Hohwachter Bucht
Hohwacht
Oldenburg in Holstein
Mecklenburger Bucht
Dahme
Dahmeshöved
Kellenhusen
Grömitz
1
Rendsburg
Büdelsdorf
Kiel
Kronshagen
Preetz
WAGRIEN
Plön
Malente
Eutin
Großer Plöner See
Neustadt in Holstein
Lübecker Bucht
Scharbeutz
Timmendorfer Strand
Travemünde
Neumünster
Nord-Ostsee-Kanal
Itzehoe
Bad Bramstedt
Kaltenkirchen
Bad Segeberg
Bad Schwartau
Lübeck
Bad Oldesloe
STORMARN
Glückstadt
Elmshorn
Quickborn
Henstedt-Ulzburg
Norderstedt
Bargteheide
Ahrensburg
Pinneberg
Uetersen
Wedel
Stade
Hamburg
Schenefeld
Halstenbek
Rellingen
Reinbek
Glinde
Barsbüttel
Buxtehude
Jork
Neu Wulmstorf
Rosengarten
Seevetal
Winsen
Geesthacht
Schwarzenbek
Mölln
Ratzeburg
Lauenburg
Boizenburg
Grevesmühlen
Wismar
Poel
Wismarbucht
Ostseebad Kühlungsborn
Bad Doberan
Ostseebad Rerik
Halbinsel Wustrow
Neubukow
Schwerin
Schweriner See
MECKLENBURG
Hagenow
Ludwigslust
Parchim
Lübtheen
Dömitz
Hitzacker
Dannenberg
WENDLAND
Lenzen
Perleberg
Wittenberge
PRIGNITZ
2
5
3
4
Buchholz in der Nordheide
Tostedt
Lüneburg
LÜNEBURGER HEIDE
Schneverdingen
Rotenburg
Soltau
Munster
Uelzen
Bad Bevensen
Salzwedel
Arendsee
D
Walsrode
Fallingbostel
Bergen
Unterlüß
Wittingen
Celle
Winsen
ALTMARK
Gardelegen
Stendal
Tangermünde
Langenhagen
Isernhagen
Hannover
Garbsen
Seelze
Burgdorf
Uetze
Gifhorn
Wolfsburg
DRÖMLING
11
12
A
B
C

DK
D
E
3
F
7
Helsinki
Wittow
Altenkirchen
Dranske
Wiek
Hiddensee
Lohme
Stubbenkammer
Jasmund
Sassnitz
Mukran
Prorer Wiek
Bergen
Rügen
Ostseebad Binz
Ostseebad Sellin
Putbus
Vilm
Ostseebad Göhren
Greifswalder Bodden
Thießow
Greifswalder Oie
Ruden
Ystad
Darß
Darßer Ort
Prerow am Darß
Ostseebad Zingst am Darß
Zingst
Bock
Klausdorf
Ostseebad Ahrenshoop
Wieck am Darß
Born am Darß
Groß Mohrdorf
Prohn
Ostseebad Wustrow
Barth
Saal
Löbnitz
Niepars
Stralsund
Altefähr
Samtens
Garz
Poseritz
Zudar
Ostseebad Dierhagen
Ostseebad Graal-Müritz
Ribnitz-Damgarten
Trinwillershagen
Velgast
Ahrenshagen
Richtenberg
Brandshagen
Miltzow
Reinberg
Wittenhagen
Koos
Gelbensande
Rövershagen
Marlow
Semlow
Franzburg
Gresenhorst
Bentwisch
Dettmannsdorf
Bad Sülze
Tribsees
Grimmen
Greifswald
Lubmin
Peenemünde
Karlshagen
Kröslin
Oderbucht
Zinnowitz
Wolgast
Koserow
Loddin
Ückeritz
Zatoka Pomorska
Dziwnów
Sanitz
Reppelin
Broderstorf
Tessin
Behren-Lübchin
Poggendorf
Glewitz
Kandelin
Sassen
Weitenhagen
Kemnitz
Hohendorf
Lühmannsdorf
Groß Kiesow
Züssow
Karlsburg
Zemitz
Lassan
Seebad Bansin
Seebad Heringsdorf
Seebad Ahlbeck
Kamień Pomorski
Międzyzdroje
Świnoujście
Usedom
Wolin
Kritzmow
Papendorf
Dummerstorf
Grammendorf
Kavelstorf
Cammin
Walkendorf
Gnoien
Nossendorf
Loitz
Görmin
Bentzin
Jarmen
Gützkow
Demmin
Tutow
Völschow
Liepen
Klein Bünzow
Murchin
Zirchow
Laage
Jördenstorf
Dargun
Verchen
Kuhs
Diekhof
Plaaz
Thürkow
Groß Roge
Groß Wüstenfelde
Neukalen
Metschow
Utzedel
Borrentin
Hohenmocker
Krien
Anklam
Pelsin
Bargischow
Oderhaff
Zalew Szczeciński
Teterow
Malchin
Remplin
Kummerow
Sarow
Burow
Gültz
Tützpatz
Spantekow
Ducherow
Leopoldshagen
Ueckermünde
Nowe Warpno
Racimierz
Gutow
Zehna
Groß Wokern
Gielow
Reuterstadt Stavenhagen
Altentreptow
Werder
Boldekow
Putzar
Liepgarten
Rieth
Ahlbeck
Trzebież
Lohmen
Krakow am See
Langhagen
Schwinkendorf
Jürgenstorf
Faulenrost
Wildberg
Knorrendorf
Rosenow
Friedland
Brunn
Schwichtenberg
Eggesin
Stepnica
Dobbertin
Hohen Wangelin
Lansen
Neddemin
Kotelow
Ferdinandshof
Wilhelmsburg
Torgelow
Hintersee
Brohm
Jatzke
Jatznick
Blumenhagen
Viereck
Tanowo
Police
Nossentiner Hütte
Jabel
Groß Plasten
Möllin
Neubrandenburg
Groß Miltzow
Strasburg
Pasewalk
Boock
Zerrenthin
Löcknitz
Szczecin
Goldberg
Gallin
Alt Schwerin
Malchow
Waren
Möllenhagen
Ankershagen
Penzlin
Cölpin
Burg Stargard
Helpter Berge
Woldegk
Wilsickow
Trebenow
Göritz
Grambow
Brüssow
Mierzyn
Plau
Karbow-Vietlübbe
Göhren-Lebbin
Klink
Sietow
Müritz
Blumenholz
Groß Nemerow
Blankensee
Fürstenwerder
Ganzlin
Röbel
Neustrelitz
Möllenbeck
Dolgen
Feldberg
Conow
Schönermark
Gollmitz
Dedelow
Prenzlau
Blindow
Drense
Krackow
Kołbaskowo
Stare Czarnowo
Meyenburg
Bütow
Vipperow
Rechlin
Roggentin
Mirow
Priborn
Freyenstein
Wredenhagen
Wulfersdorf
Wesenberg
Boitzenburg
Schmölln
Bietikow
Penkun
Gartz
Gryfino
Rohlsdorf
Falkenhagen
Dranse
Schwarz
Wustrow
Fürstenberg
Lychen
Haßleben
Seehausen
Wartin
Gramzow
Casekow
Nowe Czarnowo
Bielice
Pritzwalk
Wittstock
Schweinrich
Flecken Zechlin
Zechlinerhütte
Zechlin Dorf
Bredereiche
Densow
Templin
Mittenwalde
Gerswalde
Groß Fredenwalde
Milmersdorf
Passow
Vierraden
Widuchowa
Lubanowo
Banie
Buchholz
Herzsprung
Linow
Gühlen-Glienicke
Rheinsberg
Dannenwalde
Tornow
Hammelspring
Gollin
Wilmersdorf
Greiffenberg
Schwedt an der Oder
Felchow
Krajnik Dolny
Krzywin
Piaseczno
Swobnica
Grzybno
Tüchen
Lindenberg
Groß Welle
Schönebeck
Vehlow
Rossow
Rägelin
Gransee
Vogelsang
Friedrichswalde
Angermünde
Trzcińsko-Zdrój
Schrepkow
Gumtow
Kyritz
Walsleben
Alt Ruppin
Lindow
Schönberg
Zehdenick
Groß Dölln
Schorfheide
Joachimsthal
Groß Ziethen
Stolpe
Parstein
Piasek
Chojna
PL
Wusterhausen
Stüdenitz-Zernitz
Neuruppin
Herzberg
Löwenberg
Liebenwalde
Groß Schönebeck
Werbellin
Altenhof
Britz
Lichterfelde
Sandkrug
Lunow
Oderberg
Cedynia
Moryń
Witnica
Breddin
Neustadt
Sieversdorf
Wildberg
Nackel
Segeletz
Radensleben
Fehrbellin
Wustrau-Altfriesack
Zerpenschleuse
Finowfurt
Liepe
Niederfinow
Hohensaaten
Stara Rudnica
Mieszkowice
Rhinluch
Sommerfeld
Oranienburg
Klosterfelde
Wandlitz
Eberswalde-Finow
Bad Freienwalde
Smolnica
Rhinow
Kamern
Friesack
Melchow
Biesenthal
Heckelberg
Wriezen
Rozdowice
Neulewin
Boleszkowice
Oderbruch
Schollene
Hohennauen
Deutschhof
Paulinenaue
Velten
Birkenwerder
Berlin
Rüdnitz
Bernau
Tiefensee
Leuenberg
Schulzendorf
Neutrebbin
Kamień
Rathenow
Großwudicke
Stechow
Nennhausen
Pessin
Havelländisches Luch
Hennigsdorf
Mühlenbeck
Schönow
Seefeld
Blumberg
Werneuchen
Prötzel
Letschin
Nauen
Falkensee
Altlandsberg
Strausberg
Buckow
Märkische Schweiz
Gusow
Kostrzyn
Premnitz
Möglin
Barnewitz
Wachow
Wustermark
Dallgow
BERLIN
Neuenhagen Berlin
Fredersdorf
Vogelsdorf
Seelow
Manschnow
Kietz
Milow
Marzahne
Päwesin
Ketzin
Jahnsfelde
Rathstock
Podelzig
Pritzerbe
Fohrde
Roskow
Müncheberg
Görzyca
Bensdorf
Klein Kreutz
Töplitz
Groß Kreutz
Fahrland
Groß Glienicke
Kleinmachnow
Herzfelde
Rüdersdorf Berlin
Heinersdorf
Erkner
Grünheide
Hangelsberg
Petershagen
Lebus
13
4
2
1

8
A
B
C
1
2
3
4
16
NORTH SEA
NORDSEE
GB
F
Hull 12 hrs
Hull 12 hrs 45 mins
Rosyth
Harwich
3 hrs 30 mins
55 mins
Channel Tunnel
Dover
Strait of Dover
(Pas de Calais)
EUROPOORT
Beccles
Bungay
Lowestoft
Hopton
Oulton
Kessingland
Halesworth
Southwold
Saxmundham
Leiston
Aldeburgh
Wickham Market
Orford Ness
Hollesley Bay
Felixstowe
Landguard Point
Naze
North Foreland
Broadstairs
Ramsgate
Pegwell Bay
Deal
South Foreland
Goedereede
Scharendijke
Renesse
Burgh-Haamstede
Zierikzee
Vrouwenpolder
Domburg
Oostkapelle
Wissenkerke
Kortgene
Westkapelle
Middelburg
Goes
Koudekerke
Arnemuiden
Heinkenszand
Vlissingen
Oost-Souburg
's-Gravenpolder
Ovezande
Breskens
Westerschelde
Schoondijke
Knokke-Heist
Zeebrugge
Blankenberge
De Haan
Oostburg
Sluis
IJzendijke
Aardenburg
Hoek
Terneuzen
Sluiskil
Sas Van Gent
Assenede
Damme
Bredene
Oostende (Ostend)
Brugge (Bruges)
Maldegem
Kaprijke
Zelzate
Middelkerke
Oudenburg
Jabbeke
Oostkamp
Beernem
Eeklo
Waarschoot
Nieuwpoort
Koksijde
Gistel
Zedelgem
Knesselare
Zomergem
Evergem
Lochristi
De Panne
Veurne
Ichtegem
Koekelare
Lovendegem
Wachtebeke
St-Pol-sur-Mer
Dunkerque
Ghyvelde
Torhout
Wingene
Aalter
Gent (Gand)
Destelbergen
Grande-Synthe
Coudekerque-Branche
Diksmuide
Kortemark
Lichtervelde
Ruiselede
Tielt
Nevele
St-Martens-Latem
Melle
Laarne
Grand-Fort-Philippe
Gravelines
Hondschoote
Houthulst
Ardooie
Pittem
Dentergem
Merelbeke
Wetteren
Calais
Sangatte
Marck
Bergues
Lo
Staden
Meulebeke
Deinze
Cap Blanc Nez
Coquelles
Bourbourg
Oostvleteren
Roeselare (Roulers)
Ingelmunster
Zulte
Oosterzele
Gavere
Wissant
Audruicq
Langemark
Moorslede
Izegem
Kruishoutem
Cap Gris Nez
Guines
Wormhout
Poperinge
Ieper
Zonnebeke
Harelbeke
Waregem
Munkzwalm
Herzele
Zottegem
Marquise
Ardres
Kuurne
Anzegem
Oudenaarde
Ambleteuse
Watten
Steenvoorde
Wevelgem
Kortrijk (Courtrai)
Deerlijk
Wimereux
Cassel
Menen (Menin)
Wervik
Zwevegem
Brakel
Licques
St-Omer
Arques
Mont des Cats
Kemmel
Comines
Halluin
Mouscron
Berchem
Ronse
St-Martin-Boulogne
Longuenesse
Bailleul
Quesnoy-sur-Deûle
Tourcoing
Avelgem
Le Portel
Boulogne-sur-Mer
Outreau
Lumbres
Wizernes
Hazebrouck
Roubaix
Estaimpuis
Pecq
Ellezelles
Frasnes-lez-Buissenal
Lessines
Desvres
Armentières
Marcq-en-Barœul
Celles
Hardelot
Samer
Aire-sur-la-Lys
Merville
Lambersart
Lille
Villeneuve-d'Ascq
Isbergues
Estaires
Lomme
Tournai
Ath
Hucqueliers
Fauquembergues
Norrent-Fontes
Haubourdin
Wavrin
Lesquin
Leuze-en-Hainaut
Chièvres
Paris-Plage
Étaples
Lillers
La Bassée
Seclin
Rumes
Antoing
Bléharies
Béthune
Beuvry
Péruwelz
Belœil
Fruges
Montreuil
Bruay-en-Artois
Calonne-Ricouart
Heuchin
Carvin
Pont-à-Marcq
Bernissart
Houdain
Divion
Nœux-les-Mines
Harnes
Oignies
Orchies
St-Amand-les-Eaux
St-Ghislain
Berck
Bully-les-Mines
Liévin
Lens
Vieux-Condé
Raismes
Boussu
Campagne-lès-Hesdin
Hesdin
St-Pol-sur-Ternoise
Avion
Hénin-Beaumont
Flers-en-Escrebieux
Marchiennes
Quiévrain
Dour
Le Parcq
Aubigny-en-Artois
Vimy
Douai
Sin-le-Noble
Somain
Anzin
Valenciennes
Marly
Denain
Douchy-les-Mines
Arras
Vitry-en-Artois
Dainville
Frévent
TERNOIS
ARTOIS
FLANDRE
Canal d'Aire

D
E
F
4
9
1
2
3
4
10
17
Newcastle 14 hrs
Markermeer
NL
B
D
AMSTERDAM
Haarlem
IJmuiden
Zandvoort
Beverwijk
Zaandam
Lelystad
Almere
Hilversum
Amersfoort
Apeldoorn
Deventer
Zwolle
Kampen
Dronten
Harderwijk
Leiden
'S-GRAVENHAGE (DEN HAAG)
Zoetermeer
Delft
Rotterdam
Schiedam
Vlaardingen
Gouda
Utrecht
Nieuwegein
Arnhem
Nijmegen
Ede
Wageningen
Doetinchem
Dordrecht
Gorinchem
Breda
Tilburg
Waalwijk
's-Hertogenbosch
Oss
Eindhoven
Helmond
Venlo
Roermond
Weert
Kleve
Emmerich
Mönchengladbach
Viersen
Krefeld
Sittard
Geleen
Heerlen
Kerkrade
Maastricht
Aachen
Antwerpen (Anvers)
Mechelen (Malines)
BRUXELLES (BRUSSEL)
Leuven (Louvain)
Hasselt
Genk
Tienen
St-Truiden
Tongeren
Liège (Luik)
Verviers
Spa
Malmédy
Namur
Charleroi
Waterloo
Wavre
Nivelles
Turnhout
Roosendaal
Bergen op Zoom
Vlissingen
Middelharnis
St-Niklaas
Lokeren
Dendermonde
Aalst (Alost)
Hamont
Lommel
Mol
Geel
Herentals
Huy
Seraing
Eupen
Stolberg
Jülich
Düren
Geilenkirchen
Erkelenz
Hückelhoven

10
A
4
B
5
C
1
2
3
4
9
18
NL
Kampen
Zwolle
Hardenberg
Lingen
Apeldoorn
Deventer
Almelo
Hengelo
Enschede
Oldenzaal
Bad Bentheim
Rheine
Ibbenbüren
Osnabrück
Arnhem
Nijmegen
Doetinchem
Winterswijk
Vreden
Ahaus
Stadtlohn
Gronau
Steinfurt
Emsdetten
Greven
Münster
MÜNSTERLAND
Coesfeld
Dülmen
Borken
Bocholt
Kleve
Emmerich
Rees
Wesel
Dorsten
Recklinghausen
Gelsenkirchen
Bottrop
Herne
Essen
Bochum
Dortmund
Duisburg
Oberhausen
Moers
Mülheim an der Ruhr
Krefeld
Venlo
Mönchengladbach
Neuss
Düsseldorf
Wuppertal
Solingen
Remscheid
Hagen
Witten
Unna
Hamm
Soest
Lippstadt
Iserlohn
Lüdenscheid
Arnsberg
SAUERLAND
Leverkusen
Bergisch Gladbach
Köln
Bergheim
Düren
Aachen
Heerlen
Siegburg
BONN
Siegen
Gummersbach
Olpe
Euskirchen
Bad Neuenahr-Ahrweiler
Remagen
Neuwied
Koblenz
Andernach
Montabaur
Limburg an der Lahn
Monschau
Malmedy
Eupen
Verviers
Maastricht
Roermond
Sittard
Heinsberg
Gütersloh
Warendorf
Haltern
Lünen
Kamen
Schwerte
Velbert
Ratingen
Hilden
Dormagen
Grevenbroich
Wesseling
Troisdorf
Sankt Augustin
Königswinter
Hennef
Brühl
Hürth
Kerpen
Frechen
Erftstadt
Zülpich
Mechernich
Wipperfürth
Meinerzhagen
Attendorn
Plettenberg
Menden
Werl
Bad Iburg
Lengerich
Versmold
Telgte
Ahlen
Beckum
Oelde
Xanten
Goch
Geldern
Kevelaer
Viersen
Kempen
Willich
Kaarst
Meerbusch
Jüchen
Erkelenz
Hückelhoven
Geilenkirchen
Alsdorf
Würselen
Eschweiler
Stolberg
Schleiden
Kall
Rheinbach
Meckenheim
Sinzig
Wissen
Betzdorf
Altenkirchen
Hachenburg
Haiger
Dillenburg
Herborn
Hadamar
Bad Honnef
Linz am Rhein
Overath
Wiehl
Waldbröl
Morsbach
Kreuztal
Hilchenbach
Lennestadt
Schmallenberg
Finnentrop
Sundern
Meschede
Wetter
Herdecke
Ennepetal
Gevelsberg
Sprockhövel
Hattingen
Castrop-Rauxel
Datteln
Marl
Herten
Gladbeck
Dinslaken
Voerde
Hamminkeln
Schermbeck
Senden
Lüdinghausen
Ascheberg
Werne
Bergkamen
Selm
Olfen
Nottuln
Havixbeck
Billerbeck
Gescher
Velen
Reken
Rhede
Isselburg
Ochtrup
Metelen
Neuenkirchen
Hörstel
Mettingen
Recke
Bramsche
Lotte
Georgsmarienhütte
Hasbergen
Bissendorf
Dissen am Teutoburger Wald
Harsewinkel
Sassenberg
Herzebrock-Clarholz
Rheda
Ennigerloh
Sendenhorst
Drensteinfurt
Bönen
Fröndenberg
Holzwickede
Ense
Balve
Altena
Neuenrade
Werdohl
Herscheid
Kierspe
Halver
Radevormwald
Hückeswagen
Schwelm
Wermelskirchen
Burscheid
Leichlingen
Langenfeld
Monheim
Pulheim
Bedburg
Elsdorf
Jülich
Linnich
Baesweiler
Übach-Palenberg
Herzogenrath
Kerkrade
Nettetal
Brüggen
Schwalmtal
Niederkrüchten
Wegberg
Wassenberg
Tegelen
Straelen
Issum
Alpen
Rheinberg
Kamp-Lintfort
Neukirchen-Vluyn
Kalkar
Uedem
Weeze
Gennep
Cuijk
Boxmeer
Venray
Sevenum
Helden
Horst
Arcen
Bergen
Weert
Heythuysen
Emmen
Meppen
Dedemsvaart
Ommen
Hattem
Epe
Heerde
Raalte
Nijverdal
Rijssen
Holten
Lochem
Zutphen
Dieren
Doesburg
Didam
Zevenaar
Huissen
Elst
Bemmel
Haaksbergen
Eibergen
Neede
Borculo
Groenlo
Lichtenvoorde
Aalten
Terborg-Silvolde
Varsseveld
Ulft
Gendringen
Dinxperlo
Bad Münstereifel
Hellenthal
Nettersheim
Blankenheim
Adenau
Ahrbrück
Altenahr
Dümpelfeld
Bendorf
Vallendar
Höhr-Grenzhausen
Selters
Westerburg
Rennerod
Bad Marienberg
Puderbach
Dierdorf
Rengsdorf
Waldbreitbach
Asbach
Neustadt
Eitorf
Weyerbusch
Hamm
Kirchen
Mudersbach
Wilnsdorf
Netphen
Neunkirchen
Burbach
Breitscheid
Driedorf
Weilburg
Merenberg
Runkel
Elz
Diez
Nassau
Arzbach
Eitelborn
Spa
Stavelot
Trois-Ponts
Bütgenbach
Amel
Recht
Jalhay
Hertogenwald
Signal de Botrange
Roetgen
Simmerath
Raeren
Kelmis
Vaals
Valkenburg
Simpelveld
Brunssum
Geleen
Landgraaf
Schaesberg
Beek
Stein
Haaksbergen
Denekamp
Losser
Ootmarsum
Tubbergen
Vriezenveen
Wierden
Goor
Markelo
Bathmen
Gorssel
Twello
Vaassen
Oldebroek
Wezep
Nunspeet
Elspeet
Harderwijk
Teutoburger Wald
Haarstrang
Arnsberger Wald
Rothaargebirge
Westerwald
Sorpe Staubecken
Biggesee
Dümmer
Rhein
Ruhr
Lippe
Ems
Vechte
Maas
Niers
Sieg
Wupper
Erft
Rur

D
E
6
F
11
1
2
3
4
12
19
Nienburg
Neustadt am Rübenberge
Stolzenau
Rahden
Petershagen
Espelkamp
Hille
Minden
Lübbecke
Bad Essen
Hüllhorst
Bünde
Löhne
Hiddenhausen
Spenge
Enger
Herford
Vlotho
Bad Salzuflen
Werther
Bielefeld
Leopoldshöhe
Lemgo
Lage
Oerlinghausen
Detmold
Schloß Holte-Stukenbrock
Verl
Rheda-Wiedenbrück
Hövelhof
Rietberg
Delbrück
Paderborn
Salzkotten
Borchen
Bad Lippspringe
Horn-Bad Meinberg
Blomberg
Lügde
Bad Pyrmont
Aerzen
Barntrup
Dörentrup
Steinheim
Nieheim
Bad Driburg
Brakel
Höxter
Beverungen
Lichtenau
Büren
Wünnenberg
Rüthen
Warstein
Brilon
Olsberg
Marsberg
Warburg
Willebadessen
Borgentreich
Trendelburg
Hofgeismar
Arolsen
Volkmarsen
Korbach
Wolfhagen
Twiste
Adorf
Willingen
Winterberg
Medebach
Hallenberg
Sachsenberg
Bad Berleburg
Frankenberg
Bad Wildungen
Fritzlar
Felsberg
Melsungen
Homberg
Borken
Bad Zwesten
Frankenau
Battenberg
Biedenkopf
Wetter
Münchhausen
Marburg an der Lahn
Kirchhain
Stadtallendorf
Alsfeld
Neustadt
Amöneburg
Gladenbach
Lohra
Allendorf
Gießen
Wetzlar
Linden
Lich
Grünberg
Hungen
Laubach
Nidda
Butzbach
Langgöns
Solms
Bad Nauheim
Schotten
Herbstein
Lauterbach
Schlitz
Fulda
Künzell
Petersberg
Hünfeld
Gersfeld
Schlüchtern
Neuhof
Bad Hersfeld
Niederaula
Bebra
Rotenburg an der Fulda
Schwalmstadt-Treysa
Schwalmstadt-Ziegenhain
Neukirchen
Kassel
Vellmar
Baunatal
Lohfelden
Kaufungen
Sandershausen
Witzenhausen
Hessisch Lichtenau
Helsa
Großalmerode
Eschwege
Sontra
Waldkappel
Spangenberg
Heringen (Werra)
Friedewald
Bad Salzungen
Vacha
Tann
Eiterfeld
Rasdorf
Hannoversch Münden
Hann. Münden
Göttingen
Rosdorf
Dransfeld
Friedland
Heiligenstadt
Heilbad
EICHSFELD
Leinefelde
Worbis
Duderstadt
Gieboldehausen
Bovenden
Northeim
Uslar
Bodenfelde
Dassel
Holzminden
Einbeck
Bad Gandersheim
Seesen
Alfeld
Bockenem
Osterode am Harz
Herzberg am Harz
Bad Lauterberg im Harz
Clausthal-Zellerfeld
Braunlage
Bad Harzburg
Goslar
Langelsheim
Vienenburg
Wernigerode
Blankenburg
Ilsenburg
Nordhausen
Bleicherode
Sondershausen
Mühlhausen
Bad Langensalza
Gotha
Eisenach
Waltershausen
Ohrdruf
Arnstadt
Kurort Schmalkalden
Zella-Mehlis
Suhl
Meiningen
Schleusingen
Hildburghausen
Mellrichstadt
Bischofsheim an der Rhön
Römhild
Hannover
Langenhagen
Isernhagen
Garbsen
Seelze
Wunstorf
Hemmingen
Laatzen
Sehnde
Lehrte
Burgdorf
Uetze
Peine
Gifhorn
Wolfsburg
Braunschweig
Wolfenbüttel
Salzgitter
Hildesheim
Harsum
Sarstedt
Pattensen
Springe
Bad Münder am Deister
Hameln
Salzhemmendorf
Hessisch Oldendorf
Rinteln
Obernkirchen
Stadthagen
Bückeburg
Wennigsen
Barsinghausen
Gehrden
Ronnenberg
Bad Salzdetfurth
Ilsede
Vechelde
Cremlingen
Edemissen
WESERGEBIRGE
OBERWÄLDER LAND
SENNE
SOLLING
DÜN
HAINICH
THÜRINGER WALD
RHÖN
VOGELSBERG
BURGWALD
EGGEGEBIRGE

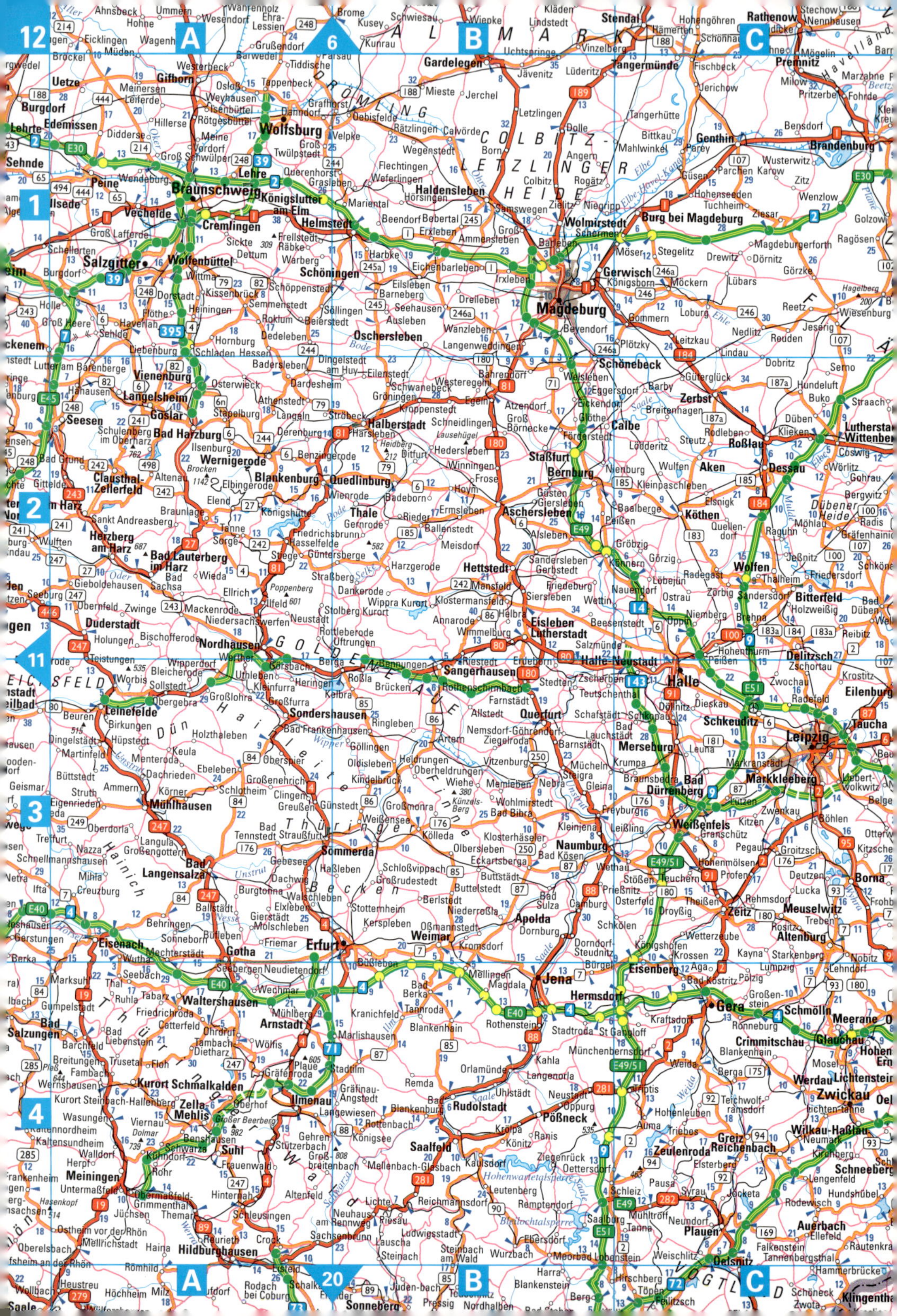
12
A
6
B
C
1
2
3
4
11
20
Braunschweig
Wolfsburg
Magdeburg
Halle
Leipzig
Erfurt
Gotha
Eisenach
Weimar
Jena
Gera
Zwickau
Plauen
Salzgitter
Goslar
Wernigerode
Quedlinburg
Halberstadt
Nordhausen
Mühlhausen
Sömmerda
Naumburg
Weißenfels
Merseburg
Dessau
Köthen
Bernburg
Aschersleben
Sangerhausen
Eisleben
Bitterfeld
Wolfen
Delitzsch
Eilenburg
Markkleeberg
Altenburg
Schmölln
Meerane
Glauchau
Crimmitschau
Greiz
Zeulenroda
Pößneck
Rudolstadt
Saalfeld
Ilmenau
Arnstadt
Suhl
Meiningen
Hildburghausen
Sonneberg
Oelsnitz
Auerbach
Apolda
Bad Langensalza
Sondershausen
Leinefelde
Duderstadt
Gardelegen
Stendal
Tangermünde
Rathenow
Premnitz
Genthin
Brandenburg
Burg bei Magdeburg
Zerbst
Roßlau
Aken
Schönebeck
Staßfurt
Oschersleben
Haldensleben
Helmstedt
Schöningen
Wolfenbüttel
Gifhorn
Peine
Sehnde
Lehrte
Burgdorf
Uetze
Seesen
Bad Harzburg
Vienenburg
Langelsheim
Clausthal-Zellerfeld
Herzberg am Harz
Bad Lauterberg im Harz
Blankenburg
Thale
Hettstedt
Querfurt
Schkeuditz
Taucha
Borna
Zeitz
Eisenberg
Hermsdorf
Waltershausen
Bad Salzungen
Kurort Schmalkalden
Zella-Mehlis
Schleiz
Wilkau-Haßlau
Werdau
Lichtenstein
Hohenstein-Ernstthal
Schneeberg
Klingenthal
A L T M A R K
D R Ö M L I N G
C O L B I T Z - L E T Z L I N G E R H E I D E
G O L D E N E A U E
H a i n l e i t e
D ü n
F i n n e
T h ü r i n g e r B e c k e n
H a i n i c h
T h ü r i n g e r W a l d
V O G T L A N D
E30
E45
E40
E49
E51
E49/51
2
4
9
14
38
39
71
72
143
395

13
7
21
D
E
F
1
2
3
4
BERLIN
Potsdam
Hennigsdorf
Nauen
Werder
Kleinmachnow
Teltow
Ludwigsfelde
Neuenhagen Berlin
Rüdersdorf Berlin
Erkner
Strausberg
Fürstenwalde
Frankfurt an der Oder
Słubice
Königs Wusterhausen
Wildau
Zossen
Luckenwalde
Jüterbog
Beelitz
Beeskow
Eisenhüttenstadt
Krosno Odrzańskie
Guben
Gubin
Lübben
Lübbenau
Luckau
Dahme
Cottbus
Forst
Spremberg
Finsterwalde
Senftenberg
Großräschen
Lauchhammer
Elsterwerda
Bad Liebenwerda
Herzberg
Torgau
Hoyerswerda
Weißwasser
Bad Muskau
Żary
Lubsko
Kamenz
Bautzen
Niesky
Görlitz
Zgorzelec
Löbau
Riesa
Oschatz
Wurzen
Grimma
Döbeln
Meißen
Großenhain
Radebeul
Coswig
Dresden
Freital
Heidenau
Pirna
Radeberg
Bischofswerda
Neustadt in Sachsen
Sebnitz
Freiberg
Mittweida
Chemnitz
Flöha
Frankenberg
Zschopau
Stollberg
Marienberg
Annaberg-Buchholz
Aue
Schwarzenberg
Olbernhau
Zittau
Bogatynia
Ebersbach
Děčín
Ústí nad Labem
Teplice
Krupka
Most
Litvínov
Bílina
Chomutov
Jirkov
Kadaň
Litoměřice
Česká Lípa
Liberec
Jablonec nad Nisou
Mladá Boleslav
Roudnice nad Labem
Mělník
SPREEWALD
NIEDERLAUSITZ
OBERLAUSITZ
SÄCHSISCHE SCHWEIZ
POJEZIERZE LUBUSKIE
Dahlener Heide
PL
D
CZ

14
A
B
C
1
2
3
4
23
GB
Poole
Bournemouth
Christchurch
Poole Bay
Wareham
Isle of Purbeck
Corfe Castle
Swanage
St Alban's Head
Weymouth
Chesil Beach
Lyme Bay
Fortuneswell
Easton
Weston
Isle of Portland
South Dorset Downs
Lytchett Minster
The Needles
St Catherine's Point
Cowes
Ryde
Seaview
Newport
Shalfleet
Brighstone
Sandown
Shanklin
Ventnor
Chale
Foreland
Portsmouth
East Wittering
Bognor Regis
E N G L I
Portsmouth
3 hrs
4 hrs 15 mins
9 hrs
2 hrs 45 mins (summer only)
5 hrs
6 hrs
5 hrs
Dublin 18 hrs
Rosslare 20 hrs
1 hr 10 mins
Alderney
St Anne
Cap de la Hague
Urville Nacqueville
Beaumont
Équerdreville-Hainneville
Octeville
Cherbourg
Tourlaville
Cap Lévy
Pte de Barfleur
St-Pierre-Eglise
Quettehou
La Glacerie
Flamanville
Les Pieux
Brix
Valognes
Montebourg
Îles St-Marcouf
BAIE DE S
Guernsey
Vale
St Sampson
Herm
St Peter in the Wood
St Peter Port
St Martin
Sark
CHANNEL ISLANDS
Passage de la Déroute
Bricquebec
COTENTIN
St-Sauveur-le-Vicomte
Ste-Mère-Eglise
Barneville-Carteret
Cap de Carteret
Portbail
Picauville
Carentan
Jersey
St John
St Ouen
St Martin
St Brelade
St Saviour
St Helier
St Clement
La Haye-du-Puits
Lessay
St-Jean-de-Daye
Créances
Périers
Pont-Hébert
St-Sauveur-Lendelin
Marigny
Agneaux
St-Lô
Grandcamp-Maisy
Vierville-sur-Mer
Isigny-sur-Mer
Trévières
Port-en-Bessin-Huppain
Courseulles-sur-Mer
Ryes
Douvres-la-Délivrande
BESSIN
Bayeux
Le Molay-Littry
Tilly-sur-Seulles
Carpiquet
Balleroy
Hérouville-St-Clair
Verson
Évrecy
Blainville-sur-Mer
Agon-Coutainville
St-Malo-de-la-Lande
Coutances
Cerisy-la-Salle
Condé-sur-Vire
Torigni-sur-Vire
Caumont-l'Éventé
Villers-Bocage
Aunay-sur-Odon
Brettville-sur-Laize
Les Minquiers
Montmartin-sur-Mer
Quettreville-sur-Seinne
Tessy-sur-Vire
Mont Pinçon
Thury-Harcourt
Îles Chausey
Bréhal
Hambye
Cérences
Gavray
Percy
Villedieu-les-Poêles
St-Sever-Calvados
BOCAGE
Clécy
Condé-sur-Noireau
Donville-les-Bains
Granville
St-Pair-sur-Mer
Jullouville
La Haye-Pesnel
Sartilly
Vire
Vassy
SUISSE NORMANDE
Athis-de-l'Orne
St-Georges-des-Groseillers
Golfe de St-Malo
Collines de Normandie
St-Pois
Tinchebray
Chanu
Flers
Messei
Pte du Grouin
Cancale
Baie du Mont-St-Michel
Brécey
Sourdeval
Ger
Cap Fréhel
Avranches
Juvigny-le-Tertre
Mortain
Lonlay-l'Abbaye
La Ferrière-aux-Étangs
Champsecret
Sables-d'Or-les-Pins
Erquy
Fréhel
Pléneuf-Val-André
Matignon
St-Lunaire
St-Briac-sur-Mer
Dinard
St-Malo
St-Méloir-des-Ondes
Le-Vivier-sur-Mer
Mont-St-Michel
Ducey
Étables-sur-Mer
Binic
Baie de St-Brieuc
Plérin
St-Brieuc
Langueux
St-Alban
Hénanbihen
Ploubalay
St-Jouan-des-Guérets
Châteauneuf-d'Ille-et-Vilaine
Dol-de-Bretagne
Pontorson
St-Hilaire-du-Harcouët
Barenton
Domfront
Plancoët
Miniac-Morvan
Pleudihen-sur-Rance
Dinan
Lamballe
Corseul
Trégueux
St-James
St-Martin-de-Landelles
Le Teilleul
Landivy
Passais
Ceaucé
Sélune
Orne
Vire
A35
A351
A352
A353
A354
A3054
A3055
A3020
E03
N13
D900
D901
D902
D903
D904
D2
D650
D971
D972
D514
E46
D11
D6
D572
D9
E401
D71
D13
A84
D999
N174
D577
D7
D33
D524
D512
D911
D962
D924
D973
E03/401
D5
D797
N175
N176
D907
D32
D977
D908
D18
D786
D768
E50
D155
D40
D36

Seaford
Eastbourne
Beachy Head
Newhaven
2 hrs
D
E
F
8
15
1
2
16
3
4
24
CHANNEL
MANCHE
St-Martin-Boulogne
Boulogne-sur-Mer
Le Portel
Outreau
Desvres
Samer
Neufchâtel-Hardelot
Hucqueliers
Étaples
Le Touquet-Paris-Plage
Montreuil
Fruges
Berck
Verton
Campagne-lès-Hesdin
Hesdin
Fort-Mahon-Plage
Baie de la Somme
Pte du Hourdel
Rue
Le Crotoy
Crécy-en-Ponthieu
Nouvion
Auxi-le-Château
St-Valery-sur-Somme
Cayeux-sur-Mer
PONTHIEU
St-Riquier
Abbeville
Domart-en-Ponthieu
Ault
Friville-Escarbotin
Feuquières-en-Vimeu
Moyenneville
Haut-Clocher
Ailly-le-Haut-Clocher
Longpré-les-Corps-Saints
Flixecourt
Mers-les-Bains
Le Tréport
Eu
Criel-sur-Mer
VIMEU
Incheville
Gamaches
Hallencourt
Airaines
Oisemont
Picquigny
Ailly-sur-Somme
Blangy-sur-Bresle
Molliens-Dreuil
Dieppe
Neuville-lès-Dieppe
Varengeville-sur-Mer
Arques-la-Bataille
Envermeu
St-Nicolas-d'Aliermont
Beaucamps-le-Vieux
Foucarmont
Hornoy-le-Bourg
Quevauvillers
Londinières
St-Valery-en-Caux
Offranville
Veulettes-sur-Mer
Néville
Fontaine-le-Dun
Bacqueville-en-Caux
Longueville-sur-Scie
PICARDIE
Aumale
Poix-de-Picardie
St-Pierre-en-Port
Cany-Barville
Fécamp
Yport
Valmont
Ourville-en-Caux
Doudeville
Auffay
Bellencombre
Neufchâtel-en-Bray
Conty
Étretat
Cap d'Antifer
PAYS DE CAUX
Tôtes
St-Saëns
Formerie
Grandvilliers
St-Jouin-Bruneval
Goderville
Fauville-en-Caux
Yerville
Criquetot-l'Esneval
Forges-les-Eaux
Feuquières
Clères
Marseille-en-Beauvaisis
Montivilliers
Bolbec
Yvetot
Pavilly
Buchy
Argueil
Songeons
Octeville-sur-Mer
Lillebonne
Barentin
Fontaine-le-Bourg
Montville
Malaunay
Cap de la Hève
Harfleur
Villers-Écalles
Gournay-en-Bray
Troissereux
Ste-Adresse
Gonfreville-l'Orcher
Notre-Dame-de-Gravenchon
Mont-St-Aignan
Bois-Guillaume
Le Havre
Tancarville
Beauvais
Seine
Quillebeuf-sur-Seine
Duclair
Maromme
Honfleur
Le Petit-Quevilly
Rouen
Lyons-la-Forêt
Le Grand-Quevilly
Sotteville-lès-Rouen
Le Coudray-St-Germer
Trouville-sur-Mer
Deauville
Fleury-sur-Andelle
Routot
Grand-Couronne
Beuzeville
Pont-Audemer
Sérifontaine
Villers-sur-Mer
Touques
St-Étienne-du-Rouvray
Oissel
Pitres
VEXIN NORMAND
Luc-sur-Mer
Lion-sur-Mer
Houlgate
Dives-sur-Mer
Bourg-Achard
St-Aubin-lès-Elbeuf
Caudebec-lès-Elbeuf
Trie-Château
Chaumont-en-Vexin
Pont-l'Évêque
Montfort-sur-Risle
Épaignes
Cléon
Elbeuf
Étrépagny
Gisors
Ouistreham
Bourgtheroulde-Infreville
St-Pierre-lès-Elbeuf
Cormeilles
St-Georges-du-Vièvre
Val-de-Reuil
Les Andelys
Méru
Colombelles
Dozulé
Louviers
Amblainville
Troarn
Brionne
Le Neubourg
Acquigny
Gaillon
VEXIN FRANÇAIS
Argences
Lisieux
Thiberville
Écos
Magny-en-Vexin
Marines
Serquigny
Vernon
L'Isle-Adam
Mézidon-Canon
Bernay
Beaumont-le-Roger
St-Marcel
Gasny
Vigny
Osny
PAYS D'AUGE
Évreux
Gravigny
Pacy-sur-Eure
Mantes-la-Jolie
Limay
Cergy
Livarot
Orbec
Broglie
St-Sébastien-de-Morsent
Meulan
Les Mureaux
St-Pierre-sur-Dives
Beaumesnil
La Bonneville-sur-Iton
Conches-en-Ouche
Mantes-la-Ville
Aubergenville
Poissy
Potigny
Plaine de St-André
St-André-de-l'Eure
La Couture-Boussey
St-Germain-en-Laye
Vimoutiers
Septeuil
Falaise
Morteaux-Coulibœuf
PAYS D'OUCHE
Ivry-la-Bataille
Rueil-Malmaison
Damville
Ézy-sur-Eure
Anet
Plaisir
NORMANDE
Trun
La Ferté-Frênel
Breteuil
Bû
Rugles
Marcilly-sur-Eure
Houdan
Gacé
St-Sulpice-sur-Risle
Nonancourt
St-Lubin-des-Joncherets
Montfort-l'Amaury
Trappes
Argentan
Exmes
St-Rémy-sur-Avre
Tillières-sur-Avre
Écouché
L'Aigle
Verneuil-sur-Avre
Dreux
Chevreuse
Aube
Vernouillet
St-Léger-en-Yvelines
Le Merlerault
Brézolles
Rambouillet
Forêt de Rambouillet
Moulins-la-Marche
Coulombs
Rânes
Mortrée
Courtomer
La Ferté-Vidame
Tréon
Nogent-le-Roi
Épernon
Tremblay-les-Villages
Pierres
St-Arnoult-en-Yvelines
Maintenon
La Ferté-Macé
Sées
Tourouvre
Châteauneuf-en-Thymerais
Carrouges
Le Mêle-sur-Sarthe
Bazoches-sur-Hoëne
Mortagne-au-Perche
Senonches
Gallardon
Ablis
Dourdan
Pré-en-Pail
A13
A28
A29
A131
A150
A151
A16
A11
E05
E44
E46
E402
N1
N12
N13
N14
N15
N26
N27
N28
N29
N31
N39
N138
N154
N158
N175

A
B
C
8
1
2
3
4
15
25
St-Omer
Bailleul
Armentières
Comines
Halluin
Tourcoing
Mouscron
Roubaix
Lille
Villeneuve-d'Ascq
Tournai
Leuze-en-Hainaut
Ath
Lessines
Enghien
Braine-le-Comte
Soignies
Étaples
Desvres
Montreuil
Hucqueliers
Fauquembergues
Aire-sur-la-Lys
Isbergues
Béthune
Bruay-en-Artois
Hazebrouck
Merville
Estaires
La Bassée
Haubourdin
Seclin
Carvin
Lens
Liévin
Bully-les-Mines
Noeux-les-Mines
Hénin-Beaumont
Douai
Oignies
Orchies
St-Amand-les-Eaux
Péruwelz
Bernissart
St-Ghislain
Mons
Frameries
Boussu
Dour
Quiévrain
Valenciennes
Anzin
Denain
Marly
Douchy-les-Mines
Maubeuge
Hautmont
Le Quesnoy
Aulnoye-Aymeries
Condé
Raismes
Somain
Sin-le-Noble
Arras
Avion
Vimy
Dainville
Achicourt
Beaumetz-lès-Loges
Avesnes-le-Comte
Frévent
St-Pol-sur-Ternoise
Hesdin
TERNOIS
ARTOIS
Campagne-lès-Hesdin
Berck
Rue
Le Crotoy
Crécy-en-Ponthieu
Nouvion
Auxi-le-Château
PONTHIEU
Abbeville
Doullens
Pas-en-Artois
Bapaume
Cambrai
Marquion
Caudry
Le Cateau-Cambrésis
Landrecies
Solesmes
Avesnes-sur-Helpe
Le Nouvion-en-Thiérache
Marcoing
St-Riquier
Bernaville
Beauval
Domart-en-Ponthieu
Flixecourt
Long
Ailly-le-Haut-Clocher
Amiens
Albert
Méaulte
Combles
Moislains
Péronne
Roisel
Vermand
VERMANDOIS
St-Quentin
Bohain-en-Vermandois
Fresnoy-le-Grand
Guise
Wassigny
Étreux
La Capelle
Vervins
Sains-Richaumont
THIÉRACHE
Hirson
Airaines
Oisemont
Picquigny
Ailly-sur-Somme
Molliens-Dreuil
Hornoy-le-Bourg
Poix-de-Picardie
Conty
Corbie
Villers-Bretonneux
Boves
Moreuil
Ailly-sur-Noye
Rosières-en-Santerre
Chaulnes
Nesle
Ham
Roye
Harly
Ribemont
Moy-de-l'Aisne
Crécy-sur-Serre
Marle
SANTERRE
PICARDIE
Aumale
Formerie
Grandvilliers
Crèvecœur-le-Grand
Breteuil
Montdidier
Tricot
Maignelay-Montigny
Ressons-sur-Matz
Lassigny
Guiscard
Noyon
Chauny
Tergnier
La Fère
Laon
Sissonne
Crépy
St-Gobain
Coucy-le-Château-Auffrique
Anizy-le-Château
St-Just-en-Chaussée
Froissy
Songeons
Marseille-en-Beauvaisis
Beauvais
Troissereux
Nivillers
Le Coudray-St-Germer
Estrées-St-Denis
Compiègne
Thourotte
Ribécourt-Dreslincourt
Clairoix
Soissons
Vailly-sur-Aisne
Craonne
Neufchâtel
Fismes
Braine
Venizel
Crouy
Pierrefonds
Cuise-la-Motte
Villers-Cotterêts
Oulchy-le-Château
Fère-en-Tardenois
TARDENOIS
Reims
Tinqueux
Cormontreuil
Ville-en-Tardenois
Châtillon-sur-Marne
Dormans
Épernay
Clermont
Liancourt
Noailles
Mouy
Nogent-sur-Oise
Pont-Ste-Maxence
Creil
Montataire
Senlis
Chantilly
Crépy-en-Valois
VALOIS
Verberie
Méru
Chaumont-en-Vexin
Gisors
Trie-Château
Persan
Beaumont-sur-Oise
L'Isle-Adam
Luzarches
Marines
Magny-en-Vexin
VEXIN FRANÇAIS
Pontoise
Cergy
Taverny
Domont
Sarcelles
Goussainville
Dammartin-en-Goële
Nanteuil-le-Haudouin
La Ferté-Milon
Neuilly-St-Front
Château-Thierry
Condé-en-Brie
Montmort-Lucy
Vertus
Mantes-la-Jolie
Limay
Meulan
Les Mureaux
Poissy
Aubergenville
St-Germain-en-Laye
Argenteuil
St-Denis
Aulnay-sous-Bois
Mitry-Mory
Meaux
Nanterre
Rueil-Malmaison
Le Raincy
Lagny-sur-Marne
Boulogne-Billancourt
PARIS
Versailles
Plaisir
Ivry-sur-Seine
Marne-la-Vallée
Crécy-la-Chapelle
Coulommiers
La Ferté-sous-Jouarre
Montmirail
Trappes
Antony
Créteil
Pontault-Combault
Ozoir-la-Ferrière
Tournan-en-Brie
Brie-Comte-Robert
Rozay-en-Brie
La Ferté-Gaucher
Sézanne
Fère-Champenoise
Esternay
CÔTE CHAMPENOISE
Rambouillet
Palaiseau
Orsay
Montgeron
Évry
Corbeil-Essonnes
Arpajon
Mennecy
Melun
Provins
Villiers-St-Georges
Nangis
Donnemarie-Dontilly
Villenauxe-la-Grande
Nogent-sur-Seine
Anglure
Méry-sur-Seine
HUREPOIX
Dourdan
Étréchy
Ablis
Gallardon
Maintenon
Épernon
St-Arnoult-en-Yvelines
Chevreuse
Montfort-l'Amaury
F

17
18
9
26
D
E
F
1
2
3
4
B
D
L
Halle
Waterloo
Braine-l'Alleud
Tubize
Nivelles
Genappe
Seneffe
Manage
Pont-à-Celles
Chapelle-lez-Herlaimont
Courcelles
Charleroi
Fleurus
Gembloux
Jemeppe
Namur
Auvelais
Farciennes
Châtelet
Montignies-le-Tilleul
Gerpinnes
Mettet
Florennes
Dinant
Ciney
Walcourt
Beaumont
Thuin
Ham-sur-Heure
Philippeville
Couvin
Chimay
Bois de Chimay
Forêt de Nismes
Givet
Fumay
Revin
Rocroi
Hirson
Signy-le-Petit
Monthermé
Renwez
Charleville-Mézières
Villers-Semeuse
Sedan
Flize
Donchery
Boulzicourt
Signy-l'Abbaye
Chaumont-Porcien
Novion-Porcien
Rethel
Sault-lès-Rethel
Asfeld
Juniville
Warmeriville
Machault
Attigny
Vouziers
Le Chesne
Tourteron
Omont
Grandpré
Monthois
Buzancy
Stenay
Montmédy
Mouzon
Carignan
Douzy
Bouillon
Florenville
Virton
Etalle
Arlon
Aubange
Longwy
Pétange
Differdange
Esch-sur-Alzette
Dudelange
Bettembourg
LUXEMBOURG
Hesperange
Mersch
Echternach
Diekirch
Ettelbruck
Wiltz
Clervaux
Vianden
Bitburg
Bastogne
Houffalize
Libramont
Neufchâteau
Martelange
Redange
Saint-Hubert
Rochefort
Marche-en-Famenne
La Roche-en-Ardenne
Durbuy
Hotton
Huy
Andenne
Wanze
Amay
Hannut
Waremme
Liège (Luik)
Herstal
Seraing
Flémalle
Chaudfontaine
Fléron
Esneux
Sprimont
Spa
Verviers
Eupen
Malmédy
Stavelot
Stoumont
Vielsalm
St-Vith
Gouvy
Trois-Ponts
Monschau
Hertogenwald
Simmerath
Visé
Soumagne
Herve
Dison
Theux
Aywaille
Hamoir
Ardennes
Famenne
Fagne
Plateau de Semois
Vallée de la Semois
Forêt d'Anlier
Forêt de Chiny
GAUME
Hohe Venn
Vallée de l'Our
Verdun
Dun-sur-Meuse
Damvillers
Forêt de Wœvre
Varennes-en-Argonne
Montfaucon-d'Argonne
Clermont-en-Argonne
Ste-Menehould
Ville-sur-Tourbe
ARGONNE
LORRAINE
Étain
Spincourt
Longuyon
Audun-le-Roman
Thionville
Yutz
Hayange
Fameck
Florange
Rombas
Woippy
Metz
Montigny-lès-Metz
Ars-sur-Moselle
Conflans-en-Jarnisy
Plaine de la Wœvre
Côtes de Moselle
Pont-à-Mousson
Dieulouard
Nancy
Laxou
Villers-lès-Nancy
Vandœuvre-lès-Nancy
Jarville-la-Malgrange
St-Max
St-Nicolas-de-Port
Toul
Commercy
St-Mihiel
Vigneulles-lès-Hattonchâtel
Bar-le-Duc
Ligny-en-Barrois
Void-Vacon
Vaucouleurs
Plateau du Barrois
St-Dizier
Vitry-le-François
Châlons-en-Champagne
Suippes
Reims
Pontfaverger-Moronvilliers
Mont Cornillet
Vaubecourt
Revigny-sur-Ornain
Sermaize-les-Bains
Pierrefitte-sur-Aire
Souilly
Dieue-sur-Meuse
Lac du Der Chantecoq
Arcis-sur-Aube
Wassy
Montiers-sur-Saulx
Eurville-Bienville
Colombey-les-Belles
CHAMPAGNE POUILLEUSE
Sarry
Ecury-sur-Coole
Fagnières
Rehlingen-Siersdorf
Bouzonville
Sierck-les-Bains
Mondorf-les-Bains
Thiaucourt-Regniéville
Château-Salins
Delme
Nomeny

A
B
C
1
2
3
4
BONN
Koblenz
Wiesbaden
Mainz
Trier
LUXEMBOURG
Saarbrücken
Kaiserslautern
Ludwigshafen
Metz
Nancy
Strasbourg
Stolberg
Kreuzau
Weilerswist
St Augustin
Königswinter
Eitorf
Eupen
Verviers
Spa
Malmedy
Monschau
Schleiden
Mechernich
Euskirchen
Rheinbach
Meckenheim
Bad Honnef
Remagen
Sinzig
Bad Neuenahr-Ahrweiler
Bad Münstereifel
Neuwied
Bendorf
Andernach
Montabaur
Hadamar
Limburg an der Lahn
Bad Ems
Lahnstein
Mayen
Boppard
Bad Schwalbach
St Goar
Eltville am Rhein
Oestrich-Winkel
Geisenheim
Ingelheim am Rhein
Bingen am Rhein
Bad Kreuznach
Alzey
Grünstadt
Bad Dürkheim
Neustadt an der Weinstraße
Landau in der Pfalz
Pirmasens
Zweibrücken
Homburg
Neunkirchen
St Wendel
Idar-Oberstein
Morbach
Wittlich
Bitburg
Daun
Gerolstein
Prüm
Clervaux
Wiltz
Diekirch
Ettelbruck
Mersch
Echternach
Konz
Merzig
Saarlouis
Dillingen
Völklingen
Forbach
St-Avold
Sarreguemines
Thionville
Hayange
Florange
Yutz
Dudelange
Differdange
Esch-sur-Alzette
Woippy
Montigny-lès-Metz
Pont-à-Mousson
Toul
Villers-lès-Nancy
Lunéville
Sarrebourg
Saverne
Haguenau
Bischwiller
Schiltigheim
Kehl
Offenburg
Rastatt
Wissembourg
Kaiserslautern
Bexbach

10
17
27

D
E
F
19
11
1
2
3
4
20
28
Gießen
Wetzlar
Fulda
Hünfeld
Meiningen
Suhl
Zella-Mehlis
Hildburghausen
Bad Neustadt an der Saale
Bad Kissingen
Hammelburg
Schweinfurt
Haßfurt
Frankfurt am Main
Offenbach am Main
Hanau
Darmstadt
Aschaffenburg
Würzburg
Kitzingen
Ochsenfurt
Wertheim
Tauberbischofsheim
Bad Mergentheim
Rothenburg ob der Tauber
Mannheim
Heidelberg
Heilbronn
Karlsruhe
Pforzheim
Stuttgart
Ludwigsburg
Esslingen am Neckar
Göppingen
Schwäbisch Hall
Schwäbisch Gmünd
Aalen
Heidenheim an der Brenz
Nördlingen
Dinkelsbühl
Crailsheim
Tübingen
Reutlingen
Böblingen
Nürtingen
Vogelsberg
Spessart
Odenwald
Bauland
Kraichgau
Schönbuch
Hohe Rhön
Hohenloher Ebene
Frankenhöhe
Steigerwald
Haßberge
Grabfeld
Welzheimer Wald
Albuch
Härtsfeld
Virngrund

20
A
12
B
C
1
2
3
4
19
D5
29
Zwickau
Plauen
Hof
VOGTLAND
Cheb
Fichtelgebirge
Schweinfurt
Bamberg
Bayreuth
Fränkische Schweiz
Erlangen
Fürth
Nürnberg
Ansbach
Schwabach
Neumarkt in der Oberpfalz
Amberg
Weiden in der Oberpfalz
Regensburg
Ingolstadt
Donauwörth
Nördlingen
Weißenburg in Bayern
Fränkische Alb
Eichstätt
Kelheim
Landshut
Straubing
Coburg
Kronach
Kulmbach
Lichtenfels
Meiningen
Suhl
Saalfeld
Dingolfing
Pfaffenhofen an der Ilm
Moosburg an der Isar
DONAUMOOS
HALLERTAU

21
13
30
D
E
F
1
2
3
4
PRAHA
Plzeň
Karlovy Vary
Mariánské Lázně
Ústí nad Labem
Teplice
Most
Chomutov
Litvínov
Bílina
Jirkov
Kadaň
Klášterec nad Ohří
Žatec
Louny
Litoměřice
Česká Lípa
Mladá Boleslav
Mělník
Roudnice nad Labem
Kralupy nad Vltavou
Kladno
Slaný
Rakovník
Beroun
Příbram
Rokycany
Benešov
Tábor
Písek
Strakonice
Klatovy
Domažlice
Sušice
Prachatice
České Budějovice
Český Krumlov
Jindřichův Hradec
Vlašim
Nymburk
Poděbrady
Říčany
Brandýs nad Labem-Stará Boleslav
Čelákovice
Neratovice
Dobříš
Horšovský Týn
Stříbro
Ostrov
Sokolov
Aue
Zwönitz
Stollberg
Marienberg
Annaberg-Buchholz
Schwarzenberg
Olbernhau
Zschopau
Deggendorf
Plattling
Osterhofen
Landau an der Isar
Vilshofen
Passau
Regen
Zwiesel
Hauzenberg
Freyung
CZ
A
BOHEMIA
Doupovské Hory
Křivoklátská Vrchovina
Rakovnická Pahorkatina
Tepelská Vrchovina
Brdy
Šumava
Novohradské Hory
Vodní nádrž Lipno
Vodní nádrž Orlík
Vodní nádrž Slapy
Vltava
Labe
Ohře

A
B
C
1
2
3
4
Cork 14 hrs (April - October)
Rosslare 15 hrs (summer only)
Plymouth 6hrs
Île de Batz
Roscoff
Baie de Morlaix
Sillon de Talbert
Île de Bréhat
Pte du Château
Plougrescant
Pleubian
Perros-Guirec
Penvénan
Pte de l'Arcouest
Ploubazlanec
Paimpol
Trégastel
Pleumeur-Bodou
Louannec
Tréguier
Plouguiel
Plouézec
Trébeurden
Lannion
La Roche-Derrien
Pte de Primel
Baie de Lannion
TRÉGORROIS
Plougasnou
Locquirec
Ploubezre
Pontrieux
Plouha
Cléder
Plouescat
St-Pol-de-Léon
Lanmeur
Ploumilliau
Plestin-les-Grèves
Pluzunet
Plouaret
Bégard
Lanvollon
Kerlouan
Guissény
Taulé
St-Martin-des-Champs
Pabu
Plouguerneau
Lannilis
PAYS DE LÉON
Plouzévédé
Plouvorn
Morlaix
Plounévez-Moëdec
Guingamp
Plélo
Châtelaudren
Lesneven
Le Folgoët
Plouigneau
Plougonven
Belle-Isle-en-Terre
Grâces
Ploumagoar
Plouagat
Ploudalmézeau
Plouguin
Landivisiau
St-Thégonnec
Pleyber-Christ
Île d'Ouessant
Porspoder
Plabennec
Lampaul-Guimiliau
Ploufragan
Lampaul-Plouarzel
Milizac
Gouesnou
Landerneau
Ploudiry
Bourbriac
Passage du Fromveur
Plouarzel
St-Renan
Bohars
Guipavas
Plouzané
Guilers
Le Relecq-Kerhuon
Sizun
Roc'h Trévézel
Berrien
Callac
Quintin
Locmaria-Plouzané
Brest
Daoulas
Huelgoat
Le Conquet
Goulet de Brest
Plougastel-Daoulas
Monts d'Arrée
Poullaouen
St-Nicolas-du-Pélem
Pte de St-Mathieu
Montagne St-Michel
Hanvec
Le Faou
Corlay
Camaret-sur-Mer
Presqu'île de Crozon
Plonévez-du-Faou
Carhaix-Plouguer
Maël-Carhaix
Plounévez-Quintin
Pte de Penhir
Pont-de-Buis-lès-Quimerch
Mer d'Iroise
Crozon
Menez Hom
Landeleau
Rostrenen
Plouguernével
Pleyben
Gouarec
Châteaulin
Châteauneuf-du-Faou
Roc de Toullaëron
Mûr-de-Bretagne
Cap de la Chèvre
Baie de Douarnenez
Plomodiern
Montagnes Noires
Gourin
Plouray
BRETAGNE
Cléguérec
Plonévez-Porzay
Briec
Guémené-sur-Scorff
Pontivy
Douarnenez
Ploaré
Ploggonnec
CORNOUAILLE
Coray
Le Faouët
Île de Sein
Le Cap
Pte du Raz
Audierne
Pont-Croix
Plouhinec
Scaër
Ergué-Gabéric
Inguiniel
Melrand
Bubry
Plumélia
Plozévet
Landudec
Quimper
Rosporden
Pouldreuzic
St-Yvy
Bannalec
Tréméven
Baie d'Audierne
Melgven
Mellac
Plouay
Plonéour-Lanvern
Pleuven
Fouesnant
Concarneau
Riec-sur-Belon
Quimperlé
Inzinzac-Lochrist
Baud
Camors
Pont-l'Abbé
Bénodet
Trégunc
Névez
Pont-Aven
Plomeur
Plobannalec
Loctudy
Moëlan-sur-Mer
Clohars-Carnoët
Guidel
Caudan
Hennebont
Languidic
St-Guénolé
Penmarch
Lesconil
Guilvinec
Pte de Penmarch
Lorient
Lanester
Pluvigner
Grand-Champ
Landévant
Anse de Pouldu
Ploemeur
Merlevenez
Riantec
Brech
Larmor-Plage
Port-Louis
Plouhinec
Pluneret
Belz
Auray
Groix
Île de Groix
Erdeven
Bono
Plouharnel
Crach
Carnac
La Trinité-sur-Mer
Locmariaquer
Presqu'île de Quiberon
St-Pierre-Quiberon
Baie de Quiberon
St-Gildas-de-Rhuys
Quiberon
Passage de la Teignouse
Le Palais
Belle-Île
E50
E60
N12
N164
N165
N24
D786
D767
D790
D789
D887
D765
D785
D768

D
E
F
14
23
1
2
3
4
24
32
Les Minquiers
Jersey
Guernsey
Portsmouth
Golfe de St-Malo
Îles Chausey
Montmartin-sur-Mer
Quettreville-sur-Sienne
Tessy-sur-Vire
Bréhal
Cérences
Villedieu-les-Poêles
Percy
St-Sever-Calvados
Vire
Condé-sur-Noireau
Vassy
Clécy
SUISSE NORMANDE
Athis-de-l'Orne
St-Georges-des-Groseillers
Flers
Messei
Tinchebray
Chanu
Collines de Normandie
Donville-les-Bains
Granville
St-Pair-sur-Mer
Jullouville
La Haye-Pesnel
Sartilly
St-Pois
Brécey
Sourdeval
Ger
Juvigny-le-Tertre
Mortain
Lonlay-l'Abbaye
La Ferrière-aux-Étangs
Champsecret
Domfront
Avranches
Ducey
Pte du Grouin
Cancale
Baie du Mont-St-Michel
Mont-St-Michel
Cap Fréhel
Sables-d'Or-les-Pins
Erquy
Fréhel
Dinard
St-Malo
St-Lunaire
St-Briac-sur-Mer
St-Méloir-des-Ondes
Le-Vivier-sur-Mer
Châteauneuf-d'Ille-et-Vilaine
Dol-de-Bretagne
Pontorson
St-Hilaire-du-Harcouët
Barenton
Juvigny-sous-Andaine
Le Teilleul
Passais
Ceaucé
Étables-sur-Mer
Binic
Baie de St-Brieuc
Pléneuf-Val-André
Matignon
St-Jouan-des-Guérets
Ploubalay
Plérin
St-Brieuc
St-Alban
Hénanbihen
Plancoët
Miniac-Morvan
Pleudihen-sur-Rance
Pleine-Fougères
St-James
St-Martin-de-Landelles
Louvigné-du-Désert
Landivy
Fougerolles-du-Plessis
Lassay-les-Châteaux
Langueux
Trégueux
Lamballe
Maroué
Corseul
Dinan
Léhon
St-Pierre-de-Plesguen
Combourg
Meillac
Antrain
St-Brice-en-Coglès
Gorron
Châtillon-sur-Colmont
Ambrières-les-Vallées
Quessoy
PENTHIÈVRE
Jugon-les-Lacs
Évran
Dingé
Lécousse
Fougères
Larchamp
St-Denis-de-Gastines
Oisseau
Mayenne
Plaintel
Moncontour
Plénée-Jugon
Yvignac
Tinténiac
Sens-de-Bretagne
Romagné
Ernée
Montenay
St-Georges-Buttavent
Aron
Plœuc-sur-Lié
Landes du Méné
Collinée
Broons
Caulnes
Bécherel
Hédé
St-Aubin-du-Cormier
Chailland
Plouguenast
Irodouër
St-Aubin-d'Aubigné
Gosné
Juvigné
La Baconnière
Martigné-sur-Mayenne
Trévé
Loudéac
Plémet
Merdrignac
Montauban-de-Bretagne
Romillé
Gévezé
La Chapelle-des-Fougeretz
Betton
Liffré
La Bouëxière
Val-d'Izé
Andouillé
St-Ouen-des-Toits
Montsûrs
St-Méen-le-Grand
Boisgervilly
Bédée
Breteil
Cesson-Sévigné
Servon-sur-Vilaine
Vitré
Port Brillet
Louverné
Laval
Argentré
La Chèze
Ménéac
La Trinité-Porhoët
Iffendic
Talensac
Montfort
Rennes
Châteaubourg
Changé
Bonchamp-lès-Laval
Mauron
Mordelles
St-Jacques-de-la-Lande
Bruz
Vern-sur-Seiche
Châteaugiron
Argentré-du-Plessis
Loiron
Le Pertre
St-Berthevin
L'Huisserie
Rohan
Bréhan
Guilliers
Forêt de Paimpont
Paimpont
Plélan-le-Grand
Goven
Bais
Entrammes
Meslay-du-Maine
Naizin
Josselin
Campénéac
Baulon
Guichen
Corps-Nuds
Janzé
La Guerche-de-Bretagne
Nuillé-sur-Vicoin
Moréac
Guégon
Ploërmel
Guer
Maure-de-Bretagne
Guignen
Le Theil-de-Bretagne
Le Sel-de-Bretagne
Retiers
Cossé-le-Vivien
Ballots
Quelaines-St-Gault
Grez-en-Bouère
Bignan
St-Jean-Brévelay
Plumelec
Sérent
Ruffiac
Carentoir
Pipriac
Guipry
Messac
Bain-de-Bretagne
Martigné-Ferchaud
Congrier
St-Aignan-sur-Roë
Renazé
Craon
Bazouges
Château-Gontier
Azé
Chemazé
Landes de Lanvaux
Malestroit
La Gacilly
Grand-Fougeray
Rougé
Pouancé
Soudan
Noyant-la-Gravoyère
Segré
Monterblanc
Elven
Rochefort-en-Terre
Peillac
Malansac
Châteaubriant
Champigné
St-Avé
Sulniac
Questembert
Redon
St-Nicolas-de-Redon
Derval
Erbray
St-Julien-de-Vouvantes
Vern-d'Anjou
SEGRÉEN
ANJOU
Le Lion-d'Angers
Vannes
Theix
Noyal-Muzillac
Allaire
Fégréac
Guémené-Penfao
Moisdon-la-Rivière
La Meilleraye-de-Bretagne
Candé
La Pouëze
Montreuil-Juigné
Avrillé
Angers
Surzur
Ambon
Muzillac
Péaule
Marzan
St-Dolay
Marsac-sur-Don
Nozay
St-Mars-la-Jaille
Le Louroux-Béconnais
Bécon-les-Granits
Beaucouzé
Sarzeau
Damgan
La Roche-Bernard
Nivillac
Missillac
Plessé
Guenrouet
St-Gildas-des-Bois
Saffré
Riaillé
Joué-sur-Erdre
Presqu'île de Rhuys
Pénestin
Férel
Herbignac
Blain
Nort-sur-Erdre
Mésanger
Ancenis
Varades
Ingrandes
Bouchemaine
St-Georges-sur-Loire
Mûrs-Erigné
Brissac
Assérac
GRANDE BRIÈRE
Pontchâteau
Campbon
Fay-de-Bretagne
Héric
Bouvron
Ligné
Petit-Mars
St-Mars-du-Désert
Oudon
Champtoceaux
Liré
St-Florent-le-Vieil
La Pommeraye
Chalonnes-sur-Loire
Piriac-sur-Mer
Mesquer
St-Joachim
Montoir-de-Bretagne
Savenay
Île de Hœdic
La Turballe
Guérande
La Baule-Escoublac
Donges
Cordemais
La Chapelle-sur-Erdre
Carquefou
St-Laurent-des-Autels
Le Fuilet
Montrevault
St-Pierre-Montlimart
La Jumellière
Thouarcé
Le Croisic
Pte de Croisic
Batz-sur-Mer
Le Pouliguen
Pornichet
St-Nazaire
Trignac
Paimbœuf
St-Étienne-de-Montluc
Orvault
Sautron
Thouaré-sur-Loire
St-Julien-de-Concelles
LES MAUGES
Valanjou
St-Brevin-les-Pins
St-Père-en-Retz
Couëron
St-Herblain
Nantes
Rezé
St-Sébastien-sur-Loire
Beaupréau
Gesté
Chemillé
Jallais
Melay
Vihiers
St-Michel-Chef-Chef
Bouguenais
Vertou
Vallet
Le Pallet
Villedieu-la-Blouère
Le May-sur-Èvre
Trémentines
Coron
Pte de St-Gildas
PAYS DE RETZ
Les Sorinières
Port-St-Père
Aigrefeuille-sur-Maine
Clisson
Montfaucon
Gétigné
St-Macaire-en-Mauges
La Séguinière
Cholet
Pornic
La Bernerie-en-Retz
Arthon-en-Retz
Ste-Pazanne
St-Philbert-de-Grand-Lieu
Cugand
Maulévrier
Baie de Bourgneuf
Pte de l'Herbaudière
Bourgneuf-en-Retz
St-Philbert-de-Bouaine
Montaigu
La Bruffière
La Verrie
Mortagne-sur-Sèvre
St-Pierre-des-Échaubrognes
Les Aubiers
Noirmoutier-en-l'Île
Île de Noirmoutier
Passage du Gois
Bouin
Machecoul
Paulx
Les Landes-Genusson
La Gaubretière
St-Laurent-sur-Sèvre
Mauléon
Nueil-sur-Argent
Barbâtre
Beauvoir-sur-Mer
St-Gervais
La Garnache
Falleron
Touvois
Rocheservière
Les Épesses
Mont des Alouettes
Les Herbiers
La Barre-de-Monts
Notre-Dame-de-Monts
Challans
Legé
Les Lucs-sur-Boulogne
St-Fulgent
Le Boupère
Pouzauges
Cerizay
St-Jean-de-Monts
Soullans
Palluau
Le Poiré-sur-Vie
Belleville-sur-Vie
Les Essarts
La Forêt-sur-Sèvre
Montournais
Aizenay
Chantonnay
Moncoutant
BOCAGE VENDÉEN
Sèvre Nantaise
Hauteurs de la Gâtine
Rance
Vilaine
Loire
Mayenne
Sélune
Seiche
Chère
Oust
Sarthe
E50
E401
E03
E60
E62
A81
A84
A11
A83
A87
E03/401

24
15
23
33
A
B
C
1
2
3
4
SUISSE NORMANDE
PAYS D'OUCHE
Collines de Normandie
Vire
Flers
Argentan
Vimoutiers
Gacé
La Ferté-Frênel
Rugles
Breteuil
Damville
Dreux
Vernouillet
Tillières-sur-Avre
Nonancourt
Verneuil-sur-Avre
L'Aigle
St-Sulpice-sur-Risle
Le Merlerault
Moulins-la-Marche
Sées
Mortrée
Courtomer
Domfront
La Ferté-Macé
Carrouges
Rânes
Briouze
Messei
Putanges-Pont-Écrepin
Écouché
Athis-de-l'Orne
Tinchebray
Condé-sur-Noireau
Falaise
Clécy
Vassy
Barenton
Juvigny-sous-Andaine
Passais
Ceaucé
Couterne
Lassay-les-Châteaux
Gorron
Ambrières-les-Vallées
Châtillon-sur-Colmont
Alençon
Damigni
Arçonnay
St-Paterne
Pervenchères
Mamers
Bellême
Mortagne-au-Perche
Le Mêle-sur-Sarthe
Bazoches-sur-Hoëne
Tourouvre
Longny-au-Perche
Senonches
La Loupe
Châteauneuf-en-Thymerais
Brézolles
Mainvilliers
Lucé
Courville-sur-Eure
Bailleau-le-Pin
Illiers-Combray
Thiron Gardais
Nogent-le-Rotrou
Rémalard
Noce
Condé-sur-Huisne
Bretoncelles
Mayenne
Aron
Les Coëvrons
Evron
Bais
Fresnay-sur-Sarthe
Beaumont-sur-Sarthe
Sillé-le-Guillaume
Marolles-les-Braults
St-Cosme-en-Vairais
La Ferté-Bernard
Bonnétable
Le Theil
Ceton
Authon-du-Perche
La Bazoche-Gouet
Unverre
Brou
Bonneval
Arrou
Châteaudun
Cloyes-sur-le-Loir
Droué
Mondoubleau
Montmirail
Vibraye
Laval
Louverné
Argentré
Bonchamp-lès-Laval
L'Huisserie
Entrammes
Nuillé-sur-Vicoin
Meslay-du-Maine
Vaiges
Ste-Suzanne
Brûlon
Loué
Le Mans
Coulaines
Allonnes
Changé
Ruaudin
Arnage
Mulsanne
Parigné-l'Évêque
Savigné-l'Évêque
La Milesse
Ballon
Beaufay
Tuffé
Connerré
Montfort-le-Gesnois
Dollon
St-Mars-la-Brière
Bouloire
St-Calais
Savigny-sur-Braye
Bessé-sur-Braye
Vendôme
St-Ouen
Morée
La Ville-aux-Clercs
Le Grand-Lucé
Écommoy
Marigné-Laillé
Jupilles
Cérans-Foulletourte
La Suze-sur-Sarthe
Noyen-sur-Sarthe
Sablé-sur-Sarthe
Parcé-sur-Sarthe
Malicorne-sur-Sarthe
Château-Gontier
Azé
Bazouges
Grez-en-Bouère
Bierné
Précigné
La Flèche
Durtal
Daumeray
Châteauneuf-sur-Sarthe
Champigné
Le Lion-d'Angers
Segré
Tiercé
Seiches-sur-le-Loir
Jarzé
Baugé
Angers
Avrillé
Trélazé
Les Ponts-de-Cé
Beaufort-en-Vallée
Longué-Jumelles
Saumur
Allonnes
Bourgueil
Château-du-Loir
Montoire-sur-le-Loir
La Chartre-sur-le-Loir
Château-la-Vallière
Neuillé-Pont-Pierre
Château-Renault
Herbault
Blois
Onzain
Chouzy-sur-Cisse
Amboise
Nazelles-Négron
Vouvray
Tours
St-Cyr-sur-Loire
St-Pierre-des-Corps
St-Avertin
Joué-lès-Tours
Chambray-lès-Tours
Montlouis
Bléré
Montrichard
Langeais
Cinq-Mars-la-Pile
Azay-le-Rideau
Chinon
Avoine
Fontevraud-l'Abbaye
L'Île-Bouchard
Ste-Maure-de-Touraine
Loches
Ligueil
Descartes
Richelieu
Loudun
Les Trois-Moutiers
Montreuil-Bellay
Doué-la-Fontaine
Thouars
Bressuire
Châtellerault
Dangé-St-Romain
Ingrandes
La Roche-Posay
Preuilly-sur-Claise
Le Grand-Pressigny
Châtillon-sur-Indre
Montrésor
Beaulieu-lès-Loches
Cholet
Maulévrier
Mauléon
Vihiers
Chemillé
Coron
Le Puy-Notre-Dame
Airvault
Argenton-Château
St-Varent
Lencloître
Mirebeau
Neuville-de-Poitou
Scorbé-Clairvaux
Pleumartin
MAINE
ANJOU
BAUGEOIS
SAUMUROIS
MAUGES
TOURAINE
GÂTINE
CHAMPAGNE
BRENNE
Les Vaux du Loir
Plateau de Ste-Maure
Hauteurs de la Gâtine

25
16
26
34
D
E
F
1
2
3
4
PARIS
Aubergenville
St-Germain-en-Laye
St-Denis
Nanterre
Le Raincy
Lagny-sur-Marne
Quincy-Voisins
Crécy-la-Chapelle
Jouarre
Rebais
Montmirail
Rueil-Malmaison
Boulogne-Billancourt
Marne-la-Vallée
Coulommiers
Septeuil
Plaisir
Versailles
Ivry-sur-Seine
Pontault-Combault
Faremoutiers
La Ferté-Gaucher
Esternay
Champenoise
Houdan
Montfort-l'Amaury
Trappes
Antony
Créteil
Ozoir-la-Ferrière
Tournan-en-Brie
Sézanne
Chevreuse
Palaiseau
Orsay
Montgeron
Brie-Comte-Robert
Rozay-en-Brie
Villiers-St-Georges
St-Léger-en-Yvelines
Forêt de Rambouillet
Rambouillet
Évry
Corbeil-Essonnes
Guignes
Mormant
Villenauxe-la-Grande
Anglure
Nogent-le-Roi
Épernon
St-Arnoult-en-Yvelines
Arpajon
Mennecy
Cesson
Melun
Vaux-le-Pénil
Nangis
Provins
Romilly-sur-Seine
Maintenon
HUREPOIX
BRIE
Montois
Gallardon
Dourdan
Étréchy
La Ferté-Alais
Perthes
Longueville
Donnemarie-Dontilly
Nogent-sur-Seine
Jouy
Ablis
Milly-la-Forêt
Fontainebleau
Avon
Champagne-sur-Seine
Bray-sur-Seine
Marigny-le-Châtel
Auneau
Béville-le-Comte
Étampes
Maisse
Forêt de Fontainebleau
Moret-sur-Loing
Montereau-Fault-Yonne
Val de Seine
Chartres
Sours
Villeneuve-la-Guyard
Sergines
Thorigny-sur-Oreuse
Marcilly-le-Hayer
Dammarie
Méréville
Sermaises
Malesherbes
La Chapelle-la-Reine
St-Pierre-lès-Nemours
Champigny
Pont-sur-Yonne
La Chapelle
Voves
Angerville
Nemours
Voulx
Lorrez-le-Bocage-Préaux
Soucy
Villeneuve-l'Archevêque
Estissac
Aix-en-Othe
BEAUCE
Toury
Outarville
Pithiviers
Bagneaux-sur-Loing
Souppes-sur-Loing
Puiseaux
Chéroy
Sens
St-Clément
Paron
Orgères-en-Beauce
Janville
Bazoches-les-Gallerandes
GÂTINAIS
Château-Landon
Dordives
St-Valérien
Cerisiers
Villeneuve-sur-Yonne
Boynes
Ferrières
Neuville-aux-Bois
Artenay
Chilleurs-aux-Bois
Beaune-La-Rolande
Corbeilles
Châlette-sur-Loing
Courtenay
St-Julien-du-Sault
PAYS D'OTHE
Forêt d'Othe
Brienon-sur-Armançon
St-Florentin
Patay
Chevilly
ORLÉANAIS
Loury
Traînou
Pannes
Ladon
Villemandeur
Montargis
Joigny
Migennes
Cheny
Vergigny
Épieds-en-Beauce
Saran
Fleury-les-Aubrais
Bellegarde
Amilly
Triguères
Douchy
Charmoy
Seignelay
Ligny-le-Châtel
St-Jean-de-la-Ruelle
Orléans
St-Jean-de-Braye
Chécy
Vimory
Châteaurenard
Montcresson
Charny
Aillant-sur-Tholon
Jargeau
Châteauneuf-sur-Loire
Lorris
Canal d'Orléans
Monéteau
Auxerre
Venoy
Chablis
Meung-sur-Loire
St-Ay
Olivet
Sandillon
Loire
St-Benoît-sur-Loire
Les Bordes
Nogent-sur-Vernisson
Châtillon-Coligny
St-Georges-sur-Baulche
Pourrain
AUXERROIS
Beaugency
Cléry-St-André
Tigy
Sully-sur-Loire
Ouzouer-sur-Loire
Champignelles
Toucy
Champs-sur-Yonne
St-Bris-le-Vineux
Lailly-en-Val
Jouy-le-Potier
Marcilly-en-Villette
Val d'Orléans
Gien
Bléneau
Coulanges-la-Vineuse
Vermenton
Mer
St-Laurent-Nouan
La Ferté-St-Aubin
Briare
Canal de Briare
St-Fargeau
St-Sauveur-en-Puisaye
Courson-les-Carrières
St-Victor
Vouzon
Coullons
Lamotte-Beuvron
Châtillon-sur-Loire
PUISAYE
Bonny-sur-Loire
Brinon-sur-Sauldre
Beaulieu-sur-Loire
Coulanges-sur-Yonne
Cour-Cheverny
SOLOGNE
Neung-sur-Beuvron
Nouan-le-Fuzelier
Argent-sur-Sauldre
Blancafort
St-Amand-en-Puisaye
Entrains-sur-Nohain
Clamecy
Vézelay
Aubigny-sur-Nère
Vailly-sur-Sauldre
Léré
Cosne-Cours-sur-Loire
Souesmes
Salbris
Soings-en-Sologne
Mur-de-Sologne
Selles-St-Denis
La Ferté-Imbault
La Chapelle-d'Angillon
Donzy
Varzy
Tannay
Pruniers-en-Sologne
Romorantin-Lanthenay
Villefranche-sur-Cher
Theillay
Neuvy-sur-Barangeon
Collines du Sancerrois
Henrichemont
Sancerre
Pouilly-sur-Loire
Brinon-sur-Beuvron
Corbigny
Lormes
Selles-sur-Cher
Gièvres
Vierzon
Menetou-Salon
Herry
Prémery
Chabris
St-Christophe-en-Bazelle
Méreau
Foëcy
Mehun-sur-Yèvre
St-Martin-d'Auxigny
Fussy
Les Aix-d'Angillon
Sancergues
La Charité-sur-Loire
Valençay
Massay
Gracay
Lury-sur-Arnon
Marmagne
St-Doulchard
St-Germain-du-Puy
Baugy
St-Saulge
Guérigny
Pougues-les-Eaux
Châtillon-en-Bazois
Lucay-le-Mâle
Vatan
Reuilly
Bourges
SEPTAINE
Garchizy
Urzy
Varennes-Vauzelles
CHAMPAGNE BERRICHONNE
La Chapelle-St-Ursin
Trouy
Avord
Nérondes
Fourchambault
Nevers
St-Benin-d'Azy
Levroux
Ste-Lizaigne
Chârost
St-Florent-sur-Cher
La Guerche-sur-l'Aubois
Imphy
La Machine
Cercy-la-Tour
Issoudun
Civray
Lunery
Levet
Dun-sur-Auron
BERRY
Vineuil
Neuvy-Pailloux
Magny-Cours
St-Parize-le-Châtel
St-Léger-des-Vignes
Decize
Fours
Déols
Châteauroux
St-Maur
Châteauneuf-sur-Cher
Chezal-Benoît
Sancoins
St-Pierre-le-Moûtier
Le Poinçonnet
Lignières
Charenton-du-Cher
Ainay-le-Château
Lurcy-Lévis
Dornes
Chevagnes
Le Châtelet
Canal du Berry
Canal latéral à la Loire
Allier
Aron
Auron
Arnon
Yonne
Vanne
Seine
Cure
Loing
Essonne
Eure
A6
A10
A11
A19
A20
A5
A71
A77
A85
E05
E09
E11
E15
E50
E54
E511
E60
E604
N4
N6
N7
N10
N12
N19
N20
N36
N60
N76
N104
N151
N152
N154
N191
N81
N77

26
A
B
C
17
1
2
3
4
25
35
Sézanne
Esternay
Fère-Champenoise
Connantre
CÔTE
Mailly-le-Camp
CHAMPAGNE POUILLEUSE
Vitry-le-François
Frignicourt
Revigny-sur-Ornain
Sermaize-les-Bains
Pargny-sur-Saulx
Thiéblemont-Farémont
Villiers-en-Lieu
St-Dizier
Bar-le-Duc
Fains-Véel
Longeville-en-Barrois
Ligny-en-Barrois
Void-Vacon
Lérouville
Commercy
St-Mihiel
Euville
Sorcy-St-Martin
Plateau du Barrois
Montois
Villenauxe-la-Grande
Anglure
Plancy-l'Abbaye
St-Just-Sauvage
Romilly-sur-Seine
Méry-sur-Seine
Seine
Aube
Canal de la Haute Seine
Arcis-sur-Aube
Nogent-sur-Seine
Marigny-le-Châtel
Marcilly-le-Hayer
Thorigny-sur-Oreuse
St-Lyé
La Chapelle-St-Luc
Ste-Savine
Pont-Ste-Marie
Troyes
St-André-les-Vergers
Estissac
Villeneuve-l'Archevêque
Aix-en-Othe
Bouilly
Vanne
Lac du Der Chantecoq
Chavanges
CHAMPAGNE HUMIDE
Eclaron-Braucourt-Ste-Livière
Ancerville
Eurville-Bienville
Wassy
Montier-en-Der
Chevillon
Montiers-sur-Saulx
Houdelaincourt
Gondrecourt-le-Château
Vaucouleurs
Joinville
Poissons
VALLAGE
Doulevant-le-Château
Soulaines-Dhuys
Brienne-le-Château
Piney
Lac du Temple
Doulaincourt-Saucourt
Liffol-le-Grand
Neufchâteau
Coussey
Vignory
Lusigny-sur-Barse
Vendeuvre-sur-Barse
Bar-sur-Aube
Juzennecourt
Andelot-Blancheville
St-Blin-Semilly
Bologne
Bourmont
Chaumont
Brottes
Biesles
Clefmont
Lamarche
Nogent
Val-de-Meuse
Plaine Lorraine
Cerisiers
Villeneuve-sur-Yonne
PAYS D'OTHE
Forêt d'Othe
Bar-sur-Seine
Essoyes
Chaource
Ervy-le-Châtel
Brienon-sur-Armançon
St-Florentin
Cheny
Vergigny
Flogny-la-Chapelle
Ligny-le-Châtel
Seignelay
Charmoy
Monéteau
Auxerre
Venoy
Chablis
Tonnerre
Tanlay
Cruzy-le-Châtel
Laignes
Mussy-sur-Seine
Montigny-sur-Aube
Châteauvillain
Semoutiers-Montsaon
Arc-en-Barrois
Rolampont
Neuilly-l'Évêque
Bourbonne-les-Bains
Langres
Laferté-sur-Amance
Chalindrey
Fayl-la-Forêt
Le Haut du Sec
Auberive
Châtillon-sur-Seine
Recey-sur-Ource
Aisey-sur-Seine
Ancy-le-Franc
AUXERROIS
Canal de Bourgogne
St-Bris-le-Vineux
Vermenton
Noyers
Coulanges-la-Vineuse
Courson-les-Carrières
Coulanges-sur-Yonne
L'Isle-sur-Serein
Montbard
Baigneux-les-Juifs
Aignay-le-Duc
Grancey-le-Château-Nouvelle
Le Vallinot-Longeau-Percey
Prauthoy
Plateau de Langres
Plateau de la Haute-Saône
Champlitte
Dampierre-sur-Salon
Selongey
Is-sur-Tille
Fontaine-Française
Autrey-lès-Gray
Arc-lès-Gray
Gray
Vézelay
Avallon
Terre Plaine
Quarré-les-Tombes
Semur-en-Auxois
Venarey-les-Laumes
Vitteaux
St-Seine-l'Abbaye
Mont Tasselot
Précy-sous-Thil
Armançon
Tannay
Brinon-sur-Beuvron
Corbigny
Lormes
Morvan
Saulieu
Pouilly-en-Auxois
Sombernon
Talant
Dijon
Chenôve
St-Apollinaire
Arc-sur-Tille
Mirebeau
Pontailler-sur-Saône
Pesmes
Marnay
Montmirey-le-Château
Genlis
Fénay
Gevrey-Chambertin
Auxonne
Massif de la Serre
Rochefort-sur-Nenon
Forêt de Chaux
Dole
Vauclaix
Montsauche-les-Settons
Liernais
Montagne de Bard
Arnay-le-Duc
Bligny-sur-Ouche
Nuits-St-Georges
Brazey-en-Plaine
Longecourt-en-Plaine
St-Jean-de-Losne
Tavaux
Saulge
Châtillon-en-Bazois
Château-Chinon
Le Télégraphe
Lucenay-l'Évêque
Haut-Folin
Moulins-Engilbert
Autun
Épinac
Nolay
Beaune
St-Aubin
Seurre
Chemin
Chaussin
Montbarrey
Mont-sous-Vaudrey
AUTUNOIS
CÔTE D'OR
BOURGOGNE
La Machine
Cercy-la-Tour
St-Léger-des-Vignes
Mont Beuvray
St-Léger-sous-Beuvray
Étang-sur-Arroux
Auxy
Chagny
Mont de Rome Château
Demigny
Rully
Gergy
Verdun-sur-le-Doubs
Doubs
St-Sernin-du-Bois
Couches
Fontaines
St-Léger-sur-Dheune
Châtenoy-le-Royal
Givry
Chalon-sur-Saône
St-Marcel
Mervans
Chaumergy
Sellières
VIGNOBLE
Poligny
Fours
Luzy
Mont Julien
Le Creusot
Montcenis
Le Breuil
Torcy
Écuisses
Montchanin
Blanzy
Montceau-les-Mines
Buxy
Ouroux-sur-Saône
St-Germain-du-Bois
Bletterans
Voiteur
Lons-le-Saunier
Conliège
Toulon-sur-Arroux
Issy-l'Évêque
Bourbon-Lancy
Gueugnon
Perrecy
St-Vallier
Canal latéral à la Loire
Beaurepaire-en-Bresse
Montret
Branges
Louhans
Simandre
Seille
A5
A6
A26
A31
A36
A38
A39
E15
E17
E21
E54
E60
E511
E607

27
18
28
36
D
E
F
1
2
3
4
Lorraine
Dieulouard
Château-Salins
Dieuze
Phalsbourg
Hochfelden
Haguenau
Bischwiller
Pompey
Liverdun
Frouard
Custines
Bouxières-aux-Dames
Vic-sur-Seille
Étang du Stock
Réding
Sarrebourg
Saverne
Marmoutier
Nancy
St-Max
Jarville-la-Malgrange
Vandœuvre-lès-Nancy
Laxou
Villers-lès-Nancy
Toul
Gondreville
Chaligny
Arracourt
Réchicourt-le-Château
Dabo
Wasselonne
Truchtersheim
Hœnheim
Bischheim
Schiltigheim
Strasbourg
Kehl
Achern
Bühl
Rheinau
St-Nicolas-de-Port
Lunéville
Abreschviller
Cirey-sur-Vezouze
St-Quirin
Blâmont
Marlenheim
Mutzig
Lingolsheim
Ostwald
Illkirch-Graffenstaden
Oberkirch
Offenburg
Ortenberg
Ohlsbach
Gengenbach
Flavigny-sur-Moselle
Blainville-sur-l'Eau
Vézelise
Haroué
Gerbéviller
Bayon
Badonviller
Baccarat
Rosheim
Bischoffsheim
Obernai
Barr
Andlau
Schirmeck
La Broque
Erstein
Benfeld
Rhinau
Gerstheim
Friesenheim
Lahr
XAINTOIS
Charmes
Mirecourt
Portieux
Vincey
Rambervillers
Châtel-sur-Moselle
Raon-l'Étape
Senones
Étival-Clairefontaine
St-Michel-sur-Meurthe
Provenchères-sur-Fave
Saales
Col de Saales
Villé
Scherwiller
Châtenois
Sélestat
Kippenheim
Mahlberg
Ettenheim
Thaon-les-Vosges
Igney
Chavelot
Golbey
Épinal
Dompaire
Vittel
Bulgnéville
Contrexéville
St-Dié
Taintrux
Brouvelieures
Bruyères
St-Léonard
Anould
Corcieux
Granges-sur-Vologne
Ste-Marie-aux-Mines
St-Hippolyte
Fraize
Col du Bonhomme
Riquewihr
Kaysersberg
Lapoutroie
Plainfaing
Ingersheim
Colmar
Horbourg-Wihr
Herbolzheim
Weisweil
Wyhl
Kenzingen
Malterdingen
Teningen
Emmendingen
Waldkirch
Elzach
Furtwangen im Schwarzwald
Marckolsheim
Sasbach
Endingen
Oberrotweil
Ihringen
Breisach am Rhein
Neuf-Brisach
Denzlingen
Gundelfingen
Freiburg im Breisgau
St Peter
Martigny-les-Bains
Darney
Monthureux-sur-Saône
Les Forges
Arches
Pouxeux
Le Tholy
Xonrupt-Longemer
Col de la Schlucht
Wintzenheim
Gérardmer
Hohneck
Munster
Xertigny
Hadol
St-Nabord
Remiremont
St-Étienne-lès-Remiremont
Vagney
La Bresse
Cornimont
La Vôge
Bains-les-Bains
Plombières-les-Bains
Aillevillers-et-Lyaumont
Rouffach
Guebwiller
Fessenheim
Hartheim
Bad Krozingen
Staufen im Breisgau
Ebringen
Kirchzarten
Hinterzarten
Feldberg
Titisee
Lenzkirch
Vauvillers
St-Loup-sur-Semouse
Fontaine-lès-Luxeuil
Luxeuil-les-Bains
Fougerolles
Rupt-sur-Moselle
Le Thillot
Bussang
Col de Bussang
St-Amarin
Soultz-Haut-Rhin
Bollwiller
Pulversheim
Ensisheim
Neuenburg am Rhein
Müllheim
Badenweiler
Todtnau
Bernau
Polaincourt-et-Clairefontaine
Amance
Froideconche
St-Sauveur
Faucogney-et-la-Mer
Servance
St-Maurice-sur-Moselle
Ballon d'Alsace
Cernay
Thann
Wittelsheim
Kingersheim
Wittenheim
Illzach
Lutterbach
Mulhouse
Riedisheim
Rixheim
Habsheim
Auggen
Bad Bellingen
Kandern
Todtmoos
Häusern
Jussey
Faverney
Mélisey
Masevaux
Giromagny
Rougemont-le-Château
Combeaufontaine
Port-sur-Saône
Saulx
Ronchamp
Plancher-Bas
Champagney
Lure
Valdoie
Belfort
Essert
Fontaine
Danjoutin
Dannemarie
Carspach
Altkirch
Hirsingue
Sierentz
Bartenheim
St-Louis
Allschwil
Basel
Riehen
Weil am Rhein
Lörrach
Efringen-Kirchen
Steinen
Schopfheim
Wehr
Bad Säckingen
Rheinfelden
Zell im Wiesental
Waldshut
Scey-sur-Saône-et-St-Albin
Vaivre-et-Montoille
Noidans-lès-Vesoul
Vesoul
Echenoz-la-Méline
Noroy-le-Bourg
Héricourt
Châtenois-les-Forges
Grandvillars
Delle
Boncourt
Ferrette
Muttenz
Pratteln
Reinach
Dornach
Liestal
Sissach
Frick
Villersexel
Montbéliard
Sochaux
Beaucourt
Audincourt
Seloncourt
Valentigney
Hérimoncourt
L'Isle-sur-le-Doubs
Rougemont
Montbozon
Porrentruy
Alle
Courgenay
Damvant
Bassecourt
Zwingen
Laufen
Breitenbach
Waldenburg
Hölstein
Delémont
Courrendlin
Mümliswil
Balsthal
Aarau
Olten
Aarburg
Zofingen
Rioz
Marchaux
Clerval
Baume-les-Dames
Lomont
Pont-de-Roide
St-Hippolyte
Doubs
Moutier
Court
Oensingen
Niederbipp
Wangen
Aarwangen
Langenthal
Solothurn
Grenchen
Biberist
Zuchwil
Miserey-Salines
Thise
Roche-lez-Beaupré
Roulans
Sancey-le-Grand
Aïssey
Besançon
Saône
Franois
Maîche
Saignelégier
Tramelan
Tavannes
Sonceboz
Damprichard
Le Noirmont
Pierrefontaine-les-Varans
Mamirolle
St-Imier
Courtelary
Chasseral
Biel
Nidau
Bätterkinden
Büren an der Aare
Lyss
Fraubrunnen
Kriegstetten
Herzogenbuchsee
Huttwil
Willisau
Boussières
Valdahon
Orchamps-Vennes
Le Russey
La Chaux-de-Fonds
Dombresson
Cernier
Cressier
La Neuveville
Erlach
Aarberg
Kirchberg
Burgdorf
Eriswil
Sumiswald
Ornans
Amancey
Morteau
Les Fins
Le Locle
St-Blaise
Neuchâtel
Ins
Kerzers
Zollikofen
Bolligen
Ostermundigen
Worb
Hasle
Langnau
Entlebuch
Montbenoît
Les Ponts-de-Martel
Colombier
Boudry
Lac de Neuchâtel
Murten
Laupen
BERN
Köniz
Belp
Münsingen
Schlosswil
Eggiwil
Escholzmatt
Pontarlier
Levier
Couvet
Travers
Môtiers
Fleurier
Le Chasseron
Estavayer-le-Lac
Avenches
MITTELLAND
Marbach
Forêt de la Joux
Frasne
La Cluse-et-Mijoux
Jougne
Le Mont d'Or
Ste-Croix
Yverdon
Payerne
Fribourg
Tafers
Schwarzenburg
Uetendorf
Steffisburg
Wattenwil
Thun
Spiez
Brienz
Nozeroy
Mont de St-Sorlin
Mouthe
Vallorbe
Orbe
Romainmôtier
Yvonand
Thierrens
Romont
Plaffeien
La Roche
La Berra
Gantrisch
Stockhorn
Bönigen
Interlaken
Schwarzhorn
Corbières
Lac de la Gruyère
Moudon
Echallens
L'Abbaye
Lac de Joux
Charmey
Jaun
Frutigen
Reichenbach
Wengen
Lauterbrunnen
Grindelwald
Eiger
Simmental
Thuner See
CH
BREISGAU
VOSGES
ALSACE
PLAINE D'ALSACE
Canal du Rhône au Rhin

28
19
37
27
A
B
C
1
2
3
4
D
CH
FL
Stuttgart
Esslingen am Neckar
Böblingen
Sindelfingen
Leonberg
Göppingen
Schwäbisch Gmünd
Aalen
Heidenheim an der Brenz
Tübingen
Reutlingen
Metzingen
Nürtingen
Rottenburg am Neckar
Nagold
Calw
Freudenstadt
Baden-Baden
Offenburg
Gengenbach
Oberkirch
Achern
Bühl
Horb am Neckar
Sulz am Neckar
Oberndorf am Neckar
Hechingen
Balingen
Albstadt
Rottweil
Schramberg
St Georgen im Schwarzwald
Villingen
Schwenningen
Trossingen
Tuttlingen
Donaueschingen
Waldkirch
Sigmaringen
Meßstetten
Spaichingen
Ulm
Neu-Ulm
Blaubeuren
Ehingen
Laupheim
Biberach an der Riß
Memmingen
Saulgau
Pfullendorf
Stockach
Ludwigshafen
Singen
Radolfzell am Bodensee
Überlingen
Konstanz
Markdorf
Friedrichshafen
Ravensburg
Weingarten
Tettnang
Lindau
Wangen im Allgäu
Isny im Allgäu
Leutkirch im Allgäu
Kempten
Bad Wurzach
Bad Waldsee
Bregenz
Dornbirn
Hohenems
Götzis
Rankweil
Feldkirch
Bludenz
VADUZ
Schaffhausen
Neuhausen
Waldshut
Tiengen
Winterthur
Frauenfeld
Kreuzlingen
Arbon
Rorschach
St Gallen
Gossau
Herisau
Wil
Bülach
Kloten
Baden
Wettingen
Zürich
Wallisellen
Dübendorf
Uster
Wetzikon
Rüti
Jona
Horgen
Wädenswil
Meilen
Stäfa
Thalwil
Adliswil
Dietikon
Schlieren
Aarau
Zofingen
Wohlen
Zug
Baar
Cham
Luzern
Emmen
Kriens
Horw
Littau
Ebikon
Schwyz
Einsiedeln
Glarus
Chur
Davos
Arosa
Bad Ragaz
Landquart
Sargans
Buchs
Altdorf
Stans
Sarnen
Engelberg
Meiringen
Andermatt
Disentis
Ilanz
Thusis
Bodensee
Zürichsee
Walensee
Vierwaldstätter See
Zuger See
SCHÖNBUCH
HEGAU
LINZGAU
TOGGENBURG
SURSELVA
Rhätikon
Silvretta Gruppe
ENGADIN

D
E
20
F
29
1
2
3
4
30
38
39
Nördlingen
Donauwörth
Ingolstadt
Neuburg an der Donau
Abensberg
Kelheim
Mainburg
Landshut
Dingolfing
Vilsbiburg
Eggenfelden
Dillingen an der Donau
Gundelfingen an der Donau
Augsburg
Gersthofen
Friedberg
Stadtbergen
Aichach
Schrobenhausen
Pfaffenhofen an der Ilm
Freising
Moosburg an der Isar
Erding
Dorfen
Mühldorf am Inn
Waldkraiburg
Dachau
Unterschleißheim
Garching bei München
Ismaning
Neufahrn bei Freising
Karlsfeld
Fürstenfeldbruck
Germering
Puchheim
Gilching
München
Haar
Vaterstetten
Unterhaching
Taufkirchen
Gräfelfing
Planegg
Ottobrunn
Neubiberg
Grafing bei München
Krumbach
Schwabmünchen
Königsbrunn
Bobingen
Mindelheim
Landsberg am Lech
Starnberg
Gauting
Wörishofen
Kaufbeuren
Marktoberdorf
Schongau
Peiting
Peißenberg
Weilheim in Oberbayern
Penzberg
Wolfratshausen
Geretsried
Holzkirchen
Bad Tölz
Miesbach
Bad Aibling
Bruckmühl
Rosenheim
Kolbermoor
Wasserburg am Inn
Trostberg
Traunreut
Traunstein
Chiemsee
Chiemgauer Alpen
Füssen
Murnau am Staffelsee
Garmisch-Partenkirchen
Mittenwald
Ammergauer Alpen
Estergebirge
Mangfallgebirge
Kufstein
Wörgl
Kitzbühel
Kaisergebirge
Karwendelgebirge
Schwaz
Jenbach
Hall in Tirol
Innsbruck
Telfs
Imst
Landeck
Zams
Reutte
Lechtaler Alpen
Kitzbüheler Alpen
Zillertaler Alpen
Stubaier Alpen
Ötztaler Alpen
Hohe Tauern
Tuxer Gebirge
Mayrhofen
Sölden
Matrei am Brenner
Steinach am Brenner
Brenner
Vipiteno
Bressanone
Brunico
Merano
OSTTIROL
St Jakob in Defereggen
Nauders
I
Großglockner

30
A
21
B
C
1
2
3
4
29
39
D
CZ
MÜHLVIERTEL
SALZKAMMERGUT
Passau
Vilshofen
Plattling
Landau an der Isar
Osterhofen
Dingolfing
Vilsbiburg
Eggenfelden
Pfarrkirchen
Hauzenberg
Český Krumlov
Linz
Leonding
Traun
Ansfelden
Enns
Steyr
Wels
Marchtrenk
Ried im Innkreis
Braunau am Inn
Mühldorf am Inn
Altötting
Burghausen
Trostberg
Traunreut
Traunstein
Freilassing
Salzburg
Bad Reichenhall
Hallein
Vöcklabruck
Gmunden
Bad Ischl
Waidhofen
Liezen
Kitzbühel
Saalfelden am Steinernen Meer
Bischofshofen
Zell am See
Lienz
Spittal an der Drau
Villach
Feldkirchen in Kärnten
St Veit an der Glan
Judenburg
Chiemsee
Traunsee
Attersee
Mondsee
Wolfgangsee
Hohe Tauern
Niedere Tauern
Dachstein Gruppe
Großglockner 3798
Großvenediger 3674
Radstädter Tauern
Gurktaler Alpen
Gailtaler Alpen
Karnische Alpen
Zillertaler Alpen
Dolomiten

D
E
F
1
2
3
4
Gmünd
Nové Hrady
Stropnice
Weitra
Zwettl
Waidhofen an der Thaya
Dietmanns
Groß-Siegharts
Raabs an der Thaya
Geras
Retz
Znojmo
Jaroslavice
Hrušovany nad Jevišovkou
Mikulov
Břeclav
Valtice
Lednice
Podivín
Lanžhot
Kostice
Brodské
Kúty
Moravský Svätý Ján
Malacky
Jakubov
Zohor
Stupava
Laa an der Thaya
Poysdorf
Mistelbach
Wilfersdorf
Zistersdorf
Drösing
Dürnkrut
Hohenau an der March
Hollabrunn
Ernstbrunn
Stockerau
Korneuburg
Tulln
Krems an der Donau
Melk
Spitz
Göttweig
Klosterneuburg
WIEN
Schwechat
Fischamend-Markt
Hainburg an der Donau
Bruck an der Leitha
Parndorf
Neusiedl am See
Neusiedler See
Purbach am Neusiedler See
Rust
Podersdorf am See
Eisenstadt
Sopron
Mattersburg
Wiener Neustadt
Neunkirchen
Ternitz
Gloggnitz
Semmering
Mürzzuschlag
Krieglach
Kindberg
Kapfenberg
Bruck an der Mur
Leoben
Trofaiach
Eisenerz
Knittelfeld
Graz
Köflach
Voitsberg
Weiz
Gleisdorf
Hartberg
Pinkafeld
Oberwart
Güssing
Fürstenfeld
Feldbach
Leibnitz
Deutschlandsberg
Wolfsberg
St Andrä
Völkermarkt
Dravograd
Pesnica
Murska Sobota
Radenci
Bad Radkersburg
Mureck
Szentgotthárd
Körmend
Szombathely
Kőszeg
Sárvár
Zalaegerszeg
Jennersdorf
Ybbs an der Donau
Amstetten
Waidhofen an der Ybbs
Scheibbs
Lilienfeld
St.Pölten
Purkersdorf
Pressbaum
Perchtoldsdorf
Mödling
Baden
Bad Vöslau
Traiskirchen
Himberg
Gänserndorf
Wolkersdorf
Marchegg
Mariazell
Gußwerk
Lunzer See
Göstling an der Ybbs
Lassing
Wildalpen
Hochschwab
Kalwang
Judenburg
Zeltweg
Frohnleiten
Peggau
Gratkorn
Bärnbach
Lannach
Wildon
Gralla
Straden
Jagerberg
Fehring
Kirchberg am Wechsel
Aspang-Markt
Friedberg
Lockenhaus
Rechnitz
Oberpullendorf
Deutschkreutz
Ebreichsdorf
Pottendorf
Ebenfurth
Neudörfl
WALDVIERTEL
WACHAU
Dunkelsteiner Wald
Buckligge Welt
Fischbacher Alpen
Gleinalpe
Koralpe
Kräuterin
Raxalpe
Leithagebirge
GORIČKO
ÖRSÉG
Marchfeld
A
H
SLO
E59
E49
E60
E58
E65
E461
A1
A2
A4
A9
A21
S6
S31
S33
S35
S36
E57
E66
E59/66
E57/59
D2

32
A
B
C
1
2
3
4
23
40
BOCAGE VENDÉEN
Hauteurs de la Gâtine
POITOU
AUNIS
SAINTONGE
ANGOU
MÉDOC
ENTRE-DEU
Plaine Seuil de
Marais Breton
Pertuis Breton
Pertuis d'Antioche
Gironde
Île de Ré
Île d'Oléron
Île d'Aix
Étang d'Hourtin et de Carcans
Étang de Lacanau
Bassin d'Arcachon
Anse de l'Aiguillon
St-Gervais
Paulx
La Garnache
Falleron
Challans
Soullans
Commequiers
St-Hilaire-de-Riez
St-Gilles-Croix-de-Vie
Coëx
Aizenay
Venansault
Palluau
Le Poiré-sur-Vie
Legé
Rocheservière
Les Lucs-sur-Boulogne
Belleville-sur-Vie
Dompierre-sur-Yon
La Roche-sur-Yon
La Chaize-le-Vicomte
La Ferrière
Landes-Genusson
La Gaubretière
La Verrie
Les Herbiers
Mont des Alouettes
St-Fulgent
Les Essarts
Le Boupère
Pouzauges
Mouchamps
Chantonnay
Montournais
Mauléon
Nueil-sur-Argent
Les Aubiers
Echaubrognes
Bressuire
Cerizay
Terves
Chiché
Courlay
La Forêt-sur-Sèvre
Moncoutant
St-Pierre-du-Chemin
L'Absie
Thouars
Ste-Radegonde
Oiron
St-Varent
Moncontour
Airvault
St-Loup-Lamairé
Mirebeau
Vendeuvre
Thénezay
Châtillon-sur-Thouet
Neuville-de-Poitou
Parthenay
Pompaire
Secondigny
Mazières-en-Gâtine
Terrier de St-Martin
Latillé
Vouillé
Ménigoute
Coulombiers
Lusignan
Rouillé
Pamproux
St-Maixent-l'École
La Crèche
La Mothe-St-Héray
Lezay
Celles-sur-Belle
Melle
Chaunay
Sauzé-Vaussais
Chef-Boutonne
Brioux-sur-Boutonne
Prahecq
Niort
Aiffres
Magné
Bessines
Echiré
Villiers-en-Plaine
St-Hilaire-des-Loges
Champdeniers-St-Denis
Coulonges-sur-l'Autize
Mervent
L'Hermenault
Fontenay-le-Comte
La Châtaigneraie
La Caillère
Ste-Hermine
Bournezeau
St-Florent-des-Bois
La Mothe-Achard
Aubigny
Mareuil-sur-Lay-Dissais
Moutiers-les-Mauxfaits
Nalliers
Luçon
Chaillé-les-Marais
Maillezais
Benet
Vix
Marans
Triaize
St-Michel-en-l'Herm
L'Aiguillon-sur-Mer
La Tranche-sur-Mer
Jard-sur-Mer
Longeville-sur-Mer
Talmont-St-Hilaire
Avrillé
Château-d'Olonne
Les Sables-d'Olonne
Pte de l'Aiguille
Olonne-sur-Mer
St-Mathurin
Brem-sur-Mer
Bretignolles-sur-Mer
Pte des Baleines
Pte de l'Aiguillon
Ars-en-Ré
St-Martin-de-Ré
La Couarde-sur-Mer
Le Bois-Plage-en-Ré
Rivedoux-Plage
St-Xandre
Lagord
La Rochelle
Dompierre-sur-Mer
Aytré
Angoulins
Châtelaillon-Plage
La Jarrie
Aigrefeuille-d'Aunis
Courçon
Frontenay-Rohan-Rohan
Mauzé-sur-le-Mignon
Beauvoir-sur-Niort
Surgères
Loulay
Aulnay
Tonnay-Boutonne
Breuil-Magné
Rochefort
Tonnay-Charente
Fouras
Port-des-Barques
St-Agnant
St-Savinien
St-Jean-d'Angély
Matha
St-Hilaire-de-Villefranche
Aigre
Villefagnan
Mansle
St-Amant-de-Boixe
Rouillac
Vars
Pte de Chassiron
St-Denis-d'Oléron
St-Georges-d'Oléron
St-Pierre-d'Oléron
Dolus-d'Oléron
Le Château-d'Oléron
St-Trojan-les-Bains
Bourcefranc-le-Chapus
Marennes
St-Just-Luzac
La Tremblade
Étaules
Pte de la Coubre
Vaux-sur-Mer
St-Palais-sur-Mer
St-Georges-de-Didonne
Pte de Grave
Royan
Saujon
Médis
Semussac
Cozes
Gémozac
St-Porchaire
Saintes
Burie
Chérac
Cherves-Richemont
Nercillac
Cognac
Jarnac
St-Yrieix-sur-Charente
Angoulême
Hiersac
Nersac
St-Michel
Puymoyen
La Couronne
Mouthiers-sur-Boëme
Blanzac-Porcheresse
Châteauneuf-sur-Charente
Segonzac
Châteaubernard
Salles-d'Angles
Barbezieux-St-Hilaire
Archiac
Pons
St-Genis-de-Saintonge
Jonzac
Baignes-Ste-Radegonde
Montmoreau-St-Cybard
Brossac
Chevanceaux
Montendre
Mirambeau
St-Fort-sur-Gironde
St-Christoly-Médoc
Le Verdon-sur-Mer
Meschers-sur-Gironde
Soulac-sur-Mer
St-Vivien-de-Médoc
Montalivet-les-Bains
Vendays-Montalivet
Queyrac
Gaillan-en-Médoc
Lesparre-Médoc
St-Germain-d'Esteuil
St-Ciers-sur-Gironde
St-Estèphe
Vertheuil
Braud-et-St-Louis
Pauillac
Étauliers
Marcillac
Reignac
Montlieu-la-Garde
Montguyon
Chalais
Aubeterre-sur-Dronne
St-Aigulin
La Roche-Chalais
Laruscade
St-Savin
Cavignac
Les Églisottes-et-Chalaures
Lagorce
Guîtres
Coutras
Les Peintures
St-Seurin-sur-l'Isle
Le Pizou
Ménesplet
St-Denis-de-Pile
Lussac
Villefranche-de-Lonchat
Hourtin-Plage
Hourtin
Carcans-Plage
Carcans
St-Laurent-Médoc
Blaye
Cars
Bourg
Peujard
Prignac-et-Marcamps
Listrac-Médoc
Moulis-en-Médoc
Castelnau-de-Médoc
Lacanau-Océan
Lacanau
Cantenac
Le Pian-Médoc
Ambès
St-André-de-Cubzac
Cubzac-les-Ponts
Parempuyre
Bassens
Ste-Hélène
Blanquefort
St-Médard-en-Jalles
Le Porge
Galgon
Fronsac
Arveyres
Libourne
Montagne
St-Magne-de-Castillon
Vélines
Castillon-la-Bataille
Branne
Génissac
St-Loubès
Bordeaux
Floirac
Pessac
Talence
Cestas
Léognan
Cambes
Langoiran
Créon
Targon
Pellegrue
Pujols
Lège-Cap-Ferret
Andernos-les-Bains
Lanton
Marcheprime
St-Jean-d'Illac
A10
A83
A837
A89
E03
E05
E62
E601
E602
E603
E606
E70
E72
N10
N11
N137
N141
N148
N149
N150
N160
N215
N250
N89
N21
D948
D949
D937
D938
D939
D950
D911
D733
D728
D730
D734
D746
D753
D743
D670
D1

D
E
F
24
33
34
41
1
2
3
4
Poitiers
Châtellerault
Châteauroux
Déols
Issoudun
Limoges
Guéret
Périgueux
Brive-la-Gaillarde
Tulle
Bergerac
Sarlat-la-Canéda
Aurillac
Montluçon
Ussel
St-Junien
Confolens
Bellac
Le Blanc
Argenton-sur-Creuse
La Châtre
Aubusson
Uzerche
Égletons
Nontron
Thiviers
Brantôme
Chauvigny
Montmorillon
Civray
Ruffec
Rochechouart
La Rochefoucauld
Eymoutiers
St-Léonard-de-Noblat
Bourganeuf
Felletin
Meymac
Lubersac
Vigeois
Terrasson-la-Villedieu
Montignac
Souillac
Martel
Gramat
Figeac
Mussidan
Ribérac
Soyaux
Chalus
Nexon
St-Yrieix-la-Perche
Ambazac
Bessines-sur-Gartempe
La Souterraine
Dun-le-Palestel
Boussac
Chambon-sur-Voueize
Évaux-les-Bains
BERRY
BOISCHAUT
BRENNE
BRANDES
CONFOLENTAIS
MARCHE
Plateaux de la Marche
Plateau de Gentioux
Plateau de Millevaches
Monts du Limousin
Monts d'Ambazac
Plateaux du Limousin
LIMOUSIN
PÉRIGORD BLANC
PÉRIGORD
PÉRIGORD NOIR
Causse de Martel
SÉGALA DU QUERCY
CHÂTAIGNERAIE
Lac de Vassivière
Barrage d'Éguzon
A10
A20
A89
E05
E09
E62
E70
E603
N10
N20
N21
N89
N120
N121
N140
N141
N145
N147
N151
D941
D943
D951

34
A
B
C
25
42
33
1
2
3
4
F
Issoudun
Lunery
Levet
Dun-sur-Auron
La Guerche-sur-l'Aubois
Nevers
Imphy
La Machine
Cercy-la-Tour
St-Léger-des-Vignes
Decize
Fours
Luzy
Neuvy-Pailloux
Châteauneuf-sur-Cher
Chezal-Benoît
Châteauroux
Ardentes
Lignières
Charenton-du-Cher
St-Amand-Montrond
Ainay-le-Château
Lurcy-Lévis
Sancoins
Magny-Cours
St-Parize-le-Châtel
St-Pierre-le-Moûtier
Dornes
Lucenay-lès-Aix
Issy-l'Évêque
Le Châtelet
Montgivray
Châteaumeillant
La Châtre
St-Denis-de-Jouhet
Saulzais-le-Potier
Forêt de Tronçais
Cérilly
Bourbon-l'Archambault
St-Menoux
Moulins
Avermes
Yzeure
Chevagnes
Beaulon
Bourbon-Lancy
Gueugnon
Neuvy-Grandchamp
Ste-Sévère-sur-Indre
Vallon-en-Sully
Hérisson
Souvigny
Toulon-sur-Allier
Neuilly-le-Réal
Dompierre-sur-Besbre
Digoin
Molinet
Aigurande
Lourdoueix-St-Pierre
Estivareilles
Cosne-d'Allier
Buxières-les-Mines
Villefranche-d'Allier
Le Montet
Bessay-sur-Allier
Jaligny-sur-Besbre
BOURBONNAIS
Huriel
Domérat
Montluçon
Désertines
Quinssaines
Prémilhat
Néris-les-Bains
Commentry
Doyet
Montmarault
St-Pourçain-sur-Sioule
Varennes-sur-Allier
St-Gérand-le-Puy
Le Donjon
Boussac
Bonnat
Châtelus-Malvaleix
Durdat-Larequille
Chantelle
Billy
Lapalisse
Semur-en-Brionnais
BRIONNAIS
Gouzon
Jarnages
Guéret
Ste-Feyre
Chambon-sur-Voueize
Évaux-les-Bains
Marcillat-en-Combraille
Montaigut
St-Éloy-les-Mines
Bellenaves
St-Germain-des-Fossés
Cusset
Vichy
La Pacaudière
COMBRAILLE
Chénérailles
Ahun
Lavaveix-les-Mines
Pionsat
Menat
Ébreuil
Gannat
Bellerive-sur-Allier
Abrest
St-Yorre
Le Mayet-de-Montagne
Ambierle
Renaison
Riorges
Roanne
Auzances
St-Gervais-d'Auvergne
Aigueperse
Randan
Monts de la Madeleine
St-Sulpice-les-Champs
Aubusson
Bellegarde-en-Marche
Manzat
Combronde
Châteldon
Bourganeuf
Châtelguyon
St-Georges-de-Mons
Maringues
St-Rémy-sur-Durolle
Bois-Noirs
Puy de Montoncel
St-Just-en-Chevalet
Crocq
Felletin
Pontaumur
Mozac
Volvic
Riom
Ennezat
Chabreloche
Royère-de-Vassivière
Gentioux-Pigerolles
Plateau de Gentioux
Giat
Pontgibaud
Cébazat
Gerzat
Thiers
La Monnerie-le-Montel
Peschadoires
Noirétable
St-Germain-Laval
Lac de Vassivière
Herment
Chamalières
Royat
Puy de Dôme
Clermont-Ferrand
Aulnat
Lezoux
Pont-du-Château
Lempdes
Cournon-d'Auvergne
Billom
Courpière
Sail-Sous-Couzan
St-Georges-en-Couzan
La Courtine
Sornac
Plateau de Millevaches
Bourg-Lastic
Rochefort-Montagne
St-Amant-Tallende
Les Martres-de-Veyre
Veyre-Monton
Vic-le-Comte
St-Dier-d'Auvergne
Olliergues
Bugeat
Meymac
Ussel
Messeix
La Bourboule
St-Sauves-d'Auvergne
Mont-Dore
Aydat
Champeix
Issoire
Sauxillanges
St-Amant-Roche-Savine
Job
Montbrison
Pierre-sur-Haute
La Tour-d'Auvergne
Tauves
Puy de Sancy
Monts Dore
Monts d'Auvergne
Besse-et-St-Anastaise
St-Germain-Lembron
Auzat-sur-Allier
St-Germain-l'Herm
Ambert
St-Anthème
Marsac-en-Livradois
Égletons
Neuvic
Barrage de Neuvic
Bort-les-Orgues
Lanobre
Barrage de Bort-les-Orgues
Champs-sur-Tarentaine-Marchal
Ydes
Champagnac
Condat
Ardes
Lempdes
Jumeaux
Auzon
Vergongheon
Arlanc
Viverols
Usson-en-Forez
St-Pal-de-Chalencon
La Chaise-Dieu
Craponne-sur-Arzon
Monts du Livradois
MASSIF
Le Luguet
Blesle
Brioude
Vieille-Brioude
Massiac
Riom-ès-Montagnes
Mauriac
Barrage de l'Aigle
La Roche-Canillac
Vallée du Falgoux
Allanche
Allègre
Retournac
Barrage du Chastang
Salers
St-Privat
Pleaux
St-Martin-Valmeroux
Massif du Cantal
Puy Mary
Murat
Neussargues-Moissac
Col de la Fageolle
Lavoûte-Chilhac
St-Paulien
Yssingeaux
Argentat
Barrage d'Enchanet
St-Cernin
Puy Griou
Plomb du Cantal
PLANÈZE
St-Flour
Ruynes-en-Margeride
Pinols
Langeac
Loudes
Espaly-St-Marcel
Le-Puy-en-Velay
VELAY
Aiguilhe
Blavozy
Jussac
Vic-sur-Cère
Polminhac
Aurillac
Naucelles
Laroquebrou
Mont Mouchet
Saugues
Coubon
Biars-sur-Cère
St-Céré
Sousceyrac
SÉGALA
DU QUERCY
Arpajon-sur-Cère
CHÂTAIGNERAIE
Neuvéglise
Pierrefort
Mur-de-Barrez
Gorges de la Truyère
Barrage de Sarrans
Chaudes-Aigues
Barrage de Grandval
Truc de la Garde
Le Malzieu-Ville
CENTRAL
Le Devès
Le Monastier-sur-Gazeille
Landos
Latronquière
Ste-Geneviève-sur-Argence
Fournels
St-Chély-d'Apcher
St-Alban-sur-Limagnole
Grandrieu
Leyme
Lacapelle-Marival
Maurs
Montsalvy
Aumont
Pradelles
Langogne
LIMAGNE
Monts du Forez
Monts de la Margeride
Plaines de la Loire et de l'Allier
A71
A72
A75
A89
E11
E62
E70
N7
N9
N79
N81
N88
N89
N102
N106
N120
N122
N144
N145
N151
N209
N1079
D588
D906
D907
D941
D942
D943
D973
D922
D921

35
36
43
26
D
E
F
1
2
3
4
CH
Autun
Le Creusot
Montceau-les-Mines
Chalon-sur-Saône
Lons-le-Saunier
Tournus
Mâcon
Bourg-en-Bresse
Oyonnax
St-Claude
Nyon
Genève
Annemasse
Bellegarde-sur-Valserine
Annecy
Aix-les-Bains
Chambéry
Villefranche-sur-Saône
Lyon
Tarare
Roanne
St-Étienne
Vienne
Bourgoin-Jallieu
Voiron
Grenoble
Romans-sur-Isère
Valence
Tournon-sur-Rhône
Privas
Annonay
Villefontaine
Ambérieu-en-Bugey
Charollais
Mâconnais
Roannais
Monts du Beaujolais
Dombes
Bresse
Bugey
Bauges
Belledonne
Massif de la Chartreuse
Oisans
Alpes du Dauphiné
Plateau de Chambaran

36
27
35
44
A
B
C
1
2
3
4
CH
F
I
Pontarlier
Bern
Köniz
Muri
Worb
Belp
Münsingen
Mittelland
Schüpfheim
Escholzmatt
Sarnen
Kerns
Wolfenschiessen
Sachseln
Flühli
Marbach
Eggiwil
Konolfingen
Schlosswil
Laupen
Murten
Bevaix
Boudry
Couvet
Môtiers
Lac de Neuchâtel
Avenches
Payerne
Düdingen
Tafers
Villars-sur-Glâne
Fribourg
Marly
Schwarzenburg
Riggisberg
Seftigen
Uetendorf
Steffisburg
Thun
Oberhofen
Interlaken
Bönigen
Brienz
Brienzer See
Giswil
Lungern
Meiringen
Innertkirchen
Gadmen
Guttannen
Thuner See
Spiez
Wimmis
Wattenwil
Plaffeien
Lac de la Gruyère
La Roche
La Berra
Gantrisch
Stockhorn
Frasne
Mignovillard
Malbuisson
Les Fourgs
Ste-Croix
Grandson
Yvonand
Yverdon
Orbe
Vallorbe
Romainmôtier
Lac de Joux
L'Abbaye
Le Sentier
Thierrens
Moudon
Romont
Corbières
Bulle
Riaz
Charmey
Boltigen
Jaun
Gruyères
Broc
Zweisimmen
Cossonay
Echallens
Epalinges
Oron-la-Ville
Châtel-St-Denis
Le Moleson
Vanil Noir
Bussigny
Renens
Lausanne
Morges
St-Prex
Cully
Vevey
Montreux
Villeneuve
Bière
Aubonne
Rolle
Nyon
Divonne-les-Bains
Lac Léman
Saanen
Gstaad
Château-d'Oex
Leuk
Adelboden
Frutigen
Reichenbach
Lauterbrunnen
Wengen
Grindelwald
Eiger
Mönch
Jungfrau
Finsteraarhorn
Oberwald
Münster
Reckingen
Fiesch
Mörel
Naters
Brig
Ried
Kandersteg
Blümlisalp
Aletschhorn
Bietschhorn
Kippel
Leukerbad
Balmhorn
Berner Alpen
Goms
Simmental
La Tornette
Gsteig
Wildhorn
Les Diablerets
Leysin
Aigle
Ollon
Bex
Collombey
Monthey
Châtel
Vouvry
Bouveret
St-Gingolph
Meillerie
Lugrin
Evian-les-Bains
Publier
Thonon-les-Bains
Allinges
Yvoire
Sciez
Douvaine
Versoix
Genève
Annemasse
Gaillard
Reignier
Bons-en-Chablais
Bellevaux
St-Cergues
La Chapelle-d'Abondance
Abondance
Vacheresse
Le Biot
Chablais
Montriond
Morzine
Avoriaz
Les Gets
Champéry
St-Maurice
Dents du Midi
Vernayaz
Martigny
Charrat
Saxon
Riddes
Leytron
Ardon
Conthey
Sion
Chalais
Chippis
Sierre
Crans-sur-Sierre
Montana
Anzère
Leuk
Raron
Visp
Stalden
Saas Fee
Saas Grund
Weissmies
Simplon
Vissoie
Val d'Anniviers
Val d'Hérens
Evolène
Verbier
Bagnes
Lac des Dix
Arolla
Dent Blanche
Weisshorn
Zermatt
Täsch
Matterhorn
Monte Rosa
Dufourspitze
Macugnaga
Vanzone
Ceppo Morelli
Pieve Vergonte
Ornavasso
Gravellona Toce
Domodossola
Villadossola
Crevoladossola
Masera
Trontano
Premosello-Chiovenda
Piedimulera
Bognanco
Varzo
Baceno
Crodo
Premia
Nendaz
Vex
Mauvoisin
Champex
Orsières
Sembrancher
Vallorcine
Grand Combin
Alpi Pennine
Grand St Bernard
St-Rhémy
Etroubles
Gignod
Valpelline
Bionaz
Valtournenche
Breuil-Cervinia
Champoluc
Gressoney-la-Trinité
Alagna Valsesia
Carcoforo
Fobello
Cravagliana
Balmuccia
Varallo
Omegna
Lago d'Orta
Campertogno
Scopello
Quarona
Borgosesia
Bonneville
Thyez
Cluses
Faucigny
Taninges
Samoëns
Mieussy
St-Jeoire
Fillinges
Sixt-Fer-à-Cheval
Flaine
Magland
Scionzier
St-Pierre-en-Faucigny
Annecy-le-Vieux
Annecy
Seynod
St-Jean-de-Sixt
Le Grand-Bornand
La Clusaz
Thônes
Col des Aravis
Talloires
Sallanches
Combloux
Passy
Servoz
Bornes
Argentière
Aiguille d'Argentière
Aiguille Verte
Mont Dolent
Grandes Jorasses
Chamonix-Mont-Blanc
Aiguille du Midi
Mont Blanc
Les Houches
St-Gervais-les-Bains
Megève
Flumet
Praz-sur-Arly
Notre-Dame-de-Bellecombe
Les Contamines-Montjoie
Ugine
Queige
Beaufort
Albertville
Gilly-sur-Isère
Grésy-sur-Isère
La Bâthie
Barrage de Roselend
Le Roignais
Bourg-St-Maurice
Séez
Bonneval
Courmayeur
Morgex
La Salle
Pré-St-Didier
La Thuile
Col du Petit St-Bernard
Aosta
St-Pierre
Sarre
Gressan
Aymavilles
Charvensod
Nus
Fenis
Châtillon
St-Vincent
Montjovet
Verrès
Issogne
Arnad
Donnas
Pont-St-Martin
Hône
Quincinetto
Settimo Vittone
Borgofranco d'Ivrea
Ivrea
Fontainemore
Gaby
Issime
Brusson
Biella
Andorno Micca
Vigliano Biellese
Cossato
Gattinara
Valle Mosso
Trivero
Coggiola
Borgomanero
Valgrisenche
Rhêmes-St-Georges
Rhêmes-Notre-Dame
Valsavarenche
Cogne
Gran Paradiso
Surier
Lago di Beauregard
Ste-Foy-Tarentaise
Les Arcs
Aime
La Plagne
Mont Pourri
Beaufortin
Feissons-sur-Isère
Cevins
Aiguebelle
Chamoux-sur-Gelon
Aiguebelanche
Argentine
Epierre
Valmorel
Moûtiers
Tarentaise
Brides-les-Bains
Bozel
Courchevel
Méribel-les-Allues
Barrage de Tignes
Tignes
Val-d'Isère
Lac du Chevril
Ceresole Reale
Noasca
Locana
Pont-Canavese
Ronco Canavese
Campiglia Soana
Cuorgnè
Valperga
Rivarolo Canavese
Castellamonte
Strambino
Bollengo
Salussola
Cavaglià
Santhià
Borgo d'Ale
Tronzano Vercellese
Carisio
Formigliana
Balocco
Arborio
Buronzo
Zubiena
Mongrando
Gaglianico
Candelo
Pralognan-la-Vanoise
St-Martin-de-Belleville
Les Menuires
Lanslebourg-Mont-Cenis
Termignon
Bonneval-sur-Arc
Groscavallo
Ala di Stura
Cantoira
Balme
Ceres
Lanzo Torinese
Canavese
Col du Mont Cenis
Lac du Mont Cenis
La Chambre
St-François-Longchamp
St-Jean-de-Maurienne
St-Michel-de-Maurienne
Maurienne
Modane
Bramans
Valloire
St-Sorlin-d'Arves
Aiguilles d'Arves
Mont Thabor
Susa
Bussoleno
Borgone Susa
Condove
Chiomonte
Exilles
Salbertrand
Oulx
Bardonecchia
Sestriere
Pragelato
Fenestrelle
Roure
Monte Orsiera
Giaveno
Avigliana
Lago Grande
Piossasco
Cumiana
Pinasca
Perosa Argentina
Pinerolo
San Germano Chisone
Bobbio Pellice
Torre Pellice
Luserna San Giovanni
Bricherasio
Cavour
Bagnolo Piemonte
Barge
Usseglio
Margone
Ciriè
Mathi
Cafasse
Fiano
Volpiano
Leinì
Chivasso
Caselle Torinese
Venaria
Collegno
Rivoli
Grugliasco
Beinasco
Orbassano
Torino
San Mauro Torinese
Settimo Torinese
Gassino Torinese
Nichelino
Moncalieri
Chieri
Castelnuovo Don Bosco
Carignano
Carmagnola
Racconigi
Poirino
Villanova d'Asti
Villafranca d'Asti
Asti
Buriasco
Vigone
Pancalieri
Airasca
None
Casalgrasso
Moretta
Sommariva del Bosco
Bra
Alba
Canale
San Damiano d'Asti
Isola d'Asti
Nizza Monferrato
Canelli
Neive
Castagnole Monferrato
Montemagno
Calliano
Montechiaro d'Asti
Buttigliera d'Asti
Montiglio
Murisengo
Moncalvo
Casale Monferrato
Morano sul Po
Crescentino
Saluggia
Livorno Ferraris
Bianzè
Cigliano
Caluso
Rondissone
Casalborgone
Robella
Trino
Desana
Briançon
Névache
Le Monêtier-les-Bains
La Salle les Alpes
Col du Lautaret
La Grave
La Meije
Barre des Ecrins
Mont Pelvoux
Pelvoux
Vallouise
St-Chaffrey
Montgenèvre
Villar-St-Pancrace
L'Argentière-la-Bessée
La Roche-de-Rame
Freissinières
Champoléon
Orcières
La Chapelle-en-Valgaudémar
Col d'Izoard
Arvieux
Abriès
Molines
Crissolo
Le Bourg-d'Oisans
La Bérarde
Besse
Mont-Dauphin
Vieux Chaillol

37
28
38
45
D
E
F
1
2
3
4
Flüelen
Altdorf
Bürglen
Unterschächen
Linthal
Elm
Ringelspitz 3247
Klosters
Silvrettahorn 3244
Piz Buin 3312
Silvretta Gruppe
Ramosch
Passo di Resia 1507
Curon Venosta
Weißkugel 3738
Erstfeld
Todi 3614
Hausstock 3158
Flims
Laax
Tamins
Bonaduz
Domat Ems
Churwalden
Arosa
Davos
Flüelepass 2383
Susch
Ardez
Scuol
Lago di Resia
Lago di Muta
Malles Venosta
Silenen
Oberalpstock 3328
Disentis Muster
Sumvitg
Trun
Breil
Ilanz
SURSELVA
Cazis
Thusis
Albula
Alvaneu
Wiesen
Filisur
Tiefencastel
Bergün
Piz Kesch 3418
Zernez
UNTER ENGADIN
Piz Pisoc 3174
Parco Nazionale del Monte
Tubre
Müstair
Sluderno
Spondigna
Lasà
Wassen
Andermatt
Vorderrhein
Piz Medel 3210
Glogn
Zillis
Piz d'Anarosa 3000
Andeer
Savognin
Piz Ela 3339
Albula Alpen
OBER ENGADIN
Zuoz
La Punt
Livigno
Lago di Livigno
Lago di San Giacomo
Santa Maria
Prato allo Stelvio
Passo dello Stelvio 2758
Cima Vertona 3544
Ortles 3905
Solda
Passo del San Gottardo 2108
Airolo
Ticino
Quinto
Olivone
Vals
Splügen
Hinterrhein
Passo dello Spluga
Rheinwaldhorn 3402
Passo di San Bernardino 2065
Piz Platta 3392
Avers
Bivio
St Moritz
Samedan
Pontresina
Silvaplana
Sils
Silvaplaner See
Lago di Cancano
Valdidentro
Bormio
Valfurva
Monte Cevedale 3757
Faido
Acquarossa
Campo Tencia 3072
Valle Leventina
Giornico
Malvaglia
Mesocco
Campodolcino
Piz Duan 3131
Mera
Lago da Segl
Piz Bernina 4049
Bernina
Piz Varuna 3453
Corno di Campo 3234
Cima de' Piazzi 3439
Valdisotto
Corno dei Tre Signori 3360
Peio
Basodino 3273
Peccia
Monte Zucchero 2736
Biasca
Bignasco
Castasegna
Poschiavo
Roasco
Sondalo
Lago Pian Palu
Pellizzano
Ossana
Cevio
Maggia
Osogna
Lostallo
Claro
Sasso della Paglia 2593
Roveredo
Gordona
Chiavenno
Bagni di Masino
Monte Disgrazia 3678
Chiesa in Valmalenco
Monte Combolo 2900
Brusio
Grosotto
Grosio
Ponte di Legno
Passo di Tonale 1883
Vermiglio
Mazzo di Valtellina
Lovero
Tirano
Vezza d'Oglio
Temù
Cima Presanella 3558
Minusio
Gordola
Arbedo
Bellinzona
Giubiasco
Locarno
Ascona
Losone
Samolaco
Novate Mezzola
Verceia
Lago di Mezzola
Dubino
Spriana
Chiuro
Teglio
Tresenda
Aprica
Corteno Golgi
Edolo
Adamello 3539
Carisolo
Pinzolo
Strembo
Sta Maria Maggiore
Malesco
Cadenazzo
Gravedona
Dongo
Colico
Cavargna
Monte Legnone 2609
Talamona
Morbegno
Sondrio
Adda
Alpi Orobie
Pizzo di Coca 3050
Malonno
Lago Dosazzo
Lago Belviso
Lago di Bissina
Vigo Rendena
Villa Rendena
Cedegolo
Capo di Ponte
Falmenta
Cannobio
Cannero Riviera
Torricella Taverne
Maccagno
Sta Maria Rezzonico
Porlezza
Dervio
Bellano
Albaredo per San Marco
Gerola Alta
Foppolo
Valbondione
Lago d'Arno
Schilpario
Ceto
Braone
Breno
Luino
Agno
Lugano
Lago di Lugano
Menaggio
Tremezzo
Varenna
Bellagio
Mezzoldo
Branzi
Carona
Introbio
Piazzatorre
Gandellino
Gromo
Pizzo della Presolana 2521
Azzone
Chiese
Roncone
Lardaro
Pieve di Bono
Bersone
Mergozzo
Ghiffa
Lago Maggiore
Lavena
Ponte Tresa
Argegno
Lago di Como
Grigna 2409
Piazza Brembana
Barzio
Lenna
Pizzo Arera 2512
Castione della Presolana
Bienno
Verbania
Baveno
Cittiglio
Campo dei Fiori 1226
Gavirate
Mendrisio
Torno
Lago di Lecco
Lambro
Mandello del Lario
Ballabio
Clusone
Darfo Boario Terme
Condino
Stresa
Laveno
Cernobbio
Asso
Valmadrera
Lecco
San Giovanni Bianco
Serina
Ponte Nossa
Costa Volpino
Artogne
Bagolino
Storo
Lesa
Besozzo
Varese
Chiasso
Como
Lago di Annone
Erba
Lago di Garlate
Oginate
Calolziocorte
Zogno
San Pellegrino Terme
Selvino
Gandino
Lovere
Pisogne
Bovegno
Collio
Mella
Lago d'Idro
Anfo
Idro
Lago di Valvestino
Ispra
Malnate
Lago di Varese
Lago di Alserio
Lago di Pusiano
Sedrina
Villa d'Almè
Albino
Nembro
Riva di Solto
Isola San Paolo
Brozzo
Vestone
Gargnano
Meina
Arona
Angera
Sesto Calende
Lago di Comabbio
Castiglione Olona
Tradate
Cantù
Mariano Comense
Merate
Caprino Bergamasco
Ponte San Pietro
Dalmine
Bergamo
Seriate
Trescore Balneario
Monte Bronzone 1334
Lago d'Iseo
Gardone Val Trompia
Barghe
Toscolano-Maderno
Gardone Riviera
Lago di Garda
Somma Lombardo
Gallarate
Cassano Magnano
Fino Mornasco
Seveso
Casatenovo
Sarnico
Iseo
Sarezzo
Lumezzane
Concesio
Salò
Torri del Benaco
Oleggio
Samarate
Busto Arsizio
Cesano Maderno
Legnano
Saronno
Seregno
Lissone
Trezzo sull'Adda
Osio Sotto
Cologno al Serio
Palazzolo sull'Oglio
Rovato
Villa Carcina
Gussago
Nave
Gavardo
Garda
Bardolino
Momo
Bellinzago Novarese
Castano Primo
Lainate
Cinisello Balsamo
Monza
Vimercate
Agrate Brianza
Treviglio
Martinengo
Romano di Lombardia
Chiari
Ospitaletto
Travagliato
Roncadelle
Brescia
Rezzato
Mazzano
Desenzano del Garda
Lonato
Caltignaga
Cameri
Rho
Pero
Sesto San Giovanni
Gorgonzola
Pioltello
Melzo
Caravaggio
Calcio
Urago d'Oglio
Calcinato
Novara
Galliate
Arluno
Cornaredo
Milano
Rivolta d'Adda
Agnadello
Roccafranca
Bagnolo Mella
Ghedi
Montichiari
Solferino
Sommacampagna
Villafranca
Biandrate
Borgo Vercelli
Trecate
Magenta
Cerano
Cesano Boscone
Corsico
San Donato Milanese
San Giuliano Milanese
Pandino
Sergnano
Canale Vacchelli
Soncino
Offanengo
Orzinuovi
Dello
Castiglione delle Stiviere
Volta Mantovana
Vercelli
Vespolate
Abbiategrasso
Borgo-lavezzaro
Buccinasco
Rozzano
Binasco
Locate di Triulzi
Melegnano
Crema
Manerbio
Leno
Carpenedolo
Guidizzolo
Robbio
Vigevano
Motta Visconti
Lodi
Lodi Vecchio
Castelleone
Soresina
Quinzano d'Oglio
Verolanuova
Pontevico
Isorella
Gambara
Castel Goffredo
Goito
Mortara
Gambolò
Bereguardo
Tromello
Garlasco
Certosa di Pavia
Sant'Angelo Lodigiano
Casalbuttano ed Uniti
Robecco d'Oglio
Ostiano
Asola
Gazoldo degli Ippoliti
Marmirolo
Candia Lomellina
San Giorgio di Lomellina
Gropello Cairoli
Dorno
Pavia
Belgioioso
Villanterio
San Colombano al Lambro
Corteolona
Pizzighettone
Casalpusterlengo
Codogno
Castelverde
Cremona
Vescovato
Canneto sull'Oglio
Acquanegra sul Chiese
Castellucchio
Borgo San Martino
Lomello
Mede
Cava Manara
Sannazzaro de' Burgondi
Bressana Bottarone
Stradella
Rottofreno
Castelvetro Piacentino
Monticelli d'Ongina
Piadena
San Giovanni in Croce
Bozzolo
Marcaria
Pieve del Cairo
Casei Gerola
Broni
Castèl San Giovanni
Piacenza
San Daniele Po
Rivarolo Mantovano
Gazzuolo
Valenza
Castelnuovo Scrivia
Voghera
Casteggio
Borgonovo Val Tidone
Pontenure
Cadeo
Busseto
Zibello
Roccabianca
Gussola
Casalmaggiore
Sabbioneta
Viadana
San Salvatore Monferrato
Sale
Pontecurone
Rivanazzano
Sta Maria della Versa
Pianello Val Tidone
Rivergaro
Podenzano
Fiorenzuola d'Arda
Soragna
Sissa
Colorno
San Secondo Parmense
Brescello
Guastalla
Alessandria
Tortona
Viguzzolo
Godiasco
Nibbiano
Carpaneto Piacentino
Alseno
Fontanellato
Quargnento
Oviglio
Casal Cermelli
Bosco Marengo
Volpedo
Ponte Nizza
Zavattarello
Monte Lazzaro 987
Ponte dell'Olio
Castell'Arquato
Lugagnano Val d'Arda
Fidenza
Salsomaggiore Terme
Noceto
Parma
Collecchio
Sorbolo
Poviglio
Castelnovo di Sotto
Cadelbosco di Sopra
Villavernia
Pozzolo Formigaro
Novi Ligure
Cassano Spinola
Bagnaria
Varzi
Travo
Bettola
Lago di Mignano
Pellegrino Parmense
Medesano
Sant'Ilario d'Enza
Cavriago
Montecchio Emilia
Acqui Terme
Predosa
Rocca Grimalda
Serravalle Scrivia
Arquata Scrivia
Gavi
Borghetto di Borbera
Cabella Ligure
Albera Ligure
Brallo di Pregola
Monte Lesima 1724
Bobbio
Farini
Monte Menegosa 1355
Morfasso
Varano de' Melegari
Fornovo di Taro
Felino
Traversetolo
Quattro Castella
Reggio nell'Emilia
Montechiarugolo
E35
E43
E62
E64
E70
E25
E26/7
A1
A2
A4
A7
A8
A9
A13
A21
A21dir
A26

38
29
37
46
A
B
C
1
2
3
4
CH
I
Chur
Klosters
Hochwang
Silvretta Gruppe
Silvrettahorn 3244
Piz Buin 3312
Davos
Arosa
Churwalden
Flüelapass
Ardez
Susch
Scuol
Ramosch
Passo di Resia
Lago di Resia
Curon Venosta
Lago di Muta
Malles Venosta
Wildspitze 3768
Obergurgl
Similaun
L'Altissima
Lago di Vernago
Senales
Val Senales
Moso in Passiria
San Leonardo in Passiria
San Martino in Passiria
Monte Altacroce 2743
Campo di Trens
Vandoies
Rio di Pusteria
Fortezza
Varna
Bressanone
UNTER ENGADIN
OBER ENGADIN
Piz Pisoc 3174
Zernez
Parco Nazionale del Monte
Tubre
Sluderno
Spondigna
Val Venosta
Lasà
Silandro
Laces
Naturno
Lagundo
Rifiano
Merano
Marlengo
Lana
Sarentino
Postal
Gargazzone
Velturno
Chiusa
Ponte Gardena
Funes
Ortisei
Castelrotto
Wiesen
Alvaneu
Filisur
Tiefencastel
Bergün
Piz Kesch 3418
Piz Ela 3339
Zillis
Savognin
Andeer
Albula Alpen
Zuoz
La Punt
Livigno
Lago di Livigno
Lago di San Giacomo
Santa Maria
Müstair
Prato allo Stelvio
Passo dello Stelvio 2758
Cima Vertana 3544
Solda
Ortles 3905
Lago di Gioveretto
Martello
Gioveretto 3439
Lago di Zoccolo
San Pancrazio
Tesimo
Monte Luco 2434
Terlano
Renòn
Bolzano
Sasso Lungo 3181
Fiè allo Sciliar
Cornedo all'Isarco
Samedan
Pontresina
St Moritz
Silvaplana
Silvaplaner See
Sils
Bivio
Avers
Piz Platta 3392
Lago di Cancano
Valdidentro
Bormio
Valfurva
Monte Cevedale 3757
Appiano sulla Strada del Vino
Caldaro sulla Strada del Vino
Laives
Nova Levante
Vigo di Fassa
Soraga
Moena
Pozza di Fassa
Lago di Caldaro
Monte Roèn 2116
Nova Ponte
Latemar 2842
Corno di Campo 3234
Cima de'Piazzi 3439
Bernina
Piz Bernina 4049
Piz Varuna 3453
Lago da Segl
Piz Duan 3131
Mera
Casaccia
Castasegna
Poschiavo
Brusio
Grosotto
Grosio
Valdisotto
Sondalo
Corno dei Tre Signori 3360
Lago Pian Palu
Peio
Bagni di Rabbi
Malè
Cles
Tuenno
Dimaro
Taio
Egna
Ora
Predazzo
Tesero
Cavalese
San Martino di Castrozza
Cima di Cece 2754
Monte Disgrazia 3678
Chiesa in Valmalenco
Monte Combolo 2900
Mazzo di Valtellina
Lovero
Vezza d'Oglio
Temù
Ponte di Legno
Passo di Tonale 1883
Vermiglio
Pellizzano
Ossana
Mezzana
Madonna di Campiglio
Lago di Tovel
Mezzocorona
Salorno
Brusago
Monte Croce 2490
Lastè delle Sute 2616
Cima d'Asta 2847
Canal San Bovo
Bagni di Masino
Novate Mezzola
Verceia
Dubino
Spriana
Chiuro
Teglio
Tirano
Tresenda
Aprica
Corteno Golgi
Edolo
Cima Presanella 3558
Carisolo
Pinzolo
Strembo
Gruppo di Brenta
Cima Tosa 3159
Molveno
Lago di Molveno
Andalo
Paganella 2098
Mezzolombardo
Cembra
Lavis
Bedollo
Baselga di Pinè
Pergine Valsugana
Roncegno
Strigno
Castello Tesino
Lamon
Talamona
Sondrio
Morbegno
Albaredo per San Marco
Gerola Alta
Alpi Orobie
Pizzo di Coca 3050
Valbondione
Foppolo
Carona
Branzi
Mezzoldo
Piazzatorre
Piazza Brembana
Lenna
Pizzo Arera 2512
Gandellino
Gromo
Pizzo della Presolana 2521
Schilpario
Azzone
Malonno
Adamello 3539
Lago Dosazzo
Lago Belviso
Cedegolo
Capo di Ponte
Ceto
Braone
Breno
Bienno
Lago di Bissina
Lago d'Arno
Vigo Rendena
Villa Rendena
Darè
Tione di Trento
Stenico
Vezzano
Trento
Lago di Caldonazzo
Caldonazzo
Levico Terme
Borgo Valsugana
Cima Dodici 2341
Grigno
Primolano
Enego
Barzio
Clusone
Castione della Presolana
Darfo Boario Terme
Costa Volpino
Artogne
Pisogne
Lovere
Bovegno
Collio
Serina
San Giovanni Bianco
San Pellegrino Terme
Ponte Nossa
Gandino
Zogno
Selvino
Albino
Nembro
Calolziocorte
Riva di Solto
Lago d'Iseo
Monte Isola
Iseo
Bagolino
Breguzzo
Roncone
Lardaro
Pieve di Bono
Bersone
Condino
Storo
Lago di Ledro
Molina di Ledro
Riva del Garda
Arco
Nago-Torbole
Dro
Fiavè
Lagarina
Villa Lagarina
Aldeno
Cornetto 2180
Becco di Filadonna 2150
Lastebasse
Folgaria
Rovereto
Mori
Tonezza del Cimone
Cima Palòn 2235
Monte Priaforà 1659
Arsiero
Cima Fonti 1519
Gallio
Asiago
Valstagna
Bassano del Grappa
Marostica
Piovene Rocchette
Raossi
Cima Carega 2259
Recoaro Terme
Schio
Thiene
Breganze
Castelfranco
Cittadella
Bergamo
Seriate
Ponte San Pietro
Dalmine
Trescore Balneario
Monte Bronzone 1334
Sarnico
Sarezzo
Villa Carcina
Gussago
Lumezzane
Concesio
Gardone Val Trompia
Brozzo
Vestone
Barghe
Idro
Anfo
Lago d'Idro
Lago di Valvestino
Tignale
Limone sul Garda
Malcesine
Brenzone
Avio
Ala
Gargnano
Toscolano-Maderno
Gardone Riviera
Salò
Lago di Garda
Torri del Benaco
Caprino Veronese
Garda
Bardolino
Lazise
Sirmione
Peschiera del Garda
Desenzano del Garda
Monti Lessini
Bosco Chiesanuova
Valdagno
Selva di Progno
Badia Calavena
Chiampo
Tregnago
Arzignano
Montebello Vicentino
Malo
Dueville
Vicenza
Caldogno
Montecchio Maggiore
Longare
Monte Alto 444
Barbarano Vicentino
Selvazzano Dentro
Abano Terme
Montegrotto Terme
Monte Venda 601
Trezzo sull'Adda
Osio Sotto
Cologno al Serio
Martinengo
Romano di Lombardia
Palazzolo sull'Oglio
Rovato
Chiari
Ospitaletto
Travagliato
Roncadelle
Brescia
Rezzato
Nave
Gavardo
Mazzano
Calcinato
Lonato
Montichiari
Castiglione delle Stiviere
Solferino
Volta Mantovana
Sona
Sommacampagna
Villafranca di Verona
Valeggio sul Mincio
Bussolengo
San Pietro in Cariano
Negrar
Pescantina
Verona
San Martino Buon Albergo
San Giovanni Lupatoto
Zevio
San Bonifacio
Soave
Lonigo
Cologna Veneta
Noventa Vicentina
Treviglio
Brianza
Calcio
Urago d'Oglio
Caravaggio
Roccafranca
Orzinuovi
Soncino
Offanengo
Crema
Bagnolo Mella
Dello
Ghedi
Manerbio
Quinzano d'Oglio
Verolanuova
Leno
Isorella
Carpenedolo
Gambara
Pontevico
Robecco d'Oglio
Castellone
Soresina
Casalbuttano ed Uniti
Guidizzolo
Castel Goffredo
Goito
Roverbella
Vigasio
Isola della Scala
Oppeano
Bovolone
Montagnana
Este
Lodi
Lodigiano
Sergnano
Pandino
Pizzighettone
Casalpusterlengo
Codogno
Castelverde
Cremona
Ostiano
Asola
Gazoldo degli Ippoliti
Marmirolo
Lago Superiore
Mantova
Castel d'Ario
Nogara
Sanguinetto
Cerea
Legnago
Merlara
Casale di Scodosia
Castagnaro
Villa Bartolomea
Gazzo Veronese
Canneto sull'Oglio
Acquanegra sul Chiese
Castellucchio
Vescovato
Piadena
San Giovanni in Croce
Bozzolo
Marcaria
Badia Polesine
Lendinara
Fratta Polesine
Castelvetro Piacentino
Monticelli d'Ongina
San Daniele Po
Rottofreno
Piacenza
Pontenure
Cadeo
Podenzano
Rivergaro
Carpaneto Piacentino
Castell'Arquato
Lugagnano Val d'Arda
Fiorenzuola d'Arda
Alseno
Busseto
Zibello
Roccabianca
Soragna
Fidenza
Salsomaggiore Terme
Noceto
Fontanellato
Gussola
Casalmaggiore
Rivarolo Mantovano
Sabbioneta
Sissa
Colorno
San Secondo Parmense
Viadana
Brescello
Guastalla
Luzzara
Suzzara
Gonzaga
Borgoforte
Gazzuolo
Bagnolo San Vito
Sustinente
San Benedetto Po
Moglia
Reggiolo
Guastalla
Novellara
Gualtieri
Ostiglia
Castelmassa
Sermide
Trecenta
Ceneselli
Bergantino
Villa Poma
Poggio Rusco
Ficarolo
Stienta
Occhiobello
Bondeno
Pontelagoscuro
Ferrara
Novi di Modena
Mirandola
Medolla
San Felice sul Panaro
Finale Emilia
Vigarano Mainarda
Cavezzo
Camposanto
Sant'Agostino
Poggio Renatico
Cento
Pieve di Cento
Malalbergo
Parma
Collecchio
Medesano
Varano de'Melegari
Fornovo di Taro
Felino
Sant'Ilario d'Enza
Montecchio Emilia
Cadelbosco di Sopra
Bagnolo in Piano
Correggio
Carpi
Soliera
San Prospero
Castelnovo di Sotto
Poviglio
Sorbolo
Cavriago
Montechiarugolo
Quattro Castella
Reggio nell'Emilia
Rubiera
Modena
Nonantola
San Giovanni in Persiceto
Crevalcore
Bomporto
Castello d'Argile
Bentivoglio
Giorgio di Piano
Travo
Bettola
Farini
Monte Menegosa 1355
Morfasso
Pellegrino Parmense
Lago di Mignano
Bore
Varsi
Bardi
Ferriere
Solignano
Langhirano
Ponte dell'Olio
Pieve

30
47
D
E
F
1
2
3
4
A
SLO
HR
Lienz
Spittal an der Drau
Villach
Feldkirchen in Kärnten
Brunico
Dobbiaco
Sesto
Cortina d'Ampezzo
Pieve di Cadore
Tolmezzo
Gemona del Friuli
Tarvisio
Jesenice
Bovec
Kobarid
Tolmin
Belluno
Feltre
Maniago
Spilimbergo
Udine
Cividale del Friuli
Nova Gorica
Gorizia
Vittorio Veneto
Conegliano
Sacile
Pordenone
Codroipo
San Vito al Tagliamento
Palmanova
Cervignano del Friuli
Monfalcone
Trieste
Muggia
Koper
Izola
Piran
Umag
Novigrad
Poreč
Rovinj
Pula
Montebelluna
Castelfranco Veneto
Treviso
Oderzo
Portogruaro
Latisana
San Donà di Piave
Jesolo
Caorle
Lignano Pineta
Bibione
Grado
Mestre
Venezia
Padova
Chioggia
Rovigo
Adria
Porto Tolle
Codigoro
Copparo
Comacchio
Golfo di Venezia
MARE ADRIATICO
Laguna Veneta
Istra
Karnische Alpen
Julijske Alpe
Gailtaler Alpen

A
B
C
32
57
56
1
2
3
4
Bordeaux
Blanquefort
St-Médard-en-Jalles
Pessac
Floirac
Talence
Cestas
Libourne
Arveyres
Génissac
Fronsac
Montagne
Lussac
Ménestérol
St-Loubès
Le Porge
Lège-Cap-Ferret
Arès
Andernos-les-Bains
Bassin d'Arcachon
Île aux Oiseaux
Arcachon
La Teste
Le Teich
Gujan-Mestras
Lanton
Audenge
Marcheprime
Biganos
Mios
Salles
Le Barp
Dune du Pilat
Étang de Cazaux et de Sanguinet
Sanguinet
Biscarrosse-Plage
Biscarrosse
Étang de Biscarrosse et de Parentis
Parentis-en-Born
Ychoux
Pontenx-les-Forges
Mimizan-Plage
Mimizan
Contis-Plage
St-Julien-en-Born
Lit-et-Mixe
St-Girons-Plage
Étang de Léon
Léon
Castets
Lesperon
Vieux-Boucau-les-Bains
Étang de Soustons
Soustons
Magescq
Tosse
St-Vincent-de-Tyrosse
Capbreton
Labenne
Bénesse-Maremne
Tarnos
Boucau
Bayonne
Biarritz
St-Martin-de-Seignanx
Urcuit
Urt
Bardos
Bidache
Briscous
Hasparren
Ustaritz
Larressore
Espelette
St-Pée-sur-Nivelle
Ascain
Sare
Mont Ursuya
PAYS DE BORN
MARENSIN
PAYS BASQUE
SOULE
LANDES DE GASCOGNE
GRANDE LANDE
GRAVES
ENTRE-DEUX-MERS
CHALOSSE
BÉARN
ARMAGNAC
ASTARAC
NEBOUZAN
BIGORRE
Léognan
La Brède
Saucats
Cabanac-et-Villagrains
Landiras
Cambes
Créon
Langoiran
Portets
Podensac
Cadillac
Rions
Barsac
Illats
St-Macaire
Langon
Fargues
Auros
Bazas
Villandraut
Belin-Béliet
St-Symphorien
Pissos
Sore
Luxey
Labouheyre
Sabres
Labrit
Morcenx
Rion-des-Landes
Captieux
Roquefort
Mont-de-Marsan
St-Pierre-du-Mont
Villeneuve-de-Marsan
Tartas
Begaar
Pontonx-sur-l'Adour
St-Paul-lès-Dax
Dax
Mées
Narrosse
Souprosse
Mugron
Hinx
Montfort-en-Chalosse
Hagetmau
St-Sever
Grenade-sur-l'Adour
Aire-sur-l'Adour
Barcelonne-du-Gers
Samadet
Geaune
Pouillon
Habas
Amou
Pomarez
Peyrehorade
Puyôo
Orthez
Salies-de-Béarn
Sauveterre-de-Béarn
Arthez-de-Béarn
Arzacq-Arraziguet
Thèze
Lagor
Artix
Mourenx
Navarrenx
Sauvagnon
Lescar
Lons
Billère
Pau
Jurançon
Bizanos
Monein
Oloron-Ste-Marie
Ledeuix
Lasseube
Gan
Bordes
Assat
Nay
Coarraze
Bénéjacq
Asson
Bourdettes
Lestelle-Bétharram
Montaut
Arudy
Louvie-Juzon
Ogeu-les-Bains
Aramits
Arette
Mauléon-Licharre
Chéraute
Tardets-Sorholus
St-Palais
Iholdy
St-Jean-Pied-de-Port
St-Étienne-de-Baïgorry
Col d'Ispéguy
Eliozondo
Oronoz
Sayoa
Puerto de Ibañeta
Pic des Escaliers
Pic d'Orhy
Sierra de Abodi
Escaroz
Zubiri
Huarte
Burlada
Pamplona (Irunea)
Villava
Mutilva Baja
Elorz
Aoiz
Sierra de Labia
Valle de Baztán
Accous
Urdos
Candanchú
Col du Somport
Col du Pourtalet
Baños de Panticosa
Hecho
Laruns
Col d'Aubisque
Aucun
Pic du Moulle de Jaut
Arrens
Argelès-Gazost
Pierrefitte-Nestalas
Cauterets
Luz-St-Sauveur
Gèdre
Gavarnie
Lourdes
Bagnères-de-Bigorre
Campan
Col du Tourmalet
Col d'Aspin
Arreau
Bordères
Vielle-Aure
St-Lary-Soulan
Tarbes
Séméac
Aureilhan
Orleix
Bordères-sur-l'Échez
Andrest
Vic-en-Bigorre
Lalouère
Ossun
Pontacq
St-Pé-de-Bigorre
Lannemezan
Capvern-les-Bains
La Barthe-de-Neste
Tournay
Galan
Pouyastruc
Trie-sur-Baïse
Miélan
Mirande
Marciac
Maubourguet
Rabastens-de-Bigorre
Lembeye
Morlaàs
Garlin
Castelnau-Rivière-Basse
Plaisance
Montesquiou
Bassoues
Riscle
Aignan
Nogaro
Le Houga
Manciet
Eauze
Vic-Fezensac
Jegun
Gondrin
Valence-sur-Baïse
Condom
Montréal
Castelnau-d'Auzan
Cazaubon
Gabarret
Mézin
Francescas
Nérac
Barbaste
Lavardac
Houeillès
Casteljaloux
Buzet-sur-Baïse
Damazan
Aiguillon
Port-Ste-Marie
Tonneins
Clairac
Castelmoron-sur-Lot
Le Mas-d'Agenais
Bouglon
Grignols
Marmande
Virazeil
Seyches
Miramont-de-Guyenne
St-Pardoux
Lauzun
Eymet
Duras
Monségur
Ste-Bazeille
La Réole
Gironde-sur-Dropt
Sauveterre-de-Guyenne
Targon
Pellegrue
Sigoulès
Ste-Foy-la-Grande
Gardonne
Bergerac
Le Fleix
La Force
Vélines
St-Magne-de-Castillon
Castillon-la-Bataille
Branne
Pujols
Garonne
Dropt
Ciron
Midouze
Douze
Adour
Gave de Pau
Gave d'Oloron
Saison
Baïse
Neste
Arros

D
E
F
33
41
42
58
1
2
3
4
Sarlat-la-Canéda
Souillac
Beaulieu-sur-Dordogne
Aurillac
Gramat
Figeac
Decazeville
Rodez
Onet-le-Château
Cahors
Villefranche-de-Rouergue
Agen
Moissac
Castelsarrasin
Montauban
Caussade
Carmaux
Albi
Gaillac
Graulhet
Castres
Mazamet
Toulouse
Blagnac
Colomiers
Plaisance-du-Touch
Cugnaux
Ramonville-St-Agne
Muret
Castelnaudary
Carcassonne
Limoux
Pamiers
Foix
Auch
St-Gaudens
Montréjeau
Bagnères-de-Luchon
Ax-les-Thermes
Tarascon-sur-Ariège
Lavelanet
Mirepoix
Quillan
Revel
Lectoure
Fleurance
Lauzerte
Cordes
Réalmont
HAUT QUERCY
BAS QUERCY
QUERCY
ROUERGUE
SÉGALA
CHÂTAIGNERAIE
PÉRIGORD NOIR
LOMAGNE
LAURAGAIS
CABARDÈS
RAZÈS
Causse de Gramat
Causse de Limogne
Forêt de la Grésigne
Montagne Noire
Monts de Lacaune
Massif de l'Arize
Montagnes du Plantaurel
Plateau de Lecamp
A20
A62
A68
A680
A61
A64
A66
E09
E72
E80
N20
N21
N113
N124
N126
N88
N140
N122
Garonne
Tarn
Lot
Dordogne
Aveyron
Ariège

42
34
41
59
A
B
C
1
2
3
4
GÉVAUDAN
Causse Comtal
Causse de Sauveterre
Causse Méjean
Causse Noir
Causse du Larzac
Causse de St-Affrique
Monts de Lacaune
Monts de l'Espinouse
Montagne de la Séranne
Monts du Vivarais
Mont Lozère
Cévennes
MINERVOIS
GARRIGUES
CAMARGUE
PETITE CAMARGUE
Golfe du Lion
Golfe d'Aigues-Mortes
Golfe de Stes Maries ou Beauduc
Étang de Vaccarès
Étang de Bages et de Sigean
Étang de l'Ayrolle
Bassin de Thau
Cap Leucate
Pointe de l'Espiguette
Pointe du Sablon
Gorges de la Truyère
Gorges du Tarn
Gorges de l'Hérault
Lac du Salagou
Lac de Pareloup
Lac de Charpal
Barrage de Sarrans
Barrage de Naussac
Lac de Laouzas
Rodez
Espalion
Laguiole
Chaudes-Aigues
St-Chély-d'Apcher
Aumont-Aubrac
Marvejols
Mende
La Canourgue
Sévérac-le-Château
Millau
St-Affrique
Florac
Langogne
Pradelles
Aubenas
Privas
Villeneuve-de-Berg
Les Vans
Alès
Uzès
Bagnols-sur-Cèze
Pont-St-Esprit
Nîmes
Beaucaire
Lunel
Vauvert
St-Gilles
Aigues-Mortes
Le Grau-du-Roi
Stes-Maries-de-la-Mer
Montpellier
Castelnau-le-Lez
Lattes
Palavas-les-Flots
Frontignan
Sète
Mèze
Agde
Cap d'Agde
Béziers
Pézenas
Clermont-l'Hérault
Lodève
Le Vigan
Ganges
Bédarieux
Lamalou-les-Bains
St-Pons-de-Thomières
Narbonne
Narbonne-Plage
Gruissan
Sigean
Port-la-Nouvelle
Leucate
Durban-Corbières
Salses-le-Château
Perpignan
Canet-en-Roussillon
A75
A9
A61
A54
E11
E15
E80
N9
N88
N106
N102
N104
N113
N110
N112
N109

43
35
44
D
E
F
1
2
3
4
Bourg-lès-Valence
Valence
St-Péray
Cornas
Portes-lès-Valence
Montmeyran
Livron-sur-Drôme
Loriol-sur-Drôme
Allex
Crest
Saulce-sur-Rhône
Grane
Saillans
Die
Châtillon-en-Diois
Luc-en-Diois
Alpes du Dauphiné
Massif du Diois
Bourdeaux
La Bégude-de-Mazenc
Marsanne
St-Marcel-lès-Sauzet
Montélimar
Allan
Dieulefit
Taulignan
Donzère
Grignan
Grillon
Valréas
La Garde-Adhémar
St-Paul-Trois-Châteaux
Visan
Tulette
Nyons
Mirabel-aux-Baronnies
Buis-les-Baronnies
BARONNIES
Rémuzat
Rosans
La Motte-Chalancon
Bollène
Mondragon
Mornas
Piolenc
Orange
Jonquières
Courthézon
Sérignan-du-Comtat
Violès
Vaison-la-Romaine
Sablet
Malaucène
Mont Ventoux 1909
Bédoin
Aubignan
Sarrians
Carpentras
Mazan
Monteux
Entraigues-sur-Sorgues
Pernes-les-Fontaines
Sorgues
Pujaut
Vedène
Le Pontet
Avignon
Le Thor
L'Isle-sur-la-Sorgue
Gordes
Roussillon
Monts de Vaucluse
Sault
St-Christol
St-Saturnin-lès-Apt
Apt
Châteaurenard
Cavaillon
Robion
Bonnieux
Goult
Noves
Caumont-sur-Durance
Rognonas
Eyragues
St-Andiol
Maillane
St-Rémy-de-Provence
Tarascon
Orgon
Alpilles
Maussane-les-Alpilles
Eygalières
Sénas
Lamanon
Mouriès
Salon-de-Provence
Mallemort
Mérindol
Lauris
Lourmarin
Cadenet
Cucuron
Montagne du Lubéron
La Roque-d'Anthéron
Alleins
Lambesc
Pélissanne
St-Cannat
Rognes
Le Puy-Ste-Réparade
Pertuis
Villelaure
La Tour-d'Aigues
Venelles
Éguilles
Meyrargues
Peyrolles-en-Provence
Jouques
Miramas
St-Chamas
Istres
Berre-l'Étang
Étang de Berre
La Fare-les-Oliviers
Velaux
Rognac
Vitrolles
Aix-en-Provence
Gardanne
Fos-sur-Mer
Port-de-Bouc
Martigues
Marignane
St-Victoret
Châteauneuf-les-Martigues
Port-St-Louis-du-Rhône
Sausset-les-Pins
Carry-le-Rouet
Ensuès-la-Redonne
Septèmes-les-Vallons
Allauch
Marseille
Golfe de Fos
Cap Couronne
Île Pomègues
Île Ratonneau
Île de Planier
Cap Croisette
Île de Riou
Cassis
La Penne-sur-Huveaune
Aubagne
Roquevaire
Auriol
Gémenos
Cuges-les-Pins
La Ciotat
Ceyreste
Bandol
Ollioules
Sanary-sur-Mer
La Seyne-sur-Mer
Toulon
Presqu'île de St-Mandrier
Cap Sicié
Le Pradet
Carqueiranne
Hyères
La Crau
Presqu'île de Giens
Golfe de Giens
Île de Porquerolles
Îles d'Hyères
Île de Port-Cros
Île du Levant
Rade d'Hyères
Le Lavandou
Rade de Bormes
Cap Bénat
Bormes-les-Mimosas
La Londe-les-Maures
Massif des Maures
Collobrières
Pierrefeu-du-Var
Cavalaire-sur-Mer
Cap Cartaya
La Croix-Valmer
Ramatuelle
Cogolin
Grimaud
St-Tropez
Cap de St-Tropez
Port Grimaud
Ste-Maxime
Golfe de St-Tropez
La Garde-Freinet
Le Cannet-des-Maures
Le Luc
Vidauban
Plan-de-la-Tour
Roquebrune-sur-Argens
Fréjus
St-Raphaël
St-Aygulf
Le Muy
Trans-en-Provence
Draguignan
Estérel
Bagnols-en-Forêt
Fayence
Callas
Seillans
Montferrat
Figanières
Flayosc
Lorgues
Taradeau
Salernes
Villecroze
Aups
Cotignac
Carcès
Le Val
Cabasse
Brignoles
Flassans-sur-Issole
Besse-sur-Issole
Carnoules
Puget-Ville
Gareoult
Néoules
La Roquebrussanne
Nans-les-Pins
Tourves
St-Maximin-la-Ste-Baume
Pourcieux
Trets
Fuveau
Rousset
St-Zacharie
Signes
Le Beausset
Solliès-Pont
Solliès-Toucas
Cuers
Belgentier
PROVENCE
Barjols
Tavernes
Rians
Vinon-sur-Verdon
Gréoux-les-Bains
Riez
Valensole
Plateau de Valensole
Moustiers-Ste-Marie
Lac de Ste-Croix
Grand Canyon du Verdon
Comps-sur-Artuby
Roumoules
Castellane
Barrême
St-Auban
Sénez
Mézel
Digne-les-Bains
Aiglun
Malijai
Les Mées
Peyruis
Château-Arnoux
L'Escale
Volonne
Peipin
Sisteron
Noyers-sur-Jabron
Montagne de Lure
St-Étienne-les-Orgues
Forcalquier
Mane
Banon
Reillanne
Villeneuve
Volx
Manosque
Pierrevert
Ste-Tulle
Sederon
St-Auban-sur-l'Ouvèze
Orpierre
Laragne-Montéglin
Serres
Aspres-sur-Buëch
Veynes
Gap
Tallard
Barcillonnette
La Motte-du-Caire
La Bâtie-Neuve
Chorges
Lac de Serre-Ponçon
Savines-le-Lac
Embrun
Le Lauzet-Ubaye
Barcelonnette
Jausiers
Seyne
La Javie
Le Seignus-d'Allos
Colmars
St-Étienne-de-Tinée
Annot
Entrevaux
St-André-les-Alpes
Grasse
St-Vallier-de-Thiey
Guillestre
Briançon
Villar-St-Pancrace
L'Argentière-la-Bessée
Massif du Pelvoux
La Bérarde
Orcières
St-Bonnet-en-Champsaur
St-Firmin
Corps
St-Étienne-en-Dévoluy
Dévoluy
BOCHAINE
Mens
Clelles
Monestier-de-Clermont
Valbonnais
La Mure
Pierre-Châtel
La Chapelle-en-Vercors
8 hrs 30 mins Ajaccio
10 hrs Bastia
12 hrs Calvi
11 hrs 30 mins L'Île Rousse
13 hrs 30 mins Porto Vecchio
8 hrs 30 mins Propriano
8 hrs 30 mins Propriano
8 hrs Ajaccio
8 hrs 30 mins Bastia
6 hrs 30 mins L'île Rousse

A
B
C
36
43
1
2
3
4
I
F
MC
Pinerolo
San Germano Chisone
Torre Pellice
Bobbio Pellice
Luserna San Giovanni
Bricherasio
Cavour
Airasca
Vigone
None
Pancalieri
Casalgrasso
Carmagnola
Racconigi
Moretta
Bagnolo Piemonte
Barge
Crissolo
Paesana
Revello
Saluzzo
Sanfront
Savigliano
Cavallermaggiore
Sommariva del Bosco
Bra
Alba
Asti
Villanova d'Asti
Villafranca d'Asti
Ferrere
San Damiano d'Asti
Monta
Canale
Isola d'Asti
Castello di Annone
Alessandria
Castellazzo-Bormida
Mombercelli
Nizza Monferrato
Calamandrana
Canelli
Cassine
Acqui Terme
Novi Ligure
Serravalle Scrivia
Arquata Scrivia
Predosa
Rocca Grimalda
Ovada
Molare
Mornese
Voltaggio
Castagnole delle Lanze
Neive
Sto Stefano Belbo
Bubbio
Bistagno
Cessole
Vesime
Melazzo
Visone
Ponzone
Cortemilia
Mombaldone
Spigno Monferrato
Rossiglione
Campo Ligure
Masone
Campomorone
Urbe
Sassello
Monte Beigua 1287
Dego
Cairo Montenotte
Albisola Superiore
Varazze
Arenzano
Cogoleto
Voltri
Pegli
Celle Ligure
Albisola Marina
Savona
Vado Ligure
Capo di Vado
Bergeggi
Spotorno
Noli
Capo di Noli
Finale Ligure
Pietra Ligure
Loano
Borghetto Sto Spirito
Ceriale
Albenga
Villanova d'Albenga
Isola Gallinara
Alassio
Laigueglia
Capo Mele
Cervo
San Bartolomeo al Mare
Diano Marina
Oneglia
Imperia
San Lorenzo al Mare
Sto Stefano al Mare
Taggia
San Remo
Bordighera
Ventimiglia
Camporosso
Dolceacqua
Menton
Roquebrune-Cap-Martin
Beausoleil
Monte-Carlo
Villefranche-sur-Mer
Nice
St-Laurent-du-Var
Cagnes-sur-Mer
Villeneuve-Loubet
Antibes
Cap d'Antibes
Juan-les-Pins
Vallauris
Cannes
Le Cannet
Mougins
Grasse
Vence
La Trinité
Carros
Gattières
Théoule-sur-Mer
Îles de Lérins
Le Trayas
Cap Roux
Anthéor
Fréjus
St-Raphaël
Boulouris
St-Aygulf
Golfe de Fréjus
Les Issambres
Pointe des Issambres
Ste-Maxime
Golfe de St-Tropez
Cap de St-Tropez
St-Tropez
Cap Camarat
Cap Cartaya
Baie des Anges
Côte d'Azur
Riviera di Ponente
MAR
Barcelona
Cuneo
Mondovì
Fossano
Centallo
Borgo San Dalmazzo
Boves
Peveragno
Beinette
Chiusa di Pesio
Vicoforte
San Michele Mondovì
Ceva
Cengio
Millesimo
Carcare
Altare
Quiliano
Bagnasco
Massimino
Osiglia
Calizzano
Garessio
Bardineto
Ormea
Erli
Toirano
Pieve di Teco
Pornassio
Cosio di Arroscia
Borghetto d'Arroscia
Ortovera
Cisano sul Neva
Cesio
Chiusavecchia
Borgomaro
Pontedassio
Badalucco
Triora
Rezzo
Pigna
Baiardo
Ceriana
Airole
Saorge
Fontan
Tende
Breil-sur-Roya
Sospel
Limone Piemonte
Vernante
Robilante
Roccavione
Entracque
Certosa di Pesio
Frabosa Soprana
Fontane
Pamparato
Dronero
Caraglio
Busca
Costigliole Saluzzo
Venasca
Verzuolo
Genola
Narzole
Bene Vagienna
Cherasco
Dogliani
Carrù
Morozzo
Murazzano
Monforte d'Alba
Diano d'Alba
Bossolasco
Monesiglio
Saliceto
Piana Crixia
Castelmagno
Demonte
Vinadio
Sambuco
Pietraporzio
Argentera
Acceglio
Stroppo
San Damiano Macra
Sampeyre
Casteldelfino
Pontechianale
Chianale
Monte Viso 3841
Monte Chersogno 3026
Monte Nebin 2510
Rocca la Meia 2831
Guillestre
Arvieux
Aiguilles
La Roche-de-Rame
Jausiers
Barcelonnette
St-Laurent-du-Verdon
St-Étienne-de-Tinée
Auron
Isola
Isola 2000
Le Boréon
St-Sauveur-sur-Tinée
Valdeblore
St-Martin-Vésubie
Roquebillière
Lantosque
Péone
Beuil
Valberg
Guillaumes
Daluis
Rigaud
Puget-Théniers
Entrevaux
Clans
Villars-sur-Var
Utelle
La Penne
Roquesteron
Gilette
Levens
Lucéram
Peïra-Cava
L'Escarène
Contes
Blausasc
Peille
St-Martin-du-Var
Coursegoules
St-Auban
St-Vallier-de-Thiey
Escragnolles
Le Bar-sur-Loup
Peymeinade
Valbonne
Biot
Mouans
Callian
Fayence
Montauroux
St-Paul-en-Forêt
Mandelieu-la-Napoule
Lago di Piastra
Bacino Chiotas
Col de Tende
Alpes Maritimes
Alpi Cozie
Montagne de Gourdan

37
38
45
46
D
E
F
1
2
3
4
Genova
Recco
Camogli
Rapallo
Zoagli
Chiavari
Lavagna
Sta Margherita Ligure
Portofino
Sestri Levante
Casarza Ligure
Moneglia
Deiva Marina
Bonassola
Levanto
Riomaggiore
La Spezia
Portovenere
Lerici
Isola Palmaria
Isola del Tino
Golfo della Spezia
Sarzana
Carrara
Massa
Marina di Carrara
Marina di Massa
Montignoso
Seravezza
Pietrasanta
Viareggio
Massarosa
Lago di Massaciuccoli
Lucca
Capannori
Porcari
Altopascio
Pescia
Montecatini Terme
Monsummano Terme
Pistoia
Quarrata
Vinci
Fucecchio
Santa Croce sull'Arno
Castelfranco di Sotto
Empoli
San Miniato
Vecchiano
San Giuliano Terme
Pisa
Cascina
Pontedera
Ponsacco
Tirrenia
Collesalvetti
Livorno
Torre della Meloria
Isola di Gorgona
Torre Nuovo Scalo
Quercianella
Castiglioncello
Rosignano Marittimo
Cecina
Marina di Cecina
Bibbona
Volterra
Pomarance
Larderello
Marina di Castagneto Donoratico
Castagneto Carducci
Sassetta
San Vincenzo
Suvereto
Campiglia Marittima
Populonia
Piombino
Golfo di Follonica
Follonica
Massa Marittima
Scarlino
Punta Ala
Castiglione della Pescaia
Marina di Grosseto
Canale di Piombino
Isola d'Elba
Portoferraio
Rio nell'Elba
Rio Marina
Porto Azzurro
Capoliveri
Marciana Marina
Marciana
Marina di Campo
Punta di Fetovaia
Punta dei Ripalti
Capo Vita
Isola Palmaiola
Isola Cerboli
Scoglio dello Sparviero
Monte Capanne
1018
Arcipelago
Capraia Isola
Isola di Capraia
CORSE
F
Cap Corse
Île de la Giraglia
Centuri
Macinaggio
Rogliano
Meria
Pino
Luri
Pietracorbara
Canari
Monte Stello
1307
Sisco
Nonza
Brando
Golfe de St-Florent
Pta di Curza
Patrimonio
St-Florent
Bastia
Désert des
Golfo di Genova
Mar Ligure
IGURE
Riviera di Levante
Parma
Collecchio
Fornovo di Taro
Salsomaggiore Terme
Fidenza
Fiorenzuola d'Arda
Reggio nell'Emilia
Modena
Carpi
Correggio
Novellara
Soliera
Scandiano
Sassuolo
Formigine
Maranello
Fiorano Modense
Vignola
Spilamberto
Pavullo nel Frignano
Castelnovo ne'Monti
Frignano
Appennino
Alpi Apuane
Barga
Castelnuovo di Garfagnana
Abetone
Cutigliano
San Marcello Pistoiese
Bagni di Lucca
Borgo a Mozzano
Fivizzano
Aulla
Pontremoli
Villafranca in Lunigiana
Sto Stefano di Magra
Bardi
Borgotaro
Berceto
Passo della Cisa
Bedonia
Varzi
Torriglia
Bobbio
Colline Metallifere
A1
A12
A15
A11
A22
E80
E33
E35
E62
E76

46
38
A
B
C
1
2
3
4
45
48
Parma
Collecchio
Reggio nell'Emilia
Scandiano
Sassuolo
Modena
Formigine
Maranello
Fiorano Modenese
Casalgrande
Correggio
Carpi
Soliera
Novellara
Novi di Modena
Mirandola
Bondeno
Ferrara
Copparo
Codigoro
Comacchio
Portomaggiore
Argenta
Cento
Crevalcore
Nonantola
San Giovanni in Persiceto
Castelfranco Emilia
San Cesario sul Panaro
Spilamberto
Vignola
Zola Predosa
Casalecchio di Reno
Bologna
San Lazzaro di Savena
Castel Maggiore
Castenaso
Budrio
Molinella
Medicina
Sasso Marconi
Pianoro
Castèl San Pietro Terme
Imola
Lugo
Bagnacavallo
Alfonsine
Ravenna
Russi
Faenza
Forlì
Forlimpopoli
Cesena
Savignano sul Rubicone
Santarcangelo di Romagna
Pavullo nel Frignano
Castelnovo ne' Monti
Castelnuovo di Garfagnana
Barga
Seravezza
Pietrasanta
Massarosa
Viareggio
Lucca
Capannori
Pescia
Montecatini Terme
Monsummano Terme
Pistoia
Montemurlo
Agliana
Prato
Calenzano
Sesto Fiorentino
Campi Bisenzio
Quarrata
Signa
Lastra a Signa
Scandicci
Fiesole
Firenze
Bagno a Ripoli
Pontassieve
Borgo San Lorenzo
Vinci
Fucecchio
Santa Croce sull'Arno
Empoli
Montelupo Fiorentino
San Miniato
Castelfranco di Sotto
Pontedera
Cascina
Pisa
San Giuliano Terme
Vecchiano
Livorno
Collesalvetti
Ponsacco
Rosignano Marittimo
Cecina
San Casciano in Val di Pesa
Impruneta
Castelfiorentino
Certaldo
Poggibonsi
Colle di Val d'Elsa
Volterra
Figline Valdarno
Greve in Chianti
San Giovanni Valdarno
Terranuova Bracciolini
Montevarchi
Bibbiena
Arezzo
Sansepolcro
Città di Castello
Castiglion Fiorentino
Cortona
Siena
Sinalunga
Montepulciano
Castiglione del Lago
Magione
Corciano
Campiglia Marittima
Piombino
Follonica
Portoferraio
Grosseto
Orvieto
FRIGNANO
MONTEFELTRO
Colline Metallifere
Golfo di Follonica
Canale di Piombino
Lago Trasimeno
E35
E45
E55
E76
E78
E80
A1
A11
A12
A13
A14
A14dir
A22

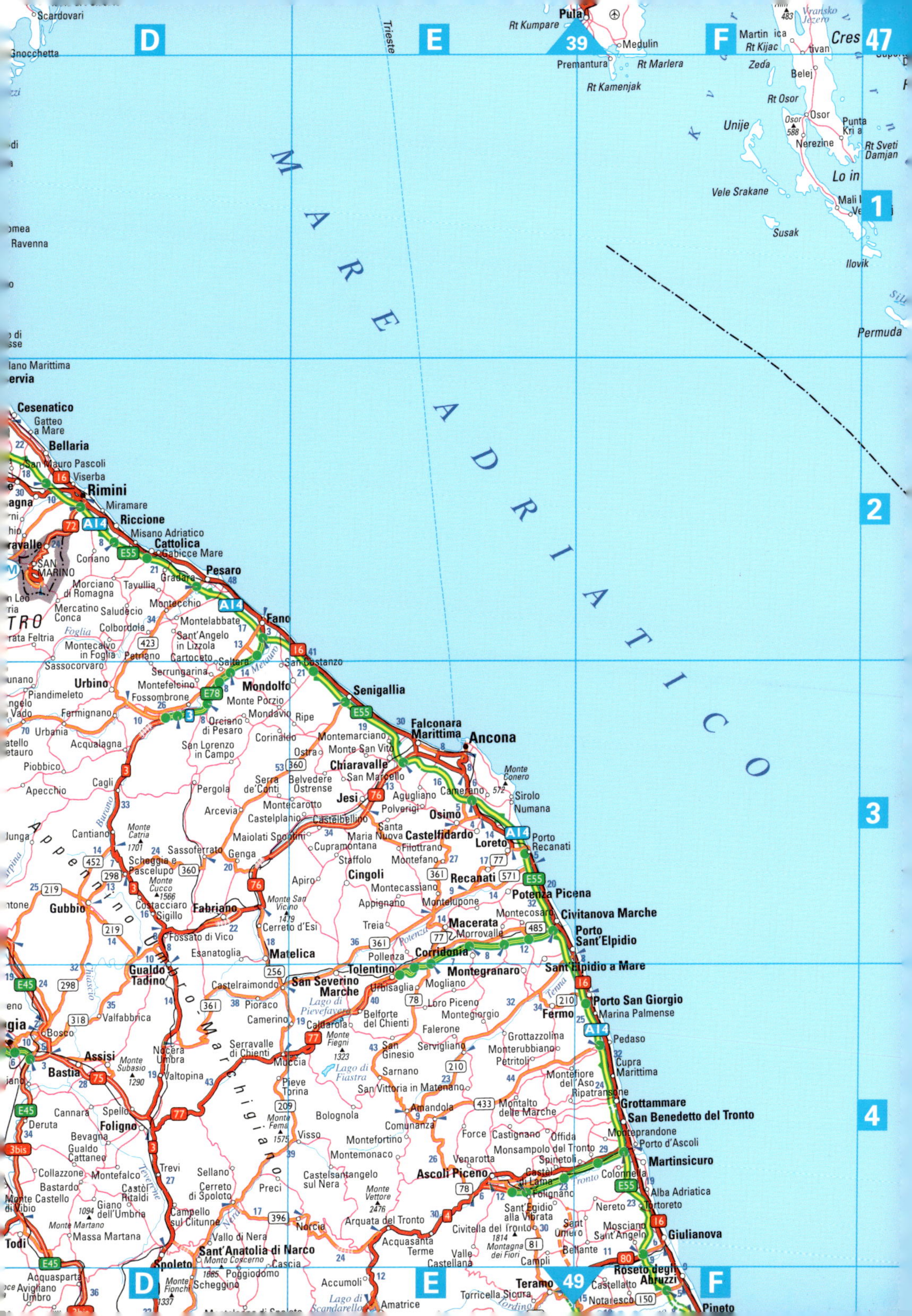
D
E
F
1
2
3
4
39
49
MARE ADRIATICO
Appennino Umbro-Marchigiano
Scardovari
Gnocchetta
Ravenna
Trieste
Pula
Rt Kumpare
Premantura
Medulin
Rt Marlera
Rt Kamenjak
Martin ica
Rt Kijac
Cres
Zeđa
Belej
Rt Osor
Osor
588
Unije
Nerezine
Punta Kri a
Rt Sveti Damjan
Lo in
Vele Srakane
Mali L
Susak
Ilovik
Permuda
Vransko Jezero
483
Cesenatico
Gatteo a Mare
Bellaria
San Mauro Pascoli
Viserba
Rimini
Miramare
Riccione
Misano Adriatico
Cattolica
Gabicce Mare
SAN MARINO
Coriano
Morciano di Romagna
Tavullia
Gradara
Pesaro
Mercatino Conca
Saludecio
Montecchio
Colbordola
Montelabbate
Fano
Sant'Angelo in Lizzola
Montecalvo in Foglia
Petriano
Cartoceto
San Costanzo
Saltara
Sassocorvaro
Serrungarina
Urbino
Montefelcino
Mondolfo
Senigallia
Piandimeleto
Fossombrone
Monte Porzio
Fermignano
Orciano di Pesaro
Mondavio
Ripe
Urbania
Acqualagna
San Lorenzo in Campo
Corinaldo
Montemarciano
Falconara Marittima
Ancona
Monte Conero
572
Sirolo
Numana
Ostra
Monte San Vito
Chiaravalle
San Marcello
Piobbico
Cagli
Pergola
Serra de'Conti
Belvedere Ostrense
Jesi
Agugliano
Camerano
Polverigi
Osimo
Apecchio
Arcevia
Montecarotto
Castelplanio
Castelbellino
Santa Maria Nuova
Castelfidardo
Loreto
Porto Recanati
Cantiano
Monte Catria 1701
Maiolati Spontini
Cupramontana
Montefano
Scheggia e Pascelupo
Sassoferrato
Genga
Staffolo
Recanati
Monte Cucco 1566
Apiro
Cingoli
Potenza Picena
Gubbio
Costacciaro
Sigillo
Fabriano
Monte San Vicino 1479
Montecassiano
Appignano
Montelupone
Montecosaro
Civitanova Marche
Porto Sant'Elpidio
Cerreto d'Esi
Treia
Macerata
Morrovalle
Fossato di Vico
Esanatoglia
Matelica
Pollenza
Corridonia
Sant'Elpidio a Mare
Gualdo Tadino
Tolentino
Montegranaro
Castelraimondo
San Severino Marche
Urbisaglia
Mogliano
Porto San Giorgio
Marina Palmense
Pioraco
Lago di Pievefavera
Loro Piceno
Fermo
Camerino
Belforte del Chienti
Montegiorgio
Valfabbrica
Caldarola
Falerone
Grottazzolina
Pedaso
Bosco
Nocera Umbra
Serravalle di Chienti
Monte Fiegni 1323
San Ginesio
Servigliano
Monterubbiano
Petritoli
Cupra Marittima
Assisi
Monte Subasio 1290
Muccia
Lago di Fiastra
Sarnano
Montefiore dell'Aso
Ripatransone
Bastia
Valtopina
Pieve Torina
San Vittoria in Matenano
Grottammare
San Benedetto del Tronto
Cannara
Spello
Amandola
Montalto delle Marche
Monteprandone
Porto d'Ascoli
Deruta
Foligno
Bolognola
Comunanza
Bevagna
Gualdo Cattaneo
Monte Fema 1575
Visso
Montefortino
Force
Castignano
Offida
Monsampolo del Tronto
Spinetoli
Martinsicuro
Montemonaco
Venarotta
Collazzone
Montefalco
Trevi
Sellano
Colonnella
Bastardo
Castel Ritaldi
Cerreto di Spoleto
Castelsantangelo sul Nera
Preci
Monte Vettore 2476
Ascoli Piceno
Castel di Lama
Folignano
Alba Adriatica
Monte Castello di Vibio
Giano dell'Umbria
1094
Tortoreto
Campello sul Clitunno
Arquata del Tronto
Sant'Egidio alla Vibrata
Nereto
Monte Martano
Massa Martana
Vallo di Nera
Norcia
Civitella del Tronto
Sant'Omero
Mosciano Sant'Angelo
Giulianova
Todi
Sant'Anatolia di Narco
Monte Coscerno 1685
Cascia
Acquasanta Terme
1814
Montagna dei Fiori
Valle Castellana
Bellante
Spoleto
Poggiodomo
Campli
Roseto degli Abruzzi
Acquasparta
Avigliano Umbro
Monte Fionchi 1337
Scheggino
Accumoli
Lago di Scandarello
Amatrice
Torricella Sicura
Teramo
Castellalto
Notaresco
Pineto
A14
E55
E78
E45
16
72
76
77
3
3bis
75
80
423
360
452
298
219
256
361
318
209
396
571
485
210
433
78
81
150

A
B
C
46
1
2
3
4
Grosseto
Marina di Grosseto
Marina di Alberese
Formiche di Grosseto
Talamone
Scansano
Sempronianò
Magliano in Toscana
Manciano
Pitigliano
Sorano
Onano
Grotte di Castro
Gradoli
Lago di Bolsena
Bolsena
Castell'Azzara
Proceno
Acquapendente
San Lorenzo Nuovo
Castel Viscardo
Orvieto
Lago di Corbara
Todi
Massa Martana
Vallo di Nera
Sant'Anatolia di Narco
Spoleto
Monte Coscerno
Poggiodomo
Scheggino
Monte Fionchi
Acquasparta
Avigliano Umbro
Baschi
Castiglione in Teverina
Bagnoregio
Guardea
Lago di Alviano
Alviano
Montecastrilli
San Gemini
Montefranco
Ferentillo
Arrone
Monteleone di Spoleto
Leonessa
Terni
Narni
Stroncone
Rivodutri
Poggio Bustone
Lago di Piediluco
Lago Lungo
Cantalice
Contigliano
Greccio
Rieti
Amelia
Penna in Teverina
Orte
Otricoli
Cottanello
Calvi dell'Umbria
Magliano Sabina
Tarano
Casperia
Monte Pizzuto
Forano
Poggio Catino
Poggio Mirteto
Montopoli di Sabina
Torricella in Sabina
Belmonte in Sabina
Rocca Sinibalda
Fara in Sabina
Poggio Moiano
Lago di Turano
Scandriglia
Orvinio
Montelibretti
Moricone
Palombara Sabina
Monti Sabini
Monterotondo
Licenza
Marcellina
Vicovaro
Mentana
Guidonia-Montecelio
Castel Madama
Tivoli
Gallicano nel Lazio
Colle Corvia
Palestrina
Cave
Valmontone
Genazzano
Farnese
Valentano
Capodimonte
Montefiascone
Graffignano
Lugnano in Teverina
Attigliano
Ischia di Castro
Cellere
Piansano
Marta
Canino
Arlena di Castro
Vitorchiano
Monte Cimino
Soriano nel Cimino
Vasanello
Gallese
Vignanello
Fabrica di Roma
Corchiano
Canepina
Viterbo
Tuscania
Vetralla
Lago di Vico
Carparola
Civita Castellana
Ronciglione
Blera
Monte Romano
Capranica
Sutri
Nepi
Faleria
Rignano Flaminio
Bassano Romano
Vejano
Oriolo Romano
Mazzano Romano
Fiano Romano
Campagnano di Roma
Castelnuovo di Porto
Riano
Formello
Trevignano Romano
Lago di Bracciano
Bracciano
Anguillara Sabazia
Lago di Martignano
Manziana
Tolfa
Allumiere
Poggio del Leccio
Capalbio
Laguna di Orbetello
Porto Santo Stefano
Orbetello
Punta Lividonia
Monte Argentario
Porto Ercole
Ansedonia
I'Isolotto
Punta del Fenaio
Punta del Capel Rosso
Isola di Giannutri
Montalto di Castro
Montalto Marina
Tarquinia
Tarquinia Lido
Civitavecchia
Santa Marinella
San Severa
Cerveteri
Ladispoli
Fregene
Fiumicino
Lido di Ostia
Ostia
CITTÀ DEL VATICANO
ROMA
Ciampino
Frascati
Grottaferrata
Rocca di Papa
Marino
Castel Gandolfo
Albano Laziale
Ariccia
Genzano di Roma
Artena
Lariano
Rocca Massima
Velletri
Lanuvio
Montelanico
Pomezia
Tor Vaianica
Ardea
Aprilia
Cori
Norma
Cisterna di Latina
Lavinio-Lido di Enea
Nettuno
Anzio
Latina
Lido di Foce Verde
Torre Astura
Lago di Fogliano
Lago di Caprolace
Sabaudia
Lago di Sabaudia
Isola Palmarola
Isole Ponziane
Isola di Ponza
Cagliari (Sardegna)
A1
A1dir
A12
A24
E35
E35/45
E45
E80
Tevere
Fiora
Arrone
Mignone
Ombrone
Albegna
Astura

49
47
50
D
E
F
1
2
3
4
Teramo
Roseto degli Abruzzi
Giulianova
Pineto
Silvi
Atri
Montesilvano
Pescara
Spoltore
Francavilla al Mare
Chieti
Ortona
Punta di Ferruccio
San Vito Chietino
Punta Cavalluccio
Rocca San Giovanni
Fossacesia
Lanciano
Guardiagrele
Punta della Penna
Vasto
San Salvo
Termoli
Campomarino
Marina di Chieuti
Penne
Amatrice
Accumoli
Lago di Scandarello
Campotosto
Lago di Campotosto
Montereale
Gran Sasso d'Italia
Isola del Gran Sasso d'Italia
Monte Corno 2912
Assergi
L'Aquila
Antrodoco
Paganica
Poggio Picenze
Barisciano
Navelli
Popoli
Tocco da Casauria
Corfinio
Raiano
Sulmona
Pratola Peligna
Pescina
Celano
Avezzano
Piana del Fucino
San Benedetto dei Marsi
Trasacco
Gioia dei Marsi
Tagliacozzo
Scurcola Marsicana
Magliano de'Marsi
Capistrello
Civitella Roveto
Balsorano
Pescasseroli
Villetta Barrea
Lago di Barrea
Alfedena
Castel di Sangro
Roccaraso
Pescocostanzo
Rivisondoli
Palena
Lama
Casoli
Atessa
Bomba
Lago di Bomba
Montenerodomo
Villa Santa Maria
Lago di Sangro
Monti dei Frentani
Agnone
Capracotta
Pescopennataro
Schiavi di Abruzzo
Trivento
Montefalcone
Torrebruna
Castelmauro
Lago di Guardialfiera
Larino
Montenero di Bisaccia
Guglionesi
Palata
Montecilfone
Casacalenda
Lucito
Bonefro
Colletorto
Santa Croce di Magliano
Sant'Elia a Pianisi
Ripalimosano
Campobasso
Ferrazzano
Vinchiaturo
Baranello
Bojano
Monti del Matese
Monti del Sannio
Jelsi
Riccia
Gambatesa
Castelvetere in Val Fortore
Pietracatella
Lago di Occhito
Isernia
Carpinone
Pescolanciano
Carovilli
Frosolone
Civitanova del Sannio
Castropignano
Limosano
Bagnoli del Trigno
Pietrabbondante
Rionero Sannitico
Cerro al Volturno
Colli a Volturno
Venafro
Monteroduni
Macchiagodena
Roccamandolfi
Capriati a Volturno
Letino
Lago del Matese
Piedimonte Matese
Alife
Cusano Mutri
Cerreto Sannita
Guardia Sanframondi
Telese
Solopaca
San Salvatore Telesino
Faicchio
Gioia Sannitica
Dragoni
Morcone
Sepino
Cercemaggiore
Sta Croce del Sannio
Colle Sannita
Circello
Baselice
San Bartolomeo in Galdo
Molinara
San Marco dei Cavoti
San Giorgio la Molara
Pesco Sannita
Buonalbergo
Paduli
Benevento
Apice
Ariano Irpino
Montesarchio
Airola
Moiano
Sant'Agata de'Goti
Frasso Telesino
Vitulano
Foglianise
Torrecuso
Ponte
Caserta
Maddaloni
Casagiove
Capua
Sta Maria Capua Vetere
Marcianise
Caianello
Teano
Sessa Aurunca
Carinola
Roccamonfina
Mondragone
Castèl Volturno
Villa Literno
San Cipriano d'Aversa
Aversa
Lusciano
Giugliano in Campania
Qualiano
Casoria
Afragola
Acerra
Caivano
Cicciano
Marigliano
Nola
Palma Campania
Avellino
Atripalda
Mercogliano
Montemiletto
Solofra
Serino
Mercato San Severino
Sarno
Pagani
Nocera Inferiore
Cava de'Tirreni
Baronissi
Salerno
Pontecagnano Faiano
Bellizzi
Battipaglia
Monti Picentini
Montecorvino Rovella
Golfo di Salerno
Vietri sul Mare
Amalfi
Praiano
Positano
Sorrento
Massa Lubrense
Vico Equense
Castellammare di Stabia
Gragnano
Torre Annunziata
Torre del Greco
Pompei
Angri
Boscotrecase
Ottaviano
San Giuseppe Vesuviano
Vesuvio 1281
Portici
Napoli
Pozzuoli
Bacoli
Monte di Procida
Capo Miseno
Procida
Isola di Procida
Ischia
Isola d'Ischia
Forio
Lacco Ameno
Barano d'Ischia
Golfo di Napoli
Capri
Isola di Capri
Anacapri
Punta Campanella
Li Galli
Golfo di Gaeta
Isola Ventotene
Isola Zannone
Gaeta
Formia
Minturno
Sperlonga
Terracina
Golfo di Terracina
San Felice Circeo
Fondi
Lago di Fondi
Monti Aurunci
Monti Ausoni
Sonnino
Priverno
Roccasecca dei Volsci
Maenza
Roccagorga
Sezze
Ceccano
Frosinone
Ferentino
Alatri
Fumone
Anagni
Fiuggi
Acuto
Piglio
Olevano Romano
Subiaco
Monti Simbruini
Veroli
Sora
Isola del Liri
Arpino
Monte San Giovanni Campano
Ceprano
Pontecorvo
Aquino
Roccasecca
Cassino
Cervaro
Sant'Elia Fiumerapido
Atina
Villa Latina
Picinisco
Alvito
San Donato Val di Comino
Campoli Appennino
Pignataro Interamna
Esperia
Ausonia
Spigno Saturnia
Castelforte
Sessa
Pietramelara
Vairano Patenora
Pratella
San Gregorio Matese
Calvi Risorta
Vitulazio
Sparanise
Grazzanise
Cancello ed Arnone
A1
A14
A16
A24
A25
A3
A30
E45
E80
E55
E842
E841

50
49
A
B
C
1
2
3
4
52
Termoli
Campomarino
Marina di Chieuti
Lago di Lesina
Lesina
Poggio Imperiale
Torre Mileto
Lago di Varano
Rodi Garganico
Ischitella
Peschici
San Menaio
Vieste
Testa del Gargano
Vico del Gargano
Carpino
Cagnano Varano
Sannicandro Garganico
Apricena
Promontorio del Gargano
Pugnochiuso
Baia della Zagare
Mattinata
Monte Sant'Angelo
San Marco in Lamis
Monte Calvo
San Giovanni Rotondo
Rignano Garganico
San Severo
Torremaggiore
San Paolo di Civitate
Serracapriola
Chieuti
San Martino in Pensilis
Ururi
Larino
Guglionesi
Montenero di Bisaccia
Montecilfone
Palata
Casacalenda
Rotello
Santa Croce di Magliano
Bonefro
Colletorto
Casalnuovo Monterotaro
Casalvecchio di Puglia
Castelnuovo della Daunia
Pietramontecorvino
Carlantino
Lago di Occhito
Celenza Valfortore
Motta Montecorvino
Volturara Appula
Volturino
Lucera
Tavoliere
Manfredonia
Lido di Siponto
Golfo di Manfredonia
Foggia
Zapponeta
Saline
Margherita di Savoia
Trinitapoli
San Ferdinando di Puglia
Barletta
Trani
Bisceglie
Molfetta
Canosa di Puglia
Andria
Corato
Terlizzi
Ruvo di Puglia
Bitonto
Palo del Colle
Grumo Appula
Mariotto
Cerignola
Stornara
Stornarella
Orta Nova
Ordona
Carapelle
Castelluccio dei Sauri
Troia
Biccari
Alberona
San Bartolomeo in Galdo
Baselice
Colle Sannita
Circello
Molinara
Roseto Valfortore
Faeto
Castelluccio Valmaggiore
Orsara di Puglia
Montefalcone di Val Fortore
San Giorgio la Molara
Greci
Buonalbergo
Casalbore
Bovino
Panni
Deliceto
Ascoli Satriano
Accadia
Monteleone di Puglia
Savignano Irpino
Montecalvo Irpino
Ariano Irpino
Sant'Agata di Puglia
Anzano di Puglia
Villanova del Battista
Grottaminarda
Flumeri
Vallata
Lacedonia
Rocchetta Sant'Antonio
Candela
Lago di Capaciotti
Posta Piana
Minervino Murge
Lavello
Montemilone
Lago del Rendina
Melfi
Rapolla
Venosa
Spinazzola
Palazzo San Gervasio
Monte Caccia
Poggiorsini
Gravina in Puglia
Altamura
Murgia Sant'Elia
Genzano di Lucania
Lago di Serra del Corvo
Banzi
Maschito
Forenza
Acerenza
Barile
Rionero in Vulture
Monte Vulture
Atella
Ripacandida
Filiano
Lago Pesole
Bradano
Monte Torretta
Pietragalla
Oppido Lucano
Irsina
Cancellara
Tolve
San Chirico Nuovo
Vaglio Basilicata
Potenza
Brindisi Montagna
Trivigno
Albano di Lucania
Tricarico
Grassano
Grottole
Miglionico
Lago di San Giuliano
Matera
Pomarico
Salandra
Garaguso
Oliveto Lucano
Accettura
San Mauro Forte
Ferrandina
Stigliano
Cirigliano
Gorgoglione
Guardia Perticara
Aliano
Missanello
Craco
Lago di Gannano
Pisticci
Bernalda
Montalbano Jonico
Tursi
Policoro
Rotondella
Nova Siri
Rocca Imperiale
Montegiordano
Canna
Valsinni
Colobraro
Senise
Lago di Monte Cotugna
San Giorgio Lucano
Noepoli
Oriolo
Cersosimo
San Costantino Albanese
San Severino Lucano
Francavilla in Sinni
Chiaromonte
Fardella
Teana
Castronuovo di Sant'Andrea
Roccanova
Sant'Arcangelo
Episcopia
Latronico
Castelsaraceno
San Chirico Raparo
Moliterno
Sarconi
Lago di Pietra del Pertusillo
Montemurro
Armento
Corleto Perticara
Viggiano
Marsico Vetere
Marsico Nuovo
Monte Volturino
Calvello
Laurenzana
Anzi
Abriola
Lago di Ponte Fontanelle
Pignola
Passo Croce dello Scrivano
Tito
Satriano di Lucania
Brienza
Sasso di Castalda
Picerno
Baragiano
Ruoti
Bella
Avigliano
Muro Lucano
San Gregorio Magno
Balvano
Vietri di Potenza
Caggiano
Auletta
Polla
Sant'Arsenio
Atena Lucana
San Rufo
Sala Consilina
Teggiano
Sassano
Padula
Monte Motola
Paterno
Tramutola
Montesano sulla Marcellana
Buonabitacolo
Casalbuono
Monte Cervati
Sanza
Caselle in Pittari
Lagonegro
Monte del Papa
Rivello
Lauria
Monte la Spina
Trecchina
Maratea
Tortora
Aieta
Praia a Mare
Scalea
Papasidero
Mormanno
Laino Borgo
Castelluccio Inferiore
Rotonda
Viggianello
Monte Pollino
Morano Calabro
Terranova di Pollino
Alessandria del Carretto
Albidona
San Lorenzo Bellizzi
Villapiana
Trebisacce
Amendolara
Golfo di Policastro
Sapri
Vibonati
Santa Marina
Roccagloriosa
Torre Orsaia
Laurito
Montano Antilia
Rofrano
San Giovanni a Piro
Scario
Camerota
Marina di Camerota
Punta degli Infreschi
Palinuro
Capo Palinuro
Centola
Pisciotta
Ascea
Ceraso
Vallo della Lucania
Gioi
Stio
Laurino
Felitto
Roscigno
Castel San Lorenzo
Roccadaspide
Capaccio
Agropoli
Ogliastro Cilento
Torchiara
Rutino
Castellabate
Santa Maria di Castellabate
Isola Licosa
Perdifumo
Sessa Cilento
Montecorice
Acciaroli
Pollica
Casal Velino
Omignano
Golfo di Salerno
Battipaglia
Bellizzi
Eboli
Pontecagnano Faiano
Salerno
Campagna
Serre
Postiglione
Controne
Castelcivita
Altavilla Silentina
Albanella
Sant'Angelo a Fasanella
Contursi Terme
Buccino
Palomonte
Oliveto Citra
Colliano
Laviano
Castelgrande
San Fele
Ruvo del Monte
Rapone
Conza della Campania
Teora
Lioni
Calitri
Andretta
Sant'Angelo dei Lombardi
Nusco
Montella
Bagnoli Irpino
Caposele
Calabritto
Acerno
Monti Picentini
Montecorvino Rovella
Baronissi
Mercato San Severino
Solofra
Serino
Atripalda
Avellino
Volturara Irpina
Castelfranci
Paternopoli
Gesualdo
Frigento
Guardia Lombardi
Taurasi
Mirabella Eclano
Montemiletto
Altavilla Irpina
Apice
Benevento
Montesarchio
San Giorgio del Sannio
Cava de' Tirreni
Nocera Inferiore
Pagani
Sarno
Forino
Bisaccia
Aquilonia
Monteverde
Carife
Monti del Sannio
Jelsi
Riccia
Gambatesa
Castelvetere in Val Fortore
Sassinoro
Pietracatella
Ferrazzano
Sepino
Guardia Sanframondi
Pesco Sannita
Paduli
Ponte Landolfo
Fragneto
Mercogliano
Trieste

D
E
F
1
2
3
4
Dubrovnik
Bar
Durrës
Durrës
Igoumenitsa
Vlorë
Kerkyra, Igoumenitsa
Paxos, Patras, Sami,
Zakynthos, Cesmé
vinazzo
San Spirito
Bari
Mola
di Bari
Modugno
Triggiano
Valenzano
Capurso
Noicattaro
Bitritto
Rutigliano
Adelfia
Polignano
a Mare
Sannicandro
di Bari
Conversano
Monopoli
Casamassima
Aquaviva
delle Fonti
Turi
Castellana Grotte
Sammichele
di Bari
Putignano
Fasano
Selva
Torre
Canne
Villanova
Gioia
del Colle
Noci
Alberobello
Locorotondo
Cisternino
Ostuni
Carovigno
anteramo
in Colle
Masseria
Risana
Martina
Franca
Ceglie
Messapica
San Vito
dei Normanni
Punta
Penne
Isole Pedagne
Brindisi
Capo di
Torre Cavallo
Laterza
Castellaneta
Mottola
Palagianello
Crispiano
Villa Castelli
San Michele
Salentino
Ginosa
Palagiano
Massafra
Montemesola
Canale Reale
Latiano
Mesagne
Capo San Gennaro
ntescaglioso
Grottaglie
Monteiasi
Francavilla
Fontana
Oria
Torre Sta
Susanna
San Pietro Vernotico
Case Perrone
Carosino
San Pancrazio
Salentino
Torchiarolo
Casa l'Abate
Borgo Grappa
Bradano
Isole
Cheradi
Taranto
Mare
Piccolo
Mare Grande
San Giorgio
Ionico
Fragagnano
Erchie
San
Donaci
Squinzano
Trepuzzi
Surbo
San
Cataldo
Talsano
Lizzano
Sava
Manduria
Campi
Salentina
Capo
San Vito
Leporano
Pulsano
Murge Tarantine
Salice Salentino
Veglie
Carmiano
Lecce
Lido di
Metaponto
Marina di
Pulsano
Torricella
Avetrano
Maruggio
Monteroni di Lecce
Lizzanello
Roca
Vecchia
Leverano
Vernole
Punta
dell'Ovo
Campomarino
Copertino
Lequile
Melendugno
Scanzano Jonico
Porto Cesareo
San Donato
di Lecce
Calimera
Soleto
Martano
Nardò
Carpignano Salentino
Galatina
Cursi
Otranto
Galatone
Cutrofiano
Maglie
Uggiano la Chiesa
Aradeo
Golfo di
Taranto
Sannicola
Neviano
Isola
Sant'Andrea
Gallipoli
Alezio
Collepasso
Scorrano
Poggiardo
Parabita
Matino
Nociglia
Sta Cesarea Terme
Supersano
Castro
Torre del Pizzo
Taviano
Casarano
Andrano
Ruffano
Melissano
Montesano Salentino
Racale
Taurisano
Tricase
Alliste
Specchia
Ugento
Presicce
Corsano
Alessano
Torre San
Giovanni
Salve
Marina di Novaglie
Morciano di Leuca
Castrignano del Capo
Gagliano del Capo
Marina
di Leuca
Capo Sta
Spulico
E55
E843
E90
A14
D
E
F

50
A
B
C
1
2
3
4
Golfo di Policastro
Golfo di Sta Eufemia
Golfo di Squillace
Golfo di Gioia
Stretta di Messina
MARE IONIO
LA SILA
Lauria
Maratea
Praia a Mare
Isola di Dino
Capo Scalea
Scalea
Tortora
Aieta
Mormanno
Papasidero
Sta Domenica Talao
Orsomarso
Verbicaro
Sta Maria del Cedro
Grisolia
Buonvicino
Diamante
Belvedere Marittimo
Bonifati
Cittadella del Capo
Cetraro
Acquappesa
Guardia Piemontese
Fuscaldo
Paola
San Lucido
Falconara Albanese
Fiumefreddo Bruzio
Longobardi
Belmonte Calabro
Amantea
Campora San Giovanni
Nocera Terinese
Capo Suvero
Castrovillari
Cassano allo Ionio
Sibari
Trebisacce
Villapiana
Amendolara
Capo Spulico
Montegiordano
Rotonda
Viggianello
Morano Calabro
Frascineto
Civita
Saracena
Lungro
Altomonte
Firmo
Spezzano Albanese
Terranova da Sibari
Tarsia
San Demetrio Corone
Corigliano Calabro
Rossano
Marina Schiavonea
Capo Trionto
Mirto Crosia
Crosia
Cropalati
Mandatoriccio
Cariati
Pta Fiume Nicà
Terravecchia
Campana
Crucoli
Cirò
Punta Alice
Cirò Marina
Bisignano
Acri
Luzzi
Rose
Montalto Uffugo
San Fili
Rende
Cosenza
San Pietro in Guarano
Celico
Camigliatello Silano
Lago di Cecita
Lago di Ariamacina
Longobucco
Bocchigliero
Savelli
Verzino
Umbriatico
Pallagorio
Melissa
Strongoli
San Nicola dell'Alto
Casabona
Rocca di Neto
San Giovanni in Fiore
Caccuri
Lago Arvo
Lago Ampollino
Cotronei
Petilia Policastro
Sta Severina
Scandale
San Mauro Marchesato
Crotone
Capo Colonna
Cutro
Isola di Capo Rizzuto
Capo Rizzuto
Steccato
Botricello
Sellia Marina
Mesoraca
Petronà
Sersale
Cropani
Simeri-Crichi
Zagarise
Pentone
Magisano
Taverna
Villaggio Mancuso
Carlopoli
Soveria Mannelli
Decollatura
Serrastretta
Platania
Gimigliano
Tiriolo
Nicastro
Feroleto Antico
Sambiase
Falerna
Gizzeria
Lamezia
Catanzaro
Catanzaro Marina
Borgia
Girifalco
Cortale
Maida
Curinga
Amaroni
Squillace
Copanello
Filadelfia
Polia
Pizzo
Monterosso Calabro
Gasperina
San Vito sullo Ionio
Soverato
Chiaravalle Centrale
Cardinale
Davoli
St Andrea Apostolo dello Ionio
Badolato
Sta Caterina dello Ionio
Punta Stilo
Stilo
Monasterace
Riace
Caulonia
Serra San Bruno
Simbario
Soriano Calabro
Vibo Valentia
Stefanaconi
Maierato
Mileto
Sant'Angelo
Tropea
Parghelia
Zungri
Spilinga
Capo Vaticano
Ricadi
Joppolo
Rombiolo
Limbadi
Nicotera
San Ferdinando
Rosarno
Gioia Tauro
Laureana di Borrello
Dinami
Acquaro
Ferdinandea
Guardavalle
Fabrizia
Melicucco
Rizziconi
Cinquefrondi
Polistena
Cittanova
Taurianova
Palmi
Bagnara Calabra
Seminara
Scilla
Sinopoli
Cosoleto
Delianuova
Grotteria
Mammola
Gioiosa Ionica
Roccella Ionica
Marina di Gioiosa Ionica
Siderno
Gerace
Locri
Platì
Ardore
Benestare
San Luca
Bovalino
St Agata del Bianco
Bianco
Capo Bruzzano
Brancaleone
Capo Spartivento
Staiti
Palizzi
Bova
Bova Marina
Condofuri
Roghudi
San Lorenzo
Bagaladi
Melito di Porto Salvo
Capo dell'Armi
Montebello Ionico
Motta San Giovanni
Pellaro
San Gregorio
Cardeto
Reggio di Calabria
Gambarie
Cerasi
Calanna
Villa San Giovanni
Messina
Capo Peloro
Mortelle
Spartà
Scaletta Zanclea
Nizza di Sicilia
Teresa di Riva
Monte Pollino 2248
Monte Botte Donato 1928
Monte Cocuzzo 1541
Monte Reventino 1417
Monte Scorda
Montalto 1955
Passo di Pietra Spada
Passo di Cancello
A3
E45
E90
E844
E846
E848
106
107
18
19
534

D
E
F
1
2
3
4
54
60
Pta da Estaca de Bares
Cabo Ortegal
Cariño
Porto do Barqueiro
Vicedo
Ría de Viveiro
Pta Candelaria
Ortigueira
Viveiro
Xove
Cervo
Cedeira
Serra da Faladoira
Vila da Igrexa
Cabo Prior
Pereiro
Ourol
Avenida do Marqués de Figueroa
Serra do Xistral
Castro de Ouro
Gándara
Neda
Ferrol
Foxas
Muras
Cabo Prioriño Grande
Mugardos
Ares
As Neves
As Pontes de García Rodríguez
Ría de Betanzos
Pontedeume
Chao
Porto da Xesta
Abadín
A Coruña (La Coruña)
Illas Sisargas
Pta Langosteira
Armada
Xermade
Malpica
A Baiuca
Real
Sada
Carreira
Caión
Carrio
Rebordelo
Pta Roncudo
Corme-Porto
BERGANTIÑOS
Tarrio
Cambre
Betanzos
Pazo de Irixoa
Vilalba
Pastoriza
Ponte-Ceso
Laracha
Carballo
AS MARIÑAS
Laxe
Bosque
Carral
San Marcos
Oza
Ponte-Aranga
Feira do Monte
Campo da Feira
Baio Grande
San Roque
Castro de Rei
Camariñas
Mesón do Vento
Cesuras
Teixeiro
Guitiriz
Begonte
Rábade
Muxía
Vimianzo
Zas
Serra da Cova da Serpe
Cabo Touriñán
Outeiro de Rei
Pontepedra
Ordes
Xanceda
Ru
Sobrado
Santa Catalina de Armada
Dumbría
Bembibre
Viaño Pequeno
Gándara
Friol
Lugo
Cée
Sigüeiro
Tambre
Corcubión
San Vicente
A Picota
Arzúa
Sierra da Cova
Souto
Negreira
Santiago de Compostela
Melide
Cabo Fisterra
Fisterra
O Pedrouzo
Palas de Rei
Carreteira
Ría de Corcubión
Pedrouzos
Fuente Díaz
Embalse de Portodemouros
Carnota
Serra de Outes
Bertamiráns
Treboile
Puebla de San Xulián
Forte
Vila de Cruces
Portomarín
Antas de Ulla
Muros
Noia
Dices
A Ramallosa
Vedra
Monterroso
Punta Carreiro
Portobravo
Ría de Muros e Noia
Padrón
Ulla
A Golada
Porto do Son
Taboada
Tallós
Enfesta
Ponte Valga
Embalse de Belesar
Boiro
Rianxo
A Estrada
Silleda
Lalín
Rodeiro
Catoira
Cuntis
Alto de Nespereira
Vilagarcía de Arousa
Puebla del Caramiñal
Caldas de Reis
Santa Lucía
Forcarei
Chantada
Bóveda
Vilanova de Arousa
Escairón
Santa Eugenia
Cabo Falcoeira
Curres
O Castro
Ría de Arousa
Campo Lameiro
Serra do Faro
A Barrela
Cambados
San Antoniño
Cercedo
Montes de Testeiro
Monforte
O Grove
Mosteiro
Irixo
Piñor
Embalse dos Peares
Illa de Salvora
Escusa
O Convento
A Chán
Beariz
Cea
Castro
As Covas
Pontevedra
Serra do Suido
A Peroxa
Sanxenxo
Boborás
Carballiño
Amoeiro
Vilarchao
Illa de Ons
Marín
Ponte Caldelas
A Lama
Igrexario
Maside
A Teixeira
Luintra
Ría de Pontevedra
Toural
Leiro
San Amaro
Embalse de Velle
Parada de Sil
Embalse San Este
Bueu
Rial
Igrexa
Carballeda de Avia
A Forxa
Pereiro de Aguiar
Castro Caldelas
Moaña
Pazos
Ourense (Orense)
Esgos
Puebla
Cangas
Redondela
Barral
Toén
Alto de Cousa
Ribadavia
Barbadás
San Cibrao das Viñas
Alto do Rodicio
Melón
Montederramo
Illas Cíes
Vigo
Ría de Vigo
Mondariz
Covelo
Paderne de Allariz
Maceda
Mondariz-Balneario
Cortegada
A Merca
Baños de Molgas
A Cañiza
Outomuro
Taboadela
Nigrán
Reguengo
Ponteareas
Crecente
Sobrado
Ramirás
Xunqueira de Ambía
Serra do San Mamede
Cabo Silleiro
Porriño
O Ribeiro
San Roque
Allariz
Vilar de Barrio
Baiona
Consistorio
Melgaço
Leirado
Celanova
Sandiás
Gondomar
Esfarrapada
As Neves
Paderne
Carballo
Vilar de Santos
Sarreaus
O Castelo
Valadares
Xinzo de Limia
Tui
Ganfei
Monção
Longos Vales
Cubalhão
Castro Laboreiro
Bande
A LIMIA
Laza
Valença
Riba de Mouro
Trasmiras
Arrabal
Gandra
Serra da Peneda
Monte del Quinxo
A Forxa
Blancos
Porto de Estivadas
O Seixo
Minho
Extremo
Vila
Cualedro
Embalse das Conchas
Castrel do Val
Candemil
Paredes de Coura
Muiños
Calvos
Baltar
A Guardia
Coura
Soajo
Pedrada
Embalse de Salas
Monterrei
Punta dos Picos
Moledo
Caminha
Serra de Arga
Arcos de Valdevez
Fondevila
Serra do Larouco
Oímbra
Vila Praia de Âncora
Orbacém
Lindoso
Barrio
Britelo
Serra do Gerês
Montealegre
Vilarelho da Raia
Afife
Cabração
Arcozelo
Jolda
Ponte da Barca
Sarraquinhos
Amonde
Ribeira
Outeiro
Carreço
Ponte de Lima
Serra Amarela
Homem
Paradela
Outeiro Seco
Águas Frias
Meadela
Boalhosa
Barragem do Alto Rabagão
Chaves
Areosa
Seara
Sobito
MINHO
Vilar da Veiga
Viana do Castelo
Darque
Vila da Ponte
Redondelo
Anha
Barroselas
Freixo
Caldelas
Caldo
Ruivães
Barragem Venda Nova
Boticas
Vidago
Lagarelhos
Castelo do Neiva
Antas
Forjães
Prado
Vila Verde
Amares
Vieira do Minho
Venda Nova
Salto
Dornelas
Loivos
Tâmega
TRÁS-OS
A55
A9
A6
A53
A52
E01
E70
E801
V1
550
552
545
543
540
634
640
641
642
646
547
525
533
541
120
554
531
536
301
202
101
304
202-2
201
IC1
303
306
305
202
203
204
13
103
307
308
308-4
311
213
314
532
205

A
B
C
1
2
3
4
53
61
Costa Verde
Cabo Burela
Cabo de Peñas
Cabo Vidio
Vicedo
Ria de Viveiro
Xove
Viveiro
Cervo
Foz
San Cosme
Tapia de Casariego
Ribadeo
Castropol
Vegadeo
La Caridad
Coaña
Navia
Luarca
Canero
Cudillero
Piedras Blancas
Salinas
Avilés
Luanco
Candás
Gijón-Xijón
Muros
Pravia
Soto
Nubledo
Posada de Llanera
Lugones
Noreña
Pola de Siero
Grullos
Santullano de las Regueras
Oviedo
Trubia
Grado
Soto de Ribera
Langreo
Santa Eulalia
Sotrondio
Mieres
Blimea
Pola de Lena
Moreda
Cabañaquinta
Proaza
Caranga
La Vega de Riosa
La Plaza
Bárzana
Ferreira
Castro de Ouro
Vilanova de Lourenzá
Trabada
Mondoñedo
Porto da Xesta
Abadín
El Llano
Rodrigas
A Pontenova
Taramundi
Pastoriza
Sierra de la Bobia
Boal
Villayón
Sierra de Rañadoiro
Bárcena del Monasterio
Tineo
La Espina
Cornellana
Salas
Belmonte
La Florida
Pola de Allande
Puerto del Palo
Berducedo
Santa Eulalia de Oscos
Grandas de Salime
Feira do Monte
Castro de Rei
Meira
Serra de Meira
A Fonsagrada
Mosteiro
Embalse de Salime
Cangas del Narcea
Venta Nueva
San Antolín de Ibias
Castroverde
O Cádabo
Paradela
Proba
O Corgo
Genestoso
Pola de Somiedo
Puerto de Somiedo
Puerto de Rañadoiro
Degaña
Puerto de Leitariegos
Piedrafita de Babia
Cabrillanes
Villaseca de Laciana
Villablino
San Emiliano
Puerto de Pajares
Cármenes
Baralla
Becerreá
San Román
Serra dos Ancares
Palacios del Sil
Sierra de Gistredo
Embalse de Barrios de Luna
Vegacervera
Ciñera
La Pola de Gordón
Puebla de San Xulián
Sarria
As Nogais
Candín
Murias de Paredes
Los Barrios de Luna
Páramo del Sil
Vegarienza
La Magdalena
La Robla
Triacastela
Samos
Pedrafita do Cebreiro
Porto de Piedrafita
Fabero
Riello
Soto y Amío
Rioseco de Tapia
Cuadros
Garrafe de Torío
Igueña
Vega de Espinareda
Toreno
Boeza
Quintana del Castillo
Las Omañas
El Bierzo
Bóveda
Escairón
A Cruz de Incio
Folgoso do Courel
Serra do Courel
Vega de Valcarce
Arganza
Villafranca del Bierzo
Cabañas Raras
Congosto
Folgoso de la Ribera
Llamas de la Ribera
Sariegos
Villaquilambre
San Andrés del Rabanedo
León
Puebla de Brollón
Monforte
Corullón
Carracedelo
Cacabelos
Camponaraya
Bembibre
Castropodame
Torre del Bierzo
Manzanal del Puerto
Puerto del Manzanal
Carrizo de la Ribera
Cimanes del Tejar
Toral de los Vados
Ponferrada
Priaranza del Bierzo
Molinaseca
Villamejil
Valverde de la Virgen
Turcia
Armunia
Onzonilla
Santa Marina del Rey
Benavides de Orbigo
Chozas de Abajo
Quiroga
San Clodio
Vilamartín de Valdeorras
Rubiá
O Barco
Carucedo
Villar de los Barrios
Montes de León
Santa Colomba de Somoza
Astorga
San Justo de la Vega
Villarejo de Orbigo
Bustillo del Páramo
Sil
A Teixeira
Embalse de San Estevan
A Rúa
Sobradelo
Puente de Domingo Flórez
Lucillo de Somoza
Santiagomillas
Riego de la Vega
Valdevimbre
Castro Caldelas
Petín
Luyego de Somoza
Soto de la Vega
Santa María del Páramo
Berciano del Páramo
Alto do Rodicio
Puebla de Trives
Manzaneda
O Bolo
Serra do Eixe
Destriana
La Bañeza
Laguna Dalga
Villamañán
Montederramo
Embalse de Chandrexa de Queixa
A Veiga
Encinedo
Truchas
Roperuelos del Páramo
Toral de los Guzmanes
Serra do San Mamede
Alto de Cevelo
Sierra de la Cabrera
Santa Elena de Jamuz
Embalse de Vao
Porto
Viana do Bolo
Castrocontrigo
Castrocalbón
Laguna de Negrillos
Embalse das Portas
Vilariño de Conso
Sanabria
Alija del Infantado
Pozuelo del Páramo
Villamandos
Villaquejida
Sarreaus
Ribadelago
Galende
Espadañedo
Ayoo de Vidriales
Arrabalde
Pobladura del Valle
Laza
Trasmiras
Alto do Canizo
A Gudiña
Puebla de Sanabria
Peque
Uña de Quintana
Santibáñez de Vidriales
Quiruelas de Vidriales
Manganeses de la Polvorosa
San Cristóbal de Entreviñas
Valderas
Porto de Estivadas
Castrelo do Val
Lubián
Portilla de Padornelo
Requejo
Palacios de Sanabria
San Pedro de Ceque
Mombuey
Camarzana de Tera
Benavente
Verín
Ríos
Hermisende
Pedralba de la Pradería
Embalse de Cernadilla
Rionegro del Puente
Melgar de Tera
Santibáñez de Tera
Santa Cristina de la Polvorosa
Castrogonzalo
Monterrei
Alto de Fumaces
Manzanal de Arriba
Rio de Onor
Embalse de Valparaíso
Burganes de Valverde
Oímbra
Vilardevós
Santalha
Mofreita
Peña Mira
Villardeciervos
Otero de Bodas
Morales de Valverde
San Esteban del Molar
Villamayor
Serra da Coroa
Parâmio
Serra de Montezinho
Aveleda
Ferreras de Abajo
Ferreras de Arriba
Bretocino
Santovenia
Vilarelho da Raia
Mauros
São Vicente
Vinhais
Mahíde
Sierra de la Culebra
Tábara
Villafáfila
Outeiro Seco
Vila Verde da Raia
Tronco
Bragança
Deilão
Figueruela de Arriba
Granja de Moreruela
Chaves
Águas Frias
Lebução
Rebordelo
Edrosa
Samil
Milhão
San Vitero
Riofrío de Aliste
Rabanales
Moreruela de Tábara
Villarrín de Campos
Manganeses de la Lampreana
Castronuevo
Sonim
Agrochão
Faílde
Trabazos
Ferreruela de Tábara
Perilla de Castro
Vilarandelo
Outeiro
Alcañices
Samir de los Caños
Embalse de Ricobayo
Losacino
Carbajales de Alba
San Cebrián de Castro
Pajares de la Lampreana
Montamarta
Lagarelhos
Vidago
Loivos
Torre de Dona Chama
Santa Comba de Rossas
A52
A6
A8
A66
E70
E801
E82
IP4

D
E
F
1
2
3
4
56
62
Plymouth (summer only)
Ría de Villaviciosa
Cabo Lastres
Cabo Mayor
Bahía de Santander
Cabo de Ajo
Villaviciosa de Asturias
Colunga
Ribadesella
Nueva
Llanes
Santander
Santoña
Noja
Laredo
Torrelavega
Muriedas
El Astillero
Renedo
Santa Cruz de Bezana
Suances
Santillana
Comillas
San Vicente de la Barquera
Pesués
Colombres
Panes
Infiesto
Arriondas
Cangas de Onís
Benia de Onís
Carreña de Cabrales
Las Arenas
Santa Eulalia
Laviana
Sames
Campo de Caso
Picos de Europa
Sotres
Tama
Potes
Camaleño
Espinama
La Vega
Posada de Valdeón
Oseja de Sajambre
Puerto de Tarna
Puerto del Pontón
Portilla de la Reina
Puerto de San Glorio
Cabezón de Liébana
Sierra de Peña Sagra
Puentenansa
Roiz
Cabezón de la Sal
Puente de San Miguel
Luzmela
Ruente
Valle
Los Corrales de Buelna
Puente Viesgo
Rivero
Cartes
Arenas de Iguña
Bárcena de Pie de Concha
Los Tojos
Molledo
Los Pandos
Puerto de Piedrasluengas
Puerto de Palombera
Espinilla
Embalse del Ebro
Reinosa
Matamorosa
Arija
Pedrosa
Soncillo
Sierra de Peña Labra
Sierra de Alba
San Salvador de Cantamunda
Triollo
Vañes
Branosera
Barruelo de Santullán
Salinas de Pisuerga
Cervera de Pisuerga
Mataporquera
Arroyal
Puerto Pozazal
Aguilar de Campóo
Embalse de Aguilar de Campóo
Polientes
Ebro
Riaño
Embalse de Riaño
Burón
Puebla de Lillo
Embalse de Porma
Crémenes
Boñar
La Collada
Vegaquemada
La Ercina
Sabero
Cistierna
Prioro
Besande
Alto de las Portillas
Velilla del Río Carrión
Santibáñez de la Peña
Guardo
Castrejón de la Peña
Respenda de la Peña
Olmos de Ojeda
Prado de la Guzpeña
Santa Columba de Curueño
Ambasaguas
Vegas del Condado
Gradefes
Almanza
Villalba de Guardo
La Puebla de Valdavia
Congosto de Valdavia
Pino del Río
Buenavista de Valdavia
Revilla de Collazos
Villaeles de Valdavia
Villanuño de Valdavia
Saldaña
Prádanos de Ojeda
Alar del Rey
Herrera de Pisuerga
Sotresgudo
Basconcillos del Tozo
Quintana del Pino
Puerto del Páramo de Masa
Villadiego
Villamayor de Treviño
Villegas
Sasamón
Rabanedo
Quintana de Rueda
Villazanzo de Valderaduey
Santervás de la Vega
Saelices del Río
Mansilla de las Mulas
El Burgo Ranero
Cea
Renedo de la Vega
Bahíllo
Villasarracino
Villaherreros
Osorno
Melgar de Fernamental
Villasandino
Villanueva de Argaño
Tardajos
Buniel
Burgos
Sahagún
Ledigos
San Mamés de Campos
Carrión de los Condes
Villalcázar de Sirga
Lantadilla
Castellanos de Castro
Castrojeriz
Estepar
Gordaliza del Pino
Grajal de Campos
Melgar de Arriba
Villada
Cervatos de la Cueza
San Román de la Cuba
Cisneros
Itero de la Vega
Frómista
Villoldo
Piña de Campos
Astudillo
Pedrosa del Príncipe
Pampliega
Saelices de Mayorga
Boadilla de Rioseco
Mayorga
Villalumbroso
Paredes de Nava
Amusco
Monzón de Campos
Palenzuela
Santa María del Campo
Villahizán
Villahoz
Becilla de Valderaduey
Villalón de Campos
Frechilla
Becerril de Campos
Villaumbrales
Grijota
Cuenca de Campos
Fuentes de Nava
Villamartín de Campos
Villarramiel
Castromocho
Palencia
Villamediana
Torquemada
Quintana del Puente
Tabanera de Cerrato
Valdunquillo
Ceinos de Campos
Pedraza de Campos
Villerías
Villamuriel de Cerrato
Magaz
Villaviudas
Baltanás
Espinosa de Cerrato
Tierra de Campos
Castroverde de Campos
Ampudia
Venta de Baños
Dueñas
Cevico de la Torre
Cevico Navero
Villafruela
Villafrechós
Medina de Rioseco
Villalpando
Morales de Campos
Tordehumos
Villabrágima
Villalba de los Alcores
La Mudarra
Trigueros del Valle
Valoria la Buena
Tórtoles de Esgueva
Castrillo de Don Juan
Villagarcía de Campos
Castromonte
San Pedro de Latarce
Urueña
Montes de Torozos
Cigales
Mucientes
Esguevillas de Esgueva
Villafuerte
Piña de Esgueva
Villardefrades
Peñaflor de Hornija
Wamba
Villanubla
Torrelobatón
Zaratán
Valladolid
Mota del Marqués
Tiedra
Renedo
Valbuena de Duero
Castrillo Tejeriego
Piñel de Abajo
Peñafiel
Castrillo de la Vega
Fuentecén
Aranda de Duero
La Horra
Roa
Villalba
Gumiel de Mercado
Gumiel de Hizán
Hontoria de Valdearados
Quemada
Baños de Valdearados
Caleruega
Olmedilla de Roa
Torresandino
Bahabón de Esgueva
Nebreda
Peñas de Cervera
Lerma
Covarrubias
Madrigal del Monte
Cogollos
Cuevas de San Clemente
Hontoria de la Cantera
Sarracín
Cardeñadijo
Arcos
Villasur de Herreros
Revilla del Campo
Ibeas de Juarros
Arlanzón
Quintanapalla
Rubena
Sotopalacios
Puerto de la Brújula
Huérmeces
Santibáñez Zarzaguda
Masa
Cernégula
Tubilla del Agua
Sedano
La Lora
La Bureba
Poza de la Sal
Briviesca
Rublacedo de Abajo
Pesadas de Burgos
Dobro
Puerto de la Mazorra
Villarcayo
Incinillas
Medina de Pomar
Manzanedo
Sierra de la Tesla
Nofuentes
Trespaderne
Oña
Cornudilla
La Cerca
Bercedo
Villasante de Montija
Espinosa de los Monteros
San Pedro del Romeral
Barcenillas de Cerezos
Vega de Pas
San Vicente de Toranzo
Selaya
Villacarriedo
Santa María de Cayón
Penagos
San Martín
La Concha
Pomaluengo
Valdecilla
Solórzano
La Cavada
Arredondo
Riba
Ramales de la Victoria
Rasines
Ampuero
Bádames
Limpias
Colindres
El Puente
Concha
Montes de Ordunte
Ajo
Carriazo
Escalante
Rubayo
Beranga
Gama

A
B
C
1
2
3
4
55
63
Plymouth (summer only)
Portsmouth (winter only)
Golfe de Gascogne
Golfo de Gascuña
Côte d'
Cabo Mayor
Bahía de Santander
Cabo de Ajo
Cabo Machichaco
Santander
El Astillero
Noja
Santoña
Laredo
Castro-Urdiales
Colindres
Ajo
Carriazo
Escalante
Rubayo
Beranga
Gama
Valdecilla
Solórzano
Bádames
Ampuero
Limpias
El Puente
La Concha
Penagos
La Cavada
Pomaluengo
Santa María de Cayón
Arredondo
Riba
Ramales de la Victoria
Rasines
Villacarriedo
Selaya
Vega de Pas
San Pedro del Romeral
Espinosa de los Monteros
Barcenillas de Cerezos
Bercedo
Villasante de Montija
Castrobarto
Pedrosa
Soncillo
Villarcayo
Medina de Pomar
La Cerca
Manzanedo
Incinillas
Nofuentes
Trespaderne
Frías
Oña
Puerto de la Mazorra
Dobro
Pesadas de Burgos
Polientes
Sedano
Tubilla del Agua
Cernégula
Masa
Poza de la Sal
Cornudilla
Cubo de Bureba
Pancorbo
Briviesca
Rublacedo de Abajo
LA LOSA
LA BUREBA
Sierra de la Tesla
Sierra Salvada
Montes Obarenes
Huérmeces
Sotopalacios
Rubena
Quintanapalla
Puerto de la Brújula
Villaescusa la Sombría
Belorado
Alcocero de Mola
Cerezo de Río Tirón
Herramélluri
Burgos
Tardajos
Buniel
Ibeas de Juarros
Arlanzón
Villasur de Herreros
Cardeñadijo
Sarracín
Arcos
Cogollos
Revilla del Campo
Hontoria de la Cantera
Cuevas de San Clemente
Madrigal del Monte
Covarrubias
Lerma
Barbadillo del Mercado
Santo Domingo de Silos
Hortigüela
Barbadillo del Pez
Barbadillo de Herreros
Nebreda
Peñas de Cervera
Valdosa 1412
Villafruela
Bahabón de Esgueva
Caleruega
Huerta del Rey
Espejón
Baños de Valdearados
Gumiel de Hizán
Hontoria de Valdearados
Gumiel de Mercado
Villalba de Duero
Quemada
Aranda de Duero
Vadocondes
Langa de Duero
Sierra de la Demanda
Sierra de Neila
Salas de los Infantes
Castrillo de la Reina
Hacinas
Canicosa de la Sierra
Quintanar de la Sierra
Duruelo de la Sierra
Covaleda
Hontoria del Pinar
Navaleno
San Leonardo de Yagüe
Casarejos
Espeja de San Marcelino
Alcubilla de Avellaneda
Ucero
Sierra de Cabrejas
Cabrejas del Pinar
Abejar
Torralba de El Burgo
Pineda de la Sierra
Mansilla
Villavelayo
Viniegra de Arriba
Picos de Urbión
Montenegro de Cameros
Ezcaray
San Millán de la Cogolla
Pradoluengo
Villafranca-Montes de Oca
Santo Domingo de la Calzada
Castañares de Rioja
San Asensio
Hormilla
Nájera
Villar de Torre
Badarán
Anguiano
Sierra de San Lorenzo
Baños de Río Tobía
Pedroso
Ortigosa
Pradillo
Villanueva de Cameros
Lumbreras
Puerto de Piqueras
Sierra Cebollera
Sotillo del Rincón
Vinuesa
El Royo
Salduero
Embalse de la Cuerda del Pozo
Cidones
Villaciervos
Carbonera de Frentes
Navalcaballo
Los Rábanos
Candilichera
Soria
Garray
Aldealafuente
CAMPO DE GÓMARA
Gomara
Torrubia
Almazán
Sestao
Portugalete
Santurtzi
Barakaldo
Bilbao (Bilbo)
Getxo
Leioa
Erandio
Sopelana
Berango
Plentzia
Bakio-Basigo
Bermeo
Mundaka
Mungia
Axpe-Busturia
Muruetа
Gernika-Lumo
Berriatúa
Ondarroa
Mutriku
Markina-Xemein
Mendaro
Deba
Zumaia
Getaria
Zarautz
Zestoa
Orio
Donostia-San Sebastián
Pasai Donibane
Hondarribia
Irun
Errenteria
Lasarte-Orio
Hernani
Andoain
Zuzurkil
Urnieta
Vera de Bidasoa
Oiartzun
St-Jean-de-Luz
Urrugne
Hendaye
Sopuerta
Zalla
Güeñes
Balmaseda
Concha
Montes de Ordunte
Gordexola
Arcentales
Villasana de Mena
Arceniega
Respaldiza
Llodio
Arrigorriaga
Basauri
Galdakao
Zaratamo
Amorebieta
Igorre
Durango
Ugarana
Mañaria
Areatza
Ceanuri-Elexondo
Ubidea
Otxandio
Zubiaur
Amurrio
Barambio
Orduña
Embalse de Urrúnaga
Gopegui
Murguía
Izarra
Bóveda
Osma
Zuazo de Cuartango
Salinas de Añana
Nanclares de la Oca
Vitoria-Gasteiz
Durana
Embalse de Ullívarri
Ozeta
Legutiano
Ermua
Eibar
Zaldivar
Abadiño
Elorrio
Elgeta
Placencia de las Armas
Elgoibar
Azpeitia
Azkoitia
Regil
Anoeta
Tolosa
Ibarra
Villabona
Arano
Goizueta
Zubieta
Leiza
Ezcurra
Lecumberri
Jaunsarás
Betelu
Sierra de Aralar
Mondragón-Arrasate
Aretxabaleta
Legazpia
Antzuola
Bergara
Urretxu
Zumarraga
Ordizia
Amezketa
Oñati
Eskoriatza
Beasain
Idiazabal
Lazkao
San Martín
Zegama
Sierra de Urquilla
Puerto Echegárate
Alsasua
Echarri-Aranaz
Lacunza
Huarte-Araquil
Irurzun
Lizarraga
Olazagutia
Sierra de Andía
Ollo
Aizpun
Berrioplano
Orcoyen
Barañáin
Echarri
Belascoáin
Gazólaz
Salvatierra
Araia
Sierra de Urbasa
Zudaire
Eulate
Puerto de Azáceta
Sierra de Lóquiz
Montes de Vitoria
La Puebla de Arganzón
Treviño
Maestu
San Vicente de Arana
Larrión
Galbarra
Arizala
Estella
Cirauqui
Puente la Reina
Mañeru
Villatuerta
Oteiza
Mendigorría
Santa Cruz de Campezo
Acedo
Ancín
Genevilla
Azuelo
Morentin
Arroniz
Los Arcos
Allo
Larraga
CONDADO DE TREVIÑO
Miranda de Ebro
Berantevilla
Peñacerrada
Bernedo
Lagrán
Sierra de Cantabria
Cripán
Laguardia
Zambrana
Villalba de Rioja
San Vicente de la Sonsierra
Haro
Briones
Treviana
Tirgo
Casalarreina
Cenicero
Fuenmayor
Elciego
Oyón
Viana
Sansol
Logroño
Lazagurría
Mendavia
Sesma
Lodosa
Lerín
Miranda de Arga
RIBERA
Navarrete
Sotés
Entrena
Lardero
Agoncillo
Villamediana de Iregua
Murillo de Río Leza
Ribafrecha
Alcanadre
Cárcar
Andosilla
Falces
San Adrián
Peralta
Sartaguda
Pradejón
Calahorra
Azagra
Funes
Alesón
Albelda de Iregua
Nalda
Santa Engracia
El Villar de Arnedo
Robres del Castillo
Ausejo
Bergasa
Arnedo
Soto en Cameros
Aldeanueva de Ebro
Milagro
Rincón de Soto
Quel
Autol
San Román de Cameros
Arnedillo
Cabezón de Cameros
Munilla
Enciso
Yanguas
Grávalos
Corella
Igea
Cintruénigo
Fitero
Cornago
San Pedro Manrique
Cervera del Río Alhama
Aguilar del Río Alhama
Hurteles
Oncala
Puerto de Oncala
La Poveda de Soria
Almarza
Magaña
Almajano
Castilruiz
Matalebreras
Sierra del Almuerzo
Sierra del Madero
Sierra del Moncayo
Ágreda
Vozmediano
Ólvega
Alto del Moncayo
Cueva de Ágreda
Aldealpozo
Noviercas
Almenar de Soria
Borobia
Ciria
Monteagudo
Tarazona
Embalse de Sobrón
Ebro
Duero
Urbel
Arga
Ega
Alhama
Araviana
Ucero
Nela
Losa
E70
A8
E804
A68
E05/80
A15
A1
E05
1718
1235
1178
1475
1175
1231
981
2132
2262
2228
2148
1710
1722
1454
1429
1215
1375
1135
1139
1412
957
658
592
890
2313

57
40
41
58
64
D
E
F
1
2
3
4
ARMAGNAC
BÉARN
BIGORRE
PAYS BASQUE
SOBRARBE
NAVARRA
BÁRDENAS REALES
CINCO VILLAS
EL CASTELLAR
LOS MONEGROS
SOMONTANO
LLANO DE PLASENCIA
Sierra de Guara
Sierra de Santo Domingo
Sierra de San Juan de la Peña
Sierra de Javierre
Sierra de Abodi
Sierra de Izco
Sierra de Labia
Sierra de Luna
Sierra de Alcubierre
Montes de Castejón
Moilets-et-Maa
Messanges
Vieux-Boucau-les-Bains
Soustons
Tosse
Soorts-Hossegor
Capbreton
Bénesse-Maremne
Labenne
Ondres
Tarnos
Boucau
Bayonne
Biarritz
Anglet
Bidart
St-Pierre-d'Irube
Villefranque
Ustaritz
Larressore
St-Pée-sur-Nivelle
Cambo-les-Bains
Espelette
Ascain
Sare
Hasparren
St-Esteben
Iholdy
St-Palais
Dax
St-Geours-de-Maremne
Saubusse
St-Vincent-de-Paul
Peyrehorade
Bidache
Orthez
Salies-de-Béarn
Sauveterre-de-Béarn
Navarrenx
Mauléon-Licharre
Oloron-Ste-Marie
Pau
Billère
Lescar
Jurançon
Gelos
Nay-Bourdettes
Tarbes
Lourdes
Bagnères-de-Bigorre
Argelès-Gazost
Pierrefitte-Nestalas
Cauterets
Luz-St-Sauveur
Barèges
Gavarnie
Lannemezan
Capvern-les-Bains
St-Lary-Soulan
Vielle-Aure
Arreau
Vic-en-Bigorre
Maubourguet
Mirande
Aire-sur-l'Adour
Barcelonne-du-Gers
Nogaro
Mont-de-Marsan
Hagetmau
Amou
Arzacq-Arraziguet
Garlin
Riscle
Plaisance
Marciac
Mont-de-Marsan
St-Sever
Tartas
Montfort-en-Chalosse
St-Jean-Pied-de-Port
St-Étienne-de-Baïgorry
Larrau
Tardets-Sorholus
Arette
Lurbe-St-Christau
Bedous
Accous
Urdos
Laruns
Col du Somport
Col d'Aubisque
Col du Tourmalet
Col du Pourtalet
Roncesvalles
Burguete
Pamplona (Iruñea)
Burlada
Huarte
Villava
Aoiz
Noáin
Mutilva Baja
Elorz
Monreal
Tiebas
Lumbier
Liédena
Yesa
Sangüesa
Javier
Aibar
Barasoain
Eslava
San Martin de Unx
Olite
Tafalla
Cáseda
Sos del Rey Católico
Carcastillo
Murillo el Fruto
Santacara
Mélida
Caparroso
Marcilla
Cadreita
Valtierra
Arguedas
Castejón
Tudela
Cabanillas
Fustiñana
Ribaforada
Fontellas
Ablitas
Cortes
Mallén
Tarazona
Malón
El Buste
Borja
Magallón
Ainzón
Ambel
Gallur
Luceni
Alagón
Grisén
Pedrola
Remolinos
Torres de Berrellén
Sobradiel
Utebo
Zaragoza
Villanueva de Gállego
Zuera
San Mateo de Gállego
Ejea de los Caballeros
Tauste
Erla
Luna
Valpalmas
Castejón de Valdejasa
Gurrea de Gállego
Alcalá de Gurrea
Las Pedrosas
Ayerbe
Loarre
Bolea
Plasencia del Monte
Lupiñón
Huesca
Alerre
Almudévar
Tardienta
Almuniente
Torralba de Aragón
Robres
Alcubierre
Leciñena
Perdiguera
Farlete
Lanaja
Grañén
Poleñino
Lalueza
Sariñena
Castelflorite
Albalatillo
Sena
Alcolea de Cinca
Ontiñena
Chalamera
Belver de Cinca
Albalate de Cinca
Binaced
Monzón
Barbastro
Berbegal
Peralta de Alcofea
Castejón del Puente
Pueyo de Santa Cruz
Alfántega
Fonz
Estadilla
El Grado
Graus
Naval
Barcabo
Adahuesca
Abiego
Bierge
Angüés
Blecua
Peraltilla
Pertusa
Albero Alto
Novales
Sesa
Huerto
Alberuela de Tubo
Arguis
Nueno
Sabiñánigo
Jaca
Santa Cruz de la Serós
Santa Cilia de Jaca
Berdún
Artieda
Biniés
Hecho
Ansó
Canfranc
Candanchú
Villanúa
Castiello de Jaca
Biescas
Sallent de Gállego
Baños de Panticosa
Panticosa
Torla
Broto
Fanlo
Sarvisé
Fiscal
Boltaña
Aínsa
Bielsa
Lafortunada
Yebra de Basa
Albella
Laguarta
Molino de Villobas
Arcusa
Rodellar
Aguas
Caldearenas
Aquilué
Santa María
Bailo
Lobera de Onsella
Isuerre
Urriés
Navardún
Pintano
Biel
Luesia
Asín
Orés
Biota
Farasdués
Layana
Uncastillo
Castiliscar
Sádaba
Bárdena
Pinsoro
Valareña
El Sabinar
Isaba
Roncal
Vidángoz
Esparza de Salazar
Escároz
Jaurrieta
Ochagavía
Navascués
Burgui
Castillo-Nuevo
Sigüés
Güesa
Burguete
Zubiri
Larrasoaña
Zunzarren
Urroz
Irurozqui
Ardanaz
Biguëzal
Idocin
Embalse de Yesa
Embalse de Sotonera
Embalse de Mediano
Embalse de Grado
Canal de Monegros
Canal de Cinca
Canal Imperial de Aragón
Gállego
Aragón
Ebro
Cinca
Flumen
Arba
Huecha
Jalón
Alcanadre
Adour
Gabas
Arros
Gave d'Oloron
Jalón
Trasobares
Tabuenca
Talamantes
Fuendejalón
Pozuelo de Aragón
Urrea de Jalón
Rueda de Jalón
Lumpiaque
Épila
Tiergo
Alfajarín
Nuez de Ebro
Villafranca de Ebro
Puebla de Alfindén
Castejón de Monegros
Castejón de Monegros
A63
A64
A15
A68
E05
E07
E7
E80
E804
N10
N117
N124
N134
N21
N935
D932
D933
D918
D920
330
232
240
260
121A
121C
135

58
A
B
C
40
41
1
2
3
4
57
65
Lourdes
Bagnères-de-Bigorre
Argelès-Gazost
Pierrefitte-Nestalas
Cauterets
Luz-St-Sauveur
Barèges
Gavarnie
Campan
Capvern-les-Bains
Lannemezan
Montréjeau
St-Gaudens
St-Bertrand-de-Comminges
Mauléon-Barousse
Arreau
Bordères-Louron
Vielle-Aure
St-Lary-Soulan
Aragnouet
Bagnères-de-Luchon
Bossòst
Vielha
Salardu
St-Girons
St-Lizier
Castillon-en-Couserans
Massif de l'Arize
Foix
Tarascon-sur-Ariège
Ax-les-Thermes
Vicdessos
Aulus-les-Bains
Massat
Seix
Oust
Sallent de Gállego
Panticosa
Biescas
Torla
Broto
Sabiñánigo
Fiscal
Boltaña
Ainsa
Bielsa
Benasque
Castejón de Sos
Campo
Montes Malditos
Esterri d'Àneu
Espot
Llavorsí
Sort
Rialb de Noguera
La Torre de Cabdella
Pont de Suert
Senterada
Sopeira
Arén
Serra de Sant Gervás
La Pobla de Segur
Serra del Boumort
Tremp
Isona
Organyà
Guardiola de Berguedà
La Seu d'Urgell
Martinet
Andorra la Vella
Les Escaldes
La Massana
Encamp
Sant Julià de Lòria
Soldeu
El Serrat
AND
Condado
Sobrarbe
Sierra de Guara
Embalse de Mediano
Embalse de El Grado
El Grado
Graus
Lascuarre
Puente de Montañana
Tolva
Benabarre
Huesca
Barbastro
Somontano
Sierra de Carrodilla
Monzón
Binéfar
Tamarite de Litera
Alfarràs
Almenar
Balaguer
Serra del Montsec
Àger
La Noguera
Ponts
Artesa de Segre
Oliana
Solsona
Cardona
Berga
Embassament de Rialp
Embassament de Canelles
Embassament de Santa Ana
Les Avellanes
Agramunt
Guissona
Calaf
Tàrrega
Cervera
Segarra
Urgell
Segrià
La Litera
Lleida (Lérida)
Alcarràs
Mollerussa
Les Borges Blanques
Igualada
Els Prats de Rei
Fraga
Mequinenza
Caspe
Alcañiz
Llanos de Cardiel
Monegros
Serreta Negra
Sierra de Mequinenza
Embalse de Mequinenza
Embalse de Caspe
Pantà de Riba-roja
Ebro
Riba-roja d'Ebre
Flix
Móra d'Ebre
Gandesa
Falset
Valls
Reus
Tarragona
Salou
Cambrils de Mar
Vila-seca de Solcina
Cap de Salou
El Vendrell
Vilafranca del Penedès
Montblanc
Santa Coloma de Queralt
Vinaixa
L'Hospitalet de l'Infant
Serra de Montsant
Valjunquera
Valdealgorfa
Calaceite

D
E
F
1
2
3
4
42
Carcassonne
Narbonne
Limoux
Lavalette
Preixan
Leuc
Trèbes
Capendu
Moux
Cazilhac
Fanjeaux
Belvèze-du-Razès
Mirepoix
Alaigne
Lauraguel
St-Hilaire
St-Pierre-des-Champs
Lagrasse
Fabrezan
Montlaur
Ferrals-les-Corbières
St-Laurent-de-la-Cabrerisse
Bizanet
Gruissan
Portel-des-Corbières
Étang de l'Ayrolle
Sigean
Port-la-Nouvelle
La Palme
Villerouge-Termenès
Durban-Corbières
Alet-les-Bains
Plateau de Lecamp
Arques
Rennes-les-Bains
Couiza
Espéraza
Puivert
Chalabre
Aigues-Vives
Léran
St-Benoît
La Bastide-sur-l'Hers
Bélesta
Nébias
Quillan
Ginoles
Montségur
Mouthoumet
Tuchan
Paziols
Opoul-Périllos
Fitou
Leucate
Cap Leucate
Port-Leucate
Port-Barcarès
Soulatgé
Caudiès-de-Fenouillèdes
Maury
Vingrau
Salses-le-Château
Espira-de-l'Agly
Belcaire
Espezel
Prades
Pays de Sault
Axat
St-Paul-de-Fenouillet
Estagel
Latour-de-France
Baixas
St-Estève
Rivesaltes
Bompas
Ste-Marie
Canet-en-Roussillon
Canet-Plage
Perpignan
Millas
Ille-sur-Têt
Sournia
Escouloubre
Quérigut
Mérens-les-Vals
Molitg-les-Bains
Marquixanes
Vinça
Thuir
Toulouges
Corneilla-del-Vercol
Alénya
St-Cyprien
Elne
Bages
St-André
Argelès-sur-Mer
Collioure
Port-Vendres
Banyuls-sur-Mer
Côte Vermeille
Cerbère
Cap Cerbère
Portbou
Formiguères
Les Angles
CONFLENT
ROUSSILLON
Prades
Fourques
Vernet-les-Bains
Olette
St-Marsal
Col de Puymorens
Porta
Font-Romeu-Odeillo-Via
Mont-Louis
Thuès-entre-Valls
Planès
Llívia
Saillagouse-Llo
Puigcerdà
Osséja
Amélie-les-Bains-Palalda
Céret
Maureillas-las-Illas
Le Boulou
Le Perthus
Col du Perthus
La Jonquera
Espolla
Llançà
El Port de la Selva
Vilajuïga
Cap de Creus
Cadaqués
Roses
Cap de Norfeu
Castelló d'Empúries
Golf de Roses
Sant Pere Pescador
L'Armentera
L'Escala
Cala Montgó
La Preste
St-Laurent-de-Cerdans
Coustouges
Prats-de-Mollo-la-Preste
Maçanet de Cabrenys
Agullana
Pantà de Boadella
Albanyà
Terrades
Figueres
Peralada
Vilanant
Navata
Queralbs
Vilallonga
Molló
Camprodon
Ribes de Freser
Coll de Merolla
La Pobla de Lillet
Sant Joan de les Abadesses
Sant Joan les Fonts
Tortellà
Esponellà
Serinyà
Bàscara
Besalú
Fluvià
Cadí
RIPOLLES
Campdevànol
Ripoll
Olot
Sant Privat d'en Bas
Santa Pau
Porqueres
Banyoles
Mieres
Les Preses
Sierra Finestres
Camallera
Viladamat
Colomers
Verges
Torroella de Montgrí
Bagà
Berguedà
Berga
Vilada
Alpens
Sant Quirze de Besora
Sant Agustí de Lluçanès
Olvan
Sant Pere de Torelló
Torelló
Sant Feliu de Pallerols
Les Planes d'Hostoles
Cornellà de Terri
Bordils
Celrà
Sarrià de Ter
Perafita
Sant Hipòlit de Voltregà
Manlleu
Santa Maria de Corcó
Pantà de Susqueda
Amer
La Cellera de Ter
Salt
Girona
(Gerona)
Bescanó
Fornells de la Selva
La Bisbal d'Empordà
Corçà
Vulpellac
Pals
Cap de Begur
Begur
Palafrugell
Mont-ras
Cap de Sant Sebastià
Calonge
Palamós
Castell d'Aro
Sant Feliu de Guíxols
Prats de Lluçanès
Olost
Vic
Roda de Ter
Tavertet
Vilanova de Sau
Serra de Vielles
Osor
Anglès
Vilobí d'Onyar
Cassà de la Selva
Serra de les Gavarres
Sant Feliu Sasserra
Oristà
Santa Eulàlia de Riuprimer
Sant Hilari Sacalm
Santa Coloma de Farners
Avinyó
Sallent
Artés
Moià
Tona
Taradell
Seva
Viladrau
Arbúcies
Riudarenes
Sils
Llagostera
Vidrieres
Lloret de Mar
Tossa
Blanes
Malgrat de Mar
Pineda de Mar
Calella
Sant Pol de Mar
Canet de Mar
Arenys de Mar
Mataró
Vilassar de Mar
Premià de Mar
Monistrol de Calders
Centelles
Aiguafreda
La Estación
Matagalls
Serra de Montseny
Montseny
Maçanet de la Selva
Hostalric
Breda
Sant Celoni
Tordera
Serra de Montnegre
Caldes d'Estrac
Manresa
Navarcles
Castellterçol
Sierra de Sant Llorenç
Caldes de Montbui
Barriada Nueva
La Garriga
Cardedeu
Matadepera
Granollers
Terrassa
Sabadell
Argentona
Mollet del Vallès
Barberà del Vallès
Cerdanyola del Vallès
Rubí
El Masnou
Martorell
Sant Cugat del Vallès
Molins de Rei
Badalona
Barcelona
Sant Vicenç dels Horts
Cornellà de Llobregat
L'Hospitalet de Llobregat
Viladecans
El Prat de Llobregat
Gavà
Castelldefels
Sitges
Costa Brava
Costa Dorada
Genova
Palma de Mallorca
Mahon

A
B
C
1
2
3
4
A Guardia
Punta dos Picos
Vila Praia de Âncora
Afife
Carreço
Areosa
Viana do Castelo
Anha
Castelo do Neiva
Antas
Mar
Marinhas
Esposende
Fão
Estela
Póvoa de Varzim
Vila do Conde
Ponte de Lima
Arcos de Valdevez
Ponte da Barca
Lindoso
Britelo
M I N H O
Serra do Gerês
Embalse de Salas
Paradela
Vila da Ponte
Barragem de Venda Nova
Salto
Dornelas
Vieira do Minho
Póvoa de Lanhoso
Serra da Cabreira
Guilhofrei
Cabeceiras de Basto
Arco de Baúlhe
Cerva
Barcelos
Barcelinhos
Vila Seca
Braga
Caldelas
Taipas
Fafe
Gandarela
Celorico de Basto
Molares
Guimarães
Caldas de Vizela
Sendim
Felgueiras
Calendário
Trofa
Santo Tirso
Vila Cova da Lixa
Amarante
Campeã
Cumieira
Maia
Leça do Bailio
Leça da Palmeira
Matosinhos
Porto
Alfena
Ermesinde
Valongo
Rio Tinto
Gondomar
Vila Nova de Gaia
Valbom
Oliveira do Douro
Avintes
Vilar de Andorinho
Pedroso
Paços de Ferreira
Carvalhosa
Lousada
Penafiel
Castelões
Marco de Canaveses
Loivos do Monte
Serra do Marão
Mesão Frio
Peso da Régua
Lamego
Resende
Cinfães
D O U R O
Castelo de Paiva
Melres
Eja
Serzedo
Espinho
Lamas
Pousadela
Canedo do Arda
Oliveira
Serra de Montemuro
Alvarenga
Mezio
Tarouca
Praia de Esmoriz
Maceda
Santa Maria da Feira
Mansores
Arouca
Parada de Ester
Pendil
São João da Madeira
Furadouro
Ovar
Válega
Vale de Cambra
Castro Daire
Figueiredo de Alva
Avanca
Oliveira de Azeméis
Pardilhó
Torreira
Estarreja
Palmaz
Santa Cruz da Tapa
Serra da Arada
São Pedro do Sul
Sever do Vouga
Oliveira de Frades
Albergaria-a-Velha
Vouzela
Mozelos
Couto de Cima
Lordosa
Ria de Aveiro
São Jacinto
Praia da Barra
Gafanha da Nazaré
Aveiro
Esgueira
Angeja
Talhadas
Cambra de Baixo
Torredeita
Viseu
Ranhados
Mourisca do Vouga
Travassô
Águeda
Caparrosa
Gafanha do Carmo
Ílhavo
Vagos
Gafanha da Boa Hora
Oiã
Caramulo
Serra do Caramulo
Belazaima do Chão
São Miguel
Vila Chã de Sá
Mangualde
Santar
Nelas
Molelos
Tondela
Oliveira do Bairro
Avelãs de Caminho
Praia de Mira
Calvão
Mira
Vilarinho do Bairro
Anadia
Moita
Cabanas de Viriato
Oliveira do Conde
Lagares da Beira
Santa Comba Dão
Carregal do Sal
Mortágua
Luso
Barragem da Aguieira
Praia da Tocha
Cantanhede
Murtede
Mealhada
Pampilhosa
Travanca do Mondego
Tábua
Oliveira do Hospital
Tocha
Arazede
BEIRA LITORAL
Botão
Vila Pouca da Beira
Coja
Quiaios
Cabo Mondego
São João do Campo
Carapinheira
Santana
Tentúgal
Taveiro
Coimbra
Penacova
São Martinho
Vila Nova de Poiares
Arganil
Cerdeira
Buarcos
Figueira da Foz
Maiorca
Vila Verde
Granja do Ulmeiro
Sebal
Ceira
Serpins
Semide
Góis
Colmeal
Fajão
Unhais-o-Velho
Condeixa-a-Nova
Almalaguês
Miranda do Corvo
Lousã
Serra da Lousã
Cabril
Barragem de Santa Luzia
Pampilhosa da Serra
Paião
Marinha das Ondas
Soure
Rabaçal
Penela
Espinhal
Castanheira de Pêra
Álvares
Campelo
Lourical
Carriço
Redinha
Pedrógão
Guia
Pombal
Avelar
Ansião
Figueiró dos Vinhos
Pedrógão Grande
Embalse del Cabril
Pedrógão Pequeno
Álvaro
Estreito
Oleiros
Coimbrão
Monte Redondo
Vieira de Leiria
Monte Real
Carreira
Vermoil
Almoster
Alvaiázere
Cernache do Bonjardim
Troviscal
Mosteiro
Isna
São Pedro de Muel
Marinha Grande
Boa Vista
Leiria
Albergaria dos Doze
Espite
Freixianda
Sertã
Sobreira Formosa
Pousos
Caxarias
Areias
Fundada
Proença-a-Nova
Moita
Maceira
Martingança
Olival
Vila Nova
Águas Belas
Ferreira do Zêzere
Cardigos
A1-IP1
A3-IP1
A14-IP3
E01
E01/80
E80
E801
E805
E82
IC1
IC2
IC3
IC7
IC8
IP3
IP4
IP5

53
66

D
E
F
54
61
1
2
3
4
62
67
Monterrei
Oimbra
Vilardevós
Alto de Fumaces
Santalha
Mofreita
Parâmio
Aveleda
Onor
Peña Mira
Villardeciervos
Ferreras de Abajo
Otero de Bodas
Morales de Valverde
Bretocino
Serra da Coroa
Serra de Montesinho
Sierra de la Culebra
Figueruela de Arriba
Tábara
Granja de Moreruela
Vilarelho da Raia
Vila Verde da Raia
São Vicente
Vinhais
Bragança
Deilão
Riofrío de Aliste
Moreruela de Tábara
Villarrín de Campos
Manganeses de la Lampreana
Castronuevo
Sarraquinhos
Outeiro Seco
Chaves
Águas Frias
Tronco
Lebução
Rebordelo
Edrosa
Samil
Milhão
San Vitero
Rabanales
Ferreruela de Tábara
Perilla de Castro
Barragem do Alto Rabagão
Redondelo
Boticas
Sonim
Vilarandelo
Agrochão
Failde
Outeiro
Trabazos
Alcañices
Samir de los Caños
Embalse de Ricobayo
San Cebrián de Castro
Pajares de la Lampreana
Losacino
Carbajales de Alba
Montamarta
Vidago
Loivos
Lagarelhos
Torre de Dona Chama
Santa Comba de Rossas
Pinela
São Martinho de Angueira
Luz
Fonfría
Constantim
Torres del Carrizal
Tâmega
Trás-os-Montes
Serra de Nogueira
Carrazedo de Montenegro
Valpaços
Vale de Salgueiro
Mascarenhas
Edroso
Izeda
Carção
Vimioso
Embalse de Castro
Andavías
La Hiniesta
Tierra del Pan
Coreses
Zamora
Rio Torto
Vinhas
Macedo de Cavaleiros
Caçarelhos
Malhadas
Miranda do Douro
Pino
Villadepera
Villalcampo
Moralina
Muelas del Pan
Villaseco del Pan
Villaralbo
Bornes de Aguiar
Vila Pouca de Aguiar
Jou
Mirandela
Romeu
Cedães
Bornes
Chacim
Morais
Algoso
Duas Igrejas
Torregamones
Luelmo
Embalse de Villalcampo
Pereruela
Morales del Vino
Moraleja del Vino
Perdigón
Teloes
Murça
Franco
Frechas
Serra de Bornes
Sambade
Peredo
Lagoa
Fariza de Sayago
Muga de Sayago
Sayago
Corgo
Vila Verde
Populo
Abreiro
Trindade
Azinhoso
Sendim
Villar del Buey
Bermillo de Sayago
Fresno de Sayago
Corrales
El Piñero
Parada de Pinhão
Sanfins do Douro
Samões
Vila Flor
Alfândega da Fé
Mogadouro
Serra de Mogadouro
Bemposta
Fermoselle
Embalse de Almendra
Peñausende
Constantim
Sabrosa
Alijó
Carvalho de Egas
Castelo Branco
Carbellino
Almeida de Sayago
Teso Santo
El Cubo de Tierra del Vino
Villanueva de los Escuderos
Favaios
Pombal
Carrazeda de Ansiães
Aldeadávila de la Ribera
Villarino de los Aires
Trabanca
Almendra
Santiz
Pinhão
Ervedosa do Douro
Vilarinho da Castanheira
Felgar
Carviçais
Lagoaça
Cabeza de Framontanos
Moraleja de Sayago
São João da Pesqueira
Torre de Moncorvo
Fornos
Mieza
Villaseco de los Reyes
Valença do Douro
Tabuaço
Embalse de Saucelle
Vilvestre
Ahigal de Villarino
Cabeza del Caballo
Aldearrodrigo
Torresmenudas
Barcos
Trevões
Vila Nova de Foz Côa
Urros
Freixo de Espada à Cinta
Barruecopardo
Brincones
Tremedal de Tormes
Villaseco de los Gamitos
Ledesma
Calzada de Valdunciel
Paradela
Touça
Villasbuenas
Villar de Peralonso
Vega de Tirados
Tormes
Florida de Liébana
Villamayor
Cosmado
Barca de Alva
Hinojosa de Duero
Guardramiro
Vitigudino
Villasdardo
Golpejas
Doñinos de Salamanca
Salamanca
Sarzedo
Penedono
Moimenta da Beira
Meda
Longroiva
Almendra
La Fregeneda
Rollán
Sando
Barragem de Vilar
Escalhão
Cerralbo
Lumbrales
Yecla de Yeltes
Santa Marta de Tormes
Rua
Ariz
Antas
Torre do Terrenho
Marialva
Figueira de Castelo Rodrigo
Abadengo
El Cubo de Don Sancho
Aldeatejada
Arapiles
Sernancelhe
Bogajo
Pelarrodríguez
Embalse de Mozárbez
Cunha
Rabaçal
San Felices de los Gallegos
Villavieja de Yeltes
Huebra
Robliza de Cojos
Vila Nova de Paiva
Aguiar da Beira
Rio de Mel
Castanheira
Vermiosa
Reigada
Bañobárez
Boada
La Fuente de San Esteban
Aldehuela de la Bóveda
Queiriga
Trancoso
Cogula
Pínhel
Puerto Seguro
Retortillo
Vecinos
San Pedro de Rozados
Póvoa do Concelho
Malta
Malpartida
Villar de Ciervo
Martín de Yeltes
Carrascal del Obispo
Cabrillas
Sátão
Beira Alta
Vila Franca das Naves
Souro Pires
Castillejo de Martín Viejo
Sancti-Spíritus
Las Veguillas
Pedrosillo de los Aires
Penalva do Castelo
Aldeia do Bispo
Villar de la Yegua
Sepulcro-Hilario
Aldehuela de Yeltes
Tamames
Frades de la Sierra
Maceira
Alverca da Beira
Lameiras
Freixedas
Bocacara
Navarredonda de la Rinconada
Figueiró da Granja
Celorico da Beira
Castelo Bom
Gallegos de Argañán
Puebla de Yeltes
Embalse de Santa Teresa
Fornos de Algodres
Lajeosa do Mondego
Fuentes de Oñoro
Vilar Formoso
Ciudad Rodrigo
Morasverdes
Linares de Riofrío
Endrinal
Pinzio
El Cabaco
Fuenterroble de Salvatierra
Carrapichana
Arrifana
Guarda
Pousada
Espeja
Serradilla del Arroyo
Peña de Francia
Sierra de la Peña de Francia
Los Santos
San Esteban de la Sierra
Valdelacasa
Linhares
Trinta
Parada
Nave de Haver
El Bodón
Sequeros
La Alberca
Cristóbal
Ledrada
Gouveia
Videmonte
Vale de Estrela
Itueiro de Azaba
Embalse de Águeda
Casares de las Hurdes
Santibáñez de la Sierra
Pinhanços
Famalicão
Adão
La Alberguería de Argañán
Agallas
Sotoserrano
Seia
Gonçalo
Pega
Rapoula do Côa
Fuenteguinaldo
Martiago
Nuñomoral
Colmenar de Montemayor
Béjar
Candelario
Manteigas
Sameiro
Valhelhas
Vila Boa
Aldeia da Ponte
El Saugo
Arrobuey
Portilla Alta
Sierra de Gata
Las Hurdes
Puerto de Béjar
Belmonte
Sabugal
Alfaiates
Casillas de Flores
Villasrubias
Caminomorisco
Lagunilla
Baños de Montemayor
Calvitero
Torre
Teixoso
Alvoco da Serra
Sortelha
Quadrazais
Souto
Lajeosa
Pinofranqueado
La Pesga
Covilhã
Caria
Casteleiro
Vale de Espinho
El Payo
Navasfrías
Descargamaría
Casar de Palomero
Embalse de Gabriel y Galán
Unhais da Serra
Escarigo
Serra da Malcata
Mezas
Puerto de Perales
Jañona
Gata
Mohedas de Granadilla
Aldeanueva del Camino
Tortozendo
Pero Viseu
Meimoa
Valverde del Fresno
Eljas
Acebo
Villanueva de la Sierra
Ahigal
Zarza de Granadilla
Casas del Monte
Cabezuela del Valle
Jerte
Capinha
Benquerença
Santibáñez el Bajo
Guijo de Granadilla
Navaconcejo
Paul
Telhado
Penamacor
Villamiel
Hoyos
Perales del Puerto
Pozuelo de Zarzón
Aceituna
Sierra de Tormantos
Jarandilla de la Vera
Fatela
Fundão
Vale de Prazeres
Aldeia do Bispo
Aranhas
Santa Olalla
Embalse del Borbollón
Embalse de Valdeobispo
El Torno
Piornal
Aldeanueva de la Vera
Souto da Casa
Serra da Gardunha
Alpedrinha
Pedrógão
Aldeia de João Pires
Cilleros
Moraleja
Guijo de Coria
Montehermoso
Valdeobispo
Garganta la Olla
Cuacos de Yuste
Jaraiz de la Vera
Orca
Medelim
Penha Garcia
Gujo de Galisteo
Carcaboso
São Vicente da Beira
São Miguel de Acha
Proença-a-Velha
Monfortinho
Calzadilla
Plasencia
Cañalizo
Tejeda de Tiétar
Foz Giraldo
Idanha-a-Velha
Barragem da Idanha
Coria
Galisteo
Malpartida de Plasencia
Embalse de Tiétar
Beira Baixa
Alcafozes
Alagón
Gargüera
Majadas de Tiétar
Tinhalhas
Idanha-a-Nova
Portaje
Riolobos
Holguera
Navalmoral de la Mata
Escalos de Cima
Salvaterra do Extremo
Torrejoncillo
Puerto de la Serrana
Casatejada
Alcains
Escalos de Baixo
Zarza la Mayor
Mirabel
Embalse de Torrejón-Tiétar
Embalse de Arrocampo
Salgueiro
Ladoeiro
Zebreira
Ceclavín
Puerto de los Castaños
Casas de Millán
Serradilla
Serrejón
Almaraz
Castelo Branco
Segura
Piedras Albas
Acehuche
Cañaveral
Torrejón el Rubio
Benquerenças
Ponsul
Monforte da Beira
Embalse de Alcántara
Garrovillas
Hinojal
Talaván
Embalse de Alcántara
Embalse de Torrejón-Tajo
Mirabete
Puerto de Miravete
Vila Velha de Ródão
Malpica
Rosmaninhal
Alcántara
Jaraicejo
E80
E801
E802
E803
E82
IP2
IP4
IP5
A52

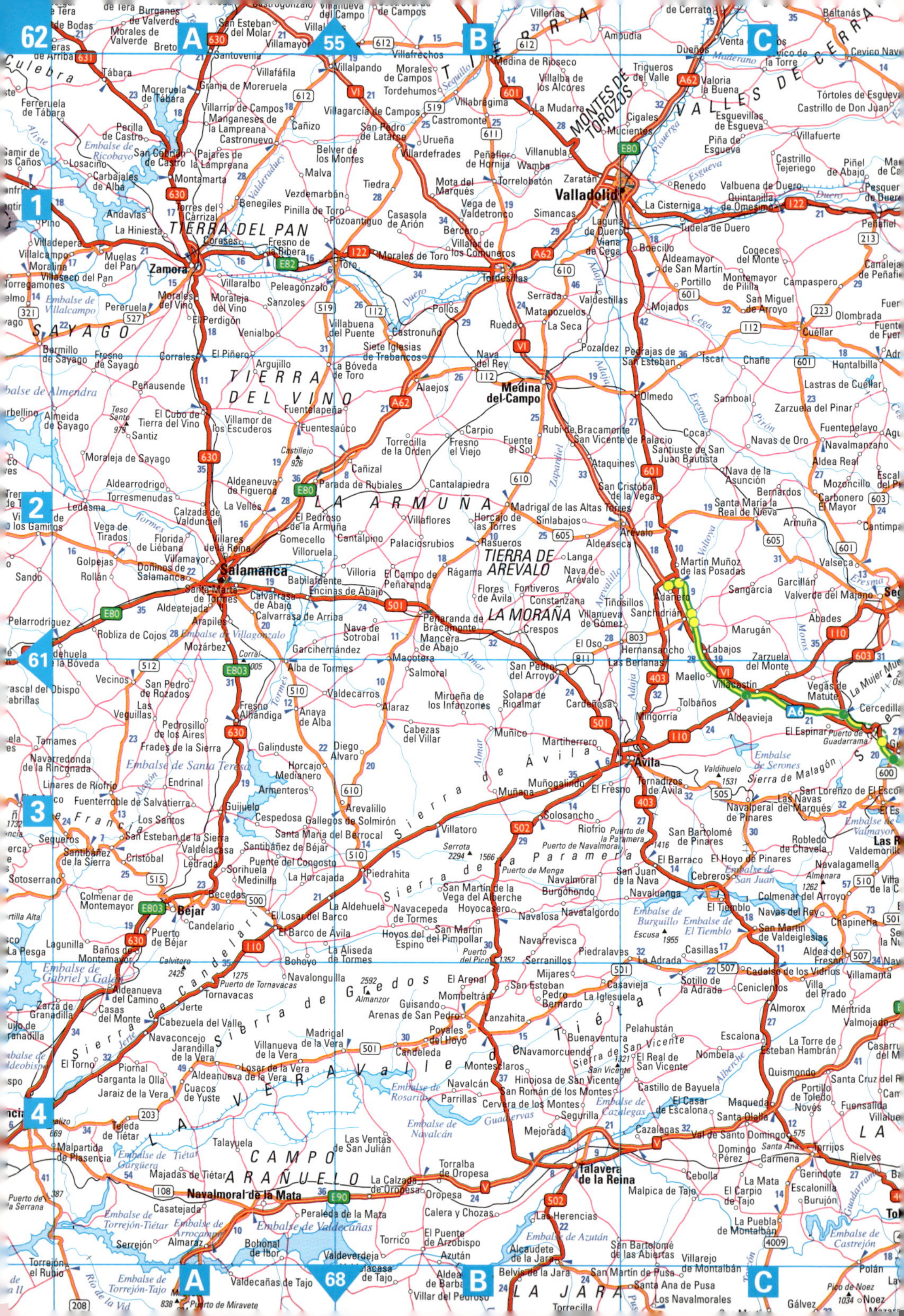
55
61
68
A
B
C
1
2
3
4
Valladolid
Zamora
Salamanca
Ávila
Medina del Campo
Tordesillas
Toro
Béjar
Talavera de la Reina
Navalmoral de la Mata
Arévalo
Peñaranda de Bracamonte
Medina de Rioseco
Cuéllar
Olmedo
Alba de Tormes
Guijuelo
Piedrahita
El Barco de Ávila
Plasencia
Oropesa
Tordehumos
Villalpando
Benavente
Tordesillas
Segovia
Las Rozas
Toledo
TIERRA DEL PAN
TIERRA DEL VINO
SAYAGO
LA ARMUÑA
TIERRA DE ARÉVALO
LA MORAÑA
MONTES DE TOROZOS
VALLES DE CERRATO
TIERRA DE CAMPOS
Sierra de Ávila
Sierra de la Paramera
Sierra de Gredos
Sierra de Malagón
Sierra de Francia
Sierra de Candelario
Sierra de San Vicente
LA VERA
Valle del Tiétar
CAMPO ARAÑUELO
LA JARA
Embalse de Almendra
Embalse de Ricobayo
Embalse de Villalcampo
Embalse de Santa Teresa
Embalse de Villagonzalo
Embalse de Gabriel y Galán
Embalse de Valdecañas
Embalse de Torrejón-Tiétar
Embalse de Rosarito
Embalse de Navalcán
Embalse de Azután
Embalse de Castrejón
Embalse de Burguillo
Embalse de El Tiemblo
Embalse de San Juan
Embalse de Cazalegas
Embalse de Serones
Embalse de Valmayor
Duero
Tormes
Eresma
Adaja
Pisuerga
Esgueva
Alberche
Tiétar
E80
E82
E90
E803
A62
A6
VI
V
630
631
122
501
502
403
110
601
610
605
Almanzor 2592
Puerto de Béjar
Puerto de Tornavacas
Puerto de Navalmoral
Puerto de Menga
Puerto del Pico
Puerto de la Paramera
Puerto de Guadarrama
Puerto de Miravete

63
56
64
69
D
E
F
1
2
3
4
Nebreda
Peñas de Cervera
Valdosa 1412
Villafruela
Canicosa de la Sierra
Covaleda
del Rincón
Almarza
Magaña
Hontoria del Pinar
Navalero
Abejar
El Royo
Almajano
Castilruiz
Matalebreras
Torresandino
Caleruega
Huerta del Rey
Espejón
San Leonardo de Yagüe
Cabrejas del Pinar
Cidones
Garray
Soria
Sierra del Almuerzo
Aldealpozo
Olmedilla de Roa
Baños de Valdearados
Espeja de San Marcelino
Casarejos
Sierra de Cabrejas
Villaciervos
Carbonera de Frentes
Los Rábanos
Candilichera
Noviergas
Gumiel de Hizán
Gumiel de Mercado
Hontoria de Valdearados
Alcubilla de Avellaneda
Ardal 1215
Ucero
Hinojedo 1375
Navalcaballo
Almenar de Soria
La Horra
Roa
Villalba de Duero
Quemada
Peñaranda de Duero
Aldealafuente
CAMPO DE GÓMARA
Gómara
Torralba de El Burgo
Aranda de Duero
Castrillo de la Vega
Fuentecén
Vadocondes
La Vid
Langa de Duero
San Esteban de Gormaz
El Burgo de Osma
Quintana Redonda
Cubo de la Solana
Torrubia de Soria
Tejado
Almazul
Fuentelcésped
Tardelcuende
Castrillo de Duero
Milagros
Castillejo de Robledo
Fuentepinilla
Matamala de Almazán
Borjabad
Moradillo de Roa
Sacramenia
Embalse de Linares
Honrubia de la Cuesta
Fuentecambrón
La Rasa
Gormaz
Bayubas de Abajo
Hortezuela
Almazán
Sierra de Perdices
Serón de Nájima
Deza
Valtiendas
Sierra de Pradales
Rubio 1313
Campo de San Pedro
Languilla
Recuerda
Berlanga de Duero
Velamazán
Barca
Coscurita
Fuentelmonge
San Miguel de Bernuy
Embalse de Las Vencías
Ayllón
Nograles
Caltojar
Sierra de Hontalbilla
Morón de Almazán
Bordalba
Liceras
MARQUESADO DE BERLANGA
Villasayas
Adradas
Monteagudo de las Vicarías
Embalse de Burgomillodo
Boceguillas
Riaza
Ribota
Arenillas
La Riba de Escalote
Ariza
Almaluez
Cetina
Cantalejo
Fuenterrebollo
Sepúlveda
Castillejo de Mesleón
Sierra de Ayllón
Sierra de Pela
Retortillo de Soria
Barcones
Barahona
Jalón
Santa María de Huertas
Campisábalos
Galve de Sorbe
Alpanseque
Arcos de Jalón
Cabolafuente
Cerezo de Arriba
Cerezo de Abajo
Atienza
Veganzones
La Matilla
Turégano
Puerto de Somosierra
Peña Cabollera 2179
Sierra de Somosierra
La Bodera 1408
Rebollosa de Jadraque
Sierra Ministra
Medinaceli
Ministra 1310
Esteras de Medinaceli
Sierra de Solorio
1290 Judes
Prádena
Torreiglesias
Matabuena
Robregordo
Montejo de la Sierra
Embalse de Matallana
Ocejón 2048
Hiendelaencina
Embalse de Pálmaces
Sigüenza
Estriégana
Alcolea del Pinar
Maranchón
Collado Hermoso
Navafría
Braojos
Embalse de Puentes Viejas
Embalse del Vado
Tamajón
Embalse del Alcorno
Negredo
Saúca
Anguita
Luzón
Cirueles del Pinar
Mazarete
Puerto de Maranchón
Torrecaballeros
Embalse de Riosequillo
Buitrago del Lozoya
Embalse de El Villar
Embalse de Beleña
Cogolludo
Mandayona
Algora
Luzaga
Anquela del Ducado
Aragoncillo 1518
Lozoya
Embalse de Pinilla
Lozoyuela
Embalse de El Atazar
Puebla de Beleña
Jadraque
Laranueva
Saelices de la Sal
Riba de Saelices
Rascafría
San Ildefonso
Peñalara 2430
La Cabrera
Embalse de Valdentales
Jarama
Humanes de Mohernando
Espinosa de Henares
Abánades
Esplegares
Cobeta
Rillo de Gallo
Miraflores de la Sierra
Cuerda Larga
Uceda
Mohernando
Hita
Badiel
Ledanca
Gajanejos
Masegoso de Tajuña
Pinoso 1250
Sacecorbo
Canredondo
Huertahernando
Corduente
Cabeza de Hierro 2383
Puerto de Navacerrada
Torrelaguna
Viñuelas
Yunquera de Henares
Torre del Burgo
Cifuentes
Armallones
Zaorejas
Soto del Real
Embalse de Santillana
Manzanares el Real
El Molar
Torija
Brihuega
Valtablado del Río
Los Molinos
Guadarrama
San Agustín de Guadalix
El Casar
Fontanar
Tórtola de Henares
LA ALCARRIA
Trillo
Arbeteta
Peñalén
Collado Villalba
Hoyo de Manzanares
Colmenar Viejo
Torrejón del Rey
Marchamalo
Valdenoches
Irueste
Villanueva de Alcorón
Fuente el Saz de Jarama
Taracena
Guadalajara
Embalse de Entrepeñas
Peralveche
El Recuenco
Galapagar
Torrelodones
Algete
Alovera
Budia
Bienvenida 1249
Carrascosa
San Sebastián de los Reyes
Daganzo de Arriba
Meco
Azuqueca de Henares
Chiloeches
Romanones
Berninches 1041
Alocén
Pareja
Alcantud
Alcobendas
Paracuellos de Jarama
Alcalá de Henares
Tendilla
Alhóndiga
Escamilla
Salmerón
Valdeolivas
Cañizares
Santa María del Val
Las Rozas de Madrid
Majadahonda
MADRID
Aranzueque
Auñón
Salmeroncillos de Abajo
Albendea
Fuertescusa
Pozuelo de Alarcón
Coslada
Torrejón de Ardoz
San Fernando de Henares
Pozo de Guadalajara
Sacedón
Alocer
San Pedro Palmiches
Priego
Cañamares
Poyatos
Boadilla del Monte
Mejorada del Campo
Torres de la Alameda
Loranca de Tajuña
Pastrana
Embalse de Buendía
Cañaveruelas
La Frontera
Villaviciosa de Odón
Loeches
Pozuelo del Rey
Escariche
Embalse de Bolarque
Buendía
Canalejas del Arroyo
Villaconejos de Trabaque
Fresneda de la Sierra
Alcorcón
Móstoles
Leganés
Getafe
Rivas-Vaciamadrid
Fuentenovilla
Yebra
Sayatón
Villalba del Rey
Tinajas
Albalate de las Nogueras
Cañaveras
Almonacid de Zorita
Albalate de Zorita
Guadamejud
Gascueña
Torralba
Las Majadas
Portilla
Fuenlabrada
Arganda
Valdilecha
Mondéjar
Orusco
Almoguera
Villalba de la Sierra
Humanes de Madrid
Pinto
Carabaña
Driebes
Embalse de Estremera
Sierra de Altomira
La Peraleja
Garcinarro
Sierra de Bascuñana
Losares 1389
Uña
El Álamo
Griñón
Parla
Morata de Tajuña
Brea de Tajo
Illana
La Ventosa
Sotos
Mariana
Buenache de la Sierra
Carranque
Valdemoro
San Martín de la Vega
Villarejo de Salvanés
Estremera
Leganiel
Huete
Ciempozuelos
Chinchón
Barajas de Melo
Vellisca
Altos de Cabrejas
Jábaga
Cedillo del Condado
Illescas
Esquivias
Titulcia
Colmenar de Oreja
Canal de Estremera
Pineda de Cigüela
Seseña
Borox
Villaconejos
Alcázar del Rey
Carrascosa del Campo
Cuenca
Palomera
Yuncos
Pantoja
Yuncler
Belinchón
Tarancón
Huelves
Naharros
LA OBISPALÍA
Villar de Olalla
Alameda de la Sagra
Cobeja
Aranjuez
Villarrubia de Santiago
Zarza de Tajo
Torrejoncillo del Rey
Abia de la Obispalía
Talayuelo 1233
Añover de Tajo
Noblejas
Ocaña
Santa Cruz de la Zarza
Uclés
Rozalén del Monte
Palomeras del Campo
Olías del Rey
Villaseca de la Sagra
Mocejón
Ciruelos
MESA DE OCAÑA
Villarrubio
Almendros
Saelices
Zafra de Záncara
La Parra de las Vegas
Yepes
Villatobas
Fuente de Pedro Naharro
Torrubia del Campo
Montalbo
Laguna de El Hito
El Hito
San Lorenzo de la Parrilla
Belmontejo
Villasequilla de Yepes
Dosbarrios
Huerta de Valdecarábanos
Horcajo de Santiago
Pozorrubio
Almonacid del Marquesado
Villares del Saz
Villaverde y Pasaconsol
Valera de Arriba
Olivares de Júcar
Villamuelas
Nambroca
Melgar
La Guardia
Cabezamesada
Puebla de Almenara
Cervera del Llano
Burguillos de Toledo
Toledo
Almonacid
Villanueva de Bogas
Mascaraque
Tembleque
Corral de Almaguer
Villamayor de Santiago
Villarejo de Fuentes
Villar de Cañas
Valverde de Júcar
Hontecillas
Ajofrín
Lillo
Tresjuncos
La Almarcha

64
57
63
70
A
B
C
1
2
3
4
Soria
Tarazona
Zaragoza
Calatayud
Teruel
Cuenca
Borja
Alagón
Cariñena
Daroca
Almazán
Medinaceli
Molina de Aragón
Monreal del Campo
Calamocha
Ademuz
Montalbán
Belchite
Ateca
Ariza
Alhama de Aragón
Agreda
Ólvega
Gómara
Épila
La Almunia de Doña Godina
Cella
Albarracín
Utrillas
Mora de Rubielos
Sarrión
Landete
Cañete
Beteta
Priego
Villar de Olalla
Sierra del Moncayo
Sierra de la Virgen
Sierra de Armantes
Sierra de Vicort
Sierra de Algairén
Sierra de Santa Cruz
Sierra de Pardos
Sierra de Solorio
Sierra de Caldereros
Sierra Menera
Sierra Palomera
Sierra de Albarracín
Serranía de Cuenca
Sierra de Javalambre
Sierra de Bascuñana
Sierra de Cabrejas
Sierra de las Cuerdas
Sierra Ministra
Sierra de San Just
Sierra del Tremedal
Sierra de Valdeminguete
Montes Universales
Cerro Moro
EL CASTELLAR
LLANO DE PLASENCIA
CAMPO DE GÓMARA
CAMPO DE CARIÑENA
RINCÓN DE ADEMUZ
LA OBISPALÍA
Laguna de Gallocanta
Laguna de Zaida
Embalse de la Tranquera
Embalse de Mezalocha
Embalse de las Torcas
Embalse de Moneva
Embalse del Arquillo de San Blás
Embalse de Loriguilla
Canal Imperial de Aragón
Duero
Jalón
Jiloca
Huerva
Tajo
Júcar
Cabriel
Guadalaviar
Alfambra
Turia
Ebro

D
E
58
F
1
2
3
4
71
Monzón
Tamarite de Litera
LA LITERA
Balaguer
SEGRIÀ
URGELL
SEGARRA
Tàrrega
Cervera
Lleida
(Lerida)
MONEGROS
Fraga
LLANOS DE CARDIEL
Mequinenza
Embalse de Mequinenza
Ebro
Sierra de Mequinenza
Caspe
Embalse de Caspe
Chiprana
DESIERTO
DE CALANDA
Alcañiz
Valdealgorfa
Calanda
Alcorisa
Embalse de Calanda
Les Borges Blanques
L'Espluga de Francolí
Montblanc
Valls
El Vendrell
Reus
Tarragona
Vilaseca de Solcina
Salou
Cap de Salou
Cambrils de Mar
L'Hospitalet de l'Infant
Cap de Terme
L'Ametlla de Mar
Golf de
Sant Jordi
Flix
Móra la Nova
Gandesa
Serra de Montsant
Serra de la Fatarrella
Tortosa
BAIX EBRE
Ports de Beseit
Amposta
La Cava
Punta del Fangar
Illa de Buda
Sant Carles de la Ràpita
Port dels Alfacs
Platja del Trabucador
Costa de Fora
Les Cases d'Alcanar
Ulldecona
Vinaròs
Benicarló
Peñíscola
Santa Magdalena de Pulpís
Alcalá de Chivert
Serra d'Irta
Alcossebre
Punta de Capicorp
Torrenostra
Torreblanca
Cabo de Oropesa
Oropesa
Benicasim
Castelló de la Plana
Almassora
Vila-real de los Infantes
Burriana
El Grau de Borriana
Nules
Platja de Nules
Moncófar
Vall de Uxó
Chilches
Islas Columbretes
Costa del Azahar
Morella
EL MAESTRAZGO
Sierra del Monte Turmell
Sant Mateu
Vilafranca del Cid
Embalse de María Cristina
Onda
Plana de Castelló
Sierra d'Espadà
A2
A7
E90
E15

60

A
B
C
1
2
3
4
Pedrógão
Vieira de Leiria
Monte Real
São Pedro de Muel
Marinha Grande
Leiria
Pombal
Martingança
Batalha
Nazaré
Fátima
São Martinho do Porto
Alfeizerão
Alcobaça
Porto de Mós
Torres Novas
Farilhões
Foz do Arelho
Lagoa de Óbidos
Berlenga
Caldas da Rainha
Cabo Carvoeiro
Peniche
Atouguia da Baleia
Óbidos
Rio Maior
Santarém
Lourinhã
Bombarral
Cadaval
Cartaxo
Torres Vedras
São Pedro da Cadeira
Ericeira
Mafra
Alenquer
Vila Franca de Xira
Alverca
Sintra
Algueirão-Mem Martins
Cabo da Roca
Cascais
Estoril
Oeiras
Queluz
Amadora
Odivelas
Sacavém
Moscavide
LISBOA
Almada
Costa do Estoril
Caparica
Costa da Caparica
Barreiro
Seixal
Moita
Montijo
Alcochete
Pinhal Novo
Palmela
Setúbal
Tróia
Costa do Sol
Cabo Espichel
Costa Bela
Baía de Setúbal
Costa da Galé
Comporta
Alcácer do Sal
Carvalhal
Grândola
Melides
Lagoa de Santo André
Santo André
Cabo de Sines
Sines
Santiago do Cacém
Porto Covo da Bandeira
Tomar
Entroncamento
Abrantes
Constância
Chamusca
Almeirim
RIBATEJO
Coruche
Benavente
Samora Correia
Montemor-o-Novo
Évora
Vendas Novas
Arraiolos
Alcáçovas
Viana do Alentejo
Alvito
ALENTEJO
Ferreira do Alentejo
Beringel
Ermidas do Sado
Alvalade
Messejana
Mora
Pavia
Ponte de Sor
Sardoal
Mação
Proença-a-Nova
Sertã
Figueiró dos Vinhos
Ourém
Barragem de Montargil
Barragem do Maranhão
Barragem de Odivelas
Barragem do Roxo
Barragem de Morgavel
A1-IP1
A2-IP7
A6-IP7
A8-IC1
A9-IC18
A10
A12-IP1
A13-IC11
A15-IP6
E01
E90
E806

72

D
E
F
61
67
68
73
1
2
3
4
BEIRA BAIXA
Serra da Gardunha
São Vicente da Beira
Foz Giraldo
Miguel de Acha
Proença-a-Velha
Idanha-a-Velha
Monfortinho
Barragem da Idanha
Alcafozes
Idanha-a-Nova
Tinalhas
Escalos de Cima
Alcains
Escalos de Baixo
Salvaterra do Extremo
Zebreira
Sarzedas
Salgueiro
Castelo Branco
Ladoeiro
Segura
Piedras Albas
Benquerenças
Monforte da Beira
Ponsul
Rosmaninhal
Alcántara
Sarnadas de Ródão
Malpica do Tejo
Perais
Vila Velha de Ródão
Cedillo
Embalse de Cedillo
La Atalaya de Santiago
Santiago de Alcántara
Fratel
Montalvão
São Miguel
Nisa
Nossa Senhora da Graça de Póvoa e Meadas
Barragem da Póvoa
Membrío
Salorino
Herreruela
Sierra de San Pedro
Torrico de San Pedro
Castelo de Vide
Beirã
Marvão
Tolosa
Gáfete
Alpalhão
Alagoa
Valencia de Alcántara
San Vicente de Alcántara
Serra de São Mamede
Portalegre
Fortios
Vale do Peso
Crato
Aldeia da Mata
Seda
Alter Pedroso
Alter do Chão
Cabeço de Vide
Assumar
Barulho
Esperança
Arronches
La Codosera
Puerto de los Conejeros
Alburquerque
Villar del Rey
Vaiamonte
Fronteira
Senhora do Rosário
Monforte
Barragem do Caia
Nossa Senhora da Graça dos Degolados
Ouguela
Campo Maior
Santa Eulália
Barbacena
Cano
Sousel
São Bento do Cortiço
Veiros
Santo Aleixo
Vila Fernando
São Lourenço de Mamporcão
Elvas
Orada
Arcos
Terrugem
Estremoz
Glória
Borba
Rio de Moinhos
Vila Viçosa
São Romão
Ossa
Serra de Ossa
Bencatel
Pardais
Azaruja
Alandroal
Redondo
São Miguel de Machede
Terena
Nossa Senhora de Machede
Santa Susana
Casas Novas de Mares
Aldeia de Ferreira
Barragem do Monte Novo
Montoito
Vendinha
São Manços
Caridade
Monsaraz
Reguengos de Monsaraz
Campinho
São Marcos do Campo
Portel
Amieira
Vera Cruz
Alqueva
Póvoa de São Miguel
Vidigueira
Marmelar
Selmes
Moura
Santo Amador
Pedrógão
Machados
Safara
Serra da Adiça
Brinches
Pias
Baleizão
Sobral da Adiça
Clara de Louredo
Quintos
Serpa
Ficalho
Rosal de la Frontera
Vila Verde de Ficalho
Vila Nova de São Bento
Cabeça Gorda
Santa Iria
São Brás
Vales Mortos
Mourão
Luz
Estrela
Granja
Amareleja
Santo Aleixo da Restauração
Barrancos
Olivenza
San Benito de la Contienda
LLANOS DE OLIVENZA
Cheles
Alconchel
Táliga
San Jorge de Alor
Almendral
Valverde de Leganés
Embalse de Piedra Aguda
Higuera de Vargas
Barcarrota
Villanueva del Fresno
Valle de Santa Ana
Zahinos
Oliva de la Frontera
Valencia del Mombuey
Badajoz
Talavera la Real
Montijo
Torremayor
La Garrovilla
Mérida
Puebla de la Calzada
Lobón
Guadajira
Arroyo de San Serván
Torremegía
Calamonte
Valverde de Mérida
Don Álvaro
Villagonzalo
Zarza de Alange
Alange
Oliva de Mérida
Embalse de Alange
La Albuera
Corte de Peleas
Solana de los Barros
Almendralejo
TIERRA DE BARROS
Torre de Miguel Sesmero
Nogales
La Morera
Salvaleón
La Parra
Santa Marta
Villalba de los Barros
Aceuchal
Villafranca de los Barros
Fuente del Maestre
Feria
Sierra de Feria
Salvatierra de los Barros
Embalse de Guadajira
Valle de Matamoros
Burguillos del Cerro
Zafra
La Lapa
Los Santos de Maimona
Puebla de Sancho Pérez
Medina de las Torres
Valverde de Burguillos
Jerez de los Caballeros
Calzadilla de los Barros
Valencia del Ventoso
Fregenal de la Sierra
Higuera la Real
Encinasola
Bodonal de la Sierra
Segura de León
Cabeza la Vaca
Fuentes de León
Cumbres de San Bartolomé
Cumbres Mayores
Cañaveral de León
Hinojales
Arroyomolinos de León
Sierra de Hinojales
Sierra de Aracena
Sierra de Aroche
La Nava
Galaroza
Jabugo
Cortegana
Aracena
Alájar
Santa Ana la Real
Almonaster la Real
Sierra Pelada
Valdelamusa
Zufre
Santa Olalla del Cala
Corteconcepción
Embalse de Aracena
Cala
Monesterio
Tentudía
Calera de León
Pallarés
Montemolín
Fuente de Cantos
Bienvenida
Usagre
Higuera de Llerena
Villagarcía de la Torre
Llerena
Valverde de Llerena
Ahillones
Casas de Reina
Reina
Puebla del Maestre
Embalse El Pintado
El Real de la Jara
Almadén de la Plata
El Pedroso
Valencia de las Torres
Llera
Hinojosa del Valle
Ribera del Fresno
Hornachos
Embalse de los Molinos de Matachel
Puebla del Prior
Puebla de la Reina
Palomas
Retamal
Valle de la Serena
Quintana de la Serena
Guareña
Manchita
Valdetorres
Medellín
Mengabril
Santa Amalia
Trujillanos
Mirandilla
Esparragalejo
Aljucén
Carmonita
La Nava de Santiago
Cordobilla de Lácara
La Roca de la Sierra
Puebla de Obando
Embalse de los Canchales
Embalse de la Peña del Águila
Puerto del Zángano
Jabarriega
Puerto del Clavín
Carqueisa
Aliseda
Arroyo de la Luz
Malpartida de Cáceres
Cáceres
Sierra de Fuentes
Torreorgaz
Embalse de Salor
Torremocha
La Cumbre
Salvatierra de Santiago
Ibahernando
Valdefuentes
Torre de Santa María
Montánchez
Sierra de Montánchez
Alcuéscar
Almoharín
Miajadas
Villar de Rena
Rena
Aldea del Cano
Estena
Casar de Cáceres
Embalse de Cáceres
Aldea de Trujillo
Trujillo
Herguijuela
Santa Cruz de la Sierra
Villamesías
Abertura
Embalse de Brozas
Brozas
Navas del Madroño
Garrovillas
Embalse de Alcántara
Acehuche
Ceclavín
Zarza la Mayor
Portaje
Torrejoncillo
Alagón
Riolobos
Holguera
Mirabel
Puerto de la Serrana
Casas de Millán
Serradilla
Cañaveral
Puerto de los Castaños
Hinojal
Talaván
Santiago del Campo
Monroy
Embalse de Alcántara II
Torrejón el Rubio
Serrejón
Embalse de Torrejón-Tiétar
Embalse de Torrejón-Tajo
Malpartida de Plasencia
Plasencia
Carcaboso
Coria
Tejeda de Tiétar
Majadas
Casatejada
Jaraicejo

68
62
67
74
A
B
C
1
2
3
4
CAMPO ARAÑUELO
LA JARA
Montes de Toledo
Sierra de Guadalupe
Sierra de Altamira
Sierra de las Villuercas
Sierra de Montánchez
Sierra de la Chimenea
Sierra de los Golondrinos
Sierra de la Rinconada
LA SERENA
TIERRA DE BARROS
Sierra de los Argallanes
VALLE DE ALCUDIA
Sierra de Alcudia
Los Pedroches
Sierra Morena
Sierra de los Santos
Sierra Chimorra
Sierra del Agua
Sierra de Córdoba
Galisteo
Plasencia
Tejeda de Tiétar
Valverde de la Vera
Navalmoral de la Mata
Majadas de Tiétar
Casatejada
Almaraz
Serrejón
Bohonal de Ibor
Peraleda de la Mata
Embalse de Valdecañas
Valdecañas de Tajo
Ventas de San Julián
La Calzada de Oropesa
Torralba de Oropesa
Oropesa
Calera y Chozas
Torrico
El Puente de Arzobispo
Azután
Valdeverdeja
Valdelacasa de Tajo
Talavera de la Reina
Segurilla
Mejorada
Cazalegas
Malpica de Tajo
Cebolla
El Carpio de Tajo
La Puebla de Montalbán
Las Herencias
Alcaudete de la Jara
Belvís de la Jara
San Bartolomé de las Abiertas
Villarejo de Montalbán
San Martín de Pusa
Santa Ana de Pusa
Los Navalmorales
San Martín de Montalbán
Torrecilla de la Jara
Espinoso del Rey
Los Navalucillos
Navahermosa
La Nava de Ricomalillo
Robledo del Mazo
Sevilleja de la Jara
El Campillo de la Jara
Puerto de San Vicente
Aldeanueva de Barbarroya
Villar del Pedroso
La Estrella
Aldeanueva de San Bartolomé
Mohedas de la Jara
Fresnedoso de Ibor
Castañar de Ibor
Navalvillar de Ibor
Deleitosa
Robledollano
Cabañas del Castillo
Navezuelas
Torrecillas de la Tiesa
Aldeacentenera
Jaraicejo
Aldea de Trujillo
Trujillo
Riolobos
Holguera
Mirabel
Casas de Millán
Serradilla
Cañaveral
Torrejón el Rubio
Embalse de Alcántara II
Embalse de Torrejón-Tiétar
Embalse de Arrocampo
Embalse de Torrejón-Tajo
Puerto de Miravete
Puerto de la Serrana
Hinojal
Talaván
Santiago del Campo
Monroy
Casar de Cáceres
Embalse de Cáceres
Cáceres
Sierra de Fuentes
Torreorgaz
Embalse de Salor
Torremocha
La Cumbre
Madroñera
Garciaz
Herguijuela
Pedro Gómez
Cañamero
Puerto Llano
Logrosán
Alía
Retuerta del Bullaque
Navas de Estrena
Horcajo de los Montes
Embalse de Cijara
Alcoba
Villarta de los Montes
Fontanarejo
Navalpino
Arroba de los Montes
Castilblanco
Embalse de García Sola
Valdecaballeros
Peloche
Herrera del Duque
Puebla de Don Rodrigo
Salvatierra de Santiago
Ibahernando
Valdefuentes
Torre de Santa María
Santa Cruz de la Sierra
Zorita
Villamesías
Abertura
Alcollarín
Campo Lugar
Montánchez
Alcuéscar
Almoharín
Miajadas
Escurial
Madrigalejo
Villar de Rena
Rena
Gargáligas
Acedera
Navalvillar de Pela
Casas de Don Pedro
Orellana la Vieja
Orellana de la Sierra
Embalse de Orellana
Talarrubias
Puerto de los Carneros
Garbayuela
Tamurejo
Agudo
Valdemanco del Esteras
Saceruela
Baterno
Siruela
Puebla de Alcocer
Esparragosa
Embalse del Zújar
Mirandilla
Santa Amalia
Trujillanos
Mérida
Medellín
Mengabril
Don Benito
Villanueva de la Serena
La Haba
La Coronada
Valdetorres
Calamonte
Villagonzalo
Zarza de Alange
Alange
Oliva de Mérida
Guareña
Manchita
Magacela
Campanario
La Guarda
Quintana de la Serena
Embalse de Alange
Palomas
Valle de la Serena
Castuera
Benquerencia de la Serena
Almorchón
Cabeza del Buey
Zarza Capilla
Peñalsordo
Capilla
Sancti-Spíritus
Garlitos
Embalse de la Serena
Chillón
Almadén
Fontanosas
Abenójar
Puerto del Rayo
Guadalmez
Almadenejos
Alamillo
Malpartida de la Serena
Higuera de la Serena
Zalamea de la Serena
Esparragosa de la Serena
Helechal
Monterrubio de la Serena
Belalcázar
Santa Eufemia
San Benito
Puebla de la Reina
Puebla del Prior
Hornachos
Retamal
Ribera del Fresno
Hinojosa del Valle
Embalse de los Molinos de Matachel
Campillo de Llerena
Peraleda del Zaucejo
Hinojosa del Duque
Villaralto
El Viso
Dos Torres
Torrecampo
Añora
Pedroche
Conquista
Los Santos de Maimona
Llera
Valencia de las Torres
Higuera de Llerena
Blázquez
Valsequillo
La Granjuela
Villanueva del Duque
Alcaracejos
Pozoblanco
Villanueva de Córdoba
Usagre
Bienvenida
Villagarcía de la Torre
Maguilla
Berlanga
Granja de Torrehermosa
Peñarroya-Pueblonuevo
Fuente Obejuna
Bélmez
Fuente de Cantos
Llerena
Ahillones
Azuaga
La Coronada
Argallón
Montemolín
Casas de Reina
Reina
Valverde de Llerena
Fuente del Arco
Pallarés
Guadalcanal
Malcocinado
Villanueva del Rey
Espiel
Villaharta
Obejo
Embalse de Puente Nuevo
Embalse de Guadalmellato
Puebla del Maestre
Alanís
San Nicolás del Puerto
Villaviciosa de Córdoba
Embalse El Pintado
El Real de la Jara
Cazalla de la Sierra
Las Navas de la Concepción
Embalse del Bembézar
Adamuz
Montoro
Villafranca de Córdoba
Alcolea
Pedro Abad
El Carpio
Bujalance
Almadén de la Plata
Constantina
El Pedroso
Embalse de Retortillo
Embalse de la Breña
Córdoba
Hornachuelos
La Puebla de los Infantes
Cardeña
E803
E90
630
521
430
502
432

69
D
E
F
1
2
3
4
63
70
75
LA SAGRA
MESA DE OCAÑA
LA OBISPALÍA
LA MANCHA
CAMPO DE CALATRAVA
CAMPO DE MONTIEL
LOMA DE CHICLANA
LOMA DE ÚBEDA
Montes de Toledo
Sierra de los Torneros
Sierra del Pocito
Sierra de la Calderina
Sierra de Yébenes
Sierra de Alhambra
Sierra Madrona
Sierra de San Andrés
Sierra de Cazorla
Sierra del Pozo
Sierra de Segura
Sierra de Alcaraz
Calar del Mundo
Noves
Fuensalida
Villaluenga de la Sagra
Yuncler
Cobeja
Alameda de la Sagra
Aranjuez
Añover de Tajo
Torrijos
Rielves
Gerindote
Escalonilla
Burujón
Olías del Rey
Bargas
Villaseca de la Sagra
Mocejón
Toledo
Embalse de Castrejón
Argés
Polán
Layos
Burguillos de Toledo
Nambroca
Almonacid de Toledo
Gálvez
Pico de Noez 1034
Noez
Ajofrín
Mazarambroz
Pulgar
Sonseca
Mascaraque
Mora
Menasalbas
Cuerva
Orgaz
Manzaneque
Las Ventas con Peña Aguilera
Amor 1379
Los Yébenes
Marjaliza
Pablo de los Montes
El Molinillo
Embalse de la Torre de Abraham
Urda
Cortijo de Arriba
La Calderina 1028
Fuente el Fresno
El Trincheto
Porzuna
Embalse de Gasset
Puerto de los Majales
Malagón
Embalse de Puente Navarro
Fernáncaballero
Embalse de El Vicario
Piedrabuena
Picón
Carrión de Calatrava
Luciana
Alcolea de Calatrava
Palo 697
Ciudad Real
Torralba de Calatrava
Poblete
Miguelturra
Pozuelos de Calatrava
Corral de Calatrava
Los Pozuelos de Calatrava
Cabezarados
El Collado 850
Villamayor de Calatrava
Caracuel de Calatrava
Ballesteros de Calatrava
Valenzuela de Calatrava
Almagro
Bolaños de Calatrava
Moral de Calatrava
Prieto 927
Granátula de Calatrava
Embalse de la Vega del Jabalón
Argamasilla de Calatrava
Aldea del Rey
Calzada de Calatrava
Puertollano
Brazatortas
Cabezarrubias del Puerto
Puerto de Mestanza 871
Hinojosas de Calatrava
Mestanza
Mojina 1067
Villanueva de San Carlos
Embalse de Montoro
Encinas 1138
San Lorenzo de Calatrava
Solana del Pino
Rebollera 1157
Fuencaliente
Azuel
Venta del Charco
Embalse del Yeguas
Marmolejo
Andújar
Villanueva de la Reina
Arjonilla
Lopera
Arjona
Higuera de Arjona
Porcuna
Cañete de las Torres
Villardompardo
Fuerte del Rey
Mengíbar
Torreblascopedro
Villargordo
Cazalilla
Bailén
Baños de la Encina
Embalse del Encinarejo
Embalse del Jándula
El Centenillo
La Carolina
Embalse del Rumblar
Guarromán
Linares
Carboneros
Embalse de la Fernandina
Vilches
Arquillos
Estación de Baeza
Jabalquinto
Lupión
Baeza
Begíjar
Ibros
Canena
Rus
Sabiote
Torreperogil
Úbeda
Embalse de Giribaile
Embalse de Pedro Marín
Embalse de Doña Aldonza
Jódar
Jimena
Santa Elena
Desfiladero de Despeñaperros
Desesperada 1146
Estrella 1300
Aldeaquemada
Embalse del Guadalén
Navas de San Juan
Santisteban del Puerto
Castellar de Santisteban
Sorihuela del Guadalimar
Chiclana de Segura
La Muela 961
Venta de los Santos
Montizón
Arroyo del Ojanco
Puente de Génave
La Puerta de Segura
Beas de Segura
Cortijos Nuevos
Hornos
Embalse de Olvera
Villacarrillo
Villanueva del Arzobispo
Mogón
Santo Tomé
Chilluévar
Peal de Becerro
Cazorla
La Iruela
Quesada
Blanquillo 1830
Embalse del Tranco de Beas
Yelmo 1809
Pontones
Santiago de la Espada
Segura de la Sierra
Orcera
Benatae
Siles
Génave
Torres de Albánchez
Villarrodrigo
Villaverde de Guadalimar
Bienservida
Villapalacios
Embalse del Guadalmena
Puebla de Don Fadrique
Empanadas 2107
Tornajuelos 2133
Sagra 2382
Embalse de San Clemente
Huéscar
Las Cabras 2106
Puerto del Pinar
Lobos 1804
Mentiras 1897
Arguellite
Yeste
Tragoncillo
Fábricas de San Juan de Alcaraz
Puerto de las Almenaras 1797
Puerto del Arenal 1180
Salobre
Vianos
Alcaraz
Povedilla
Robledo
Puerto de los Pocicos 1058
Viveros
El Ballestero
Los Barreros 1101
El Bonillo
Ossa de Montiel
Ruidera
Embalse de Peñarroya
Munera
Sotuélamos
Villarrobledo
Socuéllamos
Minaya
Casas de los Pinos
El Provencio
Las Mesas
San Clemente
Pedro Muñoz
Las Pedroñeras
El Pedernoso
Mota del Cuervo
Santa María de los Llanos
Belmonte
Rada de Haro
Santa María del Campo Rus
El Cañavate
Atalaya
La Alberca de Záncara
Canteras 852
Pinarejo
Castillo de Garcimuñoz
Villaescusa de Haro
Osa de Vega
Fuentelespino de Haro
Tresjuncos
Hontanaya
Cruz 1057
Villamayor de Santiago
La Hinojosa
Mojón Alto 1024
Villar de Cañas
Villarejo de Fuentes
Almonacid del Marquesado
Puebla de Almenara
Pozorrubio
Horcajo de Santiago
Cabezamesada
Corral de Almaguer
Lillo
El Romeral
Tembleque
Villanueva de Bogas
Turleque
Embalse de Finisterre
Villacañas
La Villa de Don Fadrique
La Puebla de Almoradiel
Villanueva de Alcardete
Los Hinojosos
Quintanar de la Orden
El Toboso
Miguel Esteban
Quero
Consuegra
Madridejos
Camuñas
Villafranca de los Caballeros
Laguna de Las Yeguas
Laguna del Retamar
Alcázar de San Juan
Campo de Criptana
Herencia
Puerto Lápice
Las Labores
Arenas de San Juan
Villarta de San Juan
Alameda de Cervera
Villarrubia de los Ojos
Cinco Casas
Argamasilla de Alba
Tomelloso
Laguna la Albuera
Daimiel
Manzanares
Membrilla
La Solana
Alhambra
Juego de Bolos 1087
Carrizosa
San Carlos del Valle
Valdepeñas
Alcubillas
Villanueva de los Infantes
Villahermosa
Montiel
Villanueva de la Fuente
Santa Cruz de los Cáñamos
Castellanos 1040
Albaladejo
Terrinches
Cózar
Almedina
Cabeza de Buey 1158
Torrenueva
Santa Cruz de Mudela
Torre de Juan Abad
Puebla del Príncipe
Villamanrique
Castellar de Santiago
Viso del Marqués
Almuradiel
Ocaña
Noblejas
Ciruelos
Yepes
Dosbarrios
Villasequilla de Yepes
Huerta de Valdecarábanos
Villamuelas
La Guardia
Villatobas
Santa Cruz de la Zarza
Zarza de Tajo
Tarancón
Belinchón
Huelves
Uclés
Rozalén del Monte
Saelices
Villarrubio
Almendros
Fuente de Pedro Naharro
Torrubia del Campo
Palomeras del Campo
Abia de la Obispalía
Naharros
Montalbo
El Hito
Laguna de El Hito
Zafra de Záncara
San Lorenzo de la Parrilla
Villares del Saz
Cervera del Llano
Olivares de Júcar
Belmonte
Canal de Trasvase
Embalse de la Fernandina
Guadiana
Cigüela
Záncara
Jabalón
Azuer
Guadalmena
Guadalimar
Guadalquivir
Guadalén
Riansares
Amarguillo
Algodor
Guadarrama
Bullaque
Montoro
Ojailén
Fresnedas
Jándula
Yeguas
Rumblar
Cañamares
Pinilla
Córcoles
Madera
Dañador
Tús
Segura
Bravatas
Salado
Guadalbullón
Torres
E05
E901
IV
III
301
400
401
403
410
420
430
310
200
3000
3103
3119
3106
3133
3129
4111
4112
4110
412
413
320
322
317
314
315
319
330
3204
302
303
305
306
311
316
323

70
64
69
76
A
B
C
1
2
3
4
LA OBISPALIA
LA MANCHA
CAMPO DE MONTIEL
VALENCIA
RINCÓN DE ADEMUZ
Cuenca
Villar de Olalla
Palomera
Cañete
Salinas del Manzano
Huérguina
Vallenca
Huelves
Torrejoncillo del Rey
Naharros
Abia de la Obispalía
Rozalén del Monte
Villarrubio
Almendros
Saelices
Palomares del Campo
Zafra de Záncara
Torrubia del Campo
Montalbo
El Hito
Laguna de El Hito
Pozorrubio
Puebla de Almenara
Almonacid del Marquesado
Villarejo de Fuentes
Villar de Cañas
San Lorenzo de la Parrilla
Villares del Saz
Cervera del Llano
Belmontejo
Olivares de Júcar
Villaverde y Pasaconsol
Valverde de Júcar
La Parra de las Vegas
Cañada del Hoyo
Talayuelo
Puerto de Tórdiga
Carboneras de Guadazaón
Arguisuelas
Monteagudo de las Salinas
Valera de Arriba
Cerro Moro
Sierra del Monje
Pajarón
Reíllo
Boniches
Campillos-Paravientos
Sierra de las Cuerdas
Fuentelespino de Moya
Villar del Humo
Henarejos
Moya
Landete
Talayuelas
Garaballa
Santa Cruz de Moya
Arcos de las Salinas
Aras de Alpuente
Alpuente
Titaguas
Tuéjar
Picaracho
Embalse del Generalísimo
Sinarcas
Mira
Sierra de Mira
Aliaguilla
Embalse de Loriguilla
Loriguilla
Cardenete
Yémeda
Villora
Almodóvar del Pinar
Paracuellos
Enguídanos
Camporrobles
Hontanaya
Tresjuncos
Fuentelespino de Haro
Osa de Vega
Villaescusa de Haro
Los Hinojosos
La Hinojosa
Mojón Alto
La Almarcha
Hontecillas
Buenache de Alarcón
Embalse de Alarcón
Honrubia
Castillo de Garcimuñoz
Pinarejo
Santa María del Campo Rus
Rada de Haro
Belmonte
Villa de Almoradiel
Quintanar de la Orden
El Toboso
Mota del Cuervo
Santa María de los Llanos
El Cañavate
Atalaya del Cañavate
La Alberca de Záncara
Alarcón
Tébar
Gabaldón
Campillo de Altobuey
Puebla del Salvador
Motilla del Palancar
Graja de Iniesta
Minglanilla
Embalse de Contreras
Caudete de las Fuentes
Utiel
Chera
Villargordo del Cabriel
San Antonio
Requena
Venta del Moro
Moluengo
Sierra de Rubial
El Peral
El Pedernoso
Las Pedroñeras
Pedro Muñoz
Las Mesas
El Provencio
San Clemente
Vara del Rey
Casas de Fernando Alonso
Sisante
El Picazo
Casasimarro
Pozoamargo
Casas de Benítez
Villanueva de la Jara
Quintanar del Rey
Iniesta
Villalpardo
Villarta
El Herrumblar
Ledaña
Villamalea
Villagarcía del Llano
Villatoya
La Portera
Sierra Martés
Los Pedrones
Casas de los Pinos
Casas de Haro
Villalgordo del Júcar
Tarazona de la Mancha
Navas de Jorquera
Casas-Ibáñez
Alborea
Casas de Ves
Balsa de Ves
Villa de Ves
Cofrentes
Socuéllamos
Villarrobledo
Minaya
La Roda
Fuensanta
Madrigueras
Fuentealbilla
Mahora
Motilleja
Alcalá del Júcar
Jorquera
Presa y Embalse del Molinar
Jalance
Casas de Juan Gil
Jarafuel
Teresa de Cofrentes
Munera
Santa Marta
La Gineta
Valdeganga
Casas de Juan Núñez
Pozo-Lorente
Alatoz
Carcelén
Zarra
Ayora
Sotuélamos
Barrax
Albacete
La Felipa
Ruidera
Ossa de Montiel
El Bonillo
Laguna de Navalcudia
Lezuza
Los Barreros
Tiriez
Balazote
Santa Ana
Chinchilla de Monte Aragón
Hoya Gonzalo
Higueruela
Molatón
Alpera
El Mugrón
Puerto Los Altos
Villar de Chinchilla
Bonete
Almansa
Embalse de Almansa
Altos de Chinchilla
El Ballestero
San Pedro
Laguna del Salobral
Argamasón
El Salobral
Pozuelo
Laguna Salada de Pétrola
Pétrola
Pozo Cañada
Corral-Rubio
La Higuera
Montealegre del Castillo
La Font de la Figuera
Villahermosa
Viveros
Robledo
Puerto de los Pocicos
Casas de Lázaro
Masegoso
Povedilla
Peñascosa
Pozohondo
Laguna de Ontalafia
Peñas de San Pedro
Fuente-Álamo
Caudete
Montiel
Villanueva de la Fuente
Alcaraz
Vianos
Alcadozo
Carro de Fuente Albilla
Tobarra
Ontur
Albatana
Yecla
Sierra de la Magdalena
Albaladejo
Terrinches
Salobre
Sierra de Alcaraz
Paterna del Madera
Bogarra
Villapalacios
Puebla del Príncipe
Almenaras
Puerto del Barrancazo
Puerto de las Crucetillas
Bienservida
Ayna
Liétor
Embalse de Talave
Villarrodrigo
Fábricas de San Juan de Alcaraz
Hellín
Isso
Minateda
Sierra de las Cabras
Jumilla
Sierra del Buey
Puerto del Arenal
Villaverde de Guadalimar
Molinicos
Torres de Albánchez
Génave
Peñarrubia
Elche de la Sierra
Porrón
Calar del Mundo
Agramón
Cancarix
Sierra del Carche
Casas del Puerto
Pinoso
Puente de Génave
La Puerta de Segura
Siles
Benatae
Orcera
Segura de la Sierra
Yeste
Embalse de la Fuensanta
Letur
Férez
Socovos
Embalse del Cenajo
Moharque
Embalse de Camarillas
Rambla del Judío
Embalse del Judío
Rambla del Moro
Algueña
Hondón de los Frailes
Barinas
Cortijos Nuevos
Hornos
Embalse del Tranco de Beas
Yelmo
Mentiras
Arguellite
Sierra de Lagos
Tragoncillo
Embalse de Taibilla
Benizar y la Tercia
Calasparra
Embalse de Almadenes
Cieza
Sierra de la Pila
Abanilla
Fortuna
Abarán
Blanca
Pontones
Sierra de Segura
Santiago de la Espada
Embalse de la Novia
Nerpio
Sierra de Taibilla
El Sabinar
Moratalla
Embalse de Argos
El Buitre
Caravaca de la Cruz
Cehegín
Archivel
Bullas
Villanueva del Río Segura
Archena
Ceutí
Alguazas
Molina de Segura
Orihuela
Redován
Santomera
Beniel
Alquerías
Mula
Embalse de la Cierva
Albudeite
Las Torres de Cotillas
Pliego
Barranda
Revolcadores
Puerto del Pinar
Las Cabras
Puerto de Almaciles
El Moral
Almudema
Javalí Viejo
Murcia
Sierra del Pozo
Empanadas
Tornajuelos
Sagra
Lobos
Puebla de Don Fadrique
Los Royos
Barqueros
Alcantarilla
El Palmar
Los Algezares
La Alberca
Sucina
Embalse de San Clemente
Huéscar
Zarcilla de Ramos
La Paca
Zarzadilla de Totana
Sierra de España
Alhama
Librilla

D
E
F
65
Manzanera
Barracas
Cirat
Argelita
Alcora
Ribesalbes
Embalse de María Cristina
Embalse de Sichar
Borriol
Oropesa
Benicasim
Castelló de la Plana
Almassora
Onda
Tales
Pavías
Caudiel
Embalse del Regajo
Jérica
Viver
Bejís
Teresa
Arteas de Abajo
Sacañet
Navajas
Altura
Segorbe
Castellnovo
Chovar
Serra d'Espada
Betxí
Artana
Villavieja
Vila-real de los Infantes
Burriana
El Grau de Borriana
Nules
Platja de Nules
Moncófar
Vall de Uxó
Chilches
Almenara
Las Casas
Barrio Mar
Soneja
Gátova
Alcublas
Villar del Arzobispo
Casinos
Olocau
Serra
Náquera
Faura
Quartell
Sagunto
El Port
Marines
Losa del Obispo
Bugarra
Pedralba
Llíria
Bétera
Rafelbunyol
Puçol
Puig
Massamagrell
La Pobla de Vallbona
Vilamarxant
Riba-roja
Moncada
Paterna
Burjassot
Meliana
Alboraya
Gestalgar
Santa María
Cheste
Chiva
Manises
Xirivella
Valencia
Alaquàs
Torrent
Catarroja
Alfafar
El Saler
Buñol
Godelleta
Turís
Macastre
Yatova
Alcácer
Picassent
Silla
Montroy
Monserrat
L'Albufera
El Perelló
Almussafes
Benifaió
Alginet
Llombai
Catadau
Dos Aguas
Millares
Cortes de Pallás
Carlet
L'Alcudia
Guadassuar
Algemesí
Sueca
Cap-Blanc
Cullera
Corbera
Alzira
Embalse de Tous
Bicorp
Tous
Massalavés
Alberic
Carcaixent
Llaurí
Favara
Quesa
Navarrés
Villanueva de Castellón
Simat de la Valldigna
Tavernes de la Valldigna
Xeraco
Xeresa
Bolbaite
Chella
Anna
Manuel
Xàtiva
Barxeta
Genovés
Mondúver
Gandía
Piles
Serra de Enguera
Enguera
Montesa
L'Alcudia de Crespins
Quatretonda
Benigánim
Bellreguard
Alquería de la Condesa
Oliva
Canals
L'Olleria
Puerto de l'Olleria
La Pobla del Duc
Montaberner
Aielo de Malferit
Moixent-Mogente
Villalonga
Castelló de Rugat
Lorcha
Pego
Vergel
Denia
Las Rotas
Cabo de San Antonio
Ontinyent
Albaidá
Adzaneta de Albaida
Beniarrés
Embalse de Beniarrés
Agullent
Benarbeig
Ondara
Montgó
Jávea-Xàbia
Cabo de San Martín
Cabo de la Nao
Orba
Alcalalí
Gata de Gorgos
Parcent
Benitachell
Bocairent
Agrés
Cocentaina
Muro de Alcoy
Castell de Castells
Benejama
Bañeres
Benilloba
Puerto de Ares
Tárbena
Benissa
Teulada
Moraira
Punta de Moraira
Alcoy-Alcoi
Benasau
Benifallim
Guadalest
Peñón de Ifach
Calpe
Cañada
Villena
Ibi
Torremanzanas-La Torre de les Maçanes
Aitana
Callosa d'En Sarrià
Sella
Polop
Biar
Relleu
La Nucía
Finestrat
Altea
Castalla
Alfaz del Pi
Sax
Tibi
Jijona-Xixona
Embalse de Amadorio
Punta de la Escaleta
Elda
Petrer
Maigmó
Embalse de Tibi
Busot
Aguas de Busot
Benidorm
Villajoyosa-La Vila Joiosa
Isolte de Benidorm
Agost
Mutxamel
Campello
San Vicente del Raspeig
San Juan de Alicante
Novelda
Monforte del Cid
Cabo de las Huertas
Aspe
Alicante-Alacant
Bahía de Alicante
Embalse de Elche
Torellano
Crevillente
Elche-Elx
Los Arenales del Sol
Cabo de Santa Pola
Santa Pola
Isla Plana o Nueva Tabarca
Catral
Dolores
Cox
Callosa de Segura
Rojales
Almoradí
Guardamar del Segura
Benejúzar
Bigastro
Laguna Salada de la Mata
Laguna Salada de Torrevieja
Embalse de la Pedrera
Torrevieja
San Miguel de Salinas
Punta Prima
Dehesa de Campoamor
Costa del Azahar
Golfo de Valencia
Costa Blanca
Islas Columbretes
Mahon
Palma del Mallorca
Eivissa
1
2
3
4
A7
E15
E901
A37

A
B
C
1
2
3
4
66
Lagoa de Santo André
Santa Margarida da Serra
Grândola
Santa Margarida do Sádão
Faro do Alentejo
Cuba
Selmes
Moura
Santo Amador
Safara
ALENTEJO
São Francisco da Serra
Azinheira dos Barros
Ferreira do Alentejo
Peroguarda
Trigaches
São Matias
Pedrógão
Santo André
Santa Cruz
São Bartolomeu da Serra
Canhestros
Beringel
São Brissos
Nossa Senhora das Neves
Brinches
Sobral da Adiça
Serra da Adiça
Cabo de Sines
Sines
Santiago do Cacém
Abela
Ermidas do Sado
Ervidel
Penedo Gordo
Santa Vitória
Beja
Baleizão
Pias
Ficalho
Rosal de la Frontera
Canal do Sado-Morgavel
São Domingos
Alvalade
Montes Velhos
Barragem do Roxo
Santa Clara de Louredo
Quintos
Serpa
Guadalupe
Vila Nova de São Bento
Vila Verde de Ficalho
Barragem de Morgavel
Barragem de Campilhas
Rio de Moinhos
Aljustrel
Albernoa
Trindade
Cabeça Gorda
São Brás
Santa Iria
Porto Covo da Bandeira
Campilhas
Messejana
P
Cercal
Bicos
Aldeia dos Elvas
Vales Mortos
Serpa
Mosteiro
Amendoeira
Serra de Serpa
Serra de Mértola
Santa Bárbara de Casa
Campo Redondo
Panóias
Casével
Entradas
Vale de Açor
Algodor
Água Negra
Chança
Paymogo
Milfontes
Serra do Cercal
Colos
Santa Luzia
Barragem do Monte da Rocha
Cobres
Terges
Cabezas Rubias
Malagon
São Luís
Relíquias
Garvão
Castro Verde
Alcaria Ruiva
São Marcos da Ataboeira
Almograve
São Martinho das Amoreiras
Aldeia dos Palheiros
Ourique
Mina de São Domingos
Moreanes
Puebla de Guzmán
Cavaleiro
Cabo Sardão
Vigia
Luzianes
Urza
São João dos Caldeireiros
Mértola
Santana de Cambas
Odemira
Mira
Aldeia dos Fernandes
Rosário
Oeiras
São Sebastião dos Carros
Pomarão
EL ANDÉVALO
Zambujeira do Mar
São Teotónio
Santa Clara-a-Velha
Santana da Serra
Barragem da Perna Seca
Almodôvar
São Miguel do Pinheiro
Espírito Santo
Granado
El Granado
El Almendro
Villanueva de los Castillejos
Barragem de Santa Clara
Gomes Aires
Santa Clara-a-Nova
São Pedro de Solis
Quintã
Martim Longo
Vascão
Giões
Pereiro
Alcoutim
Sanlúcar de Guadiana
Odeceixe
Serra da Brejeira
Pereiras
Nave Redonda
A2-IP1
Serra do Caldeirão
San Bartolomé de la Torre
Seixe
Rogil
Portela das Corchas
São Marcos da Serra
Ameixial
Vaqueiros
Mu
San Silvestre de Guzmán
Embalse
Pta da Atalaia
Serra de Espinhaço de Cão
Fóia
Alferce
São Barnabé
Cachopo
Odeleite
Aljezur
Marmelete
Monchique
Odelouca
Villablanca
Alfambras
Serra de Monchique
Nave
Barragem do Arade
Arade
Vale da Rosa
Peralva
Azinhal
Cartaya
ALGARVE
São Bartolomeu de Messines
Salir
Feiteira
Alcaria do Cume
Junqueira
Lepe
Bordeira
Barragem da Bravura
Alte
Barranco do Velho
Castro Marim
Ayamonte
Isla Cristina
La Antilla
Carrapateira
Porto de Lagos
Cumeada
Algibre
São Brás de Alportel
Santa Catarina da Fonte do Bispo
Alportel
Vila Real de Santo António
Vila Nova de Cacela
Monte Gordo
Bensafrim
Odiáxere
Cardosas
Estômbar
Algoz
Paderne
Loulé
Barão de São João
Portimão
Guia
Boliqueime
Santo Estêvão
Conceição
Tavira
Vila do Bispo
Budens
Praia da Rocha
Lagoa
Pêra
Luz
Raposeira
Lagos
Carvoeiro
Armação de Pêra
Albufeira
Vilamoura
Quarteira
Almansil
Estói
Moncarapacho
Ilha de Tavira
Cabo de São Vicente (Cape St Vincent)
Burgau
Luz
Pta da Piedade
Vale de Lobo
São João da Venda
Sagres
Pta de Sagres
Faro
Olhão
Ria Formosa
Cabo de Santa Maria
GOLFO
Islas Canarias
IP8
IC1
IC4
IP2
IP1
E01
E802

73
D
E
F
67
74
1
2
3
4
Barrancos
Higuera la Real
Bodonal de la Sierra
Segura de León
Calera de León
Pallarés
Puebla del Maestre
Malcocinado
Fuentes de León
Cabeza la Vaca
Monesterio
Tentudía 1104
Cumbres de San Bartolomé
Cumbres Mayores
Cañaveral de León
Hinojales
Arroyomolinos de León
Sierra de Aroche
Sierra del Castaño
Sierra de Hinojales
Sierra de Aracena
Sierra Pelada
Embalse El Pintado
Alanís
San Nicolás del Puerto
Hamapega 910
Las Navas de la Concepción
Tiesa 673
Embalse de Retortillo
Embalse Bembézar
Cala
El Real de la Jara
La Nava
Galaroza
Jabugo
Alájar
Aracena
Cortegana
Santa Ollala del Cala
Corteconcepción
Embalse de Aracena
Almadén de la Plata
Cazalla de la Sierra
Constantina
Gibarrayo
Almonaster la Real
Santa Ana la Real
Higuera de la Sierra
Zufre
Cabezo Gordo 613
San Telmo
Valdelamusa
Campofrío
Embalse de Zufre
Embalse de Cala
El Pedroso
Embalse de Huezna
Hornachuelos
La Puebla de los Infantes
Embalse de José Torán
Peñaflor
Palma del Río
El Cerro de Andévalo
La Granada de Riotinto
Minas de Riotinto
Padre Caro 698
Nerva
El Castillo de las Guardas
El Ronquillo
Embalse de la Minilla
Zalamea la Real
El Campillo
Calañas
Villanueva de las Cruces
Sotiel Coronada
El Garrobo
Castilblanco de los Arroyos
Villaverde del Río
Villanueva del Río y Minas
Alcolea del Río
Lora del Río
Canal del Bajo Guadalquivir
Cantillana
Burguillos
Guillena
Brenes
Guadajoz
La Campana
La Luisiana
Valverde del Camino
Embalse de Agrio
Embalse El Esparragal
Aznalcóllar
Gerena
Alcalá del Río
La Rinconada
Carmona
Fuentes de Andalucía
Los Castillejos
El Tumbalejo
Embalse de Corumbel Bajo
EL ALJARAFE
La Algaba
Santiponce
Camas
Sevilla
Embalse de Sancho
Beas
CONDADO DE NIEBLA
Villalba del Alcor
Paterna del Campo
Olivares
Salteras
Mairena del Alcor
El Viso del Alcor
Gibraleón
Trigueros
Villarrasa
Niebla
La Palma del Condado
Manzanilla
Carrión
Sanlúcar
Castilleja de la Cuesta
Tomares
San Juan de Aznalfarache
Alcalá de Guadaira
Marchena
Paradas
La Lantejuela
San Juan del Puerto
Bonares
Bollullos Par del Condado
Huévar
Benacazón
Pilas
Palomares del Río
Bellavista
Aljaraque
Huelva
Moguer
Lucena del Puerto
Rociana del Condado
Hinojos
Aznalcázar
La Puebla del Río
Coria del Río
Dos Hermanas
El Arahal
La Puebla de Cazalla
El Rompido
Palos de la Frontera
Punta Umbría
Almonte
Villamanrique de la Condesa
Utrera
Morón de la Frontera
Mazagón
El Rocío
Los Palacios y Villafranca
Villafranco del Guadalquivir
Isla Menor
Embalse de la Torre del Aguila
El Coronil
Sierra de Esparteros
Playa de Castilla
Isla Mayor
Marismas
Torre de la Higuera
Las Cabezas de San Juan
Montellano
Coripe
Sierra de San Juan
Pruna
Costa de la Luz
Lebrija
Puerto Serrano
Algodonales
Olvera
Torre-Alháquime
Setenil
Trebujena
El Cuervo
Espera
Villamartín
Gibalbín 410
Zahara
Embalse de Zahara-El Gastor
Bonanza
Nueva Jarilla
Bornos
Embalse de Bornos
Prado del Rey
Sierra Margarita
Pinar 1654
Pta de Malandar
Sanlúcar de Barrameda
Arcos de la Frontera
El Bosque
Grazalema
Montejaque
Ronda
Pta del Perro
Chipiona
Jerez de la Frontera
Jédula
Embalse de los Hurones
Benaocaz
Benaoján
Sierra de Aznar
Ubrique
Algar
Sierra de Ubrique
DE CÁDIZ
Pta Candor
Rota
El Puerto de Santa María
San José del Valle
Embalse de Guadalcacín
Sierra de las Cabras
Cortes de la Frontera
Algatocín
Bahía de Cádiz
Paterna de Rivera
Cádiz
Puerto Real
Aljibe 1092
Gaucín
Isla de León
San Fernando
Alcalá de los Gazules
Jimena de la Frontera
Casares
Estepona
Medina-Sidonia
Embalse de Barbate
Campo de Gibraltar
Chiclana de la Frontera
Isla Sancti Petri
Campano
San José de Malcocinado
Manilva
Benalup de Sidonia
Conil de la Frontera
Cabo Roche
Embalse de Celemín
Sierra Blanquilla
Castellar de la Frontera
Vejer de la Frontera
Sierra del Niño
Los Barrios
San Roque
La Línea de la Concepción
Barbate de Franco
Gibraltar
Europa Point
Cabo Trafalgar
Sierra de Retín
Facinas
Sierra de Fates
Zahara de los Atunes
Algeciras
Sierra de la Plata
Luna 788
Pta del Carnero
Pta Camarinal
Pta Palomas
Tarifa
Strait of Gibraltar
Pta Almina
GBZ
A49
E01
A4
A92
E05
E803
E15
IV

74
68
73
A
B
C
1
2
3
4
Malcocinado
Alanís
San Nicolás del Puerto
Las Navas de la Concepción
Cazalla de la Sierra
Constantina
El Pedroso
Embalse de Huezna
Embalse de Retortillo
Hornachuelos
La Puebla de los Infantes
Embalse de José Torán
Peñaflor
Palma del Río
Posadas
Almodóvar del Río
Villaviciosa de Córdoba
Embalse del Bembézar
Embalse de la Breña
Córdoba
Alcolea
Embalse de S. Rafael Navallana
Villaharta
Obejo
Embalse de Guadalmellato
Adamuz
Villafranca de Córdoba
Montoro
Pedro Abad
El Carpio
Bujalance
Villa del Río
Marmolejo
Andújar
Arjonilla
Lopera
Arjona
Embalse del Yeguas
Cañete de las Torres
Porcuna
Valenzuela
Torredonjimeno
Santiago de Calatrava
Castro del Río
Espejo
Albendín
Fernán Núñez
Montemayor
Guadalcázar
Fuente Palmera
La Carlota
San Sebastián de los Ballesteros
La Victoria
La Rambla
Montalbán de Córdoba
Montilla
Aguilar de la Frontera
Santaella
Baena
Doña Mencía
Nueva-Carteya
Luque
Alcaudete
Zuheros
Fuente-Tójar
Priego de Córdoba
Almedinilla
Carcabuey
Cabra
Lucena
Moriles
Puente-Genil
Rute
Iznájar
Algarinejo
Montefrío
Villanueva del Río y Minas
Alcolea del Río
Lora del Río
Cantillana
Villaverde del Río
Brenes
Guadajoz
La Campana
Canal del Bajo Guadalquivir
CAMPIÑA
Écija
La Luisiana
Fuentes de Andalucía
Carmona
A N D A L U C Í A
Sevilla
La Rinconada
Mairena del Alcor
El Viso del Alcor
Alcalá de Guadaira
Dos Hermanas
Marchena
Paradas
El Arahal
Utrera
La Puebla de Cazalla
Morón de la Frontera
El Coronil
Osuna
La Lantejuela
Marinaleda
El Rubio
Herrera
Estepa
Aguadulce
Gilena
Pedrera
Badolatosa
Casariche
Benamejí
Palenciana
Alameda
La Roda de Andalucía
Fuente de Piedra
Humilladero
Laguna de Fuente de Piedra
Los Corrales
Martín de la Jara
Sierra de Yeguas
El Saucejo
Villanueva de San Juan
Algámitas
Almargen
Campillos
Teba
Cañete la Real
Bobadilla
Antequera
Archidona
Loja
Villanueva de Algaidas
Villanueva de Tapia
Cuevas de San Marcos
Cuevas Bajas
Encinas Reales
Villanueva de Mesía
Huétor-Tájar
Salar
Montellano
Coripe
Pruna
Puerto Serrano
Algodonales
Olvera
Torre-Alháquime
Setenil
Alcalá del Valle
Las Cabezas de San Juan
Espera
Villamartín
Bornos
Embalse de Bornos
Zahara
Embalse de Zahara-El Gastor
Prado del Rey
El Bosque
Grazalema
Sierra Margarita
Benaocaz
Ubrique
Montejaque
Benaoján
Ronda
Arriate
Embalse de los Hurones
Algar
Sierra de Aznar
Sierra de Ubrique
San José del Valle
Paterna de Rivera
Cortes de la Frontera
Algatocín
Jubrique
Igualeja
Sierra de Tolox
Serranía de Ronda
Cuevas del Becerro
Ardales
Embalse del Conde de Guadalhorce
Carratraca
El Burgo
Yunquera
Alozaina
Tolox
Guaro
Monda
Coín
Casarabonela
Pizarra
Álora
Valle de Abdalajís
Almogía
Villanueva de la Concepción
Villanueva del Trabuco
Villanueva del Rosario
Alhama de Granada
Zafarraya
Periana
Riogordo
Colmenar
Casabermeja
Comares
Benamargosa
Almáchar
Vélez-Málaga
Benamocarra
Moclinejo
Montes de Málaga
Ventas de Zafarraya
Alcaucín
Canillas de Aceituno
Cártama
Alhaurín el Grande
Alhaurín de la Torre
Málaga
El Palo
Rincón de la Victoria
Torre del Mar
Algarrobo
Torremolinos
Benalmádena
Mijas
Fuengirola
Punta de Calaburra
Istán
Ojén
Marbella
Ensenada de Marbella
San Pedro de Alcántara
Benahavís
Sierra Bermeja
Estepona
Casares
Gaucín
Jimena de la Frontera
Manilva
Pta de la Chullera
Alcalá de los Gazules
Medina-Sidonia
Embalse de Barbate
Campo de Gibraltar
San José de Malcocinado
Embalse de Celemín
Sierra Blanquilla
Sierra del Niño
Castellar de la Frontera
Los Barrios
San Roque
La Línea de la Concepción
Gibraltar
Europa Point
Algeciras
Pta del Carnero
Strait of Gibraltar
Sierra de Retín
Sierra de la Plata
Facinas
Sierra de Fates
Tarifa
Pta Paloma
Pta de Tarifa o Marroquí
Pta Almina
Costa del Sol
Pta Mala
GBZ
E05
E15
E15/902
A7
A92
A4
IV
N340
340
351
331
359
432
431
Guadalquivir
Genil
Guadajoz
Corbones
Guadiaro
Guadalhorce
Embalse de Guadalteba
Embalse de Iznájar
Embalse de la Viñuela
Sierra de Espartero
Sierra de San Juan
Sierra de Líjar
Sierra Gorda

75
D
E
F
69
76
1
2
3
4
Bailén
Linares
Estación de Baeza
Úbeda
Baeza
LOMA DE ÚBEDA
Sabiote
Torreperogil
Mogón
Santo Tomé
Chilluévar
Villanueva del Arzobispo
Villacarrillo
Embalse de Olvera
Embalse de Giribaile
Canena
Rus
Ibros
Jabalquinto
Lupión
Begíjar
Cazalilla
Torreblascopedro
Mengíbar
Villargordo
Embalse de Mengíbar
Guadalquivir
Embalse de Pedro Marín
Embalse de Doña Aldonza
Peal de Becerro
La Iruela
Cazorla
Sierra de Cazorla
Sierra del Pozo
Quesada
Jódar
Jimena
Bedmar
Torres
Mancha Real
Pegalajar
Sierra Mágina
Mágina
2167
Bélmez de la Moraleda
Larva
Huesa
Puerto de Tíscar
1183
Cabañas
2036
Pozo Alcón
Hinojares
1183 Peña Cambrón
Cabra del Santo Cristo
Alicún de Ortega
Cuevas del Campo
Dehesas de Guadix
Villanueva de las Torres
Mencal
1447
Jaén
Torre del Campo
Jamilena
Martos
La Guardia de Jaén
Los Villares
Cambil
Carchelejo
Huelma
Embalse de Quiebrajano
Fuensanta de Martos
Valdepeñas de Jaén
Víboras
Campillo de Arenas
Castillo de Locubín
Noalejo
Frailes
Montillana
Campotéjar
Alcalá la Real
Montejícar
Guadahortuna
Torre-Cardela
Pedro-Martínez
Alamedilla
Moreda
Huélago
Fonelas
Piñar
Benalúa de las Villas
Iznalloz
Embalse de Colomera
Colomera
Moclín
Íllora
Pinos-Puente
Fuente Vaqueros
Lachar
Chauchina
Atarfe
Albolote
Santa Fe
Granada
Armilla
Deifontes
Sierra Arana
1943 Orduña
Embalse de Cubillas
Cogollos Vega
Alfacar
Beas de Granada
Darro
Diezma
Purullena
Benalúa de Guadix
Guadix
Graena
La Peza
Alcudia de Guadix
Lugros
Embalse de Quéntar
Güéjar-Sierra
Huétor Vega
Monachil
Embalse de Canales
Zubia
Alhendín
Dílar
Gabia la Grande
Malá
Ventas de Huelma
Escúzar
Chimeneas
Moraleda de Zafayona
Jerez del Marquesado
Alto de las Catifas
2329
Lacalahorra
Alquife
Sierra Nevada
Mulhacén
3482
Pico Veleta
3392
Caballo
3015
Trevélez
Puerto de la Ragua
2000
Alto de San Juan
2781
Chullo
2606
Mojón Alto
3152
2439
Bayárcal
Paterna del Río
Válor
Laroles
Laujar de Andarax
Mecina-Bombarón
Bérchules
Cádiar
Ugíjar
Alcolea
Fondón
Andarax
Embalse de Benínar
Murtas
Berja
Dalías
El Ejido
Adra
Balerma
Guardias Viejas
Punta Culo de Perro
Punta de las Entinas
Almerimar
CAMPO DE DALÍAS
Sierra de Gádor
Punta del Sabinar
2236
Félix
Vícar
Enix
Almería
Huércal de Almería
Viator
Pechina
Benahadux
Rioja
Gádor
Huécija
Alhabia
Illar
Instinción
Canjáyar
Ohanes
Alboloduy
Alhama de Almería
Aguadulce
Roquetas de Mar
La Mojonera
Punta Sabinar
Golfo de Almería
El Alquián
La Cañada de San Urbano
Punta del Río
El Cabo de Gata
Cabo de Gata
San José
Sierra del Cabo de Gata
Níjar
Sierra Alhamilla
Tabernas
Lucainena de las Torres
Sorbas
Gérgal
Abla
Abrucena
Fiñana
Nacimiento
Padul
Dúrcal
Nigüelas
Lecrín
Lanjarón
Órgiva
Capileira
Pitres
Albuñuelas
Jayena
Embalse de los Bermejales
Embalse de Béznar
Guájar-Faraguit
Otívar
Ítrabo
Molvízar
Salobreña
Motril
Vélez de Benaudalla
Torvizcón
Albondón
Albuñol
Sorvilán
Sierra de Contraviesa
Cerrón
1238
Frigiliana
Nerja
Punta de la Mona
Almuñécar
Cabo Sacratif
Calahonda
Castell de Ferro
Punta Negra
Sierra de Almijara
Navachica
1832
Suspiro del Moro
Gorafe
Gor
Freila
Zújar
Jabalcón
1494
Baza
Caniles
Sierra de Baza
Santa Bárbara
2270
2236
2061 Las Tejoneras
Dos Picos
2085
Benamaurel
Cúllar
Cúllar-Baza
Embalse de Negratín
Cortes de Baza
Castilléjar
Castril
Embalse de la Bolera
Huéscar
Galera
Orce
Sierra de Orce
1612
Perea
Argerín
1822
Chirivel
Puerto de El Contador
Sierra de María
María
Vélez-Blanco
Vélez-Rubio
Cerro Poyo
2045
El Gabar
1508
Empanadas
2107
Tornajuelos
2133
Sagra
2382
Embalse de San Clemente
Puebla de Don Fadrique
Lobos
1804
Santiago de la Espada
Pontones
Nerpio
Puerto del Pinar
1600
Las Cabras
2106
Sierra de Taibilla
Revolcadores
2001
Puerto de Almaciles
1100
El Moral
Archivel
Barranda
Los Royos
Topares
Sierra de las Estancias
Oria
Taberno
Partaloa
Albox
Cantoria
Arboleas
Olula del Río
Purchena
Somontín
Lúcar
Sierra de Lúcar
1722
Tíjola
Bayarque
Serón
Alcóntar
Sierro
Las Menas
Bacares
Tetica de Bacares
2088
Calar Alto
2168
Sierra de los Filabres
Velefique
Senés
Alcudia de Monteagud
Tahal
Benizalón
Uleila del Campo
Macael
Líjar
Albánchez
Puerto de la Virgen
1070
Lubrín
Almanzora
Blanquillo
1830
Melilla
Isla de Alborán

A
B
C
1
2
3
4
70
75
Leturo
Férez
Socovos
Benizar y la Tercia
Sierra de Lagos
Taibilla
1557
Tragoncillo
Embalse de Taibilla
Moratalla
El Sabinar
Embalse de la Novia
Nerpio
Sierra de Taibilla
Las Cabras 2106
2001
Revolcadores
Puerto del Pinar
Puerto de Almaciles
1100
El Moral
1804
Lobos
Puebla de Don Fadrique
Caravaca de la Cruz
El Buitre 1427
Archivel
Barranda
Almudema
Los Royos
Topares
Zarcilla de Ramos
La Paca
Zarzadilla de Totana
Embalse de Valdeinfierno
Caramel
El Gabar 1508
Gigante 1494
Fuensanta
Embalse de Puentes
María
Vélez-Blanco
Cerro Poyo 2045
Sierra de María
Sierra de Orce
1822 Argerín
1130
Chirivel
Puerto de El Contador
Vélez-Rubio
Corneros
Casa Alta 919
Sierra de las Estancias
Puerto de Santa María de Nieva
1085
Puerto Lumbreras
Orce
Oria
1722 Lúcar
Taberno
Santa María de Nieva
Partaloa
Somontín
Olula del Río
Albox
Cantoria
Arboleas
Huércal-Overa
Purchena
Bayarque
Sierro
Almanzora
Macael
Lijar
Zúrgena
Sa de Almagro
Cuevas de Almanzora
Alcudia de Monteagud
Albánchez
1070
Puerto de la Virgen
Tahal
Senés
Benizalón
Velefique
Uleila del Campo
Lubrín
Antas
Bédar
Los Gallardos
Vera
Garrucha
Turre
Mojácar
Sorbas
Tabernas
Lucainena de las Torres
Sierra Alhamilla
Sierra Cabrera
Níjar
Carboneras
Punta de la Media Naranja
Benahadux
Pechina
Viator
El Alquián
La Cañada de San Urbano
Punta del Río
Las Negras
Punta de la Polacra
Punta de Loma Pelada
Sierra del Cabo de Gata
El Cabo de Gata
San José
Cabo de Gata
Golfo de Almería
Embalse de Camarillas
Calasparra
Embalse de Almadenes
Cieza
Abarán
Blanca
Cehegín
Embalse de Argos
Argos
Bullas
Mula
Almeces 1121
Embalse de la Cierva
Archena
Las Torres de Cotillas
Pliego
Barqueros
Sierra de Espuña
1583 Espuña
Alhama de Murcia
Las Terreras
Aledo
Totana
La Manilla 991
Lorca
Guadalentín
Cantareros
Almenara 893
Sierra de la Almenara
881 Talayón
El Cabildo y la Campana
Almendricos
Pulpí
Águilas
Cabo Cope
Calabardina
Atalaya Árabe 367
Mazarrón
Puerto de Mazarrón
Isla Plana
La Azohía
Cabo Tiñoso
Golfo de Mazarrón
Embalse del Judío
Rambla del Moro
Sierra de la Pila
Pila 1264
Fortuna
Villanueva del Río Segura
Embalse de Santomera
Ceutí
Alguazas
Albudeite
Molina de Segura
Javalí Viejo
Alcantarilla
El Palmar
Murcia
Los Algezares
La Alberca
609 Relojero
647 Columbares
Puerto de la Cadena
Librilla
Carrascoy 1066
Sierra de Carrascoy
Corvera
Valladolises
Los Maldonados
Fuente Álamo
Cánovas
Balsa Pintada
Albujón
La Pinilla
Algarrobo 713
Las Palas
La Aljorra
Los Dolores
Canteras
Cartagena
Escombreras
La Unión
La Romana
Novelda
Algueña
Hondón de las Nieves
Hondón de los Frailes
Barinas
Abanilla
Crevillente 835
Crevillente
Aspe
Embalse de Elche
Elche-Elx
Albatera
Cox
Catral
Dolores
Redován
Orihuela
Callosa de Segura
Almoradí
Rojales
Santomera
Beniel
Alquerías
Bigastro
Benejúzar
Embalse de la Pedrera
Guardamar del
Santa Pola
Laguna Salada
Laguna Salada de T
Torrevieja
San Miguel de Salinas
Punta Prima
Cabo Roig
Dehesa de Campoamor
Sucina
Balsicas
San Pedro del Pinatar
Santiago de la Ribera
San Javier
Canal del Campo de Cartagena
Torre-Pacheco
Mar Menor
Los Alcázares
Isla Grosa
La Palma
Barrio del Peral
El Algar
La Manga del Mar Menor
El Estrecho
Cabo de Palos
Los Belones
Portman
Cabo Negrete
Cabo del Agua
E15
A7
A37
A92N
301
302
312
330
332
340
341
342
343
344
3317
3314
3211
3315
3319
3223
415
552
330
350
399
317
327
334
349
370
414
603
602
910
95
865

INDEX

A

Aachen **10** A4
Aadorf **28** B3
Aalen **19** F4
Aalsmeer **9** D1
Aalst **9** D3
Aalten **10** A2
Aalter **8** C3
Aarau **27** F3
Aarberg **27** E4
Aarburg **27** F3
Aardenburg **8** C3
Aarle **9** F2
Aarschot **9** E3
Aartselaar **9** D3
Aarwangen **27** F3
Abades **62** C2
Abadín **54** A1
Abadiño **56** B2
A Baiuca **53** E1
Abánades **63** F2
Abanilla **76** C1
Abano Terme **39** D3
Abarán **76** B1
A Barrela **53** F3
Abbadia San Salvatore **46** B4
Abbeville **16** A2
Abbiategrasso **37** D3
Abcoude **9** E1
Abejar **56** B4
Abejuela **64** C4
Abela **66** B4
Abenberg **20** A3
Abenójar **68** C3
Åbenrå **2** B3
Abensberg **20** B4
Abertura **68** A2
Abetone **46** A2
Abfaltersbach **30** A4
Abia de la Obispalía **63** F4
Abiego **58** A2
Abild **2** A4
Abilly **24** C4
Abla **75** E2
Ablis **25** D1
Ablitas **57** D4
Abondance **36** A2
Abragão **60** C2
Abrantes **66** C1
Abreiro **61** D1
Abrera **59** D4
Abreschviller **27** E1
Abrest **34** C2
Abrigada **66** B2
Abriola **50** B3
Abrucena **75** E2
Absam **29** E3
Absberg **20** A3
Absdorf **31** E1
Abtenau **30** B3
Abtsgmünd **19** F4
Åbybro **1** F2
Åbyen **1** F1
A Cañiza **53** E4
Accadia **50** A2
Acceglio **44** A1
Accettura **50** C3
Acciano **49** E1
Acciaroli **50** A4
Accous **40** B4
Accumoli **49** D1
Acebo **61** E4
Acedera **68** B2
Acedo **56** C3
Acehuche **67** E1
Aceituna **61** F4
Acered **64** B2
Acerenza **50** B3
Acerno **50** A3
Acerra **49** F4
Aceuchal **67** F3
Ach **30** A2
A Chán **53** E3
Achenkirch **29** E3
Achern **27** F1
Acheux-en-Amiénois **16** B2
Achicourt **16** B1
Achim **5** F3
Achstetten **28** C2
Achtrup **2** B4
A Coruña **53** E1
Acqualagna **47** D3
Acquanegra sul Chiese **38** B4
Acquapendente **46** C4
Acquappesa **52** A1
Acquaro **52** B3
Acquarossa **37** D1
Acquasanta Terme **47** E4
Acquasparta **48** C1
Acquigny **15** E3
Acqui Terme **44** C1
Acri **52** B1
A Cruz de Incio **54** A3
Acuto **49** D2
Adahuesca **58** A2
Adamuz **68** C4
Adanero **62** C2
Adão **61** D3
Adaúfe **60** C1
Adelboden **36** B1
Adelebsen **11** E2
Adelfia **51** D2
Adelschlag **20** B4
Adelsheim **19** E3
Adelsried **29** D1
Ademuz **64** B4
Adenau **18** B1
Adendorf **6** B3
Adenstedt **11** E2
Adliswil **28** A3
Adlkofen **29** F1
Admont **30** C3
Adorf **20** C1
Adorf (Diemelsee) **11** D3
Adoufe **60** C2
Adra **75** E3
Adradas **63** F1
Adrados **62** C1
Adria **39** D4
Ådum **2** A2
Adzaneta **65** D4
Adzaneta de Albaida **71** D3
Ærøskøbing **2** C4
Aerzen **11** E1
A Estrada **53** E3
Affing **29** D1
Afife **60** B1
Aflenz Kurort **31** D3
A Fonsagrada **54** A2
A Forxa *Spain* **53** F3
A Forxa *Spain* **53** F4
Afragola **49** F4
Afritz **30** B4
Aga **12** C4
Agallas **61** E3
Agde **42** B3
Agen **41** D2
Ager **58** B3
Agerbæk **2** A2
Agerskov **2** B3
Agersted **1** F2
Ågerup **3** E2
Aggersund **1** E2
Aggsbach Markt **31** D1
Aglasterhausen **19** D3
Agliana **46** B2
Agnadello **37** E3
Agneaux **14** B3
Agno **37** D2
Agnone **49** F2
A Golada **53** F2
Agoncillo **56** C3
Agon-Coutainville **14** B4
Agordo **39** D2
Agost **71** D4
Agramón **70** B4
Agramunt **58** B3
Agrate Brianza **37** E3
Agreda **56** C4
Agrés **71** D3
Agrochão **61** E1
Agropoli **50** A4
Aguadulce *Spain* **74** B2
Aguadulce *Spain* **75** F3
A Guardia **53** D4
Aguarón **64** B2
Aguas **58** A2
Águas Belas **66** C1
Aguas de Busot **71** D3
Águas de Moura **66** B3
Águas Frias **61** D1
Aguaviva **65** D3
A Gudiña **54** A4
Agudo **68** C2
Águeda **60** B3
Agugliano **47** E3
Aguiar **66** C4
Aguiar da Beira **61** D2
Aguilafuente **62** C2
Aguilar de Alfambra **64** C3
Aguilar de Campóo **55** E2
Aguilar de la Frontera **74** B2
Aguilar del Río Alhama **56** C4
Águilas **76** B2
Agullana **59** E2
Agullent **71** D3
Aham **30** A1
Ahaus **10** B1
Ahigal **61** F4
Ahigal de Villarino **61** F2
Ahillones **68** A4
Ahlbeck **7** F2
Ahlen **10** C2
Ahlerstedt **5** F3
Ahlhorn **5** E4
Ahnsbeck **6** A4
Ahorn **20** A1
Ahrbrück **10** B4
Ahrensbök **6** B2
Ahrensburg **6** A2
Ahrenshagen **7** D1
Ahun **33** F2
Aibar **57** D3
Aibl **31** D4
Aichach **29** E1
Aichhalden **28** A2
Aichstetten **28** C2
Aidenbach **30** A1
Aidt **2** B1
Aiello Calabro **52** B2
Aielo de Malferit **71** D3
Aieta **52** A1
Aiffres **32** C2
Aigen im Ennstal **30** C3
Aigen im Mühlkreis **30** C1
Aigle **36** B2
Aiglun **43** F2
Aignan **40** C3
Aignay-le-Duc **26** B3
Aigre **32** C2
Aigrefeuille-d'Aunis **32** B2
Aigrefeuille-sur-Maine **23** E4
Aiguafreda **59** D3
Aiguebelle **36** A3
Aigueblanche **36** A3
Aigueperse **34** B2
Aigues-Mortes **42** C3
Aigues-Vives **42** C3
Aiguilhe **34** C4
Aiguilles **44** A1
Aiguillon **40** C2
Aigurande **33** F1
Aillant-sur-Tholon **25** F2
Aillevillers-et-Lyaumont **27** D2
Ailly-le-Haut-Clocher **16** A2
Ailly-sur-Noye **16** A2
Ailly-sur-Somme **16** A2
Aimargues **42** C3
Aime **36** A3
Ainay-le-Château **34** B1
Aindling **29** D1
Ainet **30** A4
Ainsa **58** A2
Ainzón **57** D4
Airaines **16** A2
Airasca **36** B4
Aire-sur-l'Adour **40** B3
Aire-sur-la-Lys **16** A1
Airola **49** F4
Airole **44** B2
Airolo **37** D1
Airvault **32** C1
Aisey-sur-Seine **26** B3
Aïssey **27** D3
Aiterhofen **20** C4
Aitona **58** B4
Aitrach **28** C2
Aitrang **29** D2
Aix-en-Othe **25** F2
Aix-en-Provence **43** E3
Aixe-sur-Vienne **33** E3
Aix-les-Bains **35** F3
Aizenay **32** A1
Aizpun **56** C2
Ajo **55** F1
Ajofrín **69** D1
Aken **12** C2
Akkrum **4** B3
Ala **38** B3
Ala di Stura **36** B3
Alaejos **62** B2
Alagna Valsesia **36** C2
Alagoa **67** D2
Alagón **57** E4
Alaigne **41** F4
Alájar **67** E4
A Lama **53** E3
Alameda **74** B2
Alameda de Cervera **69** E2
Alameda de la Sagra **63** D4
Alamedilla **75** E1
Alamillo **68** C3
Alandroal **67** D3
Alange **67** F3
Alanís **68** A4
Alaquàs **71** D2
Alaraz **62** B3
Alarcón **70** B1
Alar del Rey **55** E3
Alassio **44** C2
Alatoz **70** C2
Alatri **49** D2
Alba **44** B1
Alba Adriatica **47** F4
Albacete **70** B2
Alba de Tormes **62** A3
Ålbæk **1** F1
Albaida **71** D3
Albaladejo **70** A3
Albalate de Arzobispo **65** D2
Albalate de Cinca **58** A3
Albalate de las Nogueras **63** F3
Albalate de Zorita **63** E3
Albalatillo **58** A3
Alban **41** F2
Albánchez **76** A3
Albanella **50** A3
Albano di Lucania **50** C3
Albano Laziale **48** C2
Albano Vercellese **36** C3
Albanyà **59** E2
Albaredo per San Marco **38** A2
Albareto **45** E1
Albarracín **64** B3
Albatana **70** C3
Albatàrrec **58** B3
Albatera **76** C1
Albbruck **28** A3
Albelda **58** B3
Albelda de Iregua **56** B3
Albella **58** A2
Albendea **63** F3
Albendín **74** C1
Albenga **44** C2
Albens **35** F3
Albentosa **64** C4
Albergaria-a-Velha **60** B3
Albergaria dos Doze **66** B1
Alberic **71** D2
Alberndorf in der Riedmark **30** C1
Albernoa **72** B1
Albero Alto **57** F4
Alberobello **51** D3
Alberona **50** A2
Alberoni **39** D3
Alberschwende **28** C3
Albersdorf **5** F1
Albert **16** B2
Alberta Ligure **45** D1
Albertville **36** A3
Alberuela de Tubo **58** A3
Albesa **58** B3
Albestroff **18** B4
Albi **41** F2
Albias **41** E2
Albignasego **39** D3
Albino **38** A3
Albires **55** D4
Albisheim (Pfrimm) **18** C2
Albisola Marina **44** C2
Albisola Superiore **44** C1
Alblasserdam **9** D2
Albocácer **65** D3
Alboloduy **75** F3
Albolote **75** D2
Albon **35** E4
Albondón **75** E3
Alboraya **71** D1
Alborea **70** C2
Ålborg **1** F2
Albox **76** A2
Albstadt **28** B2
Albudeite **76** B1
Albufeira **72** B2
Albujón **76** C2
Albuñol **75** E3
Albuñuelas **75** D3
Alburquerque **67** E2
Alby-sur-Chéran **35** F3
Alcácer **71** D2

Alcácer do Sal 66 B4
Alcáçovas 66 C4
Alcadozo 70 B3
Alcafozes 67 E1
Alcaine 64 C2
Alcains 67 D1
Alcalá de Chivert 65 E3
Alcalá de Guadaira 74 A2
Alcalá de Gurrea 57 E4
Alcalá de Henares 63 E3
Alcalá del Júcar 70 C2
Alcalá de los Gazules 74 A4
Alcalá del Río 73 E2
Alcalá del Valle 74 B3
Alcalá la Real 75 D2
Alcalalí 71 E3
Alcampell 58 B3
Alcanadre 56 C3
Alcanede 66 B2
Alcanena 66 B1
Alcanhões 66 B2
Alcañices 61 F1
Alcañiz 65 D2
Alcántara 67 E1
Alcantarilla 76 B1
Alcantud 63 F3
Alcaracejos 68 C4
Alcaraz 70 A3
Alcaria Ruiva 72 B1
Alcarràs 58 B3
Alcaucín 74 C3
Alcaudete 74 C1
Alcaudete de la Jara 62 B4
Alcázar del Rey 63 E4
Alcázar de San Juan 69 E2
Alcoba 68 C2
Alcobaça 66 B1
Alcobendas 63 D3
Alcocer 63 F3
Alcocero de Mola 56 A3
Alcochete 66 B3
Alcoentre 66 B2
Alcolea *Spain* 68 C4
Alcolea *Spain* 75 E3
Alcolea de Calatrava 69 D2
Alcolea de Cinca 58 A3
Alcolea del Pinar 63 F2
Alcolea del Río 74 A1
Alcollarín 68 A2
Alconchel 67 E3
Alcóntar 75 F2
Alcora 65 D4
Alcorcón 63 D3
Alcorisa 65 D2
Alcoroches 64 B3
Alcossebre 65 E4
Alcoutim 72 C2
Alcover 58 C4
Alcoy-Alcoi 71 D3
Alcubierre 57 E4
Alcubilla de Avellaneda 56 A4
Alcubillas 69 E3
Alcublas 64 C4
Alcudia de Guadix 75 E2
Alcudia de Monteagud 76 A3
Alcuéscar 67 F2
Aldeacentenera 68 B1
Aldeadávila de la Ribera 61 E2
Aldea del Cano 67 F2
Aldea del Fresno 62 C3
Aldea del Obispo 61 E3
Aldea del Rey 69 D3
Aldea de Trujillo 67 F1
Aldealafuente 63 F1
Aldealpozo 56 C4
Aldeamayor de San Martín 62 C1
Aldeaneuva de Figueroa 62 A2
Aldeanueva de Barbarroya 68 B1
Aldeanueva de Ebro 56 C3
Aldeanueva de la Vera 62 A4
Aldeanueva del Camino 62 A4
Aldeanueva de San Bartolomé 68 B1
Aldeaquemada 69 E4
Aldea Real 62 C2
Aldearrodrigo 62 A2
Aldeaseca 62 B2
Aldeatejada 62 A2
Aldeavieja 62 C3
Aldehuela de la Bóveda 62 A2
Aldehuela de Yeltes 61 F3
Aldeia da Mata 67 D2
Aldeia da Ponte 61 E3
Aldeia de Ferreira 67 D3
Aldeia de João Pires 61 D4
Aldeia do Bispo 61 D4
Aldeia dos Elvas 72 B1
Aldeia dos Fernandes 72 B1
Aldeia dos Palheiros 72 B1
Aldeia Velha 66 C2
Aldenhoven 10 A4
Aldeno 38 C2
Aldersbach 30 A1
Aldover 65 E2
Åle 2 B2
Aledo 76 B2
Alençon 24 B1
Alenquer 66 B2
Alénya 59 E1
Alerheim 20 A4
Alerre 57 E4
Alès 42 C2
Alesón 56 B3
Alessandria 37 D4
Alessano 51 F4
Ålestrup 1 E3
Alezio 51 F4
Alf 18 B2
Alfacar 75 D2
Alfafar 71 D2
Alfaiates 61 E3
Alfajarín 64 C1
Alfambra 64 C3
Alfambras 72 A2
Alfamén 64 B1
Alfândega da Fé 61 E2
Alfántega 58 A3
Alfarim 66 A3
Alfaro 57 D4
Alfarràs 58 B3
Alfaz del Pi 71 E3
Alfdorf 19 E4
Alfedena 49 E2
Alfeizerão 66 B1
Alfeld (Leine) 11 E2
Alfena 60 B2
Alferce 72 A2
Alfhausen 10 C1
Alfonsine 46 C1
Alforja 58 B4
Alfundão 66 C4
Algámitas 74 B3
Algar 74 A3
Algarinejo 74 C2
Algarrobo 74 C3
Algatocín 74 A3
Algeciras 74 A4
Algemesí 71 D2
Algermissen 11 E1
Algerri 58 B3
Algestrup 3 E3
Algete 63 D3
Alginet 71 D2
Algodonales 74 A3
Algodor 72 B1
Algora 63 F2
Algoso 61 E1
Algoz 72 B2
Algrange 17 F3
Alguaire 58 B3
Alguazas 76 B1
Algueirão-Mem Martins 66 A3
Algueña 76 C1
Alhabia 75 F3
Alhama de Almería 75 F3
Alhama de Aragón 64 A2
Alhama de Granada 74 C3
Alhama de Murcia 76 B2
Alhambra 69 E3
Alhaurín de la Torre 74 C3
Alhaurín el Grande 74 B3
Alhendín 75 D2
Alhóndiga 63 E3
Alía 68 B1
Aliaga 64 C3
Aliaguilla 70 C1
Aliano 50 C4
Alicante-Alacant 71 D4
Alicún de Ortega 75 E1
Alife 49 E3
Alija del Infantado 54 C4
Alijó 61 D2
Aliseda 67 E2
Aljaraque 73 D2
Aljezur 72 A2
Aljubarrota 66 B1
Aljucén 67 F2
Aljustrel 72 B1
Alken 9 E4
Alkmaar 4 A4
Allaire 23 D3
Allan 43 D1
Allanche 34 B4
Allariz 53 F4
Allassac 33 E4
Allauch 43 E3
Alle 27 E3
Alleghe 39 D1
Allègre 34 C4
Alleins 43 D3
Allemond 35 F4
Allendorf (Eder) 11 D3
Allendorf (Lumda) 11 D4
Allensbach 28 B3
Allentsteig 31 D1
Allepuz 64 C3
Allerona 46 C4
Allersberg 20 B3
Allershausen 29 E1
Allerslev 3 E3
Allevard 35 F3
Allex 43 D1
Alling 29 E2
Allingåbro 2 C1
Allinges 36 A1
Alliste 51 F4
Allmendingen 28 C1
Allo 56 C3
Allonnes *France* 24 B2
Allonnes *France* 24 B3
Alloza 64 C2
Allschwil 27 F3
Allstedt 12 B3
Allumiere 48 B2
Almacelles 58 B3
Almáchar 74 C3
Almada 66 A3
Almadén 68 C3
Almadenejos 68 C3
Almagro 69 D3
Almajano 56 C4
Almalaguês 60 C4
Almaluez 63 F2
Almansa 70 C3
Almansil 72 B2
Almanza 55 D3
Almaraz 62 A4
Almargen 74 B3
Almarza 56 C4
Almassora 65 D4
Almazán 63 F1
Almazul 63 F1
Almedina 69 F3
Almedinilla 74 C2
Almeida de Sayago 62 A2
Almeirim 66 B2
Almelo 10 A1
Almenar 58 B3
Almenara 71 E1
Almenar de Soria 56 C4
Almendra *Port.* 61 E2
Almendra *Spain* 61 F2
Almendral 67 E3
Almendralejo 67 F3
Almendricos 76 A2
Almendros 63 E4
Almere 9 E1
Almería 75 F3
Almerimar 75 E3
Almind 2 B2
Almkerk 9 E2
Almodôvar 72 B2
Almodóvar del Campo 69 D3
Almodóvar del Pinar 70 B1
Almodóvar del Río 74 B1
Almofala 60 C2
Almogía 74 C3
Almograve 72 A1
Almoguera 63 E4
Almoharín 67 F2
Almonacid de la Sierra 64 B1
Almonacid del Marquesado 63 F4
Almonacid del Zorita 63 E3
Almonacid de Toledo 69 D1
Almonaster la Real 73 D1
Almonte 73 E2
Almoradí 76 C1
Almorchón 68 B3
Almorox 62 C4
Almoster 66 C1
Almstedt 11 E1
Almudema 76 A1
Almudévar 57 E4
Almuñécar 75 D3
Almuniente 57 E4
Almünster 30 B2
Ámuradiel 69 E3
Almussafes 71 D2
Alobras 64 B4
Alocén 63 E3
Álora 74 B3
Alós d'Ensil 58 C1
Alosno 73 D2
Alovera 63 E3
Alozaina 74 B3
Alp 59 D2
Alpalhão 67 D2
Alpanseque 63 F2
Alpbach 29 F3
Alpedrinha 61 D4
Alpedriz 66 B1
Alpen 10 A2
Alpenrod 10 C4
Alpens 59 D2
Alpera 70 C2
Alphen 9 E2
Alphen aan den Rijn 9 D1
Alpiarça 66 B2
Alpirsbach 28 A1
Alpnach 28 A4
Alpuente 64 C4
Alquería de la Condesa 71 E3
Alquerías 76 C1
Alqueva 67 D4
Alquife 75 E2
Als 1 F3
Alsasua 56 C2
Alsdorf 10 A4
Alseno 38 A4
Alsenz 18 C2
Alsfeld 11 E4
Alsheim 19 D2
Alsleben (Saale) 12 B2
Alslev 2 A2
Ålsrode 3 D1
Altafulla 58 C4
Altamura 50 C3
Altare 44 C1
Altaussee 30 B3
Altavilla Irpina 50 A2
Altavilla Silentina 50 A3
Altdöbern 13 E2
Altdorf *Ger.* 29 F1
Altdorf *Switz.* 28 A4
Altdorf bei Nürnberg 20 B3
Alt Duvenstedt 6 A1
Alte 72 B2
Altea 71 E3
Altefähr 7 E1
Alteglofsheim 20 C4
Altena 10 C3
Altenahr 10 B4
Altenau 11 F2
Altenberg 13 E4
Altenberge 10 B1
Altenbruch-Westerende 5 E2
Altenbuch 19 E2
Altenburg 12 C3
Altenfeld 12 A4
Altenfelden 30 C1
Altenglan 18 B3
Altenhagen 6 C2
Altenhof 7 E4
Altenholz 6 A1
Altenkirchen 7 E1
Altenkirchen (Westerwald) 10 C4
Altenkrempe 6 B1
Altenkunstadt 20 B2
Altenmarkt an der Triesting 31 E2
Altenmarkt bei St Gallen 31 D2
Altenmarkt im Pongau 30 B3
Altenmedingen 6 B3
Altenmünster 29 D1
Altenstadt *Ger.* 28 C2
Altenstadt *Ger.* 29 D2
Altenstadt *Ger.* 19 D1
Altensteig 28 A1
Altentreptow 7 E2
Alter do Chão 67 D2
Altes Lager 13 D2
Altfraunhofen 29 F1
Altheim *Austria* 30 B1
Altheim *Ger.* 28 B2
Althofen 30 C4
Altkirch 27 E3
Alt Krenzlin 6 C3
Altlandsberg 7 E4
Altmannstein 20 B4
Altomonte 52 B1
Altomünster 29 E1
Altopascio 46 A2
Altorricón 58 B3
Altötting 30 A2
Alt Ruppin 7 D4
Alt Schwerin 7 D3

Altshausen **28** C2
Altstätten **28** C3
Altura **64** C4
Altusried **28** C2
Alustante **64** B3
Alvaiázere **66** C1
Alvalade **66** C4
Alvaneu **28** C4
Alvarenga **60** C2
Álvares **60** C4
Álvaro **60** C4
Alvega **66** C1
Alvelos **60** B1
Alverca **66** B3
Alverca da Beira **61** D3
Alviano **48** B1
Alvito *Italy* **49** E2
Alvito *Port.* **66** C4
Alvoco da Serra **61** D3
Alzenau in Unterfranken **19** D2
Alzey **18** C2
Alzira **71** D2
Alzon **42** B2
Alzonne **41** F4
Amadora **66** A3
Amalfi **49** F4
Amance **27** D2
Amancey **27** D4
Amandola **47** E4
Amantea **52** A2
Amarante **60** C2
Amareleja **67** D4
Amares **60** C1
Amaroni **52** B3
Amaseno **49** D3
Amatrice **49** D1
Amay **17** E1
Ambasaguas **55** D3
Ambazac **33** E2
Ambel **57** D4
Amberg **20** C3
Ambérieu-en-Bugey **35** E2
Amberloup **17** E2
Ambert **34** C3
Ambès **32** B4
Ambierle **34** C2
Ambillou **24** B3
Amblainville **16** A3
Ambleteuse **8** A4
Amboise **24** C3
Ambon **23** D3
Ambrières-les-Vallées **23** F1
Ambronay **35** E2
Ameglia **45** E2
Ameixial **72** B2
Amel **17** F1
Amelia **48** C1
Amélie-les-Bains-Palalda **59** E2
Amelinghausen **6** A3
Amêndoa **66** C1
Amendoeira **72** C1
Amer **59** E3
Amerang **29** F2
A Merca **53** F3
Amersfoort **9** E1
Amezketa **56** C2
Amieira **67** D4
Amiens **16** A2
Amilly **25** E2
Ammern **11** F3
Ammersbek **6** A2
Amoeiro **53** F3
Amonde **60** B1
Amöneburg **11** D4
Amorbach **19** E2
Amorebieta **56** B2
Amou **40** B3
Ampezzo **39** E1
Ampfing **30** A1
Ampflwang im Hausruckwald **30** B2
Amplepuis **35** D2
Amposta **65** E3
Ampudia **55** E4
Ampuero **55** F1
Amriswil **28** B3
Amstelveen **9** E1
Amsterdam **9** E1
Amstetten **31** D2
Amurrio **56** B2
Amusco **55** E4
Anacapri **49** E4
Anadia **60** B3
Anagni **49** D2
Anaya de Alba **62** A3
Ancenis **23** F3
Ancerville **17** E4
Ancín **56** C3
Ancona **47** E3
Ancy-le-Franc **26** A2
Andalo **38** B2
Andance **35** E4
Andavías **62** A1
Andechs **29** E2
Andeer **37** E1
Andelfingen **28** A3
Andelot-Blancheville **26** C2
Andelst **9** F2
Andenne **17** E1
Anderlecht **9** D4
Anderlues **17** D1
Andermatt **37** D1
Andernach **10** B4
Andernos-les-Bains **40** A1
Andijk **4** A4
Andlau **27** F1
Andoain **56** C2
Andolsheim **27** F2
Andorf **30** B1
Andorno Micca **36** C3
Andorra **65** D2
Andorra la Vella **58** C2
Andosilla **56** C3
Andouillé **23** F2
Andrano **51** F4
Andrest **40** C4
Andretta **50** A3
Andrézieux-Bouthéon **35** D3
Andria **50** C2
Andrup **2** A3
Andújar **69** D4
Anduze **42** B2
Anet **24** C1
Anfo **38** B3
Angeja **60** B3
Anger **30** A2
Angera **37** D3
Angermünde **7** F4
Angern **12** B1
Angern an der March **31** F1
Angers **24** A3
Angerville **25** D2
Anghiari **46** C3
Anglès *France* **41** F3
Anglès *Spain* **59** E3
Anglesona **58** B3
Anglure **16** C4
Angoulême **32** C3
Angoulins **32** B2
Angri **49** F4
Angüés **58** A2
Anguiano **56** B3
Anguillara Sabazia **48** B2
Anguillara Veneta **39** D4
Anguita **63** F2
Anha **60** B1
Anhée **17** D1
Aniane **42** B3
Anif **30** A2
Anizy-le-Château **16** C3
Anjum **4** B3
Ankershagen **7** E3
Anklam **7** E2
Ankum **5** D4
Anna **71** D2
Annaberg **31** D2
Annaberg-Buchholtz **13** D4
Annaburg **13** D2
Annahütte **13** E2
Anna Paulowna **4** A4
Annarode **12** B2
Annecy **35** F2
Annecy-le-Vieux **35** F2
Annemasse **35** F2
Annen **4** C3
Anneyron **35** E4
Annonay **35** D4
Annot **43** F2
Annweiler am Trifels **18** C3
Anoeta **56** C2
Añón **57** D4
Anor **17** D2
Añora **68** C3
Anould **27** E2
Añover de Tajo **63** D4
Anquela del Ducado **63** F2
Anras **30** A4
Ans *Belgium* **17** E1
Ans *Denmark* **2** B1
Ansager **2** A2
Ansbach **20** A3
Anse **35** D2
Ansedonia **48** A1
Ansfelden **30** C2
Ansião **66** C1
Ansó **57** E2
Ansprung **13** D4
Antanhol **60** B4
Antas *Port.* **60** B1
Antas *Port.* **61** D2
Antas *Spain* **76** A3
Antas de Ulla **53** F2
Antequera **74** C3
Anterselva di Sopra **29** F4
Anthéor **44** A3
Antibes **44** A3
Antoing **16** C1
Antonne-et-Trigonant **33** E4
Antony **16** A4
Antraigues-sur-Volane **42** C1
Antrain **23** E1
Antrodoco **49** D1
Antwerpen **9** D3
Antzuola **56** C2
Anzano di Puglia **50** A2
Anzegem **8** C4
Anzère **36** B2
Anzi **50** B3
Anzin **16** C1
Anzing **29** F2
Anzio **48** C3
Aoiz **57** D2
Aos **57** D2
Aosta **36** B3
Aoste **35** F3
Apače **31** E4
Apecchio **47** D3
Apeldoorn **10** A1
Apelern **11** E1
Apen **5** D3
Apenburg **6** B4
Apensen **6** A3
A Peroxa **53** F3
Apice **50** A2
A Picota **53** D2
Apiro **47** E3
Apolda **12** B3
A Pontenova **54** A1
Appelscha **4** B4
Appenzell **28** B3
Appiano sulla Strada del Vino **38** C1
Appignano **47** E3
Apprieu **35** E3
Aprica **38** A2
Apricena **50** B1
Aprigliano **52** B2
Aprilia **48** C3
Apt **43** D2
Aquaviva delle Fonti **51** D3
Aquilonia **50** B2
Aquilué **57** E3
Aquino **49** E3
Aracena **67** E4
Aradeo **51** F4
Aragnouet **58** A1
Aragoncillo **64** A2
Araia **56** C2
A Ramallosa **53** E2
Aramits **40** B4
Aramon **42** C2
Aranda de Duero **63** D1
Aranda de Moncayo **64** B1
Aranhas **61** D4
Aranjuez **63** D4
Arano **56** C2
Aranzueque **63** E3
Arapiles **62** A2
Aras **56** C3
Aras de Alpuente **64** C4
Arazede **60** B3
Arbeca **58** B4
Arbedo **37** D2
Arberg **20** A3
Arbesbach **31** D1
Arbeteta **63** F3
Arbois **26** C4
Arboleas **76** A2
Arbon **28** B3
Arborio **36** C3
Arbúcies **59** E3
Årby **3** D2
Arcachon **40** A1
Arce **49** D3
Arcen **10** A2
Arc-en-Barrois **26** B2
Arceniega **56** B2
Arc-et-Senans **26** C4
Arcevia **47** D3
Archena **76** B1
Arches **27** D2
Archiac **32** C3
Archidona **74** C2
Archivel **76** A1
Arcidosso **46** B4
Arcis-sur-Aube **26** A1
Arc-lès-Gray **26** C3
Arco **38** B2
Arco de Baúlhe **60** C1
Arcola **45** E2
Arconnay **24** B1
Arcos *Port.* **67** D3
Arcos *Spain* **55** F3
Arcos de Jalón **63** F2
Arcos de la Frontera **73** F3
Arcos de las Salinas **64** C4
Arcos de Valdevez **60** C1
Arcozelo *Port.* **60** B1
Arcozelo *Port.* **60** B1
Arc-sur-Tille **26** C3
Arcusa **58** A2
Ardagger Markt **31** D2
Ardales **74** B3
Ardanaz **57** D3
Ardea **48** C3
Arden **1** F3
Ardentes **33** F1
Ardes **34** B3
Ardez **38** A1
Ardon **36** B2
Ardooie **8** C3
Ardore **52** B4
Ardres **8** A4
Areatza **56** B2
Areias **66** C1
Arén **58** B2
Arenas de Iguña **55** F2
Arenas del Rey **75** D3
Arenas de San Juan **69** F2
Arenas de San Pedro **62** B4
Arendonk **9** E3
Arendsee (Altmark) **6** C4
Arenillas **63** E2
Arenshausen **11** E3
Arentsminde **1** E2
Arenys de Mar **59** E4
Arenzano **44** C1
Areosa **60** B1
Arès **40** A1
Ares **53** E1
Ares del Maestre **65** D3
Aresing **29** E1
Arette **40** B4
Aretxabaleta **56** B2
Arevalillo **62** B3
Arévalo **62** B2
Arezzo **46** C3
Argallón **68** B4
Argamasilla de Alba **69** E2
Argamasilla de Calatrava **69** D3
Argamasón **70** B3
Arganda **63** D4
Arganil **60** C4
Arganza **54** B3
Argegno **37** D2
Argelès-Gazost **40** C4
Argelès-sur-Mer **59** E2
Argeliers **42** A3
Argelita **65** D4
Argenbühl **28** C3
Argences **15** D3
Argenta **46** C1
Argentan **24** B1
Argentat **33** F4
Argente **64** C3
Argentera **44** A1
Argenteuil **16** A4
Argenthal **18** C2
Argentière **36** A2
Argentine **36** A3
Argentona **59** D4
Argenton-Château **24** A4
Argenton-sur-Creuse **33** E1
Argentre **23** F2
Argentré-du-Plessis **23** F2
Argent-sur-Sauldre **25** E3
Argés **63** D4
Argonay **35** F2
Arguedas **57** D4
Argueil **15** F3
Arguís **57** E3
Arguisuelas **64** A4
Argujillo **62** A2
Århus **2** C1
Ariano Irpino **50** A2
Ariano nel Polesine **39** D4
Ariccia **48** C2
Arija **55** F2
Ariño **64** C2
Arinsal **58** C2
Arinthod **35** E1
Arive **57** D2
Ariz **61** D2
Arizola **56** C3
Arjona **69** D4
Arjonilla **69** D4
Arlanc **34** C3
Arlanzón **55** F3
Arlena di Castro **48** B1
Arles **42** C3

Arleux 16 B1
Arlon 17 F2
Arluno 37 D3
Armação de Pêra 72 B2
Armada 53 F1
Armallones 63 F3
Armamar 61 D2
Armeno 36 C3
Armenteros 62 A3
Armentières 16 B1
Armento 50 C4
Armilla 75 D2
Armissan 42 A4
Armuña 62 C2
Armunia 54 C3
Arnac-Pompadour 33 E3
Arnad 36 C3
Arnage 24 B2
Arnay-le-Duc 26 B4
Arnborg 2 B2
Arnbruck 21 D3
Arneburg 6 C4
Arnedillo 56 C4
Arnedo 56 C3
Arnemuiden 8 C2
Arnes 65 E2
Arnfels 31 E4
Arnhem 10 A1
Arnoldstein 39 F1
Arnsberg 10 C3
Arnschwang 21 D3
Arnstadt 12 A4
Arnstein 19 F2
Arnstorf 30 A1
Arnum 2 A3
Arolla 36 B2
Arolsen 11 D3
Aron 23 F2
Arona 37 D3
Arosa *Port.* 60 C1
Arosa *Switz.* 28 C4
Arouca 60 C2
Arpajon 16 A4
Arpajon-sur-Cère 34 A4
Arpino 49 D2
Arquata del Tronto 47 E4
Arquata Scrivia 45 D1
Arques 8 A4
Arques-la-Bataille 15 E2
Arquillos 69 E4
Arrabal 53 D4
Arrabalde 54 C4
Arracourt 27 D1
Arradon 23 D3
Arraiolos 66 C3
Arranhó 66 A2
Arras 16 B1
Årre 2 A2
Arreau 40 C4
Arredondo 55 F2
Arriach 30 B4
Arriate 74 B3
Arrifana 61 D3
Arrigorriaga 56 B2
Arrild 2 A3
Arriondas 55 D1
Arroba de los Montes 68 C2
Arronches 67 D2
Arrone 48 C1
Arroniz 56 C3
Arrou 24 C2
Arroyal 55 F2
Arroyo de la Luz 67 E1
Arroyo del Ojanco 69 F4
Arroyo de San Serván 67 F3
Arroyomolinos de León 67 F4
Arruda dos Vinhos 66 B2
Års 1 E2
Ars-en-Ré 32 A2
Arsiè 38 C2
Arsiero 38 C2
Årslev 2 C3
Arsoli 49 D2
Ars-sur-Moselle 17 F3
Artajona 56 C3
Artana 65 D4
Artannes-sur-Indre 24 B4
Artèn 39 D2
Artena 48 C2
Artenay 25 D2
Artern (Unstrut) 12 B3
Artés 59 D3
Artesa de Segre 58 B3
Arth 28 A4
Arthez-de-Béarn 40 B3
Arthon-en-Retz 23 E4
Artieda 57 E3
Artix 40 B3
Artlenburg 6 B3
Artogne 38 A2
A Rúa 54 A3
Arudy 40 B4
Årup 2 C3
Arveyres 32 C4
Arvieux 44 A1
Arvillé 32 A1
Arzacq-Arraziguet 40 B3
Arzbach 18 C1
Arzberg *Ger.* 20 C2
Arzberg *Ger.* 13 D2
Arzfeld 17 F2
Arzignano 38 C3
Arzl im Pitztal 29 D3
Arzúa 53 E2
As 9 F3
Aså 1 F2
Asbach 10 B4
Ascea 50 A4
Aschach an der Donau 30 C1
Aschaffenburg 19 E2
Aschbach Markt 31 D2
Ascheberg 10 C2
Ascheberg (Holstein) 6 B1
Aschersleben 12 B2
Asciano 46 B4
Ascó 58 B4
Ascoli Piceno 47 E4
Ascoli Satriano 50 B2
Ascona 37 D2
Ascou 59 D1
As Covas 53 E3
Asendorf 5 F4
Asfeld 17 D3
Asferg 2 C1
Asiago 38 C2
Asín 57 E3
Asnæs 3 D2
As Neves *Spain* 53 E4
As Neves *Spain* 53 F1
As Nogais 54 A2
Asola 38 B4
Asolo 39 D2
Asp 2 A1
Aspach 30 B2
Aspang-Markt 31 E3
Asparn an der Zaya 31 F1
Aspe 76 C1
Aspet 41 D4
As Pontes de García Rodríguez 53 F1
Aspres-sur-Buëch 43 E1
Assamstadt 19 E3
Assat 40 B4
Asse 9 D3
Asseiceira 66 C1
Assen 4 C4
Assendelft 9 D1
Assenede 8 C3
Assens *Denmark* 1 F3
Assens *Denmark* 2 C3
Assentoft 2 C1
Assérac 23 D3
Assergi 49 D1
Assesse 17 E1
Assisi 47 D4
Aßlar 11 D4
Assling 30 A4
Asso 37 E2
Asson 40 B4
Assumar 67 D2
Astaffort 41 D2
Asten *Austria* 30 C2
Asten *Neth.* 9 F3
Asti 36 C4
Astorga 54 C3
Astrup *Denmark* 1 F1
Astrup *Denmark* 1 F3
Astrup *Denmark* 2 A2
Astudillo 55 E4
Atalaia *Port.* 66 C2
Atalaia *Port.* 66 C1
Atalaya del Cañavate 70 A1
Ataquines 62 B2
Atarfe 75 D2
Atea 64 B2
Ateca 64 B2
A Teixeira 54 A3
Ateleta 49 E2
Atella 50 B3
Atena Lucana 50 B3
Atessa 49 F2
Ath 16 C1
Athenstedt 12 A2
Athies-sous-Laon 16 C3
Athis-de-l'Orne 24 A1
Atienza 63 E2
Atina 49 E3
Atouguia da Baleia 66 A2
Atri 49 E1
Atripalda 50 A3
Attendorn 10 C3
Attenkirchen 29 E1
Attersee 30 B2
Attert 17 F2
Attigliano 48 B1
Attignat 35 E2
Attigny 17 D3
Attnang 30 B2
Atur 33 D4
Atzenbrugg 31 E1
Atzendorf 12 B2
Au *Austria* 28 C3
Au *Switz.* 28 C3
Aub 19 F3
Aubagne 43 E3
Aubais 42 C3
Aubange 17 F3
Aube 24 B1
Aubenas 42 C1
Aubenton 17 D2
Aubergenville 16 A4
Auberive 26 B2
Aubeterre-sur-Dronne 33 D4
Aubiet 41 D3
Aubignan 43 D2
Aubigné-Racan 24 B3
Aubigny 32 A1
Aubigny-en-Artois 16 B1
Aubigny-sur-Nère 25 E3
Aubin 41 F1
Aubonne 36 A1
Aubord 42 C3
Auboué 17 F3
Aubusson 33 F2
Auby 16 B1
Auch 41 D3
Aucun 40 C4
Audenge 40 A1
Audeux 27 D3
Audierne 22 A2
Audincourt 27 E3
Audruicq 8 A4
Audun-le-Roman 17 F3
Aue 13 D4
Auerbach 12 C4
Auerbach in der Oberpfalz 20 B2
Auersthal 31 F1
Auffay 15 E2
Aufhausen 20 C4
Auggen 27 F2
Augsburg 29 D1
Augustenborg 2 C4
Augustusburg 13 D4
Aukrug 6 A1
Aulendorf 28 C2
Auletta 50 B3
Aulla 45 E2
Aulnat 34 B3
Aulnay 32 C2
Aulnay-sous-Bois 16 A4
Aulnoye-Aymeries 16 C1
Aulosen 6 C4
Ault 15 F2
Auma 12 C4
Aumale 16 A2
Aumetz 17 F3
Aumont-Aubrac 42 B1
Aumühle 6 A2
Aunay-sur-Odon 14 C4
Auneau 25 D1
Auning 2 C1
Auñón 63 E3
Aups 43 F3
Aurach 20 A3
Aurach bei Kitzbühel 30 A3
Aura im Sinngrund 19 E1
Auray 22 C3
Aureilhan 40 C4
Aurich 5 D3
Aurignac 41 D4
Aurillac 34 A4
Auriol 43 E3
Aurisina 39 F2
Aurolzmünster 30 B2
Auron 44 A2
Auronzo di Cadore 39 D1
Auros 40 C1
Ausa-Corno 39 E3
Ausejo 56 C3
Ausleben 12 B1
Ausonia 49 E3
Außervillgraten 39 D1
Aussillon 41 F3
Auterive 41 E3
Authon-du-Perche 24 C2
Autol 56 C4
Autrans 35 F4
Autrey-lès-Gray 26 C3
Autun 26 A4
Auvelais 17 D1
Auvers-le-Hamon 24 A2
Auvillar 41 D2
Auxerre 25 F2
Auxi-le-Château 16 A1
Auxonne 26 C4
Auxy 26 B4
Auzances 34 A2
Auzat 58 C1
Auzat-sur-Allier 34 B3
Auzon 34 C3
Availles-Limouzine 33 D2
Avallon 26 A3
Avanca 60 B2
A Veiga 54 A3
Aveiras de Cima 66 B2
Aveiro 60 B3
Avelar 66 C1
Avelãs de Caminho 60 B3
Aveleda *Port.* 60 B1
Aveleda *Portugal* 54 B4
Avelgem 8 C4
Avella 49 F4
Avellino 50 A3
Avenches 27 E4
Avenhorn 4 A4
Avenida do Marqués de Figueroa 53 F1
Avermes 34 B1
Avers 37 E1
Aversa 49 E4
Avesnes-le-Comte 16 B1
Avesnes-sur-Helpe 16 C2
Avetrano 51 E4
Avezzano 49 D2
Avia 59 D2
Aviano 39 E2
Avigliana 36 B4
Avigliano 50 B3
Avigliano Umbro 48 C1
Avignon 43 D2
Ávila 62 C3
Avilés 54 C1
Avintes 60 B2
Avinyó 59 D3
Avio 38 B3
Avion 16 B1
Avis 66 C2
Avize 16 C4
Avlum 2 A1
Avoine 24 B4
Avon 25 E1
Avord 25 E4
Avoriaz 36 A2
Avranches 23 E1
Avrillé 24 A3
Axams 29 E3
Axat 41 F4
Axel 8 C3
Ax-les-Thermes 59 D1
Axpe-Busturia 56 B1
Ayamonte 72 C2
Aydat 34 B3
Ayen 33 E4
Ayerbe 57 E3
Aying 29 E2
Ayllón 63 E1
Aymavilles 36 B3
Ayna 70 B3
Ayoo de Vidriales 54 C4
Ayora 70 C2
Aytré 32 B2
Aywaille 17 E1
Azagra 56 C3
Azaila 65 D2
Azambuja 66 B2
Azanúy 58 A3
Azaruja 67 D3
Azay-le-Ferron 33 E1
Azay-le-Rideau 24 B4
Azé 23 F3
Azerables 33 E2
Azinhaga 66 B2
Azinhal 72 C2
Azinheira dos Barros 66 C4
Azinhoso 61 E1
Azkoitia 56 C2
Aznalcázar 73 E2
Aznalcóllar 73 E2
Azóia 66 A3
Azpeitia 56 C2
Azuaga 68 A4
Azuara 64 C2
Azuel 69 D4
Azuelo 56 C3
Azuqueca de Henares 63 E3
Azután 62 B4
Azzano Decimo 39 E2
Azzone 38 A2

B

Baalberge 12 C2
Baar 28 A4
Baarle-Hertog 9 E3
Baarle-Nassau 9 E2
Baarn 9 E1

Babenhausen **19** D2
Babilafuente **62** A2
Bacares **75** F2
Baccarat **27** E1
Baceno **36** C2
Bach **29** D3
Backnang **19** E4
Bacoli **49** E4
Bacqueville-en-Caux **15** E2
Bad Abbach **20** C4
Bad Aibling **29** F2
Badajoz **67** E3
Badalona **59** D4
Badalucco **44** B2
Bádames **55** F1
Badarán **56** B3
Bad Aussee **30** B3
Bad Bellingen **27** F3
Bad Bentheim **10** B1
Badbergen **5** D4
Bad Bergzabern **18** C3
Bad Berka **12** B4
Bad Berleburg **11** D3
Bad Berneck im Fichtelgebirge **20** B2
Bad Bertrich **18** B2
Bad Bevensen **6** B3
Bad Bibra **12** B3
Bad Birnbach **30** A1
Bad Blankenburg **12** B4
Bad Bocklet **19** F1
Bad Brambach **20** C1
Bad Bramstedt **6** A2
Bad Breisig **10** B4
Bad Brückenau **19** E1
Bad Buchau **28** C2
Bad Camberg **18** C1
Bad Doberan **6** C1
Bad Driburg **11** D2
Bad Düben **12** C2
Bad Dürkheim **18** C3
Bad Dürrenberg **12** C3
Bad Dürrheim **28** A2
Badeborn **12** B2
Bad Elster **20** C1
Bad Ems **18** C1
Baden *Austria* **31** F2
Baden *France* **22** C3
Baden *Switz.* **28** A3
Badenas **64** C2
Baden-Baden **28** A1
Bad Endbach **11** D4
Bad Endorf **29** F2
Badenweiler **27** F2
Badersleben **12** A2
Bad Essen **11** D1
Bad Feilnbach **29** F2
Bad Frankenhausen (Kyffhäuser) **12** B3
Bad Freienwalde **7** F4
Bad Friedrichshall **19** E3
Bad Füssing **30** B1
Bad Gams **31** D4
Bad Gandersheim **11** F2
Badgastein **30** A4
Bad Goisern **30** B3
Bad Großpertholz **31** D1
Bad Grund (Harz) **11** F2
Bad Hall **30** C2
Bad Harzburg **11** F2
Bad Herrenalb **19** D4
Bad Hersfeld **11** E4
Bad Hofgastein **30** A4
Bad Homburg vor der Höhe **19** D1
Bad Honnef **10** B4
Bad Hönningen **10** B4
Badia **39** D1
Badia Calavena **38** C3
Badia Polesine **38** C4
Badia Tedalda **46** C3
Bad Iburg **10** C1
Bad Ischl **30** B3
Bad Karlshafen **11** E2
Bad Kissingen **19** F1
Bad Kleinen **6** C2
Bad Kleinkirchheim **30** B4
Bad König **19** D2
Bad Königshofen im Grabfeld **20** A1
Bad Kösen **12** B3
Bad Köstritz **12** C4
Bad Kreuzen **31** D1
Bad Kreuznach **18** C2
Bad Krozingen **27** F2
Bad Laasphe **11** D4
Bad Langensalza **11** F3
Bad Lauchstädt **12** C3
Bad Lausick **13** D3
Bad Lauterberg im Harz **11** F2
Bad Leonfelden **30** C1
Bad Liebenstein **11** F4
Bad Liebenwerda **13** D2
Bad Liebenzell **28** A1
Bad Lippspringe **11** D2
Bad Marienberg (Westerwald) **10** C4
Bad Mergentheim **19** E3
Bad Mitterndorf **30** C3
Bad Münder am Deister **11** E1
Bad Münstereifel **10** B4
Bad Muskau **13** F2
Bad Nauheim **19** D1
Bad Nenndorf **11** E1
Bad Neuenahr-Ahrweiler **10** B4
Bad Neustadt an der Saale **19** F1
Badolato **52** B3
Badolatosa **74** B2
Bad Oldesloe **6** B2
Badonviller **27** E1
Bad Orb **19** E1
Bad Peterstal **28** A1
Bad Pirawarth **31** F1
Bad Pyrmont **11** E2
Bad Radkersburg **31** E4
Bad Ragaz **28** B4
Bad Reichenhall **30** A2
Bad Rothenfelde **10** C1
Bad Saarow-Pieskow **13** E1
Bad Sachsa **11** F2
Bad Säckingen **27** F3
Bad Salzdetfurth **11** E1
Bad Salzuflen **11** D1
Bad Salzungen **11** F4
Bad Sassendorf **10** C2
Bad Schandau **13** E4
Bad Schmiedeberg **13** D2
Bad Schönborn **19** D3
Bad Schussenried **28** C2
Bad Schwalbach **18** C2
Bad Schwartau **6** B2
Bad Segeberg **6** A2
Bad Soden-Salmünster **19** E1
Bad Sooden-Allendorf **11** E3
Bad Steben **20** B1
Bad St Leonhard im Lavanttal **31** D4
Bad Sulza **12** B3
Bad Sülze **7** D1
Bad Tennstedt **12** A3
Bad Tölz **29** E2
Badules **64** B2
Bad Urach **28** B1
Bad Vilbel **19** D1
Bad Vöslau **31** F2
Bad Waldsee **28** C2
Bad Wildungen **11** D3
Bad Wilsnack **6** C4
Bad Wimpfen **19** E3
Bad Windsheim **20** A3
Bad Wörishofen **29** D2
Bad Wurzach **28** C2
Bad Zell **31** D1
Bad Zwesten **11** E3
Bad Zwischenahn **5** D3
Bække **2** B2
Bækmarksbro **2** A1
Bælum **1** F2
Baena **74** C1
Baesweiler **10** A4
Baeza **69** E4
Baflo **4** C3
Bagà **59** D2
Bagaladi **52** A4
Bagard **42** C2
Bâgé-le-Châtel **35** E2
Bagenkop **2** C4
Bages **59** E2
Bagnacavallo **46** C1
Bagnac-sur-Célé **41** F1
Bagnara Calabra **52** A4
Bagnaria **45** D1
Bagnaria Arsa **39** F2
Bagnasco **44** B2
Bagneaux-sur-Loing **25** E2
Bagnères-de-Bigorre **40** C4
Bagnères-de-Luchon **58** B1
Bagni di Lucca **46** A2
Bagni di Masino **38** A2
Bagni di Rabbi **38** B1
Bagno a Ripoli **46** B3
Bagno di Romagna **46** C2
Bagnoli del Trigno **49** F2
Bagnoli di Sopra **39** D4
Bagnoli Irpino **50** A3
Bagnolo in Piano **38** B4
Bagnolo Mella **38** A3
Bagnolo Piemonte **44** A1
Bagnolo San Vito **38** B4
Bagnols-en-Forêt **43** F3
Bagnols-sur-Cèze **42** C2
Bagnoregio **48** B1
Bagolino **38** B2
Báguena **64** B2
Bahabón de Esgueva **55** F4
Bahíllo **55** E3
Bahrenborstel **5** E4
Bahrendorf **12** B2
Baia della Zagare **50** C1
Baiano **49** F4
Baiardo **44** B2
Baiersbronn **28** A1
Baiersdorf **20** A2
Baignes-Ste-Radegonde **32** C3
Baigneux-les-Juifs **26** B3
Bailén **69** D4
Baillargues **42** C3
Bailleau-le-Pin **24** C1
Bailleul **8** B4
Baillonville **17** E1
Bailo **57** E3
Bain-de-Bretagne **23** E3
Baindt **28** C2
Bains **34** C4
Bains-les-Bains **27** D2
Baio Grande **53** D2
Baiona **53** D4
Bais *France* **23** F2
Bais *France* **24** A2
Baiso **46** A1
Baixa da Banheira **66** B3
Baixas **59** E1
Bakel **9** F2
Bakio-Basigo **56** B1
Bakum **5** E4
Balaguer **58** B3
Balan **17** E2
Balaruc-les-Bains **42** B3
Balazote **70** B3
Balbigny **35** D3
Baleizão **67** D4
Balen **9** E3
Balerma **75** E3
Balingen **28** B2
Balje **5** F2
Balk **4** B4
Balkbrug **4** C4
Ballabio **37** E2
Balle **3** D1
Ballen **2** C2
Ballenstedt **12** B2
Balleroy **14** C3
Ballerup **3** E2
Ballesteros de Calatrava **69** D3
Ballobar **58** A3
Ballon **24** B2
Ballots **23** F2
Ballstädt **11** F3
Ballum *Denmark* **2** A3
Ballum *Neth.* **4** B3
Balmaseda **56** A2
Balme **36** B3
Balmuccia **36** C2
Balocco **36** C3
Balow **6** C3
Balsa de Ves **70** C2
Balsa Pintada **76** C2
Balsareny **59** D3
Balsicas **76** C2
Balsorano **49** D2
Balsthal **27** F3
Baltanás **55** E4
Baltar **53** F4
Balvano **50** B3
Balve **10** C3
Balzers **28** C4
Bamberg **20** A2
Bammental **19** D3
Bande **53** F4
Bandenitz **6** C3
Bandholm **3** D4
Bandol **43** E4
Bañeres **71** D3
Bannalec **22** B2
Bannesdorf auf Fehmarn **6** C1
Bannewitz **13** E3
Bañobárez **61** E2
Banon **43** E2
Bañón **64** B2
Baños de la Encina **69** D4
Baños de Molgas **53** F3
Baños de Montemayor **62** A3
Baños de Panticosa **58** A1
Baños de Río Tobía **56** B3
Baños de Valdearados **55** F4
Bant **4** B4
Banteln **11** E1
Banyeres del Penedès **58** C4
Banyoles **59** E2
Banyuls-sur-Mer **59** E2
Banzi **50** B3
Banzkow **6** C3
Bapaume **16** B2
Baragiano **50** B3
Barahona **63** F2
Barajas de Melo **63** E4
Barakaldo **56** B2
Baralla **54** A2
Barambio **56** B2
Barañain **57** D2
Baranello **49** F3
Barano d'Ischia **49** E4
Barão de São João **72** A2
Baraqueville **41** F2
Barasoain **57** D3
Barbacena **67** D2
Barbadás **53** F3
Barbadillo de Herreros **56** A4
Barbadillo del Mercado **56** A4
Barbadillo del Pez **56** A4
Barbarano Vicentino **38** C3
Barbaste **40** C2
Barbastro **58** A3
Barbate de Franco **73** E4
Barbâtre **23** D4
Barbazan **41** D4
Barberá del Vallès **59** D4
Barberino di Mugello **46** B2
Barbezieux-St-Hilaire **32** C3
Barby (Elbe) **12** C2
Barca **63** F1
Barcabo **58** A2
Barca de Alva **61** E2
Barcarrota **67** E3
Barcelinhos **60** B1
Barcelona **59** D4
Barcelonne-du-Gers **40** B3
Barcelonnette **43** F1
Barcelos **60** B1
Bárcena del Monasterio **54** B1
Bárcena de Pie de Concha **55** F2
Barcenillas de Cerezos **55** F2
Barchfeld **11** F4
Barcillonnette **43** E1
Barcis **39** E2
Barcones **63** E2
Barcos **61** D2
Barde **2** A1
Bárdena **57** D4
Bardenitz **13** D1
Bårdesø **2** C2
Bardi **45** E1
Bardineto **44** B2
Bardolino **38** B3
Bardonecchia **36** A4
Bardos **40** A3
Bardowick **6** B3
Barenburg **5** E4
Barendorf **6** B3
Bärenklau **13** F2
Bärenstein *Ger.* **13** D4
Bärenstein *Ger.* **13** E4
Barentin **15** E3
Barenton **23** F1
Barga **46** A2
Bargagli **45** D1
Bargas **63** D4
Barge **44** A1
Bargen **28** A2
Bargenstedt **5** F1
Barghe **38** B3
Bargischow **7** E2
Bargstedt **5** F3
Bargteheide **6** A2
Bari **51** D2
Barile **50** B3
Barinas **76** C1
Båring **2** C3
Barisciano **49** D1
Barjac **42** C2
Barjols **43** E3
Barkelsby **6** A1
Barleben **12** B1
Bar-le-Duc **17** E4
Barletta **50** C2
Barmstedt **6** A2
Bärnau **20** C2
Barnbach **31** D4
Barneberg **12** B1

Barneveld 9 E1
Barneville-Carteret 14 B3
Barnewitz 13 D1
Barnstädt 12 B3
Barnstorf 5 E4
Barntrup 11 D2
Baronissi 50 A3
Baronville 18 A4
Barqueros 76 B1
Barquinha 66 C1
Barr 27 F1
Barracas 64 C4
Barrachina 64 C2
Barral 53 F3
Barranco do Velho 72 B2
Barrancos 67 E4
Barranda 76 A1
Barrax 70 B2
Barre-des-Cévennes 42 B2
Barreiro 66 B3
Barrême 43 F2
Barriada Nueva 59 D3
Bárrio 60 B1
Barrio del Peral 76 C2
Barrio Mar 71 E1
Barrit 2 C2
Barroca 61 D4
Barroselas 60 B1
Barruecopardo 61 E2
Barruelo de Santullan 55 E2
Barsac 40 B1
Barsbüttel 6 A2
Bârse 3 E3
Barsinghausen 11 E1
Barßel 5 D3
Bar-sur-Aube 26 B2
Bar-sur-Seine 26 B2
Bartenheim 27 F3
Bartenstein 19 E3
Barth 7 D1
Bartholomä 28 C1
Bartholomäberg 28 C4
Barulho 67 D2
Baruth 13 E1
Barver 5 E4
Barwedel 11 F1
Barxeta 71 D2
Bárzana 54 C2
Barzio 37 E2
Basauri 56 B2
Bàscara 59 E2
Bascharage 17 F3
Baschi 48 B1
Basciano 49 E1
Basconcillos del Tozo 55 F3
Basdahl 5 F3
Basel 27 F3
Baselga di Pinè 38 C2
Baselice 50 A2
Basiliano 39 E2
Bassano del Grappa 38 C2
Bassano Romano 48 B1
Bassecourt 27 E3
Bassenge 9 F4
Bassens 32 C4
Bassiano 49 D3
Bassoues 40 C3
Bassum 5 E4
Bastardo 47 D4
Bastia 47 D4
Bastogne 17 F2
Bastorf 6 C1
Batalha 66 B1
Batea 58 A4
Baterno 68 C2
Bathmen 10 A1
Battenberg (Eder) 11 D3
Bätterkinden 27 F4
Battipaglia 50 A3
Batz-sur-Mer 23 D4
Baud 22 C3
Bauen 28 A4
Baugé 24 A3
Baugy 25 E4
Baulon 23 E2
Baume-les-Dames 27 D3
Baumholder 18 B3
Baunach 20 A2
Bausendorf 18 B2
Bautzen 13 F3
Bavay 16 C1
Baveno 37 D2
Bawinkel 5 D4
Bayárcal 75 E3
Bayarque 75 F2
Bayerbach 30 B1
Bayerisch Eisenstein 21 D3
Bayersoien 29 D3
Bayeux 14 C3
Bayon 27 D1
Bayonne 40 A3
Bayreuth 20 B2
Bayrischzell 29 F3
Bayubas de Abajo 63 E1
Baza 75 E2
Bazas 40 B1
Bazièqe 41 E3
Bazoches-les-Gallerandes 25 D2
Bazoches-sur-Hoëne 24 B1
Bazouges 23 F2
Bazzano 46 B1
Beamub 64 B4
Beariz 53 E3
Beas 73 D2
Beasain 56 C2
Beas de Granada 75 D2
Beas de Segura 69 F4
Beaucaire 42 C2
Beaucourt 27 E3
Beaucouzé 23 F3
Beaufay 24 B2
Beaufort *France* 35 E1
Beaufort *France* 36 A3
Beaufort-en-Vallée 24 A3
Beaugency 25 D3
Beaujeu 35 D2
Beaulieu-lès-Loches 24 C4
Beaulieu-sur-Dordogne 33 F4
Beaulieu-sur-Loire 25 E3
Beaulon 34 C1
Beaumesnil 15 E4
Beaumetz-lès-Loges 16 B1
Beaumont *Belgium* 17 D1
Beaumont *France* 41 D1
Beaumont *France* 14 B2
Beaumont *France* 33 D1
Beaumont-de-Lomagne 41 D2
Beaumont-en-Véron 24 B4
Beaumont-le-Roger 15 E4
Beaumont-sur-Oise 16 A3
Beaumont-sur-Sarthe 24 B2
Beaune 26 B4
Beaune-La Rolande 25 E2
Beaupréau 23 F4
Beauquesne 16 A2
Beauraing 17 E2
Beaurepaire 35 E3
Beaurepaire-en-Bresse 35 E1
Beausoleil 44 A3
Beautor 16 C2
Beauvais 16 A3
Beauval 16 A2
Beauville 41 D2
Beauvoir-sur-Mer 23 E4
Beauvoir-sur-Niort 32 C2
Beauzac 35 D4
Beauzelle 41 E3
Bebertal 12 B1
Bebra 11 E4
Becedas 62 A3
Beceite 65 E2
Becerreá 54 A2
Becerril de Campos 55 E4
Bécherel 23 E2
Bechhofen 20 A3
Bechtheim 18 C2
Becilla de Valderaduey 55 D4
Beckdorf 6 A3
Beckedorf 11 E1
Beckeln 5 E4
Beckingen 18 A3
Beckum 10 C2
Bécon-les-Granits 23 F3
Bédar 76 A3
Bédarieux 42 A3
Bedburg 10 A3
Bédée 23 E2
Beder 2 C2
Bederkesa 5 E2
Bedmar 75 D1
Bédoin 43 D2
Bedollo 38 C2
Bedonia 45 E1
Bedsted 2 B3
Bedsted Stationsby 1 D2
Bedum 4 C3
Beedenbostel 6 A4
Beek *Neth.* 10 A2
Beek *Neth.* 9 F2
Beelitz 13 D1
Beendorf 12 B1
Beenz 7 E3
Beerfelden 19 D3
Beernem 8 C3
Beers 9 F2
Beerse 9 E3
Beersel 9 D4
Beerta 4 C3
Beesenstedt 12 B2
Beeskow 13 E1
Beetsterzwaag 4 B3
Beetzendorf 6 B4
Bégaar 40 B3
Bégard 22 C1
Begíjar 69 E4
Begijnendijk 9 E3
Begonte 53 F2
Begur 59 F3
Behren-lès-Forbach 18 B3
Behren-Lübchin 7 D2
Behringen 11 F3
Beierfeld 13 D4
Beierstedt 12 A1
Beilen 4 C4
Beilngries 20 B4
Beilstein 19 E4
Beinasco 36 B4
Beinette 44 B1
Beinwil 28 A3
Beirã 67 D2
Beja 66 C4
Béjar 62 A3
Bejís 64 C4
Bélâbre 33 E1
Belalcázar 68 B3
Belascoáin 56 C2
Belazaima do Chão 60 C3
Belcaire 41 F4
Belchite 64 C2
Bélesta 41 F4
Belfeld 10 A3
Belfort 27 E3
Belforte del Chienti 47 E4
Belgentier 43 E4
Belgern 13 D3
Belgershain 12 C3
Belgioioso 37 E4
Belianes 58 B3
Belin-Béliet 40 B1
Belinchón 63 E4
Bell 18 B1
Bella 50 B3
Bellac 33 E2
Bellagio 37 E2
Bellano 37 E2
Bellante 47 F4
Bellaria 47 D2
Bellavista 73 E2
Bellclaire d'Urgell 58 B3
Bellegarde *France* 25 E2
Bellegarde *France* 42 C3
Bellegarde-en-Marche 33 F2
Bellegarde-sur-Valserine 35 F2
Belle-Isle-en-Terre 22 C1
Bellême 24 B1
Bellenaves 34 B2
Bellenberg 28 C2
Bellencombre 15 F2
Bellerive-sur-Allier 34 C2
Belleu 16 C3
Bellevaux 36 A2
Belleville 35 D2
Belleville-sur-Meuse 17 E3
Belleville-sur-Vie 32 A1
Belley 35 F3
Bellinge 2 C3
Bellingwolde 4 C3
Bellinzago Novarese 37 D3
Bellinzona 37 D2
Bellizzi 50 A3
Bell-Lloc d'Urgell 58 B3
Bello 64 B2
Bellpuig d'Urgell 58 B3
Bellreguard 71 E3
Belluno 39 D2
Bellver de Cerdanya 59 D2
Belm 10 C1
Bélmez 68 B4
Bélmez de la Moraleda 75 D1
Belmont-de-la-Loire 35 D2
Belmonte *Port.* 61 D3
Belmonte *Spain* 54 B2
Belmonte *Spain* 70 A1
Belmonte Calabro 52 A2
Belmonte in Sabina 48 C1
Belmontejo 63 F4
Belmont-sur-Rance 42 A2
Belœil 16 C1
Belorado 56 A3
Belp 27 F4
Belpech 41 E4
Beltheim 18 B2
Beltrum 10 A1
Belvedere Marittimo 52 A1
Belvedere Ostrense 47 E3
Belver de Cinca 58 A3
Belver de los Montes 62 A1
Belvès 41 D1
Belvís de la Jara 68 C1
Belz 22 C3
Belzig 12 C1
Bembibre *Spain* 54 B3
Bembibre *Spain* 53 E2
Bemmel 10 A2
Bemposta *Port.* 61 E2
Bemposta *Port.* 66 C2
Benabarre 58 B2
Benacazón 73 E2
Benahadux 75 F3
Benahavís 74 B4
Benalmádena 74 B3
Benalúa de Guadix 75 E2
Benalúa de las Villas 75 D2
Benalup de Sidonia 73 F4
Benamargosa 74 C3
Benamaurel 75 F1
Benamejí 74 C2
Benamocarra 74 C3
Benaocaz 74 A3
Benaoján 74 A3
Benasal 65 D3
Benasau 71 D3
Benasque 58 B2
Benatae 70 A4
Benavente *Port.* 66 B2
Benavente *Spain* 54 C4
Benavides de Orbigo 54 C3
Benavila 66 C2
Bencatel 67 D3
Bendorf 10 C4
Beneden-Leeuwen 9 E2
Benediktbeuren 29 E3
Benedita 66 B1
Benegiles 62 A1
Bénéjacq 40 B4
Benejama 71 D3
Benejúzar 76 C1
Bénesse-Maremne 40 A3
Benestare 52 B4
Bénestroff 18 B4
Benet 32 B2
Bene Vagienna 44 B1
Bénévent-l'Abbaye 33 E2
Benevento 50 A2
Benfeld 27 F1
Benfica do Ribatejo 66 B2
Benia de Onís 55 D1
Beniarbeig 71 E3
Beniarrés 71 D3
Benicarló 65 E3
Benicasim 65 D4
Benidorm 71 E3
Beniel 76 C1
Benifaió 71 D2
Benifallet 65 E2
Benifallim 71 D3
Benigánim 71 D3
Benilloba 71 D3
Benissa 71 E3
Benissanet 58 B4
Benitachell 71 E3
Benizalón 76 A3
Benizar y la Tercia 76 A1
Benken 28 B4
Benlloch 65 D4
Bennewitz 13 D3
Bennungen 12 B3
Bénodet 22 B3
Benquerença 61 D4
Benquerenças 67 D1
Benquerencia de la Serena 68 B3
Bensafrim 72 A2
Bensdorf 12 C1
Benshausen 11 F4
Bensheim 19 D2
Bentivoglio 46 B1
Bentwisch 7 D1
Bentzin 7 E2
Benzingerode 12 A2
Beranga 55 F1
Berango 56 B1
Berantevilla 56 B3
Bérat 41 D3
Beratzhausen 20 B4
Berbegal 58 A3
Bercedo 55 F2
Bercero 62 B1
Berceto 45 E1
Berchem 8 C4
Berching 20 B3
Berchtesgaden 30 A3
Bérchules 75 E3

Bercianos del Páramo **54** C3
Berck **15** F1
Berducedo **54** B2
Berdún **57** E3
Bereguardo **37** D4
Berg *Ger.* **28** C2
Berg *Ger.* **20** B1
Berg *Lux.* **17** F2
Berg *Neth.* **9** F3
Berg (Pfalz) **18** C4
Berga *Ger.* **12** B3
Berga *Ger.* **12** C4
Berga *Spain* **59** D2
Bergamo **38** A3
Bergantino **38** C4
Bergara **56** C2
Bergasa **56** C3
Bergatreute **28** C2
Berg bei Neumarkt in der Oberpfalz **20** B3
Berge *Ger.* **6** C3
Berge *Ger.* **5** D4
Berge *Spain* **65** D2
Bergeggi **44** C2
Bergen *Ger.* **30** A2
Bergen *Ger.* **7** E1
Bergen *Ger.* **6** A4
Bergen *Neth.* **4** A4
Bergen (Dumme) **6** B4
Bergen op Zoom **9** D2
Bergerac **33** D4
Bergeyk **9** E3
Bergheim *Austria* **30** A2
Bergheim *Ger.* **20** B4
Bergheim (Edertal) **11** D3
Bergheim (Erft) **10** A3
Berghem **9** E2
Berghülen **28** C1
Berg im Drautal **30** A4
Bergisch Gladbach **10** B3
Bergkamen **10** C2
Bergtheim **19** F2
Bergues **8** B3
Bergum **4** B3
Bergün **38** A1
Bergwitz **12** C2
Beringel **66** C4
Beringen **9** E3
Berja **75** E3
Berka **11** F4
Berkel **9** D1
Berkel-Enschot **9** E2
Berkenthin **6** B2
Berkheim **28** C2
Berkhout **4** A4
Berlanga **68** A4
Berlanga de Duero **63** E1
Berlin **13** D1
Berlingerode **11** F3
Berlstedt **12** B3
Bermatingen **28** B2
Bermeo **56** B1
Bermillo de Sayago **61** F1
Bern **27** F4
Bernalda **51** D3
Bernardos **62** C2
Bernau *Ger.* **27** F2
Bernau *Ger.* **7** E4
Bernau am Chiemsee **30** A2
Bernaville **16** A2
Bernay **15** E4
Bernbeuren **29** D2
Bernburg (Saale) **12** B2
Berndorf **31** E2
Berne **5** E3
Bernedo **56** B3
Bernhardsthal **31** F1
Bernhardswald **20** C4
Bernis **42** C3
Bernissart **16** C1
Bernitt **6** C2
Bernkastel-Kues **18** B2
Bernsdorf **13** E3
Bernstadt *Ger.* **28** C1
Bernstadt *Ger.* **13** F3
Bernstein **31** F3
Beromünster **28** A4
Berra **39** D4
Berre-l'Étang **43** D3
Berriatúa **56** B1
Berrien **22** B2
Berriozar **57** D2
Bersenbrück **5** D4
Bersone **38** B2
Bertamirans **53** E2
Bertinoro **46** C2
Bertogne **17** E2
Bertrix **17** E2
Besalú **59** E2
Besançon **27** D3
Besande **55** D2
Bescanó **59** E3
Besigheim **19** E4
Besozzo **37** D2
Bessan **42** B3
Bessay-sur-Allier **34** C1
Besse **35** F4
Besse-et-St-Anastaise **34** B3
Bessèges **42** C2
Bessé-sur-Braye **24** C2
Besse-sur-Issole **43** F3
Bessières **41** E3
Bessines-sur-Gartempe **33** E2
Best **9** E2
Bestensee **13** E1
Bestwig **11** D3
Betanzos **53** E1
Betelu **56** C2
Bétera **71** D1
Beteta **64** A3
Betheln **11** E1
Béthune **16** B1
Bettembourg **17** F3
Bettingen **17** F2
Bettola **45** E1
Betton **23** E2
Betxi **65** D4
Betz **16** B3
Betzdorf **10** C4
Betzenstein **20** B2
Betzigau **29** D2
Beucha **12** C3
Beuil **44** A2
Beuningen **9** F2
Beuren **11** F3
Beuron **28** B2
Beuvry **16** B1
Beuzeville **15** D3
Bevagna **47** D4
Beveren **9** D3
Bevern **11** E2
Beverstedt **5** E3
Beverungen **11** E2
Beverwijk **9** D1
Béville-le-Comte **25** D1
Bex **36** B2
Bexbach **18** B3
Beyendorf **12** B1
Beynat **33** F4
Bezas **64** B3
Bezau **28** C3
Béziers **42** A3
Bezouce **42** C2
Bianco **52** B4
Biandrate **37** D3
Bianzè **36** C3
Biar **71** D3
Biarritz **40** A3
Biars-sur-Cère **33** F4
Bias **41** D1
Biasca **37** D1
Bibbiena **46** C3
Bibbona **46** A3
Biberach **27** F1
Biberach an der Riß **28** C2
Biberbach **29** D1
Biberist **27** F4
Bibione **39** E3
Biblis **19** D2
Biccari **50** A2
Bichl **29** E2
Bichlbach **29** D3
Bicorp **71** D2
Bicos **72** A1
Bidache **40** A3
Biddinghuizen **9** F1
Bieber **19** E1
Biebesheim am Rhein **19** D2
Biedenkopf **11** D4
Biel *Spain* **57** E3
Biel *Switz.* **27** E4
Bielefeld **11** D2
Biella **36** C3
Bielsa **58** A1
Bienenbüttel **6** B3
Bienno **38** B2
Bienservida **70** A3
Bienvenida **67** F4
Bière **36** A1
Bierge **58** A2
Bierné **24** A3
Biersted **1** F2
Biescas **57** F3
Biesenthal **7** E4
Biesles **26** C2
Biessenhofen **29** D2
Bietigheim **18** C4
Bietigheim-Bissingen **19** E4
Bietikow **7** F3
Bièvre **17** E2
Biganos **40** A1
Bigastro **76** C1
Bignan **23** D3
Bignasco **37** D2
Bigüezal **57** D3
Bilbo **56** B2
Billerbeck **10** B2
Billère **40** B4
Billigheim **19** E3
Billom **34** B3
Billum **2** A2
Billund **2** B2
Billy **34** C2
Bilthoven **9** E1
Bilzen **9** E4
Binaced **58** A3
Binasco **37** D3
Binche **17** D1
Bindlach **20** B2
Bindslev **1** F1
Binefar **58** A3
Bingen **28** B2
Bingen am Rhein **18** C2
Binic **23** D1
Biniés **57** E3
Binnen **5** F4
Biol **35** E3
Bionaz **36** B2
Biosca **58** C3
Biot **44** A3
Biota **57** D3
Bippen **5** D4
Birgittelyst **2** B1
Birkelse **1** E2
Birkenau **19** D3
Birkenfeld *Ger.* **19** D4
Birkenfeld *Ger.* **19** E2
Birkenfeld *Ger.* **18** B2
Birkenwerder Berlin **7** E4
Birkerød **3** E2
Birket **3** D4
Birkfeld **31** E3
Birkungen **11** F3
Birnbaum **30** A4
Birresborn **18** A1
Birstein **19** E1
Bisaccia **50** B2
Biscarrosse **40** A1
Biscarrosse-Plage **40** A1
Bisceglie **50** C2
Bischberg **20** A2
Bischhausen (Waldkappel) **11** E3
Bischheim **27** F1
Bischofferode **11** F2
Bischoffsheim **27** F1
Bischofsheim an der Rhön **19** F1
Bischofshofen **30** B3
Bischofsmais **21** D4
Bischofswerda **13** E3
Bischofswiesen **30** A3
Bischofszell **28** B3
Bischwiller **27** F1
Bisenti **49** E1
Bisignano **52** B1
Bisingen **28** B1
Bislev **1** E2
Bismark (Altmark) **6** C4
Bispingen **6** A3
Bissen **17** F2
Bissendorf **10** C1
Bissendorf (Wedemark) **11** E1
Bissingen **29** D1
Bistagno **44** C1
Bitburg **18** A2
Bitche **18** B4
Bitetto **51** D2
Bitonto **51** D2
Bitritto **51** D2
Bitterfeld **12** C2
Bittkau **12** C1
Bitz **28** B2
Biurrun **57** D3
Bivio **38** A1
Bizanet **42** A4
Bizanos **40** B4
Bjæverskov **3** E3
Bjergby **1** F1
Bjerge **3** D2
Bjerreby **2** C4
Bjerregrav **2** B1
Bjerringbro **2** B1
Bladel **9** E3
Blagnac **41** E3
Blåhøj **2** B2
Blaibach **21** D3
Blain **23** E3
Blainville-sur-l'Eau **27** D1
Blainville-sur-Mer **14** B4
Blâmont **27** E1
Blanca **76** B1
Blancafort **25** E3
Blancas **64** B2
Blancos **53** F4
Blanes **59** E3
Blangy-sur-Bresle **15** F2
Blankenberg **6** C2
Blankenberge **8** B3
Blankenburg (Harz) **12** A2
Blanken-felde **13** D1
Blankenhain *Ger.* **12** C4
Blankenhain *Ger.* **12** B4
Blankenheim **10** A4
Blankensee **7** E3
Blankenstein **20** B1
Blanquefort **32** B4
Blans **2** B4
Blanzac-Porcheresse **32** C3
Blanzy **26** B4
Blaubeuren **28** C1
Blaufelden **19** F3
Blausasc **44** A2
Blavozy **34** C4
Blaye **32** B4
Blázquez **68** B3
Bleckede **6** B3
Blecua **58** A3
Blegny **17** F1
Bléharies **16** C1
Bleialf **17** F1
Bleicherode **11** F3
Blekendorf **6** B1
Blender **5** F4
Bléneau **25** E3
Blenstrup **1** F2
Blera **48** B1
Blérancourt **16** B3
Bléré **24** C3
Blerick **10** A3
Blesa **64** C2
Blesle **34** B4
Bletterans **26** C4
Blieskastel **18** B3
Bligny-sur-Ouche **26** B4
Blimea **54** C2
Blindow **7** F3
Blistrup **3** E2
Blois **24** C3
Blokhus **1** E2
Blokzijl **4** B4
Blomberg **11** D2
Blönsdorf **13** D2
Blowatz **6** C2
Bludenz **28** C4
Blumau in Steiermark **31** E4
Blumberg *Ger.* **28** A2
Blumberg *Ger.* **7** E4
Blumenhagen **7** F2
Blumenholz **7** E3
Boada **61** F2
Boadilla del Monte **63** D3
Boadilla de Rioseco **55** D4
Boal **54** B1
Boalhosa **60** B1
Boara Pisani **39** D4
Boavista **66** A2
Boa Vista **66** B1
Bobadilla **74** B3
Bobbio **45** D1
Bobbio Pellice **44** A1
Böbing **29** D2
Bobingen **29** D1
Bobitz **6** C2
Böblingen **28** B1
Boborás **53** E3
Bobrowice **13** F2
Bocacara **61** F3
Bocairent **71** D3
Bocchigliero **52** B2
Boceguillas **63** D2
Bocholt *Belgium* **9** E3
Bocholt *Ger.* **10** A2
Bochum **10** B3
Bockenem **11** F2
Bockhorn *Ger.* **29** F1
Bockhorn *Ger.* **5** D3
Bockhorst **5** D3
Boczów **13** F1
Boddin **6** B2
Bodenfelde **11** E2
Bodenheim **19** D2
Bodenkirchen **30** A1
Bodenmais **21** D4
Bodenteich **6** B4
Bodenwerder **11** E2
Bodenwöhr **20** C3
Bodman **28** B2
Bodnegg **28** C3
Bodonal de la Sierra **67** E4
Boé **41** D2
Boechout **9** D3
Boecillo **62** C1
Boekel **9** F2
Boën **34** C3
Boeslunde **3** D3

Boeza **54** B3
Boffzen **11** E2
Bogajo **61** E2
Bogarra **70** B3
Bogatynia **13** F4
Bogen **20** C4
Bogense **2** C2
Bogliasco **45** D1
Bognanco **36** C2
Bogø **3** E4
Bohain-en-Vermandois **16** C2
Bohars **22** A1
Böheimkirchen **31** E2
Böhlen **12** C3
Böhme **5** F4
Bohmte **10** C1
Böhne **7** D4
Bohonal de Ibor **62** A4
Bohoyo **62** A4
Boiro **53** D3
Bois-d'Amont **35** F1
Boisgervilly **23** E2
Bois-Guillaume **15** E3
Boisset-et-Gaujac **42** B2
Boitzenburg **7** E3
Boizenburg **6** B3
Bojano **49** F3
Bøjden **2** C3
Bokel **5** E3
Böklund **2** B4
Bolaños de Calatrava **69** E3
Bolbaite **71** D2
Bolbec **15** E3
Boldekow **7** E2
Bolderslev **2** B4
Bolea **57** E3
Boleszkowice **7** F4
Boliqueime **72** B2
Bölkow **6** C2
Boll **28** C1
Bollène **43** D2
Bollengo **36** C3
Bolligen **27** F4
Bolling **2** A2
Bollingstedt **2** B4
Bollullos Par del Condado **73** D2
Bollwiller **27** E2
Bologna **46** B1
Bologne **26** C2
Bolognola **47** E4
Bolsena **48** B1
Bolsward **4** B3
Boltañá **58** A2
Boltigen **36** B1
Bolzano **38** C1
Bomba **49** E2
Bombarral **66** A2
Bomlitz **6** A4
Bompas **59** E1
Bomporto **38** C4
Bonaduz **28** B4
Bonanza **73** E3
Boñar **55** D2
Bonares **73** D2
Bonassola **45** E2
Bonchamp-lès-Laval **23** F2
Boncourt **27** E3
Bondeno **38** C4
Bonderup **1** E2
Bönebüttel **6** A1
Bonefro **50** A1
Bönen **10** C2
Bonete **70** C3
Bonheiden **9** D3
Boniches **64** B4
Bonifati **52** A1
Bönigen **27** F4
Bonn **10** B4
Bonnat **33** F2
Bonndorf im Schwarzwald **28** A2
Bønnerup Strand **3** D1
Bonnet **2** A1
Bonnétable **24** B2
Bonneuil-Matours **33** D1
Bonneval *France* **24** C2
Bonneval *France* **36** A3
Bonneval-sur-Arc **36** B3
Bonneville **36** A2
Bonnieux **43** D2
Bönnigheim **19** E4
Bonny-sur-Loire **25** E3
Bono **22** C3
Bons-en-Chablais **36** A2
Bonson **35** D3
Boock **7** F3
Boom **9** D3
Boortmeerbeek **9** D3
Boos **15** F3
Boostedt **6** A2
Bopfingen **20** A4
Boppard **18** C1
Borba **67** D3
Borbjerg **2** A1
Borchen **11** D2
Borculo **10** A1
Bordalba **63** F1
Bordeaux **32** B4
Bordeira **72** A2
Bordelum **2** A4
Bordères-Louron **40** C4
Bordères-sur-l'Échez **40** C4
Bordes **40** B4
Bordesholm **6** A1
Bordighera **44** B3
Bordils **59** E3
Bording **2** B1
Bordón **65** D3
Bore **38** A4
Borg **18** A3
Borgentreich **11** E2
Börger **5** D4
Borger **4** C4
Borghetto d'Arroscia **44** B2
Borghetto di Borbera **45** D1
Borghetto di Vara **45** E2
Borghetto Sto Spirito **44** C2
Borgia **52** B3
Borgloon **9** E4
Børglum **1** F1
Borgo a Mozzano **46** A2
Borgo d'Ale **36** C3
Borgoforte **38** B4
Borgofranco d'Ivrea **36** C3
Borgo Grappa **51** F3
Borgo-lavezzaro **37** D3
Borgomanero **37** D3
Borgomaro **44** B2
Borgone Susa **36** B4
Borgonovo Val Tidone **37** E4
Borgo Pace **46** C3
Borgorose **49** D1
Borgo San Dalmazzo **44** B1
Borgo San Lorenzo **46** B2
Borgo San Martino **37** D4
Borgosesia **36** C3
Borgo Tossignano **46** B2
Borgo Val di Taro **45** E1
Borgo Valsugana **38** C2
Borgo Velino **49** D1
Borgo Vercelli **37** D3
Borgstedt **6** A1
Borja **57** D4
Borjabad **63** F1
Borken **10** B2
Borken (Hessen) **11** E3
Børkop **2** B2
Borkum **4** C2
Bormes-les-Mimosas **43** F4
Bormio **38** B1
Born **12** B1
Borna *Ger.* **12** C3
Borna *Ger.* **13** D3
Born am Darß **7** D1
Borne **10** B1
Bornem **9** D3
Bornes **61** E1
Bornes de Aguiar **61** D1
Bornheim **10** B4
Bornhöved **6** A1
Bornos **74** A3
Börnsen **6** A3
Borobia **64** A1
Borox **63** D4
Borre **3** E4
Borrentin **7** E2
Borriol **65** D4
Borris **2** A2
Borsbeek **9** D3
Borstel **5** F4
Bort-les-Orgues **34** A3
Borum **2** C1
Borup **3** E3
Borzonasca **45** D1
Bosau **6** B1
Bosco **47** D4
Bosco Chiesanuova **38** C3
Bosco Marengo **44** C1
Boscotrecase **49** F4
Bösdorf **6** B1
Bösel **5** D3
Boskoop **9** D1
Bosque **53** D2
Bossolasco **44** B1
Bòssost **58** B1
Botão **60** C3
Boticas **61** D1
Botorrita **64** C1
Botricello **52** C3
Bottrop **10** B2
Boucau **40** A3
Bouchain **16** C1
Boudry **27** E4
Bougion **40** C2
Bouguenais **23** E4
Bouillargues **42** C3
Bouillon **17** E2
Bouilly **26** A2
Bouin **23** E4
Boulay-Moselle **18** A3
Boulazac **33** D4
Boulbon **42** C2
Bouligny **17** F3
Boulogne-Billancourt **16** A4
Boulogne-sur-Gesse **41** D4
Boulogne-sur-Mer **8** A4
Bouloire **24** B2
Boulouris **44** A3
Boulzicourt **17** D2
Bourbon-Lancy **34** C1
Bourbon-l'Archambault **34** B1
Bourbonne-les-Bains **26** C2
Bourbourg **8** A3
Bourbriac **22** C1
Bourcefranc-le-Chapus **32** B2
Bourdeaux **43** D1
Bourg **32** B4
Bourg-Achard **15** E3
Bourganeuf **33** F2
Bourg-Argental **35** D4
Bourg-de-Péage **35** E4
Bourg-de-Visa **41** D2
Bourg-en-Bresse **35** E2
Bourges **25** E4
Bourg-Lastic **34** A3
Bourg-lès-Valence **35** E4
Bourgneuf-en-Retz **23** E4
Bourgogne **17** D3
Bourgoin-Jallieu **35** E3
Bourg-St-Andéol **42** C1
Bourg-St-Maurice **36** A3
Bourgtheroulde-Infreville **15** E3
Bourguébus **15** D3
Bourgueil **24** B3
Bourmont **26** C2
Bournezeau **32** B1
Bourtange **4** C3
Boussac **33** F2
Boussières **27** D4
Boussois **16** C1
Boussu **16** C1
Boutersem **9** E4
Bouveret **36** A1
Bouvron **23** E3
Bouxières-aux-Dames **17** F4
Bouxwiller **18** B4
Bouzonville **18** A3
Bova **52** A4
Bovalino **52** B4
Bova Marina **52** A4
Bóveda *Spain* **54** A3
Bóveda *Spain* **56** A2
Bovegno **38** A2
Bovenden **11** E2
Boves *France* **16** A2
Boves *Italy* **44** B2
Boville Ernica **49** D2
Bovino **50** A2
Bøvlingbjerg **2** A1
Bovolone **38** C3
Bovrup **2** B4
Boxberg **13** F3
Boxdorf **13** E3
Boxmeer **10** A2
Boxtel **9** E2
Boynes **25** E2
Bozel **36** A3
Bozouls **42** A1
Bozzolo **38** B4
Bra **44** B1
Bracciano **48** B2
Bracieux **25** D3
Brackenheim **19** E3
Brædstrup **2** B2
Bràfim **58** C4
Braga **60** C1
Bragança **61** E1
Brahlstorf **6** B3
Braine **16** C3
Braine-l'Alleud **17** D1
Braine-le-Comte **17** D1
Braives **17** E1
Brake (Unterweser) **5** E3
Brakel *Belgium* **8** C4
Brakel *Ger.* **11** D2
Brallo di Pregola **45** D1
Bramans **36** A4
Bramberg am Wildkogel **29** F3
Bramdrupdam **2** B3
Bramming **2** A3
Bramsche *Ger.* **10** B1
Bramsche *Ger.* **10** C1
Bramstedt **5** E3
Brancaleone **52** A4
Brand *Austria* **28** C4
Brand *Ger.* **20** C2
Brande **2** B2
Brande-Hörnerkirchen **6** A2
Brandenberg **29** F3
Brandenburg **12** C1
Brand-Erbisdorf **13** D4
Branderup **2** B3
Brandis **13** D2
Brandshagen **7** E1
Branges **35** E1
Branne **32** C4
Branõsera **55** E2
Brantôme **33** D3
Branzi **38** A2
Braojos **63** D2
Braone **38** B2
Brassac **41** F3
Brasschaat **9** D3
Braubach **18** C1
Braud-et-St-Louis **32** B4
Braunau am Inn **30** A1
Braunfels **11** D4
Braunlage **11** F2
Bräunlingen **28** A2
Braunsbedra **12** C3
Braunschweig **11** F1
Bray-sur-Seine **25** F1
Bray-sur-Somme **16** B2
Brazatortas **69** D3
Brazey-en-Plaine **26** C4
Brea **64** B1
Brea de Tajo **63** E4
Brécey **23** F1
Brech **22** C3
Brecht **9** D3
Breda *Neth.* **9** E2
Breda *Spain* **59** E3
Breddenberg **5** D4
Breddin **7** D4
Bredebro **2** A3
Bredene **8** B3
Bredereiche **7** E3
Bredstedt **2** A4
Bredsten **2** B2
Bree **9** F3
Breese **6** C4
Breganze **38** C3
Bregenz **28** C3
Bregninge **2** C4
Breguzzo **38** B2
Bréhal **23** E1
Bréhan **23** D2
Brehna **12** C2
Breidenbach *France* **18** B3
Breidenbach *Ger.* **11** D4
Breiholz **6** A1
Breil **28** B4
Breil-sur-Roya **44** B2
Breisach am Rhein **27** F2
Breitenbach **27** F3
Breitenbach (Schauenburg) **11** E3
Breitenbach am Herzberg **11** E4
Breitenbach am Inn **29** F3
Breitenberg **30** B1
Breitenbrunn **20** B3
Breitenburg **6** A2
Breitenfelde **6** B2
Breitengüßbach **20** A2
Breitenhagen **12** C2
Breitnau **28** A2
Breitscheid **10** C4
Breitungen **11** F4
Brejning **2** B2
Breklum **2** A4
Brelingen (Wedemark) **6** A4
Bremdal **2** A1
Bremen **5** E3
Bremerhaven **5** E2
Bremervörde **5** F3
Bremgarten **28** A3
Bremm **18** B2
Brem-sur-Mer **32** A1
Brenderup **2** C3
Brenes **73** F2
Brennero **29** E4
Breno **38** A2
Brénod **35** F2

Brens **41** F2
Brensbach **19** D2
Brenzone **38** B3
Brescello **38** B4
Brescia **38** A3
Breskens **8** C3
Bressana Bottarone **37** E4
Bressanone **38** C1
Bressols **41** E2
Bressuire **32** C1
Brest **22** A2
Breteil **23** E2
Bretenoux **33** F4
Breteuil *France* **24** C1
Breteuil *France* **16** A3
Brétignolles-sur-Mer **32** A1
Bretnig **13** E3
Bretocino **54** C4
Bretoncelles **24** C1
Bretten **19** D4
Brettville-sur-Laize **15** D4
Bretzenheim **18** C2
Breuberg-Neustadt **19** D2
Breuil-Cervinia **36** B2
Breuil-Magné **32** B2
Breukelen **9** E1
Breum **1** E3
Breuna **11** E3
Brevörde **11** E2
Brézolles **24** C1
Briançon **36** A4
Briare **25** E3
Briatexte **41** F3
Bricherasio **44** A1
Bricquebec **14** B3
Brides-les-Bains **36** A3
Brie **33** D3
Briec **22** B2
Brie-Comte-Robert **16** B4
Briedel **18** B2
Brielle **9** D2
Brienne-le-Château **26** B1
Briennon **35** D2
Brienon-sur-Armançon **25** F2
Brienz **27** F4
Brienza **50** B3
Briesen **13** E1
Brieske **13** E3
Brieskow-Finkenheerd **13** F1
Briesnig **13** F2
Brietlingen **6** B3
Briey **17** F3
Brig **36** C2
Brignais **35** D3
Brignoles **43** E3
Brihuega **63** E3
Brilon **11** D3
Brinches **67** D4
Brincones **61** F2
Brindisi **51** E3
Brindisi Montagna **50** B3
Brinkum *Ger.* **5** D3
Brinkum *Ger.* **5** E3
Brinon-sur-Beuvron **25** F3
Brinon-sur-Sauldre **25** E3
Briones **56** B3
Brionne **15** E3
Brioude **34** C4
Brioux-sur-Boutonne **32** C2
Briouze **24** A1
Briscous **40** A3
Brisighella **46** C2
Brissac-Quince **24** A3
Britelo **60** C1
Britz **7** F4
Brive-la-Gaillarde **33** E4
Briviesca **56** A3
Brix **14** B3
Brixen im Thale **29** F3
Broager **2** B4
Brobyværk **2** C3
Broc **36** B1
Bröckel **11** F1
Brockum **11** D1
Broderstorf **7** D2
Brody **13** F2
Broglie **15** E4
Brohm **7** E2
Brokdorf **5** F2
Brokstedt **6** A2
Brome **6** B4
Bronchales **64** B3
Brønderslev **1** F2
Broni **37** E4
Bronice **13** F2
Brøns **2** A3
Broons **23** D2
Brørup **2** B3
Brossac **32** C4
Brotas **66** C3
Broto **58** A2
Brottes **26** C2
Brou **24** C2
Brouvelieures **27** E2
Brouwershaven **8** C2
Brovst **1** E2
Brozas **67** E1
Brozzo **38** A3
Bruay-en-Artois **16** B1
Bruchhausen-Vilsen **5** F4
Bruchköbel **19** D1
Bruchsal **19** D3
Brück **13** D1
Bruck an der Großglocknerstraße **30** A3
Bruck an der Leitha **31** F2
Bruck an der Mur **31** D3
Brücken **18** B3
Brücken (Helme) **12** B3
Brücken (Pfalz) **18** B3
Brückl **30** C4
Bruckmühl **29** F2
Brüel **6** C2
Brugg **28** A3
Brugge **8** C3
Brüggen *Ger.* **11** E1
Brüggen *Ger.* **10** A3
Brugnato **45** E2
Brugnera **39** E2
Brühl *Ger.* **19** D3
Brühl *Germany* **10** B4
Bruinisse **9** D2
Brûlon **24** A2
Brumath **27** F1
Brunau **6** C4
Brundby **2** C2
Brunete **63** D3
Brunico **39** D1
Brunn **7** E2
Brunnen **28** A4
Brunsbüttel **5** F2
Brunssum **10** A3
Brusago **38** C2
Brüsewitz **6** C2
Brusio **38** A2
Brussel **9** D4
Brusson **36** C3
Brüssow **7** F3
Bruttig-Fankel **18** B2
Bruyères **27** E2
Bruz **23** E2
Bryrup **2** B2
Bû **25** D1
Buarcos **60** B4
Bubbio **44** C1
Bubry **22** C2
Bucchianico **49** E1
Buccinasco **37** D3
Buccino **50** B3
Bucelas **66** A3
Buch **28** C2
Buch am Erlbach **29** F1
Buchbach **29** F1
Buch bei Jenbach **29** E3
Buchboden **28** C3
Büchel **18** B1
Büchen **6** B3
Buchen (Odenwald) **19** E3
Büchenbeuren **18** B2
Buchholz **7** D3
Buchholz (Aller) **6** A4
Buchkirchen **30** C2
Büchlberg **30** B1
Buchloe **29** D2
Bucholz in der Nordheide **6** A3
Buchs **28** B4
Buchy **15** F3
Bucine **46** B3
Bücken **5** F4
Buckow Märkische Schweiz **7** F4
Bückwitz **7** D4
Budel **9** E3
Büdelsdorf **6** A1
Budens **72** A2
Budia **63** F3
Büdingen **19** E1
Budoia **39** E2
Budrio **46** B1
Bueña **64** B3
Buenache de Alarcón **70** B1
Buenache de la Sierra **64** A4
Buenaventura **62** B4
Buenavista de Valdavia **55** E3
Buendía **63** F3
Bueu **53** E3
Bufleben **11** F3
Bugarra **71** D1
Bugeat **33** F3
Bugnara **49** E2
Bühl **28** A1
Bühlertal **28** A1
Bühlertann **19** F4
Bühlerzell **19** F4
Buia **39** E2
Buis-les-Baronnies **43** D2
Buitenpost **4** B3
Buitrago del Lozoya **63** D2
Bujalance **68** C4
Bujaraloz **58** A4
Buko **12** C2
Bülach **28** A3
Bulgnéville **27** D2
Bülkau **5** F2
Bullas **76** B1
Bulle **36** B1
Bullerup **2** C3
Bully-les-Mines **16** B1
Bünde **11** D1
Bunde **5** D3
Bundenbach **18** B2
Bunderhee **5** D3
Buniel **55** F3
Buñol **71** D2
Bunschoten-Spakenburg **9** E1
Buochs **28** A4
Buonabitacolo **50** B4
Buonalbergo **50** A2
Buonconvento **46** B4
Buonvicino **52** A1
Bur **2** A1
Burbach **10** C4
Burbáguena **64** B2
Burdinne **17** E1
Büren **11** D2
Büren an der Aare **27** F4
Burg **13** E2
Burg (Dithmarschen) **5** F2
Burganes de Valverde **54** C4
Burgau *Austria* **31** E4
Burgau *Ger.* **29** D1
Burgau *Port.* **72** A2
Burg auf Fehmarn **6** C1
Burg bei Magdeburg **12** C1
Burgberg im Allgäu **29** D3
Burgbernheim **20** A3
Burgdorf *Ger.* **11** F1
Burgdorf *Ger.* **11** F1
Burgdorf *Switz.* **27** F4
Burgebrach **20** A2
Bürgel **12** B4
Burghausen **30** A2
Burgh-Haamstede **8** C2
Burgkirchen an der Alz **30** A2
Burgkunstadt **20** B1
Bürglen *Switz.* **28** B3
Bürglen *Switz.* **28** A4
Burglengenfeld **20** C3
Burgohondo **62** B3
Burgos **55** F3
Burgsalach **20** B4
Burgsinn **19** E1
Burgstädt **13** D4
Bürgstadt **19** E2
Burg Stargand **7** E3
Burgthann **20** B3
Burgtonna **12** A3
Burguete **57** D2
Burgui **57** E3
Burguillos **73** E1
Burguillos del Cerro **67** E3
Burguillos de Toledo **63** D4
Burgwindheim **20** A2
Burhave (Butjadingen) **5** E3
Buriasco **36** B4
Burie **32** C3
Burjassot **71** D1
Burkardroth **19** F1
Burkhardtsdorf **13** D4
Burlada **57** D2
Burladingen **28** B1
Burlats **41** F3
Bürmoos **30** A2
Burón **55** D2
Buronzo **36** C3
Buros **40** B3
Burow **7** E2
Burriana **65** D4
Bürs **28** C4
Bursfelde **11** E2
Bürstadt **19** D2
Burujón **62** C4
Busalla **45** D1
Busana **46** A1
Busca **44** B1
Busdorf **6** A1
Busigny **16** C2
Busot **71** D3
Bussang **27** E2
Busseto **38** A4
Bussière-Badil **33** D3
Bussière-Galant **33** E3
Bussière-Poitevine **33** E2
Bussigny **36** A1
Bussi sul Tirino **49** E1
Büßleben **12** B4
Bussolengo **38** B3
Bussoleno **36** B4
Bussum **9** E1
Bustillo del Páramo **54** C3
Busto Arsizio **37** D3
Büsum **5** E1
Bütgenbach **10** A4
Bützow **7** D3
Bütschwil **28** B3
Buttelstedt **12** B3
Buttigliera d'Asti **36** C4
Buttstädt **12** B3
Büttstedt **11** F3
Butzbach **11** D4
Bützow **6** C2
Buurse **10** B1
Buxerolles **33** D1
Buxheim **28** C2
Buxières-les-Mines **34** B1
Buxtehude **6** A3
Buxy **26** B4
Buzançais **33** E1
Buzancy **17** E3
Buzet-sur-Baïse **40** C2
Buzet-sur-Tarn **41** E3
Bybjerg **3** E2
Byhleguhre **13** E2
Bylderup-Bov **2** B4

C

Cabanac-et-Villagrains **40** B1
Cabañaquinta **54** C2
Cabañas del Castillo **68** B1
Cabanas de Viriato **60** C3
Cabañas Raras **54** B3
Cabanes **65** D4
Cabanillas **57** D4
Cabasse **43** F3
Cabassers **58** B4
Cabeça Gorda **67** D4
Cabeção **66** C2
Cabeceiras de Basto **60** C1
Cabeço de Vide **67** D2
Cabella Ligure **45** D1
Cabeza de Framontanos **61** E2
Cabeza del Buey **68** B3
Cabeza del Caballo **61** E2
Cabeza la Vaca **67** F4
Cabezamesada **63** E4
Cabezarados **69** D3
Cabezarrubias del Puerto **69** D3
Cabezas del Villar **62** B3
Cabezas Rubias **73** D1
Cabezón de Cameros **56** B4
Cabezón de la Sal **55** E1
Cabezón de Liébana **55** E2
Cabezuela del Valle **62** A4
Cabo de Palos **76** C2
Cabolafuente **64** A2
Cabra **74** C2
Cabração **60** B1
Cabra del Camp **58** C4
Cabra del Santo Cristo **75** E1
Cabra de Mora **64** C3
Cabrejas del Pinar **56** B4
Cabrela **66** C3
Cabril **60** C4
Cabrillanes **54** B2
Cabrillas **61** F3
Cacabelos **54** B3
Caçarelhos **61** E1
Caccuri **52** C2
Cacém **66** A3
Cáceres **67** F1
Cachopo **72** B2
Cacín **75** D2
Cadalso de los Vidrios **62** C4
Cadaqués **59** F2
Cadaval **66** B2
Cadelbosco di Sopra **38** B4
Cadenazzo **37** D2
Cadenberge **5** F2
Cadenet **43** D3
Cadeo **38** A4
Cádiar **75** E3
Cadillac **40** B1

Cádiz **73** E4
Cadolzburg **20** A3
Cadoneghe **39** D3
Cadours **41** D3
Cadreita **57** D3
Cadrete **64** C1
Caen **15** D3
Cafasse **36** B4
Caggiano **50** B3
Cagli **47** D3
Cagnac-les-Mines **41** F2
Cagnano Varano **50** B1
Cagnes-sur-Mer **44** A3
Cahors **41** E1
Cahuzac-sur-Vère **41** F2
Caiazzo **49** F3
Caión **53** E1
Cairo Montenotte **44** C1
Caissargues **42** C3
Caivano **49** E4
Cajarc **41** E1
Cala **67** F4
Calabardina **76** B2
Calabritto **50** A3
Calaceite **65** E2
Calaf **58** C3
Calafell **58** C4
Calahonda **75** D3
Calahorra **56** C3
Calais **8** A3
Calalzo di Cadore **39** D1
Calamandrana **44** C1
Calamocha **64** B2
Calamonte **67** F3
Calañas **73** D1
Calanda **65** D2
Calanna **52** A4
Calasparra **76** B1
Calatayud **64** B2
Calatorao **64** B1
Calau **13** E2
Calbe (Saale) **12** B2
Calcinato **38** B3
Calcio **38** A3
Caldarola **47** E4
Caldaro sulla Strada del Vino **38** C1
Caldas da Rainha **66** B2
Caldas de Reis **53** E3
Caldas de Vizela **60** C1
Caldearenas **57** E3
Caldelas **60** C1
Caldelas Taipas **60** C1
Calden **11** E3
Caldes de Montbui **59** D3
Caldes d'Estrac **59** E3
Caldogno **38** C3
Caldonazzo **38** C2
Calella **59** E3
Calendário **60** B1
Calenzano **46** B2
Calera de León **67** F4
Calera y Chozas **62** B4
Caleruega **55** F4
Càlig **65** E3
Calimera **51** F4
Calitri **50** B3
Calizzano **44** B2
Callac **22** C2
Callantsoog **4** A4
Callas **43** F3
Callian **43** F3
Calliano **36** C4
Callosa d'En Sarrià **71** E3
Callosa de Segura **76** C1
Calmont *France* **41** E4
Calmont *France* **41** F2
Calolziocorte **37** E2
Calomarde **64** B3
Calonge **59** E3
Calonne-Ricouart **16** A1
Calpe **71** E3
Caltignaga **37** D3
Caltojar **63** E1
Caluire-et-Cuire **35** E3
Caluso **36** C3
Calvão **60** B3
Calvarrasa de Abajo **62** A2
Calvarrasa de Arriba **62** A2
Calvello **50** B3
Calvi dell'Umbria **48** C1
Calvi Risorta **49** E3
Calvisson **42** C3
Calvörde **12** B1
Calvos **53** F4
Calw **28** A1
Calzada de Calatrava **69** D3
Calzada de Valdunciel **62** A2
Calzadilla **61** E4
Calzadilla de los Barros **67** F4
Camaldoli **46** C2
Camaleño **55** E2
Camallera **59** E2
Camañas **64** C3
Camarasa **58** B3
Camarena **62** C4
Camarena de la Sierra **64** C4
Camarès **42** A2
Camaret-sur-Mer **22** A2
Camarillas **64** C3
Camariñas **53** D2
Camarles **65** E3
Camarzana de Tera **54** C4
Camas **73** E2
Cambados **53** E3
Cambes **40** B1
Cambil **75** D1
Cambon **41** F2
Cambra de Baixo **60** C3
Cambrai **16** B2
Cambre **53** E1
Cambrils de Mar **58** B4
Cambs **6** C2
Camburg **12** B3
Camerano **47** E3
Cameri **37** D3
Camerino **47** E4
Camerota **50** B4
Camigliatello Silano **52** B2
Camin **6** B3
Caminha **53** E4
Caminomorisco **61** F3
Caminreal **64** B2
Cammer **13** D1
Cammin **7** D2
Camogli **45** D1
Camon **16** A2
Camors **22** C3
Campagna **50** A3
Campagnano di Roma **48** C2
Campagnatico **46** B4
Campagne-lès-Hesdin **16** A1
Campan **40** C4
Campana **52** C2
Campanario **68** B3
Campano **73** E4
Campaspero **62** C1
Campbon **23** E3
Campdevànol **59** D2
Campeã **60** C2
Campello **71** D4
Campello sul Clitunne **47** D4
Campelo **60** C4
Campelos **66** A2
Campénéac **23** D2
Campertogno **36** C3
Campi Bisenzio **46** B2
Campiglia Marittima **46** A4
Campiglia Soana **36** B3
Campillo de Alto Buey **70** B1
Campillo de Arenas **75** D2
Campillo de Dueñas **64** B2
Campillo de Llerena **68** A3
Campillos **74** B3
Campillos-Paravientos **64** B4
Campinho **67** D4
Campisábalos **63** E2
Campi Salentina **51** F3
Campli **47** E4
Campo *Port.* **60** C1
Campo *Spain* **58** B2
Campobasso **49** F3
Campo da Feira **53** E2
Campodarsego **39** D3
Campo de Caso **55** D2
Campo de Criptana **69** E2
Campo de San Pedro **63** D1
Campodimele **49** D3
Campo di Trens **29** E4
Campodolcino **37** E1
Campoformido **39** E2
Campofrío **73** D1
Campo Lameiro **53** E3
Campoli Appennino **49** D2
Campo Ligure **44** C1
Campolongo Maggiore **39** D3
Campo Lugar **68** A2
Campo Maior **67** E2
Campomarino *Italy* **50** A1
Campomarino *Italy* **51** E4
Campomorone **45** D1
Camponaraya **54** B3
Camponogara **39** D3
Campora San Giovanni **52** A2
Campo Redondo **72** A1
Camporgiano **46** A2
Camporosso **44** B2
Camporrells **58** B3
Camporrobles **70** C1
Campos **60** C1
Camposampiero **39** D3
Camposanto **38** C4
Campotéjar **75** D2
Campotosto **49** D1
Campo Tures **29** F4
Camprodon **59** D2
Camuñas **69** E2
Cañada **71** D3
Cañada de Benatanduz **64** C3
Cañada del Hoyo **64** A4
Cañada Vellida **64** C3
Canale **44** B1
Canalejas del Arroyo **63** F3
Canalejas de Peñafiel **63** D1
Canals **71** D3
Canàl San Bovo **38** C2
Cañamares **63** F3
Cañamero **68** B2
Canaro **38** C4
Cañaveral **67** F1
Cañaveral de León **67** F4
Cañaveras **63** F3
Cañaveruelas **63** F3
Canazei **39** D1
Cancale **23** E1
Cancarix **70** B4
Cancellara **50** B3
Cancello ed Arnone **49** E4
Cancon **41** D1
Candanchú **57** E2
Candás **54** C1
Candasnos **58** A4
Candé **23** F3
Candela **50** B2
Candelario **62** A3
Candeleda **62** B4
Candelo **36** C3
Candemil **53** E4
Candia Lomellina **37** D4
Candilichera **56** C4
Candín **54** B2
Canedo **60** B2
Canelli **44** C1
Canena **69** E4
Canepina **48** B1
Canero **54** B1
Canet **42** B3
Canet de Mar **59** E3
Cañete **64** B4
Cañete de las Torres **74** C1
Cañete la Real **74** B3
Canet-en-Roussillon **59** E1
Canet lo Roig **65** E3
Canet-Plage **59** E1
Cangas **53** E3
Cangas del Narcea **54** B2
Cangas de Onís **55** D1
Canha **66** B3
Canhestros **66** C4
Canicosa de la Sierra **56** B4
Caniles **75** E2
Canillas de Aceituno **74** C3
Canino **48** B1
Cañizal **62** B2
Cañizares **63** F3
Cañizo **54** C4
Canjáyar **75** E3
Canna **50** C4
Cannara **47** D4
Cannero Riviera **37** D2
Cannes **44** A3
Canneto **46** A4
Canneto sull'Oglio **38** B4
Cannobio **37** D2
Cano **67** D2
Canolo **52** B4
Canosa di Puglia **50** C2
Cánovas **76** B2
Canredondo **63** F3
Cansano **49** E2
Cantagallo **46** B2
Cantalapiedra **62** B2
Cantalejo **63** D2
Cantalice **48** C1
Cantalpino **62** B2
Cantanhede **60** B3
Cantavieja **65** D3
Cantenac **32** B4
Canteras **76** C2
Cantiano **47** D3
Cantillana **74** A1
Cantimpalos **62** C2
Cantoira **36** B3
Cantoria **76** A2
Cantù **37** D3
Cany-Barville **15** E2
Caorle **39** E3
Capaccio **50** A3
Capalbio **48** A1
Capannoli **46** A3
Capannori **46** A2
Caparica **66** A3
Caparrosa **60** C3
Caparroso **57** D3
Cap-Blanc **71** E2
Capbreton **40** A3
Cap d'Agde **42** B4
Capdenac-Gare **41** F1
Capelle aan de IJssel **9** D2
Capellen **17** F2
Capendu **41** F4
Capestang **42** A3
Capestrano **49** E1
Capileira **75** D3
Capilla **68** B3
Capinha **61** D4
Capistrello **49** D2
Capodimonte **48** B1
Capo di Ponte **38** B2
Capoliveri **46** A4
Capolona **46** C3
Caposele **50** A3
Cappadocia **49** D2
Cappeln (Oldenburg) **5** E4
Capracotta **49** E2
Capraia Isola **45** E4
Capranica **48** B1
Capri **49** E4
Capriati a Volturno **49** E3
Caprino Bergamasco **37** E3
Caprino Veronese **38** B3
Captieux **40** B2
Capua **49** E3
Capurso **51** D2
Capvern-les-Bains **40** C4
Carabaña **63** E4
Caracuel de Calatrava **69** D3
Caraglio **44** B1
Caraman **41** E3
Caramanico Terme **49** E1
Caramulo **60** C3
Caranga **54** C2
Caranguejeira **66** B1
Carapelle **50** B2
Carapinheira **60** B4
Carasco **45** D1
Caravaca de la Cruz **76** A1
Caravaggio **38** A3
Carbajales de Alba **62** A1
Carballeda de Avia **53** E3
Carballiño **53** F3
Carballo *Spain* **53** E2
Carballo *Spain* **53** F4
Carbellino **61** F2
Carbonera de Frentes **56** B4
Carboneras **76** A3
Carboneras de Guadazaón **64** A4
Carbonero El Mayor **62** C2
Carboneros **69** E4
Carbonìn **39** D1
Carbonne **41** E4
Carcaboso **61** F4
Carcabuey **74** C2
Carcaixent **71** D2
Carcans **32** B4
Carcans-Plage **32** B4
Carção **61** E1
Cárcar **56** C3
Carcare **44** C1
Carcassonne **41** F4
Carcastillo **57** D3
Carcelén **70** C2
Carcès **43** F3
Carchelejo **75** D1
Carcoforo **36** C2
Cardedeu **59** D3
Cardeña **69** D4
Cardeñadijo **55** F3
Cardenete **64** B4
Cardeñosa **62** B3
Cardeto **52** A4
Cardigos **66** C1
Cardinale **52** B3
Cardito **49** E3
Cardona **58** C3
Cardosas **72** A2
Carenas **64** B2
Carentan **14** B3
Carentoir **23** D3
Carhaix-Plouguer **22** C2
Caria **61** D4

Cariati **52** C1
Caridade **67** D3
Carife **50** A2
Carignan **17** E2
Carignano **36** C4
Cariñena **64** C2
Cariño **53** F1
Carinola **49** E3
Carisio **36** C3
Carisolo **38** B2
Carlantino **50** A1
Carlet **71** D2
Carlopoli **52** B2
Carlow **6** B2
Carlsberg **18** C3
Carlux **33** E4
Carmagnola **44** B1
Carmaux **41** F2
Carmena **62** C4
Cármenes **54** C2
Carmiano **51** F4
Carmona **74** A2
Carmonita **67** F2
Carnac **22** C3
Carnières **16** C1
Carnota **53** D2
Carnoules **43** F3
Carolei **52** B2
Carona **38** A2
Carosino **51** E3
Carovigno **51** E3
Carovilli **49** E2
Carpaneto Piacentino **38** A4
Carparola **48** B1
Carpegna **47** D3
Carpenedolo **38** B3
Carpentras **43** D2
Carpi **38** B4
Carpignano Salentino **51** F4
Carpignano Sesia **37** D3
Carpineti **46** A1
Carpineto Romano **49** D3
Carpino **50** B1
Carpinone **49** E2
Carpio **62** B2
Carpiquet **14** C3
Carquefou **23** E4
Carqueiranne **43** F4
Carracedelo **54** B3
Carral **53** E2
Carranque **63** D4
Carrapateira **72** A2
Carrapichana **61** D3
Carrara **45** E2
Carrascal del Obispo **62** A3
Carrascosa **63** F3
Carrascosa del Campo **63** F4
Carratraca **74** B3
Carrazeda de Ansiães **61** D2
Carrazedo de Montenegro **61** D1
Carreço **60** B1
Carregado **66** B2
Carregal do Sal **60** C3
Carregueiros **66** C1
Carreira *Port.* **66** B1
Carreira *Spain* **53** F1
Carreña de Cabrales **55** D2
Carreteira **53** F2
Carriazo **55** F1
Carriço **60** B4
Carrio **53** E1
Carrión de Calatrava **69** D2
Carrión de los Céspedes **73** E2
Carrión de los Condes **55** E3
Carrizo de la Ribera **54** C3
Carrizosa **69** F3
Carros **44** A3
Carrouges **24** A1
Carrù **44** B1
Carry-le-Rouet **43** D3
Cars **32** B4
Carsac-Aillac **33** E4
Carsoli **49** D2
Carspach **27** E3
Cartagena **76** C2
Cártama **74** B3
Cartaxo **66** B2
Cartaya **72** C2
Cartes **55** F1
Cartoceto **47** D2
Carucedo **54** B3
Carunchio **49** F2
Carvalhal *Port.* **66** C1
Carvalhal *Port.* **66** B4
Carvalho de Egas **61** D2
Carvalhosa **60** C2
Carviçais **61** E2
Carvin **16** B1
Carvoeira **66** A2
Carvoeiro **72** A2
Casabermeja **74** C3
Casabona **52** C2
Casa Branca *Port.* **66** C3
Casa Branca *Port.* **67** D2
Casacalenda **50** A1
Casagiove **49** E3
Casa l'Abate **51** F3
Casalanguida **49** F2
Casalarreina **56** B3
Casalbordino **49** F1
Casalbore **50** A2
Casalborgone **36** C4
Casalbuono **50** B4
Casalbuttano ed Uniti **38** A4
Casàl Cermelli **44** C1
Casàl di Principe **49** E4
Casalecchio di Reno **46** B1
Casale Monferrato **37** D4
Casaletto Spartano **50** B4
Casalfiumanese **46** B2
Casalgrande **46** A1
Casalgrasso **44** B1
Casalmaggiore **38** B4
Casalnuovo Monterotaro **50** A1
Casalpusterlengo **38** A4
Casalvecchio di Puglia **50** A1
Casàl Velino **50** A4
Casamassima **51** D2
Casarabonela **74** B3
Casarano **51** F4
Casar de Cáceres **67** F1
Casar de Palomero **61** F3
Casarejos **56** B4
Casares **74** A4
Casares de las Hurdes **61** F3
Casariche **74** B2
Casarrubios del Monte **63** D4
Casarsa della Delizia **39** E2
Casarza Ligure **45** D2
Casas Altas **64** B4
Casas Bajas **64** B4
Casas de Benitez **70** B2
Casas de Don Pedro **68** B2
Casas de Fernando Alonso **70** A2
Casas de Haro **70** A2
Casas de Juan Gil **70** C2
Casas de Juan Núñez **70** C2
Casas de Lázaro **70** A3
Casas del Monte **62** A4
Casas de los Pinos **70** A2
Casas del Puerto **70** C4
Casas de Millán **67** F1
Casas de Reina **67** F4
Casas de Ves **70** C2
Casas-Ibáñez **70** C2
Casasimarro **70** B2
Casas Novas de Mares **67** D3
Casasola de Arión **62** B1
Casatejada **62** A4
Casatenovo **37** E3
Casavieja **62** B4
Cascais **66** A3
Cascante **57** D4
Cascante del Río **64** C4
Casciana Terme **46** A3
Cascina **46** A3
Casebres **66** B3
Cáseda **57** D3
Casei Gerola **37** D4
Casekow **7** F3
Casella **45** D1
Caselle in Pittari **50** B4
Caselle Torinese **36** B4
Case Perrone **51** D3
Caseras **65** E2
Caserras **59** D3
Caserta **49** F4
Casével **72** B1
Casillas **62** C3
Casillas de Flores **61** E3
Casina **46** A1
Casinos **71** D1
Casola in Lunigiana **45** E2
Casola Valsenio **46** B2
Casole d'Elsa **46** B3
Casoli **49** E2
Casoria **49** E4
Caspe **58** A4
Casperia **48** C1
Cassà de la Selva **59** E3
Cassagnes-Bégonhès **41** F2
Cassano allo Ionio **52** B1
Cassano delle Murge **51** D3
Cassano Magnano **37** D3
Cassano Spinola **45** D1
Cassel **8** B4
Casseneuil **41** D1
Cassine **44** C1
Cassino **49** E3
Cassis **43** E4
Cassola **39** D3
Castagliona Olona **37** D3
Castagnaro **38** C4
Castagneto Carducci **46** A4
Castagnole delle Lanze **44** C1
Castagnole Monferrato **36** C4
Castañar de Ibor **68** B1
Castañares de Rioja **56** B3
Castanet-Tolosan **41** E3
Castanheira **61** D2
Castanheira de Pêra **60** C4
Castano Primo **37** D3
Castasegna **37** E1
Casteggio **37** E4
Castejón **57** D4
Castejón del Puente **58** A3
Castejón de Monegros **65** D1
Castejón de Sos **58** B2
Castejón de Valdejasa **57** E4
Castelbellino **47** E3
Castèl Bolognese **46** C1
Castelcivita **50** A3
Castèl d'Ario **38** B4
Castel de Cabra **64** C3
Casteldelfino **44** A1
Castèl del Monte **49** D1
Castèl del Piano **46** B4
Castèl del Rio **46** B2
Castèl di Lama **47** E4
Castèl di Sangro **49** E2
Casteleiro **61** D4
Castelfidardo **47** E3
Castelfiorentino **46** B3
Castelflorite **58** A3
Castèl Focognano **46** C3
Castelforte **49** E3
Castelfranci **50** A3
Castelfranco di Sopra **46** B3
Castelfranco di Sotto **46** A3
Castelfranco Emilia **46** B1
Castelfranco Veneto **39** D3
Castèl Frentano **49** E1
Castèl Gandolfo **48** C2
Castelginest **41** E3
Castèl Giorgio **48** B1
Castèl Goffredo **38** B3
Castelgrande **50** B3
Casteljaloux **40** C2
Castell **20** A2
Castellabate **50** A4
Castell'Alfero **36** C4
Castellalto **47** F4
Castellammare di Stabia **49** F4
Castellamonte **36** B3
Castellana Grotte **51** D3
Castellane **43** F2
Castellaneta **51** D3
Castellanos de Castro **55** F3
Castellarano **46** A1
Castellar de la Frontera **74** A4
Castellar de la Muela **64** B3
Castellar de la Ribera **58** C3
Castellar de Santiago **69** E3
Castellar de Santisteban **69** E4
Castell'Arquato **38** A4
Castell'Azzara **46** C4
Castellazzo Bormida **44** C1
Castelldans **58** B4
Castell d'Aro **59** E3
Castell de Cabres **65** D3
Castell de Castells **71** E3
Castelldefels **59** D4
Castell de Ferro **75** D3
Castelleone **38** A3
Castelletto sopra Ticino **37** D3
Castellfort **65** D3
Castellina in Chianti **46** B3
Castellina Marittima **46** A3
Castelliri **49** D2
Castellnou de Bassella **58** C3
Castellnovo **65** D4
Castello d'Argile **46** B1
Castelló de Farfanya **58** B3
Castelló de la Plana **65** D4
Castelló d'Empúries **59** E2
Castelló de Rugat **71** D3
Castello di Annone **36** C4
Castellote **65** D3
Castello Tesino **38** C2
Castellserà **58** B3
Castellterçol **59** D3
Castellucchio **38** B4
Castelluccio dei Sauri **50** B2
Castelluccio Inferiore **50** B4
Castellucio Valmaggiore **50** A2
Castèl Madama **48** C2
Càstel Maggiore **46** B1
Castelmagno **44** A1
Castelmassa **38** C4
Castelmauro **50** A1
Castelmoron-sur-Lot **40** C1
Castelnaudary **41** F3
Castelnau-d'Auzan **40** C2
Castelnau-de-Brassac **41** F3
Castelnau-de-Médoc **32** B4
Castelnau-de-Montmiral **41** E2
Castelnau d'Estréfonds **41** E3
Castelnau-le-Lez **42** B3
Castelnau-Magnoac **41** D4
Castelnau-Montratier **41** E2
Castelnau-Rivière-Basse **40** C3
Castelnovo di Sotto **38** B4
Castelnovo ne'Monti **46** A1
Castelnuovo Berardenga **46** B3
Castelnuovo della Daunia **50** A1
Castelnuovo di Garfagnana **46** A2
Castelnuovo di Porto **48** C2
Castelnuovo di Val di Cecina **46** A4
Castelnuovo Don Bosco **36** C4
Castelnuovo Rangone **46** A1
Castelnuovo Scrivia **37** D4
Castelo Bom **61** E3
Castelo Branco *Port.* **61** E2
Castelo Branco *Port.* **67** D1
Castelo de Paiva **60** C2
Castelo de Vide **67** D2
Castelo do Neiva **60** B1
Castelões **60** C2
Castelplanio **47** E3
Castelraimondo **47** D4
Castèl Ritaldi **47** D4
Castelrotto **38** C1
Castèl San Giovanni **37** E4
Castel San Lorenzo **50** A4
Castèl San Niccolò **46** C3
Castèl San Pietro Terme **46** B1
Castèl Sant'Angelo **49** D1
Castelsantangelo sul Nera **47** E4
Castelsaraceno **50** B4
Castelsarrasin **41** D2
Castelseras **65** D2
Castelverde **38** A4
Castelvetere in Val Fortore **50** A1
Castelvetro Placentino **38** A4
Castèl Viscardo **46** C4
Castèl Volturno **49** E4
Castenaso **46** B1
Castets **40** A2
Castielfabib **64** B4
Castiello de Jaca **57** E3
Castiglioncello **46** A3
Castiglione dei Pepoli **46** B2

Castiglione del Lago 46 C4
Castiglione della Pescaia 46 A4
Castiglione della Stiviere 38 B3
Castiglione d'Orcia 46 B4
Castiglione in Teverina 48 B1
Castiglione Messer Marino 49 F2
Castiglion Fiorentino 46 C3
Castignano 47 E4
Castilblanco 68 B2
Castilblanco de los Arroyos 73 E1
Castiliscar 57 D3
Castilleja de la Cuesta 73 E2
Castillejar 75 F1
Castillejo de Martin Viejo 61 E3
Castillejo de Mesleón 63 D2
Castillejo de Robledo 63 D1
Castillo de Bayuela 62 C4
Castillo de Garcimuñoz 70 A1
Castillo de Locubín 75 D2
Castillon-en-Couserans 41 D4
Castillon-la-Bataille 32 C4
Castillonnès 41 D1
Castillo-Nuevo 57 E3
Castilruiz 56 C4
Castione della Presolana 38 A2
Castiòns di Strada 39 E2
Castrejón de la Peña 55 E2
Castrelo do Val 54 A4
Castres 41 F3
Castricum 9 D1
Castries 42 B3
Castrignano del Capo 51 F4
Castril 75 E1
Castrillo de Don Juan 55 F4
Castrillo de Duero 63 D1
Castrillo de la Reina 56 A4
Castrillo de la Vega 63 D1
Castrillo Tejeriego 62 C1
Castro *Italy* 51 F4
Castro *Spain* 53 F3
Castrobarto 56 A2
Castrocalbón 54 C4
Castro Caldelas 54 A3
Castrocaro Terme 46 C2
Castrocontrigo 54 B4
Castro Daire 60 C2
Castro dei Volsci 49 D3
Castro del Río 74 C1
Castro de Ouro 54 A1
Castro de Rei 54 A2
Castrogonzalo 54 C4
Castrojeriz 55 E3
Castro Laboreiro 53 E4
Castro Marim 72 C2
Castromocho 55 D4
Castromonte 55 D4
Castronuevo 54 C4
Castronuño 62 B1
Castronuovo di St'Andrea 50 C4
Castropignano 49 F2
Castropodame 54 B3
Castropol 54 A1
Castrop-Rauxel 10 B2
Castro-Urdiales 56 A1
Castro Verde 72 B1
Castroverde 54 A2
Castroverde de Campos 55 D4
Castrovillari 52 B1
Castuera 68 B3
Catadau 71 D2
Catanzaro 52 B3
Catanzaro Marina 52 B3
Catarroja 71 D2
Catí 65 D3
Catignano 49 E1
Cativelos 61 D3
Catoira 53 E3
Catral 76 C1
Cattenom 17 F3
Catterfeld 11 F4
Cattolica 47 D2
Catus 41 E1
Caudan 22 C3
Caudebec-lès-Elbeuf 15 E3
Caudete 70 C3
Caudete de las Fuentes 70 C1
Caudiel 64 C4
Caudry 16 C2
Caulnes 23 D2
Caulonia 52 B4
Caumont-l'Éventé 14 C4
Caumont-sur-Durance 43 D2
Caunes-Minervois 41 F3
Caussade 41 E2
Cautano 49 F3
Cauterets 40 C4
Cava de'Tirreni 50 A3
Cavaglià 36 C3
Cavaillon 43 D2
Cavalaire-sur-Mer 43 F4
Cavaleiro 72 A1
Cavalese 38 C2
Cavallermaggiore 44 B1
Cavallino 39 E3
Cava Manara 37 D4
Cavargna 37 D2
Cavarzere 39 D4
Cavazzo Carnico 39 E1
Cave 48 C2
Cave del Predil 39 F1
Caveirac 42 C2
Cavezzo 38 B4
Cavignac 32 C4
Cavour 44 A1
Cavriago 46 A1
Cavriglia 46 B3
Caxarias 66 B1
Cayeux-sur-Mer 15 F1
Caylus 41 E2
Cazalegas 62 C4
Cazalilla 69 D4
Cazalla de la Sierra 68 A4
Cazals 41 E1
Cazaubon 40 C2
Cazères 41 D4
Cazes-Mondenard 41 E2
Cazilhac 41 F4
Cazis 28 B4
Cazorla 69 F4
Cea *Spain* 55 D3
Cea *Spain* 53 F3
Ceanuri 56 B2
Ceaucé 23 F1
Cebazat 34 B3
Cebolla 62 C4
Cebreros 62 C3
Ceccano 49 D3
Cecina 46 A3
Ceclavín 67 E1
Cedães 61 D1
Cedegolo 38 B2
Cedeira 53 F1
Cedillo 67 D1
Cedillo del Condado 63 D4
Cedrillas 64 C3
Cedynia 7 F4
Cée 53 D2
Ceggia 39 E3
Ceglie Messapica 51 E3
Cehegín 76 A1
Ceinos de Campos 55 D4
Ceira 60 C4
Celadas 64 C3
Celano 49 D2
Celanova 53 F4
Celeiros 60 B1
Celenza Valfortore 50 A1
Celico 52 B2
Cella 64 B3
Celle 6 A4
Celle Ligure 44 C1
Cellere 48 B1
Celles 8 C4
Celles-sur-Belle 32 C2
Cellettes 24 C3
Cellino Attanasio 49 E1
Cellole 49 E3
Celorico da Beira 61 D3
Celorico de Basto 60 C1
Celrà 59 E3
Cembra 38 C2
Cénac-et-St-Julien 33 E4
Cencenighe Agordino 39 D1
Cendras 42 C2
Ceneselli 38 C4
Cengio 44 C1
Cenicero 56 B3
Ceniclentos 62 C4
Centallo 44 B1
Centelles 59 D3
Cento 38 C4
Centola 50 A4
Cepagatti 49 E1
Ceppaloni 50 A2
Ceppo Morelli 36 C2
Ceprano 49 D3
Cerano 37 D3
Cérans-Foulletourte 24 B2
Cerasi 52 A4
Ceraso 50 A4
Cerbère 59 F2
Cercal *Port.* 66 B2
Cercal *Port.* 72 A1
Cercedilla 62 C3
Cercedo 53 E3
Cercemaggiore 50 A2
Cerchiara di Calabria 52 B1
Cerchio 49 D2
Cercy-la-Tour 25 F4
Cerdanyola del Vallès 59 D4
Cerdeira 60 C4
Cerea 38 C4
Ceregnano 39 D4
Cérences 23 E1
Ceres 36 B3
Ceresole Reale 36 B3
Céret 59 E2
Cerezo de Abajo 63 D2
Cerezo de Arriba 63 D2
Cerezo de Riotirón 56 A3
Cerfontaine 17 D1
Cergy 16 A4
Ceriale 44 C2
Ceriana 44 B2
Cerignola 50 B2
Cérilly 34 B1
Cerisano 52 B2
Cerisiers 25 F2
Cerisy-la-Salle 14 B4
Cerizay 32 B1
Cermignano 49 E1
Cernache do Bonjardim 66 C1
Cernay 27 E2
Cernégula 55 F3
Cernier 27 E4
Cernobbio 37 D2
Cerralbo 61 E2
Cerreto d'Esi 47 D3
Cerreto di Spoleto 47 D4
Cerreto Sannita 49 F3
Cerro al Volturno 49 E2
Cersay 24 A4
Cersosimo 50 C4
Certaldo 46 B3
Certosa di Pavia 37 E4
Certosa di Pesio 44 B2
Cerva 60 C1
Cervaro 49 E3
Cervatos de la Cueza 55 D3
Cervera 58 C3
Cervera de la Cañada 64 B1
Cervera del Llano 63 F4
Cervera del Maestre 65 E3
Cervera de los Montes 62 B4
Cervera del Río Alhama 56 C4
Cervera de Pisuerga 55 E2
Cerveteri 48 B2
Cervia 46 C2
Cervignano del Friuli 39 F2
Cervinara 49 F4
Cervo *Italy* 44 B2
Cervo *Spain* 54 A1
Cerzeto 52 B1
Cesano Boscone 37 D3
Cesano Maderno 37 E3
Cesena 46 C2
Cesenatico 47 D2
Cesio 44 B2
Cespedosa 62 A3
Cessalto 39 E3
Cessenon-sur-Orb 42 A3
Cessole 44 C1
Cesson-Sévigné 23 E2
Cestas 40 B1
Cesuras 53 F2
Cetina 64 A2
Ceto 38 B2
Ceton 24 C2
Cetona 46 C4
Cetraro 52 A1
Ceutí 76 B1
Ceva 44 B1
Cevico de la Torre 55 E4
Cevico Navero 55 E4
Cevins 36 A3
Cevio 37 D2
Ceyreste 43 E4
Ceyzériat 35 E2
Chã 60 C1
Chaam 9 E2
Chabanais 33 D3
Chabeuil 35 E4
Chablis 26 A2
Chabreloche 34 C2
Chabris 25 D4
Chacim 61 E1
Chagny 26 B4
Chaillac 33 E1
Chailland 23 F2
Chaillé-les-Marais 32 B1
Chalabre 41 F4
Chalais *France* 32 C4
Chalais *Switz.* 36 B2
Chalamera 58 A3
Chalamont 35 E2
Châlette-sur-Loing 25 E2
Chaligny 17 F4
Chalindrey 26 C2
Challans 32 A1
Chalonnes-sur-Loire 23 F3
Châlons-en-Champagne 17 D4
Chalon-sur-Saône 26 B4
Châlus 33 E3
Cham *Ger.* 20 C3
Cham *Switz.* 28 A4
Chamalières 34 B3
Chamberet 33 F3
Chambéry 35 F3
Chambley-Bussières 17 F3
Chambon-sur-Voueize 34 A2
Chamboulive 33 F3
Chambray-lès-Tours 24 C3
Chamonix-Mont-Blanc 36 A2
Chamoux-sur-Gelon 35 F3
Champagnac 34 A3
Champagnac-de-Belair 33 D3
Champagne-Mouton 33 D2
Champagne-sur-Seine 25 E1
Champagney 27 E3
Champagnole 27 D4
Champdeniers-St-Denis 32 C1
Champeix 34 B3
Champéry 36 A2
Champex 36 B2
Champigné 24 A3
Champignelles 25 F3
Champigny 25 F2
Champlitte 26 C3
Champniers 32 C3
Champoluc 36 C2
Champsecret 23 F1
Champs-sur-Tarentaine-Marchal 34 A3
Champs-sur-Yonne 25 F3
Champtoceaux 23 F4
Chamusca 66 C2
Chanac 42 B1
Chanas 35 E4
Chança 67 D2
Chanceaux-sur-Choisille 24 C3
Chancelade 33 D4
Chancelaria 66 B1
Chañe 62 C2
Changé *France* 24 B2
Changé *France* 23 F2
Chantada 53 F3
Chantelle 34 B2
Chantilly 16 A3
Chantonnay 32 B1
Chanu 23 F1
Chao 53 F1
Chaource 26 A2
Chapareillan 35 F3
Chapelle-lez-Herlaimont 17 D1
Chapinería 62 C3
Charenton-du-Cher 25 E4
Charleroi 17 D1
Charleville-Mézières 17 D2
Charlieu 35 D2
Charly 16 B4
Charmes 27 D1
Charmes-sur-Rhône 43 D1
Charmey 36 B1
Charmoy 25 F2
Charny 25 F2
Charolles 35 D1
Chârost 25 D4
Charrat 36 B2
Charroux 33 D2
Chartres 25 D1
Charvensod 36 B3
Charvieu-Chavagneux 35 E3
Chasseneuil-sur-Bonnieure 33 D3
Chasse-sur-Rhône 35 E3

Chastre 17 D1
Château-Arnoux 43 E2
Châteaubernard 32 C3
Châteaubourg 23 E2
Châteaubriant 23 E3
Château-Chinon 26 A4
Château-d'Oex 36 B1
Château-d'Olonne 32 A1
Château-du-Loir 24 B3
Châteaudun 24 C2
Châteaugiron 23 E2
Château-Gontier 23 F3
Château-Landon 25 E2
Château-la-Vallière 24 B3
Châteaulin 22 B2
Châteaumeillant 33 F1
Châteauneuf-de-Galaure 35 E4
Châteauneuf-de-Randon 42 B1
Châteauneuf-d'Ille-et-Vilaine 23 E1
Châteauneuf-du-Faou 22 B2
Châteauneuf-en-Thymerais 24 C1
Châteauneuf-la-Forêt 33 E3
Châteauneuf-les-Martigues 43 D3
Châteauneuf-sur-Charente 32 C3
Châteauneuf-sur-Cher 33 F1
Châteauneuf-sur-Loire 25 D2
Châteauneuf-sur-Sarthe 24 A3
Châteauponsac 33 E2
Château-Porcien 17 D3
Châteaurenard *France* 25 E2
Châteaurenard *France* 43 D2
Château-Renault 24 C3
Châteauroux 33 F1
Château-Thierry 16 C4
Châteauvillain 26 B2
Châtel 36 A2
Châtelaillon-Plage 32 B2
Châtelaudren 22 C1
Châteldon 34 C2
Châtelet 17 D1
Châtelguyon 34 B2
Châtellerault 33 D1
Châtel-St-Denis 36 A1
Châtel-sur-Moselle 27 D1
Châtelus-Malvaleix 33 F2
Châtenois *France* 27 F1
Châtenois *France* 27 D1
Châtenois-les-Forges 27 E3
Châtenoy-le-Royal 26 B4
Châtillon *Belgium* 17 F2
Châtillon *Italy* 36 B3
Châtillon-Coligny 25 E2
Châtillon-en-Bazois 25 F4
Châtillon-en-Diois 43 E1
Châtillon-sur-Chalaronne 35 E2
Châtillon-sur-Colmont 23 F1
Châtillon-sur-Indre 24 C4
Châtillon-sur-Loire 25 E3
Châtillon-sur-Marne 16 C3
Châtillon-sur-Seine 26 B2
Châtillon-sur-Thouet 32 C1
Chatuzange-le-Goubet 35 E4
Chauchina 75 D2
Chaudes-Aigues 42 A1
Chaudfontaine 17 E1
Chauffailles 35 D2
Chaulnes 16 B2
Chaumergy 26 C4
Chaumont 26 C2
Chaumont-en-Vexin 16 A3
Chaumont-Porcien 17 D2
Chaunay 32 C2
Chauny 16 B2
Chaussin 26 C4
Chauvigny 33 D1
Chavanay 35 D3
Chavanges 26 B1
Chavelot 27 D2
Chaves 61 D1
Chazelles-sur-Lyon 35 D3
Checa 64 B3
Chécy 25 D2
Chef-Boutonne 32 C2
Cheles 67 D3
Chella 71 D2
Chelva 70 C1
Chemazé 23 F3
Chemillé 23 F4
Chemin 26 C4
Chemnitz 13 D4
Chénérailles 33 F2
Chenôve 26 B3
Cheny 25 F2
Chera 70 C1
Chérac 32 C3
Cherasco 44 B1
Chéraute 40 B4
Cherbourg 14 B2
Chéroy 25 E2
Chert 65 E3
Cherves-Richemont 32 C3
Cheste 71 D2
Chevagnes 34 C1
Chevanceaux 32 C4
Chevillon 26 C1
Chevilly 25 D2
Chevreuse 16 A4
Chezal-Benoît 33 F1
Chiampo 38 C3
Chianciano Terme 46 C4
Chianni 46 A3
Chiaravalle 47 E3
Chiaravalle Centrale 52 B3
Chiari 38 A3
Chiaromonte 50 C4
Chiasso 37 D2
Chiavari 45 D2
Chiavenno 37 E2
Chiché 32 C1
Chiclana de la Frontera 73 E4
Chiclana de Segura 69 F4
Chieming 30 A2
Chienes 39 D1
Chieri 36 C4
Chiesa in Valmalenco 38 A2
Chiesina Uzzanese 46 A2
Chieti 49 E1
Chieuti 50 A1
Chièvres 16 C1
Chilches 65 D4
Chilleurs-aux-Bois 25 D2
Chillón 68 C3
Chilluévar 69 F4
Chiloeches 63 E3
Chimay 17 D2
Chimeneas 75 D2
Chinanale 44 A1
Chinchilla de Monte Aragón 70 B3
Chinchón 63 E4
Chindrieux 35 F3
Chinon 24 B4
Chioggia 39 D4
Chiomonte 36 B4
Chipiona 73 E3
Chippis 36 B2
Chiprana 58 A4
Chirivel 76 A2
Chitignano 46 C3
Chiuro 38 A2
Chiusa 38 C1
Chiusa di Pesio 44 B1
Chiusaforte 39 F1
Chiusavecchia 44 B2
Chiusdino 46 B4
Chiusi 46 C4
Chiusi della Verna 46 C3
Chiva 71 D2
Chivasso 36 C4
Chlebowo 13 F1
Choisy 35 F2
Chojna 7 F4
Cholet 23 F4
Chomérac 42 C1
Chorges 43 F1
Chouto 66 C2
Chouzy-sur-Cisse 24 C3
Chovar 65 D4
Chozas de Abajo 54 C3
Christiansfeld 2 B3
Chulilla 71 D1
Chur 28 C4
Churwalden 28 C4
Chuzelles 35 E3
Ciadoux 41 D4
Ciampino 48 C2
Ciborro 66 C3
Ciboure 57 D1
Cicagna 45 D1
Cicciano 49 F4
Cicerale 50 A4
Cidones 56 B4
Ciempozuelos 63 D4
Cieza 76 B1
Cifuentes 63 F3
Cigales 55 E4
Cigliano 36 C3
Cillas 64 B2
Cilleros 61 E4
Cimanes del Tejar 54 C3
Cimballa 64 B2
Cimolais 39 D1
Cinco Casas 69 E2
Cinctorres 65 D3
Ciñera 54 C2
Ciney 17 E1
Cinfães 60 C2
Cingoli 47 E3
Cinigiano 46 B4
Cinisello Balsamo 37 E3
Cinq-Mars-la-Pile 24 B3
Cinquefrondi 52 A3
Cintegabelle 41 E4
Cintruénigo 56 C4
Cirat 65 D4
Ciraugui 56 C3
Circello 50 A2
Cirey-sur-Vezouze 27 E1
Ciria 64 A1
Ciriè 36 B4
Cirigliano 50 C4
Cirò 52 C2
Cirò Marina 52 C2
Ciruelos 63 D4
Ciruelos del Pinar 63 F2
Ciry-le-Noble 35 D1
Cisano sul Neva 44 C2
Cisneros 55 D4
Cisòn di Valmarino 39 D2
Cissé 33 D1
Cisterna di Latina 48 C3
Cisternino 51 E3
Cistierna 55 D2
Citerna 46 C3
Cittadella 39 D3
Città della Pieve 46 C4
Citta del Vaticano 48 C2
Città di Castello 46 C3
Cittanova 52 A4
Cittareale 49 D1
Città Sant'Angelo 49 E1
Cittiglio 37 D2
Ciudad Real 69 D2
Ciudad Rodrigo 61 E3
Cividale del Friuli 39 F2
Civita 52 B1
Civita Castellana 48 C1
Civita d'Antino 49 D2
Civitanova del Sannio 49 F2
Civitanova Marche 47 E3
Civitaquana 49 E1
Civitavecchia 48 B2
Civitella Casanova 49 E1
Civitella del Tronto 47 E4
Civitella di Romagna 46 C2
Civitella in Val di Chiana 46 C3
Civitella Roveto 49 D2
Civray *France* 25 D4
Civray *France* 33 D2
Clairac 40 C2
Clairoix 16 B3
Clairvaux-les-Lacs 35 F1
Clamecy 25 F3
Clans 44 A2
Claro 37 D2
Clary 16 C2
Clausnitz 13 E4
Claußnitz 13 D4
Clausthal-Zellerfeld 11 F2
Claut 39 E2
Clauzetto 39 E2
Clavier 17 E1
Clécy 14 C4
Cléder 22 B1
Clefmont 26 C2
Cléguérec 22 C2
Clelles 43 E1
Clémency 17 F3
Clenze 6 B4
Cléon 15 E3
Cléré-les-Pins 24 B3
Clères 15 E3
Clermont 16 A3
Clermont-en-Argonne 17 E3
Clermont-Ferrand 34 B3
Clermont-l'Hérault 42 B3
Clerval 27 D3
Clervaux 17 F2
Cléry-St-André 25 D3
Cles 38 B1
Clinge 9 D3
Clingen 12 A3
Clion 24 C4
Clisson 23 F4
Clohars-Carnoët 22 C3
Cloppenburg 5 D4
Cloyes-sur-le-Loir 24 C2
Cluis 33 F1
Cluny 35 D1
Cluses 36 A2
Clusone 38 A2
Coaña 54 B1
Coarraze 40 B4
Cobeja 63 D4
Cobeta 63 F2
Coburg 20 A1
Coca 62 C2
Cocentaina 71 D3
Cochem 18 B2
Codevigo 39 D3
Codigoro 39 D4
Codogno 38 A4
Codos 64 B2
Codroipo 39 E2
Coesfeld 10 B2
Coevorden 4 C4
Coëx 32 A1
Cofrentes 70 C2
Cogeces del Monte 62 C1
Coggiola 36 C3
Cognac 32 C3
Cogne 36 B3
Cognin 35 F3
Cogoleto 44 C1
Cogolin 43 F4
Cogollos 55 F4
Cogollos Vega 75 D2
Cogolludo 63 E2
Cogula 61 D3
Coimbra 60 B4
Coimbrão 66 B1
Coín 74 B3
Coincy 16 C3
Coja 60 C4
Colares 66 A3
Colayrac-St-Cirq 41 D2
Cölbe 11 D4
Colbitz 12 B1
Colbordola 47 D2
Colditz 13 D3
Colico 37 E2
Coligny 35 E1
Colindres 55 F1
Collado Hermoso 63 D2
Collado Villalba 63 D3
Collagna 46 A1
Collanzo 54 C2
Collarmele 49 D2
Collazzone 47 D4
Collecchio 38 A4
Collecorvino 49 E1
Colledara 49 E1
Colle di Val d'Elsa 46 B3
Colleferro 49 D2
Collegno 36 B4
Colle Isarco 29 E4
Collelongo 49 D2
Collepardo 49 D2
Collepasso 51 F4
Collesalvetti 46 A3
Colle Sannita 50 A2
Colletorto 50 A1
Colliano 50 A3
Colli a Volturno 49 E2
Collinée 23 D2
Collinghorst (Rhauderfehn) 5 D3
Collio 38 B2
Collioure 59 E2
Collobrières 43 F4
Collombey 36 A2
Collonges 35 F2
Colmar 27 F2
Colmars 43 F2
Colmberg 20 A3
Colmeal 60 C4
Colmenar 74 C3
Colmenar del Arroyo 62 C3
Colmenar de Montemayor 62 A3
Colmenar de Oreja 63 E4
Colmenar Viejo 63 D3
Colobraro 50 C4
Cologna Veneta 38 C3
Cologne 41 D3
Cologno al Serio 38 A3
Colombelles 15 D3
Colombey-les-Belles 27 D1
Colombier 27 E4
Colombiès 41 F2
Colombres 55 E1
Colomers 59 E2
Colomiers 41 E3
Colonnella 47 F4
Colorno 38 B4
Colos 72 A1
Cölpin 7 E3
Colunga 55 D1
Comacchio 46 C1
Comares 74 C3
Combeaufontaine 27 D3

Comblain-au-Pont **17** E1
Combles **16** B2
Combloux **36** A2
Combourg **23** E2
Combronde **34** B2
Comeglіàns **39** E1
Comèlico Superiore **39** D1
Comillas **55** E1
Comines **8** B4
Commentry **34** B2
Commequiers **32** A1
Commercy **17** E4
Como **37** D2
Cómpeta **74** C3
Compiano **45** E1
Compiègne **16** B3
Comporta **66** B3
Compreignac **33** E2
Comps-sur-Artuby **43** F3
Comunanza **47** E4
Cona **39** D4
Concarneau **22** B3
Conceição **72** C2
Concesio **38** A3
Concha **56** A2
Conches-en-Ouche **15** E4
Concordia Sagittaria **39** E3
Condat **34** B3
Condé-en-Brie **16** C4
Condeixa-a-Nova **60** B4
Condé-sur-Huisne **24** C1
Condé-sur-Noireau **23** F1
Condé-sur-Vire **14** C4
Condino **38** B2
Condofuri **52** A4
Condom **40** C2
Condove **36** B4
Condrieu **35** D3
Conegliano **39** D2
Conflans-en-Jarnisy **17** F3
Conflenti **52** B2
Confolens **33** D2
Congosto **54** B3
Congosto de Valdavia **55** E3
Congrier **23** F3
Conil de la Frontera **73** E4
Conlie **24** B2
Conliège **35** F1
Connantre **16** C4
Connaux **42** C2
Connerré **24** B2
Conow **7** E3
Conques **41** F1
Conques-sur-Orbiel **41** F4
Conquista **68** C3
Consandolo **46** C1
Conselice **46** C1
Conselve **39** D4
Consistorio **53** E4
Constância **66** C1
Constantí **58** C4
Constantim *Port.* **61** F1
Constantim *Port.* **61** D2
Constantina **74** A1
Constanzana **62** B2
Consuegra **69** E1
Contarina **39** D4
Contes **44** A2
Conthey **36** B2
Contigliano **48** C1
Contis-Plage **40** A2
Contres **24** C3
Contrexéville **27** D2
Controne **50** A3
Contursi Terme **50** A3
Conty **16** A2
Conversano **51** D2
Conza della Campania **50** A3
Copanello **52** B3
Copertino **51** F4
Copons **58** C3
Copparo **39** D4
Corato **50** C2
Coray **22** B2
Corbalán **64** C3
Corbeil-Essonnes **16** A4
Corbeilles **25** E2
Corbelin **35** F3
Corbera **71** D2
Corbera de Terra Alta **58** B4
Corbie **16** B2
Corbières **36** B1
Corbigny **25** F3
Corçà **59** E3
Corchiano **48** C1
Corciano **46** C4
Corcieux **27** E2
Corcubión **53** D2
Cordemais **23** E4
Cordenòns **39** E2
Cordes **41** F2
Córdoba **74** B1
Cordobilla de Lácara **67** F2
Corduente **64** A2
Coreglia Antelminelli **46** A2
Corella **56** C4
Coreses **62** A1
Corfinio **49** E2
Cori **48** C3
Coria **61** E4
Coria del Río **73** E2
Coriano **47** D2
Corigliano Calabro **52** B1
Corinaldo **47** D3
Coripe **74** A3
Corlay **22** C2
Corleto Perticara **50** C4
Cormeilles **15** D3
Corme-Porto **53** D1
Cormons **39** F2
Cormontreuil **17** D3
Cornago **56** C4
Cornaredo **37** D3
Cornas **35** E4
Cornau **5** E4
Cornedo all'Isarco **38** C1
Cornedo Vicentino **38** C3
Corneilla-del-Vercol **59** E1
Cornellá de Llobregat **59** D4
Cornellà de Terri **59** E3
Cornellana **54** B1
Corniglio **45** E1
Cornimont **27** E2
Cornuda **39** D2
Cornudella de Montsant **58** B4
Cornudilla **55** F3
Cornus **42** A2
Coron **23** F4
Corps **35** F4
Corps-Nuds **23** E2
Corral de Calatrava **69** D3
Corrales **62** A2
Corral-Rubio **70** C3
Correggio **38** B4
Corrèze **33** F3
Corridonia **47** E3
Corsano **51** F4
Corseul **23** D1
Corsico **37** D3
Cortale **52** B3
Corteconcepción **67** F4
Corte de Peleas **67** E3
Cortegada **53** F3
Cortegana **67** E4
Cortemilia **44** C1
Corteno Golgi **38** A2
Corteolona **37** E4
Cortes **57** D4
Cortes de Aragón **64** C2
Cortes de Arenoso **64** C4
Cortes de Baza **75** E1
Cortes de la Frontera **74** A3
Cortes de Pallás **70** C2
Cortiçadas do Lavre **66** C3
Cortijo de Arriba **69** D2
Cortijos Nuevos **70** A4
Cortina d'Ampezzo **39** D1
Cortona **46** C3
Coruche **66** B2
Corullón **54** B3
Corvara in Badia **39** D1
Corvera **76** B2
Cosa **64** C3
Coscurita **63** F1
Cosenza **52** B2
Cosio di Arroscia **44** B2
Coslada **63** D3
Cosne-Cours-sur-Loire **25** E3
Cosne-d'Allier **34** B1
Cosoleto **52** A4
Cossato **36** C3
Cossé-le-Vivien **23** F2
Cossonay **36** A1
Costacciaro **47** D3
Costa da Caparica **66** A3
Costa di Rovigo **38** C4
Costa Volpino **38** A2
Costigliole Saluzzo **44** B1
Cosuenda **64** B1
Coswig *Ger.* **13** E3
Coswig *Ger.* **12** C2
Cothen **9** E1
Cotignac **43** F3
Cotignola **46** C1
Cotronei **52** C2
Cottanello **48** C1
Cottbus **13** F2
Coubon **34** C4
Couches **26** B4
Couço **66** C2
Coucy-le-Château-Auffrique **16** C3
Coudekerque-Branche **8** B3
Couëron **23** E4
Couflens **58** C1
Couhé **32** C2
Couiza **41** F4
Coulaines **24** B2
Coulanges-la-Vineuse **25** F3
Coulanges-sur-Yonne **25** F3
Coulaures **33** E4
Coullons **25** E3
Coulogne **8** A3
Coulombiers **32** C1
Coulombs **25** D1
Coulommiers **16** B4
Coulonges-sur-l'Autize **32** B1
Coulounieix-Chamiers **33** D4
Couptrain **24** A1
Coura **53** E4
Courcelles **17** D1
Courcelles-Chaussy **17** F3
Courchevel **36** A3
Cour-Cheverny **25** D3
Courçon **32** B2
Courcy **16** C3
Courgenay **27** E3
Courlay **32** C1
Courmayeur **36** B3
Courmelles **16** C3
Cournon-d'Auvergne **34** B3
Cournonterral **42** B3
Courpière **34** C3
Courrendlin **27** F3
Coursac **33** D4
Coursan **42** A4
Coursegoules **44** A2
Courseulles-sur-Mer **14** C3
Cours-la-Ville **35** D2
Courson-les-Carrières **25** F3
Court **27** F3
Courtelary **27** E4
Courtenay **25** F2
Courthézon **43** D2
Courtisols **17** D4
Courtomer **24** B1
Courville-sur-Eure **24** C1
Cousance **35** E1
Coussac-Bonneval **33** E3
Coussey **26** C1
Coustouges **59** E2
Coutances **14** B4
Couterne **24** A1
Couto de Cima **60** C3
Coutras **32** C4
Couvet **27** E4
Couvin **17** D2
Couzeix **33** E2
Covaleda **56** B4
Covarrubias **55** F4
Covelo **53** E3
Covilhã **61** D4
Cox **76** C1
Cózar **69** E3
Cozes **32** B3
Crach **22** C3
Craco **50** C4
Crailsheim **19** F3
Cran-Gevrier **35** F2
Crans-sur-Sierre **36** B2
Craon **23** F2
Craonne **16** C3
Craponne-sur-Arzon **34** C4
Crato **67** D2
Cravagliana **36** C2
Créances **14** B3
Crecente **53** E4
Crêches-sur-Saône **35** D2
Crécy-en-Ponthieu **16** A1
Crécy-la-Chapelle **16** B4
Crécy-sur-Serre **16** C2
Creglingen **19** F3
Creil *France* **16** A3
Creil *Neth.* **4** B4
Creissels **42** A2
Crema **38** A3
Crémenes **55** D2
Crémieu **35** E3
Cremlingen **11** F1
Cremona **38** A4
Créon **40** B1
Crépy **16** C3
Crépy-en-Valois **16** B3
Crescentino **36** C4
Crespina **46** A3
Crespino **39** D4
Crespos **62** B2
Cressier **27** E4
Crest **43** D1
Cretas **65** E2
Créteil **16** A4
Creußen **20** B2
Creutzwald **18** A3
Creuzburg **11** F3
Crèvecœur-le-Grand **16** A2
Crevillente **76** C1
Crevoladossola **36** C2
Criel-sur-Mer **15** F2
Crimmitschau **12** C4
Crinitz **13** E2
Cripán **56** B3
Criquetot-l'Esneval **15** D2
Crispiano **51** D3
Crissolo **44** A1
Cristóbal **62** A3
Crivitz **6** C2
Crock **12** A4
Crocq **33** F2
Crodo **36** C2
Crognaleto **49** D1
Croisilles **16** B1
Crolles **35** F3
Cropalati **52** B1
Cropani **52** C2
Crosia **52** C1
Crotone **52** C2
Crottendorf **13** D4
Crouy **16** C3
Crouy-sur-Ourcq **16** B4
Crozon **22** A2
Cruas **43** D1
Crucoli **52** C2
Cruseilles **35** F2
Crusnes **17** F3
Cruzy-le-Châtel **26** A2
Cuacos de Yuste **62** A4
Cuadros **54** C3
Cualedro **53** F4
Cuarte de Huerva **64** C1
Cuba **66** C4
Cubalhão **53** E4
Cubells **58** B3
Cubla **64** C4
Cubo de Bureba **56** A3
Cubo de la Solana **63** F1
Cubzac-les-Ponts **32** C4
Cucalón **64** B2
Cucuron **43** E3
Cudillero **54** C1
Cuéllar **62** C1
Cuenca **63** F4
Cuenca de Campos **55** D4
Cuers **43** E4
Cuerva **69** D1
Cueva de Agreda **56** C4
Cuevas Bajas **74** C2
Cuevas de Almanzora **76** A3
Cuevas del Becerro **74** B3
Cuevas del Campo **75** E1
Cuevas de San Clemente **55** F4
Cuevas de San Marcos **74** C2
Cuevas de Vinromá **65** D3
Cuevas Labradas **64** C3
Cugand **23** F4
Cuges-les-Pins **43** E4
Cugnaux **41** E3
Cuijk **9** F2
Cuiseaux **35** E1
Cuise-la-Motte **16** B3
Cuisery **35** E1
Culemborg **9** E2
Culla **65** D3
Cúllar-Baza **75** F2
Cullera **71** E2
Cully **36** A1
Culoz **35** F2
Cumbres de San Bartolomé **67** E4
Cumbres Mayores **67** E4
Cumeada **72** B2
Cumiana **36** B4
Cumieira **60** C2
Cumlosen **6** C3
Cuneo **44** B1
Cunewalde **13** F3
Cunha **61** D2
Cunit **58** C4
Cuntis **53** E3
Cuorgnè **36** B3
Cupello **49** F2
Cupra Marittima **47** F4
Cupramontana **47** E3
Cuq-Toulza **41** F3
Cureggio **37** D3
Curinga **52** B3

Curon Venosta 38 B1
Currás 53 E3
Cursi 51 F4
Cusano Mutri 49 F3
Cussac 33 D3
Cusset 34 C2
Custines 17 F4
Cutigliano 46 A2
Cutro 52 C2
Cutrofiano 51 F4
Cuxac-Cabardès 41 F3
Cuxac-d'Aude 42 A4
Cuxhaven 5 E2
Cybinka 13 F1
Czarnów 13 F1

D

Dabel 6 C2
Dabo 27 E1
Dachau 29 E1
Dachrieden 11 F3
Dachwig 12 A3
Daganzo de Arriba 63 D3
Dagebüll 2 A4
Dagmersellen *Switz.* 27 F3
Dagmersellen *Switzerland* 28 A3
Dahlem 18 A1
Dahlen 13 D3
Dahlenburg 6 B3
Dahme *Ger.* 13 D2
Dahme *Ger.* 6 B1
Dahn 18 C3
Dähre 6 B4
Daimiel 69 E2
Dainville 16 B1
Dalaas 28 C4
Dalberg-Wendelstorf 6 C2
Dalby *Denmark* 2 C3
Dalby *Denmark* 3 E3
Dalbyover 1 F3
Dalen 4 C4
Dalfsen 10 A1
Dalhem 9 F4
Dalías 75 E3
Dallgow 13 D1
Dall Villaby 1 F2
Dalmine 38 A3
Dalmose 3 D3
Damazan 40 C2
Dambeck 6 C3
Damery 16 C4
Damgan 23 D3
Damigni 24 B1
Dammarie 25 D1
Dammartin-en-Goële 16 B4
Damme *Belgium* 8 C3
Damme *Ger.* 10 C1
Damp 2 C4
Dampierre 26 C4
Dampierre-sur-Salon 26 C3
Damprichard 27 E3
Damshagen 6 B2
Damsholte 3 E4
Damüls 28 C3
Damvant 27 E3
Damville 24 C1
Damvillers 17 E3
Damwoude 4 B3
Dangé-St-Romain 24 B4
Dänischenhagen 6 A1
Danjoutin 27 E3
Dankerode 12 B2
Danndorf 12 A1
Dannemare 3 D4
Dannemarie 27 E3
Dannenberg (Elbe) 6 B3
Dannenwalde 7 E3
Daoulas 22 B2
Dardesheim 12 A2
Darè 38 B2
Darfo Boario Terme 38 A2
Dargun 7 D2
Darmstadt 19 D2
Darney 27 D2
Daroca 64 B2
Darque 60 B1
Darro 75 E2
Dasing 29 D1
Dassel 11 E2
Dassendorf 6 B3
Dassow 6 B2
Datteln 10 B2
Datterode (Ringgau) 11 F3
Daugård 2 B2
Daumeray 24 A3
Daun 18 B1
Dautphetal-Friedensdorf 11 D4
Davoli 52 B3
Davos 28 C4
Dax 40 A3
Deauville 15 D3
Deba 56 C2
De Bilt 9 E1
Decazeville 41 F1
Decize 25 F4
De Cocksdorp 4 A3
Decollatura 52 B2
Dedeleben 12 A1
Dedelow 7 F3
Dedelstorf 6 B4
Dedemsvaart 4 C4
Deensen 11 E2
Deerlijk 8 C4
Degaña 54 B2
Deggendorf 21 D4
Deggingen 28 C1
Dego 44 C1
De Haan 8 B3
Dehesa de Campoamor 76 C1
Dehesas de Guadix 75 E1
Deifontes 75 D2
Deilão 61 E1
Deining 20 B3
Deiningen 20 A4
Deinste 5 F2
Deinze 8 C3
Deiva Marina 45 D2
De Koog 4 A3
De Kooy 4 A4
Delbrück 11 D2
Deleitosa 68 B1
Delémont 27 F3
Delft 9 D1
Delfzijl 4 C3
Delianuova 52 A4
Deliceto 50 B2
Delingsdorf 6 A2
Delitzsch 12 C3
Delle 27 E3
Delligsen 11 E2
Dello 38 A3
Delme 17 F4
Delmenhorst 5 E3
Demen 6 C2
Demigny 26 B4
Demmin 7 E2
Demonte 44 A2
Denain 16 C1
Den Burg 4 A3
Dendermonde 9 D3
Den Dungen 9 E2
Denekamp 10 B1
Denguin 40 B3
Den Ham 10 A1
Den Helder 4 A4
Denia 71 E3
Denkendorf *Ger.* 28 B1
Denkendorf *Ger.* 20 B4
Denkingen *Ger.* 28 A2
Denkingen *Ger.* 28 B2
Denklingen 29 D2
Dennewitz 13 D2
Dennhausen (Fuldabrück) 11 E3
Den Oever 4 A4
Densow 7 E3
Dentergem 8 C3
Dentlein am Forst 20 A3
Denzlingen 27 F2
Déols 33 F1
De Panne 8 B3
Derenburg 12 A2
De Rijp 4 A4
Dermbach 11 F4
Dersum 5 D4
Deruta 47 D4
Derval 23 E3
Dervio 37 E2
Désaignes 35 D4
Desana 36 C4
Descargamaría 61 E4
Descartes 24 C4
Desenzano del Garda 38 B3
Désertines 34 B2
Dessau 12 C2
Dessel 9 E3
De Steeg 10 A1
Destelbergen 8 C3
Destriana 54 C3
Desvres 16 A1
Detern 5 D3
Detmold 11 D2
Dettelbach 19 F2
Dettmannsdorf 7 D1
Dettum 11 F1
Deurne 9 F2
Deutsch Evern 6 B3
Deutschfeistritz 31 D3
Deutsch Goritz 31 E4
Deutschhof 7 D4
Deutschkreutz 31 F3
Deutschlandsberg 31 D4
Deutschneudorf 13 E4
Deutsch-Wagram 31 F1
Deutzen 12 C3
Deventer 10 A1
De Wijk 4 B4
Deza 64 A1
Diamante 52 A1
Dianalund 3 D3
Diano d'Alba 44 B1
Diano Marina 44 B2
Dices 53 E2
Dicomano 46 B2
Didam 10 A2
Didderse 11 F1
Die 43 D1
Dieblich 18 B1
Dieburg 19 D2
Diedorf 29 D1
Diego Alvaro 62 B3
Diekhof 7 D2
Diekholzen 11 E1
Diekirch 17 F2
Dielmissen 11 E2
Dielsdorf 28 A3
Diemen 9 E1
Diémoz 35 E3
Diepenau 11 D1
Diepenbeek 9 E3
Diepholz 5 E4
Dieppe 15 E2
Dierdorf 10 C4
Dieren 10 A1
Diesdorf 6 B4
Dieskau 12 C3
Diespeck 20 A2
Dießen am Ammersee 29 E2
Diessenhofen 28 A3
Diest 9 E3
Dietachdorf 30 C2
Dietenheim 28 C2
Dietersburg 30 A1
Dietfurt an der Altmühl 20 B4
Dietikon 28 A3
Dietingen 28 A2
Dietmanns 31 D1
Dietmannsried 28 C2
Dieue-sur-Meuse 17 E4
Dieulefit 43 D1
Dieulouard 17 F4
Dieuze 18 A4
Diever 4 B4
Diex 30 C4
Diez 18 C1
Diezma 75 E2
Differdange 17 F3
Dignac 33 D3
Dignano 39 E2
Digne-les-Bains 43 F2
Digoin 34 C1
Dijon 26 C3
Diksmuide 8 B3
Dilar 75 D2
Dillenburg 10 C4
Dillingen (Saar) 18 A3
Dillingen an der Donau 29 D1
Dilsen 9 F3
Dimaro 38 B2
Dinami 52 B3
Dinan 23 E1
Dinant 17 E1
Dinard 23 E1
Dingé 23 E2
Dingelstädt 11 F3
Dingelstedt am Huy 12 B2
Dingolfing 30 A1
Dinkelsbühl 19 F3
Dinkelscherben 29 D1
Dinklage 5 E4
Dinslaken 10 B2
Dinteloord 9 D2
Dinxperlo 10 A2
Diou 34 C1
Dipignano 52 B2
Dippach 17 F3
Dippoldiswalde 13 E4
Dirkshorn 4 A4
Dirksland 9 D2
Dirlewang 29 D2
Dischingen 29 D1
Disentis Muster 28 B4
Dison 17 F1
Dissay 33 D1
Dissen am Teutoburger Wald 10 C1
Ditfurt 12 B2
Ditzingen 19 E4
Dives-sur-Mer 15 D3
Divion 16 B1
Divonne-les-Bains 35 F1
Dizy 16 C4
Dobbertin 7 D2
Dobbiaco 39 D1
Döbeln 13 D3
Doberlug-Kirchhain 13 E2
Döbern 13 F2
Doberschütz 13 D3
Dobritz 12 C2
Dobro 55 F2
Dockweiler 18 B1
Doesburg 10 A1
Doetinchem 10 A2
Dogliani 44 B1
Dohna 13 F4
Dohren 5 D4
Doische 17 D2
Dokkedal 1 F2
Dokkum 4 B3
Dolceacqua 44 B2
Dol-de-Bretagne 23 E1
Dole 26 C4
Dolgen 7 E3
Dolle 12 B1
Dollern 6 A2
Döllnitz 12 C3
Dollnstein 20 A4
Dollon 24 B2
Dolo 39 D3
Dolores 76 C1
Dölsach 30 A4
Dolus-d'Oléron 32 A2
Domart-en-Ponthieu 16 A2
Domat Ems 28 B4
Dombresson 27 E4
Domburg 8 C2
Domegge di Cadore 39 D1
Domène 35 F4
Domérat 34 A2
Domèvre-en-Haye 17 F4
Domfront 23 F1
Domingo Pérez 62 C4
Dömitz 6 C3
Dommitzsch 13 D2
Domodossola 36 C2
Domont 16 A4
Dompaire 27 D2
Dompierre-sur-Besbre 34 C1
Dompierre-sur-Mer 32 B2
Dompierre-sur-Yon 32 A1
Domsühl 6 C3
Donada 39 D4
Don Álvaro 67 F3
Doña Mencía 74 C1
Donaueschingen 28 A2
Donauwörth 29 D1
Don Benito 68 A2
Donchery 17 D2
Dongen 9 E2
Donges 23 E4
Dongo 37 E2
Doñinos de Salamanca 62 A2
Donkerbroek 4 B4
Donnas 36 C3
Donnemarie-Dontilly 25 F1
Donnersbach 30 C3
Donnersdorf 20 A2
Donostia-San Sebastián 56 C1
Donville-les-Bains 23 E1
Donzdorf 28 C1
Donzenac 33 E4
Donzère 43 D1
Donzy 25 F3
Doorn 9 E1
Dordives 25 E2
Dordrecht 9 D2
Dörentrup 11 D1
Dorfen 29 F1
Dorfgastein 30 A3
Dorfmark 6 A4
Dorf Mecklenburg 6 C2
Dormagen 10 B3
Dormans 16 C4
Dornach 27 F3
Dörnberg (Habichtswald) 11 E3
Dornbirn 28 C3
Dornburg (Saale) 12 B3
Dornburg-Frickhofen 10 C4
Dornbusch 5 F2
Dorndorf 11 F4
Dorndorf-Steudnitz 12 B3
Dornelas 60 C1
Dornes 25 F4
Dörnitz 12 C1
Dorno 37 D4
Dornstadt 28 C1
Dornstetten 28 A1
Dornum 5 D2
Dornumersiel 5 D2
Dörpen 5 D4
Dorstadt 11 F1

Dorsten 10 B2
Dortan 35 F2
Dortmund 10 B2
Dorum 5 E2
Dörverden 5 F4
Dörzbach 19 E3
Dos Aguas 71 D2
Dosbarrios 63 D4
Dos Hermanas 73 E2
Dossenheim 19 D3
Dos Torres 68 C3
Døstrup 2 A3
Dotternhausen 28 B2
Döttingen 28 A3
Douai 16 B1
Douarnenez 22 B2
Douchy 25 F2
Douchy-les-Mines 16 C1
Doucier 35 F1
Doudeville 15 E2
Doué-la Fontaine 24 A4
Doulaincourt-Saucourt 26 C1
Doullens 16 A2
Dour 16 C1
Dourdan 25 D1
Dourgne 41 F3
Doussard 35 F3
Douvaine 36 A2
Douvres-la-Déliverande 14 C3
Douzy 17 E2
Dovadola 46 C2
Doyet 34 B2
Dozulé 15 D3
Dråby 2 C1
Drachhausen 13 F2
Drachselsried 21 D3
Drachten 4 B3
Drage 6 A3
Dragoni 49 E3
Dragør 3 F3
Draguignan 43 F3
Drahnsdorf 13 E2
Drakenburg 5 F4
Drangstedt 5 E2
Dranse 7 D3
Dransfeld 11 E3
Dranske 7 E1
Draßmarkt 31 F3
Drebber 5 E4
Drebkau 13 E2
Dreieich 19 D2
Dreileben 12 B1
Dreis 18 B2
Drelsdorf 2 B4
Drenchia 39 F2
Drense 7 F3
Drensteinfurt 10 C2
Drentwede 5 E4
Dresden 13 E3
Dreux 24 C1
Drewitz 12 C1
Driebergen 9 E1
Driebes 63 E4
Dro 38 B2
Drochtersen 5 F2
Dronero 44 A1
Dronninglund 1 F2
Dronrijp 4 B3
Dronten 4 B4
Drösing 31 F1
Droué 24 C2
Droyßig 12 C3
Drulingen 18 B4
Drumettaz-Clarafond 35 F3
Drusenheim 27 F1
Duas Igrejas 61 F1
Düben 12 C2
Duben 13 E2
Dübendorf 28 A3
Dubino 37 E2
Ducey 23 E1
Ducherow 7 F2
Duclair 15 E3
Dudelange 17 F3
Dudeldorf 18 A2
Duderstadt 11 F2
Dueñas 55 E4
Dueville 38 C3
Duffel 9 D3
Dugny-sur-Meuse 17 E3
Duino 39 F2
Duisburg 10 B2
Dülmen 10 B2
Dumbría 53 D2
Dummerstorf 7 D2
Dümpelfeld 10 B4
Düngenheim 18 B1
Dunières 35 D4
Dunkerque 8 B3
Dun-le-Palestel 33 E2
Dun-sur-Auron 25 E4
Dun-sur-Meuse 17 E3
Durach 29 D3
Durana 56 B2
Durango 56 B2
Duras 40 C1
Durbach 27 F1
Durban-Corbières 42 A4
Durbuy 17 E1
Dúrcal 75 D3
Durdat-Larequille 34 B2
Düren 10 A4
Dürmentingen 28 B2
Durmersheim 18 C4
Dürnkrut 31 F1
Dürrlauingen 29 D1
Dürrwangen 20 A3
Durtal 24 A3
Duruelo de la Sierra 56 B4
Durup 1 E3
Düsseldorf 10 B3
Dussen 9 E2
Düßnitz 13 D2
Dwingeloo 4 B4
Dybvad 1 F2
Dychów 13 F2

E

Eaunes 41 E3
Eauze 40 C3
Ebberup 2 C3
Ebbs 29 F3
Ebeleben 11 F3
Ebelsbach 20 A2
Ebeltoft 2 C1
Ebene Reichenau 30 B4
Ebenfurth 31 F2
Eben im Pongau 30 B3
Ebensee 30 B2
Ebensfeld 20 A2
Ebenweiler 28 B2
Eberau 31 F4
Eberbach 19 D3
Ebergötzen 11 F2
Ebermannsdorf 20 C3
Ebermannstadt 20 B2
Ebern 20 A2
Ebersbach *Ger.* 13 E3
Ebersbach *Ger.* 13 F3
Ebersbach an der Fils 28 B1
Ebersberg 29 F2
Eberschwang 30 B2
Ebersdorf *Austria* 31 E3
Ebersdorf *Ger.* 5 F2
Ebersdorf *Ger.* 12 B4
Eberstein 30 C4
Eberswalde-Finow 7 F4
Ebhausen 28 A1
Ebikon 28 A4
Ebnat-Kappel 28 B3
Eboli 50 A3
Ebrach 20 A2
Ebreichsdorf 31 F2
Ébreuil 34 B2
Ebringen 27 F2
Ebstorf 6 B3
Echallens 36 A1
Echarri 56 C2
Echarri-Aranaz 56 C2
Échenoz-la-Méline 27 D3
Eching *Ger.* 29 E1
Eching *Ger.* 29 F1
Échiré 32 C1
Echsenbach 31 D1
Echt 9 F3
Echte 11 F2
Echternach 17 F2
Echzell 19 D1
Écija 74 B2
Eckartsberga 12 B3
Eckental 20 B3
Eckernförde 6 A1
Éclaron-Braucourt-Ste-Livière 17 E4
Écommoy 24 B2
Écos 15 F3
Écouché 24 A1
Écouflant 24 A3
Écrouves 17 F4
Écueillé 24 C4
Écuisses 26 B4
Écury-sur-Coole 17 D4
Edam 4 A4
Eddelak 5 F2
Ede 9 F1
Edegem 9 D3
Edelschrott 31 D4
Edemissen 11 F1
Edenkoben 18 C3
Edermünde 11 E3
Edesheim 18 C3
Edewecht 5 D3
Edewechterdamm 5 D3
Edling 29 F2
Edlitz 31 E3
Edolo 38 B2
Edrosa 61 E1
Edroso 61 E1
Eeklo 8 C3
Eerbeek 10 A1
Eersel 9 E3
Eferding 30 C1
Effelder 20 B1
Effeltrich 20 B2
Effretikon 28 A3
Efringen-Kirchen 27 F3
Egebæk 2 A3
Egebjerg *Denmark* 2 C2
Egebjerg *Denmark* 3 E2
Egeln 12 B2
Egense 1 F2
Egernsund 2 B4
Egeskov 2 B2
Egestorf 6 A3
Eggebek 2 B4
Eggenburg 31 E1
Eggenfelden 30 A1
Eggenstein-Leopoldshafen 19 D3
Eggersdorf 12 B2
Eggesin 7 F2
Eggingen 28 A3
Eggiwil 27 F4
Egglham 30 A1
Eggolsheim 20 A2
Eggstätt 30 A2
Eghezée 17 E1
Eging am See 30 B1
Égletons 33 F3
Egling 29 E2
Eglisau 28 A3
Egmond aan Zee 4 A4
Egna 38 C2
Egsmark 2 C1
Egtved 2 B2
Éguilles 43 D3
Éguzon-Chantôme 33 E1
Ehekirchen 29 E1
Ehingen 20 A3
Ehingen (Donau) 28 C1
Ehlen (Habichtswald) 11 E3
Ehra-Lessien 6 B4
Ehrenberg-Wüstensachsen 11 F4
Ehrenfriedersdorf 13 D4
Ehringshausen 11 D4
Eibar 56 B2
Eibelstadt 19 F2
Eibenstock 12 C4
Eibergen 10 A1
Eibiswald 31 D4
Eich 19 D2
Eichenbarleben 12 B1
Eichenbühl 19 E2
Eichendorf 30 A1
Eichenzell 11 E4
Eichigt 20 C1
Eichstätt 20 B4
Eichwalde 13 E1
Eickendorf 12 B2
Eicklingen 6 A4
Eigeltingen 28 B2
Eigenrieden 11 F3
Eilenburg 12 C3
Eilenstedt 12 B2
Eilsleben 12 B1
Eime 11 E1
Eimen 11 E2
Eimke 6 A4
Einbeck 11 E2
Eindhoven 9 E2
Einsiedeln 28 A4
Eiselfing 29 F2
Eisenach 11 F3
Eisenberg 12 C4
Eisenberg (Pfalz) 18 C3
Eisenerz 31 D3
Eisenhüttenstadt 13 F1
Eisenstadt 31 F2
Eisfeld 20 A1
Eisleben Lutherstadt 12 B2
Eislingen (Fils) 28 C1
Eitelborn 18 C1
Eiterfeld 11 E4
Eitorf 10 B4
Eja 60 C2
Ejby *Denmark* 2 C3
Ejby *Denmark* 3 E2
Ejby *Denmark* 3 E3
Ejea de los Caballeros 57 D4
Ejsing 2 A1
Ejstrupholm 2 B2
Ejulve 64 C3
El Álamo 63 D4
El Algar 76 C2
El Almendro 72 C2
El Alquián 76 A3
El Arahal 74 A2
El Arenal 62 B4
El Astillero 55 F1
El Ballestero 70 A3
El Barco de Ávila 62 A3
El Barraco 62 C3
Elbeuf 15 E3
Elbigenalp 29 D3
Elbingerode (Harz) 11 F2
El Bodón 61 E3
El Bonillo 70 A2
El Bosque 74 A3
El Bullaque 69 D2
El Burgo 74 B3
El Burgo de Ebro 64 C1
El Burgo de Osma 63 E1
El Burgo Ranero 55 D3
El Buste 57 D4
El Cabaco 61 F3
El Cabildo y la Campana 76 A2
El Cabo de Gata 76 A4
El Campillo 73 D1
El Campillo de la Jara 68 B1
El Campo de Peñaranda 62 B2
El Cañavate 70 A1
El Carpio 68 C4
El Carpio de Tajo 62 C4
El Casar 63 D3
El Casar de Escalona 62 C4
El Castellar 64 C3
El Castillo de las Guardas 73 E1
El Catllar de Gaià 58 C4
El Centenillo 69 D4
El Cerro de Andévalo 73 D1
Elche de la Sierra 70 B3
Elche-Elx 71 D4
Elciego 56 B3
El Coronil 74 A2
El Cubo de Don Sancho 61 F2
El Cubo de Tierra del Vino 62 A2
El Cuervo *Spain* 73 E3
El Cuervo *Spain* 64 B4
Elda 71 D3
Eldena 6 C3
Eldingen 6 A4
El Ejido 75 E3
Elend 11 F2
El Escorial 62 C3
El Espinar 62 C3
El Estrecho 76 C2
El Fresno 62 B3
El Garrobo 73 E1
Elgershausen (Schauenburg) 11 E3
Elgeta 56 B2
Elgoibar 56 C2
El Grado 58 A2
El Granado 72 C2
El Grau de Borriana 65 D4
El Herrumblar 70 B2
El Hito 63 F4
El Hoyo de Pinares 62 C3
Elice 49 E1
Eliozondo 57 D2
Eljas 61 E4
Elkenroth 10 C4
Ellefeld 12 C4
Ellerau 6 A2
Ellerbek 6 A2
Ellezelles 8 C4
Ellidshøj 1 F2
Elling 1 F1
Ellingen 20 A3
El Llano 54 A1
Ellmau 29 F3
El Losar del Barco 62 A3
Ellrich 11 F2
Ellwangen (Jagst) 19 F4
Ellwürden 5 E3
Elm *Ger.* 5 F2
Elm *Switz.* 28 B4
El Masnou 59 D4
El Masroig 58 B4
Elmen 29 D3
Elmenhorst *Ger.* 6 B2
Elmenhorst *Ger.* 6 C1
Elmenhorst *Ger.* 6 A2
Elmenhorst *Ger.* 6 B2
El Molar 63 D3
El Molinillo 69 D1
El Moral 76 A1
El Morell 58 C4
Elmshorn 6 A2
Elmstein 18 C3

Elne **59** E2
Elorrio **56** B2
Elorz **57** D2
El Oso **62** B2
El Palau d'Anglesola **58** B3
El Palmar **76** B1
El Palo **74** C3
El Payo **61** E3
El Pedernoso **70** A2
El Pedroso **74** A1
El Pedroso de la Armuña **62** A2
El Peral **70** B1
El Perdigón **62** A1
El Perelló *Spain* **65** E2
El Perelló *Spain* **71** E2
Elpersbüttel **5** F1
El Picazo **70** B2
El Pinell de Bray **65** E2
El Piñero **62** A2
El pla de Santa Maria **58** C4
El Pobo **64** C3
El Pobo de Dueñas **64** B3
El Pont d'Armentera **58** C4
El Port **71** E1
El Port de la Selva **59** F2
El Prat de Llobregat **59** D4
El Provencio **70** A2
El Puente **56** A1
El Puente de Arzobispo **62** B4
El Puerto de Santa María **73** E3
El Real de la Jara **67** F4
El Real de San Vicente **62** C4
El Recuenco **63** F3
El Robledo **69** D2
El Rocío **73** E2
El Romeral **69** E1
El Rompido **73** D2
El Ronquillo **73** E1
El Royo **56** B4
El Rubio **74** B2
El Sabinar *Spain* **57** D4
El Sabinar *Spain* **76** A1
El Saler **71** D2
El Salobral **70** B3
Els Arcs **58** B3
El Saucejo **74** B2
El Saugo **61** E3
Elsdorf **10** A4
Elsendorf **29** E1
Elsenfeld **19** E2
El Serrat **58** C1
Elsfleth **5** E3
Elsnig **13** D2
Elsnigk **12** C2
El Soleràs **58** B4
Elspeet **9** F1
Els Prats de Rei **58** C3
Elst **9** F2
Elster **13** D2
Elsterberg **12** C4
Elsterwerda **13** E3
Elstra **13** E3
El Tiemblo **62** C3
Eltmann **20** A2
El Toboso **69** F1
El Torno **62** A4
El Trincheto **69** D2
El Tumbalejo **73** D2
Eltville am Rhein **18** C2
Elvas **67** E3
Elven **23** D3
El Vendrell **58** C4
El Villar de Arnedo **56** C3
El Viso **68** C3
El Viso del Alcor **74** A2
Elxleben **12** A3
Elz **18** C1
Elzach **27** F2
Elze **11** E1
Elze (Wedemark) **6** A4
Embid **64** B2
Embid de Ariza **64** A1
Embrun **43** F1
Emden **4** C3
Emlichheim **4** C4
Emmeloord **4** B4
Emmelsbüll-Horsbüll **2** A4
Emmelshausen **18** C1
Emmen *Neth.* **4** C4
Emmen *Switz.* **28** A4
Emmendingen **27** F2
Emmer-Compascuum **4** C4
Emmer-Erfscheidenveen **4** C4
Emmerich **10** A2
Empoli **46** A3
Emsbüren **10** B1
Emsdetten **10** C1
Emskirchen **20** A3
Emst **10** A1
Emstek **5** E4
Emtinghausen **5** F4
Encamp **58** C2
Encinas de Abajo **62** A2
Encinasola **67** E4
Encinas Reales **74** C2
Encinedo **54** B3
Enciso **56** C4
Endingen **27** F2
Endrinal **62** A3
Enego **38** C2
Enfesta **53** E3
Engelberg **28** A4
Engelhartstetten **31** F2
Engelhartszell **30** B1
Engeln **5** F4
Engelsberg **30** A2
Engelskirchen **10** B3
Engen **28** A2
Enger **11** D1
Engersen **6** C4
Engesvang **2** B1
Enghien **16** C1
Engis **17** E1
Englefontaine **16** C1
Engstingen **28** B1
Enguera **71** D2
Enguidanos **70** B1
Enix **75** F3
Enkhuizen **4** A4
Ennezat **34** B2
Ennigerloh **10** C2
Enns **30** C2
Ens **4** B4
Enschede **10** B1
Ensdorf **20** C3
Ense **10** C3
Ensheim **18** B3
Ensisheim **27** F2
Ensuès-la-Redonne **43** D3
Entlebuch **28** A4
Entracque **44** A2
Entradas **72** B1
Entraigues-sur-Sorgues **43** D2
Entrains-sur-Nohain **25** F3
Entrammes **23** F2
Entraygues-sur-Truyère **41** F1
Entre-Deux-Guiers **35** F3
Entrena **56** B3
Entrevaux **44** A2
Entroncamento **66** B2
Envendos **66** C1
Envermeu **15** F2
Enzersdorf an der Fischa **31** F2
Enzklösterle **28** A1
Épaignes **15** E3
Epalignes **36** A1
Epe **10** A1
Épernay **16** C4
Épernon **25** D1
Epfendorf **28** A2
Épieds-en-Beauce **25** D2
Épierre **36** A3
Épila **64** B1
Épinac **26** B4
Épinal **27** D2
Episcopia **50** C4
Eppelborn **18** B3
Eppelheim **19** D3
Eppenbrunn **18** C3
Eppertshausen **19** D2
Eppeville **16** B2
Eppingen **19** D3
Eppishausen **29** D2
Eppstein **19** D1
Équerdreville-Hainneville **14** B2
Eraclea **39** E3
Eraclea Mare **39** E3
Erandio **56** B1
Erba **37** E2
Erbach *Ger.* **28** C1
Erbach *Ger.* **19** D2
Erbendorf **20** C2
Erbray **23** F3
Erchie **51** E3
Erdeborn **12** B3
Erdeven **22** C3
Erding **29** F1
Erdweg **29** E1
Erfde **5** F1
Erftstadt **10** A4
Erfurt **12** B3
Ergersheim **20** A3
Ergoldsbach **29** F1
Ergué-Gabéric **22** B2
Erharting **30** A1
Erica **4** C4
Erice **56** C2
Ericeira **66** A2
Ering **30** B1
Eriswil **27** F4
Erkelenz **10** A3
Erkheim **29** D2
Erkner **13** E1
Erla **57** E4
Erlach **27** E4
Erlangen **20** A3
Erlauf **31** D2
Erlbach **20** C1
Erli **44** B2
Ermelo *Neth.* **9** F1
Ermelo *Port.* **60** C1
Ermesinde **60** B2
Ermidas do Sado **66** C4
Ermsleben **12** B2
Ermua **56** B2
Erndtebrück **10** C3
Ernée **23** F2
Ernstbrunn **31** F1
Erp **9** E2
Erquelinnes **17** D1
Erquy **23** D1
Errindlev **3** D4
Erritsø **2** B2
Erstein **27** F1
Erstfeld **28** A4
Ertingen **28** B2
Erto **39** D2
Ervedosa do Douro **61** D2
Ervidel **66** C4
Ervy-le-Châtel **26** A2
Erwitte **10** C2
Erxleben *Ger.* **12** B1
Erxleben *Ger.* **6** C4
Esanatoglia **47** D3
Esbjerg **2** A3
Esbønderup **3** E2
Escairón **53** F3
Escalante **55** F1
Escalhão **61** E2
Escaló **58** C2
Escalona **62** C4
Escalona del Prado **62** C2
Escalonilla **62** C4
Escalos de Baixo **67** D1
Escalos de Cima **67** D1
Escamilla **63** F3
Escañuela **74** C1
Escariche **63** E3
Escarigo **61** D4
Escaroz **57** D2
Escatrón **65** D2
Eschborn **19** D1
Escheburg **6** A3
Eschede **6** A4
Eschenbach **28** A4
Eschenstruth (Helsa) **11** E3
Eschershausen **11** E2
Eschlkam **21** D3
Escholzmatt **27** F4
Esch-sur-Alzette **17** F3
Esch-sur-Sûre **17** F2
Eschwege **11** F3
Eschweiler **10** A4
Escombreras **76** C2
Escorihuela **64** C3
Escouloubre **59** D1
Escragnolles **44** A3
Escucha **64** C3
Escurial **68** A2
Escusa **53** E3
Escúzar **75** D2
Esens **5** D2
Esfarrapada **53** E4
Esgos **53** F3
Esgueira **60** B3
Esguevillas de Esgueva **55** E4
Eskilstrup **3** E4
Eskoriatza **56** B2
Eslarn **20** C3
Eslava **57** D3
Eslohe (Sauerland) **10** C3
Esneux **17** E1
Espadañedo **54** B4
Espalion **42** A1
Espaly-St-Marcel **34** C4
Esparragalejo **67** F2
Esparragosa **68** B2
Esparragosa de la Serena **68** B3
Esparraguera **59** D4
Esparza de Salazar **57** D2
Espe **2** C3
Espeja **61** E3
Espeja de San Marcelino **56** A4
Espejo **74** C1
Espejón **56** A4
Espel **4** B4
Espelette **40** A3
Espelkamp **11** D1
Espenau **11** E3
Espera **74** A3
Esperança **67** D2
Espéraza **41** F4
Espergærde **3** F2
Esperia **49** D3
Espiel **68** B4
Espinama **55** D2
Espinhal **60** C4
Espinho **60** B2
Espinilla **55** E2
Espinosa de Cerrato **55** F4
Espinosa de Henares **63** E2
Espinosa de los Monteros **55** F2
Espinoso del Rey **68** C1
Espira-de-l'Agly **42** A4
Espírito Santo **72** C2
Espite **66** B1
Esplegares **63** F2
Esplús **58** A3
Espolla **59** E2
Esponellà **59** E2
Esposende **60** B1
Espot **58** C2
Esquivias **63** D4
Essel **6** A4
Essen *Belgium* **9** D2
Essen *Ger.* **10** B2
Essen (Oldenburg) **5** D4
Essenbach **29** F1
Essert **27** E3
Essingen **19** F4
Esslingen am Neckar **28** B1
Essoyes **26** B2
Estación de Baeza **69** E4
Estadilla **58** A3
Estagel **42** A4
Estaimpuis **8** C4
Estaing **42** A1
Estaires **16** B1
Estarreja **60** B3
Estavayer-le-Lac **27** E4
Este *Italy* **38** C4
Este *Port.* **60** C1
Estela **60** B1
Estella **56** C3
Estepa **74** B2
Estepar **55** F3
Estepona **74** B4
Esteras de Medinaceli **63** F2
Estercuel **64** C2
Esternay **16** C4
Esterri d'Aneu **58** C2
Esterwegen **5** D4
Estissac **26** A2
Estivareilles **34** B1
Estói **72** B2
Estômbar **72** A2
Estorf *Ger.* **5** F2
Estorf *Ger.* **5** F4
Estoril **66** A3
Estrées-St-Denis **16** B3
Estreito **67** D1
Estrela **67** D4
Estremera **63** E4
Estremoz **67** D3
Estriégala **63** F2
Esvres **24** C3
Étables-sur-Mer **23** D1
Étain **17** E3
Étalle **17** E2
Étampes **25** D1
Étang-sur-Arroux **26** A4
Étaples **15** F1
Étaules **32** B3
Étauliers **32** B4
Ethe **17** E3
Étival-Clairefontaine **27** E1
Étoile-sur-Rhône **43** D1
Étréchy **25** D1
Étrépagny **15** F3
Étretat **15** D2
Étreux **16** C2
Etrín Bajo **67** E3
Etroubles **36** B3
Ettelbruck **17** F2
Ettenheim **27** F2
Etten-Leur **9** D2
Ettlingen **19** D4
Etxalar **57** D2
Eu **15** F2
Eubigheim **19** E3
Euerdorf **19** F1
Eulate **56** C2
Eupen **17** F1
Euper **13** D2
Eurasburg **29** E2
Eurville-Bienville **17** E4

Euskirchen **10** B4
Eußenheim **19** E2
Eutin **6** B1
Eutzsch **13** D2
Euville **17** F4
Évaux-les-Bains **34** A2
Everdrup **3** E3
Evergem **8** C3
Évian-les-Bains **36** A1
Evolène **36** B2
Évora **66** C3
Évora-Monte **67** D3
Évran **23** E2
Évrecy **14** C4
Évreux **15** E4
Évron **24** A2
Évry **16** A4
Excideuil **33** E4
Exilles **36** A4
Exloo **4** C4
Exmes **24** B1
Extremo **53** E4
Eydelstedt **5** E4
Eyguières **43** D3
Eymet **40** C1
Eymoutiers **33** F3
Eyragues **43** D2
Ezcaray **56** B3
Ezcurra **56** C2
Ézy-sur-Eure **24** C1

F

Fabara **58** A4
Fabero **54** B3
Fåborg *Denmark* **2** C3
Fåborg *Denmark* **2** A2
Fabrègues **42** B3
Fabrezan **42** A4
Fabriano **47** D3
Fabrica di Roma **48** B1
Fábricas de San Juan de Alcaraz **70** A3
Fabrizia **52** B3
Fabro **46** C4
Facinas **74** A4
Faedis **39** F2
Faenza **46** C2
Faeto **50** A2
Fafe **60** C1
Fagagna **39** E2
Fagnano Castello **52** A1
Fagnières **17** D4
Fahrdorf **6** A1
Fahrenkrug **6** A2
Fahrenzhausen **29** E1
Fahrland **13** D1
Faicchio **49** F3
Faid **18** B2
Faido **37** D1
Failde **61** E1
Faimes **17** E1
Fains-Véel **17** E4
Fajão **60** C4
Fajarda **66** B2
Fakse **3** E3
Fakse Ladeplads **3** E3
Falaise **15** D4
Falcade **39** D1
Falces **56** C3
Falconara Albanese **52** A2
Falconara Marittima **47** E3
Faldsled **2** C3
Faleria **48** C1
Falerna **52** B2
Falerone **47** E4
Falkenberg *Ger.* **30** A1
Falkenberg *Ger.* **20** C2
Falkenberg *Ger.* **13** D2
Falkenhagen **7** D3
Falkenhain **13** D3
Falkensee **7** E4
Falkenstein *Ger.* **20** C3
Falkenstein *Ger.* **12** C4
Falleron **32** A1
Fallingbostel **6** A4
Falmenta **37** D2
Falset **58** B4
Famalicão **61** D3
Fambach **11** F4
Fameck **17** F3
Fanano **46** A2
Fanjeaux **41** F4
Fanlo **58** A2
Fano **47** D2
Fão **60** B1
Fara Filiorum Petri **49** E1
Fara in Sabina **48** C1
Fara San Martino **49** E2
Farasdues **57** D3
Farchant **29** E3
Farciennes **17** D1
Fardella **50** C4
Faremoutiers **16** B4
Fårevejle **3** D2
Fårevejle Stationsby **3** D2
Fargues **40** B1
Fårhus **2** B4
Farini **45** E1
Fariza de Sayago **61** F1
Farlete **57** E4
Farnese **48** B1
Farnstädt **12** B3
Faro **72** B3
Faro do Alentejo **66** C4
Farra d'Alpago **39** D2
Farre *Denmark* **2** C1
Farre *Denmark* **2** B2
Farsø **1** E2
Farstrup **1** E2
Fårup **2** C1
Fårvang **2** B1
Fasano **51** E3
Fasterholt **2** B2
Fatela **61** D4
Fátima **66** B1
Faucogney-et-la-Mer **27** E2
Fauglia **46** A3
Faulenrost **7** D2
Faulquemont **18** A4
Fauquembergues **16** A1
Faura **71** D1
Fauville-en-Caux **15** E2
Favaios **61** D2
Favale di Malvaro **45** D1
Favara **71** E2
Faverges **36** A3
Faverney **27** D3
Fay-de-Bretagne **23** E3
Fayence **43** F3
Fayl-la-Forêt **26** C2
Fayón **58** A4
Fay-sur-Lignon **35** D4
Fécamp **15** D2
Fégréac **23** E3
Fehrbellin **7** D4
Fehring **31** E4
Feijó **66** A3
Feilitzsch **20** C1
Feillens **35** E2
Feira do Monte **53** F2
Feissons-sur-Isère **36** A3
Feiteira **72** B2
Felchow **7** F3
Feld am See **30** B4
Feldbach **31** E4
Feldballe **2** C1
Feldberg **7** E3
Felde **6** A1
Feldkirch **28** C3
Feldkirchen in Kärnten **30** C4
Feldkirchen-Westerham **29** F2
Felgar **61** E2
Felgueiras **60** C1
Felino **46** A1
Felitto **50** A4
Félix **75** F3
Felixdorf **31** F2
Felizzano **37** D4
Fell **18** B2
Fellbach **19** E4
Felletin **33** F2
Felsberg **11** E3
Felsted **2** B4
Feltre **39** D2
Fénay **26** C3
Fenestrelle **36** B4
Fénétrange **18** B4
Feneu **24** A3
Fenis **36** B3
Fensmark **3** E3
Ferdinandea **52** B3
Ferdinandshof **7** F2
Fère-Champenoise **16** C4
Fère-en-Tardenois **16** C3
Férel **23** D3
Ferentillo **48** C1
Ferentino **49** D2
Férez **76** A1
Feria **67** E3
Fermignano **47** D3
Fermo **47** E4
Fermoselle **61** F2
Fernáncaballero **69** D2
Fernán Núñez **74** B1
Ferney-Voltaire **35** F2
Fernitz **31** E4
Feroleto Antico **52** B2
Ferrandina **50** C3
Ferrara **38** C4
Ferrazzano **49** F3
Ferreira **54** A1
Ferreira do Alentejo **66** C4
Ferreira do Zêzere **66** C1
Ferrel **66** A2
Ferreras de Abajo **54** B4
Ferreras de Arriba **54** C4
Ferrere **36** C4
Ferreruela de Huerva **64** B2
Ferreruela de Tábara **54** C4
Ferrette **27** E3
Ferriere **45** D1
Ferrières *Belgium* **17** E1
Ferrières *France* **25** E2
Ferritslet **2** C3
Ferrol **53** E1
Ferwerd **4** B3
Fessenheim **27** F2
Feucht **20** B3
Feuchtwangen **20** A3
Feuquières **16** A2
Feuquières-en-Vimeu **15** F2
Feurs **35** D3
Feytiat **33** E3
Fiamignano **49** D1
Fiano **36** B4
Fiano Romano **48** C2
Fiavè **38** B2
Ficarolo **38** C4
Fichtelberg **20** B2
Fichtenberg **19** E4
Ficulle **46** C4
Fidenza **38** A4
Fiè allo Sciliar **38** C1
Fieberbrunn **30** A3
Fiera di Primiero **39** D2
Fiesch **36** C1
Fiesole **46** B2
Fiesso Umbertiano **38** C4
Figanières **43** F3
Figeac **41** F1
Figline Valdarno **46** B3
Figueira da Foz **60** B4
Figueira de Castelo Rodrigo **61** E2
Figueira e Barros **67** D2
Figueiredo de Alva **60** C2
Figueiró da Granja **61** D3
Figueiró dos Vinhos **66** C1
Figueres **59** E2
Figueroles **65** D4
Figueruela de Arriba **54** B4
Filadelfia **52** B3
Filattiera **45** E1
Filettino **49** D2
Filiano **50** B3
Filisur **38** A1
Fillinges **36** A2
Filottrano **47** E3
Filskov **2** B2
Filsum **5** D3
Filzmoos **30** B3
Finale Emilia **38** C4
Finale Ligure **44** C2
Fiñana **75** E2
Finestrat **71** E3
Finkenstein **39** F1
Finnentrop **10** C3
Fino Mornasco **37** D3
Finowfurt **7** E4
Finsterwalde **13** E2
Finsterwolde **4** C3
Fintel **6** A3
Fiorano Modense **46** A1
Fiorenzuola d'Arda **38** A4
Firenze **46** B3
Firenzuola **46** B2
Firmi **41** F1
Firminy **35** D3
Firmo **52** B1
Fiscal **58** A2
Fischach **29** D1
Fischamend Markt **31** F2
Fischbach *Austria* **31** E3
Fischbach *Ger.* **18** B2
Fischbachau **29** F2
Fischbach bei Dahn **18** C4
Fischbeck **12** C1
Fischen im Allgäu **28** C3
Fismes **16** C3
Fisterra **53** D2
Fitero **56** C4
Fitz-James **16** A3
Fiuggi **49** D2
Fiumalbo **46** A2
Fiumefreddo Bruzio **52** A2
Fiumicino **48** B2
Fivizzano **45** E2
Fjellerup **2** C1
Fjelsø **1** E3
Fjelsted **2** C3
Fjelstervang **2** A1
Fjelstrup **2** B3
Fjenneslev **3** E3
Fjerritslev **1** E2
Flachau **30** B3
Flachsmeer **5** D3
Fladungen **11** F4
Flaine **36** A2
Flakkebjerg **3** D3
Flamanville **14** B3
Flassans-sur-Issole **43** F3
Flattach **30** A4
Flattnitz **30** C4
Flauenskjold **1** F2
Flavigny-sur-Moselle **17** F4
Flavin **41** F2
Flawil **28** B3
Flayosc **43** F3
Flechtingen **12** B1
Flecken Zechlin **7** D3
Fleetmark **6** C4
Flein **19** E3
Flémalle **17** E1
Flensburg **2** B4
Fléron **17** E1
Flers **23** F1
Flers-en-Escrebieux **16** B1
Flessau **6** C4
Fleurance **41** D3
Fleurie **35** D2
Fleurier **27** E4
Fleurus **17** D1
Fleury **42** A4
Fleury-les-Aubrais **25** D2
Fleury-sur-Andelle **15** F3
Flieden **19** E1
Fließ **29** D4
Flims **28** B4
Flintbek **6** A1
Flix **58** B4
Flixecourt **16** A2
Flize **17** D2
Flogny-la-Chapelle **26** A2
Floh **11** F4
Flöha **13** D4
Floing **17** E2
Floirac **32** C4
Florac **42** B2
Florange **17** F3
Floreffe **17** D1
Florennes **17** D1
Florenville **17** E2
Flores de Ávila **62** B2
Florida de Liébana **62** A2
Flörsbach **19** E2
Flörsheim am Main **19** D2
Flörsheim-Dalsheim **18** C2
Flossenbürg **20** C2
Flöthe **11** F1
Flüelen **28** A4
Flumeri **50** A2
Flumet **36** A2
Flums **28** B4
Fly **2** B1
Fobello **36** C2
Foëcy **25** D4
Foggia **50** B2
Foglianise **49** F3
Fohnsdorf **31** D3
Fohrde **12** C1
Föhren **18** B2
Foiano della Chiana **46** C3
Foix **41** E4
Fole **2** B3
Folgaria **38** C2
Folgoso de Courel **54** A3
Folgoso de la Ribera **54** B3
Folignano **47** E4
Foligno **47** D4
Føllenslev **3** D2
Follina **39** D2
Follonica **46** A4
Folschviller **18** A4
Fondevila **53** F4
Fondi **49** D3
Fondón **75** E3
Fonelas **75** E2
Fonfría *Spain* **64** C2
Fonfría *Spain* **61** F1
Fontaine *France* **27** E3
Fontaine *France* **35** F4
Fontainebleau **25** E1
Fontaine-Française **26** C3
Fontaine-le-Bourg **15** E3
Fontaine-le-Dun **15** E2
Fontaine-lès-Luxeuil **27** D2
Fontainemore **36** C3
Fontaines **26** B4
Fontan **44** B2
Fontanar **63** E3
Fontanarejo **68** C2
Fontane **44** B2
Fontanelice **46** B2
Fontanellato **38** A4
Fontanigorda **45** D1
Fontanosas **68** C3

Fontecchio **49** D1
Fontellas **57** D4
Fontenay-le-Comte **32** B1
Fontes **66** C1
Fontevrault-l'Abbaye **24** B4
Fontiveros **62** B2
Font-Romeu-Odeillo-Via **59** D2
Fontvieille **43** D3
Fonz **58** A3
Fonzaso **39** D2
Foppolo **38** A2
Forano **48** C1
Forbach *France* **18** B3
Forbach *Ger.* **28** A1
Forcall **65** D3
Forcalquier **43** E2
Forcarei **53** E3
Forcc **47** E4
Forchheim **20** B2
Forchtenstein **31** F2
Förderstedt **12** B2
Forenza **50** B3
Forges-les-Eaux **15** F3
Forino **50** A3
Forio **49** E4
Föritz **20** B1
Forjães **60** B1
Forlev **3** D3
Forlì **46** C2
Forlimpopoli **46** C2
Formazza **36** C1
Formello **48** C2
Formerie **16** A2
Formia **49** D3
Formiche Alto **64** C3
Formicola **49** E3
Formigine **46** A1
Formigliana **36** C3
Formignana **39** D4
Formiguères **59** D2
Fornells de la Selva **59** E3
Forni Avoltri **39** E1
Forni di Sopra **39** E1
Forni di Sotto **39** E1
Forno Alpi Graie **36** B3
Forno di Zoldo **39** D1
Fornos **61** E2
Fornos de Algodres **61** D3
Foros de Vale Figueira **66** C3
Foros do Arrão **66** C2
Førslev **3** E3
Forst *Ger.* **19** D3
Forst *Ger.* **13** F2
Forstinning **29** F2
Fortanete **65** D3
Forte **53** E2
Fortezza **38** C1
Fortios **67** D2
Fort-Mahon-Plage **15** F1
Fortuna **76** C1
Fosdinovo **45** E2
Fossacesia **49** F1
Fossalta di Portogruaro **39** E2
Fossano **44** B1
Fossato di Vico **47** D3
Fosses-la-Ville **17** D1
Fossiat **35** E1
Fossombrone **47** D3
Fos-sur-Mer **43** D3
Foucarmont **15** F2
Fouesnant **22** B3
Foug **17** F4
Fougères **23** F2
Fougerolles **27** D2
Fougerolles-du-Plessis **23** F1
Fouilloy **16** B2
Foulayronnes **41** D2
Fouras **32** B2
Fourchambault **25** F4
Fourmies **16** C2
Fournels **42** A1
Fourques *France* **42** C3
Fourques *France* **59** E2
Fours **26** A4
Foxas **53** F1
Foz *Port.* **66** C2
Foz *Spain* **54** A1
Foz do Arelho **66** A1
Foz Giraldo **61** D4
Frabosa Soprana **44** B2
Frades de la Sierra **62** A3
Fraga **58** A4
Fragagnano **51** E3
Fraham **30** C1
Frailes **75** D2
Fraisans **26** C4
Fraize **27** E2
Frameries **16** C1
Framlev **2** C1
Francavilla al Mare **49** E1
Francavilla Fontana **51** E3
Francavilla in Sinni **50** C4
Francescas **40** C2
Franco **61** D1
Franeker **4** B3
Frangy **35** F2
Frankenau **11** D3
Frankenberg **13** D4
Frankenberg (Eder) **11** D3
Frankenburg am Hausruck **30** B2
Frankenfels **31** D2
Frankenheim **11** F4
Frankenmarkt **30** B2
Frankenthal (Pfalz) **19** D3
Frankfurt am Main **19** D2
Frankfurt an der Oder **13** F1
Franois **27** D3
Franzburg **7** D1
Frascati **48** C2
Frascineto **52** B1
Frasne **27** D4
Frasnes-lez-Buissenal **16** C1
Frasnes-lez-Gosselies **17** D1
Frassinoro **46** A2
Frasso Telesino **49** F3
Frastanz **28** C3
Fratel **67** D1
Fratta Polesine **38** C4
Fratta Todina **47** D4
Fraubrunnen **27** F4
Frauenau **21** D4
Frauenfeld **28** B3
Frauental an der Laßnitz **31** D4
Frauenwald **12** A4
Fraunberg **29** F1
Frayssinet-le-Gélat **41** D1
Frechas **61** D1
Frechen **10** B4
Frechilla **55** D4
Fredensborg **3** E2
Fredericia **2** B2
Frederiks **2** B1
Frederiksberg *Denmark* **3** E2
Frederiksberg *Denmark* **3** D3
Frederikshavn **1** F1
Frederikssund **3** E2
Frederiksværk **3** E2
Fredersdorf **13** E1
Fregenal de la Sierra **67** E4
Fregene **48** B2
Freginals **65** E3
Fréhel **23** D1
Freiberg **13** D4
Freiburg (Elbe) **5** F2
Freiburg im Breisgau **27** F2
Freiensteinau **19** E1
Freienwill **2** B4
Freihung **20** C3
Freila **75** E2
Freilassing **30** A2
Freisen **18** B3
Freising **29** E1
Freistadt **30** C1
Freistroff **18** A3
Freital **13** E3
Freixedas **61** D3
Freixianda **66** C1
Freixiosa **61** D3
Freixo **60** B1
Freixo de Espada à Cinta **61** E2
Frejlev **1** F2
Fréjus **43** F3
Frellstedt **12** A1
Fremdingen **20** A4
Frensdorf **20** A2
Freren **10** C1
Fresach **30** B4
Fresnay-sur-Sarthe **24** B2
Fresneda de la Sierra **63** F3
Fresnedoso de Ibor **68** B1
Fresnes-en-Woëvre **17** F3
Fresne-St-Mamès **27** D3
Fresno Alhándiga **62** A3
Fresno de la Ribera **62** A1
Fresno de Sayago **62** A2
Fresno el Viejo **62** B2
Fresnoy-le-Grand **16** C2
Freudenberg **10** C4
Freudenstadt **28** A1
Frévent **16** A1
Freyburg (Unstrut) **12** B3
Freyenstein **7** D3
Freyming-Merlebach **18** B3
Freyung **21** E4
Frías **56** A2
Fribourg **27** E4
Frick **27** F3
Fridingen an der Donau **28** B2
Fridolfing **30** A2
Frieda (Meinhard) **11** F3
Friedberg *Austria* **31** E3
Friedberg *Ger.* **29** D1
Friedberg (Hessen) **19** D1
Friedeburg **5** D3
Friedeburg (Saale) **12** B2
Friedenfels **20** C2
Friedersdorf *Ger.* **13** E1
Friedersdorf *Ger.* **12** C2
Friedewald **11** E4
Friedland *Ger.* **13** E1
Friedland *Ger.* **7** E2
Friedland *Ger.* **11** E3
Friedrichroda **11** F4
Friedrichsbrunn **12** B2
Friedrichsdorf **19** D1
Friedrichshafen **28** C3
Friedrichskoog **5** E2
Friedrichsruhe **6** C2
Friedrichstadt **5** F1
Friedrichswalde **7** E3
Frielendorf **11** E3
Friemar **12** A3
Friesach **30** C4
Friesack **7** D4
Friesenheim **27** F1
Friesenried **29** D2
Friesoythe **5** D3
Frifelt **2** A3
Frigento **50** A2
Frigiliana **75** D3
Frignicourt **17** D4
Friol **53** F2
Frisange **17** F3
Fritzens **29** E3
Fritzlar **11** E3
Friville-Escarbotin **15** F2
Froges **35** F4
Frohburg **12** C3
Frohnleiten **31** D3
Froideconche **27** D2
Froissy **16** A3
Frómista **55** E3
Fröndenberg **10** C2
Fronhausen **11** D4
Fronsac **32** C4
Fronteira **67** D2
Frontenay-Rohan-Rohan **32** B2
Frontenhausen **30** A1
Frontignan **42** B3
Fronton **41** E3
Frose **12** B2
Frosinone **49** D2
Frøslev **1** D2
Frosolone **49** F3
Frøstrup **1** E2
Frouard **17** F4
Fruges **16** A1
Frutigen **36** B1
Fubine **37** D4
Fucecchio **46** A3
Fuchstal **29** D2
Fuencaliente **69** D4
Fuendejalón **57** D4
Fuengirola **74** B4
Fuenlabrada **63** D4
Fuenmayor **56** B3
Fuensalida **62** C4
Fuensanta *Spain* **70** B2
Fuensanta *Spain* **76** A2
Fuensanta de Martos **75** D1
Fuente Álamo **76** B2
Fuente-Álamo **70** C3
Fuentealbilla **70** C2
Fuentecambrón **63** E1
Fuentecén **63** D1
Fuente de Cantos **67** F4
Fuente del Arco **68** A4
Fuente del Maestre **67** F3
Fuente de Pedro Naharro **63** E4
Fuente de Piedra **74** B2
Fuente Díaz **53** E2
Fuente el Fresno **69** D2
Fuente el Saz de Jarama **63** D3
Fuente el Sol **62** B2
Fuenteguinaldo **61** E3
Fuentelapeña **62** B2
Fuentelcésped **63** D1
Fuentelespino de Haro **70** A1
Fuentelespino de Moya **64** B4
Fuentelmonge **63** F1
Fuentenovilla **63** E3
Fuente Obejuna **68** B4
Fuente Palmera **74** B1
Fuentepelayo **62** C2
Fuentepinilla **63** E1
Fuenterodos **64** C2
Fuenterrebollo **63** D2
Fuenterroble de Salvatierra **62** A3
Fuentesaúco **62** A2
Fuentesaúco de Fuentidueña **62** C1
Fuentes-Claras **64** B2
Fuentes de Andalucía **74** A2
Fuentes de Ebro **64** C1
Fuentes de Jiloca **64** B2
Fuentes de León **67** F4
Fuentes de Nava **55** D4
Fuentes de Oñoro **61** E3
Fuentes de Ropel **54** C4
Fuentespalda **65** D3
Fuente-Tójar **74** C2
Fuente Vaqueros **75** D2
Fuentidueña **63** D1
Fuerte del Rey **75** D1
Fuertescusa **63** F3
Fügen **29** F3
Fuglebjerg **3** D3
Fuhrberg (Burgwedel) **6** A4
Fulda **11** E4
Fumay **17** D2
Fumel **41** D1
Fumone **49** D2
Fundada **66** C1
Fundão **61** D4
Funder Kirkeby **2** B1
Funes *Italy* **38** C1
Funes *Spain* **56** C3
Furadouro **60** B2
Furci **49** F2
Fürstenau **10** C1
Fürstenberg *Ger.* **7** E3
Fürstenberg *Ger.* **11** E2
Fürstenberg (Lichtenfels) **11** D3
Fürstenfeld **31** E4
Fürstenfeldbruck **29** E2
Fürstenwalde **13** E1
Fürstenwerder **7** E3
Fürstenzell **30** B1
Fürth *Ger.* **20** A3
Fürth *Ger.* **19** D2
Furth **29** F1
Furth bei Göttweig **31** E1
Furth im Wald **21** D3
Furtwangen im Schwarzwald **28** A2
Fuscaldo **52** A2
Fusignano **46** C1
Fußach **28** C3
Füssen **29** D3
Fussy **25** E4
Fustiñana **57** D4
Fuveau **43** E3
Fynshav **2** C4

G

Gaal **30** C3
Gabaldón **70** B1
Gabarret **40** C2
Gabia la Grande **75** D2
Gabicce Mare **47** D2
Gablingen **29** D1
Gablitz **31** E2
Gaby **36** C3
Gacé **24** B1
Gadbjerg **2** B2
Gadebusch **6** B2
Gadmen **28** A4
Gádor **75** F3
Gadstrup **3** E3
Gaeiras **66** B2
Gærum **1** F1
Gaeta **49** D3
Gafanha da Boa Hora **60** B3
Gafanha da Nazaré **60** B3
Gafanha do Carmo **60** B3
Gafanhoeira **66** C3
Gáfete **67** D2
Gaggenau **19** D4
Gaggio Montano **46** A2
Gaglianico **36** C3
Gagliano del Capo **51** F4
Gaildorf **19** E4
Gaillac **41** E2
Gaillard **35** F2
Gaillon **15** F3
Gaimersheim **20** B4

Gaiole in Chianti **46** B3
Gais *Italy* **29** F4
Gais *Switz.* **28** B3
Gaishorn **30** C3
Gajanejos **63** E2
Galan **40** C4
Galapagar **63** D3
Galaroza **67** E4
Galatina **51** F4
Galatone **51** F4
Galbarra **56** C3
Galdakao **56** B2
Galeata **46** C2
Galende **54** B4
Galera **75** F1
Galgon **32** C4
Galinduste **62** A3
Galisteo **61** F4
Gallarate **37** D3
Gallardon **25** D1
Gallegos de Argañan **61** E3
Gallegos de Solmirón **62** A3
Galleno **46** A3
Gallese **48** C1
Gallian-en-Médoc **32** B3
Galliate **37** D3
Gallicano **46** A2
Gallicano nel Lazio **48** C2
Gallin *Ger.* **6** B3
Gallin *Ger.* **7** D3
Gallio **38** C2
Gallipoli **51** F4
Gallneukirchen **30** C1
Galluccio **49** E3
Gallur **57** D4
Galten **2** C1
Galtür **28** C4
Galve **64** C3
Galve de Sorbe **63** E2
Galveias **66** C2
Gálvez **69** D1
Gama **55** F1
Gamaches **15** F2
Gambara **38** A3
Gambarie **52** A4
Gambassi Terme **46** A3
Gambatesa **50** A1
Gambettola **47** D2
Gambolò **37** D4
Gambsheim **27** F1
Gaming **31** D2
Gamlitz **31** E4
Gammel Rye **2** B1
Gammelsdorf **29** F1
Gammertingen **28** B2
Gams **28** B3
Gan **40** B4
Gand **8** C3
Gándara *Spain* **53** F1
Gándara *Spain* **53** F2
Gandarela **60** C1
Gandellino **38** A2
Ganderkesee **5** E3
Gandesa **58** B4
Gandesbergen **5** F4
Gandía **71** E3
Gandino **38** A2
Gandra **53** E4
Gandrup **1** F2
Ganfei **53** E4
Ganges **42** B2
Gangkofen **30** A1
Ganløse **3** E2
Gannat **34** B2
Gänserndorf **31** F1
Ganshoren **9** D4
Ganzlin **7** D3
Gap **43** E1
Garaballa **64** B4
Garaguso **50** C3
Garbayuela **68** C2
Garbsen **11** E1
Garching an der Alz **30** A2
Garching bei München **29** E1
Garchizy **25** F4
Garcia **58** B4
Garciaz **68** B2
Garcihernández **62** A2
Garcillán **62** C2
Garcinarro **63** F4
Garda **38** B3
Gardanne **43** E3
Gardelegen **12** B1
Garding **5** E1
Gardone Riviera **38** B3
Gardone Val Trompia **38** A3
Gardonne **33** D4
Garéoult **43** E3
Garessio **44** B2
Gargáligas **68** A2
Gargallo **64** C3
Garganta la Olla **62** A4
Gargazzone **38** C1
Gargnano **38** B3
Garijp **4** B3
Garlasco **37** D4
Garlenz **31** D2
Garlin **40** B3
Garlitos **68** B3
Garlstorf **6** A3
Garmisch-Partenkirchen **29** E3
Garons **42** C3
Garrafe de Torio **54** C3
Garralda **57** D2
Garray **56** C4
Garrel **5** D4
Garrovillas **67** E1
Garrucha **76** A3
Gars am Inn **29** F2
Gars am Kamp **31** E1
Gårslev **2** B2
Garstedt **6** A3
Gartow **6** C3
Gärtringen **28** B1
Gartz **7** F3
Garvão **72** B1
Garz **7** E1
Gaschurn **28** C4
Gascueña **63** F3
Gasny **15** F4
Gasperina **52** B3
Gaspoltshofen **30** B2
Gasselte **4** C4
Gasselternijveen **4** C4
Gassino Torinese **36** C4
Gassum **2** C1
Gata **61** E4
Gata de Gorgos **71** E3
Gátova **71** D1
Gatteo a Mare **47** D2
Gattières **44** A3
Gattinara **36** C3
Gau-Algesheim **18** C2
Gauchy **16** B2
Gaucín **74** A4
Gaukönigshofen **19** F2
Gauting **29** E2
Gavà **59** D4
Gavardo **38** B3
Gavarnie **58** A1
Gavere **8** C3
Gavi **44** C1
Gavião **66** C1
Gavirate **37** D2
Gavorrano **46** A4
Gavray **14** B4
Gaweinstal **31** F1
Gazolaz **57** D2
Gazoldo degli Ippoliti **38** B4
Gazzo Veronese **38** C4
Gazzuolo **38** B4
Geaune **40** B3
Gebesee **12** A3
Gedern **19** E1
Gedinne **17** E2
Gèdre **58** A1
Gedser **3** E4
Gedsted **1** E3
Gedved **2** C2
Geel **9** E3
Geertruidenberg **9** E2
Geeste **5** D4
Geestgottberg **6** C4
Geesthacht **6** B3
Geetbets **9** E4
Gefrees **20** B2
Gehrden **11** E1
Gehren **12** A4
Geilenkirchen **10** A3
Geisa **11** E4
Geiselhöring **20** C4
Geiselwind **20** A2
Geisenfeld **29** E1
Geisenheim **18** C2
Geising **13** E4
Geisingen **28** A2
Geislingen an der Steige **28** C1
Geismar **11** F3
Geistthal **31** D4
Geithain **13** D3
Gelbensande **7** D1
Gelchsheim **19** F3
Geldermalsen **9** E2
Geldern **10** A2
Geldersheim **19** F2
Geldrop **9** E3
Geleen **9** F3
Gelnhausen **19** E1
Gelsa **65** D1
Gelsenkirchen **10** B2
Gelsted *Denmark* **2** C3
Gelsted *Denmark* **3** E3
Geltendorf **29** D2
Gelting **2** C4
Geltow **13** D1
Gembloux **17** D1
Gémenos **43** E3
Gemert **9** F2
Gemmingen **19** D3
Gemona del Friuli **39** E1
Gémozac **32** B3
Gemünden **18** B2
Gemünden (Wohra) **11** D4
Gemünden am Main **19** E2
Genappe **17** D1
Génave **70** A3
Genazzano **48** C2
Gençay **33** D2
Gendt **10** A2
Génelard **35** D1
Genemuiden **4** B4
Genestoso **54** B2
Genève **35** F2
Genevilla **56** C3
Genga **47** D3
Gengenbach **27** F1
Génissac **32** C4
Genk **9** E3
Genlis **26** C3
Gennep **10** A2
Genner **2** B3
Gennes **24** A3
Genola **44** B1
Génolhac **42** B1
Genova **45** D1
Genovés **71** D2
Genthin **12** C1
Gentioux-Pigerolles **33** F3
Genzano di Lucania **50** C3
Genzano di Roma **48** C2
Georgensgmünd **20** A3
Georgsdorf **4** C4
Georgsheil **5** D3
Georgsmarienhütte **10** C1
Ger *France* **23** F1
Ger *Spain* **59** D2
Gera **12** C4
Geraardsbergen **8** C4
Gerabronn **19** F3
Gerace **52** B4
Gérardmer **27** E2
Gerasdorf bei Wien **31** F1
Gerbéviller **27** D1
Gerbstedt **12** B2
Gerchsheim **19** E2
Gerdau **6** B4
Gerena **73** E2
Geretsberg **30** A2
Geretsried **29** E2
Gérgal **75** F2
Gergy **26** B4
Gerhardshofen **20** A2
Gerindote **62** C4
Geringswalde **13** D3
Gerlev **3** E2
Gerlingen **28** B1
Gerlos **29** F3
Germering **29** E2
Germersheim **19** D3
Gernika-Lumo **56** B1
Gernrode **12** B2
Gernsbach **28** A1
Gernsheim **19** D2
Gerola Alta **37** E2
Gerolsbach **29** E1
Gerolstein **18** A1
Gerolzhofen **20** A2
Gerpinnes **17** D1
Gersau **28** A4
Gersfeld (Rhön) **11** E4
Gersheim **18** B3
Gersten **5** D4
Gerstetten **28** C1
Gerstheim **27** F1
Gersthofen **29** D1
Gerstungen **11** F3
Gerswalde **7** E3
Gerwisch **12** B1
Gerzat **34** B3
Gerzen **30** A1
Gescher **10** B2
Gespunsart **17** D2
Gesserts-hausen **29** D1
Gestalgar **71** D1
Gesté **23** F4
Gesten **2** B2
Gesualdo **50** A2
Getafe **63** D4
Getaria **56** C1
Gétigné **23** F4
Gettorf **6** A1
Gevelsberg **10** B3
Gévezé **23** E2
Gevrey-Chambertin **26** B4
Gex **35** F2
Gexto **56** B1
Geyer **13** D4
Gföhl **31** E1
Ghedi **38** A3
Ghemme **37** D3
Ghiffa **37** D2
Ghyvelde **8** B3
Giano dell'Umbria **47** D4
Giat **34** A3
Giaveno **36** B4
Gibraleón **73** D2
Gibraltar **74** A4
Giebelstadt **19** F2
Gieboldehausen **11** F2
Gielow **7** D2
Gien **25** E3
Giengen an der Brenz **28** C1
Giersleben **12** B2
Gierstädt **12** A3
Gießen **11** D4
Gieten **4** C4
Gièvres **25** D4
Gifhorn **11** F1
Gigean **42** B3
Gignac **42** B3
Gignod **36** B3
Gijón-Xijón **54** C1
Gilching **29** E2
Gilena **74** B2
Gilette **44** A2
Gilleleje **3** E1
Gillenfeld **18** B2
Gilly-sur-Isère **36** A3
Gilserberg **11** D4
Gilten **6** A4
Gilze **9** E2
Gimigliano **52** B2
Gimont **41** D3
Ginestas **42** A4
Gingelom **9** E4
Gingst **7** E1
Ginosa **51** D3
Giões **72** C2
Gioi **50** A4
Gioia dei Marsi **49** E2
Gioia del Colle **51** D3
Gioia Sannitica **49** F3
Gioia Tauro **52** A3
Gioiosa Ionica **52** B4
Giornico **37** D1
Giovinazzo **50** C2
Girifalco **52** B3
Girod **10** C4
Giromagny **27** E2
Girona **59** E3
Gironde-sur-Dropt **40** C1
Gironella **59** D3
Gislev **2** C3
Gislinge **3** D2
Gisors **16** A3
Gissi **49** F2
Gistel **8** B3
Gistrup **1** F2
Giswil **28** A4
Gittelde **11** F2
Giubiasco **37** D2
Giugliano in Campania **49** E4
Giuliano di Roma **49** D3
Giulianova **47** F4
Giuncugnano **45** E2
Give **2** B2
Givet **17** D2
Givors **35** D3
Givry *Belgium* **16** C1
Givry *France* **26** B4
Givry-en-Argonne **17** E4
Givskud **2** B2
Gizzeria **52** B2
Gjerlev **2** C1
Gjern **2** B1
Gjerrild **3** D1
Gjesing **2** C1
Gjøl **1** E2
Gladbeck **10** B2
Gladenbach **11** D4
Gladsakse **3** E2
Glamsbjerg **2** C3
Glandorf **10** C1
Glanegg **30** C4
Glarus **28** B4
Glashütten **20** B2
Glaubitz **13** D3
Glauchau **12** C4
Gleina **12** B3
Gleisdorf **31** E4
Gleizé **35** D2
Glejbjerg **2** A2
Glesborg **3** D1
Gletsch **36** C1
Glewitz **7** E2
Glinde **6** A2

Glindow **13** D1
Glödnitz **30** C4
Gloggnitz **31** E3
Glonn **29** F2
Glória **67** D3
Glória do Ribatejo **66** B2
Glöthe **12** B2
Glowe **7** E1
Glöwen **7** D4
Glücksburg (Ostsee) **2** B4
Glückstadt **5** F2
Glud **2** C2
Gludsted **2** B2
Glumsø **3** E3
Glyngøre **1** E2
Gmünd *Austria* **30** B4
Gmünd *Austria* **31** D1
Gmund am Tegernsee **29** E2
Gmunden **30** B2
Gnarrenburg **5** F3
Gneisenaustadt Schildau **13** D3
Gniebing **31** E4
Gnocchetta **39** D4
Gnoien **7** D2
Gnotzheim **20** A4
Gnutz **6** A1
Goch **10** A2
Gochsheim **20** A2
Goddelsheim (Lichtenfels) **11** D3
Godega di Sant'Urbano **39** D2
Godelleta **71** D2
Goderville **15** D2
Godiasco **37** E4
Goedereede **9** D2
Goes **8** C2
Göfritz an der Wild **31** D1
Göhl **6** B1
Gohrau **12** C2
Göhrde **6** B3
Göhren-Lebbin **7** D3
Goirle **9** E2
Góis **60** C4
Goito **38** B4
Goizueta **56** C2
Gokels **6** A1
Golbey **27** D2
Goldach **28** B3
Goldbeck **6** C4
Goldberg **7** D2
Goldegg **30** A3
Goldelund **2** B4
Goldenstedt **5** E4
Golegã **66** B2
Göllersdorf **31** E1
Göllin **6** C2
Gollin **7** E3
Golling an der Salzach **30** B3
Göllingen **12** B3
Gollmitz **7** E3
Golmes **58** B3
Gøløse **3** E2
Golpejas **62** A2
Gols **31** F2
Golßen **13** E2
Golzow **12** C1
Gomadingen **28** B1
Gómara **63** F1
Gomecello **62** A2
Gomes Aires **72** B2
Gommern **12** C1
Gonçalo **61** D3
Goncelin **35** F3
Gondershausen **18** B1
Gondomar *Port.* **60** B2
Gondomar *Spain* **53** E4
Gondorf **18** B1
Gondrecourt-le-Château **26** C1
Gondreville **17** F4
Gondrin **40** C2
Gonfreville-l'Orcher **15** D3
Gonzaga **38** B4
Goor **10** A1
Gopegui **56** B2
Göppingen **28** C1
Gor **75** E2
Gorafe **75** E2
Gordaliza del Pino **55** D3
Gordes **43** D2
Gordexola **56** B2
Gørding **2** A3
Gordola **37** D2
Gordona **37** E2
Gorgoglione **50** C4
Gorgonzola **37** E3
Gorinchem **9** E2
Gorino **39** D4
Görisried **29** D3
Göritz **7** F3
Gorizia **39** F2
Gorleben **6** C3
Gørlev **3** D3
Görlitz **13** F3
Gorlosen **6** C3
Gormaz **63** E1
Görmin **7** E2
Gornau **13** D4
Goro **39** D4
Gorredijk **4** B3
Gorreto **45** D1
Gorron **23** F1
Görsbach **12** A3
Gorssel **10** A1
Görwihl **28** A3
Gorxheimertal **19** D3
Gorze **17** F4
Görzig **12** C2
Görzke **12** C1
Górzyca **13** F1
Górzyn **13** F2
Gosaldo **39** D2
Gosau **30** B3
Goslar **11** F2
Gosné **23** E2
Gossau **28** B3
Gössendorf **31** E4
Gößl **30** C3
Göstling an der Ybbs **31** D2
Gotha **11** F3
Gotteszell **21** D4
Gottfrieding **30** A1
Göttingen **11** E2
Gottmadingen **28** B2
Gøttrup **1** E2
Götzis **28** C3
Gouarec **22** C2
Gouda **9** D1
Gouesnou **22** A1
Goult **43** D2
Gourdon **41** E1
Gourin **22** C2
Gournay-en-Bray **15** F3
Goussainville **16** A4
Gouveia **61** D3
Gouvieux **16** A3
Gouvy **17** F1
Gouzon **33** F2
Gove **60** C2
Goven **23** E2
Gozdowice **7** F4
Gozzano **36** C3
Graben-Neudorf **19** D3
Grabow **6** C3
Grabs **28** B4
Graçay **25** D4
Grâce-Hollogne **17** E1
Grâces **22** C1
Gradara **47** D2
Gradefes **55** D3
Grado *Italy* **39** F3
Grado *Spain* **54** C1
Gradoli **48** B1
Graena **75** E2
Græsted **3** E2
Gräfelfing **29** E2
Grafenau **21** D4
Gräfenberg **20** B2
Gräfendorf **19** E2
Grafendorf bei Hartberg **31** E3
Gräfenhainichen **12** C2
Gräfenhausen **28** A2
Gräfenroda **12** A4
Grafenwöhr **20** C2
Grafenworth **31** E1
Graffignano **48** B1
Grafhorst **12** A1
Gräfinau-Angstedt **12** B4
Grafing bei München **29** F2
Grafrath **29** E2
Gragnano **49** F4
Grainau **29** D3
Grainet **21** E4
Graja de Iniesta **70** B1
Grajal de Campos **55** D3
Gralla **31** E4
Gram **2** B3
Gramastettan **30** C1
Gramat **41** E1
Gramatneusiedl **31** F2
Grambow **7** F3
Gramkow **6** C2
Grammendorf **7** D2
Gramsbergen **4** C4
Gramzow **7** F3
Granada **75** D2
Granarolo dell'Emilia **46** B1
Granátula de Calatrava **69** D3
Grancey-le-Château-Nouvelle **26** B3
Grandas de Salime **54** A2
Grandcamp-Maisy **14** C3
Grand-Champ **23** D3
Grand-Couronne **15** E3
Grande-Synthe **8** A3
Grand-Fort-Philippe **8** A3
Grand-Fougeray **23** E3
Grândola **66** B4
Grandpré **17** E3
Grandrieu **42** B1
Grandris **35** D2
Grandvillars **27** E3
Grandvilliers **16** A2
Grane **43** D1
Grañén **57** F4
Granges-sur-Vologne **27** E2
Granja **67** D4
Granja de Moreruela **54** C4
Granja de Torrehermosa **68** B4
Granja do Ulmeiro **60** B4
Granollers **59** D3
Granschütz **12** C3
Gransee **7** E4
Granville **23** E1
Grasleben **12** B1
Grassano **50** C3
Grassau **30** A2
Grasse **44** A3
Gråsten **2** B4
Gratallops **58** B4
Gratentour **41** E3
Gratkorn **31** D4
Gratwein **31** D4
Grauballe **2** B1
Graulhet **41** F3
Graupa **13** E3
Graus **58** A2
Grávalos **56** C4
Grave **9** F2
Gravedona **37** E2
Gravelines **8** A3
Gravellona Toce **37** D2
Gravens **2** B2
Grävenwiesbach **19** D1
Gravigny **15** E4
Gravina in Puglia **50** C3
Gray **26** C3
Graz **31** E4
Grazalema **74** A3
Grazzanise **49** E3
Grea de Albarracín **64** B3
Grebendorf (Meinhard) **11** F3
Grebenhain **11** E4
Grebenstein **11** E3
Grebin **6** B1
Greccio **48** C1
Greci **50** A2
Greding **20** B4
Gredstedbro **2** A3
Greene **11** E2
Greggio **36** C3
Greifenburg **30** B4
Greifendorf **13** D3
Greifenstein **10** C4
Greiffenberg **7** F3
Greifswald **7** E1
Grein **31** D2
Greiz **12** C4
Grejs **2** B2
Gremersdorf **6** B1
Grenå **3** D1
Grenade **41** E3
Grenade-sur-l'Adour **40** B3
Grenchen **27** F4
Grenoble **35** F4
Gréoux-les-Bains **43** E3
Gresenhorst **7** D1
Gressan **36** B3
Gresse **6** B3
Gressoney-la-Trinite **36** C3
Gresten **31** D2
Grésy-sur-Aix **35** F3
Grésy-sur-Isère **35** F3
Greußen **12** A3
Greve in Chianti **46** B3
Greven *Ger.* **6** B3
Greven *Ger.* **10** C1
Grevenbroich **10** A3
Grevenmacher **18** A2
Grevesmühlen **6** B2
Grevinge **3** D2
Grez-Doiceau **9** D4
Grez-en-Bouère **24** A2
Griegos **64** B3
Gries **27** F1
Gries am Brenner **29** E4
Griesbach **28** A1
Griesbach im Rottal **30** B1
Griesheim **19** D2
Grieskirchen **30** B1
Grießen **13** F2
Griesstätt **29** F2
Griffen **31** D4
Grignan **43** D1
Grigno **38** C2
Grignols **40** C2
Grijota **55** E4
Grijpskerk **4** B3
Grillon **43** D1
Grimaldi **52** B2
Grimaud **43** F3
Grimbergen **9** D3
Grimma **13** D3
Grimmen **7** E1
Grimstrup **2** A2
Grindelwald **36** C1
Grindsted *Denmark* **1** F2
Grindsted *Denmark* **2** B2
Griñón **63** D4
Grins **29** D4
Grisén **57** D4
Grisolia **52** A1
Grisolles **41** E3
Grobbendonk **9** D3
Gröbenzell **29** E2
Gröbming **30** B3
Gröbzig **12** C2
Gröden **13** E3
Grödig **30** A2
Gröditz **13** E3
Groenlo **10** A1
Grohnde (Emmerthal) **11** E2
Groitzsch **12** C3
Groix **22** C3
Grömitz **6** B1
Gromo **38** A2
Gronau (Westfalen) **10** B1
Grønbjerg **2** A1
Grönenbach **28** C2
Grønhøj **2** B1
Gröningen **12** B2
Groningen **4** C3
Grønnemose **2** C3
Grootegast **4** B3
Gropello Cairoli **37** D4
Groscavallo **36** B3
Grosio **38** A2
Grosotto **38** A2
Großaitingen **29** D2
Groß Ammensleben **12** B1
Großarl **30** B3
Groß-Bieberau **19** D2
Groß Börnecke **12** B2
Großbothen **13** D3
Groß-breitenbach **12** A4
Großburgwedel (Burgwedel) **11** E1
Groß Dölln **7** E4
Grosselfingen **28** B1
Großenaspe **6** A2
Großenbrode **6** B1
Großenehrich **12** A3
Groß Engersdorf **31** F1
Großengottern **11** F3
Großenhain **13** E3
Großenkneten **5** E4
Großenlüder **11** E4
Großensee **6** B2
Großen-stein **12** C4
Großenwiehe **2** B4
Groß-Enzersdorf **31** F2
Grosseto **46** B4
Groß Fredenwalde **7** F3
Großfurra **12** A3
Groß-Gerau **19** D2
Groß-Gerungs **31** D1
Groß Glienicke **13** D1
Großgmain **30** A2
Groß Grönau **6** B2
Groß-habersdorf **20** A3
Großhansdorf **6** A2
Großharras **31** F1
Großhart-mannsdorf **13** D4
Groß Heere (Heere) **11** F1
Groß-hennersdorf **13** F3
Groß-Hesepe **5** D4
Großkarolinenfeld **29** F2
Groß Kiesow **7** E2
Großklein **31** E4
Groß Köris **13** E1
Groß Kreutz **13** D1
Großkrut **31** F1
Groß Lafferde (Lahstedt) **11** F1
Groß Leine **13** E2
Groß Leuthen **13** E1
Großlittgen **18** B2
Großlohra **11** F3
Großmehlen **13** E3

Groß Miltzow **7** E2
Groß Mohrdorf **7** E1
Großmonra **12** B3
Groß Naundorf **13** D2
Großnaundorf **13** E3
Groß Nemerow **7** E3
Groß Oesingen **6** B4
Großolbersdorf **13** D4
Groß Oßnig **13** F2
Großostheim **19** D2
Großpetersdorf **31** F3
Groß Plasten **7** D2
Großraming **30** C2
Großräschen **13** E2
Großrinderfeld **19** E2
Groß Roge **7** D2
Großröhrsdorf **13** E3
Großrudestedt **12** B3
Großrußbach **31** F1
Groß Särchen **13** F3
Großschirma **13** D4
Großschönau **31** D1
Groß Schönebeck **7** E4
Groß Schwechten **6** C4
Groß Schwülper (Schwülper) **11** F1
Groß St Florian **31** D4
Groß Stieten **6** C2
Großthiemig **13** E3
Großtreben **13** D2
Groß-Umstadt **19** D2
Grosswangen **27** F4
Groß Warnow **6** C3
Großweikersdorf **31** E1
Groß Welle **7** D3
Groß Wittensee **6** A1
Groß Wokern **7** D2
Großwudicke **7** D4
Groß Wüstenfelde **7** D2
Groß Ziethen **7** F4
Groß-Zimmern **19** D2
Grostenquin **18** A4
Grottaferrata **48** C2
Grottaglie **51** E3
Grottaminarda **50** A2
Grottammare **47** F4
Grottazzolina **47** E4
Grotte di Castro **48** B1
Grotteria **52** B4
Grottole **50** C3
Grouw **4** B3
Grub am Forst **20** A1
Grube **6** B1
Grugliasco **36** B4
Gruissan **42** A4
Grullos **54** C1
Grumbach **13** E3
Grumo Appula **51** D2
Grünau *Austria* **31** E2
Grünau *Austria* **30** C2
Grünberg **11** D4
Grünburg **30** C2
Grünendeich **6** A2
Grünewald **13** E3
Grünewalde **13** E2
Grünheide **13** E1
Grünkraut **28** C2
Grunow **13** F1
Grünsfeld **19** E2
Grünstadt **18** C3
Grünwald **29** E2
Grußendorf (Sassenburg) **6** B4
Gruyères **36** B1
Gryfino **7** F3
Grzybno **7** F3
Gschnitz **29** E4
Gschwandt **30** B2
Gschwend **19** E4
Gstaad **36** B1
Gsteig **36** B1
Guadahortuna **75** D2
Guadajoz **74** A1
Guadalajara **63** E3
Guadalaviar **64** B3
Guadalcanal **68** A4
Guadalcázar **74** B1
Guadalest **71** E3
Guadalmez **68** C3
Guadarrama **62** C3
Guadassuar **71** D2
Guadix **75** E2
Guájar-Faraguit **75** D3
Gualdo Cattaneo **47** D4
Gualdo Tadino **47** D4
Gualtieri **38** B4
Guarcino **49** D2
Guarda **61** D3
Guardamar del Segura **71** D4
Guardavalle **52** B3
Guardea **48** B1
Guardiagrele **49** E1
Guardia Lombardi **50** A2
Guardia Perticara **50** C4
Guardia Piemontese **52** A1
Guardia Sanframondi **49** F3
Guardias Viejas **75** E3
Guardiola de Bergueda **59** D2
Guardo **55** D2
Guardramiro **61** E2
Guareña **67** F3
Guaro **74** B3
Guarromán **69** E4
Guastalla **38** B4
Gubbio **47** D3
Guben **13** F2
Gubin **13** F2
Gudar **64** C3
Gudbjerg **2** C3
Guderup **2** B4
Gudme **2** C3
Gudow **6** B2
Gudum **2** A1
Gudumholm **1** F2
Guebwiller **27** E2
Guégon **23** D2
Güéjar-Sierra **75** D2
Guémené-Penfao **23** E3
Guémené-sur-Scorff **22** C2
Guénange **17** F3
Güeñes **56** B2
Guenrouet **23** E3
Guer **23** D2
Guérande **23** D4
Guéret **33** F2
Guérigny **25** F4
Guerri de la Sal **58** B2
Güesa **57** D2
Gueugnon **34** C1
Güglingen **19** D4
Guglionesi **50** A1
Gühlen-Glienicke **7** D3
Guia *Port.* **72** B2
Guia *Port.* **66** B1
Guichen **23** E2
Guidel **22** C3
Guidizzolo **38** B3
Guidonia-Montecelio **48** C2
Guiglia **46** B1
Guignen **23** E2
Guignes **16** B4
Guignicourt **16** C3
Guijo de Coria **61** E4
Guijo de Galisteo **61** F4
Guijo de Granadilla **61** F4
Guijuelo **62** A3
Guilers **22** A2
Guilherand **35** E4
Guilhofrei **60** C1
Guilhovai **60** B2
Guillaumes **44** A2
Guillena **73** E2
Guillestre **43** F1
Guilliers **23** D2
Guilvinec **22** B3
Guimarães **60** C1
Guînes **8** A4
Guingamp **22** C1
Guipavas **22** A1
Guipry **23** E3
Guisando **62** B4
Guiscard **16** B2
Guise **16** C2
Guissény **22** A1
Guissona **58** C3
Guitiriz **53** F2
Guîtres **32** C4
Gujan-Mestras **40** A1
Guldager **2** A2
Guldborg **3** E4
Gülitz **6** C3
Gültz **7** E2
Gülzow **6** C2
Gumiel de Hizán **55** F4
Gumiel de Mercado **55** F4
Gummersbach **10** B3
Gumpelstadt **11** F4
Gumtow **7** D4
Gundelfingen **27** F2
Gundelfingen an der Donau **29** D1
Gundelsheim **19** E3
Gundershoffen **18** C4
Gundsømagle **3** E2
Günstedt **12** B3
Güntersberge **12** B2
Guntersdorf **31** E1
Günzburg **28** C1
Gunzenhausen **20** A3
Gurk **30** C4
Gurrea de Gállego **57** E4
Gusborn **6** B3
Güsen **12** C1
Gusow **7** F4
Gussago **38** A3
Güssing **31** F4
Gussola **38** B4
Gußwerk **31** D2
Güsten **12** B2
Gusterath **18** B2
Güstrow **7** D2
Gutau **30** C1
Gutenstein **31** E2
Güterfelde **13** D1
Güterglück **12** C2
Gütersloh **11** D2
Gutow **7** D2
Guttannen **36** C1
Guttaring **30** C4
Gützkow **7** E2
Guxhagen **11** E3
Gy **27** D3
Gyhum **5** F3
Gylling **2** C2
Gyrstinge **3** E3

H

Haacht **9** D3
Haag **30** C2
Haag am Hausruck **30** B2
Haag in Oberbayern **29** F2
Haaksbergen **10** B1
Haaltert **9** D4
Haar **29** E2
Haarbach **30** B1
Haarlem **9** D1
Haastrecht **9** D1
Habas **40** A3
Habay-la-Neuve **17** E2
Habsheim **27** F3
Hachenburg **10** C4
Hacinas **56** A4
Hadamar **10** C4
Haderslev **2** B3
Haderup **2** B1
Hadol **27** D2
Hadres **31** E1
Hadsten **2** C1
Hadsund **1** F3
Hafnerbach **31** E2
Hagen **10** B3
Hagenbach **18** C4
Hagenburg **11** E1
Hagenow **6** C3
Hagenwerder **13** F3
Hagetmau **40** B3
Hagondange **17** F3
Haguenau **18** C4
Hahausen **11** F2
Hahnbach **20** B3
Hahnstätten **18** C1
Haibach *Ger.* **21** D4
Haibach *Ger.* **19** E2
Haidmühle **21** E4
Haiger **10** C4
Haigerloch **28** B1
Haiming **30** A2
Haina **11** F4
Haina (Kloster) **11** D3
Hainburg an der Donau **31** F2
Hainfeld **31** E2
Hainichen **13** D4
Halbe **13** E1
Halbenrain **31** E4
Halberstadt **12** B2
Halbjerg **1** F1
Halblech **29** D3
Hald *Denmark* **2** C1
Hald *Denmark* **1** E3
Hald Ege **2** B1
Haldensleben **12** B1
Halfing **29** F2
Halfweg **9** D1
Halle *Belgium* **9** D4
Halle *Ger.* **11** E2
Halle (Saale) **12** C3
Halle (Westfalen) **11** D1
Hallein **30** A3
Hallenberg **11** D3
Hallencourt **16** A2
Halle-Neustadt **12** C3
Hallerndorf **20** A2
Hall in Tirol **29** E3
Hallstatt **30** B3
Halluin **8** B4
Hallund **1** F2
Hals **1** F2
Halsskov **3** D3
Halstenbek **6** A2
Halsteren **9** D2
Halstroff **18** A3
Haltern **10** B2
Halver **10** B3
Halvrimmen **1** E2
Ham **16** B2
Hambergen **5** E3
Hambrücken **19** D3
Hambühren **6** A4
Hamburg **6** A2
Hambye **14** B4
Hämelhausen **5** F4
Hameln **11** E1
Hämerten **6** C4
Hamm **10** C2
Hamm (Sieg) **10** C4
Hamme **9** D3
Hammel **2** C1
Hammelburg **19** F2
Hammelev **2** B3
Hammelspring **7** E3
Hammerbrücke **20** C1
Hammershøj **2** B1
Hammerum **2** B1
Hamminkeln **10** A2
Hamoir **17** E1
Hamois **17** E1
Hamont **9** E3
Hampen **2** B2
Hampont **18** A4
Ham-sur-Heure **17** D1
Hanau **19** D1
Handbjerg **2** A1
Handeloh **6** A3
Handest **2** C1
Handewitt **2** B4
Hanerau-Hademarschen **5** F1
Hangelsberg **13** E1
Hankensbüttel **6** B4
Hannover **11** E1
Hannoversch Münden **11** E3
Hannut **17** E1
Hanshagen **6** B2
Hanstedt **6** A3
Hanstholm **1** D2
Han-sur-Nied **18** A4
Hanvec **22** B2
Happburg **20** B3
Harbke **12** B1
Harboør **1** D3
Harburg (Schwaben) **29** D1
Hårby **2** C3
Hard **28** C3
Hardegsen **11** E2
Hardenberg **4** C4
Harderwijk **9** F1
Hardheim **19** E2
Hardt **28** A2
Harelbeke **8** C4
Haren **4** C3
Haren (Ems) **5** D4
Harfleur **15** D3
Harka **31** F3
Hårlev **3** E3
Harlingen **4** A3
Harly **16** C2
Harmannsdorf **31** F1
Harmsdorf **6** B2
Harnes **16** B1
Haro **56** B3
Haroué **27** D1
Harpstedt **5** E4
Harra **20** B1
Harre **1** E3
Harridslev **2** C1
Harrislee **2** B4
Harsefeld **6** A3
Harsewinkel **10** C2
Harsleben **12** B2
Hårslev **2** C3
Harsum **11** E1
Hartberg **31** E3
Hartenholm **6** A2
Hartha **13** D3
Hartheim **27** F2
Hart im Zillertal **29** F3
Hartkirchen **30** C1
Harzgerode **12** B2
Haselünne **5** D4
Haslach an der Mühl **30** C1
Haslach im Kinzigtal **27** F2
Hasle **27** F4
Haslev **3** E3
Hasloh **6** A2
Haslund **2** C1
Hasparren **40** A3
Haßbergen **5** F4
Hassel (Weser) **5** F4
Hasselfelde **12** A2
Hasselt *Belgium* **9** E3
Hasselt *Neth.* **4** B4
Haßfurt **20** A2
Haßleben *Ger.* **7** E3
Haßleben *Ger.* **12** B3
Haßloch **18** C3
Hastière-Lavaux **17** D1
Håstrup **2** C3

Hattem **10** A1
Hattersheim am Main **19** D2
Hatting **2** B2
Hattingen **10** B3
Hattstedt **5** F1
Hatzendorf **31** E4
Haubourdin **16** B1
Haulerwijk **4** B3
Haus **30** B3
Hausen **20** C4
Häusern **28** A2
Hausham **29** F2
Hausleiten **31** E1
Hautefort **33** E4
Hauteville-Lompnes **35** F2
Hautmont **16** C1
Hauzenberg **30** B1
Havbro **1** E2
Havelange **17** E1
Havelberg **7** D4
Havelte **4** B4
Haverlah **11** F1
Haverslev **1** E2
Havixbeck **10** B2
Havndal **1** F3
Havneby **2** A3
Havnebyen **3** D2
Havnsø **3** D2
Havrebjerg **3** D3
Hayange **17** F3
Haybes **17** D2
Hayingen **28** B2
Hazebrouck **8** B4
Hebenhausen (Neu-Eichenberg) **11** E3
Hebertsfelden **30** A1
Hechingen **28** B1
Hecho **57** E2
Hechtel **9** E3
Hechthausen **5** F2
Heckelberg **7** F4
Hédé **23** E2
Hedel **9** E2
Heden **2** C3
Hedensted **2** B2
Hedersleben **12** B2
Hee **2** A1
Heeg **4** B4
Heek **10** B1
Heemsen **5** F4
Heemskerk **9** D1
Heemstede **9** D1
Heerde **10** A1
Heerenveen **4** B4
Heerhugowaard **4** A4
Heerlen **10** A4
Heers **9** E4
Heesch **9** E2
Heeslingen **5** F3
Heeßen **11** D1
Heeswijk **9** E2
Heeze **9** E3
Hehlen **11** E2
Heide **5** F1
Heideck **20** B3
Heidelberg **19** D3
Heiden **10** B2
Heidenau **13** E4
Heidenheim **20** A4
Heidenheim an der Brenz **28** C1
Heikendorf **6** A1
Heilbronn **19** E3
Heilbrunn **31** E3
Heiligenberg **28** B2
Heiligenfelde **6** C4
Heiligenhafen **6** B1
Heiligenhaus **10** B3
Heiligenkreuz im Lafnitztal **31** F4
Heiligenstadt Heilbad **11** F3
Heiligenstedten **6** A2
Heiloo **4** A4
Heilsbronn **20** A3
Heimertingen **28** C2
Heinade **11** E2
Heinebach (Alheim) **11** E3
Heinersbrück **13** F2
Heinersdorf **13** E1
Heinersreuth **20** B2
Heiningen **11** F1
Heinkenszand **8** C2
Heinsberg **10** A3
Heinsen **11** E2
Heist-op-den-Berg **9** D3
Hejls **2** B3
Hejnsvig **2** B2
Hejsager **2** B3
Hekelgem **9** D3
Helbra **12** B2
Heldburg **20** A1
Heldrungen **12** B3
Helechal **68** B3
Helfenberg **30** C1
Hellebæk **3** F2
Hellenthal **10** A4
Hellested **3** E3
Hellevad **2** B3
Hellevoetsluis **9** D2
Hellín **70** B3
Helmbrechts **20** B1
Helmond **9** F2
Helmstadt **19** E2
Helmstedt **12** B1
Helse **5** F2
Helsinge **3** E2
Helsingør **3** F2
Hem **1** E3
Hemau **20** B4
Hemhofen **20** A2
Hemme **5** F1
Hemmet **2** A2
Hemmingen **11** E1
Hemmoor **5** F2
Hemsbach **19** D3
Hemsbünde **5** F3
Hemslingen **6** A3
Hénanbihen **23** D1
Henarejos **64** B4
Hendaye **56** C1
Hengelo *Neth.* **10** A1
Hengelo *Neth.* **10** B1
Hengersberg **21** D4
Henggart **28** A3
Hénin-Beaumont **16** B1
Henndorf am Wallersee **30** B2
Hennebont **22** C3
Hennef (Sieg) **10** B4
Henne Stationsby **2** A2
Hennickendorf **13** D1
Hennigsdorf Berlin **7** E4
Hennstedt **5** F1
Henrichemont **25** E3
Henstedt-Ulzburg **6** A2
Heppenheim (Bergstraße) **19** D2
Herbault **24** C3
Herbertingen **28** B2
Herbés **65** D3
Herbignac **23** D3
Herbolzheim **27** F2
Herborn **10** C4
Herbrechtingen **28** C1
Herbstein **11** E4
Herdecke **10** B3
Herdorf **10** C4
Herencia **69** E2
Herent **9** D3
Herentals **9** E3
Hérépian **42** A3
Herford **11** D1
Hergatz **28** C3
Hergiswil **28** A4
Herguijuela **68** A2
Héric **23** E3
Héricourt **27** E3
Hérimoncourt **27** E3
Heringen (Helme) **12** A3
Heringen (Werra) **11** F4
Heringsdorf **6** B1
Herisau **28** B3
Hérisson **34** B1
Herk-de-Stad **9** E3
Herleshausen **11** F3
Herlev **3** E2
Herlufmagle **3** E3
Hermagor **39** F1
Hermannsburg **6** A4
Herment **34** A3
Hermersberg **18** C3
Hermeskeil **18** B2
Hermisende **54** A4
Hermsdorf **12** C4
Hernani **56** C2
Hernansancho **62** C2
Herne *Belgium* **9** D4
Herne *Ger.* **10** B2
Herning **2** B1
Heroldsbach **20** A2
Héron **17** E1
Hérouville-St-Clair **15** D3
Herpf **11** F4
Herramélluri **56** B3
Herrenberg **28** B1
Herrera **74** B2
Herrera del Duque **68** B2
Herrera de los Navarros **64** C2
Herrera de Pisuerga **55** E3
Herrería **64** A2
Herreruela **67** E1
Herrieden **20** A3
Herrlisheim **27** F1
Herrnhut **13** F3
Herrsching am Ammersee **29** E2
Herry **25** E4
Hersbruck **20** B3
Herscheid **10** C3
Herselt **9** E3
Herslev **2** B2
Herstal **9** F4
Herten **10** B2
Herve **17** F1
Herxheim bei Landau (Pfalz) **18** C3
Herzberg *Ger.* **13** D2
Herzberg *Ger.* **7** E4
Herzberg *Ger.* **6** C3
Herzberg am Harz **11** F2
Herzebrock-Clarholz **10** C2
Herzele **8** C4
Herzfelde **13** E1
Herzhorn **5** F2
Herzlake **5** D4
Herzogenaurach **20** A3
Herzogenbuchsee **27** F4
Herzogenburg **31** E1
Herzsprung **7** D3
Hesdin **16** A1
Hesel **5** D3
Hespérange **17** F3
Heßdorf **20** A2
Hesselager **2** C3
Hessen **11** F1
Hessisch Lichtenau **11** E3
Hessisch Oldendorf **11** E1
Hetlingen **6** A2
Hettenleidelheim **18** C3
Hettenshausen **29** E1
Hettingen **28** B2
Hettstedt **12** B2
Hetzerath **18** B2
Heuchin **16** A1
Heukelum **9** E2
Heusden **9** E3
Heustreu **19** F1
Heyrieux **35** E3
Heythuysen **9** F3
Hiddenhausen **11** D1
Hiddensee **7** E1
Hieflau **31** D3
Hiendelaencina **63** E2
Hiersac **32** C3
Higuera de Arjona **69** D4
Higuera de la Serena **68** A3
Higuera de la Sierra **73** E1
Higuera de Llerena **67** F4
Higuera de Vargas **67** E3
Higuera la Real **67** E4
Higueruela **70** C3
Higueruelas **64** C4
Híjar **65** D2
Hilbersdorf **13** D4
Hilchenbach **10** C3
Hildburghausen **20** A1
Hilden **10** B3
Hilders **11** F4
Hildesheim **11** E1
Hilgertshausen **29** E1
Hille **11** D1
Hillegom **9** D1
Hillerød **3** E2
Hillerse **11** F1
Hillerslev *Denmark* **2** C3
Hillerslev *Denmark* **1** D2
Hillesheim **18** A1
Hilpoltstein **20** B3
Hiltpoltstein **20** B2
Hilversum **9** E1
Himberg **31** F2
Himbergen **6** B3
Himmelberg **30** C4
Himmelpforten **5** F2
Hindelang **29** D3
Hindenburg **6** C4
Hinnerup **2** C1
Hinojal **67** F1
Hinojales **67** E4
Hinojares **75** E1
Hinojasas de Calatrava **69** D3
Hinojos **73** E2
Hinojosa **64** A2
Hinojosa de Duero **61** E2
Hinojosa de Jarque **64** C3
Hinojosa del Duque **68** B3
Hinojosa del Valle **67** F3
Hinojosa de San Vicente **62** B4
Hinte **4** C3
Hinterhermsdorf **13** F4
Hinternah **12** A4
Hinterrhein **37** D1
Hintersee *Austria* **30** B3
Hintersee *Ger.* **7** F2
Hinterweidenthal **18** C3
Hinterzarten **28** A2
Hinwil **28** B3
Hinx **40** A3
Hippolytushoef **4** A4
Hirrlingen **28** B1
Hirschaid **20** A2
Hirschau **20** C3
Hirschberg **20** B1
Hirschfeld **13** E3
Hirschhorn (Neckar) **19** D3
Hirsingue **27** E3
Hirson **17** D2
Hirtshals **1** F1
Hirzenhain **19** E1
Hita **63** E3
Hittisau **28** C3
Hitzacker **6** B3
Hitzendorf **31** D4
Hitzhusen **6** A2
Hjallerup **1** F2
Hjarup **2** B3
Hjerm **2** A1
Hjordkær **2** B3
Hjørring **1** F1
Hobro **1** F3
Hochdonn **5** F2
Hochdorf *Ger.* **28** C2
Hochdorf *Switz.* **28** A4
Hochfelden **27** F1
Höchheim **20** A1
Höchstadt an der Aisch **20** A2
Höchstädt an der Donau **29** D1
Hochstetten-Dhaun **18** B2
Hockenheim **19** D3
Hodenhagen **6** A4
Hodsager **2** A1
Hoek **8** C3
Hoek van Holland **9** D1
Hœnheim **27** F1
Hoensbroek **9** F3
Hoeselt **9** E4
Hoevelaken **9** E1
Hoeven **9** D2
Hof **20** C1
Hofbieber **11** E4
Hofgeismar **11** E3
Hofheim am Taunus **19** D2
Hofheim in Unterfranken **20** A1
Høgild **2** B2
Hohen-Altheim **29** D1
Hohenaspe **6** A2
Hohenau **21** E4
Hohenau an der March **31** F1
Hohenberg **31** E2
Hohenbocka **13** E3
Hohenbrunn **29** E2
Hohenbucko **13** E2
Hohenburg **20** B3
Hohendorf **7** E2
Hoheneich **31** D1
Hohenems **28** C3
Hohenfels **20** B3
Hohenfurch **29** D2
Hohengöhren **6** C4
Hohenhameln **11** F1
Hohenkammer **29** E1
Hohenkirchen **5** D2
Höhenkirchen-Siegertsbrunn **29** E2
Hohenleuben **12** C4
Hohenlockstedt **6** A2
Hohenmocker **7** E2
Hohenmölsen **12** C3
Hohennauen **7** D4
Hohenpeißenberg **29** D2
Hohenroth **19** F1
Hohensaaten **7** F4
Hohenseeden **12** C1
Hohenstein-Ernstthal **13** D4
Hohenthann **29** F1
Hohenthurm **12** C2
Hohen Wangelin **7** D2
Hohenwart **29** E1
Hohenwarth **21** D3
Hohenwestedt **6** A1
Hohn **6** A1
Hohne **6** A4
Hohnhorst **11** E1
Hohnstorf (Elbe) **6** B3
Hohwacht (Ostsee) **6** B1
Hoisdorf **6** A2
Højby *Denmark* **2** C3
Højby *Denmark* **3** D2
Højer **2** A4
Højmark **2** A2
Højslev **1** E3
Højslev Stationsby **2** B1
Holbæk *Denmark* **2** C1

Holbæk *Denmark* 3 E2
Holbøl 2 B4
Holeby 3 D4
Holguera 67 F1
Hollabrunn 31 E1
Holle 11 F1
Hollenbach 29 E1
Hollenbek 6 B2
Hollenegg 31 D4
Hollenstedt 6 A3
Hollenstein an der Ybbs 31 D2
Hollern-Twielenfleth 6 A2
Hollfeld 20 B2
Hollingstedt 5 F1
Hollum 4 B3
Holm *Denmark* 2 B3
Holm *Ger.* 6 A2
Holme-Olstrup 3 E3
Holstebro 2 A1
Holsted 2 A3
Hölstein 27 F3
Holte 3 E2
Holten 10 A1
Holtgast 5 D2
Holthusen 6 C2
Holtsee 6 A1
Holungen 11 F2
Holwerd 4 B3
Holzen 11 E2
Holzhausen an der Haide 18 C1
Holzheim *Ger.* 28 C1
Holzheim *Ger.* 29 D1
Holzheim *Ger.* 29 D1
Holzkirchen 29 E2
Holzminden 11 E2
Holzthaleben 11 F3
Holzweißig 12 C2
Holzwickede 10 C2
Høm 3 E3
Homberg (Efze) 11 E3
Homberg (Ohm) 11 D4
Homburg 18 B3
Homécourt 17 F3
Hondarribia 56 C1
Hondón de las Nieves 76 C1
Hondón de los Frailes 76 C1
Hondschoote 8 B3
Hône 36 C3
Honfleur 15 D3
Høng 3 D3
Honrubia 70 A1
Honrubia de la Cuesta 63 D1
Hontacillas 70 B1
Hontalbilla 62 C2
Hontanaya 70 A1
Hontoria de la Cantera 55 F4
Hontoria del Pinar 56 A4
Hontoria de Valdearados 55 F4
Hoofddorp 9 D1
Hoogerheide 9 D3
Hoogersmilde 4 C4
Hoogeveen 4 C4
Hoogezand-Sappemeer 4 C3
Hoogkarspel 4 A4
Hoogkerk 4 C3
Hoogstede 4 C4
Hoogstraten 9 E3
Hoogvliet 9 D2
Hooksiel 5 D2
Hoorn 4 A4
Hopfgarten im Brixental 29 F3
Hopfgarten in Defereggen 30 A4
Hoppstädten 18 B2
Hopsten 10 C1
Hoptrup 2 B3
Horb am Neckar 28 A1
Horbourg-Wihr 27 F2
Hörbranz 28 C3
Hørby 1 F1
Horcajo de las Torres 62 B2
Horcajo de los Montes 68 C2
Horcajo de Santiago 63 E4
Horcajo Medianero 62 A3
Hordum 1 D2
Horgen 28 A3
Horgenzell 28 B2
Horitschon 31 F3
Horka 13 F3
Hörlitz 13 E2
Hormilla 56 B3
Horn 31 E1
Hornachos 67 F3
Hornachuelos 74 A1
Hornbach 18 B3
Horn-Bad Meinberg 11 D2
Hornbæk 3 E2
Hornburg 11 F1
Horne *Denmark* 2 C3
Horne *Denmark* 1 F1
Horne *Denmark* 2 A2
Horneburg 6 A2
Hørning 2 C2
Hornos 70 A4
Hornow 13 F2
Hornoy-le-Bourg 16 A2
Hornslet 2 C1
Hornstorf 6 C2
Hornsyld 2 C2
Hornum 1 E2
Hörnum 2 A4
Horreby 3 E4
Hörsching 30 C2
Horsens 2 C2
Hørsholm 3 E2
Hörsingen 12 B1
Horslunde 3 D4
Horst 10 A3
Horst (Holstein) 6 A2
Horstedt 5 F3
Hörstel 10 C1
Horstmar 10 B1
Hortezuela 63 E1
Hortigüela 55 F4
Høruphav 2 C4
Hørve 3 D2
Horw 28 A4
Hösbach 19 E2
Hosena 13 E3
Hosenfeld 11 E4
Hosingen 17 F2
Hoßkirch 28 B2
Hostalríc 59 E3
Hostrupskov 2 B3
Hotton 17 E1
Hou 1 F2
Houdain 16 B1
Houdan 25 D1
Houdelaincourt 26 C1
Houeillès 40 C2
Houffalize 17 F2
Houlbjerg 2 C1
Houlgate 15 D3
Hourtin 32 B4
Hourtin-Plage 32 B4
Houten 9 E1
Houthalen 9 E3
Houthulst 8 B3
Hov 2 C2
Hovborg 2 B2
Hovedgård 2 C2
Hövelhof 11 D2
Hoven 2 A2
Hovslund Stationsby 2 B3
Höxter 11 E2
Hoya 5 F4
Hoya Gonzalo 70 C2
Hoyerswerda 13 F3
Hoym 12 B2
Hoyocasero 62 B3
Hoyo de Manzanares 63 D3
Hoyos 61 E4
Hoyos del Espino 62 B3
Huarte 57 D2
Huarte-Araquil 56 C2
Hückelhoven 10 A3
Hückeswagen 10 B3
Hucqueliers 16 A1
Hude (Oldenburg) 5 E3
Huécija 75 F3
Huélago 75 E2
Huelgoat 22 B2
Huelma 75 D1
Huelva 73 D2
Huelves 63 E4
Huércal de Almería 75 F3
Huércal-Overa 76 A2
Huérguina 64 B4
Huérmeces 55 F3
Huerta del Marquesada 64 B4
Huerta de Valdecarábanos 63 D4
Huertahernando 63 F2
Huerto 58 A3
Huesa 75 E1
Huesa del Común 64 C2
Huesca 57 E4
Huéscar 75 F1
Huete 63 F4
Huétor-Tájar 74 C2
Huétor-Vega 75 D2
Huévar 73 E2
Hüfingen 28 A2
Huisheim 20 A4
Huissen 10 A2
Huizen 9 E1
Hüllhorst 11 D1
Hulst 9 D3
Humanes de Madrid 63 D4
Humanes de Mohernando 63 E2
Humble 2 C4
Humilladero 74 B2
Humlebæk 3 F2
Humlum 2 A1
Hundborg 1 D2
Hundeluft 12 C2
Hunderdorf 21 D4
Hundested 3 E2
Hundshübel 12 C4
Hundslund 2 C2
Hune 1 E2
Hünfeld 11 E4
Hungen 11 D4
Hunsel 9 F3
Hunspach 18 C4
Huntlosen 5 E4
Hüpstedt 11 F3
Huriel 34 A1
Hurteles 56 C4
Hürth 10 B4
Hurup 1 D3
Husby 2 B4
Husum *Ger.* 5 F4
Husum *Ger.* 5 F1
Hüttau 30 B3
Hüttenberg 30 C4
Hüttisheim 28 C1
Hüttlingen 19 F4
Hüttschlag 30 B3
Huttwil 27 F4
Hüven 5 D4
Huy 17 E1
Hvalpsund 1 E3
Hvalsø 3 E2
Hvam 1 E3
Hvidbjerg 1 D3
Hvide Sande 2 A2
Hvidovre 3 E2
Hvilsom 1 E3
Hvorslev 2 B1
Hyères 43 F4
Hyllinge 3 D3

I

Ibahernando 67 F2
Ibarra 56 C2
Ibbenbüren 10 C1
Ibdes 64 B2
Ibeas de Juarros 55 F3
Ibi 71 D3
Ibros 69 E4
Ichenhausen 28 C1
Ichtegem 8 B3
Icking 29 E2
Idanha-a-Nova 67 D1
Idanha-a-Velha 61 D4
Idar-Oberstein 18 B2
Iden 6 C4
Idestrup 3 E4
Idiazabal 56 C2
Idocin 57 D3
Idom 2 A1
Idro 38 B3
Idstedt 2 B4
Idstein 18 C1
Ieper 8 B4
Iffendic 23 E2
Ifs 15 D3
Ifta 11 F3
Igea 56 C4
Igensdorf 20 B2
Igersheim 19 E3
Iggensbach 30 B1
Igis 28 C4
Igling 29 D2
Igney 27 D2
Igorre 56 B2
Igrejinha 66 C3
Igrexa 53 E3
Igrexario 53 E3
Igualada 58 C3
Igualeja 74 B3
Igueña 54 B3
Ihlienworth 5 E2
Ihlowerhörn (Ihlow) 5 D3
Iholdy 40 A4
Ihrhove 5 D3
Ihringen 27 F2
Ihrlerstein 20 B4
IJlst 4 B4
IJmuiden 9 D1
IJsselmuiden 4 B4
IJsselstein 9 E1
IJzendijke 8 C3
Ikast 2 B1
Ilanz 28 B4
Ilfeld 11 F2
Ílhavo 60 B3
Illana 63 E4
Illar 75 F3
Illats 40 B1
Illerrieden 28 C2
Illertissen 28 C2
Illescas 63 D4
Ille-sur-Têt 59 E1
Illiers-Combray 24 C2
Illingen 18 B3
Illkirch-Graffenstaden 27 F1
Illmensee 28 B2
Illmitz 31 F2
Íllora 75 D2
Illschwang 20 B3
Illueca 64 B1
Illzach 27 F2
Ilmenau 12 A4
Ilmmünster 29 E1
Ilsede 11 F1
Ilsenburg (Harz) 11 F2
Ilsfeld 19 E4
Ilskov 2 B1
Ilz 31 E4
Imèr 39 D2
Immendingen 28 A2
Immenhausen 11 E3
Immenreuth 20 B2
Immenstaad am Bodensee 28 B3
Immenstadt im Allgäu 28 C3
Imola 46 C1
Imperia 44 B2
Imphy 25 F4
Impruneta 46 B3
Imst 29 D3
Incheville 15 F2
Incinillas 55 F2
Incisa in Val d'Arno 46 B3
Incourt 9 E4
Infiesto 55 D1
Ingelheim am Rhein 18 C2
Ingelmunster 8 C3
Ingersheim 27 E2
Ingolstadt 29 E1
Ingrandes *France* 23 F3
Ingrandes *France* 33 D1
Ingstrup 1 F1
Inguiniel 22 C2
Ingwiller 18 B4
Iniesta 70 B2
Innerbraz 28 C4
Innernzell 21 D4
Innertkirchen 28 A4
Innervillgraten 39 D1
Innsbruck 29 E3
Ins 27 E4
Insming 18 B4
Instinción 75 F3
Interlaken 27 F4
Introbio 37 E2
Inzell 30 A2
Inzigkofen 28 B2
Inzing 29 E3
Inzinzac-Lochrist 22 C3
Ippesheim 19 F2
Ipsheim 20 A3
Irdning 30 C3
Irigny 35 E3
Irixo 53 F3
Irlbach 21 D4
Irnsum 4 B3
Irodouër 23 E2
Irsch 18 A3
Irsee 29 D2
Irsina 50 C3
Irueste 63 E3
Irún 56 C1
Irurita 57 D2
Irurozqui 57 D2
Irurzun 56 C2
Irxleben 12 B1
Isaba 57 E2
Isbergues 16 A1
Íscar 62 C2
Ischgl 29 D4
Ischia 49 E4
Ischia di Castro 48 B1
Ischitella 50 B1
Isen 29 F2
Isenbüttel 11 F1
Isenvad 2 B1
Iseo 38 A3
Iserlohn 10 C3
Isernhagen 11 E1
Isernia 49 E3
Isigny-sur-Mer 14 C3
Isla Cristina 72 C2
Isla Plana 76 B2
Isle 33 E3
Ismaning 29 E2
Isna 66 C1

Isny im Allgäu **28** C3
Isola 2000 **44** A2
Isola **44** A2
Isola d'Asti **44** C1
Isola del Gran Sasso d'Italia **49** D1
Isola della Scala **38** B3
Isola del Liri **49** D2
Isola di Capo Rizzuto **52** C2
Isole del Cantone **45** D1
Isona **58** B2
Isorella **38** A3
Ispra **37** D3
Ispringen **19** D4
Isselburg **10** A2
Issigeac **41** D1
Issime **36** C3
Isso **70** B3
Issogne **36** B3
Issoire **34** B3
Issoudun **25** D4
Issum **10** A2
Is-sur-Tille **26** C3
Issy-l'Évêque **34** C1
Istán **74** B3
Istres **43** D3
Isuerre **57** E3
Itero de la Vega **55** E3
Iteuil **33** D1
Itrabo **75** D3
Itri **49** D3
Itterbeck **10** B1
Ittre **17** D1
Ituero de Azaba **61** E3
Itzehoe **6** A2
Itzstedt **6** A2
Ivars d'Urgell **58** B3
Ivrea **36** C3
Ivry-la-Bataille **15** F4
Ivry-sur-Seine **16** A4
Ixelles **9** D4
Izarra **56** B2
Izeda **61** E1
Izegem **8** C4
Izernore **35** E2
Iznájar **74** C2
Iznalloz **75** D2

J

Jabaga **63** F4
Jabaloyas **64** B4
Jabalquinto **69** D4
Jabbeke **8** B3
Jabel **7** D3
Jabugo **67** E4
Jaca **57** E3
Jachenau **29** E3
Jadraque **63** E2
Jægerspris **3** E2
Jaén **75** D1
Jagerberg **31** E4
Jagsthausen **19** E3
Jagstzell **19** F4
Jahnsfelde **13** E1
Jakubov **31** F1
Jalance **70** C2
Jalhay **17** F1
Jaligny-sur-Besbre **34** C2
Jallais **23** F4
Jameln **6** B3
Jamilena **75** D1
Jandels-brunn **30** B1
Janderup **2** A2
Jänickendorf **13** D1
Janville **25** D2
Janzó **23** E2
Jaraba **64** A2
Jarafuel **70** C2
Jaraicejo **68** A1
Jaraiz de la Vera **62** A4
Jarandilla de la Vera **62** A4
Jardin **35** E3
Jard sur-Mer **32** A1
Jargeau **25** D2
Jarmen **7** E2
Jarnac **32** C3
Jarnages **33** F2
Jarny **17** F3
Jarplund-Weding **2** B4
Jarque **64** B1
Jarville-la-Malgrange **17** F4
Jarzé **24** A3
Jasień **13** F2
Jassans-Riottier **35** D2
Jasseron **35** E2
Jatar **75** D3
Jatzke **7** E2
Jatznick **7** F2
Jaulín **64** C1
Jaun **36** B1
Jaunay-Clan **33** D1
Jaunsaras **56** C2
Jaurrieta **57** D2
Jausiers **44** A1
Javalí Viejo **76** B1
Jávea-Xábia **71** E3
Jävenitz **12** B1
Javerlhac-et-la-Chapelle-St-Robert **33** D3
Javier **57** D3
Javron-les-Chapelles **24** A1
Jayena **75** D3
Jebjerg **1** E3
Jédula **73** E3
Jegun **40** C3
Jejsing **2** A4
Jelling **2** B2
Jels **2** B3
Jelsi **50** A1
Jemeppe **17** D1
Jemgum **5** D3
Jena **12** B4
Jenbach **29** E3
Jengen **29** D2
Jennersdorf **31** E4
Jerchel **12** B1
Jerez de la Frontera **73** E3
Jerez del Marquesado **75** E2
Jerez de los Caballeros **67** E4
Jérica **64** C4
Jerichow **12** C1
Jernved **2** A3
Jerslev *Denmark* **1** F2
Jerslev *Denmark* **3** D2
Jerte **62** A4
Jerup **1** F1
Jerzens **29** D4
Jesenwang **29** E2
Jeserig *Ger.* **12** C1
Jeserig *Ger.* **13** D1
Jesi **47** E3
Jesolo **39** E3
Jessen **13** D2
Jeßnitz **12** C2
Jesteburg **6** A3
Jettingen-Scheppach **29** D1
Jeumont **17** D1
Jevenstedt **6** A1
Jever **5** D2
Jijona-Xixona **71** D3
Jimena **75** D1
Jimena de la Frontera **74** A4
Joachimsthal **7** E4
Joane **60** C1
Job **34** C3
Jochberg **30** A3
Jocketa **12** C4
Jódar **75** D1
Jodoigne **9** E4
Jœuf **17** F3
Johanniskirchen **30** A1
Jöhstadt **13** D4
Joigny **25** F2
Joinville **26** C1
Jolanda di Savoia **39** D4
Jolda **60** B1
Jona **28** B3
Jonquières **43** D2
Jonzac **32** C3
Joppolo **52** A3
Jorba **58** C3
Jorcas **64** C3
Jördenstorf **7** D2
Jork **6** A2
Jorquera **70** C2
Josselin **23** D2
Jou **61** D1
Jouarre **16** B4
Joué-lès-Tours **24** B3
Joué-sur-Erdre **23** E3
Jougne **27** D4
Jouques **43** E3
Joure **4** B4
Jouy **25** D1
Jouy-aux-Arches **17** F4
Jouy-le-Potier **25** D3
Joyeuse **42** C1
Juan-les-Pins **44** A3
Jübek **5** F1
Jubrique **74** A3
Jüchen **10** A3
Jüchsen **11** F4
Juden-bach **20** B1
Judenburg **31** D4
Juelsminde **2** C2
Jugon-les-Lacs **23** D2
Juillac **33** E4
Juist **4** C2
Jujurieux **35** E2
Julbach **30** B1
Jülich **10** A4
Jullouville **23** E1
Jumeaux **34** C3
Jumilhac-le-Grand **33** E3
Jumilla **70** C3
Juncal **66** B1
Juncosa **58** B4
Juneda **58** B4
Jungingen **28** B1
Junglinster **17** F2
Juniville **17** D3
Junqueira **72** C2
Jupilles **24** B3
Juprelle **9** E4
Jurançon **40** B4
Jurbise **16** C1
Jürgenshagen **6** C2
Jürgenstorf **7** D2
Jussac **34** A4
Jussey **27** D2
Jüterbog **13** D2
Juvigné **23** F2
Juvigny-le-Tertre **23** F1
Juvigny-sous-Andaine **24** A1
Juzennecourt **26** B2
Jyderup **3** D2
Jyllinge **3** E2
Jystrup **3** E3

K

Kaarßen **6** B3
Kaarst **10** A3
Kaatsheuvel **9** E2
Kahla **12** B4
Kaisersesch **18** B1
Kaiserslautern **18** C3
Kaisheim **29** D1
Kakenstorf **6** A3
Kakerbeck **6** C4
Kalbe (Milde) **6** C4
Kalefeld **11** F2
Kalkar **10** A2
Kalkhorst **6** B2
Kall **10** A4
Kallham **30** B1
Kallmünz **20** C3
Kalmthout **9** D3
Kals am Großglockner **30** A4
Kaltbrunn **28** B3
Kaltenkirchen **6** A2
Kaltennordheim **11** F4
Kaltensundheim **11** F4
Kalundborg **3** D2
Kalwang **31** D3
Kamen **10** C2
Kamenz **13** E3
Kamern **7** D4
Kamp **18** C1
Kampen *Ger.* **2** A4
Kampen *Neth.* **4** B4
Kamp-Lintfort **10** A2
Kandel **18** C3
Kandelin **7** E2
Kandern **27** F3
Kandersteg **36** C1
Kapelle **9** D2
Kapellen **9** D3
Kapfenberg **31** D3
Kapfenstein **31** E4
Kappel **18** B2
Kappeln **2** C4
Kappelrodeck **27** F1
Kappl **29** D4
Kaprijke **8** C3
Kaprun **30** A3
Karben **19** D1
Karbow-Vietlübbe **7** D3
Karby *Denmark* **1** D2
Karby *Ger.* **2** C4
Karden **18** B1
Karise **3** E3
Karlsbad **19** D4
Karlsburg **7** E2
Karlsfeld **29** E2
Karlshagen **7** F1
Karlshöfen **5** F3
Karlsruhe **19** D4
Karlstadt **19** E2
Karlstetten **31** E2
Karow *Ger.* **7** D3
Karow *Ger.* **12** C1
Karrebæksminde **3** E3
Karrenzin **6** C3
Karstädt *Ger.* **6** C3
Karstädt *Ger.* **6** C3
Kartitsch **30** A4
Karup **2** B1
Kås **1** E2
Kasendorf **20** B2
Kasseedorf **6** B1
Kassel **11** E3
Kastellaun **18** B2
Kasterlee **9** E3
Kastl **20** B3
Kastorf **6** B2
Kathlow **13** F2
Katlenburg-Lindau **11** F2
Katsdorf **30** C1
Katwijk aan Zee **9** D1
Katzenelnbogen **18** C1
Katzweiler **18** C3
Kaub **18** C2
Kaufbeuren **29** D2
Kaufungen **11** E3
Kaulsdorf **12** B4
Kavelstorf **7** D2
Kayna **12** C3
Kaysersberg **27** E2
Kefenrod **19** E1
Kefermarkt **30** C1
Kehl **27** F1
Kehlen **17** F2
Kelberg **18** B1
Kelbra (Kyffhäuser) **12** B3
Kelheim **20** B4
Kelkheim (Taunus) **19** D2
Kell **18** B2
Kellenhusen **6** B1
Kellinghusen **6** A2
Kellmünz an der Iller **28** C2
Kelmis **10** A4
Kemberg **13** D2
Kemeten **31** F3
Kemmel **8** B4
Kemnath **20** C2
Kemnitz *Ger.* **13** F3
Kemnitz *Germany* **7** E2
Kempen **10** A3
Kempenich **10** B4
Kempten (Allgäu) **29** D3
Kenn **18** B2
Kenzingen **27** F2
Kerkdriel **9** E2
Kerken **10** A3
Kerkrade **10** A4
Kerlouan **22** B1
Kernhof **31** E2
Kerns **28** A4
Kerpen **10** A4
Kerspleben **12** B3
Kerteminde **2** C3
Kerzers **27** E4
Kettershausen **28** C2
Kettinge **3** E4
Ketzin **13** D1
Keula **11** F3
Kevelaer **10** A2
Kibæk **2** A2
Kiefersfelden **29** F3
Kiel **6** A1
Kienberg **29** F2
Kierspe **10** C3
Kieselbach **11** F4
Kietz **13** F1
Kilb **31** E2
Kilden **1** F1
Kindberg **31** E3
Kindelbrück **12** B3
Kinding **20** B4
Kingersheim **27** F2
Kinrooi **9** F3
Kipfenberg **20** B4
Kippel **36** C1
Kippenheim **27** F1
Kirchanschöring **30** A2
Kirchardt **19** D3
Kirchbach **39** E1
Kirchberg *Ger.* **21** D4
Kirchberg *Ger.* **12** C4
Kirchberg *Switz.* **27** F4
Kirchberg *Switz.* **28** B3
Kirchberg (Hunsrück) **18** B2
Kirchberg am Wagram **31** E1
Kirchberg am Walde **31** D1
Kirchberg am Wechsel **31** E3
Kirchberg an der Jagst **19** F3
Kirchberg an der Pielach **31** D2
Kirchbichl **29** F3
Kirchdorf *Ger.* **6** C2
Kirchdorf *Ger.* **5** E4
Kirchdorf an der Iller **28** C2
Kirchdorf an der Krems **30** C2
Kirchdorf im Wald **21** D4
Kirchdorf in Tirol **30** A3
Kirchehrenbach **20** B2
Kirchen (Sieg) **10** C4

Kirchenlamitz 20 C1
Kirchen-thumbach 20 B2
Kirchgellersen 6 A3
Kirchhain 11 D4
Kirchheim *Ger.* 19 F2
Kirchheim *Ger.* 11 E4
Kirchheim bei München 29 E2
Kirchheim-Bolanden 18 C2
Kirchhundem 10 C3
Kirchlauter 20 A2
Kirchlinteln 5 F4
Kirch Mulsow 6 C2
Kirchohsen (Emmerthal) 11 E1
Kirchroth 20 C4
Kirchschlag in der Buckligen Welt 31 F3
Kirchseelte 5 E4
Kirchtimke 5 F3
Kirchwalsede 5 F3
Kirchweidach 30 A2
Kirchwistedt 5 E3
Kirchzarten 27 F2
Kirchzell 19 E3
Kirkeby 2 C3
Kirke Helsinge 3 D3
Kirke Hyllinge 3 E2
Kirke Såby 3 E2
Kirke Stillinge 3 D3
Kirn 18 B2
Kirschweiler 18 B2
Kirtorf 11 D4
Kissenbrück 11 F1
Kißlegg 28 C2
Kitzbühel 30 A3
Kitzen 12 C3
Kitzingen 19 F2
Kitzscher 12 C3
Kjellerup 2 B1
Klaaswaal 9 D2
Kläden 6 C4
Klanxbüll 2 A4
Klarup 1 F2
Klaus an der Pyhrnbahn 30 C2
Klausdorf *Ger.* 13 D1
Klausdorf *Ger.* 7 E1
Klausen 18 B2
Klausen Leopoldsdorf 31 E2
Klazienaveen 4 C4
Kleinarl 30 B3
Klein Berßen 5 D4
Kleinblittersdorf 18 B3
Klein Bünzow 7 E2
Kleinfurra 11 F3
Kleinheubach 19 E2
Kleinjena 12 B3
Klein Kreutz 12 C1
Kleinlobming 31 D4
Kleinmachnow 13 D1
Kleinpaschleben 12 C2
Kleinreifling 30 C2
Klein Rönnau 6 A2
Klein St Paul 30 C4
Kleinwallstadt 19 E2
Kleinwelka 13 F3
Klejtrup 2 B1
Klettwitz 13 E2
Kleve 10 A2
Klieken 12 C2
Klietz 6 C4
Klim 1 E2
Klingenberg 13 E4
Klingenberg am Main 19 E2
Klingenthal 20 C1
Klink 7 D3
Klinkby 1 D3
Klintebjerg 2 C3
Kliplev 2 B4
Klippinge 3 E3
Klitmøller 1 D2
Klitten 13 F3
Klixbüll 2 A4
Klöch 31 E4
Kloetinge 8 C2
Klokkerholm 1 F2
Kloosterhaar 10 B1
Kloosterzande 9 D3
Kloster 2 A1
Klosterfelde 7 E4
Klosterhäseler 12 B3
Klösterle 28 C4
Klosterlechfeld 29 D2
Klostermansfeld 12 B2
Klosterneuburg 31 F1
Klosters 28 C4
Kloster Zinna 13 D2
Kloten 28 A3
Klotten 18 B1
Klötze (Altmark) 6 B4
Klovborg 2 B2
Klundert 9 D2
Kluse 5 D4
Klütz 6 B2
Knebel 2 C1
Knesebeck 6 B4
Knesselare 8 C3
Knetzgau 20 A2
Knittelfeld 31 D3
Knittlingen 19 D4
Knokke-Heist 8 C3
Knorrendorf 7 E2
Knud 2 B1
København 3 F2
Kobenz 31 D3
Kobersdorf 31 F3
Koblenz 18 C1
Kobrow 6 C2
Kochel am See 29 E3
Kodersdorf 13 F3
Köditz 20 B1
Koekelare 8 B3
Köflach 31 D4
Køge 3 E3
Koglhof 31 E3
Kohlberg 20 C3
Köhlen 5 E2
Kohren-Sahlis 12 C3
Koksijde 8 B3
Kołbaskowo 7 F3
Kolbermoor 29 F2
Kølby 1 E2
Koldby 1 D2
Kolding 2 B3
Kolind 2 C1
Kolitzheim 19 F2
Kølkær 2 B1
Kolkwitz 13 F2
Kölleda 12 B3
Kölln-Reisiek 6 A2
Kollund 2 B4
Köln 10 B3
Kolochau 13 D2
Kolt 2 C1
Kølvrå 2 B1
Køng 3 E3
Kongens Lyngby 3 E2
Kongerslev 1 F2
Königsberg in Bayern 20 A2
Königsborn 12 B1
Königsbronn 28 C1
Königsbrück 13 E3
Königsbrunn 29 D1
Königsdorf 29 E2
Königsee 12 B4
Königsfeld im Schwarzwald 28 A2
Königshofen 12 C3
Königshütte 11 F2
Königslutter am Elm 11 F1
Königsmoos 29 E1
Königssee 30 A3
Königstein *Ger.* 20 B3
Königstein *Ger.* 13 E4
Königstein im Taunus 19 D1
Königswartha 13 F3
Königswiesen 31 D1
Königswinter 10 B4
Königs Wusterhausen 13 E1
Könitz 12 B4
Köniz 27 F4
Könnern 12 B2
Konstanz 28 B3
Konz 18 A2
Konzell 21 D4
Koog aan de Zaan 9 E1
Kootstertille 4 B3
Koppl 30 A2
Korbach 11 D3
Körchow 6 B3
Korinth 2 C3
Körle 11 E3
Körner 11 F3
Korneuburg 31 F1
Kornwestheim 19 E4
Körperich 17 F2
Korsør 3 D3
Kortemark 8 B3
Kortenhoef 9 E1
Kortessem 9 E4
Kortgene 8 C2
Kortrijk 8 C4
Kösching 20 B4
Kosel 6 A1
Koserow 7 F2
Koßdorf 13 D3
Kössen 29 F3
Kotelow 7 E2
Köthen (Anhalt) 12 C2
Kötschach 30 A4
Kottes 31 D1
Kötzting 21 D3
Koudekerke 8 C2
Koudum 4 A4
Kowalów 13 F1
Krabbendijke 9 D3
Krackow 7 F3
Kraftsdorf 12 C4
Kragelund 2 B1
Krajnik Dolny 7 F3
Krakow am See 7 D2
Kramsach 29 F3
Kranenburg 10 A2
Kranichfeld 12 B4
Krauchenwies 28 B2
Krauschwitz 13 F2
Krautheim 19 E3
Krefeld 10 A3
Kreiensen 11 E2
Krempe 6 A2
Kremperheide 6 A2
Krems an der Donau 31 E1
Kremsbrücke 30 B4
Kremsmünster 30 C2
Kressbronn am Bodensee 28 C3
Kreuth 29 E3
Kreuzau 10 A4
Kreuzlingen 28 B3
Kreuztal 10 C4
Kreuzwert-heim 19 E2
Krieglach 31 E3
Kriegstetten 27 F4
Krien 7 E2
Kriens 28 A4
Krimpen aan de IJssel 9 D2
Kritzmow 7 D2
Krögis 13 D3
Krölpa 12 B4
Krommenie 4 A4
Kromsdorf 12 B3
Kronach 20 B1
Kronberg im Taunus 19 D1
Kronprinzenkoog 5 E2
Kronshagen 6 A1
Kronstorf 30 C2
Kröpelin 6 C2
Kropp 6 A1
Kroppenstedt 12 B2
Kropstädt 13 D2
Kröslin 7 E1
Krosno Odrzańskie 13 F1
Krossen 12 C3
Krostitz 12 C3
Krottendorf 31 E3
Kröv 18 B2
Krüden 6 C4
Kruibeke 9 D3
Kruiningen 9 D3
Kruishoutem 8 C4
Krumbach *Austria* 31 F3
Krumbach *Austria* 28 C3
Krumbach (Schwaben) 29 D2
Krummesse 6 B2
Krumpa (Geiseltal) 12 B3
Krün 29 E3
Krunderup 2 A1
Kruså 2 B4
Krzywin 7 F3
Küblis 28 C4
Kuchen 28 C1
Kuchl 30 B3
Kufstein 29 F3
Kühbach 29 E1
Kuhbier 7 D3
Kuhfelde 6 B4
Kühndorf 11 F4
Kühren 13 D3
Kuhs 7 D2
Kuhstedt 5 F3
Kuinre 4 B4
Kukmirn 31 F4
Kulmain 20 C2
Kulmbach 20 B2
Külsheim 19 E2
Kumberg 31 E4
Kumhausen 29 F1
Kummer 6 C3
Kummerow 7 D2
Kummersdorf-Alexanderdorf 13 D1
Kummersdorf Gut 13 D1
Kunowice 13 F1
Kunrau 6 B4
Künzell 11 E4
Künzelsau 19 E3
Künzing 30 A1
Kupferberg 20 B2
Kupferzell 19 E3
Kuppenheim 18 C4
Küps 20 B1
Kürnbach 19 D4
Kurort Bad Gottleuba 13 E4
Kurort Kipsdorf 13 E4
Kurort Oberwiesenthal 13 D4
Kurort Schmalkalden 11 F4
Kurort Steinbach-Hallenberg 11 F4
Kusel 18 B3
Kusey 6 B4
Küsnacht 28 A3
Küssnacht 28 A4
Küsten 6 B4
Kusterdingen 28 B1
Kutenholz 5 F3
Kuurne 8 C4
Kværkeby 3 E3
Kværndrup 2 C3
Kvorning 2 B1
Kwaadmechelen 9 E3
Kyllburg 18 A2
Kyndby Huse 3 E2
Kyritz 7 D4

L

Laa an der Thaya 31 F1
Laaber 20 B4
La Adrada 62 C4
Laage 7 D2
La Alberca *Spain* 61 F3
La Alberca *Spain* 76 B1
La Alberca de Záncara 70 A1
La Alberguería de Argañán 61 E3
La Albuera 67 E3
La Aldehuela 62 A3
La Algaba 73 E2
La Aliseda de Tormes 62 A3
La Aljorra 76 C2
La Almarcha 70 A1
La Almolda 58 A4
La Almunia de Doña Godina 64 B1
La Antilla 72 C2
Laarkirchen 30 B2
Laarne 8 C3
Laaslich 6 C3
Laatzen 11 E1
Laax 28 B4
La Azohía 76 B2
La Baconnière 23 F2
Labajos 62 C2
La Bañeza 54 C3
La Barre-de-Monts 23 E4
La Barthe-de-Neste 40 C4
La Bassée 16 B1
La Bastide-Clairence 40 A3
La Bastide-de-Sérou 41 E4
Labastide-Murat 41 E1
Labastide-Rouairoux 42 A3
Labastide-St-Pierre 41 E2
La Bâthie 36 A3
La Bâtie-Neuve 43 F1
La Baule-Escoublac 23 D4
La Bazoche-Gouet 24 C2
La Bazoge 24 B2
L'Abbaye 36 A1
Labégude 42 C1
La Bégude-de-Mazenc 43 D1
Labenne 40 A3
La Bérarde 36 A4
La Bernerie-en-Retz 23 E4
Laberweinting 20 C4
La Biolle 35 F3
La Bisbal de Falset 58 B4
La Bisbal del Penedès 58 C4
La Bisbal d'Empordà 59 E3
Lablachère 42 C1
Laboe 6 A1
La Bonneville-sur-Iton 15 E4
La Bouëxière 23 E2
Labouheyre 40 B2
La Bourboule 34 B3
La Bóveda de Toro 62 A2
La Brède 40 B1
La Bresse 27 E2
La Bridoire 35 F3
Labrit 40 B2
La Broque 27 E1
La Bruffière 23 F4
Labruguière 41 F3
L'Absie 32 B1
La Cabrera 63 D2
La Caillère 32 B1
Lacalahorra 75 E2
La Calmette 42 C2

La Calzada de Oropesa **62** B4
La Campana **74** A1
La Cañada de San Urbano **75** F3
La Cañada de Verich **65** D2
Lacanau **32** B4
Lacanau-Océan **32** B4
La Canourgue **42** A1
La Capelle **16** C2
Lacapelle-Marival **41** E1
La Caridad **54** B1
La Carlota **74** B1
La Carolina **69** E4
Lacaune **42** A3
La Cava **65** E3
La Cavada **55** F1
Lacco Ameno **49** E4
Lacedonia **50** B2
La Cellera de Ter **59** E3
La Celle-St-Avant **24** B4
La Cerca **55** F2
La Cerollera **65** D2
Laces **38** B1
La Chaise-Dieu **34** C3
La Chaize-le-Vicomte **32** A1
La Chambre **36** A3
La Chapelle-d'Abondance **36** A2
La Chapelle-d'Aligné **24** A3
La Chapelle-d'Angillon **25** E3
La Chapelle-de-Guinchay **35** D2
La Chapelle-des-Fougeretz **23** E2
La Chapelle-en-Vercors **35** E4
La Chapelle-la-Reine **25** E1
Lachapelle-sous-Aubenas **42** C1
La Chapelle-St-Luc **26** A1
La Chapelle-St-Ursin **25** E4
La Chapelle-sur-Erdre **23** E4
Lachar **75** D2
La Charité-sur-Loire **25** F4
La Chartré-sur-le-Loir **24** B3
La Châtaigneraie **32** B1
La Châtre **33** F1
La Chaussée-St-Victor **24** C3
La Chaux-de-Fonds **27** E4
Lachendorf **6** A4
La Chèze **23** D2
La Cierva **64** A4
La Ciotat **43** E4
La Cisterniga **62** C1
La Clayette **35** D2
La Clusaz **36** A2
La Cluse-et-Mijoux **27** D4
La Codosera **67** E2
La Concha **55** F1
La Coquille **33** E3
La Coronada *Spain* **68** B4
La Coronada *Spain* **68** A2
La Côte-St-André **35** E3
La-Couarde-sur-Mer **32** A2
La Couronne **32** C3
La Courtine **33** F3
La Couture-Boussey **15** F4
La Crau **43** F4
La Crèche **32** C2
La Croix-Valmer **43** F4
Lacrouzette **41** F3
La Cumbre **67** F2
Lacunza **56** C2
Ladbergen **10** C1
Ladelund **2** B4
Ladenburg **19** D3
Ladignac-le-Long **33** E3
Ladispoli **48** B2
Ladoeiro **67** D1
Ladon **25** E2
Ładzin **7** F2
La Encina **70** C3
Laer **10** B1
La Ercina **55** D2
La Espina **54** B1
La Estación **59** D3
La Estrella **68** B1
La Fare-les-Oliviers **43** D3
La Fatarrella **58** B4
La Felipa **70** B2
La Fère **16** C2
La Ferrière **32** A1
La Ferrière-aux-Etangs **23** F1
La Ferté-Alais **25** E1
La Ferté-Bernard **24** B2
La Ferté-Frênel **24** B1
La Ferté-Gaucher **16** C4
La Ferté-Imbault **25** D3
La Ferté-Macé **24** A1
La-Ferté-Milon **16** B3
La Ferté-sous-Jouarre **16** B4
La Ferté-St-Aubin **25** D3
Laferté-sur-Amance **26** C2
La Férte-Vidame **24** C1
La Flèche **24** A3
La Florida **54** B1
Lafnitz **31** E3
La Font de la Figuera **71** D3
La Force **33** D4
La Forêt-sur-Sèvre **32** B1
Lafortunada **58** A2
La Fouillade **41** F2
Lafrançaise **41** E2
La Fregeneda **61** E2
La Fresneda **65** D2
La Frontera **63** F3
La Fuente de San Esteban **61** F2
La Fuliola **58** B3
La Gacilly **23** D3
La Galera del pla **65** E3
La Garde-Adhémar **43** D1
La Garde-Freinet **43** F3
Lagardelle-sur-Lèze **41** E3
Lagarelhos **61** D1
Lagares da Beira **60** C3
La Garnache **23** E4
La Garriga **59** D3
Lagarrigue **41** F3
La Garrovilla **67** F3
La Gaubretière **23** F4
Lage **11** D2
Lage Mierde **9** E3
La Gineta **70** B2
La Glacerie **14** B3
Lagnieu **35** E2
Lagny-sur-Marne **16** B4
Lago **52** B2
Lagoa *Port.* **61** E1
Lagoa *Port.* **72** A2
Lagoaça **61** E2
Lagonegro **50** B4
Lagor **40** B3
Lagorce **32** C4
Lagord **32** B2
La Gornal **58** C4
Lagos **72** A2
Lagosanto **39** D4
Lagrán **56** B3
La Granada de Riotinto **73** E1
La Granadella **58** B4
La Grand-Croix **35** D3
La Grande-Combe **42** C2
La Grande-Motte **42** C3
La Granja d'Escarp **58** A4
La Granjuela **68** B4
Lagrasse **42** A4
La Grave **36** A4
La Guarda **68** A3
Laguardia **56** B3
La Guardia **63** D4
La Guardia de Jaén **75** D1
Laguarta **58** A2
Laguenne **33** F4
La Guerche-de-Bretagne **23** F2
La Guerche-sur-l'Aubois **25** E4
Laguiole **42** A1
Laguna Dalga **54** C3
Laguna de Duero **62** C1
Laguna de Negrillos **54** C4
Lagundo **38** C1
Lagunilla **62** A3
La Haba **68** A2
La Haye-du-Puits **14** B3
La Haye-Pesnel **23** E1
Lähden **5** D4
La Higuera **70** C3
La Hiniesta **62** A1
La Hinojosa **70** A1
Lahnstein **18** C1
Lahntal-Goßfelden **11** D4
La Horcajada **62** A3
La Horra **55** F4
Lahr (Schwarzwald) **27** F1
Laichingen **28** C1
L'Aigle **24** B1
La Iglesuela **62** B4
La Iglesuela del Cid **65** D3
Laignes **26** B2
Laigueglia **44** C2
L'Aiguillon-sur-Mer **32** A2
Lailly-en-Val **25** D3
Lainate **37** D3
La Iruela **69** F4
Laissac **42** A1
Laives **38** C1
La Jana **65** E3
La Jarrie **32** B2
Lajatico **46** A3
La Javie **43** F2
Lajeosa **61** E3
Lajeosa do Mondego **61** D3
La Jonquera **59** E2
La Jumellière **23** F4
La Lantejuela **74** B2
La Lapa **67** F3
L'Albagés **58** B4
Lalbenque **41** E2
L'Alcudia **71** D2
L'Alcudia de Crespins **71** D3
Lalevade-d'Ardèche **42** C1
Lalín **53** F3
Lalinde **33** D4
La Línea de la Concepción **74** A4
La Londe-les-Maures **43** F4
Laloubère **40** C4
La Loupe **24** C1
La Louvière **17** D1
L'Alpe-d'Huez **35** F4
La Luisiana **74** A2
Lam **21** D3
Lama **49** E2
La Machine **25** F4
La Magdalena **54** C2
Lamagistère **41** D2
Lamalou-les-Bains **42** A3
Lama Mocogno **46** A1
La Manga del Mar Menor **76** C2
Lamanon **43** D3
Lamarche **26** C2
Lamas **60** B2
La Massana **58** C2
Lamastre **35** D4
La Mata **62** C4
La Mata de los Olmos **65** D2
La Matilla **63** D2
Lambach **30** B2
Lamballe **23** D1
Lambersart **16** B1
Lambesc **43** D3
Lambrecht (Pfalz) **18** C3
Lamego **60** C2
La Meilleraye-de-Bretagne **23** E3
Lameiras **61** D3
Lamerdingen **29** D2
L'Ametlla de Mar **65** E2
Lamezia **52** B3
La Milesse **24** B2
La Mojonera **75** F3
Lamon **38** C2
La Monnerie-le-Montel **34** C2
La Morera **67** E3
La Mothe-Achard **32** A1
La Mothe-St-Héray **32** C2
Lamotte-Beuvron **25** D3
La Motte-Chalancon **43** D1
La Motte-du-Caire **43** E1
La Motte-Servolex **35** F3
Lampaul-Guimilau **22** B1
Lampaul-Plouarzel **22** A1
Lampertheim **19** D3
Lampertswalde **13** E3
Lamprechtshausen **30** A2
Lamsfeld-Groß Liebitz **13** E2
Lamspringe **11** E2
Lamstedt **5** F2
La Mudarra **55** D4
La Muela **64** C1
La Mure **35** F4
Lamure-sur-Azergues **35** D2
Lana **38** C1
Lanaken **9** F3
La Nava **67** E4
La Nava de Ricomalillo **68** C1
La Nava de Santiago **67** F2
Lanciano **49** E1
Lancy **35** F2
Landau an der Isar **30** A1
Landau in der Pfalz **18** C3
Landeck **29** D4
Landeleau **22** B2
Landerneau **22** B1
Landete **64** B4
Landévant **22** C3
Landgraaf **10** A4
Landiras **40** B1
Landivisiau **22** B1
Landivy **23** F1
Landkirchen auf Fehmarn **6** B1
Landos **42** B1
Landquart **28** C4
Landrecies **16** C2
Landres **17** F3
Landsberg am Lech **29** D2
Landshut **29** F1
Landstuhl **18** C3
Landudec **22** B2
Lanester **22** C3
La Neuveville **27** E4
Langå **2** C1
Langa **62** B2
Langa de Duero **63** E1
Langballig **2** B4
Langburkersdorf **13** F3
Langdorf **21** D4
Langeac **34** C4
Langeais **24** B3
Langebæk **3** E4
Langedijk **4** A4
Langeln **11** F2
Langelsheim **11** F2
Langemark **8** B4
Langen **5** E2
Langenaltheim **20** A4
Langenau **28** C1
Langenberg **10** C2
Langenburg **19** F3
Langenenslingen **28** B2
Längenfeld **29** D4
Langenfeld (Rheinland) **10** B3
Langenhagen **11** E1
Langenhahn **10** C4
Langenhorn **2** A4
Langenleuba-Oberhain **13** D4
Langenlois **31** E1
Langenlonsheim **18** C2
Langennaundorf **13** D2
Langen-neufnach **29** D2
Langenorla **12** B4
Langenpreising **29** F1
Langenselbold **19** D1
Langenthal **27** F3
Langenwang **31** E3
Langenweddingen **12** B1
Langenzenn **20** A3
Langenzersdorf **31** F1
Langeoog **5** D2
Langeskov **2** C3
Langewiesen **12** A4
Langgöns **11** D4
Langhagen **7** D2
Langhirano **46** A1
Langnau **27** F4
Langø **3** D4
Langogne **42** B1
Langoiran **40** B1
Langon **40** B1
Langreo **54** C1
Langres **26** C2
Langschlag **31** D1
Langueux **23** D1
Languidic **22** C3
Languilla **63** D1
Langula **11** F3
Langwarden (Butjadingen) **5** E2
Langwedel *Ger.* **5** F3
Langwedel *Ger.* **6** A1
Langweid am Lech **29** D1
Lanjarón **75** D3
Lanmeur **22** B1
Lannach **31** D4
Lannemezan **40** C4
Lannilis **22** A1
Lannion **22** C1
Lannoy **16** B1
Lanobre **34** A3
L'Anoia **59** D4
Lanouaille **33** E3
Lansen **7** D2
Lanslebourg-Mont-Cenis **36** A3
Lanta **41** E3
Lantadilla **55** E3
Lanton **40** A1
Lantosque **44** A2
Lantriac **34** C4
La Nucía **71** E3
Lanuvio **48** C2
Lanvollon **22** C1
Lanz **6** C3

Lanzahita **62** B4
Lanžhot **31** F1
Lanzo Torinese **36** B4
Laon **16** C3
La Paca **76** A1
La Pacaudière **34** C2
Lapalisse **34** C2
La Palma **76** C2
La Palma del Condado **73** D2
La Palme **42** A4
Lapalud **42** C2
La Parra **67** E3
La Parra de Las Vegas **63** F4
La Penne **44** A2
La Penne-sur-Huveaune **43** E4
La Peraleja **63** F4
La Pesga **61** F3
La Petite-Pierre **18** B4
La Peza **75** E2
La Pinilla **76** B2
La Plage **36** A3
La Plaza **54** C2
Laplume **41** D2
La Pobla del Duc **71** D3
La Pobla de Lillet **59** D2
La Pobla de Montornès **58** C4
La Pobla de Segur **58** B2
La Pobla de Vallbona **71** D1
La Pola de Gordón **54** C2
La Pommeraye **23** F3
La Portellada **65** D2
La Portera **70** C2
La Pouëze **23** F3
Lapoutroie **27** E2
Lappersdorf **20** C4
La Preste **59** D2
La Proveda de Soria **56** B4
La Puebla de Almoradiel **69** E1
La Puebla de Arganzón **56** B2
La Puebla de Cazalla **74** A2
La Puebla de los Infantes **74** A1
La Puebla del Río **73** E2
La Puebla de Montalbán **62** C4
La Puebla de Valdavia **55** E3
La Puebla de Valverde **64** C4
La Puerta de Segura **70** A4
La Punt **38** A1
L'Aquila **49** D1
Laracha **53** E2
Laragne-Montéglin **43** E2
La Rambla **74** B1
Laranueva **63** F2
La Rasa **63** E1
La Ravoire **35** F3
L'Arboç **58** C4
L'Arbresle **35** D3
Larchamp **23** F2
Larche **33** E4
Lardaro **38** B2
Larderello **46** A4
Lardero **56** B3
Laredo **55** F1
Laren *Neth.* **10** A1
Laren *Neth.* **9** E1
La Réole **40** C1
L'Argentière-la-Bessée **36** A4
Lari **46** A3
Lariano **48** C2
La Riba **58** C4
La Riba de Escalote **63** E2
La Ricamarie **35** D3
La Riche **24** B3
La Rinconada **73** E2
Larino **50** A1
L'Armentera **59** E2
Larmor-Plage **22** C3
La Robla **54** C2
La Roca de la Sierra **67** E2
La Roche **27** E4
La Roche-Bernard **23** D3
La Roche-Canillac **33** F4
La Roche-Chalais **32** C4
La Roche-Derrien **22** C1
La Roche-en-Ardenne **17** E1
La Rochefoucauld **33** D3
La Rochelle **32** B2
La Roche-Posay **33** D1
La Roche-sur-Yon **32** A1
La Rochette **35** F3
La Roda **70** B2
La Roda de Andalucía **74** B2
Laroles **75** E3
La Romana **76** C1
Laroquebrou **33** F4
La Roquebrussanne **43** E3
La Roque-d'Anthéron **43** D3
Laroque-d'Olmes **41** E4
La Roque-Ste-Marguerite **42** A2
Laroque-Timbaut **41** D2
Larraga **56** C3
Larrasoaña **57** D2
Larressore **40** A3
Larrión **56** C3
Laruns **40** B4
Laruscade **32** C4
Larva **75** E1
Lasà **38** B1
Lasalle **42** B2
La Salle **36** B3
La Salle les Alpes **36** A4
La Salvetat-Peyralès **41** F2
La Salvetat-sur-Agout **42** A3
Las Arenas **55** D2
Lasarte-Orio **56** C2
Lasberg **30** C1
Las Berlanas **62** B3
Låsby **2** C1
Las Cabezas de San Juan **73** E3
Las Casas **71** E1
Lascuarre **58** B2
La Seca **62** B1
La Secuita **58** C4
La Séguinière **23** F4
La Selva del Camp **58** B4
La Sènia **65** E3
La Seyne-sur-Mer **43** E4
Las Herencias **62** B4
Las Labores **69** E2
Las Majadas **64** A3
Las Menas **75** F2
Las Mesas **70** A2
Las Navas de la Concepción **68** B4
Las Navas del Marqués **62** C3
Las Negras **76** A3
La Solana **69** E2
La Souterraine **33** E2
Las Palas **76** B2
Las Pedroñeras **70** A2
Las Pedrosas **57** E4
La Spezia **45** E2
Las Rotas **71** E3
Las Rozas de Madrid **63** D3
Lassahn **6** B2
Lassan **7** F2
Lassay-les-Châteaux **24** A1
Lasseube **40** B4
Lassigny **16** B3
Lassing *Austria* **31** D2
Lassing *Austria* **30** C3
Laßnitzhöhe **31** E4
Lastebasse **38** C2
Las Terreras **76** A2
Las Torres de Cotillas **76** B1
Lastra a Signa **46** B3
Lastras de Cuéllar **62** C2
Lastrup **5** D4
La Suze-sur-Sarthe **24** B2
Las Veguillas **62** A3
Las Ventas con Peña Aguilera **69** D1
Las Ventas de San Julián **62** B4
La Talaudière **35** D3
Laterza **51** D3
La Teste **40** A1
Lathen **5** D4
La Thuile **36** A3
Lathus **33** E2
Latiano **51** E3
Latillé **32** C1
Latina **48** C3
Latisana **39** E2
La Torre de Cabdella **58** B2
La Torre de Esteban Hambrán **62** C4
La Tour-d'Aigues **43** E3
La Tour-d'Auvergne **34** B3
Latour-de-France **59** E1
La Tour-du-Crieu **41** E4
La Tour-du-Pin **35** E3
La Tranche-sur-Mer **32** A2
La Tremblade **32** B3
La Trimouille **33** E1
La Trinité **44** A3
La Trinité-Porhoët **23** D2
La Trinité-sur-Mer **22** C3
Latronico **50** B4
Latronquière **33** F4
Lattarico **52** B1
Lattes **42** B3
La Turballe **23** D4
Laubach **11** D4
Lauben **29** D2
Laubusch **13** E3
Lauchhammer **13** E3
Lauchringen **28** A3
Lauda-Königshofen **19** E3
Laudun **42** C2
Lauenau **11** E1
Lauenbrück **6** A3
Lauenburg (Elbe) **6** B3
Lauenförde **11** E2
Lauf an der Pegnitz **20** B3
Laufen **27** F3
Laufenberg **28** A3
Lauingen (Donau) **29** D1
Laujar de Andarax **75** E3
La Unión **76** C2
Laupen **27** E4
Laupheim **28** C2
Laurbjerg **2** C1
Laureana di Borrello **52** A3
Laurens **42** A3
Laurenzana **50** B3
Lauria **50** B4
Laurière **33** E2
Laurino **50** A4
Lauris **43** D3
Laurito **50** B4
Lausanne **36** A1
Lauscha **12** B4
Laußig **13** D2
Laußnitz **13** E3
Laussonne **34** C4
Lauta **13** E3
Lautenbach **28** A1
Lauter **13** D4
Lauterbourg **18** C4
Lauterbrunnen **36** C1
Lauterecken **18** C2
Lauterhofen **20** B3
Lautersbach (Hessen) **11** E4
Lautertal **20** A1
Lautrec **41** F3
Lauzerte **41** D2
Lauzès **41** E1
Lauzun **40** C1
Lavagna **45** D2
Laval **23** F2
La Valle **39** D1
Lavamünd **31** D4
Lavardac **40** C2
Lavaur **41** E3
Lavaveix-les-Mines **33** F2
La Vecilla **55** D2
La Vega **55** E2
La Vega de Riosa **54** C2
La Vega de Sariego **54** C1
Lavelanet **41** E4
La Vellés **62** A2
Lavello **50** B2
Laven **2** B1
Lavena Ponte Tresa **37** D2
Laveno **37** D2
La Ventosa **63** F4
La Verpillière **35** E3
La Verrie **23** F4
Laviano **50** A3
La Victoria **74** B1
La Vid **63** D1
La Villa de Don Fadrique **69** E1
La Ville-aux-Clercs **24** C2
Lavilledieu **42** C1
La Villedieu-du-Clain **33** D1
Lavinio-Lido di Enea **48** C3
Lavìs **38** C2
Lavit **41** D2
La Voulte-sur-Rhône **43** D1
Lavoûte-Chilhac **34** C4
Lavradio **66** B3
Lavre **66** C3
Laxe **53** D2
Laxou **17** F4
Layana **57** D3
La Yesa **64** C4
Layos **69** D1
Layrac **41** D2
Laza **54** A4
Lazagurría **56** C3
Lazise **38** B3
Lazkao **56** C2
Lebach **18** B3
Le Barp **40** B1
Le Bar-sur-Loup **44** A3
Lebbeke **9** D3
Le Beausset **43** E4
Le Biot **36** A2
Le Blanc **33** E1
Le Bleymard **42** B1
Le Bois-d'Oingt **35** D2
Le Bois-Plage-en-Ré **32** A2
Le Boréon **44** A2
Le Boulou **59** E2
Le Boupère **32** B1
Le Bourg-d'Oisans **35** F4
Le Bourget-du-Lac **35** F3
Le Breuil **26** B4
Lebrija **73** E3
Lebução **61** D1
Le Bugue **33** E4
Le Buisson-de-Cadouin **33** E4
Lebus **13** F1
Lebusa **13** D2
Leça da Palmeira **60** B2
Leça do Bailio **60** B2
Le Cannet **44** A3
Le Cannet-des-Maures **43** F3
Le Cateau-Cambrésis **16** C2
Le Catelet **16** B2
Le Caylar **42** B2
Lecce **51** F4
Lecco **37** E2
Lécera **64** C2
Lech **28** C3
Le Chambon-Feugerolles **35** D3
Lechaschau **29** D3
Le Château-d'Oléron **32** B2
Le Châtelard **35** F3
Le Châtelet **33** F1
Lechbruck **29** D3
Le Chesne **17** D3
Le Cheylard **35** D4
Lechtingen (Wallenhorst) **10** C1
Leciñena **57** E4
Leck **2** A4
Le Conquet **22** A2
Le Coudray-St-Germer **16** A3
Lécousse **23** F2
Le Crès **42** B3
Le Creusot **26** B4
Lecrín **75** D3
Le Croisic **23** D4
Le Crotoy **15** F1
Lectoure **41** D2
Lecumberri **56** C2
Ledaña **70** B2
Ledanca **63** E2
Lede **9** D3
Ledesma **62** A2
Ledeuix **40** B4
Lédignan **42** C2
Ledigos **55** D3
Le Donjon **34** C2
Le Dorat **33** E2
Ledrada **62** A3
Leek **4** C3
Leende **9** E3
Leer (Ostfriesland) **5** D3
Leerdam **9** E2
Leese **11** D1
Leeuwarden **4** B3
Leezen *Ger.* **6** C2
Leezen *Ger.* **6** A2
Le Faou **22** B2
Le Faouët **22** C2
Le Fleix **33** D4
Le Folgoët **22** B1
Le Fossat **41** E4
Le Fousseret **41** D4
Le Fuilet **23** F4
Leganés **63** D4
Leganiel **63** E4
Legau **28** C2
Legazpia **56** C2
Legde **6** C4
Legden **10** B1
Legé **32** A1
Lège-Cap-Ferret **32** B4
Léglise **17** E2
Legnago **38** C4
Legnano **37** D3
Le Gond-Pontouvre **32** C3
Le Grand-Bornand **36** A2
Le Grand-Bourg **33** E2
Le Grand-Lemps **35** E3
Le Grand-Lucé **24** B2

Le Grand-Pressigny **24** C4
Le Grand-Quevilly **15** E3
Le Grand-Serre **35** E4
Le Grau-du-Roi **42** C3
Léguevin **41** E3
Legutiano **56** B2
Le Havre **15** D3
Lehe **5** F1
Lehndorf **12** C4
Lehnin **13** D1
Léhon **23** E1
Le Horps **24** A1
Le Houga **40** C3
Lehrberg **20** A3
Lehre **11** F1
Lehrte **11** E1
Lehsen **6** B3
Leibertingen **28** B2
Leiblfing **20** C4
Leibnitz **31** E4
Leiden **9** D1
Leiderdorp **9** D1
Leidschendam **9** D1
Leiferde **11** F1
Leimen **19** D3
Leinburg **20** B3
Leinefelde **11** F3
Leinì **36** C4
Leinzell **19** F4
Leioa **56** B1
Leipheim **28** C1
Leipzig **12** C3
Leirado **53** F4
Leiria **66** B1
Leiro **53** F3
Leisach **30** A4
Leisnig **13** D3
Leißling **12** C3
Leitzkau **12** C1
Leiwen **18** B2
Leiza **56** C2
Łęknica **13** F2
Le Lardin-St-Lazare **33** E4
Le Lauzet-Ubaye **43** F1
Le Lavandou **43** F4
Le Lion-d'Angers **23** F3
Le Locle **27** E4
Le Louroux-Béconnais **23** F3
Le Luc **43** F3
Le Lude **24** B3
Lelystad **4** A4
Lem **2** A2
Le Malzieu-Ville **42** B1
Le Mans **24** B2
Le Mas-d'Agenais **40** C1
Le Mas-d'Azil **41** E4
Le Massegros **42** A2
Le Mayet-de-Montagne **34** C2
Le May-sur-Èvre **23** F4
Lembach im Mühlkreis **30** C1
Lemberg *France* **18** B4
Lemberg *Ger.* **18** C3
Lembeye **40** C3
Lembras **33** D4
Lembruch **11** D1
Lemele **10** A1
Le Mêle-sur-Sarthe **24** B1
Le Merlerault **24** B1
Le Mesnil-sur-Oger **16** C4
Lemgo **11** D1
Lemmer **4** B4
Le Molay-Littry **14** C3
Le Monastier-sur-Gazeille **34** C4
Le Monêtier-les-Bains **36** A4
Le Montet **34** B1
Lempdes *France* **34** B3
Lempdes *France* **34** B3
Le Muy **43** F3
Lemvig **2** A1
Lemwerder **5** E3
Lencloître **33** D1
Lend **30** A3
Lendinara **38** C4
Lendum **1** F1
Le Neubourg **15** E3
Lengau *Austria* **30** B2
Lengau *Austria* **30** A3
Lengdorf **29** F1
Lengefeld **13** D4
Lengenfeld **12** C4
Lengenwang **29** D3
Lengerich *Ger.* **5** D4
Lengerich *Ger.* **10** C1
Lenggries **29** E3
Lengnau **27** F4
Léning **18** B4
Lenna **38** A2
Lenne **11** E2
Lennestadt **10** C3
Lenningen **28** B1
Leno **38** A3
Le Noirmont **27** E4
Lenola **49** D3
Le Nouvion-en-Thiérache **16** C2
Lens *Belgium* **16** C1
Lens *France* **16** B1
Lensahn **6** B1
Lent **35** E2
Lentiai **39** D2
Lenting **20** B4
Lenzburg **28** A3
Lenzen **6** C3
Lenzing **30** B2
Lenzkirch **28** A2
Leoben *Austria* **30** B4
Leoben *Austria* **31** D3
Leobersdorf **31** F2
Leogang **30** A3
Léognan **40** B1
Léon **40** A2
León **54** C3
Leonberg **19** D4
Leonding **30** C1
Leonessa **48** C1
Leopoldsburg **9** E3
Leopoldsdorf im Marchfelde **31** F2
Leopoldshagen **7** F2
Leopoldshöhe **11** D2
Le Palais **22** C4
Le Palais-sur-Vienne **33** E2
Le Pallet **23** F4
Le Parcq **16** A1
Le Passage **41** D2
Lepe **72** C2
Le Péage-de-Roussillon **35** D3
Le Perthus **59** E2
Le Pertre **23** F2
Le Petit-Quevilly **15** E3
Le Pian-Médoc **32** B4
Le Pizou **32** C4
Le Plessis-Belleville **16** B4
Le Poinçonnet **33** F1
Le Poiré-sur-Vie **32** A1
Le Pont-de-Claix **35** F4
Le Pont-de-Monvert **42** B1
Le Pontet **43** D2
Leporano **51** D4
Le Porge **32** B4
Le Portel **8** A4
Le Pouliguen **23** D4
Le Pouzin **43** D1
Le Pradet **43** E4
Le-Puy-en-Velay **34** C4
Le Puy-Notre-Dame **24** A4
Le Puy-Ste-Réparade **43** E3
Le Quesnoy **16** C1
Lequile **51** F4
Le Raincy **16** B4
Léré **25** E3
Le Relecq-Kerhuon **22** A2
Lerici **45** E2
Lerín **56** C3
Lerma **55** F4
Lermoos **29** D3
Lérouville **17** E4
Le Russey **27** E4
Lesa **37** D2
Les Abrets **35** F3
Lesaca **57** D2
Les Aix-d'Angillon **25** E4
Les Andelys **15** F3
Les Angles *France* **59** D2
Les Angles *France* **43** D2
Les Arcs **36** A3
Les Aubiers **24** A4
Les Avellanes **58** B3
Les Avenières **35** F3
Les Bordes **25** E2
Les Borges Blanques **58** B4
Les Borges del Camp **58** B4
Les Bouchoux **35** F2
Les Cabannes **58** C1
L'Escala **59** E2
L'Escale **43** E2
Lescar **40** B3
L'Escarène **44** A2
Les Cases d'Alcanar **65** E3
Lesconil **22** B3
Les Contamines-Montjoie **36** A3
Lescure-d'Albigeois **41** F2
Les Diablerets **36** B2
Les Échelles **35** F3
Les Églisottes-et-Chalaures **32** C4
Le Seignus-d'Allos **43** F2
Le Sel-de-Bretagne **23** E2
Le Sentier **35** F1
Les Escaldes **58** C2
Les Essarts **32** B1
Le Seu d'Urgell **58** C2
Les Fins **27** E4
Les Forges **27** D2
Les Gets **36** A2
Les Herbiers **32** B1
Les Houches **36** A2
Lesina **50** B1
Les Landes-Genusson **23** F4
Les Lucs-sur-Boulogne **32** A1
Les Marches **35** F3
Les Martres-de-Veyre **34** B3
Les Matelles **42** B3
Les Mées **43** E2
Les Menuires **36** A3
Les Mureaux **16** A4
Lesneven **22** B1
Lesparre-Médoc **32** B4
Les Peintures **32** C4
Lesperon **40** A2
Les Pieux **14** B3
Les Planes d'Hostoles **59** E3
L'Espluga Calba **58** B4
L'Espluga de Francolí **58** B4
Les Ponts-de-Cé **24** A3
Les Ponts-de-Martel **27** E4
Les Preses **59** E2
Les Rosiers **24** A3
Les Rousses **35** F1
Les Sables-d'Olonne **32** A1
Lessach **30** B3
Les Salles-du-Gardon **42** C2
Lessay **14** B3
Lessines **8** C4
Les Sorinières **23** E4
Lestelle-Bétharram **40** B4
Les Trois-Moutiers **24** B4
Les Useres **65** D4
Les Vans **42** C1
Les Vignes **42** A2
Le Teich **40** A1
Le Teil **42** C1
Le Teilleul **23** F1
Le Theil **24** B2
Le-Theil-de-Bretagne **23** E2
Le Thillot **27** E2
Le Tholy **27** E2
Le Thor **43** D2
Letino **49** E3
Le Touquet-Paris-Plage **15** F1
Le Touvet **35** F3
L'Étrat **35** D3
Le Trayas **44** A3
Le Tréport **15** F2
Letschin **7** F4
Letur **76** A1
Letzlingen **12** B1
Leucate **42** A4
Leuchtenberg **20** C3
Leuenberg **7** F4
Leuk *Switz.* **36** B1
Leuk *Switz.* **36** B2
Leukerbad **36** B1
Leuna **12** C3
Leusden **9** E1
Leutasch **29** E3
Leutenberg **12** B4
Leutershausen **20** A3
Leutesdorf **10** B4
Leutkirch im Allgäu **28** C2
Leuven **9** D4
Leuze-en-Hainaut **16** C1
Le Val **43** F3
Le Vallinot-Longeau-Percey **26** C2
Levanto **45** E2
Levens **44** A2
Leverano **51** F4
Le-Verdon-sur-Mer **32** B3
Leverkusen **10** B3
Lèves **25** D1
Levet **25** E4
Levico Terme **38** C2
Levier **27** D4
Le Vigan **42** B2
Le Ville **46** C3
Le-Vivier-sur-Mer **23** E1
Levroux **25** D4
Leyme **41** E1
Leysin **36** B1
Leytron **36** B2
Lézat-sur-Lèze **41** E4
Lezay **32** C2
Lézignan-Corbières **42** A4
Lezoux **34** C3
Lezuza **70** A2
Lherm **41** E3
L'Hermenault **32** B1
L'Honor-de-Cos **41** E2
L'Horme **35** D3
L'Hospitalet de l'Infant **65** F2
L'Hospitalet de Llobregat **59** D4
L'Hospitalet-près-l'Andorre **59** D1
L'Hostal del Alls **65** E3
L'Huisserie **23** F2
Liancourt **16** A3
Libin **17** E2
Libourne **32** C4
Libramont **17** E2
Librilla **76** B1
Libros **64** B4
Licciana Nardi **45** E2
Licenza **48** C2
Liceras **63** E1
Lich **11** D4
Lichte **12** B4
Lichtenau *Ger.* **27** F1
Lichtenau *Ger.* **11** D2
Lichtenau im Waldviertel **31** E1
Lichtenfels **20** B2
Lichtenstein **13** D4
Lichten-tanne **12** C4
Lichtenvoorde **10** A2
Lichtenwörth **31** F2
Lichterfelde **7** E4
Lichtervelde **8** C3
Licques **8** A4
Lido **39** D3
Lido Adriano **46** C1
Lido di Classe **46** C1
Lido di Foce Verde **48** C3
Lido di Jesolo **39** E3
Lido di Metaponto **51** D4
Lido di Ostia **48** B2
Lido di Siponto **50** B1
Lido di Spina **46** C1
Liebenau *Ger.* **11** E2
Liebenau *Ger.* **5** F4
Liebenburg **11** F2
Liebenfels **30** C4
Liebenwalde **7** E4
Lieberose **13** F2
Liebert-wolkwitz **12** C3
Lieboch **31** D4
Liebstadt **13** E4
Liédena **57** D3
Liège **17** E1
Lienen **10** C1
Lienz **30** A4
Liepe **7** F4
Liepen **7** E2
Liepgarten **7** F2
Lier **9** D3
Liernais **26** A4
Lierneux **17** F1
Liessel **9** F2
Liestal **27** F3
Liétor **70** B3
Liévin **16** B1
Liezen **30** C3
Liffol-le-Grand **26** C1
Liffré **23** E2
Ligist **31** D4
Lignano Pineta **39** E3
Lignano Sabbiadoro **39** E3
Lignan-sur-Orb **42** A3
Ligné **23** E3
Lignières **33** F1
Ligny-en-Barrois **17** E4
Ligny-le-Châtel **26** A2
Ligonchio **46** A1
Ligueil **24** C4
Lihme **1** D3
Lijar **76** A3
L'Île-Bouchard **24** B4
Lilienfeld **31** E2
Lilienthal **5** E3
Lille *Belgium* **9** E3
Lille *France* **16** B1
Lillebonne **15** E3
Lillers **16** A1
Lille Skensved **3** E3
Lille Værløse **3** E2
Lillo **69** E1
Limana **39** D2
Limatola **49** F3
Limay **15** F4
Limbach **19** E3
Limbach-Oberfrohna **13** D4

Limbadi **52** A3
Limbourg **17** F1
Limburg an der Lahn **18** C1
Lime **2** C1
Limmen **4** A4
Limoges **33** E3
Limogne-en-Quercy **41** E1
Limone Piemonte **44** B2
Limone sul Garda **38** B2
Limosano **49** F2
Limoux **41** F4
Limpias **55** F1
Linå **2** B1
Linards **33** E3
Linares **69** E4
Linares de Mora **64** C3
Linares de Riofrío **62** A3
Lincent **9** E4
Lind **2** B1
Lindau *Ger.* **12** C2
Lindau *Ger.* **2** B4
Lindau (Bodensee) **28** C3
Lindberg **21** D4
Linde **2** A1
Lindelse **2** C4
Linden *Ger.* **11** D4
Linden *Ger.* **5** F1
Lindenberg *Ger.* **7** D3
Lindenberg *Ger.* **13** E1
Lindenberg im Allgäu **28** C3
Lindern (Oldenburg) **5** D4
Lindewitt **2** B4
Lindknud **2** B2
Lindlar **10** B3
Lindoso **60** C1
Lindow **7** E4
Lindstedt **6** C4
Lindved **2** B2
Lindwedel **6** A4
Lingen (Ems) **10** B1
Lingolsheim **27** F1
Linhares **61** D3
Linkenheim-Hochstetten **19** D3
Linnich **10** A3
Linow **7** D3
Linthal **28** B4
Linthe **13** D1
Lintig **5** E2
Lintrup **2** B3
Linum **7** D4
Linyola **58** B3
Linz **30** C1
Linz am Rhein **10** B4
Linzoáin **57** D2
Lioni **50** A3
Lion-sur-Mer **15** D3
Lipinki Łużyckie **13** F2
Lippoldsberg (Wahlsburg) **11** E2
Lippstadt **10** C2
Liré **23** F3
Lisboa **66** A3
Lisciano Niccone **46** C3
Liseleje **3** E2
Lisieux **15** D3
L'Isle-Adam **16** A3
L'Isle-d'Espagnac **32** C3
L'Isle-en-Dodon **41** D3
L'Isle-Jourdain *France* **41** D3
L'Isle-Jourdain *France* **33** D2
L'Isle-sur-la-Sorgue **43** D2
L'Isle-sur-le-Doubs **27** E3
L'Isle-sur-Serein **26** A3
Lisle-sur-Tarn **41** E2
Lisse **9** D1
Lissone **37** E3
List **2** A3
Listrac-Médoc **32** B4
Lit-et-Mixe **40** A2
Littau **28** A4
Litzendorf **20** A2
Livarot **15** D4
Liverdun **17** F4
Livernon **41** E1
Livigno **38** A1
Livorno **46** A3
Livorno Ferraris **36** C4
Livron-sur-Drôme **43** D1
Lizarraga **56** C2
Lizy-sur-Ourcq **16** B4
Lizzanello **51** F4
Lizzano **51** E3
Llagostera **59** E3
Llamas de la Ribera **54** C3
Llançà **59** F2
Llanes **55** E1
Llardecans **58** B4
Llaurí **71** D2
Llavorsí **58** C2
Lleida (Lérida) **58** B3
Llera **67** F3
Llerena **67** F4
Llíria **71** D1
Llívia **59** D2
Llodio **56** B2
Llombai **71** D2
Llorenç del Penedès **58** C4
Lloret de Mar **59** E3
Lo **8** B3
Loano **44** C2
Loarre **57** E3
Löbau **13** F3
Löbejün **12** C2
Lobera de Onsella **57** E3
Löbnitz **7** D1
Lobón **67** E3
Loburg **12** C1
Locana **36** B3
Locarno **37** D2
Locate di Triulzi **37** E3
Loccum (Rehburg-Loccum) **11** D1
Lochau **28** C3
Lochem **10** A1
Lochen **30** B2
Loches **24** C4
Lochristi **8** C3
Lockenhaus **31** F3
Löcknitz **7** F3
Locmaria-Plouzané **22** A2
Locmariaquer **22** C3
Locminé **23** D3
Locorotondo **51** E3
Locquirec **22** B1
Locri **52** B4
Loctudy **22** B3
Lödderitz **12** C2
Loddin **7** F2
Lodève **42** B3
Lodi **37** E3
Lodi Vecchio **37** E3
Lodosa **56** C3
Loeches **63** E3
Löf **18** B1
Lofer **30** A3
Löffingen **28** A2
Logroño **56** C3
Logrosán **68** B2
Løgstør **1** E2
Løgstrup **2** B1
Løgten **2** C1
Løgumkloster **2** A3
Lohals **3** D3
Lohberg **21** D3
Lohe-Rickelshof **5** F1
Lohfelden **11** E3
Lohmar **10** B4
Lohme **7** E1
Lohmen *Ger.* **7** D2
Lohmen *Ger.* **13** E3
Löhne **11** D1
Lohne (Oldenburg) **5** E4
Lohra **11** D4
Lohr am Main **19** E2
Lohsa **13** F3
Loiano **46** B2
Loire-sur-Rhône **35** D3
Loiron **23** F2
Loitz **7** E2
Loivos **61** D1
Loivos do Monte **60** C2
Loja **74** C2
Løjt Kirkeby **2** B3
Lokeren **9** D3
Løkken **1** E1
Lollar **11** D4
L'Ollería **71** D3
Lombez **41** D3
Lomborg **2** A1
Lomello **37** D4
Lommatzsch **13** D3
Lomme **16** B1
Lommel **9** E3
Lonato **38** B3
Lønborg **2** A2
Londa **46** B2
Londerzeel **9** D3
Londinières **15** F2
Longages **41** E3
Longare **38** C3
Longares **64** C1
Longarone **39** D2
Longecourt-en-Plaine **26** C4
Longeville-en-Barrois **17** E4
Longeville-sur-Mer **32** A1
Longny-au-Perche **24** C1
Longobardi **52** A2
Longobucco **52** B2
Longomel **66** C2
Longos Vales **53** E4
Longpré-les-Corps-Saints **16** A2
Longroiva **61** D2
Longueau **16** A2
Longué-Jumelles **24** A3
Longuenesse **8** A4
Longueville **25** F1
Longueville-sur-Scie **15** E2
Longuyon **17** E3
Longwy **17** F3
Lonigo **38** C3
Löningen **5** D4
Lonlay-l'Abbaye **23** F1
Lons **40** B4
Lonsee **28** C1
Lons-le-Saunier **35** E1
Lønstrup **1** F1
Loon op Zand **9** E2
Loosdorf **31** D2
Lopera **69** D4
Loppersum **4** C3
Lora del Río **74** A1
Loranca de Tajuña **63** E3
Lorca **76** B2
Lorch *Ger.* **19** E4
Lorch *Ger.* **18** C2
Lorcha **71** E3
Lordelo **60** C2
Lordosa **60** C3
Loreo **39** D4
Loreto **47** E3
Loreto Aprutino **49** E1
Lorgues **43** F3
Lorient **22** C3
Loriguilla **70** C1
Loriol-sur-Drôme **43** D1
Lormes **26** A3
Loro Ciuffenna **46** B3
Loro Piceno **47** E4
Lorp-Sentaraille **41** D4
Lörrach **27** F3
Lorrez-le-Bocage-Préaux **25** E2
Lorris **25** E2
Lorsch **19** D2
Lørslev **1** F1
Lorup **5** D4
Losacino **62** A1
Losa del Obispo **71** D1
Los Alcázares **76** C2
Los Algezares **76** C1
Los Arcos **56** C3
Losar de la Vera **62** A4
Los Arenales del sol **71** D4
Los Barrios **74** A4
Los Barrios de Luna **54** C2
Los Belones **76** C2
Los Cantareros **76** B2
Los Corrales **74** B2
Los Corrales de Buelna **55** F2
Loscos **64** C2
Los Dolores **76** C2
Los Gallardos **76** A3
Losheim **18** B3
Los Hinojosos **70** A1
Los Maldonados **76** B2
Los Molinos **63** D3
Los Navalmorales **68** C1
Los Navalucillos **68** C1
Løsning **2** B2
Losone **37** D2
Los Palacios y Villafranca **73** E2
Los Pandos **55** F2
Los Pedrones **70** C2
Los Pozuelos de Calatrava **69** D3
Los Rábanos **56** C4
Los Royos **76** A1
Los Santos **62** A3
Los Santos de Maimona **67** F3
Loßburg **28** A1
Losser **10** B1
Lößnitz **13** D4
Lostallo **37** D2
Los Tojos **55** E2
Los Villares **75** D1
Los Yébenes **69** D1
Lotte **10** C1
Lottstetten **28** A3
Louannec **22** C1
Loudéac **23** D2
Loudes **34** C4
Loudun **24** B4
Loué **24** A2
Louhans **35** E1
Loulay **32** C2
Loulé **72** B2
Lourdes **40** C4
Lourdoueix-St-Pierre **33** F1
Louriçal **60** B4
Lourinhã **66** A2
Lourmarin **43** D3
Loury **25** D2
Lousa **66** A3
Lousã **60** C4
Lousada **60** C2
Louverné **23** F2
Louvie-Juzon **40** B4
Louviers **15** E3
Louvigné-du-Désert **23** F1
Louvroil **16** C1
Lov **3** E3
Løve **3** D3
Løvel **2** B1
Lovendegem **8** C3
Lovere **38** A2
Lovero **38** A2
Löwenberg **7** E4
Löwenstein **19** E3
Loxstedt **5** E3
Loyettes **35** E3
Lozoya **63** D2
Lozoyuela **63** D2
Lozzo di Cadore **39** D1
Luanco **54** C1
Luarca **54** B1
Lubanowo **7** F3
Lübars **12** C1
Lübbecke **11** D1
Lubbeek **9** E4
Lübben **13** E2
Lübbenau **13** E2
Lübbow **6** B4
Lübeck **6** B2
Lubersac **33** E3
Lübesse **6** C3
Lubián **54** A4
Lubmin **7** E1
Lubrín **76** A3
Lubsko **13** F2
Lübstorf **6** C2
Lübtheen **6** B3
Lübz **6** C3
Luc **41** F2
Lucainena de las Torres **76** A3
Lúcar **75** F2
Luçay-le-Mâle **25** D4
Lucca **46** A2
Lucé **24** C1
Lucena **74** C2
Lucena de Jalón **64** B1
Lucena del Cid **65** D4
Lucena del Puerto **73** D2
Lucenay-lès-Aix **34** C1
Lucenay-l'Évêque **26** A4
Luc-en-Diois **43** E1
Luceni **57** D4
Lucera **50** A1
Lucéram **44** A2
Luché-Pringé **24** B3
Lüchow **6** B4
Luciana **69** D2
Lucignano **46** C3
Lucillo de Somoza **54** B3
Lucito **49** F2
Lucka **12** C3
Luckau **13** E2
Luckenwalde **13** D1
Lückstedt **6** C4
Luco dei Marsi **49** D2
Luçon **32** B1
Luc-sur-Mer **15** D3
Lüdenscheid **10** C3
Lüderitz **12** B1
Lüdersdorf **6** B2
Lüdinghausen **10** B2
Ludwigsau-Friedlos **11** E4
Ludwigsburg **19** E4
Ludwigsfelde **13** D1
Ludwigshafen **28** B2
Ludwigshafen am Rhein **19** D3
Ludwigslust **6** C3
Ludwigsstadt **12** B4
Luelmo **61** F1
Lüerdissen **11** E2
Luesia **57** E3
Lugagnano Val d'Arda **38** A4
Lugano **37** D2
Lugau **13** D4
Lügde **11** E2
Lugnano in Teverina **48** B1
Lugo *Italy* **46** C1
Lugo *Spain* **53** F2
Lugones **54** C1
Lugrin **36** A1
Lugros **75** E2
Luhden **11** D1
Luhe-Wildenau **20** C3
Lühmannsdorf **7** E2
Luino **37** D2
Luintra **53** F3
Luisant **24** C1

Lumbier 57 D3
Lumbrales 61 E2
Lumbreras 56 B4
Lumbres 8 A4
Lumby 2 C3
Lumezzane 38 A3
Lummen 9 E3
Lumpiaque 64 B1
Lumpzig 12 C4
Luna 57 E4
Lunano 47 D3
Lunas 42 A3
Lund 2 B2
Lundby Denmark 2 C4
Lundby Denmark 3 E3
Lunde Denmark 2 C3
Lunde Denmark 2 A2
Lundeborg 3 D3
Lunden 5 F1
Lüneburg 6 B3
Lunel 42 C3
Lünen 10 B2
Lunery 25 E4
Lunéville 27 D1
Lungern 28 A4
Lungro 52 B1
Lünne 10 B1
Lunow 7 F4
Lupiñén 57 E4
Lupión 69 E4
Luppa 13 D3
Luque 74 C1
Lurcy-Lévis 25 E4
Lure 27 D3
Lury-sur-Arnon 25 D4
Lusciano 49 E4
Luserna San Giovanni 44 A1
Lusignan 32 C1
Lusigny-sur-Barse 26 A2
Luso 60 C3
Lussac 32 C4
Lussac-les-Châteaux 33 D2
Lussan 42 C2
Lüssow 7 D2
Lustenau 28 C3
Lutago 29 F4
Lütau 6 B3
Lütetsburg 5 D2
Lutherstadt Wittenberg 13 D2
Lütjenburg 6 B1
Lutter am Barenberge 11 F2
Lutterbach 27 E2
Lützelbach 19 E2
Lützen 12 C3
Lutzingen 29 D1
Lutzmannsburg 31 F3
Lützow 6 B2
Luxembourg 17 F3
Luxeuil-les-Bains 27 D2
Luxey 40 B2
Luyego de Somoza 54 B3
Luz Port. 67 D4
Luz Port. 72 A2
Luz Port. 72 C2
Luzaga 63 F2
Luzarches 16 A4
Luzech 41 E1
Luzenac 59 D1
Luzern 28 A4
Luzianes 72 A1
Luzmela 55 E2
Luzón 63 F2
Luz-St-Sauveur 40 C4
Luzy 26 A4
Luzzara 38 B4
Luzzi 52 B2
Lychen 7 E3
Lyderslev 3 E3
Lyne 2 A2
Lyngby 3 D1
Lyngså 1 F2
Lyon 35 E3
Lyons-la-Forêt 15 F3
Lysabild 2 C4
Lyss 27 F4

M

Maarssen 9 E1
Maasbracht 9 F3
Maasbree 10 A3
Maaseik 9 F3
Maasen 5 E4
Maasland 9 D2
Maasmechelen 9 F3
Maassluis 9 D2
Maastricht 9 F4
Macael 76 A3
Maçanet de Cabrenys 59 E2
Maçanet de la Selva 59 E3
Mação 66 C1
Macastre 71 D2
Maccagno 37 D2
Macchiagodena 49 F3
Maceda Port. 60 B2
Maceda Spain 53 F3
Macedo de Cavaleiros 61 E1
Maceira Port. 61 D3
Maceira Port. 66 B1
Macerata 47 E3
Macerata Feltria 47 D2
Machados 67 D4
Machault 17 D3
Machecoul 23 E4
Machern 13 D3
Mackenrode 11 F2
Mâcon 35 E2
Macotera 62 B3
Macugnaga 36 C2
Maddaloni 49 F4
Made 9 E2
Mäder 28 C3
Madonna di Campiglio 38 B2
Madrid 63 D3
Madridejos 69 E1
Madrigal de las Altas Torres 62 B2
Madrigal de la Vera 62 B4
Madrigal del Monte 55 F4
Madrigalejo 68 B2
Madrigueras 70 B2
Madroñera 68 A2
Maël-Carhaix 22 C2
Maella 58 A4
Maello 62 C3
Maenza 49 D3
Maestu 56 B3
Mafra 66 A2
Magacela 68 A3
Magalas 42 A3
Magallón 57 D4
Magaña 56 C4
Magaz 55 E4
Magdala 12 B4
Magdeburg 12 B1
Magdeburgerforth 12 C1
Magenta 37 D3
Magescq 40 A3
Maggia 37 D2
Magione 46 C4
Magisano 52 B2
Magland 36 A2
Magliano de'Marsi 49 D2
Magliano in Toscana 48 A1
Magliano Sabina 48 C1
Maglie 51 F4
Magnac-Laval 33 E2
Magné 32 B2
Magny-Cours 25 F4
Magny-en-Vexin 16 A3
Magstrup 2 B3
Magueija 60 C2
Maguilla 68 A4
Mahíde 54 B4
Mahlberg 27 F1
Mahlsdorf 6 C4
Mahlwinkel 12 C1
Mahora 70 B2
Mähring 20 C2
Maia 60 B2
Maials 58 B4
Maîche 27 E3
Maida 52 B3
Maienfeld 28 C4
Maierato 52 B3
Maierhöfen 28 C3
Maignelay-Montigny 16 A3
Maillanc 43 D2
Maillezais 32 B2
Mailly-le-Camp 17 D4
Mainbernheim 19 F2
Mainburg 29 E1
Mainhardt 19 E4
Maintenon 25 D1
Mainvilliers 24 C1
Mainz 18 C2
Maiolati Spontini 47 E3
Maiorca 60 B4
Maiorga 66 B1
Mairena del Alcor 74 A2
Maisach 29 E2
Maishofen 30 A3
Maissau 31 E1
Maisse 25 E1
Majadahonda 63 D3
Majadas de Tiétar 62 A4
Makkum 4 A3
Malá 75 D2
Málaga 74 C3
Malagón 69 D2
Malalbergo 46 B1
Malamocco 39 D3
Malansac 23 D3
Malaucène 43 D2
Malaunay 15 E3
Malborn 18 B2
Malcesine 38 B3
Malchin 7 D2
Malchow 7 D3
Malcocinado 68 A4
Maldegem 8 C3
Malden 9 F2
Malè 38 B1
Malején 57 D4
Malemort-sur-Corrèze 33 E4
Malente 6 B1
Malesco 37 D2
Malesherbes 25 E2
Malestroit 23 D3
Malgersdorf 30 A1
Malgrat de Mar 59 E3
Malhadas 61 F1
Malicorne-sur-Sarthe 24 A3
Malijai 43 E2
Malissard 35 E4
Mallemort 43 D3
Mallén 57 D4
Mallentin 6 B2
Mallersdorf 20 C4
Malles Venosta 38 B1
Malling 2 C2
Malliß 6 C3
Mallnitz 30 A4
Malmédy 17 F1
Malnate 37 D3
Malo 38 C3
Malón 57 D4
Malonno 38 A2
Malpartida 61 E3
Malpartida de Cáceres 67 F1
Malpartida de la Serena 68 A3
Malpartida de Plasencia 61 F4
Malpica 53 E1
Malpica de Tajo 62 C4
Malpica do Tejo 67 D1
Malsch 19 D4
Malsfeld 11 E3
Malta Austria 30 B4
Malta Port. 61 E3
Malterdingen 27 F2
Malters 28 A4
Maluenda 64 B2
Malva 62 A1
Malvaglia 37 D1
Malveira 66 A2
Mamarrosa 60 B3
Mambrilla de Castejón 63 D1
Mamer 17 F2
Mamers 24 B1
Mamirolle 27 D4
Mammendorf 29 E2
Mammola 52 B4
Manage 17 D1
Mañaria 56 B2
Mancera de Abajo 62 B2
Mancha Real 75 D1
Manching 29 E1
Manchita 67 F3
Manciano 48 A1
Manciet 40 C3
Mandatoriccio 52 C1
Mandayona 63 E2
Mandelieu-la-Napoule 44 A3
Mandello del Lario 37 E2
Manderscheid 18 B2
Manduel 42 C2
Manduria 51 E4
Mane France 41 D4
Mane France 43 E2
Manerbio 38 A3
Mañeru 56 C3
Manfredonia 50 B1
Manganeses de la Lampreana 54 C4
Manganeses de la Polvorosa 54 C4
Mangualde 60 C3
Manhay 17 E1
Maniago 39 E2
Manilva 74 A4
Manises 71 D2
Mank 31 D2
Manlleu 59 D3
Mannersdorf an der Rabnitz 31 F3
Mannheim 19 D3
Manoppello 49 E1
Manosque 43 E2
Manresa 59 D3
Manschnow 13 F1
Mansfeld 12 B2
Mansilla 56 B4
Mansilla de las Mulas 55 D3
Mansle 32 C2
Mansores 60 C2
Manteigas 61 D3
Mantel 20 C2
Mantes-la-Jolie 15 F4
Mantes-la-Ville 15 F4
Manthelan 24 C4
Mantova 38 B4
Manuel 71 D2
Manzanal de Arriba 54 B4
Manzanal del Puerto 54 B3
Manzanares 69 E2
Manzanares el Real 63 D3
Manzaneda 54 A3
Manzanedo 55 F2
Manzaneque 69 D1
Manzanera 64 C4
Manzanilla 73 E2
Manzano 39 F2
Manzat 34 B2
Manziana 48 B2
Manziat 35 E2
Maqueda 62 C4
Mar 60 B1
Maranchón 63 F2
Maranello 46 A1
Maranhão 66 C2
Marano 46 B2
Marano di Napoli 49 E4
Marano sul Panaro 46 B1
Marans 32 B2
Maratea 50 B4
Marateca 66 B3
Maraussan 42 A3
Marbach 27 F4
Marbach am Neckar 19 E4
Marbella 74 B4
Marboz 35 E2
Marburg an der Lahn 11 D4
Marça 58 B4
Marcaria 38 B4
Marcellina 48 C2
Marchamalo 63 E3
Marchaux 27 D3
Marche-en-Famenne 17 E1
Marchegg 31 F1
Marchena 74 A2
Marchenoir 24 C2
Marcheprime 40 B1
Marchiennes 16 B1
Marchin 17 E1
Marchtrenk 30 C2
Marciac 40 C3
Marciana 45 E4
Marciana Marina 45 E4
Marcianise 49 F4
Marciano della Chiana 46 C3
Marcigny 34 C2
Marcilla 57 D3
Marcillac 32 C4
Marcillac-Vallon 41 F1
Marcillat-en-Combraille 34 A2
Marcilly-en-Villette 25 D3
Marcilly-le-Hayer 25 F1
Marcilly-sur-Eure 24 C1
Marck 8 A3
Marckolsheim 27 F2
Marco de Canaveses 60 C2
Marcoing 16 B2
Marcòn 39 D3
Marcq-en-Barœul 16 B1
Mardeuil 16 C4
Marebbe 39 D1
Marennes 32 B3
Mareuil 33 D3
Mareuil-sur-Ay 16 C4
Mareuil-sur-Lay-Dissais 32 B1
Margherita di Savoia 50 C2
Margone 36 B4
Margraten 9 F4
Marguerittes 42 C2
María 76 A2
Maria Anzbach 31 E2
Mariager 1 F3
Maria Lankowitz 31 D4
Maria Luggau 30 A4

Marialva **61** D2
Mariana **63** F4
Mariano Comense **37** E3
Mariapfarr **30** B4
Maria Saal **30** C4
Mariazell **31** D2
Maribo **3** D4
Marienberg **13** D4
Marienhafe **5** D3
Marienhagen **11** E1
Marienheide **10** B3
Mariental **12** B1
Marigliano **49** F4
Marignane **43** D3
Marigné-Laillé **24** B3
Marigny **14** B3
Marigny-le-Châtel **25** F1
Marín **53** E3
Marina di Alberese **48** A1
Marina di Camerota **50** B4
Marina di Campo **45** F4
Marina di Carrara **45** E2
Marina di Castagneto Donoratico **46** A4
Marina di Cecina **46** A3
Marina di Chieuti **50** A1
Marina di Gioiosa Ionica **52** B4
Marina di Grosseto **46** A4
Marina di Leuca **51** F4
Marina di Massa **45** E2
Marina di Novaglie **51** F4
Marina di Pulsano **51** E4
Marina di Ravenna **46** C1
Marinaleda **74** B2
Marina Palmense **47** F4
Marina Romea **46** C1
Marina Schiavonea **52** B1
Marines *France* **16** A3
Marines *Spain* **71** D1
Maringues **34** B2
Marinha das Ondas **60** B4
Marinha Grande **66** B1
Marinhas **60** B1
Marino **48** C2
Mariotto **50** C2
Marjaliza **69** D1
Markdorf **28** B3
Markelo **10** A1
Markgröningen **19** E4
Markina-Xemein **56** B2
Märkisch Buchholz **13** E1
Markkleeberg **12** C3
Marklohe **5** F4
Marknesse **4** B4
Markneukirchen **20** C1
Markranstädt **12** C3
Marksuhl **11** F4
Markt Allhau **31** E3
Marktbergel **20** A3
Markt Berolzheim **20** A4
Markt Bibart **20** A2
Markt Erlbach **20** A3
Markt Hartmannsdorf **31** E4
Marktheidenfeld **19** E2
Markt Indersdorf **29** E1
Marktl **30** A1
Marktleugast **20** B1
Marktoberdorf **29** D2
Marktoffingen **20** A4
Marktredwitz **20** C2
Markt Rettenbach **29** D2
Markt Schwaben **29** F2
Marktseft **19** F2
Markt St Martin **31** F3
Markt Wald **29** D2
Marl **10** B2
Marle **16** C2
Marlengo **38** C1
Marlenheim **27** F1
Marlhes **35** D4
Marlishausen **12** B4
Marlow **7** D1
Marly *France* **17** F4
Marly *France* **16** C1
Marmagne **25** E4
Marmande **40** C1
Marmelar **67** D4
Marmeleira **66** B2
Marmelete **72** A2
Marmirolo **38** B4
Marmolejo **69** D4
Marmoutier **27** F1
Marnay **26** C3
Marne **5** F2
Marne-la-Vallée **16** B4
Marnitz **6** C3
Maroldsweisach **20** A1
Marolles-les-Braults **24** B2
Maromme **15** E3
Marostica **38** C3
Maroué **23** D1
Marpingen **18** B3
Marquion **16** B1
Marquise **8** A4
Marquixanes **59** E1
Marradi **46** B2
Marrum **4** B3
Marsac-en-Livradois **34** C3
Marsac-sur-Don **23** E3
Marsaglia **45** D1
Marsanne **43** D1
Marsberg **11** D3
Marsciano **46** C4
Marseillan **42** B3
Marseille **43** D3
Marseille-en-Beauvaisis **16** A3
Marsico Nuovo **50** B3
Marsico Vetere **50** B4
Mårslet **2** C2
Marssac-sur-Tarn **41** F2
Marstal **2** C4
Märstetten **28** B3
Marstrup **2** B3
Marta **48** B1
Martano **51** F4
Martel **33** E4
Martelange **17** F2
Martellago **39** D3
Martello **38** B1
Martfeld **5** F4
Martiago **61** E3
Martignacco **39** E2
Martigné-Briand **24** A4
Martigné-Ferchaud **23** F3
Martigné-sur-Mayenne **23** F2
Martigny **36** B2
Martigny-les-Bains **27** D2
Martiherrero **62** B3
Martim Longo **72** C2
Martimporra **54** C1
Martina Franca **51** D3
Martinchel **66** C1
Martín de la Jara **74** B2
Martín del Río **64** C2
Martín de Yeltes **61** F3
Martinengo **38** A3
Martinet **58** C2
Martinfeld **11** F3
Martingança **66** B1
Martín Muñoz de las Posadas **62** C2
Martinsberg **31** D1
Martinsicuro **47** F4
Martizay **33** E1
Martorell **59** D4
Martos **75** D1
Marugán **62** C2
Maruggio **51** E4
Marum **4** B3
Marvão **67** D2
Marvejols **42** B1
Marxheim **29** D1
Marxzell **19** D4
Marzabotto **46** B1
Marzahna **13** D2
Marzahne **12** C1
Marzan **23** D3
Marzling **29** E1
Masa **55** F3
Masalavés **71** D2
Mas-Cabardès **41** F3
Mascaraque **69** D1
Mascarenhas **61** D1
Maschito **50** B3
Mas de Barberans **65** E3
Mas de las Matas **65** D3
Masegosa **64** A3
Masegoso **70** A3
Masegoso de Tajuña **63** F2
Maselheim **28** C2
Masera **36** C2
Maserada sul Piave **39** D3
Masevaux **27** E2
Maside **53** F3
Masi Torello **39** D4
Masone **44** C1
Masquefa **59** D4
Massa **45** E2
Massa Fiscaglia **39** D4
Massafra **51** D3
Massa Lombarda **46** C1
Massa Lubrense **49** F4
Massamagrell **71** D1
Massa Marittimo **46** A4
Massa Martana **47** D4
Massarosa **46** A2
Massat **41** E4
Massay **25** D4
Maßbach **19** F1
Masseube **41** D3
Massiac **34** B4
Massimino **44** B2
Massing **30** A1
Mastershausen **18** B2
Maszewo **13** F1
Matabuena **63** D2
Matadepera **59** D3
Matalebreras **56** C4
Matallana de Valmadrigal **55** D3
Matamala de Almazán **63** F1
Matamorosa **55** E2
Mataporquera **55** E2
Matapozuelos **62** B1
Mataró **59** D4
Matelica **47** D3
Matera **50** C3
Matha **32** C2
Mathi **36** B4
Matignon **23** D1
Matino **51** F4
Matosinhos **60** B2
Matour **35** D2
Matrei am Brenner **29** E4
Matrei in Osttirol **30** A4
Matt **28** B4
Mattersburg **31** F2
Mattighofen **30** B2
Mattinata **50** C1
Maubeuge **16** C1
Maubourguet **40** C3
Mauerkirchen **30** B2
Mauerstetten **29** D2
Mauguio **42** C3
Maulbronn **19** D4
Mauléon **23** F4
Mauléon-Barousse **41** D4
Mauléon-Licharre **40** B4
Maulévrier **24** A4
Maure-de-Bretagne **23** E2
Maureillas-las-Illas **59** E2
Mauriac **33** F4
Mauron **23** D2
Maurs **41** F1
Maussanne-les-Alpilles **43** D3
Mauterndorf **30** B4
Mautern in Steiermark **31** D3
Mauth **21** E4
Mauthausen **30** C1
Mauthen **30** A4
Mauves **35** E4
Mauvezin **41** D3
Mauvoisin **36** B2
Mauzé-sur-le-Mignon **32** B2
Maxial **66** A2
Maxieira **66** C1
Maya **57** D2
Mayen **18** B1
Mayenne **23** F2
Mayet **24** B3
Mayorga **55** D4
Mayrhofen **29** F3
Mazagón **73** D2
Mazaleón **65** D2
Mazamet **41** F3
Mazan **43** D2
Mazarambroz **69** D1
Mazarete **63** F2
Mazarrón **76** B2
Mazé **24** A3
Mazères **41** E4
Mazet-St-Voy **35** D4
Mazières-en-Gâtine **32** C1
Mazzano **38** B3
Mazzano Romano **48** C1
Mazzo di Valtellina **38** A2
Meadela **60** B1
Mealhada **60** B3
Méaulte **16** B2
Meaux **16** B4
Mechelen **9** D3
Mechernich **10** A4
Mechterstädt **11** F3
Mecina-Bombarón **75** E3
Meckenbeuren **28** C3
Meckenheim **10** B4
Meco **63** E3
Meda **61** D2
Meddersheim **18** C2
Mede **37** D4
Medebach **11** D3
Medelim **61** D4
Medellín **67** F2
Medemblik **4** A4
Medesano **38** A4
Mediana **64** C1
Medicina **46** B1
Medinaceli **63** F2
Medina de las Torres **67** F4
Medina del Campo **62** B2
Medina de Pomar **55** F2
Medina de Rioseco **55** D4
Medina-Sidonia **73** E4
Medinilla **62** A3
Mediona **58** C4
Médis **32** B3
Medolla **38** C4
Meduno **39** E2
Meerane **12** C4
Meerbeck **11** D1
Meerbusch **10** A3
Meersburg **28** B3
Meerssen **9** F3
Mées **40** A3
Meeuwen **9** E3
Megève **36** A2
Mehren **18** B1
Mehring **18** B2
Mehrstetten **28** B1
Mehun-sur-Yèvre **25** E4
Meijel **9** F3
Meilen **28** A3
Meillac **23** E1
Meillerie **36** A1
Meimoa **61** D4
Meina **37** D3
Meine **11** F1
Meinersen **11** F1
Meinerzhagen **10** C3
Meiningen **11** F4
Meira **54** A2
Meiringen **28** A4
Meisdorf **12** B2
Meisenheim **18** C2
Meißen **13** E3
Meitingen **29** D1
Meix-devant-Virton **17** E3
Mejlby **2** C1
Mejorada **62** B4
Mejorada del Campo **63** D3
Mejrup **2** A1
Mel **39** D2
Melay **23** F4
Melazzo **44** C1
Melchow **7** E4
Meldola **46** C2
Meldorf **5** F1
Mele **44** C1
Melegnano **37** E3
Melendugno **51** F4
Melfi **50** B2
Melgaço **53** E4
Melgar de Arriba **55** D3
Melgar de Fernamental **55** E3
Melgar de Tera **54** C4
Melgven **22** B2
Meliana **71** D1
Melick **10** A3
Melicucco **52** A3
Mélida **57** D3
Melide **53** F2
Melides **66** B4
Mélisey **27** E2
Melissa **52** C2
Melissano **51** F4
Melito di Porto Salvo **52** A4
Melk **31** D2
Mellac **22** C2
Mellach **31** E4
Mellau **28** C3
Melle *Belgium* **8** C3
Melle *France* **32** C2
Melle *Ger.* **10** C1
Mellen **6** C3
Mellenbach-Glasbach **12** B4
Mellendorf (Wedemark) **6** A4
Mellensee **13** D1
Mellerup **2** C1
Mellin **6** B4
Mellingen **12** B4
Mellrichstadt **11** F4
Melón **53** E3
Melrand **22** C2
Melres **60** C2
Mels **28** B4
Melsdorf **6** A1
Melsungen **11** E3
Melun **25** E1
Melzo **37** E3
Membrilla **69** E2
Membrío **67** E1
Memleben **12** B3
Memmelsdorf **20** A2
Memmingen **28** C2
Memmingerberg **28** C2
Menaggio **37** E2
Menaldum **4** B3
Menasalbas **69** D1

Menat **34** B2
Menata **46** C1
Mendaro **56** C2
Mendavia **56** C3
Mende **42** B1
Menden (Sauerland) **10** C3
Mendig **18** B1
Mendiga **66** B1
Mendigorría **56** C3
Mendrisio **37** D2
Ménéac **23** D2
Menen **8** B4
Ménesplet **32** C4
Menetou-Salon **25** E4
Mengabril **67** F2
Mengen **28** B2
Mengerskirchen **10** C4
Mengíbar **69** D4
Ménigoute **32** C1
Mens **43** E1
Mensignac **33** D4
Menslage **5** D4
Mentana **48** C2
Menteroda **11** F3
Menton **44** B3
Méntrida **62** C4
Menznau **27** F4
Meolo **39** D3
Meppel **4** B4
Meppen **5** D4
Mequinenza **58** A4
Mer **25** D3
Merano **38** C1
Merate **37** E3
Merbes-le-Château **17** D1
Mercatale **46** C4
Mercatello sul Metauro **46** C3
Mercatino Conca **47** D2
Mercato San Severino **50** A3
Mercato Saraceno **46** C2
Merching **29** D2
Merchtem **9** D3
Mercœur **33** F4
Mercogliano **50** A3
Merdrignac **23** D2
Mere **9** D3
Méreau **25** D4
Merelbeke **8** C3
Merenberg **10** C4
Mérens-les-Vals **59** D1
Méréville **25** D2
Mergozzo **37** D2
Méribel-les-Allues **36** A3
Mérida **67** F3
Mérindol **43** D3
Mering **29** D2
Merkendorf **20** A3
Merklingen **28** C1
Merlara **38** C4
Mer-les-Bains **15** F2
Merlevenez **22** C3
Mern **3** E3
Mersch **17** F2
Merseburg (Saale) **12** C3
Mertert **18** A2
Mertingen **29** D1
Mértola **72** C1
Méru **16** A3
Mervans **26** C4
Mervent **32** B1
Merville *France* **41** E3
Merville *France* **16** B1
Méry-sur-Seine **26** A1
Merzen **10** C1
Merzig **18** A3
Mesagne **51** E3
Mésanger **23** F3
Mesão Frio **60** C2
Meschede **10** C3
Meschers-sur-Gironde **32** B3
Mesinge **2** C3
Meslay-du-Maine **24** A2
Mesocco **37** E1
Mesola **39** D4
Mesón do Vento **53** E2
Mesoraca **52** C2
Mesquer **23** D3
Messac **23** E3
Meßdorf **6** C4
Messei **23** F1
Messeix **34** A3
Messejana **72** B1
Messina **52** A4
Messingen **10** B1
Meßkirch **28** B2
Meßstetten **28** B2
Mestanza **69** D3
Mestlin **6** C2
Mestre **39** D3
Meta **49** F4
Metelen **10** B1
Metnitz **30** C4
Metschow **7** E2
Metslawier **4** B3
Mettendorf **17** F2
Mettenheim **30** A1
Mettet **17** D1
Mettingen **10** C1
Mettlach **18** A3
Mettmann **10** B3
Mettray **24** B3
Metz **17** F3
Metzervisse **17** F3
Metzingen **28** B1
Meudt **10** C4
Meulan **16** A4
Meulebeke **8** C3
Meung-sur-Loire **25** D2
Meuselwitz **12** C3
Meximieux **35** E2
Meyenburg **7** D3
Meymac **33** F3
Meyrargues **43** E3
Meyrueis **42** B2
Meyssac **33** F4
Meythet **35** F2
Meyzieu **35** E3
Mèze **42** B3
Mézel **43** F2
Mézidon-Canon **15** D4
Mézières-en-Brenne **33** E1
Mézières-sur-Issoire **33** D2
Mézilhac **42** C1
Mézin **40** C2
Mezio **60** C2
Mezquita de Jarque **64** C3
Mezzana **38** B2
Mezzanego **45** D1
Mezzano **39** D2
Mezzocorona **38** C2
Mezzoldo **38** A2
Mezzolombardo **38** C2
Miajadas **67** F2
Michelau in Oberfranken **20** B1
Michelbach an der Bilz **19** E4
Micheldorf **30** C4
Micheldorf in Oberösterreich **30** C2
Michelfeld **19** E3
Michelstadt **19** D2
Michendorf **13** D1
Middelburg **8** C2
Middelfart **2** B3
Middelharnis **9** D2
Middelkerke **8** B3
Middelstum **4** C3
Middenbeemster **4** A4
Middenmeer **4** A4
Midlum **5** E2
Midwolda **4** C3
Miedes **64** B2
Międzyzdroje **7** F2
Miehlen **18** C1
Miélan **40** C3
Mieming **29** D3
Mieres *Spain* **54** C2
Mieres *Spain* **59** E2
Mierlo **9** F2
Mierzyn **7** F3
Miesau **18** B3
Miesbach **29** F2
Miesenbach **18** C3
Mieste **12** B1
Mieszkowice **7** F4
Mietingen **28** C2
Mieussy **36** A2
Mieza **61** E2
Migennes **25** F2
Miglianico **49** E1
Migliarino **39** D4
Migliaro **39** D4
Miglionica **50** C3
Mignaloux-Beauvoir **33** D1
Mignano Monte Lungo **49** E3
Miguel Esteban **69** E1
Miguelturra **69** D3
Mihla **11** F3
Mijares **62** B4
Mijas **74** B3
Mijdrecht **9** E1
Milagro **56** C3
Milagros **63** D1
Milano **37** E3
Milano Marittima **46** C2
Mildstedt **5** F1
Mileto **52** A3
Milfontes **72** A1
Milhão **61** E1
Milhaud **42** C3
Milizac **22** A1
Milkel **13** F3
Mill **9** F2
Millares **71** D2
Millas **59** E1
Millau **42** A2
Millesimo **44** C1
Millstatt **30** B4
Milly-la-Forêt **25** E1
Milmarcos **64** A2
Milmersdorf **7** E3
Milow *Ger.* **12** C1
Milow *Ger.* **6** C3
Miltach **21** D3
Miltenberg **19** E2
Miltzow **7** E1
Milz **20** A1
Mimizan **40** A2
Mimizan-Plage **40** A2
Mina de São Domingos **72** C1
Minas de Riotinto **73** D1
Minateda **70** B3
Minaya **70** A2
Minde **66** B1
Mindelheim **29** D2
Mindelstetten **20** B4
Minden **11** D1
Minerbio **46** B1
Minervino Murge **50** C2
Minglanilla **70** C1
Mingorría **62** C3
Miniac-Morvan **23** E1
Minnertsga **4** B3
Mintraching **20** C4
Minturno **49** E3
Minucciano **45** E2
Minusio **37** D2
Mionnay **35** E2
Mios **40** B1
Mira *Italy* **39** D3
Mira *Port.* **60** B3
Mira *Spain* **70** C1
Mirabel **67** F1
Mirabel-aux-Baronnies **43** D2
Mirabella Eclano **50** A2
Miradoux **41** D2
Miraflores de la Sierra **63** D2
Miralcamp **58** B3
Miramare **47** D2
Miramas **43** D3
Mirambeau **32** B3
Mirambel **65** D3
Miramont-de-Guyenne **40** C1
Miranda de Arga **56** C3
Miranda de Ebro **56** B3
Miranda do Corvo **60** C4
Miranda do Douro **61** F1
Mirande **40** C3
Mirandela **61** D1
Mirandilla **67** F2
Mirandola **38** C4
Mirandol-Bourgnounac **41** F2
Mirano **39** D3
Miravet **65** E2
Miravete de la Sierra **64** C3
Mirebeau *France* **26** C3
Mirebeau *France* **33** D1
Mirecourt **27** D1
Mirepoix **41** F4
Miribel **35** E3
Mirow **7** D3
Mirto Crosia **52** C1
Mirueña de los Infanzones **62** B3
Misano Adriatico **47** D2
Miserey-Salines **27** D3
Missanello **50** C4
Missillac **23** D3
Mistelbach **31** F1
Mistelgau **20** B2
Misurina **39** D1
Mitry-Mory **16** B4
Mittelberg *Austria* **29** D4
Mittelberg *Austria* **28** C3
Mittelbiberach **28** C2
Mittelkalbach **19** E1
Mittenwald **29** E3
Mittenwalde *Ger.* **13** E1
Mittenwalde *Ger.* **7** E3
Mitterbach am Erlaufsee **31** D2
Mitterding **30** B1
Mitterdorf im Mürztal **31** E3
Mittersheim **18** B4
Mittersill **30** A3
Mitterskirchen **30** A1
Mitterteich **20** C2
Mittweida **13** D3
Mitwitz **20** B1
Moaña **53** E3
Moçarria **66** B2
Mocejón **63** D4
Mochales **64** A2
Möckern **12** C1
Möckmühl **19** E3
Mockrehna **13** D3
Moclín **75** D2
Moclinejo **74** C3
Modane **36** A4
Modave **17** E1
Modena **46** A1
Modigliana **46** C2
Mödling **31** F2
Modriach **31** D4
Modugno **51** D2
Moëlan-sur-Mer **22** B3
Moena **38** C1
Moergestel **9** E2
Moers **10** A3
Mofreita **54** A4
Mogadouro **61** E2
Mögelin **12** C1
Møgeltønder **2** A4
Mogenstrup **3** E3
Moggio Udinese **39** E1
Moglia **38** B4
Mogliano **47** E4
Mogliano Veneto **39** D3
Mogón **69** F4
Moguer **73** D2
Moharque **76** B1
Mohedas de Granadilla **61** F4
Mohedas de la Jara **68** B1
Mohernando **63** E3
Möhlau **12** C2
Möhlin **27** F3
Mohorn **13** E3
Moià **59** D3
Moiano **49** F3
Moimenta da Beira **61** D2
Moingt **34** C3
Moirans **35** F3
Moirans-en-Montagne **35** F1
Moisburg **6** A3
Moisdon-la-Rivière **23** F3
Moislains **16** B2
Moissac **41** D2
Moita *Port.* **60** C3
Moita *Port.* **66** B1
Moita *Port.* **66** B3
Moixent-Mogente **71** D3
Mojácar **76** A3
Mojados **62** C1
Mol **9** E3
Mola di Bari **51** D2
Molare **44** C1
Molares **60** C1
Molbergen **5** D4
Mölbling **30** C4
Mølby **2** B3
Møldrup **1** E3
Moledo *Port.* **60** B1
Moledo *Port.* **60** C3
Molelos **60** C3
Molfetta **50** C2
Molfsee **6** A1
Molières **41** E2
Molina Aterno **49** E2
Molina de Aragón **64** A2
Molina de Segura **76** B1
Molina di Ledro **38** B2
Molinara **50** A2
Molinaseca **54** B3
Molinella **46** B1
Molinet **34** C1
Molinicos **70** A3
Molini di Tures **29** F4
Molino de Villobas **58** A2
Molinos **65** D3
Molins de Rei **59** D4
Moliterno **50** B4
Molitg-les-Bains **59** D1
Molledo **55** F2
Möllenbeck **7** E3
Möllenhagen **7** D3
Mollerussa **58** B3
Mollet del Vallès **59** D4
Molliens-Dreuil **16** A2
Mollis **28** B4
Molln **30** C2
Mölln *Ger.* **7** F2
Mölln *Ger.* **6** B2
Molló **59** D2
Molschleben **11** F3
Molveno **38** B2
Molvízar **75** D3
Mombaldone **44** C1

Mombeltrán **62** B4
Mombercelli **44** C1
Mömbris **19** E2
Mombuey **54** B4
Momignies **17** D2
Momo **37** D3
Monachil **75** D2
Monasterace **52** B3
Monbazillac **33** D4
Moncada **71** D1
Moncalieri **36** C4
Moncalvo **36** C4
Monção **53** E4
Moncarapacho **72** B2
Mönchengladbach **10** A3
Monchio delle Corti **45** E1
Monchique **72** A2
Mönchsdeggingen **29** D1
Monclar **41** D1
Monclar-de-Quercy **41** E2
Moncófar **65** D4
Moncontour *France* **23** D2
Moncontour *France* **32** C1
Moncoutant **32** B1
Monda **74** B3
Mondariz **53** E3
Mondariz-Balneario **53** E3
Mondavio **47** D3
Mondéjar **63** E4
Mondeville **15** D3
Mondolfo **47** E3
Mondoñedo **54** A1
Mondorf-les-Bains **17** F3
Mondoubleau **24** C2
Mondovì **44** B1
Mondragon **43** D2
Mondragón-Arrasate **56** B2
Mondragone **49** E3
Mondsee **30** B2
Moneglia **45** D2
Monegrillo **65** D1
Monein **40** B4
Monesiglio **44** C1
Monesterio **67** F4
Monestier-de-Clermont **35** F4
Monestiés **41** F2
Monéteau **25** F2
Monfalcone **39** F2
Monfecorvino Rovella **50** A3
Monflanquin **41** D1
Monforte **67** D2
Monforte da Beira **67** D1
Monforte d'Alba **44** B1
Monforte del Cid **76** C1
Monforte de Moyuela **64** C2
Monfortinho **61** E4
Monghidoro **46** B2
Mongrando **36** C3
Monguelfo **39** D1
Monheim **20** A4
Monistrol de Calders **59** D3
Monistrol de Montserrat **59** D3
Monistrol-sur-Loire **35** D4
Mönkeberg **6** A1
Monnaie **24** C3
Monopoli **51** D2
Monóvar **71** D4
Monpazier **41** D1
Monreal **57** D3
Monreal del Campo **64** B3
Monroy **67** F1
Monroyo **65** D3
Mons **16** C1
Monsampolo del Tronto **47** F4
Monsaraz **67** D3
Monschau **10** A4
Monségur **40** C1
Monselice **39** D3
Monsempron-Libos **41** D1
Monserrat **71** D2
Mønsted **2** B1
Monster **9** D1
Monsummano Terme **46** A2
Monta **44** B1
Montabaur **10** C4
Montaberner **71** D3
Montady **42** A3
Montagnac **42** B3
Montagnana **38** C4
Montagne **32** C4
Montagny **35** D2
Montagrier **33** D4
Montaigu **23** F4
Montaigu-de-Quercy **41** D2
Montaigut **34** B2
Montaione **46** A3
Montalbán **64** C2
Montalbán de Córdoba **74** B1
Montalbano Jonico **50** C4
Montalbo **63** F4
Montalcino **46** B4
Montale **46** B2
Montalegre **60** C1
Montalieu-Vercieu **35** E3
Montalivet-les-Bains **32** B3
Montalto delle Marche **47** E4
Montalto di Castro **48** A1
Montalto Marina **48** A1
Montalto Uffugo **52** B2
Montalvão **67** D1
Montamarta **62** A1
Montana **36** B2
Montanejos **64** C4
Montano Antilia **50** A4
Montaquila **49** E3
Montargil **66** C2
Montargis **25** E2
Montastruc-la-Conseillère **41** E3
Montataire **16** A3
Montauban **41** E2
Montauban-de-Bretagne **23** E2
Montauroux **44** A3
Montaut **40** C4
Montayral **41** D1
Montbard **26** B3
Montbarrey **26** C4
Montbazens **41** F1
Montbazin **42** B3
Montbazon **24** B4
Montbéliard **27** E3
Montbenoît **27** D4
Montbeton **41** E2
Montblanc **58** C4
Montbozon **27** D3
Montbrió del Camp **58** B4
Montbrison **34** C3
Montbron **33** D3
Montceau-les-Mines **35** D1
Montcenis **26** B4
Montchanin **26** B4
Montcornet **16** C2
Montcresson **25** E2
Montcuq **41** E2
Montcy-Notre-Dame **17** D2
Mont-de-Marsan **40** B2
Montdidier **16** B2
Mont-Dore **34** B3
Monteagudo **57** D4
Monteagudo de las Salinas **64** A4
Monteagudo de las Vicarías **63** F1
Montealegre del Castillo **70** C3
Montebello Ionico **52** A4
Montebello Vicentino **38** C3
Montebelluna **39** D3
Montebourg **14** B3
Montebruno **45** D1
Montecalvo in Foglia **47** D2
Montecalvo Irpino **50** A2
Monte-Carlo **44** A3
Montecarotto **47** E3
Montecassiano **47** E3
Monte Castello di Vibio **47** D4
Montecastrilli **48** C1
Montecatini Terme **46** A2
Montecatini Val di Cecina **46** A3
Montecchio **47** D2
Montecchio Maggiore **38** C3
Montech **41** E2
Montechiaro d'Asti **36** C4
Montechiarugolo **46** A1
Montecilfone **50** A1
Montecorice **50** A4
Montecosaro **47** E3
Montecreale Valcellina **39** E2
Montecreto **46** A2
Monte da Pedra **67** D2
Monte das Flores **66** C3
Montederramo **54** A3
Monte di Procida **49** E4
Monte do Trigo **67** D4
Montefalco **47** D4
Montefalcone **49** F2
Montefalcone di Val Fortore **50** A2
Montefano **47** E3
Montefelcino **47** D3
Montefiascone **48** B1
Montefiore dell'Aso **47** F4
Montefiorino **46** A1
Montefortino **47** E4
Montefranco **48** C1
Montefrío **74** C2
Montegiordano **50** C4
Montegiorgio **47** E4
Monte Gordo **72** C2
Montegranaro **47** E4
Montegrotto Terme **39** D3
Montehermoso **61** F4
Monteiasi **51** E3
Monteils **41** E2
Montejaque **74** A3
Montejícar **75** D2
Montejo de la Sierra **63** D2
Montelabbate **47** D2
Montelanico **49** D2
Montelavar **66** A3
Monteleone di Puglia **50** A2
Monteleone di Spoleto **48** C1
Monteleone d'Orvieto **46** C4
Montelibretti **48** C2
Montélier **35** E4
Montélimar **43** D1
Montella **50** A3
Montellano **74** A3
Montelupo Fiorentino **46** B3
Montelupone **47** E3
Montemagno **36** C4
Montemarciano **47** E3
Montemayor **74** B1
Montemayor de Pililla **62** C1
Montemboeuf **33** D3
Montemesola **51** E3
Montemiletto **50** A2
Montemilone **50** B2
Montemolín **67** F4
Montemonaco **47** E4
Montemor-o-Novo **66** C3
Montemurlo **46** B2
Montemurro **50** B4
Montenay **23** F2
Montendre **32** C4
Montenegro de Cameros **56** B4
Montenero di Bisaccia **50** A1
Montenerodomo **49** E2
Monte Porzio **47** D3
Monteprandone **47** F4
Montepulciano **46** C4
Monterblanc **23** D3
Monterchi **46** C3
Monte Real **66** B1
Montereale **49** D1
Montereau-faut-Yonne **25** E1
Monte Redondo **66** B1
Monterenzio **46** B1
Monteriggioni **46** B3
Monteroduni **49** E3
Monte Romano **48** B1
Monteroni d'Arbia **46** B4
Monteroni di Lecce **51** F4
Monterosso Calabro **52** B3
Monterotondo **48** C2
Monterotondo Marittimo **46** A4
Monterrei **54** A4
Monterroso **53** F2
Monterrubio de la Serena **68** B3
Monterubbiano **47** E4
Montesa **71** D3
Monte San Biagio **49** D3
Monte San Giovanni Campano **49** D2
Montesano Salentino **51** F4
Montesano sulla Marcellana **50** B4
Monte San Savino **46** C3
Monte Santa Maria Tiberina **46** C3
Monte Sant'Angelo **50** B1
Monte San Vito **47** E3
Montesarchio **49** F4
Montescaglioso **50** C3
Montesclaros **62** B4
Montescudaio **46** A3
Montese **46** A2
Montesilvano **49** E1
Montespertoli **46** B3
Montesquieu-Volvestre **41** E4
Montesquiou **40** C3
Montestruc-sur-Gers **41** D3
Montes Velhos **66** C4
Monteux **43** D2
Montevarchi **46** B3
Monteverde **50** B2
Montevil **66** B4
Montfaucon **23** F4
Montfaucon-d'Argonne **17** E3
Montfaucon-en-Velay **35** D4
Montferrat **43** F3
Montfort **23** E2
Montfort-en-Chalosse **40** B3
Montfort-l'Amaury **16** A4
Montfort-le-Gesnois **24** B2
Montfort-sur-Risle **15** E3
Montgai **58** B3
Montgenèvre **36** A4
Montgeron **16** A4
Montgiscard **41** E3
Montgivray **33** F1
Montguyon **32** C4
Monthermé **17** D2
Monthey **36** A2
Monthois **17** D3
Monthureux-sur-Saône **27** D2
Monticelli d'Ongina **38** A4
Montichiari **38** B3
Monticiano **46** B4
Montiel **69** F3
Montier-en-Der **26** B1
Montieri **46** B4
Montiers-sur-Saulx **26** C1
Montiglio **36** C4
Montignac **33** E4
Montignies-le-Tilleul **17** D1
Montignoso **45** E2
Montigny-lès-Metz **17** F3
Montigny-sur-Aube **26** B2
Montijo *Port.* **66** B3
Montijo *Spain* **67** E2
Montilla **74** B1
Montillana **75** D2
Montivilliers **15** D3
Montizón **69** E4
Montjovet **36** B3
Montlieu-la-Garde **32** C4
Mont-Louis **59** D2
Montluçon **34** A2
Montluel **35** E2
Montmarault **34** B2
Montmartin-sur-Mer **14** B4
Montmédy **17** E3
Montmélian **35** F3
Montmerle-sur-Saône **35** D2
Montmeryran **43** D1
Montmirail *France* **16** C4
Montmirail *France* **24** C2
Montmirey-le-Château **26** C3
Montmoreau-St-Cybard **32** C3
Montmorillon **33** D1
Montmort-Lucy **16** C4
Montoir-de-Bretagne **23** D3
Montoire-sur-le-Loir **24** C3
Montoito **67** D3
Montón **64** B2
Montone **46** C3
Montopoli di Sabina **48** C1
Montorio al Vomano **49** D1
Montoro **68** C4
Montournais **32** B1
Montpellier **42** B3
Montpezat-de-Quercy **41** E2
Montpezat-sous-Bauzon **42** C1
Montpon-Ménestérol **32** C4
Montpont-en-Bresse **35** E1
Mont-ras **59** E3
Montréal *France* **41** F4
Montréal *France* **40** C2
Montréal-la-Cluse **35** F2
Montredon-Labessonnié **41** F3
Montréjeau **41** D4
Montrésor **24** C4
Montret **35** E1

Montreuil **16** A1
Montreuil-Bellay **24** A4
Montreuil-Juigné **23** F3
Montreux **36** A1
Montrevault **23** F4
Montrevel-en-Bresse **35** E2
Montrichard **24** C3
Montriond **36** A2
Mont-roig del Camp **58** B4
Montrond-les-Bains **35** D3
Montroy **71** D2
Monts **24** B4
Montsalvy **41** F1
Montsauche-les-Settons **26** A3
Montseny **59** D3
Mont-sous-Vaudrey **26** C4
Monts-sur-Guesnes **24** B4
Mont-St-Aignan **15** E3
Mont-St-Martin **17** F3
Mont-St-Michel **23** E1
Montsûrs **24** A2
Montville **15** E3
Monza **37** E3
Monzelfeld **18** B2
Monzón **58** A3
Monzón de Campos **55** E4
Moorbad Lobenstein **12** B4
Moordorf (Südbrookmerland) **5** D3
Moorenweis **29** E2
Moorrege **6** A2
Moorslede **8** B4
Moorweg **5** D2
Moos **30** A1
Moosbach **20** C3
Moosburg **30** C4
Moosburg an der Isar **29** F1
Moosinning **29** F1
Mora *Port.* **66** C2
Mora *Spain* **69** D1
Mora de Rubielos **64** C4
Moradillo de Roa **63** D1
Moraira **71** E3
Morais **61** E1
Móra la Nova **58** B4
Moral de Calatrava **69** E3
Moraleda de Zafayona **75** D2
Moraleja **61** E4
Moraleja del Vino **62** A1
Moraleja de Sayago **62** A2
Morales de Campos **55** D4
Morales del Vino **62** A1
Morales de Toro **62** B1
Morales de Valverde **54** C4
Moralina **61** F1
Morano Calabro **52** B1
Morano sul Po **36** C4
Morasverdes **61** F3
Morata de Jalón **64** B1
Morata de Tajuña **63** D4
Moratalla **76** A1
Morbach **18** B2
Morbegno **38** A2
Morbier **35** F1
Mörbisch am See **31** F2
Morcenx **40** A2
Morciano di Leuca **51** F4
Morciano di Romagna **47** D2
Morcone **49** F3
Mordelles **23** E2
Moréac **23** D2
Moreanes **72** C1
Moreda *Spain* **75** E2
Moreda *Spain* **54** C2
Morée **24** C2
Mörel **36** C1
Morella **65** D3
Morentín **56** C3
Moreruela de Tábara **54** C4
Morestel **35** E3
Moret-sur-Loing **25** E1
Moretta **44** B1
Moreuil **16** A2
Morez **35** F1
Morfasso **38** A4
Morges **36** A1
Morgex **36** B3
Morhange **18** A4
Mori **38** B2
Moricone **48** C2
Morienval **16** B3
Moriles **74** B2
Moringen **11** E2
Morino **49** D2
Moritzburg **13** E3
Mørke **2** C1
Mørkøv **3** D2
Morlaàs **40** B3
Morlaix **22** B1
Morlanwelz **17** D1
Mormanno **52** A1
Mormant **16** B4
Mornas **43** D2
Mornese **44** C1
Morolo **49** D3
Morón de Almazán **63** F1
Morón de la Frontera **74** A2
Moros **64** B1
Morozzo **44** B1
Morrovalle **47** E3
Morsbach **10** C4
Morschen **11** E3
Morsum **5** F4
Mortagne-au-Perche **24** B1
Mortagne-sur-Sèvre **23** F4
Mortágua **60** C3
Mortain **23** F1
Mortara **37** D4
Morteau **27** E4
Morteaux-Coulibœuf **15** D4
Mortegliano **39** E2
Mortelle **52** A4
Mortrée **24** B1
Mörtschach **30** A4
Mortsel **9** D3
Morud **2** C3
Moryń **7** F4
Morzine **36** A2
Mosbach **19** E3
Mosbjerg **1** F1
Moscavide **66** B3
Mosciano Sant'Angelo **47** F4
Moseby **1** E2
Mosel **12** C4
Möser **12** C1
Moso in Passiria **38** C1
Mosqueruela **65** D3
Mössingen **28** B1
Mosteiro *Port.* **72** C1
Mosteiro *Port.* **66** C1
Mosteiro *Spain* **54** A2
Mosteiro *Spain* **53** E3
Móstoles **63** D3
Mota del Cuervo **70** A1
Mota del Marqués **62** B1
Môtiers **27** E4
Motilla del Palancar **70** B1
Motilleja **70** B2
Motril **75** D3
Motta Montecorvino **50** A1
Motta San Giovanni **52** A4
Motta Visconti **37** D3
Motten **19** E1
Möttingen **20** A4
Mottola **51** D3
Mötz **29** D3
Mou **1** F2
Mouchamps **32** B1
Mouchard **27** D4
Moudon **36** A1
Mougins **44** A3
Mouleydier **33** D4
Moulins **34** B1
Moulins-Engilbert **26** A4
Moulins-la-Marche **24** B1
Moulis-en-Médoc **32** B4
Moura **67** D4
Mourão **67** D4
Mourenx **40** B3
Mouriès **43** D3
Mourisca do Vouga **60** B3
Mouriscas **66** C1
Mouscron **8** C4
Moustiers-Ste-Marie **43** F2
Mouthe **27** D4
Mouthiers-sur-Boëme **32** C3
Mouthoumet **41** F4
Moutier **27** F3
Moûtiers **36** A3
Moutiers-les-Mauxfaits **32** A1
Mouy **16** A3
Mouzon **17** E2
Moya **64** B4
Moy-de-l'Aisne **16** C2
Moyenneville **16** A2
Mozac **34** B2
Mozárbez **62** A2
Mozelos **60** C3
Mozoncillo **62** C2
Muccia **47** E4
Much **10** B4
Mücheln (Geiseltal) **12** B3
Muchow **6** C3
Mucientes **55** E4
Mücka **13** F3
Mücke Große-Eichen **11** D4
Mücke-Nieder-Ohmen **11** D4
Müden (Aller) **11** F1
Müden (Örtze) **6** A4
Mudersbach **10** C4
Muel **64** C1
Muelas del Pan **62** A1
Muga de Sayago **61** F1
Mugardos **53** E1
Muge **66** B2
Mügeln *Ger.* **13** D3
Mügeln *Ger.* **13** D2
Muggia **39** F3
Mugron **40** B3
Mühlacker **19** D4
Mühlanger **13** D2
Mühlbachl **29** E4
Mühlberg *Ger.* **13** D3
Mühlberg *Ger.* **12** A4
Mühldorf **30** B4
Mühldorf am Inn **30** A1
Mühldorf bei Feldbach **31** E4
Mühlen **30** C4
Mühlenbeck **7** E4
Mühlhausen *Ger.* **19** D3
Mühlhausen *Ger.* **20** B3
Mühlhausen (Thüringen) **11** F3
Mühltroff **12** C4
Muhr am See **20** A3
Muiños **53** F4
Muizon **16** C3
Mula **76** B1
Mulfingen **19** E3
Mülheim an der Ruhr **10** B3
Mülheim-Kärlich **18** B1
Mulhouse **27** F3
Müllheim **27** F2
Müllrose **13** F1
Mulsanne **24** B2
Mümliswil **27** F3
Muñana **62** B3
Münchberg **20** B1
Müncheberg **13** E1
München **29** E2
Münchenbernsdorf **12** C4
Münchhausen **11** D4
Münch-steinach **20** A2
Münchwilen **28** B3
Mundaka **56** B1
Munebrega **64** B2
Munera **70** A2
Mungia **56** B1
Muñico **62** B3
Muniesa **64** C2
Munilla **56** C4
Munkebo **2** C3
Munkzwalm **8** C4
Münnerstadt **19** F1
Munningen **20** A4
Muñogalindo **62** B3
Münsingen *Ger.* **28** B1
Münsingen *Switz.* **27** F4
Münster *Austria* **29** F3
Munster **27** E2
Münster *Ger.* **19** D2
Münster *Ger.* **6** A3
Münster *Ger.* **10** C2
Münster *Switz.* **36** C1
Münsterdorf **6** A2
Münsterhausen **29** D1
Muntendam **4** C3
Münzkirchen **30** B1
Muotathal **28** B4
Muras **53** F1
Murat **34** B4
Murat-sur-Vèbre **42** A3
Murau **30** C4
Murazzano **44** B1
Murça **61** D1
Murchante **57** D4
Murchin **7** E2
Murcia **76** C1
Mur-de-Barrez **42** A1
Mûr-de-Bretagne **22** C2
Mur-de-Sologne **25** D3
Mureck **31** E4
Muret **41** E3
Murg **27** F3
Murgenthal **27** F3
Murguía **56** B2
Muri **28** A3
Murias de Paredes **54** B2
Muriedas **55** F1
Murillo de Río Leza **56** C3
Murillo el Fruto **57** D3
Murisengo **36** C4
Murlo **46** B4
Murnau am Staffelsee **29** E3
Muro **60** B2
Muro de Alcoy **71** D3
Muro Lucano **50** B3
Muros *Spain* **54** C1
Muros *Spain* **53** D2
Murrhardt **19** E4
Mûrs-Erigné **24** A3
Murtas **75** E3
Murtede **60** B3
Murten **27** E4
Murueta **56** B1
Murviel-lès-Béziers **42** A3
Mürzsteg **31** E3
Mürzzuschlag **31** E3
Musile di Piave **39** E3
Musselkanaal **4** C4
Mussidan **33** D4
Musson **17** F3
Mussy-sur-Seine **26** B2
Müstair **38** B1
Mutilva Baja **57** D2
Mutriku **56** C1
Muttenz **27** F3
Mutterstadt **19** D3
Mutxamel **71** D4
Mutzig **27** F1
Mutzschen **13** D3
Muxía **53** D2
Muzillac **23** D3

N

Naaldwijk **9** D1
Naarn im Machlande **30** C2
Nabburg **20** C3
Nackel **7** D4
Næsbjerg **2** A2
Næstved **3** E3
Näfels **28** B4
Nagele **4** B4
Nagold **28** A1
Nagore **57** D2
Nago-Torbole **38** B2
Naharros **63** F4
Nahe **6** A2
Nahrendorf **6** B3
Naila **20** B1
Nailloux **41** E3
Naizin **23** D2
Najac **41** F2
Nájera **56** B3
Nakskov **3** D4
Nalda **56** B3
Nalliers **32** B1
Namborn **18** B3
Nambroca **63** D4
Namur **17** D1
Nanclares de la Oca **56** B2
Nancy **17** F4
Nangis **25** E1
Nans-les-Pins **43** E3
Nant **42** B2
Nanterre **16** A4
Nantes **23** E4
Nanteuil-le-Haudouin **16** B3
Nantiat **33** E2
Nantua **35** F2
Napoli **49** E4
Náquera **71** D1
Narbonne **42** A4
Narbonne-Plage **42** A4
Nardò **51** F4
Narni **48** C1
Narrosse **40** A3
Narzole **44** B1
Nasbinals **42** A1
Nassau **18** C1
Nassereith **29** D3
Nassogne **17** E2
Naters **36** C2
Nattheim **28** C1
Naturno **38** B1
Naucelle **41** F2
Naucelles **34** A4
Nauders **29** D4
Nauen **7** D4
Nauendorf **12** C2
Naumburg (Hessen) **11** D3
Naumburg (Saale) **12** B3
Naundorf *Ger.* **13** D3
Naundorf *Ger.* **13** D4
Naunhof **12** C3
Nava **54** C1
Navacepeda de Tormes **62** B3
Navaconcejo **62** A4
Nava de Arévalo **62** B2

Nava de la Asunción **62** C2
Nava del Rey **62** B2
Nava de Sotrobal **62** B2
Navafría **63** D2
Navahermosa **68** C1
Navajas **65** D4
Naval **58** A2
Navalagamella **62** C3
Navalcaballo **56** B4
Navalcán **62** B4
Navalcarnero **63** D4
Navalero **56** B4
Navalmanzano **62** C2
Navalmoral **62** B3
Navalmoral de la Mata **62** A4
Navalonguilla **62** A4
Navalosa **62** B3
Navalperal de Pinares **62** C3
Navalpino **68** C2
Navaluenga **62** C3
Navalvillar de Ibor **68** B1
Navalvillar de Pela **68** B2
Navamorcuende **62** B4
Navarcles **59** D3
Navardún **57** D3
Navarredonda de la Rinconada **62** A3
Navarrenx **40** B3
Navarrés **71** D2
Navarrete **56** B3
Navarrevisca **62** B3
Navàs **59** D3
Navas de Estrena **68** C1
Navas de Jorquera **70** B2
Navas del Madroño **67** E1
Navas del Rey **62** C3
Navas de Oro **62** C2
Navas de San Juan **69** E4
Navaseués **57** D3
Navasfrías **61** E4
Navata **59** E2
Navatalgordo **62** B3
Nave *Italy* **38** A3
Nave *Port.* **72** A2
Nave de Haver **61** E3
Navelli **49** E1
Nave Redonda **72** A2
Naves **33** F4
Navès **58** C3
Navezuelas **68** B1
Navia **54** B1
Nay-Bourdettes **40** B4
Nazaré **66** B1
Nazelles-Négron **24** C3
Nazza **11** F3
Nebel **2** A4
Nebra (Unstrut) **12** B3
Nebreda **55** F4
Neckargemünd **19** D3
Neckarsulm **19** E3
Neckartenzlingen **28** B1
Neda **53** F1
Neddemin **7** E2
Nederby **1** E2
Neder Hvam **2** B1
Neder Vindinge **3** E4
Nederweert **9** F3
Nedlitz **12** C1
Neermoor **5** D3
Neerpelt **9** E3
Neetze **6** B3
Negenborn **11** E2
Negrar **38** B3
Negredo **63** E2
Negreira **53** E2
Nègrepelisse **41** E2
Neiderbronn-les-Bains **18** C4
Neive **44** B1
Nelas **60** C3
Nellingen **28** C1
Nembro **38** A3
Nemours **25** E2
Nemsdorf-Göhrendorf **12** B3
Nendaz **36** B2
Nennhausen **7** D4
Nennslingen **20** B4
Nentershausen **11** E3
Nenzing **28** C4
Néoules **43** E3
Nepi **48** C1
Nérac **40** C2
Nerchau **13** D3
Nercillac **32** C3
Neresheim **28** C1
Nereto **47** F4
Néris-les-Bains **34** B2
Nerja **75** D3
Néronde **35** D3
Nérondes **25** E4
Nerpio **76** A1
Nersac **32** C3
Nersingen **28** C1
Nerva **73** D1
Nervesa della Battaglia **39** D2
Nes **4** B3
Neschwitz **13** F3
Nesle **16** B2
Nesse **5** D2
Nesselwang **29** D3
Nesslau **28** B3
Netphen **10** C4
Netra (Ringgau) **11** F3
Netstal **28** B4
Nettersheim **10** A4
Nettetal **10** A3
Nettuno **48** C3
Neu-Anspach **19** D1
Neuberend **2** B4
Neuberg an der Mürz **31** E3
Neubeuern **29** F2
Neubiberg **29** E2
Neubrandenburg **7** E2
Neubruchhausen **5** E4
Neubukow **6** C2
Neubulach **28** A1
Neuburg an der Donau **29** E1
Neuburg-Steinhausen **6** C2
Neuburxdorf **13** D3
Neuchâtel **27** E4
Neu Darchau **6** B3
Neudietendorf **12** A4
Neudorf **31** F2
Neudrossenfeld **20** B2
Neuenbürg **19** D4
Neuenburg am Rhein **27** F2
Neuendettelsau **20** A3
Neuenhagen Berlin **13** E1
Neuenhaus **10** B1
Neuenhof **28** A3
Neuenkirch **28** A4
Neuenkirchen *Ger.* **7** E1
Neuenkirchen *Ger.* **7** E1
Neuenkirchen *Ger.* **6** A3
Neuenkirchen *Ger.* **10** C1
Neuenkirchen *Ger.* **5** E2
Neuenkirchen *Ger.* **5** E4
Neuenkirchen *Ger.* **10** B1
Neuenkirchen *Ger.* **5** F1
Neuenkirchen (Oldenburg) **10** C1
Neuenkirchen-Seelscheid **10** B4
Neuenstadt am Kocher **19** E3
Neuenwalde **5** E2
Neuerburg **17** F2
Neufahrn bei Freising **29** E1
Neufahrn in Niederbayern **29** F1
Neuf-Brisach **27** F2
Neufchâteau *Belgium* **17** E2
Neufchâteau *France* **26** C1
Neufchâtel-en-Bray **15** F2
Neufchâtel-Hardelot **15** F1
Neufchâtel-sur-Aisne **17** D3
Neufeld **5** F2
Neufeld an der Leitha **31** F2
Neuffen **28** B1
Neufra **28** B2
Neugersdorf **13** F3
Neuharlingersiel **5** D2
Neuhaus **31** D2
Neuhaus (Oste) **5** F2
Neuhaus am Inn **30** B1
Neuhaus am Rennweg **12** B4
Neuhaus an der Pegnitz **20** B2
Neuhausen *Ger.* **13** E4
Neuhausen *Switz.* **28** A3
Neuhausen ob Eck **28** B2
Neuhof **19** E1
Neuhof an der Zenn **20** A3
Neuhofen an der Krems **30** C2
Neuillé-Pont-Pierre **24** B3
Neuilly-en-Thelle **16** A3
Neuilly-le-Réal **34** C1
Neuilly-l'Évêque **26** C2
Neuilly-St-Front **16** B3
Neu-Isenburg **19** D2
Neukalen **7** D2
Neu Kaliß **6** C3
Neukirch **13** F3
Neukirchen *Ger.* **11** E4
Neukirchen *Ger.* **13** D4
Neukirchen *Ger.* **2** A4
Neukirchen *Ger.* **6** B1
Neukirchen am Großvenediger **29** F3
Neukirchen an der Enknach **30** A2
Neukirchen an der Vöckla **30** B2
Neukirchen-Balbini **20** C3
Neukirchen beim Heiligen Blut **21** D3
Neukirchen vorm Wald **30** B1
Neukloster **6** C2
Neulengbach **31** E2
Neuler **19** F4
Neulewin **7** F4
Neulise **35** D2
Neu Lübbenau **13** E1
Neumark **12** C4
Neumarkt im Mühlkreis **30** C1
Neumarkt in der Oberpfalz **20** B3
Neumarkt in Steiermark **30** C4
Neumarkt-St Veit **30** A1
Neumünster **6** A1
Neunburg vorm Wald **20** C3
Neundorf **12** C4
Neung-sur-Beuvron **25** D3
Neunkirch **28** A3
Neunkirchen *Austria* **31** E2
Neunkirchen *Ger.* **10** C4
Neunkirchen *Ger.* **18** B3
Neunkirchen am Brand **20** B2
Neunkirchen am Sand **20** B3
Neuötting **30** A1
Neupetershain **13** E2
Neupölla **31** E1
Neureichenau **30** B1
Neuruppin **7** D4
Neuschönau **21** E4
Neusiedl am See **31** F2
Neusorg **20** C2
Neuss **10** A3
Neussargues-Moissac **34** B4
Neustadt *Ger.* **28** A2
Neustadt *Ger.* **7** D4
Neustadt *Ger.* **12** B4
Neustadt (Harz) **12** A2
Neustadt (Hessen) **11** D4
Neustadt (Wied) **10** B4
Neustadt am Kulm **20** B2
Neustadt am Rübenberge **11** E1
Neustadt an der Aisch **20** A3
Neustadt an der Donau **20** B4
Neustadt an der Waldnaab **20** C2
Neustadt an der Weinstraße **18** C3
Neustadt bei Coburg **20** B1
Neustadt-Glewe **6** C3
Neustadt in Holstein **6** B1
Neustadt in Sachsen **13** E3
Neustift im Stubaital **29** E4
Neustrelitz **7** E3
Neutraubling **20** C4
Neutrebbin **7** F4
Neu-Ulm **28** C1
Neuvéglise **34** B4
Neuvic *France* **33** D4
Neuvic *France* **33** F3
Neuville-aux-Bois **25** D2
Neuville-de-Poitou **33** D1
Neuville-les-Dames **35** E2
Neuville-lès-Dieppe **15** E2
Neuville-sur-Saône **35** E2
Neuvy-Grandchamp **34** C1
Neuvy-le-Roi **24** B3
Neuvy-Pailloux **33** F1
Neuvy-St-Sépulchre **33** F1
Neuvy-sur-Barangeon **25** E3
Neuweiler **28** A1
Neuwied **10** B4
Neuwittenbek **6** A1
Neu Wulmstorf **6** A3
Neu Zauche **13** E2
Neuzelle **13** F1
Neu Zittau **13** E1
Névache **36** A4
Nevele **8** C3
Nevers **25** F4
Névez **22** B3
Neviano **51** F4
Néville **15** E2
Newel **18** A2
Newmarkt am Wallersee **30** B2
Nexon **33** E3
Nibbiano **37** E4
Nibe **1** E2
Nicastro **52** B2
Nice **44** A3
Nichelino **36** B4
Nicotera **52** A3
Nidau **27** E4
Nidda **19** D1
Niebla **73** D2
Niebüll **2** A4
Niederaichbach **29** F1
Niederanven **17** F2
Niederau **13** E3
Niederaula **11** E4
Niederbipp **27** F3
Niederfinow **7** F4
Nieder-görsdorf **13** D2
Niederkassel **10** B4
Niederkirchen **18** C3
Niederkrüchten **10** A3
Niederndorf **29** F3
Niedernhall **19** E3
Niederoderwitz **13** F4
Nieder-Olm **18** C2
Nieder-Rodenbach **19** D1
Niederroßla **12** B3
Niedersachswerfen **11** F2
Niederselters **18** C1
Niederstetten **19** F3
Niederurnen **28** B4
Niederviehbach **30** A1
Niederwerrn **19** F2
Niederzissen **10** B4
Niefern-Öschelbronn **19** D4
Niegripp **12** B1
Nieheim **11** D2
Niemberg **12** C2
Niemegk **13** D1
Nienburg (Saale) **12** B2
Nienburg (Weser) **5** F4
Niepars **7** D1
Nierstein **19** D2
Niesky **13** F3
Nieul **33** E2
Nieuw-Bergen **10** A2
Nieuwegein **9** E1
Nieuwe-Niedorp **4** A4
Nieuwe Pekela **4** C3
Nieuwerkerk **9** D2
Nieuwerkerk aan de IJssel **9** D2
Nieuwerkerken **9** E4
Nieuwe-Tonge **9** D2
Nieuwkoop **9** E1
Nieuwolda **4** C3
Nieuwpoort **8** B3
Nieuw-Vennep **9** D1
Nigrán **53** E4
Nigüelas **75** D3
Níjar **76** A3
Nijkerk **9** E1
Nijlen **9** D3
Nijmegen **9** F2
Nijverdal **10** A1
Nikolsdorf **30** A4
Nilvange **17** F3
Nim **2** B2
Nîmes **42** C2
Nimis **39** F2
Nimtofte **2** C1
Nindorf **5** F1
Ninove **9** D4
Niort **32** C2
Nisa **67** D1
Nismes **17** D2
Nispen **9** D2
Nissan-lez-Enserune **42** A3
Nissumby **1** D3
Nissum Seminarieby **2** A1
Nistelrode **9** E2
Nittel **18** A2
Nittenau **20** C3
Nittendorf **20** C4
Nivå **3** E2
Nivelles **17** D1
Nivillac **23** D3
Nivillers **16** A3
Nivolas-Vermelle **35** E3
Nizza Monferrato **44** C1
No **2** A1
Noailles **16** A3
Noain **57** D2

Noale 39 D3
Noalejo 75 D2
Noasca 36 B3
Nobitz 12 C4
Noblejas 63 D4
Nocé 24 B1
Nocera Inferiore 49 F4
Nocera Terinese 52 B2
Nocera Umbra 47 D4
Noceto 38 A4
Noci 51 D3
Nociglia 51 F4
Nødebo 3 E2
Noé 41 E3
Noepoli 50 C4
Noer 6 A1
Nœux-les-Mines 16 B1
Noez 69 D1
Nofuentes 55 F2
Nogales 67 E3
Nogara 38 C4
Nogaro 40 C3
Nogent 26 C2
Nogent-le-Roi 25 D1
Nogent-le-Rotrou 24 C2
Nogent-sur-Oise 16 A3
Nogent-sur-Seine 25 F1
Nogent-sur-Vernisson 25 E2
Nograles 63 E1
Noguera 64 B3
Noguerueles 64 C4
Nohfelden 18 B3
Noia 53 D2
Noicattaro 51 D2
Noidans-lès-Vesoul 27 D3
Noirétable 34 C3
Noirmoutier-en-l'Île 23 D4
Noisseville 17 F3
Noja 55 F1
Nolay 26 B4
Noli 44 C2
Nombela 62 C4
Nomeny 17 F4
Nonancourt 24 C1
Nonantola 46 B1
Nonaspe 58 A4
None 36 B4
Nonnweiler 18 B3
Nontron 33 D3
Noordwijk-Binnen 9 D1
Noordwijkerhout 9 D1
Noordwolde 4 B4
Nørager 1 E3
Norcia 47 E4
Nordborg 2 B3
Nordby *Denmark* 2 C2
Nordby *Denmark* 2 A3
Norddeich 4 C2
Norddorf 2 A4
Norden 4 C2
Nordendorf 29 D1
Nordenham 5 E3
Nordenskov 2 A2
Norderney 4 C2
Norderstedt 6 A2
Nordhalben 20 B1
Nordhastedt 5 F1
Nordhausen 11 F2
Nordheim 19 E3
Nordholz 5 E2
Nordhorn 10 B1
Nordkirchen 10 C2
Nördlingen 20 A4
Nordstemmen 11 E1
Nordwalde 10 C1
Noreña 54 C1
Norg 4 C3
Norma 48 C3
Noroy-le-Bourg 27 D3
Nørre Åby 2 C3
Nørre Alslev 3 E4
Nørreballe 3 D4
Nørre Bork 2 A2
Nørre Broby 2 C3
Nørre Felding 2 A1
Nørre Halne 1 F2
Nørre Kongerslev 1 F2
Nørre Nebel 2 A2
Norrent-Fontes 16 A1
Nørre Snede 2 B2
Nørresundby 1 F2
Nørre Vejrup 2 A2
Nørre Vorupør 1 D2
Nors 1 D2
Nörten-Hardenberg 11 E2
Northeim 11 F2
Nortmoor 5 D3
Nortorf 6 A1
Nortrup 5 D4
Nort-sur-Erdre 23 E3
Norup 1 F3
Nossa Senhora da Boa Fé 66 C3
Nossa Senhora da Graça de Póvoa e Meadas 67 D1
Nossa Senhora da Graça do Divor 66 C3
Nossa Senhora da Graça dos Degolados 67 E2
Nossa Senhora das Neves 67 D4
Nossa Senhora de Machede 67 D3
Nossen 13 D3
Nossendorf 7 E2
Nossentiner Hütte 7 D2
Notaresco 49 E1
Notre-Dame-de-Bellecombe 36 A3
Notre-Dame-de-Gravenchon 15 E3
Notre-Dame-de-Monts 23 E4
Notre-Dame-d'Oé 24 C3
Nötsch im Gailtal 39 F1
Nottensdorf 6 A3
Nottuln 10 B2
Nouan-le-Fuzelier 25 D3
Nouvion 16 A1
Nouzilly 24 C3
Nouzonville 17 D2
Novafeltria 46 C2
Novales *Spain* 57 F4
Novales *Spain* 55 E1
Nova Levante 38 C1
Novallas 57 D4
Novara 37 D3
Nova Siri 50 C4
Novate Mezzola 37 E2
Novelda 71 D4
Novellara 38 B4
Noventa di Piave 39 E3
Noventa Vicentina 38 C3
Noves 43 D2
Novés 62 C4
Novi di Modena 38 B4
Noviergas 56 C4
Novi Ligure 44 C1
Novion-Porcien 17 D3
Nowe Czarnowo 7 F3
Nowe Warpno 7 F2
Noyal-Muzillac 23 D3
Noyal-Pontivy 22 C2
Noyant 24 B3
Noyen-sur-Sarthe 24 A2
Noyers 26 A3
Noyers-sur-Cher 24 C4
Noyers-sur-Jabron 43 E2
Noyon 16 B3
Nozay 23 E3
Nozeroy 27 D4
Nubledo 54 C1
Nudersdorf 12 C2
Nüdlingen 19 F1
Nueil-sur-Argent 24 A4
Nuenen 9 E2
Nueno 57 E3
Nueva 55 D1
Nueva-Carteya 74 C1
Nueva Jarilla 73 E3
Nuez de Ebro 64 C1
Nuillé-sur-Vicoin 23 F2
Nuits-St-Georges 26 B4
Nules 65 D4
Numana 47 E3
Numansdorp 9 D2
Nünchritz 13 D3
Nuñomoral 61 F3
Nunsdorf 13 D1
Nunspeet 9 F1
Nürnberg 20 A3
Nürtingen 28 B1
Nus 36 B3
Nusco 50 A3
Nusplingen 28 B2
Nußbach 30 C2
Nußdorf 30 A2
Nußdorf am Inn 29 F2
Nußloch 19 D3
Nustrup 2 B3
Nuth 9 F3
Nüziders 28 C4
Nyborg 3 D3
Ny Højen 2 B2
Nykøbing 3 E4
Nykøbing Mors 1 E2
Nykøbing Sjælland 3 E2
Nymindegab 2 A2
Ny Nørup 2 B2
Nyoiseau 23 F3
Nyon 35 F1
Nyons 43 D1
Nyråd 3 E4
Nysted 3 E4

O

O Barco 54 A3
Obdach 31 D4
Obejo 68 C4
Oberaich 31 D3
Oberalm 30 A2
Oberammergau 29 E3
Oberasbach 20 A3
Oberau 29 E3
Oberaudorf 29 F3
Obercunnersdorf 13 F3
Oberding 29 F1
Oberdorla 11 F3
Oberdrauburg 30 A4
Oberegg 28 C3
Oberelsbach 11 F4
Oberfell 18 B1
Obergebra 11 F3
Obergösgen 27 F3
Ober-Grafendorf 31 E2
Obergriesbach 29 D1
Obergünzburg 29 D2
Obergurgl 29 E4
Obergurig 13 F3
Oberhaag 31 D4
Oberhaid 20 A2
Oberharmersbach 28 A1
Oberhausen *Ger.* 29 E1
Oberhausen *Ger.* 10 B3
Oberheldrungen 12 B3
Oberhof 11 F4
Oberkirch 27 F1
Oberkochen 28 C1
Oberkotzau 20 C1
Oberlangen 5 D4
Oberlung-witz 13 D4
Obermarchtal 28 C2
Obermaßfeld-Grimmenthal 11 F4
Obermoschel 18 C2
Obernai 27 F1
Obernberg am Inn 30 B1
Oberndorf 5 F2
Oberndorf am Lech 29 D1
Oberndorf am Neckar 28 A1
Oberndorf bei Salzburg 30 A2
Oberneukirchen 30 C1
Obernfeld 11 F2
Obernheim 28 B2
Obernheim-Kirchenarnbach 18 C3
Obernkirchen 11 D1
Obernzell 30 B1
Oberpullendorf 31 F3
Ober-Ramstadt 19 D2
Oberrieden 29 D2
Oberriet 28 C3
Ober-Roden 19 D2
Oberrotweil 27 F2
Oberschneiding 20 C4
Oberschützen 31 F3
Obersiebenbrunn 31 F1
Obersinn 19 E1
Oberspier 12 A3
Oberstadion 28 C2
Oberstaufen 28 C3
Oberstdorf 28 C3
Oberstenfeld 19 E4
Oberthal 18 B3
Obertilliach 30 A4
Obertraubling 20 C4
Obertrubach 20 B2
Obertshausen 19 D2
Obervellach 30 B4
Oberviechtach 20 C3
Oberwald 36 C1
Oberwart 31 F3
Oberwölbling 31 E1
Oberwölz 30 C3
Óbidos 66 A2
Obing 29 F2
Objat 33 E4
Öblarn 30 C3
O Bolo 54 A3
Obón 64 C2
Obrigheim 19 E3
O Cádabo 54 A2
Ocaña 63 D4
O Castelo 53 E4
O Castro 53 F3
Occhiobello 38 C4
Occimiano 37 D4
Ochagavía 57 D2
Ocholt 5 D3
Ochsenfurt 19 F2
Ochsenhausen 28 C2
Ochtrup 10 B1
Ockholm 2 A4
O Convento 53 E3
O Corgo 54 A2
Octeville 14 B2
Octeville-sur-Mer 15 D3
Oddense 1 E3
Odder 2 C2
Odeceixe 72 A2
Odeleite 72 C2
Odelouca 72 A2
Odelzhausen 29 E1
Odemira 72 A1
Odena 58 C3
Odense 2 C3
Oderberg 7 F4
Oderin 13 E1
Oderzo 39 D2
Odiáxere 72 A2
Ødis 2 B3
Odivelas *Port.* 66 C4
Odivelas *Port.* 66 A3
Odón 64 B2
Odoorn 4 C4
Ødsted 2 B2
Oebisfelde 12 B1
Oedelsheim (Oberweser) 11 E2
Oederan 13 D4
Oeffelt 10 A2
Oegstgeest 9 D1
Oeiras 66 A3
Oelde 10 C2
Oelixdorf 6 A2
Oelsnitz *Ger.* 20 C1
Oelsnitz *Ger.* 13 D4
Oenkerk 4 B3
Oensingen 27 F3
Oerel 5 F3
Oering 6 A2
Oerlenbach 19 F1
Oerlinghausen 11 D2
Oestrich-Winkel 18 C2
Oettersdorf 12 B4
Oettingen in Bayern 20 A4
Oetz 29 D3
Oetzen 6 B3
Oeversee 2 B4
Œyréluy 40 A3
Ofena 49 E1
Offanengo 38 A3
Offenbach am Main 19 D1
Offenberg 21 D4
Offenburg 27 F1
Offida 47 E4
Offingen 29 D1
Offranville 15 E2
Ofterdingen 28 B1
Ogenbargen 5 D3
Ogeu-les-Bains 40 B4
Ogliastro Cilento 50 A4
Ogrosen 13 E2
O Grove 53 D3
Ohanes 75 E3
Ohey 17 E1
Ohlsbach 27 F1
Ohlstadt 29 E3
Ohne 10 B1
Ohorn 13 E3
Ohrdruf 11 F4
Öhringen 19 E3
Oiã 60 B3
Oiartzun 56 C1
Oignies 16 B1
Oímbra 54 A4
Oiron 24 A4
Oisemont 16 A2
Oisseau 23 F2
Oissel 15 E3
Ojén 74 B3
Ojos Negros 64 B3
Oksbøl *Denmark* 2 A2
Oksbøl *Denmark* 2 B3
Olague 57 D2
Olalhas 66 C1
Olargues 42 A3
Olave 57 D2
Olazagutía 56 C2
Olba 64 C4
Olbendorf 31 F3
Olbernhau 13 D4
Olbersdorf 13 F4
Olbersleben 12 B3
Oldebroek 10 A1
Oldehove 4 C3
Oldemarkt 4 B4
Oldenbrok 5 E3
Oldenburg 5 E3
Oldenburg in Holstein 6 B1
Oldendorf 5 F2
Oldenswort 5 E1
Oldenzaal 10 B1
Oldisleben 12 B3
Oldsum 2 A4
Oleggio 37 D3
Oleiros 66 C1
Olemps 41 F2
Olen 9 E3

Olesa de Montserrat **59** D4
Olette **59** D2
Olevano Romano **49** D2
Olfen **10** B2
Olginate **37** E2
Ølgod **2** A2
Olhalvo **66** B2
Olhão **72** B3
Ølholm **2** B2
Olho Marinho **66** A2
Oliana **58** C3
Olías del Rey **63** D4
Oliete **64** C2
Oligastro Marina **50** A4
Oliola **58** C3
Olite **57** D3
Oliva **71** E3
Oliva de la Frontera **67** E4
Oliva de Mérida **67** F3
Olival **66** B1
Olivares **73** E2
Olivares de Júcar **63** F4
Oliveira de Azeméis **60** B2
Oliveira de Frades **60** C3
Oliveira do Arda **60** C2
Oliveira do Bairro **60** B3
Oliveira do Conde **60** C3
Oliveira do Douro **60** B2
Oliveira do Hospital **60** C3
Olivenza **67** E3
Olivet **25** D2
Oliveto Citra **50** A3
Oliveto Lucano **50** C3
Olivone **37** D1
Ollerup **2** C3
Olliergues **34** C3
Ollioules **43** E4
Ollo **56** C2
Ollon **36** B2
Olmedilla de Roa **55** F4
Olmedo **62** C2
Olmos de Ojeda **55** E3
Olocau **71** D1
Olocau del Rey **65** D3
Olombrada **62** C1
Olonne-sur-Mer **32** A1
Olonzac **42** A3
Oloron-Ste-Marie **40** B4
Olost **59** D3
Olot **59** E2
Olpe **10** C3
Olsberg **11** D3
Olst **10** A1
Ølsted *Denmark* **3** E2
Ølsted *Denmark* **2** B2
Ølstykke **3** E2
Olten **27** F3
Olula del Río **76** A2
Olvan **59** D3
Ólvega **56** C4
Olvena **58** A2
Olvera **74** A3
Omegna **36** C2
Ommen **4** C4
Omont **17** D3
Oña **55** F3
Onano **48** B1
Oñati **56** C2
Oncala **56** C4
Onda **65** D4
Ondara **71** E3
Ondarroa **56** B1
Oneglia **44** B2
Onet-le-Château **41** F1
Onsbjerg **2** C2
Ønslev **3** E4
Onstmettingen **28** B2
Onstwedde **4** C3
Ontiñena **58** A3
Ontinyent **71** D3
Ontur **70** C3
Onzain **24** C3
Onzonilla **54** C3
Ooltgensplaat **9** D2
Oostakker **8** C3
Oostburg **8** C3
Oostende **8** B3
Oostendorp **10** A1
Oosterend **4** A3
Oosterhesselen **4** C4
Oosterhout **9** E2
Oosterland **9** D2
Oosterwolde **4** B4
Oosterzele **8** C3
Oosthuizen **4** A4
Oostkamp **8** C3
Oostkapelle **8** C2
Oost-Souburg **8** C2
Oostvleteren **8** B3
Oost-Vlieland **4** A3
Ootmarsum **10** B1
O Pedrouzo **53** E2
Opeinde **4** B3
Opfenbach **28** C3
Opi **49** E2
Opmeer **4** A4
Oppach **13** F3
Oppeano **38** C3
Oppenau **28** A1
Oppenheim **19** D2
Oppido Lucano **50** B3
Oppido Mamertina **52** A4
Oppin **12** C2
Opponitz **31** D2
Oppurg **12** B4
Opwijk **9** D3
Ora **38** C1
Orada **67** D3
Oradour-sur-Glane **33** E2
Oradour-sur-Vayres **33** D3
Oraison **43** E2
Orange **43** D2
Oranienburg **7** E4
Orba **71** E3
Orbacém **60** B1
Ørbæk **2** C3
Orbara **57** D2
Orbassano **36** B4
Orbe **27** D4
Orbec **15** D4
Orbetello **48** A1
Orca **61** D4
Orce **75** F1
Orcera **70** A4
Orchamps-Vennes **27** D4
Orchies **16** B1
Orciano di Pesaro **47** D3
Orcières **43** F1
Ordes **53** E2
Ordizia **56** C2
Ordona **50** B2
Orduña **56** B2
Orea **64** B3
Orehoved **3** E4
Orellana de la Sierra **68** B2
Orellana la Vieja **68** B2
Orés **57** E3
Oreye **9** E4
Organyà **58** C2
Orgaz **69** D1
Orgelet **35** F1
Orgères-en-Beauce **25** D2
Orgiva **75** D3
Orgon **43** D3
Oria *Italy* **51** E3
Oria *Spain* **76** A2
Origny-Ste-Benoite **16** C2
Orihuela **76** C1
Orihuela del Tremedal **64** B3
Orio **56** C2
Oriola **66** C4
Oriolo **50** C4
Oriolo Romano **48** B1
Oristà **59** D3
Orlamünde **12** B4
Orléans **25** D2
Orleix **40** C4
Ormea **44** B2
Ornans **27** D4
Ornavasso **36** C2
Ornbau **20** A3
Ørnhøj **2** A1
Oron-la-Ville **36** A1
Oronoz **57** D2
Oropa **36** C3
Oropesa *Spain* **62** B4
Oropesa *Spain* **65** D4
Ororbia **56** C2
Orpierre **43** E2
Orrios **64** C3
Orsara di Puglia **50** A2
Orsay **16** A4
Orsières **36** B2
Ørslev **3** E3
Orsogna **49** E1
Orsomarso **52** A1
Ørsted **2** C1
Orta Nova **50** B2
Orte **48** C1
Ortenberg *Ger.* **27** F1
Ortenberg *Ger.* **19** D1
Ortenburg **30** B1
Orth an der Donau **31** F2
Orthez **40** B3
Ortigosa **56** B4
Ortigueira **53** F1
Ørting **2** C2
Ortisei **38** C1
Ortona **49** F1
Ortovera **44** B2
Ortrand **13** E3
Ørum *Denmark* **2** C1
Ørum *Denmark* **2** B1
Orusco **63** E4
Orvalho **60** C4
Orvault **23** E4
Orvieto **46** C4
Orvinio **48** C2
Orzinuovi **38** A3
Osa de Vega **70** A1
Øsby **2** B3
Oschatz **13** D3
Oschersleben (Bode) **12** B1
Osdorf **6** A1
O Seixo **53** E4
Oseja de Sajambre **55** D2
Osera **64** C1
Osiglia **44** C2
Osimo **47** E3
Osio Sotto **38** A3
Osloß **11** F1
Osma **56** B2
Osnabrück **10** C1
Osno Lubuskie **13** F1
Osny **16** A4
Osogna **37** D2
Osoppo **39** E2
Osor **59** E3
Osorno **55** E3
Ospitaletto **38** A3
Oss **9** E2
Ossa de Montiel **70** A2
Ossana **38** B2
Osséja **59** D2
Ossiach **30** C4
Oßmannstedt **12** B3
Ossun **40** C4
Ostbevern **10** C1
Østbirk **2** B2
Osted **3** E3
Ostellato **39** D4
Osten **5** F2
Ostenfeld (Husum) **5** F1
Østengård **2** B2
Øster Assels **1** D3
Øster Bjerregrav **2** C1
Øster Brønderslev **1** F2
Osterburg (Altmark) **6** C4
Osterburken **19** E3
Østerby **1** E2
Osterby **6** A1
Osterfeld **12** C3
Osterhever **5** E1
Osterhofen **30** A1
Øster Højst **2** B3
Osterholz-Scharmbeck **5** E3
Øster Hornum **1** E2
Øster Hurup **1** F2
Østerild **1** E2
Øster Jølby **1** D2
Øster Lindet **2** B3
Ostermiething **30** A2
Ostermundigen **27** F4
Osterode am Harz **11** F2
Osterrönfeld **6** A1
Øster Tørslev **2** C1
Øster Ulslev **3** E4
Øster Vedsted **2** A3
Øster Vrå **1** F1
Øster Vrøgum **2** A2
Osterwieck **11** F2
Ostheim vor der Rhön **11** F4
Osthofen **18** C2
Ostia **48** B2
Ostiano **38** A4
Ostiglia **38** C4
Ostiz **57** D2
Ostra **47** E3
Ostrach **28** B2
Ostrau *Ger.* **13** D3
Ostrau *Ger.* **12** C2
Ostrhauderfehn **5** D3
Ostritz **13** F3
Østrup **1** E3
Ostseebad Ahrenshoop **7** D1
Ostseebad Binz **7** E1
Ostseebad Boltenhagen **6** C2
Ostseebad Dierhagen **7** D1
Ostseebad Göhren **7** E1
Ostseebad Graal-Müritz **7** D1
Ostseebad Kühlungsborn **6** C1
Ostseebad Prerow am Darß **7** D1
Ostseebad Rerik **6** C1
Ostseebad Sellin **7** E1
Ostseebad Wustrow **7** D1
Ostseebad Zingst am Darß **7** D1
Ostuni **51** E3
Ostwald **27** F1
Osuna **74** B2
Oteiza **56** C3
Otero de Bodas **54** B4
Ötigheim **18** C4
Ötisheim **19** D4
Otívar **75** D3
Otranto **51** F4
Otricoli **48** C1
Ottaviano **49** F4
Ottendorf-Okrilla **13** E3
Ottenhöfen im Schwarzwald **28** A1
Ottenschlag **31** D1
Ottensheim **30** C1
Ottenstein **11** E2
Otterfing **29** E2
Otterlo **9** F1
Otterndorf **5** E2
Ottersberg **5** F3
Ottersweier **27** F1
Otterup **2** C3
Otterwisch **12** C3
Ottignies **17** D1
Ottobeuren **29** D2
Ottobrunn **29** E2
Ottone **45** D1
Ottrau **11** E4
Ottweiler **18** B3
Otxandio **56** B2
Otzing **21** D4
Ouca **60** B3
Oucques **24** C2
Oud-Beijerland **9** D2
Oudehaske **4** B4
Oudemirdum **4** A4
Oudenaarde **8** C4
Oudenbosch **9** D2
Oudenburg **8** B3
Oude Pekela **4** C3
Oudeschild **4** A3
Oude-Tonge **9** D2
Oud-Gastel **9** D2
Oudon **23** F3
Oud-Turnhout **9** E3
Oud-Vossemeer **9** D2
Ouffet **17** E1
Ouguela **67** E2
Ouistreham **15** D3
Oulchy-le-Château **16** C3
Oulx **36** A4
Oupeye **9** F4
Oure **2** C3
Ourense **53** F3
Ourique **72** B1
Ourol **53** F1
Ouroux-sur-Saône **35** E1
Ourville-en-Caux **15** E2
Oust **41** E4
Outarville **25** D2
Outeiro *Port.* **60** B1
Outeiro *Portugal* **61** E1
Outeiro de Rei **53** F2
Outeiro Seco **61** D1
Outomuro **53** F4
Outreau **8** A4
Ouveillan **42** A3
Ouzouer-le-Marché **25** D2
Ouzouer-sur-Loire **25** E3
Ovada **44** C1
Ovar **60** B2
Ovaro **39** E1
Ove **1** F3
Ovelgönne **5** E3
Overath **10** B4
Over Feldborg **2** B1
Over Hornbæk **2** C1
Overijse **9** D4
Over Jerstal **2** B3
Overlade **1** E2
Overpelt **9** E3
Over Simmelkær **2** B1
Ovezande **8** C3
Oviedo **54** C1
Oviglio **37** D4
Ovindoli **49** D2
Ovtrup **2** A2
Owen **28** B1
Owingen **28** B2
Owschlag **6** A1
Oy-Mittelberg **29** D3
Oyón **56** B3
Oyonnax **35** F2
Oyten **5** F3
Oza **53** F2
Ozeta **56** B2
Ozoir-le-Ferrière **16** B4
Ozzano dell'Emilia **46** B1
Ozzano Monferrato **37** D4

P

Pabneukirchen **31** D1
Pabu **22** C1
Paciano **46** C4
Pack **31** D4

Pacos de Ferreira 60 C2
Pacy-sur-Eure 15 F4
Padborg 2 B4
Paderborn 11 D2
Paderne Port. 72 B2
Paderne Port. 53 E4
Paderne de Allariz 53 F3
Padova 39 D3
Padrón 53 E2
Padul 75 D3
Padula 50 B4
Paduli 50 A2
Paesana 44 A1
Paese 39 D3
Pagani 49 F4
Paganica 49 D1
Paganico 46 B4
Paglieta 49 F1
Pagny-sur-Moselle 17 F4
Pähl 29 E2
Pahlen 5 F1
Paião 60 B4
Paimbœuf 23 E4
Paimpol 22 C1
Paimpont 23 D2
Painten 20 B4
Pajares de la Lampreana 62 A1
Pajarón 64 B4
Palacios del Sil 54 B2
Palacios de Sanabria 54 B4
Palaciosrubios 62 B2
Palafrugell 59 F3
Palagianello 51 D3
Palagiano 51 D3
Palaia 46 A3
Palaiseau 16 A4
Palamós 59 E3
Palanzano 45 E1
Palas de Rei 53 F2
Palata 50 A1
Palavas-les-Flots 42 B3
Palazzolo sull'Oglio 38 A3
Palazzo San Gervasio 50 C2
Palena 49 E2
Palencia 55 E4
Palenciana 74 B2
Palenzuela 55 E4
Palestrina 48 C2
Palhaça 60 B3
Paliano 49 D2
Palinuro 50 A4
Paliseul 17 E2
Palizzi 52 A4
Pallagorio 52 C2
Pallarés 67 F4
Palling 30 A2
Palluau 32 A1
Palma 66 B3
Palma Campania 49 F4
Palma del Río 74 A1
Palmanova 39 F2
Palmaz 60 B3
Palmeira 60 B1
Palmela 66 B3
Palmi 52 A4
Palo del Colle 50 C2
Palomar de Arroyos 64 C3
Palomares del Río 73 E2
Palomas 67 F3
Palombara Sabina 48 C2
Palombaro 49 E2
Palomera 64 A4
Palomeras del Campo 63 F4
Palomonte 50 A3
Palos de la Frontera 73 D2
Pals 59 F3
Paludi 52 B1
Paluzza 39 E1
Palzem 17 F3
Pamhagen 31 F2
Pamiers 41 E4
Pamparato 44 B2
Pampelonne 41 F2
Pampilhosa 60 B3
Pampilhosa da Serra 60 C4
Pampliega 55 F4
Pamplona (Iruñea) 57 D2
Pampow 6 C2
Pamproux 32 C2
Panazol 33 E3
Pancalieri 44 B1
Pancorbo 56 B3
Pancrudo 64 C3
Pandino 37 E3
Pandrup 1 E2
Panes 55 E1
Panissières 35 D3
Paniza 64 C2
Panker 6 B1
Pannarano 49 F4
Pannes 25 E2
Panni 50 A2
Panningen 10 A3
Panóias 72 B1
Panschwitz-Kuckau 13 E3
Panticosa 58 A1
Pantoja 63 D4
Paola 52 A2
Papasidero 52 A1
Papenburg 5 D3
Papendorf 7 D2
Papendrecht 9 D2
Pappenheim 20 A4
Parabita 51 F4
Paracuellos 70 B1
Paracuellos de Jarama 63 D3
Parada 61 E3
Parada de Ester 60 C2
Parada de Pinhão 61 D1
Parada de Rubiales 62 A2
Parada de Sil 53 F3
Paradas 74 A2
Paradela Port. 60 C1
Paradela Port. 61 D2
Paradela Spain 54 A2
Parâmio 54 A4
Páramo del Sil 54 B2
Paranhos 60 C3
Parcent 71 E3
Parcé-sur-Sarthe 24 A2
Parchen 12 C1
Parchim 6 C3
Pardais 67 D3
Pardilhó 60 B3
Paredes de Coura 53 E4
Paredes de Nava 55 E4
Pareja 63 F3
Parempuyre 32 B4
Parenti 52 B2
Parentis-en-Born 40 A2
Parey 12 C1
Parghelia 52 A3
Pargny-sur-Saulx 17 D4
Parigné-l'Évêque 24 B2
Paris 16 A4
Parkstein 20 C2
Parla 63 D4
Parma 38 A4
Parndorf 31 F2
Paron 25 F2
Parrillas 62 B4
Parsau 12 A1
Parsberg 20 B3
Parstein 7 F4
Partaloa 76 A2
Partenen 28 C4
Partenstein 19 E2
Parthenay 32 C1
Pårup 2 B1
Pasai Donibane 56 C1
Pasching 30 C1
Pas-en-Artois 16 A2
Pasewalk 7 F3
Pasiàn di Prato 39 E2
Pasiano di Pordenone 39 E2
Passail 31 E3
Passais 23 F1
Passau 30 B1
Passignano sul Trasimeno 46 C4
Passow 7 F3
Passy 36 A2
Pastoriza 54 A1
Pastrana 63 E3
Pataias 66 B1
Patay 25 D2
Patergassen 30 B4
Paterna 71 D1
Paterna del Campo 73 E2
Paterna del Madera 70 A3
Paterna del Río 75 E3
Paterna de Rivera 73 F3
釋Paternion 30 B4
Paterno 50 B4
Paternopoli 50 A2
Patersdorf 21 D4
Patrica 49 D3
Pattensen 11 E1
Pâturages 16 C1
Pau 40 B4
Pauillac 32 B4
Paul 61 D4
Paularo 39 E1
Paulhan 42 B3
Paulinenaue 7 D4
Paüls dels Ports 65 E2
Paulx 23 E4
Pausa 12 C4
Pavia Italy 37 E4
Pavia Port. 66 C3
Pavia di Udine 39 F2
Pavías 65 D4
Pavie 41 D3
Pavilly 15 E3
Pavullo nel Frignano 46 A1
Päwesin 13 D1
Payerbach 31 E3
Payerne 27 E4
Paymogo 72 C1
Payrac 33 E4
Payzac 33 E3
Pazo de Irixoa 53 F1
Pazos 53 E3
Peal de Becerro 69 E4
Péaule 23 D3
Peccia 37 D1
Peccioli 46 A3
Pechina 75 F3
Pecq 16 C1
Pedaso 47 F4
Pederobba 39 D2
Pedrafita do Cebreiro 54 A3
Pedrajas de San Esteban 62 C1
Pedralba 71 D1
Pedralba de la Pradería 54 B4
Pedraza de Campos 55 E4
Pedrera 74 B2
Pedro Abad 68 C4
Pedro Bernardo 62 B4
Pedroche 68 C4
Pedrógão Port. 67 D4
Pedrógão Port. 61 D4
Pedrógão Port. 66 B1
Pedrógão Grande 66 C1
Pedrógão Pequeno 66 C1
Pedro-Martínez 75 E2
Pedro Muñoz 69 F2
Pedrosa 55 F2
Pedrosa del Príncipe 55 E3
Pedrosillo de los Aires 62 A3
Pedroso Port. 60 B2
Pedroso Spain 56 B3
Pedrouzos 53 E2
Peenemünde 7 E1
Peer 9 E3
Pega 61 D3
Pegalajar 75 D1
Pegau 12 C3
Peggau 31 D3
Pegli 44 C1
Pegnitz 20 B2
Pego Port. 66 C1
Pego Spain 71 E3
Pegões 66 B3
Peillac 23 D3
Peille 44 B2
Peine 11 F1
Peio 38 B1
Peipin 43 E2
Peïra-Cava 44 A2
Peißen Ger. 12 B2
Peißen Ger. 12 C3
Peißenberg 29 E2
Peiting 29 D2
Peitz 13 F2
Pelago 46 B3
Pelahustán 62 C4
Pelarrodríguez 61 F2
Peleagonzalo 62 A1
Pélissanne 43 D3
Pellaro 52 A4
Pellegrino Parmense 38 A4
Pellegrue 40 C1
Pellestrina 39 D3
Pellizzano 38 B1
Pelm 18 A1
Peloche 68 B2
Pelsin 7 E2
Pélussin 35 D3
Pelvoux 36 A4
Pemfling 20 C3
Peñacerrada 56 B3
Penacova 60 C4
Penafiel 60 C2
Peñafiel 62 C1
Peñaflor 74 A1
Peñaflor de Hornija 62 B1
Penagos 55 F1
Peñalba 58 A4
Peñalsordo 68 B3
Penalva do Castelo 61 D3
Penamacor 61 D4
Peñaranda de Bracamonte 62 B2
Peñaranda de Duero 63 D1
Peñarroya de Tastavins 65 D3
Peñarroya-Pueblonuevo 68 B4
Peñarrubia 70 B4
Peñascosa 70 A3
Peñas de San Pedro 70 B3
Peñausende 62 A2
Pendilhe 60 C2
Penedo Gordo 66 C4
Penedono 61 D2
Penela 60 C4
Pénestin 23 D3
Penha Garcia 61 E4
Peniche 66 A2
Peñíscola 65 E3
Penkun 7 F3
Penmarch 22 B3
Pennabilli 46 C2
Penna in Teverina 48 C1
Pennapiedimonte 49 E1
Pennautier 41 F4
Penne 49 E1
Penne-d'Agenais 41 D1
Pentone 52 B2
Penvénan 22 C1
Penzberg 29 E2
Penzlin 7 E3
Péone 44 A2
Pepingen 9 D4
Pepinster 17 F1
Peque 54 B4
Pêra 72 B2
Perafita 59 D3
Perais 67 D1
Peralada 59 E2
Peraleda de la Mata 62 A4
Peraleda del Zaucejo 68 B3
Peralejos 64 C3
Peralejos de las Truchas 64 A3
Perales del Alfambra 64 C3
Perales del Puerto 61 E4
Peralta 56 C3
Peralta de Alcofea 58 A3
Peralta de la Sal 58 A3
Peraltilla 58 A3
Peralva 72 C2
Peralveche 63 F3
Peramola 58 C3
Perarolo di Cadore 39 D1
Perchtoldsdorf 31 F2
Percy 23 F1
Perdifumo 50 A4
Perdiguera 57 E4
Peredo 61 E1
Pereiras 72 A2
Pereiro Port. 72 C2
Pereiro Spain 53 F1
Pereiro de Aguiar 53 F3
Pereruela 62 A1
Perg 30 C1
Pergine Valdarno 46 C3
Pergine Valsugana 38 C2
Pergola 47 D3
Periana 74 C3
Périers 14 B3
Périgueux 33 D4
Perilla de Castro 54 C4
Perl 17 F3
Perleberg 6 C3
Pernegg an der Mur 31 D3
Pernersdorf 31 E1
Pernes 66 B2
Pernes-les-Fontaines 43 D2
Pernitz 31 E2
Pero 37 D3
Peroguarda 66 C4
Pérols 42 B3
Péron 35 F2
Péronnas 35 E2
Péronne 16 B2
Perosa Argentina 36 B4
Pero Viseu 61 D4
Perpignan 59 E1
Perrecy-les-Forges 35 D1
Perreux 35 D2
Perros-Guirec 22 C1
Persan 16 A3
Persenbeug 31 D2
Perthes 25 E1
Pertuis 43 E3
Pertusa 58 A3
Perugia 47 D4
Péruwelz 16 C1
Pervenchères 24 B1
Pesadas de Burgos 55 F2
Pesaro 47 D2
Pescaglia 46 A2
Pescantina 38 B3

Pescara **49** E1
Pescasseroli **49** E2
Peschadoires **34** C3
Peschici **50** B1
Peschiera del Garda **38** B3
Pescia **46** A2
Pescina **49** D2
Pescocostanzo **49** E2
Pescolanciano **49** E2
Pescopennataro **49** E2
Pescorocchiano **49** D1
Pesco Sannita **50** A2
Pesmes **26** C3
Peso da Régua **60** C2
Pesquera de Duero **62** C1
Pessac **32** B4
Pesse **4** C4
Pessin **7** D4
Pesués **55** E1
Petacciato **49** F2
Pétange **17** F3
Petersberg **11** E4
Petersdorf **29** D1
Petersdorf auf Fehmarn **6** B1
Petershagen *Ger.* **13** F1
Petershagen *Ger.* **11** D1
Petilia Policastro **52** C2
Petín **54** A3
Petit-Mars **23** E3
Petkus **13** D2
Petrella Salto **49** D1
Petrella Tifernina **50** A1
Petrer **71** D3
Petriano **47** D2
Petritoli **47** E4
Pétrola **70** C3
Petronà **52** B2
Petten **4** A4
Petting **30** A2
Pettneu am Arlberg **28** C4
Pettorano sul Gizio **49** E2
Peuerbach **30** B1
Peujard **32** C4
Peveragno **44** B1
Pewsum (Krummhörn) **4** C3
Peymeinade **44** A3
Peyrat-le-Château **33** F3
Peyrehorade **40** A3
Peyriac-Minervois **41** F4
Peyrolles-en-Provence **43** E3
Peyruis **43** E2
Pézenas **42** B3
Pfaffenberg **20** C4
Pfaffendorf **13** E1
Pfaffenhausen **29** D2
Pfaffenhofen an der Ilm **29** E1
Pfaffenhoffen **18** C4
Pfäffikon **28** B4
Pfaffing **29** F2
Pfalzgrafenweiler **28** A1
Pfarrkirchen **30** A1
Pfarrweisach **20** A1
Pfarrwerfen **30** B3
Pfedelbach **19** E3
Pflach **29** D3
Pfons **29** E3
Pförring **20** B4
Pforzen **29** D2
Pforzheim **19** D4
Pfreimd **20** C3
Pfronstetten **28** B1
Pfronten **29** D3
Pfullendorf **28** B2
Pfullingen **28** B1
Pfunds **29** D4
Pfungstadt **19** D2
Pfyn **28** B3
Phalsbourg **27** E1
Philippeville **17** D1
Philippsburg **19** D3
Philippsreut **21** E4
Piacenza **38** A4
Piadena **38** B4
Piana Crixia **44** C1
Piancastagnaio **46** C4
Piandimeleto **47** D3
Piàn di Scò **46** B3
Pianella **49** E1
Pianello Val Tidone **37** E4
Piano del Voglio **46** B2
Pianoro **46** B1
Piansano **48** B1
Pias **67** D4
Piasek **7** F4
Piau-Engaly **58** A1
Piazza al Serchio **46** A2
Piazza Brembana **38** A2
Piazzatorre **38** A2
Piazzola sul Brenta **39** D3
Picassent **71** D2
Picauville **14** B3
Picerno **50** B3
Picher **6** C3
Pichl bei Wels **30** C2
Pico **49** D3
Picón **69** D2
Picquigny **16** A2
Piedimonte Matese **49** F3
Piedimulera **36** C2
Piedrabuena **69** D2
Piedrafita de Babia **54** B2
Piedrahita **62** B3
Piedralaves **62** C3
Piedras Albas **67** E1
Piedras Blancas **54** C1
Piegaro **46** C4
Piégut-Pluviers **33** D3
Piennes **17** F3
Pieńsk **13** F3
Pienza **46** B4
Piera **58** C4
Pierre-Buffière **33** E3
Pierre-Châtel **35** F4
Pierrefeu-du-Var **43** F4
Pierrefitte-Nestalas **40** C4
Pierrefitte-sur-Aire **17** E4
Pierrefonds **16** B3
Pierrefontaine-les-Varans **27** D4
Pierrefort **34** B4
Pierrelatte **42** C1
Pierrepont **17** F3
Pierres **25** D1
Pierrevert **43** E2
Piesau **12** B4
Piesendorf **30** A3
Pietrabbondante **49** E2
Pietracatella **50** A1
Pietragalla **50** B3
Pietra Ligure **44** C2
Pietralunga **47** D3
Pietramelara **49** E3
Pietramontecorvino **50** A1
Pietraporzio **44** A1
Pietrasanta **45** E2
Pieve d'Alpago **39** D2
Pieve del Cairo **37** D4
Pieve di Bono **38** B2
Pieve di Cadore **39** D1
Pieve di Cento **38** C4
Pieve di Soligo **39** D2
Pieve di Teco **44** B2
Pieve Fosciana **46** A2
Pievepelago **46** A2
Pieve Santo Stefano **46** C3
Pieve Torina **47** D4
Pieve Vergonte **36** C2
Piglio **49** D2
Pigna **44** B2
Pignataro Interamna **49** E3
Pignataro Maggiore **49** E3
Pignola **50** B3
Pijnacker **9** D1
Pila **39** E4
Pilas **73** E2
Piles **71** E3
Pill **29** E3
Pilsach **20** B3
Pilsting **30** A1
Piña de Campos **55** E4
Piña de Esgueva **55** E4
Piñar **75** D2
Pinarejo **70** A1
Pinasca **36** B4
Pindstrup **2** C1
Pineda de Cigüela **63** F4
Pineda de la Sierra **56** A4
Pineda de Mar **59** E3
Pinela **61** E1
Piñel de Abajo **62** C1
Pinerolo **36** B4
Pineto **49** E1
Piney **26** B1
Pinggau **31** E3
Pinhal Novo **66** B3
Pinhanços **61** D3
Pinhão **61** D2
Pinheiro **66** B3
Pinheiro Grande **66** C2
Pinhel **61** E3
Pinilla de Molina **64** A3
Pinilla de Toro **62** B1
Pinkafeld **31** E3
Pinneberg **6** A2
Pinnow **13** F2
Pino **61** F1
Pino del Río **55** D3
Pinofranqueado **61** F3
Pinols **34** C4
Piñor **53** F3
Pinoso **70** C4
Pinos-Puente **75** D2
Pinsoro **57** D4
Pintano **57** E3
Pinto **63** D4
Pinzano al Tagliamento **39** E2
Pinzio **61** E3
Pinzolo **38** B2
Piobbico **47** D3
Piolenc **43** D2
Pioltello **37** E3
Piombino **46** A4
Piombino Dese **39** D3
Pionsat **34** B2
Pioraco **47** D4
Piornal **62** A4
Piossasco **36** B4
Piove di Sacco **39** D3
Piovene Rocchette **38** C3
Pipriac **23** E3
Piriac-sur-Mer **23** D3
Pirmasens **18** C3
Pirna **13** E3
Pisa **46** A3
Pischelsdorf in der Steiermark **31** E4
Pisciotta **50** A4
Pisogne **38** A2
Pissos **40** B2
Pisticci **50** C4
Pistoia **46** A2
Pitarque **64** C3
Pithiviers **25** E2
Pitigliano **48** A1
Pîtres **15** F3
Pitres **75** D3
Pittem **8** C3
Pitten **31** F3
Pizarra **74** B3
Pizzighettone **38** A4
Pizzo **52** B3
Pizzoferrato **49** E2
Pizzoli **49** D1
Pjedsted **2** B2
Plaaz **7** D2
Plabennec **22** A1
Placencia de las Armas **56** C2
Plaffeien **27** F4
Plainfaing **27** E2
Plaintel **23** D2
Plaisance **40** C3
Plaisance-du-Touch **41** E3
Plaisir **16** A4
Plancher-Bas **27** E3
Plancoët **23** D1
Plancy-l'Abbaye **16** C4
Plan-de-la-Tour **43** F3
Planegg **29** E2
Planès **59** D2
Plankenfels **20** B2
Plasencia **61** F4
Plasencia del Monte **57** E3
Platania **52** B2
Plate **6** C2
Platì **52** A4
Platja de Nules **65** D4
Plattling **21** D4
Plau **7** D3
Plaue **12** A4
Plauen **12** C4
Pleaux **33** F4
Plech **20** B2
Pleine-Fougères **23** E1
Plélan-le-Grand **23** D2
Plélo **22** C1
Plémet **23** D2
Plénée-Jugon **23** D2
Pléneuf-Val-André **23** D1
Plentzia **56** B1
Plérin **23** D1
Plescop **23** D3
Plessa **13** E3
Plessé **23** E3
Plestin-les-Grèves **22** B1
Plettenberg **10** C3
Pleubian **22** C1
Pleudihen-sur-Rance **23** E1
Pleumartin **33** D1
Pleumeur-Bodou **22** C1
Pleuven **22** B2
Pleyben **22** B2
Pleyber-Christ **22** B1
Pliego **76** B1
Plobannalec **22** B3
Ploemeur **22** C3
Ploeren **22** C3
Ploërmel **23** D2
Plœuc-sur-Lié **23** D2
Plogonnec **22** B2
Plogshagen **7** E1
Plombières-les-Bains **27** D2
Plomeur **22** B3
Plomodiern **22** B2
Plön **6** B1
Plonéour-Lanvern **22** B2
Plonévez-du-Faou **22** B2
Plonevez-Porzay **22** B2
Plößberg **20** C2
Plötzin **13** D1
Plötzky **12** C1
Plou **64** C2
Plouagat **22** C1
Plouaret **22** C1
Plouarzel **22** A2
Plouay **22** C2
Ploubalay **23** D1
Ploubazlanec **22** C1
Ploubezre **22** C1
Ploudalmézeau **22** A1
Ploudiry **22** B1
Plouescat **22** B1
Plouézec **22** C1
Ploufragan **23** D1
Plougasnou **22** B1
Plougastel-Daoulas **22** B2
Plougonven **22** B1
Plougrescant **22** C1
Plouguenast **23** D2
Plouguerneau **22** A1
Plouguernével **22** C2
Plouguiel **22** C1
Plouguin **22** A1
Plouha **22** C1
Plouharnel **22** C3
Plouhinec *France* **22** A2
Plouhinec *France* **22** C3
Plouigneau **22** B1
Ploumagoar **22** C1
Ploumilliau **22** C1
Plounévez-Moëdec **22** C1
Plounévez-Quintin **22** C2
Plouray **22** C2
Plouvorn **22** B1
Plouzané **22** A2
Plouzévédé **22** B1
Plozévet **22** A2
Plumelec **23** D3
Pluméliau **22** C2
Plumergat **22** C3
Pluneret **22** C3
Pluvigner **22** C3
Pluzunet **22** C1
Pobladura del Valle **54** C4
Poblete **69** D3
Poboleda **58** B4
Poceirão **66** B3
Pöchlarn **31** D2
Pocking **30** B1
Pöcking **29** E2
Podelzig **13** F1
Podensac **40** B1
Podenzana **45** E2
Podenzano **38** A4
Podersdorf am See **31** F2
Pofi **49** D3
Poggendorf **7** E2
Poggiardo **51** F4
Poggibonsi **46** B3
Poggio Berni **47** D2
Poggio Bustone **48** C1
Poggio Catino **48** C1
Poggiodomo **47** D4
Poggio Imperiale **50** A1
Poggio Mirteto **48** C1
Poggio Moiano **48** C1
Poggio Picenze **49** D1
Poggio Renatico **38** C4
Poggiorsini **50** C3
Poggio Rusco **38** C4
Pöggstall **31** D1
Poing **29** F2
Poirino **36** C4
Poissons **26** C1
Poissy **16** A4
Poitiers **33** D1
Poix-de-Picardie **16** A2
Pola de Allande **54** B1
Pola de Laviana **54** C2
Pola de Lena **54** C2
Pola de Siero **54** C1
Pola de Somiedo **54** B2
Polaincourt-et-Clairefontaine **27** D2
Polán **62** C4
Polch **18** B1
Polesella **39** D4
Polia **52** B3
Police **7** F3
Policoro **51** D4
Polientes **55** F2
Polignano a Mare **51** D2
Poligny **26** C4
Polistena **52** A4
Pölitz **6** B2
Polla **50** B3
Pöllau **31** E3

Pöllauberg **31** E3
Polle **11** E2
Pollenfeld **20** B4
Pollenza **47** E3
Polliat **35** E2
Pollica **50** A4
Pollitz **6** C4
Pollos **62** B1
Polminhac **34** A4
Polop **71** E3
Pöls **30** C3
Polsingen **20** A4
Polverigi **47** E3
Pölzig **12** C4
Pomaluengo **55** F1
Pomarance **46** A3
Pomarão **72** C2
Pomarez **40** B3
Pomarico **50** C3
Pombal *Port.* **61** D2
Pombal *Port.* **66** B1
Pomer **64** B1
Pomezia **48** C2
Pommelsbrunn **20** B3
Pommersfelden **20** A2
Pompaire **32** C1
Pompei **49** F4
Pompey **17** F4
Poncin **35** E2
Ponferrada **54** B3
Pons **32** B3
Ponsacco **46** A3
Pont-à-Celles **17** D1
Pontacq **40** C4
Pontailler-sur-Saône **26** C3
Pont-à-Marcq **16** B1
Pont-à-Mousson **17** F4
Pontarion **33** F2
Pontarlier **27** D4
Pontassieve **46** B2
Pont-Audemer **15** E3
Pontault-Combault **16** B4
Pontaumur **34** B2
Pont-Aven **22** B3
Pont-Canavese **36** B3
Pontcharra **35** F3
Pontchâteau **23** E3
Pont-Croix **22** A2
Pont-d'Ain **35** E2
Pont-de-Buis-lès-Quimerch **22** B2
Pont-de-Larn **41** F3
Pont-de-Roide **27** E3
Pont-de-Salars **42** A2
Pont de Suert **58** B2
Pont-de-Vaux **35** E1
Pont-de-Veyle **35** E2
Pont-d'Ouilly **14** C4
Pont-du-Casse **41** D2
Pont-du-Château **34** B3
Pont-du-Navoy **26** C4
Ponte **49** F3
Ponte-Aranga **53** F2
Ponteareas **53** E4
Pontebba **39** F1
Pontecagnano Faiano **50** A3
Ponte Caldelas **53** E3
Ponte-Ceso **53** D2
Pontecorvo **49** D3
Pontecurone **37** D4
Ponte da Barca **60** C1
Pontedassio **44** B2
Pontedecimo **45** D1
Ponte de Lima **60** B1
Ponte dell'Olio **38** A4
Pontedera **46** A3
Ponte de Sor **66** C2
Pontedeume **53** F1
Ponte di Legno **38** B2
Ponte di Piave **39** E3
Ponte do Rol **66** A2
Ponte Gardena **38** C1
Pontelagoscuro **38** C4
Pontelongo **39** D3
Ponte nelle Alpi **39** D2
Ponte Nizza **45** D1
Ponte Nossa **38** A2
Ponte Nova **38** C1
Pont-en-Royans **35** E4
Pontenure **38** A4
Pontenx les-Forges **40** A2
Pontepedra **53** E2
Ponte San Nicolò **39** D3
Ponte San Pietro **38** A3
Ponte Valga **53** E3
Pontevedra **53** E3
Pontével **66** B2
Pont-Évêque **35** E3
Pontevico **38** A3
Pontfaverger-Moronvilliers **17** D3
Pontgibaud **34** B3
Pont-Hébert **14** B3
Pontinha **66** A3
Pontinia **49** D3
Pontivy **22** C2
Pont-l'Abbé **22** B3
Pont-l'Évêque **15** D3
Pontlevoy **24** C3
Pontoise **16** A4
Pontones **70** A4
Pontonx-sur-l'Adour **40** A3
Pontorson **23** E1
Pontpoint **16** B3
Pontremoli **45** E1
Pontresina **38** A1
Pontrieux **22** C1
Ponts **58** C3
Pont-Ste-Marie **26** A1
Pont-Ste-Maxence **16** B3
Pont-St-Esprit **42** C2
Pont-St-Martin **36** C3
Pont-sur-Yonne **25** F2
Pontvallain **24** B3
Ponza **48** C4
Ponzone **44** C1
Poperinge **8** B4
Popoli **49** E1
Poppenricht **20** B3
Poppi **46** C3
Pópulo **61** D1
Populonia **46** A4
Porcari **46** A2
Porcia **39** E2
Porcuna **74** C1
Pordenone **39** E2
Porlezza **37** D2
Pornassio **44** B2
Pornic **23** E4
Pornichet **23** D4
Porqueres **59** E2
Porrentruy **27** E3
Porretta Terme **46** B2
Porriño **53** E4
Porspoder **22** A1
Porta **59** D2
Portaje **67** E1
Portalegre **67** D2
Portbail **14** B3
Portbou **59** F2
Port Brillet **23** F2
Port-de-Bouc **43** D3
Port-des-Barques **32** B2
Portel **67** D4
Portell de Morella **65** D3
Port-en-Bessin-Huppain **14** C3
Portes-lès-Valence **35** E4
Portets **40** B1
Port Grimaud **43** F3
Portici **49** F4
Portieux **27** D1
Portilla **64** A4
Portilla de la Reina **55** D2
Portillo **62** C1
Portillo de Toledo **62** C4
Portimão **72** A2
Port-la-Nouvelle **42** A4
Port-Louis **22** C3
Portman **76** C2
Porto *Port.* **60** B2
Porto *Spain* **54** A4
Porto Alto **66** B3
Porto Azzurro **46** A4
Portobravo **53** D2
Porto Cesareo **51** E4
Porto Covo da Bandeira **72** A1
Porto d'Ascoli **47** F4
Porto de Lagos **72** A2
Porto de Mós **66** B1
Porto do Barqueiro **53** F1
Porto do Son **53** D3
Porto Ercole **48** A1
Portoferraio **46** A4
Portofino **45** D2
Porto Garibaldi **46** C1
Portogruaro **39** E2
Porto Levante **39** D4
Portomaggiore **46** C1
Portomarín **53** F2
Porto Recanati **47** E3
Porto San Giorgio **47** F4
Porto Sant'Elpidio **47** F3
Porto Santo Stefano **48** A1
Porto Tolle **39** D4
Portovenere **45** E2
Port-Ste-Marie **40** C2
Port-St-Louis-du-Rhône **43** D3
Port-St-Père **23** E4
Port-sur-Saône **27** D3
Portugalete **56** B1
Port-Vendres **59** E2
Porzuna **69** D2
Posada de Llanera **54** C1
Posada de Valdeón **55** D2
Posadas **74** B1
Poschiavo **38** A1
Poseritz **7** E1
Pösing **20** C3
Positano **49** F4
Possagno **39** D2
Possendorf **13** E4
Pößneck **12** B4
Posta **49** D1
Postal **38** C1
Posta Piana **50** B2
Postau **29** F1
Posterholt **10** A3
Postiglione **50** A3
Potenza **50** B3
Potenza Picena **47** E3
Potes **55** E2
Potigny **15** D4
Potsdam **13** D1
Pottendorf **31** F2
Pottenstein *Austria* **31** E2
Pottenstein *Ger.* **20** B2
Pöttmes **29** E1
Pöttsching **31** F2
Pouancé **23** F3
Pougues-les-Eaux **25** F4
Pouillon **40** A3
Pouilly-en-Auxois **26** B3
Pouilly-sous-Charlieu **35** D2
Pouilly-sur-Loire **25** F3
Pouldreuzic **22** B2
Poullaouen **22** B2
Poulstrup **1** F1
Pourrain **25** F3
Pousada **61** D3
Pousadela **60** B2
Pousos **66** B1
Poussan **42** B3
Pouxeux **27** D2
Pouyastruc **40** C4
Pouzauges **32** B1
Povedilla **70** A3
Poviglio **38** B4
Póvoa de Lanhoso **60** C1
Póvoa de São Miguel **67** D4
Póvoa de Varzim **60** B1
Póvoa do Concelho **61** D3
Povoletto **39** F2
Poyales del Hoyo **62** B4
Poyatos **64** A3
Poysdorf **31** F1
Poza de la Sal **55** F3
Pozaldez **62** B1
Pozo Alcón **75** E1
Pozoamargo **70** B2
Pozoantiguo **62** A1
Pozoblanco **68** C4
Pozo Cañada **70** B3
Pozo de Guadalajara **63** E3
Pozohondo **70** B3
Pozo-Lorente **70** C2
Pozondón **64** B3
Pozorrubio **63** E4
Pozuel del Campo **64** B3
Pozuelo **70** B3
Pozuelo de Alarcón **63** D3
Pozuelo de Aragón **57** D4
Pozuelo del Páramo **54** C4
Pozuelo del Rey **63** E3
Pozuelo de Zarzón **61** F4
Pozuelos de Calatrava **69** D3
Pozza di Fasso **38** C1
Pozzolo Formigaro **44** C1
Pozzuoli **49** E4
Pozzuolo del Friuli **39** E2
Prackenbach **21** D3
Prádanos de Ojeda **55** E3
Pradejón **56** C3
Pradelles **42** B1
Prádena **63** D2
Prades **59** D2
Pradillo **56** B4
Pradines **41** E1
Prado **60** B1
Prado de la Guzpeña **55** D3
Prado del Rey **74** A3
Pradoluengo **56** A3
Præstbro **1** F2
Præstø **3** E3
Pragelato **36** A4
Prägraten **29** F4
Prahecq **32** C2
Praia a Mare **52** A1
Praia da Barra **60** B3
Praia da Rocha **72** A2
Praia da Tocha **60** B3
Praia de Esmoriz **60** B2
Praia de Mira **60** B3
Praiano **49** F4
Pralognan-la-Vanoise **36** A3
Prambachkirchen **30** C1
Prata di Pordenone **39** E2
Pratau **13** D2
Prat de Comte **65** E2
Pratdip **58** B4
Pratella **49** E3
Prato **46** B2
Prato allo Stelvio **38** B1
Pratola Peligna **49** E2
Pratovecchio **46** C3
Prats de Lluçanes **59** D3
Prats-de-Mollo-la-Preste **59** E2
Pratteln **27** F3
Prauthoy **26** C3
Pravia **54** C1
Prayssas **41** D2
Praz-sur-Arly **36** A2
Preci **47** D4
Précigné **24** A3
Précy-sous-Thil **26** B3
Predappio **46** C2
Predazzo **38** C1
Preding **31** E4
Predlitz **30** C4
Predosa **44** C1
Pré-en-Pail **24** A1
Preetz **6** A1
Preganziòl **39** D3
Pregarten **30** C1
Preitenegg **31** D4
Prémery **25** F4
Premia **36** C2
Premià de Mar **59** D4
Premilcuore **46** C2
Prémilhat **34** A2
Premnitz **12** C1
Premosello Chiovenda **36** C2
Prenzlau **7** F3
Presicce **51** F4
Pressath **20** C2
Pressbaum **31** E2
Presseck **20** B1
Pressel **13** D2
Pressig **20** B1
Pre-St-Didier **36** B3
Prettin **13** D2
Pretzfeld **20** B2
Pretzier **6** C4
Pretzsch **13** D2
Pretzschendorf **13** E4
Preuilly-sur-Claise **33** D1
Priaranza del Bierzo **54** B3
Priborn **7** D3
Prichsenstadt **20** A2
Priego **63** F3
Priego de Córdoba **74** C2
Prien am Chiemsee **29** F2
Prieros **13** E1
Prießnitz *Ger.* **12** C3
Prießnitz *Ger.* **12** B3
Priestewitz **13** E3
Prignac-et-Marcamps **32** C4
Primolano **38** C2
Prinsenbeek **9** D2
Prioro **55** D2
Prittriching **29** D2
Pritzerbe **12** C1
Pritzier **6** B3
Pritzwalk **7** D3
Privas **42** C1
Priverno **49** D3
Proaza **54** C2
Proba **54** A2
Probsteierhagen **6** B1
Proceno **46** C4
Procida **49** E4
Proença-a-Nova **66** C1
Proença-a-Velha **61** D4
Profen **12** C3
Profondeville **17** D1
Prohn **7** E1
Prossedi **49** D3
Prötzel **7** F4
Provenchères-sur-Fave **27** E1
Provins **25** F1
Prüm **17** F1
Pruna **74** A3
Pruniers-en-Sologne **25** D3
Prutz **29** D4
Przewóz **13** F3
Publier **36** A1
Puchheim **29** E2
Puçol **71** D1
Puderbach **10** C4
Puebla de Albortón **64** C1

Puebla de Alcocer 68 B2
Puebla de Alfindén 64 C1
Puebla de Almenara 63 E4
Puebla de Beleña 63 E2
Puebla de Brollón 54 A3
Puebla de Don Fadrique 70 A4
Puebla de Don Rodrigo 68 C2
Puebla de Guzmán 72 C1
Puebla de la Calzada 67 E3
Puebla de la Reina 67 F3
Puebla del Caramiñal 53 D3
Puebla de Lillo 55 D2
Puebla del Maestre 67 F4
Puebla del Príncipe 69 F3
Puebla del Prior 67 F3
Puebla del Salvador 70 B1
Puebla de Obando 67 E2
Puebla de Sanabria 54 B4
Puebla de Sancho Pérez 67 F4
Puebla de San Miguel 64 C4
Puebla de San Xulián 54 A2
Puebla de Trives 54 A3
Puebla de Yeltes 61 F3
Puente de Domingo Flórez 54 B3
Puente de Génave 70 A4
Puente del Congosto 62 A3
Puente de Montañana 58 B2
Puente de San Miguel 55 E1
Puente-Genil 74 B2
Puente la Reina 56 C3
Puentenansa 55 E2
Puente Viesgo 55 F2
Puerto de Béjar 62 A3
Puerto de Mazarrón 76 B2
Puerto de San Vicente 68 B1
Puerto Lápice 69 E2
Puertollano 69 D3
Puerto Lumbreras 76 A2
Puertomingalvo 65 D4
Puerto Real 73 E4
Puerto Seguro 61 E3
Puerto Serrano 74 A3
Pueyo 57 D3
Pueyo de Santa Cruz 58 A3
Puget-Théniers 44 A2
Puget-Ville 43 F3
Pugnochiuso 50 C1
Puig 71 D1
Puigcerdà 59 D2
Puig-reig 59 D3
Puiseaux 25 E2
Puisserguier 42 A3
Pujaut 43 D2
Pujols *France* 32 C4
Pujols *France* 41 D2
Pulfero 39 F2
Pulgar 69 D1
Pulheim 10 B3
Pulkau 31 E1
Pulpí 76 B2
Pulsano 51 E4
Pulsen 13 D3
Pulsnitz 13 E3
Pulversheim 27 E2
Punta Ala 46 A4
Punta Sabbioni 39 D3
Punta Umbría 73 D2
Purbach am Neusiedler See 31 F2
Purchena 75 F2
Purgstall an der Erlauf 31 D2
Purkersdorf 31 E2
Purmerend 4 A4
Purujosa 64 B1
Purullena 75 E2
Puschendorf 20 A3
Pusterwald 30 C3
Putanges-Pont-Écrepin 24 A1
Putbus 7 E1
Putignano 51 D3
Putlitz 6 C3
Putte *Belgium* 9 D3
Putte *Neth.* 9 D3
Puttelange-aux-Lacs 18 B4
Putten 9 F1
Puttgarden 6 C1
Püttlingen 18 B3
Putzar 7 E2
Putzkau 13 E3
Puurs 9 D3
Puygouzon 41 F2
Puylaroque 41 E2
Puylaurens 41 F3
Puy-l'Évêque 41 D1
Puymirol 41 D2
Puymoyen 33 D3
Puyôo 40 B3
Pyhra 31 E2
Pyrbaum 20 B3

Q

Quadrazais 61 E3
Quadri 49 E2
Quakenbrück 5 D4
Qualiano 49 E4
Quargnento 37 D4
Quarona 36 C3
Quarrata 46 B2
Quarré-les-Tombes 26 A3
Quarteira 72 B2
Quartell 71 E1
Quarten 28 B4
Quatretonda 71 D3
Quattro Castella 46 A1
Quedlinburg 12 B2
Queidersbach 18 C3
Queige 36 A3
Queiriga 61 D3
Quel 56 C4
Quelaines-St-Gault 23 F2
Quellen-dorf 12 C2
Queluz 66 A3
Quemada 63 D1
Queralbs 59 D2
Quercianella 46 A3
Querfurt 12 B3
Quérigut 59 D1
Quern 2 B4
Quero *Italy* 39 D2
Quero *Spain* 69 E1
Querol 58 C4
Quesa 71 D2
Quesada 75 E1
Quesnoy-sur-Deûle 8 B4
Quessoy 23 D1
Questembert 23 D3
Quettehou 14 B3
Quettreville-sur-Seinne 14 B4
Quevauvillers 16 A2
Queyrac 32 B3
Quiaios 60 B4
Quiberon 22 C3
Quickborn 6 A2
Quiévrain 16 C1
Quiliano 44 C2
Quillan 41 F4
Quillebeuf-sur-Seine 15 E3
Quimper 22 B2
Quimperlé 22 C3
Quincinetto 36 C3
Quincy-Voisins 16 B4
Quingey 27 D4
Quinssaines 34 A2
Quintana de la Serena 68 A3
Quintana del Castillo 54 C3
Quintana del Pino 55 F3
Quintana del Puente 55 E4
Quintana de Rueda 55 D3
Quintana-Martín Galíndez 56 A2
Quintanapalla 55 F3
Quintanar de la Orden 69 F1
Quintanar de la Sierra 56 B4
Quintanar del Rey 70 B2
Quintana Redonda 63 F1
Quintanilla de Omesimo 62 C1
Quintenas 35 D4
Quintin 22 C2
Quinto *Spain* 65 D1
Quinto *Switz.* 37 D1
Quintos 67 D4
Quinzano d'Oglio 38 A3
Quiroga 54 A3
Quiruelas de Vidriales 54 C4
Quismondo 62 C4
Quissac 42 C2

R

Raab 30 B1
Raalte 10 A1
Raamsdonksveer 9 E2
Rabaçal *Port.* 61 D2
Rabaçal *Portugal* 60 B4
Rábade 53 F2
Rabanales 54 B4
Rabastens 41 E3
Rabastens-de-Bigorre 40 C3
Rabenstein an der Pielach 31 E2
Raben Steinfeld 6 C2
Räbke 12 A1
Racale 51 F4
Racconigi 44 B1
Rada de Haro 70 A1
Raddestorf 11 D1
Raddi in Chianti 46 B3
Radeberg 13 E3
Radebeul 13 E3
Radeburg 13 E3
Radefeld 12 C3
Radegast 12 C2
Radensleben 7 E4
Radenthein 30 B4
Radevormwald 10 B3
Radibor 13 F3
Radicofani 46 C4
Radicondoli 46 B3
Radis 12 C2
Radolfzell am Bodensee 28 B2
Radstadt 30 B3
Radzików 13 F1
Ræhr 1 D2
Rækker Mølle 2 A2
Raeren 10 A4
Raesfeld 10 B2
Rafelbunyol 71 D1
Rágama 62 B2
Rägelin 7 D3
Ragösen 12 C1
Raguhn 12 C2
Rahden 11 D1
Raiano 49 E2
Rain *Ger.* 20 C4
Rain *Ger.* 29 D1
Rainbach im Mühlkreis 30 C1
Raisdorf 6 A1
Raismes 16 C1
Rakkeby 1 F1
Ralingen 18 A2
Ramales de la Victoria 55 F2
Ramalhal 66 A2
Ramatuelle 43 F4
Rambervillers 27 E1
Rambin 7 E1
Rambouillet 16 A4
Rambrouch 17 F2
Ramingstein 30 B4
Ramirás 53 F4
Ramløse 3 E2
Ramme 2 A1
Rammelsbach 18 B3
Rammingen 28 C1
Ramonville-St-Agne 41 E3
Ramsau im Zillertal 29 F3
Ramsen 28 A3
Ramsing 1 D3
Ramsloh (Saterland) 5 D3
Ramstein 18 C3
Randan 34 C2
Randegg 31 D2
Randers 2 C1
Rânes 24 A1
Rangersdorf 30 A4
Rangsdorf 13 D1
Ranhados 60 C3
Ranis 12 B4
Rankweil 28 C3
Ransbach-Baumbach 10 C4
Ranten 30 C4
Rantum 2 A4
Rantzausminde 2 C3
Ranum 1 E2
Raon-l'Étape 27 E1
Raossi 38 C3
Rapallo 45 D1
Rapice 13 F1
Rapolano Terme 46 B3
Rapolla 50 B2
Raposa 66 B2
Raposeira 72 A2
Rapoula do Côa 61 D3
Rapperswil 28 B3
Raron 36 C2
Rascafría 63 D2
Raschau 13 D4
Rasdorf 11 E4
Rasines 55 F1
Rask Mølle 2 B2
Rasquera 65 E2
Rastatt 18 C4
Rastdorf 5 D4
Råsted 2 C1
Rastede 5 E3
Rastenfeld 31 D1
Rastow 6 C3
Rasueros 62 B2
Ratekau 6 B2
Rathenow 7 D4
Rathstock 13 F1
Ratingen 10 B3
Rattelsdorf 20 A2
Ratten 31 E3
Rattenberg 29 F3
Ratzeburg 6 B2
Rätzlingen 12 B1
Rauen 13 E1
Rauris 30 A3
Rauschenberg 11 D4
Rautenkranz 12 C4
Ravels 9 E3
Ravelsbach 31 E1
Ravenna 46 C1
Ravensburg 28 C2
Ravenstein 9 F2
Ravnkilde 1 E3
Ravnshøj 1 F1
Ravnstrup 2 B1
Ravsted 2 B3
Real *Port.* 60 C2
Real *Spain* 53 E1
Réalmont 41 F3
Réalville 41 E2
Rebais 16 B4
Rebecq 17 D1
Rebild 1 F2
Rebollosa de Jadraque 63 E2
Rebordelo *Port.* 61 D1
Rebordelo *Spain* 53 F1
Recanati 47 E3
Recco 45 D1
Recey-sur-Ource 26 B2
Réchicourt-le-Château 27 E1
Rechlin 7 D3
Rechnitz 31 F3
Rechtenbach 19 E2
Recke 10 C1
Reckingen 36 C1
Recklinghausen 10 B2
Recoaro Terme 38 C3
Recuerda 63 E1
Redange 17 F2
Reddelich 6 C1
Redefin 6 B3
Réding 27 E1
Redinha 60 B4
Rednitzhembach 20 A3
Redon 23 E3
Redondela 53 E3
Redondelo 61 D1
Redondo 67 D3
Redován 76 C1
Redsted 1 D3
Rees 10 A2
Reeßum 5 F3
Reetz *Ger.* 12 C1
Reetz *Ger.* 6 C3
Regen 21 D4
Regensburg 20 C4
Regensdorf 28 A3
Regenstauf 20 C3
Reggello 46 B3
Reggio di Calabria 52 A4
Reggiolo 38 B4
Reggio nell'Emilia 46 A1
Regil 56 C2
Regnitzlosau 20 C1
Régny 35 D2
Regstrup 3 D2
Reguengo 53 E4
Reguengos de Monsaraz 67 D3
Rehau 20 C1
Rehburg (Rehburg-Loccum) 11 E1
Rehden 5 E4
Rehling 29 D1
Rehlingen-Siersburg 18 A3
Rehmsdorf 12 C3
Rehna 6 B2
Reibitz 12 C2
Reichenau an der Rax 31 E2
Reichenbach *Ger.* 12 C4
Reichenbach *Switz.* 36 C1
Reichenberg 19 F2
Reichenfels 31 D4
Reichenthal 30 C1
Reichertsheim 29 F2
Reichling 29 D2
Reichmannsdorf 12 B4
Reicholzheim 19 E2
Reichraming 30 C2
Reichshoffen 18 C4
Reiden 27 F3

Reigada 61 E3
Reignac 32 C4
Reillanne 43 E2
Reillo 64 A4
Reims 16 C3
Reina 68 A4
Reinach *Switz.* 28 A3
Reinach *Switz.* 27 F3
Reinbek 6 A3
Reinberg 7 E1
Reinfeld (Holstein) 6 B2
Reinheim 19 D2
Reinosa 55 E2
Reinsfeld 18 B2
Reisbach 30 A1
Reischach 30 A1
Reiskirchen 11 D4
Reith bei Seefeld 29 E3
Reit im Winkl 30 A3
Rejsby 2 A3
Reken 10 B2
Rekken 10 B1
Relíquias 72 A1
Relleu 71 D3
Rellingen 6 A2
Remagen 10 B4
Rémalard 24 C1
Remda 12 B4
Remels (Uplengen) 5 D3
Remich 17 F3
Remiremont 27 E2
Remolinos 57 D4
Remoulins 42 C2
Remplin 7 D2
Remptendorf 12 B4
Remscheid 10 B3
Rémuzat 43 D1
Rena 68 A2
Renaison 34 C2
Renazé 23 F3
Renchen 27 F1
Rende 52 B2
Rendsburg 6 A1
Renedo *Spain* 55 F1
Renedo *Spain* 62 C1
Renedo de la Vega 55 E3
Renens 36 A1
Renesse 8 C2
Rengsdorf 10 B4
Rennerod 10 C4
Rennertshofen 29 E1
Rennes 23 E2
Renningen 28 B1
Rennweg 30 B4
Renòn 38 C1
Rens 2 B4
Rentería 56 C1
Rentweins-dorf 20 A2
Renwez 17 D2
Renzow 6 B2
Reppelin 7 D1
Reppenstedt 6 A3
Requejo 54 B4
Requena 70 C2
Réquista 41 F2
Resana 39 D3
Resenbro 2 B1
Resende 60 C2
Respaldiza 56 B2
Respenda de la Peña 55 E3
Resse (Wedemark) 11 E1
Ressons-sur-Matz 16 B3
Retamal 68 A3
Rethel 17 D3
Rethem (Aller) 5 F4
Retie 9 E3
Retiers 23 E2
Retortillo 61 F3
Retortillo de Soria 63 E2
Retournac 34 C4
Retuerta del Bullaque 68 C2
Retz 31 E1
Reuden 12 C1
Reuilly 25 D4
Reurieth 11 F4
Reus 58 B4
Reusel 9 E3
Reut 30 A1
Reute 27 F2
Reuterstadt Stavenhagen 7 D2
Reutlingen 28 B1
Reutte 29 D3
Reuver 10 A3
Revel 41 F3
Revello 44 A1
Revigny-sur-Ornain 17 E4
Revilla de Collazos 55 E3
Revilla del Campo 55 F3
Revin 17 D2
Revine-Lago 39 D2
Revò 38 C1
Reyrieux 35 E2
Rezé 23 E4
Rezzato 38 A3
Rezzo 44 B2
Rezzoaglio 45 D1
Rhade 5 F3
Rhaunen 18 B2
Rheda-Wiedenbrück 10 C2
Rhede 10 A2
Rhede (Ems) 5 D3
Rheinau 27 F1
Rheinbach 10 B4
Rheinberg 10 A2
Rheinböllen 18 C2
Rheinbreitbach 10 B4
Rheine 10 B1
Rheinfelden 27 F3
Rheinsberg 7 D3
Rheinstetten 19 D4
Rheinzabern 18 C3
Rhêmes-Notre-Dame 36 B3
Rhêmes-St-Georges 36 B3
Rhenen 9 E2
Rhinau 27 F1
Rhinow 7 D4
Rho 37 D3
Rhoden (Diemelstadt) 11 D3
Riace 52 B3
Riachos 66 B2
Riaillé 23 F3
Rial 53 E3
Rialb de Noguera 58 C2
Riano 48 C2
Riaño 55 D2
Rians 43 E3
Riantec 22 C3
Rianxo 53 E3
Riaz 36 B1
Riba 55 F2
Ribadavia 53 F3
Ribadelago 54 B4
Riba de Mouro 53 E4
Ribadeo 54 A1
Riba de Saelices 63 F2
Ribadesella 55 D1
Ribaforada 57 D4
Ribafrecha 56 C3
Riba-roja d'Ebre 58 B4
Riba-roja de Turia 71 D1
Ribe 2 A3
Ribécourt-Dreslincourt 16 B3
Ribeira 60 B1
Ribeira de Pena 60 C1
Ribemont 16 C2
Ribérac 33 D4
Ribera del Fresno 67 F3
Ribesalbes 65 D4
Ribes de Freser 59 D2
Ribnitz-Damgarten 7 D1
Ribota 63 D1
Ricadi 52 A3
Riccia 50 A1
Riccio 46 C4
Riccione 47 D2
Riccò del Golfo di Spezia 45 E2
Richelieu 24 B4
Richtenberg 7 D1
Rickling 6 A2
Ricla 64 B1
Ridderkerk 9 D2
Riddes 36 B2
Riec-sur-Belon 22 B3
Ried 36 C2
Riede 5 F4
Riedenburg 20 B4
Rieder 12 B2
Ried im Innkreis 30 B2
Ried im Oberinntal 29 D4
Ried im Zillertal 29 F3
Ried in der Riedmark 30 C1
Riedisheim 27 F3
Riedlingen 28 B2
Riegelsberg 18 B3
Riegersburg 31 E4
Riego de la Vega 54 C3
Riehe (Suthfeld) 11 E1
Riehen 27 F3
Rielasingen-Worblingen 28 B3
Riello 54 C3
Rielves 62 C4
Riemst 9 F4
Riepsdorf 6 B1
Riesa 13 D3
Rieseby 2 B4
Riestedt 12 B3
Rietberg 11 D2
Rieth 7 F2
Rieti 48 C1
Rietschen 13 F3
Rieumes 41 D3
Rieupeyroux 41 F2
Rieux *France* 23 D3
Rieux *France* 41 E4
Riez 43 F2
Rifiano 38 C1
Rigaud 44 A2
Rignac 41 F1
Rignano Flaminio 48 C1
Rignano Garganico 50 B1
Rignano sull'Arno 46 B3
Rijen 9 E2
Rijkevorsel 9 E3
Rijnsburg 9 D1
Rijsbergen 9 D2
Rijssen 10 A1
Rijswijk 9 D1
Rilhac-Rancon 33 E2
Rillieux-la-Pape 35 E2
Rillo 64 C3
Rillo de Gallo 64 A2
Rimbach *Ger.* 19 D2
Rimbach *Germany* 21 D3
Rimini 47 D2
Rimpar 19 F2
Rimsting 29 F2
Rinchnach 21 D4
Rincón de la Victoria 74 C3
Rincón de Soto 56 C3
Rindsholm 2 B1
Ringe 2 C3
Ringkøbing 2 A1
Ringleben 12 B3
Ringsted 3 E3
Rinkenæs 2 B4
Rinteln 11 D1
Rio Caldo 60 C1
Rio de Mel 61 D2
Rio de Moinhos *Port.* 66 C4
Rio de Moinhos *Port.* 67 D3
Rio de Moinhos *Port.* 66 C4
Rio de Onor 54 B4
Rio di Pusteria 38 C1
Riofrío 62 B3
Riofrío de Aliste 54 B4
Ríogordo 74 C3
Rioja 75 F3
Riolobos 67 F1
Riolo Terme 46 C2
Riom 34 B2
Riomaggiore 45 E2
Rio Maior 66 B2
Rio Marina 46 A4
Riom-ès-Montagnes 34 B4
Rion-des-Landes 40 B2
Rionegro del Puente 54 B4
Rio nell'Elba 46 A4
Rionero in Vulture 50 B3
Rionero Sannitico 49 E2
Rions 40 B1
Riorges 34 C2
Ríos 54 A4
Rioseco de Tapia 54 C3
Rio Tinto 60 B2
Rio Torto 61 D1
Rioz 27 D3
Ripacandida 50 B3
Ripalimosano 49 F2
Riparbella 46 A3
Ripatransone 47 F4
Ripe 47 E3
Ripi 49 D3
Ripoll 59 D2
Riquewihr 27 E2
Riscle 40 C3
Risum-Lindholm 2 A4
Ritterhude 5 E3
Rittersdorf 18 A2
Rittersgrün 13 D4
Riudarenes 59 E3
Riudecols 58 B4
Riudoms 58 B4
Riva del Garda 38 B2
Riva di Solto 38 A2
Riva di Tures 29 F4
Rivanazzano 37 D4
Rivardo Ligure 45 D1
Rivarolo Canavese 36 C3
Rivarolo Mantovano 38 B4
Rivas-Vaciamadrid 63 D3
Rive-de-Gier 35 D3
Rivedoux-Plage 32 A2
Rivello 50 B4
Rivergaro 37 E4
Rivero 55 F2
Rivery 16 A2
Rives 35 E3
Rivesaltes 42 A4
Rivignano 39 E2
Rivodutri 48 C1
Rivoli 36 B4
Rivolta d'Adda 37 E3
Rixensart 9 D4
Rixheim 27 F3
Rizziconi 52 A3
Ro 39 D4
Roa 55 F4
Roager 2 A3
Roanne 34 C2
Robbio 37 D3
Robecco d'Oglio 38 A4
Röbel 7 D3
Robella 36 C4
Robilante 44 B2
Robion 43 D2
Robledo 70 A3
Robledo de Chavela 62 C3
Robledo del Mazo 68 C1
Robledollano 68 B1
Robles de la Valcueva 54 C2
Robliza de Cojos 62 A2
Robregordo 63 D2
Robres 57 E4
Robres del Castillo 56 C3
Rocafort de Queralt 58 C4
Rocamadour 33 E4
Roca Vecchia 51 F4
Roccabianca 38 A4
Roccadaspide 50 A3
Rocca d'Evandro 49 E3
Rocca di Cambio 49 D1
Rocca di Mezzo 49 D1
Rocca di Neto 52 C2
Rocca di Papa 48 C2
Roccafranca 38 A3
Roccagloriosa 50 B4
Roccagorga 49 D3
Rocca Grimalda 44 C1
Rocca Imperiale 50 C4
Roccalbegna 46 B4
Roccamandolfi 49 E3
Rocca Massima 48 C2
Roccamonfina 49 E3
Roccamontepiano 49 E1
Roccanova 50 C4
Rocca Pia 49 E2
Roccaraso 49 E2
Rocca San Casciano 46 C2
Rocca San Giovanni 49 F1
Roccasecca 49 E3
Roccasecca dei Volsci 49 D3
Rocca Sinibalda 48 C1
Roccastrada 46 B4
Roccavione 44 B2
Roccella Ionica 52 B4
Rocchetta Sant'Antonio 50 B2
Rochechouart 33 D3
Rochefort *Belgium* 17 E2
Rochefort *France* 32 B2
Rochefort-en-Terre 23 D3
Rochefort-Montagne 34 B3
Rochefort-sur-Nenon 26 C4
Roche-la-Molière 35 D3
Roche-lez-Beaupré 27 D3
Rochemaure 42 C1
Rocheservière 23 E4
Rochin 16 B1
Rochlitz 13 D3
Rociana del Condado 73 D2
Rockenberg 11 D4
Rockenhausen 18 C3
Röcknitz 13 D3
Rocroi 17 D2
Rodach bei Coburg 20 A1
Roda de Ter 59 D3
Rodalben 18 C3
Rødby 3 D4
Rødbyhavn 3 D4
Rødding *Denmark* 2 B3
Rødding *Denmark* 2 B1
Rødding *Denmark* 1 D3
Rodeiro 53 F3
Rødekro 2 B3
Rodellar 58 A2
Roden 4 C3
Ródenas 64 B3
Rodenkirchen (Stadland) 5 E3
Rödental 20 A1
Rodewald 5 F4
Rodewisch 12 C4
Rodez 41 F1
Rodheim-Bieber 11 D4
Rodi Garganico 50 B1
Roding 20 C3
Rødkærsbro 2 B1
Rodleben 12 C2

Rødovre **3** E2
Rodrigas **54** A1
Rødvig **3** E3
Roermond **10** A3
Roeselare **8** B3
Roetgen **10** A4
Rofrano **50** B4
Rogätz **12** B1
Roggenburg **28** C1
Roggendorf **6** B2
Roggentin **7** D3
Roggiano Gravina **52** B1
Roghudi **52** A4
Rogil **72** A2
Rogliano **52** B2
Rognac **43** D3
Rognes **43** D3
Rognonas **43** D2
Rohan **23** D2
Röhlingen **19** F4
Rohlsdorf *Ger.* **6** C3
Rohlsdorf *Ger.* **7** D3
Rohr **11** F4
Rohrau **31** F2
Rohrbach **29** E1
Rohrbach in Oberösterreich **30** C1
Rohrbach-lès-Bitche **18** B4
Rohrberg **6** B4
Röhrmoos **29** E1
Röhrnbach **30** B1
Rohrsen **5** F4
Roisel **16** B2
Roiz **55** E1
Rojales **76** C1
Roklum **11** F1
Rolampont **26** C2
Rold **1** F3
Rolde **4** C4
Rollán **62** A2
Rolle **36** A1
Rolsted **2** C3
Rom **6** C3
Roma **48** C2
Romagnano Sesia **36** C3
Romagné **23** F2
Romainmôtier **27** D4
Romano d'Ezzelino **38** C2
Romano di Lombardia **38** A3
Romanones **63** E3
Romanshorn **28** B3
Romans-sur-Isère **35** E4
Rombas **17** F3
Rombiolo **52** A3
Romeira **66** B2
Romeu **61** E1
Römhild **20** A1
Romillé **23** E2
Romilly-sur-Seine **25** F1
Rommerskirchen **10** A3
Romont **27** E4
Romorantin-Lanthenay **25** D3
Romrod **11** E4
Rønbjerg **2** B1
Roncade **39** D3
Roncadelle **38** A3
Roncal **57** E2
Roncegno **38** C2
Roncesvalles **57** D2
Ronchamp **27** E3
Ronchi dei Legionari **39** F2
Ronciglione **48** B1
Ronco Canavese **36** B3
Roncone **38** B2
Ronco Scrivia **45** D1
Ronda **74** B3
Rønde **2** C1
Rondissone **36** C4
Rønnebæk **3** E3
Ronneburg **12** C4
Rønnede **3** E3
Ronnenberg **11** E1
Ronsberg **29** D2
Ronse **8** C4
Ronshausen **11** E4
Roordahuizum **4** B3
Roosendaal **9** D2
Roperuelos del Páramo **54** C3
Roquebillière **44** A2
Roquebrune-Cap-Martin **44** B3
Roquebrune-sur-Argens **43** F3
Roquecourbe **41** F3
Roquefort **40** B2
Roquemaure **43** D2
Roquesteron **44** A2
Roquetas **65** E2
Roquetas de Mar **75** F3
Roquevaire **43** E3
Rørby **3** D2
Rorschach **28** C3
Rørvig **3** E2
Rosà **38** C3
Rosal de la Frontera **67** D4
Rosans **43** E1
Rosário **72** B2
Rosarno **52** A3
Rosbach vor der Höhe **19** D1
Rosche **6** B4
Roscigno **50** B4
Roscoff **22** B1
Rosdorf **11** E2
Rose **52** B2
Rosell **65** E3
Rosenfeld **28** A1
Rosengarten **6** A3
Rosenheim **29** F2
Rosenow **7** E2
Roses **59** F2
Roseto Capo Spulico **50** C4
Roseto degli Abruzzi **47** F4
Roseto Valfortore **50** A2
Rosheim **27** F1
Rosières **34** C4
Rosières-en-Santerre **16** B2
Rosignano Marittimo **46** A3
Rositz **12** C3
Roskilde **3** E2
Roskow **13** D1
Röslau **20** C2
Roslev **1** E3
Rosmalen **9** E2
Rosmaninhal **67** E1
Rosolina **39** D4
Rosolina Mare **39** D4
Rosporden **22** B2
Rösrath **10** B4
Rossano **52** B1
Rossano Veneto **39** D3
Roßbach **30** A1
Rosselló **58** B3
Roßhaupten **29** D3
Rossiglione **44** C1
Rössing (Nordstemmen) **11** E1
Rossio ao Sul do Tejo **66** C2
Roßla **12** B3
Roßlau **12** C2
Roßleithen **30** C3
Rossow **7** D3
Roßtal **20** A3
Roßwein **13** D3
Rostock **7** D2
Rostrenen **22** C2
Rostrup **1** F3
Rota **73** E3
Rota Greca **52** B1
Rot am See **19** F3
Rot an der Rot **28** C2
Rotello **50** A1
Rotenburg (Wümme) **5** F3
Rotenburg an der Fulda **11** E3
Rötgesbüttel **11** F1
Rotgülden **30** B4
Roth **20** B3
Röthenbach an der Pegnitz **20** B3
Rothenberg **19** D3
Rothenbuch **19** E2
Rothenburg (Oberlausitz) **13** F3
Rothenburg ob der Tauber **19** F3
Rothenfels **19** E2
Rothenschirmbach **12** B3
Rothenstein **12** B4
Rotheux-Rimière **17** E1
Rothwesten (Fuldatal) **11** E3
Rotondella **50** C4
Rotselaar **9** D3
Rott **29** D2
Rottach-Egern **29** E3
Rott am Inn **29** F2
Rottenacker **28** C2
Röttenbach **20** A3
Rottenbach **12** B4
Rottenbuch **29** D2
Rottenburg am Neckar **28** B1
Rottenburg an der Laaber **29** F1
Rottendorf **19** F2
Rottenmann **30** C3
Rotterdam **9** D2
Rotthalmünster **30** B1
Röttingham **19** F3
Rottleberode **12** A2
Rottofreno **37** E4
Rottweil **28** A2
Rötz **20** C3
Roubaix **16** B1
Rouen **15** E3
Rouffach **27** E2
Rouffignac **33** E4
Rougé **23** E3
Rougemont **27** D3
Rougemont-le-Château **27** E3
Rouillac **32** C3
Rouillé **32** C1
Roujan **42** B3
Roulans **27** D3
Roumazières-Loubert **33** D2
Roumoules **43** F2
Roure **36** B4
Rousset **43** E3
Roussillon *France* **43** D2
Roussillon *France* **35** E3
Rousson **42** C2
Routot **15** E3
Rovato **38** A3
Rovegno **45** D1
Roverbella **38** B3
Roveredo **37** D2
Rovereto **38** C2
Rövershagen **7** D1
Roviano **48** C2
Rovigo **39** D4
Royan **32** B3
Royat **34** B3
Roybon **35** E4
Roye **16** B2
Royère-de-Vassivière **33** F3
Royuela **64** B3
Rozalén del Monte **63** E4
Rozay-en-Brie **16** B4
Rozoy-sur-Serre **17** D2
Rozzano **37** D3
Ru **53** F2
Rua **61** D2
Ruaudin **24** B2
Rubano **38** C3
Rubayo **55** F1
Rubena **55** F3
Rübenau **13** D4
Rubí **59** D4
Rubiá **54** A3
Rubí de Bracamonte **62** B2
Rubielos de la Cérida **64** B3
Rubielos de Mora **64** C4
Rubiera **46** A1
Rublacedo de Abajo **55** F3
Rückersdorf **13** E2
Rudelzhausen **29** E1
Rudersberg **19** E4
Rudersdorf **31** E4
Rüdersdorf Berlin **13** E1
Rüdesheim am Rhein **18** C2
Rudkøbing **2** C4
Rüdnitz **7** E4
Rudolstadt **12** B4
Ruds Vedby **3** D3
Rue **15** F1
Rueda **62** B1
Rueda de Jalón **64** B1
Rueil-Malmaison **16** A4
Ruelle-sur-Touvre **33** D3
Ruente **55** E2
Ruffano **51** F4
Ruffec **33** D2
Ruffiac **23** D3
Ruffieux **35** F2
Rufina **46** B2
Rügland **20** A3
Rugles **24** C1
Ruhla **11** F4
Ruhland **13** E3
Ruhmannsfelden **21** D4
Rühn **6** C2
Ruhpolding **30** A2
Ruhstorf an der Rott **30** B1
Ruidera **69** F2
Ruinen **4** B4
Ruinerwold **4** B4
Ruiselede **8** C3
Ruivães **60** C1
Rully **26** B4
Rum **29** E3
Rumelange **17** F3
Rumes **16** C1
Rumigny **17** D2
Rumilly **35** F2
Rumst **9** D3
Rungsted **3** F2
Runkel **18** C1
Ruoms **42** C1
Ruoti **50** B3
Rupt-sur-Moselle **27** E2
Rus **69** E4
Rüsselsheim **19** D2
Russi **46** C1
Rust **31** F2
Ruswil **28** A4
Rute **74** C2
Rüthen **11** D2
Rüti **28** B3
Rutigliano **51** D2
Rutino **50** A4
Rutten **4** B4
Ruurlo **10** A1
Ruvo del Monte **50** B3
Ruvo di Puglia **50** C2
Ruynes-en-Margeride **34** B4
Ry **2** B1
Ryde **2** A1
Ryes **14** C3
Rynkeby **2** C3
Ryomgård **2** C1
Ryslinge **2** C3
Rysum (Krummhörn) **4** C3
Rzepin **13** F1

S

Saal **7** D1
Saal an der Donau **20** C4
Saalbach-Hinterglemm **30** A3
Saalburg **12** B4
Saales **27** E1
Saalfeld **12** B4
Saalfelden am Steinernen Meer **30** A3
Saanen **36** B1
Saarbrücken **18** B3
Saarburg **18** A3
Saarlouis **18** B3
Saarwellingen **18** B3
Saas **28** C4
Saas Fee **36** C2
Saas Grund **36** C2
Sabadell **59** D4
Sabaudia **49** D3
Sabbionetta **38** B4
Sabero **55** D2
Sabiñánigo **57** F3
Sabiote **69** E4
Sables-d'Or-les-Pins **23** D1
Sablé-sur-Sarthe **24** A2
Sablet **43** D2
Sabres **40** B2
Sabro **2** C1
Sabrosa **61** D2
Sabugal **61** D3
Sabugueiro *Port.* **66** C3
Sabugueiro *Port.* **61** D3
Sacañet **64** C4
Sacavém **66** B3
Sacecorbo **63** F2
Sacedón **63** F3
Saceruela **68** C2
Sachseln **28** A4
Sachsenberg (Lichtenfels) **11** D3
Sachsenbrunn **12** A4
Sachsenburg **30** B4
Sachsenhagen **11** E1
Sachsenhausen (Waldeck) **11** D3
Sachsenheim **19** D4
Sacile **39** E2
Sacramenia **63** D1
Sada **53** E1
Sádaba **57** D3
Sæby *Denmark* **1** F1
Sæby *Denmark* **3** D3
Sæd **2** A4
Saelices **63** E4
Saelices de la Sal **63** F2
Saelices del Rio **55** D3
Saelices de Mayorga **55** D4
Saerbeck **10** C1
Særslev **2** C3
Saeul **17** F2
Safara **67** D4
Saffré **23** E3
Sagard **7** E1
Sage **5** E4
Sagres **72** A3
Sagunto **71** D1
Sagy **35** E1
Sahagún **55** D3
Sahl **2** B1
Sahún **58** B2
Saillagouse-Llo **59** D2
Saillans **43** D1

Sail-Sous-Couzan **34** C3
Sains-Richaumont **16** C2
St Aegyd am Neuwalde **31** E2
St-Affrique **42** A2
St Agata de'Goti **49** F3
St Agata del Bianco **52** A4
St Agata di Esaro **52** A1
St-Agnant **32** B2
St-Agnant-de-Versillat **33** E2
St-Agrève **35** D4
St-Aignan **24** C4
St-Aignan-sur-Roë **23** F2
St-Aigulin **32** C4
St-Alban **23** D1
St-Alban-d'Ay **35** D4
St-Alban-sur-Limagnole **42** B1
St-Amand-en-Puisaye **25** F3
St-Amand-les-Eaux **16** C1
St-Amand-Longpré **24** C3
St-Amand-Montrond **34** A1
St-Amans **42** B1
St-Amans-des-Cots **42** A1
St-Amans-Soult **41** F3
St-Amant-de-Boixe **32** C3
St-Amant-Roche-Savine **34** C3
St-Amant-Tallende **34** B3
St-Amarin **27** E2
St-Ambroix **42** C2
St-Amour **35** E1
St-Andiol **43** D2
St Andrä **31** D4
St-André **59** E2
St Andrea Apostolo dello Ionio **52** B3
St-André-de-Corcy **35** E2
St-André-de-Cubzac **32** C4
St-André-de-l'Eure **15** F4
St-André-de-Sangonis **42** B3
St-André-de-Valborgne **42** B2
St-André-le-Gaz **35** F3
St-André-les-Alpes **43** F2
St-André-les-Vergers **26** A2
St Anna am Aigen **31** E4
St Annaland **9** D2
St Annaparochie **4** B3
St-Anthème **34** C3
St Anton an der Jeßnitz **31** D2
St-Antonin-Noble-Val **41** E2
St-Apollinaire **26** C3
St Arcangelo **50** C4
St-Arnoult-en-Yvelines **16** A4
St-Astier **33** D4
St-Auban **43** F2
St-Auban-sur-l'Ouvèze **43** D2
St-Aubin **26** C4
St-Aubin-d'Aubigné **23** E2
St-Aubin-du-Cormier **23** E2
St-Aubin-lès-Elbeuf **15** E3
St-Aubin-sur-Mer **14** C3
St Augustin **10** B4
St-Aulaye **32** C4
St-Avé **23** D3
St-Avertin **24** C3
St-Avold **18** A3
St-Ay **25** D2
St-Aygulf **43** F3
St-Barthélemy-de-Vals **35** E4
St-Bauzille-de-Putois **42** B2
St-Béat **41** D4
St-Beauzély **42** A2
St-Benin-d'Azy **25** F4
St-Benoît **33** D1
St-Benoît-du-Sault **33** E1
St-Benoît-sur-Loire **25** E2
St-Béron **35** F3
St-Berthevin **23** F2
St-Blaise **27** E4
St-Blin-Semilly **26** C2
St-Bonnet-de-Joux **35** D1
St-Bonnet-en-Champsaur **43** E1
St-Bonnet-le-Château **34** C3
St-Branchs **24** C4
St-Brevin-les-Pins **23** D4
St-Briac-sur-Mer **23** D1
St-Brice-en-Coglès **23** E1
St-Brieuc **23** D1
St-Bris-le-Vineux **25** F3
St-Calais **24** C2
St-Cannat **43** D3
St-Céré **33** F4
St-Cergue **35** F1
St-Cergues **36** A2
St-Cernin **34** A4
St-Chaffrey **36** A4
St-Chamas **43** D3
St-Chamond **35** D3
St-Chaptes **42** C2
St-Chef **35** E3
St-Chély-d'Apcher **42** A1
St-Chély-d'Aubrac **42** A1
St-Chinian **42** A3
St-Christol **43** E2
St-Christol-lès-Alès **42** C2
St-Christoly-Médoc **32** B3
St-Christophe **36** B3
St-Christophe-en-Bazelle **25** D4
St-Ciers-sur-Gironde **32** B4
St-Clair-du-Rhône **35** D3
St-Clar **41** D2
St-Claud **33** D2
St-Claude **35** F1
St-Clément **25** F2
St-Cosme-en-Vairais **24** B2
St-Cyprien *France* **33** E4
St-Cyprien *France* **59** E2
St-Cyr-sur-Loire **24** B3
St-Denis **16** A4
St-Denis-d'Anjou **24** A3
St-Denis-de-Gastines **23** F2
St-Denis-de-Jouhet **33** F1
St-Denis-de-Pile **32** C4
St-Denis-d'Oléron **32** A2
St-Didier-en-Velay **35** D4
St-Dié **27** E2
St-Dier-d'Auvergne **34** C3
St-Dizier **17** E4
St-Dolay **23** D3
St-Doulchard **25** E4
Sainte-Adresse **15** D3
Sainte-Bazeille **40** C1
Ste-Croix **27** D4
Sainte-Croix-Volvestre **41** D4
Sainte-Énimie **42** B1
Sainte-Feyre **33** F2
Sainte-Foy-de-Peyrolières **41** D3
Sainte-Foy-la-Grande **32** C4
Sainte-Foy-l'Argentière **35** D3
Sainte-Foy-Tarentaise **36** A3
Sainte-Geneviève **16** A3
Sainte-Geneviève-sur-Argence **42** A1
Sainte-Hélène **32** B4
Sainte-Hermine **32** B1
Sainte-Livrade-sur-Lot **41** D1
Sainte-Lizaigne **25** D4
St-Éloy-les-Mines **34** B2
Sainte-Marie **59** E1
Sainte-Marie-aux-Mines **27** E2
Sainte-Maure-de-Touraine **24** B4
Sainte-Maxime **43** F3
Sainte-Menehould **17** E3
Sainte-Mère-Église **14** B3
Sainte-Pazanne **23** E4
Sainte-Radegonde **24** A4
St Erme-Outre-et-Ramecourt **16** C3
Saintes **32** B3
Sainte-Savine **26** A1
Sainte-Sévère-sur-Indre **33** F1
St-Estèphe **32** B4
St-Estève **59** E1
Sainte-Suzanne **24** A2
St-Étienne **35** D3
St-Étienne-de-Baïgorry **40** A4
St-Étienne-de-Montluc **23** E4
St-Étienne-de-St-Geoirs **35** E3
St-Étienne-de-Tinée **44** A2
St-Étienne-du-Bois **35** E2
St-Étienne-du-Rouvray **15** E3
St-Étienne-en-Dévoluy **43** E1
St-Étienne-les-Orgues **43** E2
St-Étienne-lès-Remiremont **27** E2
Sainte-Tulle **43** E3
St-Fargeau **25** F3
St-Félicien **35** D4
St-Félix-Lauragais **41** F3
St-Firmin **35** F4
St-Florent-des-Bois **32** A1
St-Florentin **25** F2
St-Florent-le-Vieil **23** F3
St-Florent-sur-Cher **25** E4
St-Flour **34** B4
St-Fons **35** E3
St-Fort-sur-Gironde **32** B3
St-François-Longchamp **36** A3
St-Front-de-Pradoux **33** D4
St-Fulgent **32** B1
St Gallenkirch **28** C4
St-Galmier **35** D3
St Gangloff **12** C4
St-Gaudens **41** D4
St-Gaultier **33** E1
St-Gély-du-Fesc **42** B3
St-Genest-Malifaux **35** D3
St-Geniez-d'Olt **42** A1
St-Genis-de-Saintonge **32** B3
St-Genis-Pouilly **35** F2
St-Genix-sur-Guiers **35** F3
St-Genou **24** C4
St Georgen am Walde **31** D1
St Georgen im Schwarzwald **28** A2
St-Georges-Buttavent **23** F2
St-Georges-de-Didonne **32** B3
St-Georges-de-Luzençon **42** A2
St-Georges-de-Mons **34** B2
St-Georges-des-Groseillers **23** F1
St-Georges-d'Espéranche **35** E3
St-Georges-d'Oléron **32** A2
St-Georges-du-Vièvre **15** E3
St-Georges-en-Couzan **34** C3
St-Georges-lès-Baillargeaux **33** D1
St-Georges-sur-Baulche **25** F2
St-Georges-sur-Cher **24** C3
St-Georges-sur-Loire **23** F3
St-Gérand-le-Puy **34** C2
St-Germain-de-Calberte **42** B2
St-Germain-des-Fossés **34** C2
St-Germain-d'Esteuil **32** B4
St-Germain-du-Bel-Air **41** E1
St-Germain-du-Bois **26** C4
St-Germain-du-Corbeis **24** B1
St-Germain-du-Plain **26** B4
St-Germain-du-Puy **25** E4
St-Germain-du-Teil **42** A1
St-Germain-en-Laye **16** A4
St-Germain-Laval **34** C3
St-Germain-Lembron **34** B3
St-Germain-les-Belles **33** E3
St-Germain-l'Herm **34** C3
St-Gervais **23** E4
St-Gervais-d'Auvergne **34** B2
St-Gervais-la-Forêt **24** C3
St-Gervais-les-Bains **36** A2
St-Gervais-les-Trois-Clochers **33** D1
St-Gervais-sur-Mare **42** A3
St-Géry **41** E1
St-Ghislain **16** C1
St-Gildas-de-Rhuys **23** D3
St-Gildas-des-Bois **23** E3
St Gilgen **30** B2
St-Gilles **42** C3
St-Gilles-Croix-de-Vie **32** A1
St-Gillis-Waas **9** D3
St-Gingolph **36** A1
St-Girons **41** D4
St-Girons-Plage **40** A2
St Goar **18** C2
St Goarshausen **18** C1
St-Gobain **16** C3
St-Guénolé **22** A3
St-Haon-le-Châtel **34** C2
St-Héand **35** D3
St-Herblain **23** E4
St-Hilaire **41** F4
St-Hilaire-de-Brethmas **42** C2
St-Hilaire-de-Riez **32** A1
St-Hilaire-des-Loges **32** B1
St-Hilaire-de-Villefranche **32** C2
St-Hilaire-du-Harcouët **23** F1
St-Hilaire-du-Rosier **35** E4
St-Hilaire-St-Florent **24** A4
St-Hippolyte *France* **27** F2
St-Hippolyte *France* **27** E3
St-Hippolyte-du-Fort **42** B2
St-Hubert **17** E2
St-Imier **27** E4
St Ingbert **18** B3
St-Jacques-de-la-Lande **23** E2
St Jakob im Walde **31** E3
St Jakob in Defereggen **29** F4
St-James **23** E1
St-Jean-Brévelay **23** D3
St-Jean-d'Angély **32** C2
St-Jean-d'Assé **24** B2
St-Jean-de-Bournay **35** E3
St-Jean-de-Braye **25** D2
St-Jean-de-Daye **14** B3
St-Jean-de-la-Ruelle **25** D2
St-Jean-de-Losne **26** C4
St-Jean-de-Luz **57** D1
St-Jean-de-Maurienne **36** A3
St-Jean-de-Muzols **35** E4
St-Jean-de-Sixt **36** A2
St-Jean-de-Védas **42** B3
St-Jean-d'Illac **32** B4
St-Jean-du-Bruel **42** B2
St-Jean-du-Falga **41** E4
St-Jean-du-Gard **42** B2
St-Jean-Pied-de-Port **40** A4
St-Jeoire **36** A2
St-Joachim **23** D3
St Johann am Tauern **30** C3
St Johann im Pongau **30** B3
St Johann im Walde **30** A4
St Johann in Tirol **30** A3
St-Jory **41** E3
St-Jouan-des-Guérets **23** E1
St-Jouin-Bruneval **15** D2
St-Julien **35** E1
St-Julien-Chapteuil **34** C4
St-Julien-de-Concelles **23** E4
St-Julien-de-Vouvantes **23** F3
St-Julien-du-Sault **25** F2
St-Julien-en-Born **40** A2
St-Julien-en-Genevois **35** F2
St-Julien-l'Ars **33** D1
St-Julien-les-Rosiers **42** C2
St-Junien **33** E2
St-Just **42** C2
St-Just-en-Chaussée **16** A3
St-Just-en-Chevalet **34** C2
St-Just-la-Pendue **35** D2
St-Just-Luzac **32** B3
St-Just-Sauvage **25** F1
St-Just-St-Rambert **35** D3
St-Katelijne-Waver **9** D3
St-Lambert-des-Levées **24** A3
St Lambrecht **30** C4
St-Lary-Soulan **58** A1
St-Laurent-d'Aigouze **42** C3
St-Laurent-de-Cerdans **59** E2
St-Laurent-de-Chamousset **35** D3

St-Laurent-de-la-Cabrerisse **42** A4
St-Laurent-de-Neste **40** C4
St-Laurent-des-Autels **23** F4
St-Laurent-du-Pont **35** F3
St-Laurent-du-Var **44** A3
St-Laurent-en-Grandvaux **35** F1
St-Laurent-Médoc **32** B4
St-Laurent-Nouan **25** D3
St-Laurent-sur-Gorre **33** E3
St-Laurent-sur-Sèvre **23** F4
St-Léger **17** F2
St-Léger-des-Vignes **25** F4
St-Léger-en-Yvelines **16** A4
St-Léger-sous-Beuvray **26** A4
St-Léger-sur-Dheune **26** B4
St-Léonard **27** E2
St-Léonard-de-Noblat **33** E3
St Leonhard am Forst **31** D2
St Leonhard am Hornerwald **31** E1
St Leonhard im Pitztal **29** D4
St-Lizier **41** D4
St-Lô **14** C3
St Lorenz **30** B2
St Lorenzen im Gitschtal **30** B4
St Lorenzen im Lesachtal **30** A4
St Lorenzen im Mürztal **31** D3
St Lorenzen ob Murau **30** C4
St-Loubès **32** C4
St-Louis **27** F3
St-Loup-Lamairé **32** C1
St-Loup-sur-Semouse **27** D2
St-Lubin-des-Joncherets **24** C1
St-Lunaire **23** D1
St-Lyé **26** A1
St-Lys **41** D3
St Maartensdijk **9** D2
St-Macaire **40** B1
St-Macaire-en-Mauges **23** F4
St-Magne-de-Castillon **32** C4
St-Maixent-l'École **32** C1
St-Malo **23** E1
St-Malo-de-la-Lande **14** B4
St-Mamert-du-Gard **42** C2
St-Marcel *France* **26** B4
St-Marcel *France* **33** E1
St-Marcel *France* **15** F4
St-Marcel-d'Ardèche **42** C2
St-Marcel-lès-Sauzet **43** D1
St-Marcellin **35** E4
St Marein im Mürztal **31** D3
St Margarethen **5** F2
St Margarethen an der Raab **31** E4
St Margarethen bei Knittelfeld **31** D3
St Margarethen im Burgenland **31** F2
St Märgen **28** A2
St-Maria-Lierde **8** C4
St-Marsal **59** E2
St-Mars-d'Outillé **24** B2
St-Mars-du-Désert **23** E3
St-Mars-la-Brière **24** B2
St-Mars-la-Jaille **23** F3
St-Martens-Latem **8** C3
St-Martin-Boulogne **8** A4
St-Martin-d'Ablois **16** C4
St-Martin-d'Auxigny **25** E4
St-Martin-de-Belleville **36** A3
St-Martin-de-Crau **43** D3
St-Martin-de-Landelles **23** F1
St-Martin-de-Londres **42** B3
St-Martin-de-Ré **32** A2
St-Martin-des-Champs **22** B1
St-Martin-de-Seignanx **40** A3
St-Martin-de-Valamas **35** D4
St-Martin-de-Valgalgues **42** C2
St-Martin-du-Mont **35** E2
St-Martin-du-Var **44** A2
St-Martin-en-Haut **35** D3
St Martin im Mühlkreis **30** C1
St-Martin-le-Beau **24** C3
St-Martin-Valmeroux **34** A4
St-Martin-Vésubie **44** A2
St-Martory **41** D4
St-Mathieu **33** D3
St-Mathurin **32** A1
St-Maur **33** E1
St-Maurice **36** B2
St-Maurice-de-Lignon **35** D4
St-Maurice-des-Lions **33** D2
St-Maurice-la-Souterraine **33** E2
St-Maurice-l'Exil **35** D3
St-Maurice-Navacelles **42** B2
St-Maurice-sur-Moselle **27** E2
St-Max **17** F4
St-Maximin-la-Ste-Baume **43** E3
St-Médard-en-Jalles **32** B4
St-Méen-le-Grand **23** D2
St-Méloir-des-Ondes **23** E1
St-Memmie **17** D4
St-Menoux **34** B1
St Michael im Burgenland **31** F4
St Michael im Lungau **30** B4
St Michael in Obersteiermark **31** D3
St Michaelisdonn **5** F2
St-Michel *France* **17** D2
St-Michel *France* **32** C3
St-Michel-Chef-Chef **23** D4
St-Michel-de-Maurienne **36** A4
St-Michel-en-l'Herm **32** B1
St-Michel-sur-Meurthe **27** E1
St-Mihiel **17** E4
St-Montant **42** C1
St Moritz **38** A1
St-Nabord **27** D2
St-Nazaire **23** D4
St-Nazaire-en-Royans **35** E4
St Nicolaasga **4** B4
St-Nicolas **16** B1
St-Nicolas-d'Aliermont **15** F2
St-Nicolas-de-la-Grave **41** D2
St-Nicolas-de-Port **17** F4
St-Nicolas-de-Redon **23** E3
St-Nicolas-du-Pélem **22** C2
St-Niklaas **9** D3
St Nikolai im Saustal **31** E4
St Nikolai im Sölktal **30** C3
St-Oedenrode **9** E2
St-Omer **8** A4
St-Orens-de-Gameville **41** E3
St Oswald bei Freistadt **30** C1
St Oswald ob Eibiswald **31** D4
St-Ouen **24** C2
St-Ouen-des-Toits **23** F2
St-Pair-sur-Mer **23** E1
St-Palais **40** A4
St-Palais-sur-Mer **32** B3
St-Pal-de-Chalancon **34** C3
St-Pal-de-Mons **35** D4
St Pankraz **30** C2
St-Pardoux-Issac **40** C1
St-Pardoux-la-Rivière **33** D3
St-Parize-le-Châtel **25** F4
St-Paterne **24** B1
St-Paterne-Racan **24** B3
St-Paul-Cap-de-Joux **41** F3
St-Paul-de-Fenouillet **41** F4
St-Paul-de-Jarrat **41** E4
St-Paulien **34** C4
St Paul im Lavanttal **31** D4
St-Paul-lès-Dax **40** A3
St-Paul-Trois-Châteaux **43** D2
St-Pé-de-Bigorre **40** C4
St-Pée-sur-Nivelle **40** A3
St-Péray **35** E4
St-Père-en-Retz **23** E4
St Peter am Kammersberg **30** C3
St Peter am Ottersbach **31** E4
St Peter-Freienstein **31** D3
St Peter in der Au **30** C2
St Peter-Ording **5** E1
St-Philbert-de-Bouaine **23** E4
St-Philbert-de-Grand-Lieu **23** E4
St Philipsland **9** D2
St-Pierre **36** B3
St-Pierre-d'Albigny **35** F3
St-Pierre-de-Chignac **33** D4
St-Pierre-de-Plesguen **23** E1
St-Pierre-des-Corps **24** C3
St-Pierre-des-Échaubrognes **24** A4
St-Pierre-des-Nids **24** A1
St-Pierre-d'Oléron **32** A2
St-Pierre-du-Chemin **32** B1
St-Pierre-du-Mont **40** B2
St-Pierre-Église **14** B2
St-Pierre-en-Faucigny **36** A2
St-Pierre-en-Port **15** E2
St-Pierre-le-Moûtier **25** F4
St-Pierre-lès-Elbeuf **15** E3
St-Pierre-lès-Nemours **25** E2
St-Pierre-Montlimart **23** F4
St-Pierre-Quiberon **22** C3
St-Pierre-sur-Dives **15** D4
St-Pieters-Leeuw **9** D4
St-Pois **23** F1
St-Pol-de-Léon **22** B1
St-Pol-sur-Mer **8** A3
St-Pol-sur-Ternoise **16** A1
St Pölten **31** E2
St-Pons-de-Thomières **42** A3
St-Porchaire **32** B3
St-Pourçain-sur-Sioule **34** B2
St-Prex **36** A1
St-Priest-Taurion **33** E2
St-Privat **33** F4
St-Privat-des-Vieux **42** C2
St-Quentin **16** B2
St-Quirin **27** E1
St Radegund **30** A2
St-Rambert-d'Albon **35** E4
St-Rambert-en-Bugey **35** E2
St-Raphaël **44** A3
St-Rémy-de-Provence **43** D3
St-Rémy-sur-Avre **24** C1
St-Rémy-sur-Durolle **34** C2
St-Renan **22** A1
St-Rhemy **36** B2
St-Riquier **16** A2
St-Romain-sur-Cher **24** C3
St-Romans **35** E4
St-Rome-de-Tarn **42** A2
St Ruprecht an der Raab **31** E4
St-Saëns **15** F2
St-Saturnin-lès-Apt **43** D2
St-Saulge **25** F4
St-Sauves-d'Auvergne **34** B3
St-Sauveur **27** D2
St-Sauveur-en-Puisaye **25** F3
St-Sauveur-Lendelin **14** B3
St-Sauveur-le-Vicomte **14** B3
St-Sauveur-sur-Tinée **44** A2
St-Savin *France* **32** C4
St-Savin *France* **33** D1
St-Savinien **32** B2
St-Sébastien-de-Morsent **15** E4
St-Sébastien-sur-Loire **23** E4
St-Seine-l'Abbaye **26** B3
St-Semin **42** C1
St-Sernin-du-Bois **26** B4
St-Sernin-sur-Rance **41** F2
St-Seurin-sur-l'Isle **32** C4
St-Sever **40** B3
St-Sever-Calvados **23** F1
St-Simon **16** B2
St-Sorlin-d'Arves **36** A4
St-Soupplets **16** B4
St Stefan im Gailtal **39** F1
St Stefan im Rosental **31** E4
St Stefan ob Leoben **31** D3
St Stefan ob Stainz **31** D4
St-Sulpice **41** E3
St-Sulpice-Laurière **33** E2
St-Sulpice-les-Champs **33** F2
St-Sulpice-les-Feuilles **33** E2
St-Sulpice-sur-Lèze **41** E4
St-Sulpice-sur-Risle **24** B1
St-Symphorien **40** B1
St-Symphorien-de-Lay **35** D2
St-Symphorien-d'Ozon **35** E3
St-Symphorien-sur-Coise **35** D3
St-Thégonnec **22** B1
St-Thibéry **42** B3
St-Trivier-de-Courtes **35** E1
St-Trivier-sur-Moignans **35** E2
St-Trojan-les-Bains **32** B3
St-Tropez **43** F3
St-Truiden **9** E4
St Ulrich bei Steyr **30** C2
St-Uze **35** E4
St Valentin **30** C2
St-Valérien **25** F2
St-Valery-en-Caux **15** E2
St-Valery-sur-Somme **15** F1
St-Vallier *France* **35** D1
St-Vallier *France* **35** D4
St-Vallier-de-Thiey **44** A3
St-Varent **32** C1
St-Vaury **33** F2
St Veit am Vogau **31** E4
St Veit an der Glan **30** C4
St Veit an der Gölsen **31** E2
St Veit im Pongau **30** B3
St Veit in Defereggen **30** A4
St-Victoret **43** D3
St-Victor-la-Coste **42** C2
St-Vincent **36** B3
St-Vincent-de-Tyrosse **40** A3
St-Vit **26** C4
St-Vite **41** D1
St-Vith **17** F1
St-Vivien-de-Médoc **32** B3
St Wendel **18** B3
St Willebrord **9** D2
St Wolfgang **29** F1
St Wolfgang im Salzkammergut **30** B2
St-Xandre **32** B2
St-Yan **34** C1
St-Yorre **34** C2
St-Yrieix-la-Perche **33** E3
St-Yrieix-sur-Charente **32** C3
St-Yvy **22** B2
St-Zacharie **43** E3
Saissac **41** F3
Saksild **2** C2
Sakskøbing **3** D4
Sala Consilina **50** B4
Salagnac **33** E4
Salamanca **62** A2
Salandra **50** C3
Salar **74** C2
Salardu **58** B1
Salas **54** B1
Salas de los Infantes **56** A4
Salbertrand **36** A4
Salbris **25** D3
Salching **20** C4
Saldaña **55** E3
Saldón **64** B3
Salduero **56** B4
Sale **37** D4
Salem *Ger.* **28** B2
Salem *Ger.* **6** B2
Salernes **43** F3

Salerno **50** A3
Salers **34** A4
Saleux **16** A2
Salgueiro **67** D1
Salice Salentino **51** E4
Saliceto **44** C1
Salies-de-Béarn **40** B3
Salies-du-Salat **41** D4
Salignac-Eyvignes **33** E4
Salillas de Jalón **64** B1
Salinas *Spain* **54** C1
Salinas *Spain* **70** C3
Salinas de Añana **56** B2
Salinas del Manzano **64** B4
Salinas de Pamplona **57** D2
Salinas de Pisuerga **55** E2
Salindres **42** C2
Saline di Volterra **46** A3
Salins-les-Bains **27** D4
Salir **72** B2
Sall **2** C1
Sallanches **36** A2
Sallent **59** D3
Sallent de Gállego **57** E2
Salles **40** B1
Salles-Curan **42** A2
Salles-d'Angles **32** C3
Salles-d'Aude **42** A4
Salles-la-Source **41** F1
Salles-sur-l'Hers **41** E4
Sallgast **13** E2
Sallingberg **31** D1
Salmerón **63** F3
Salmeroncillos de Abajo **63** F3
Salmoral **62** B3
Salmtal **18** B2
Salò **38** B3
Salobre **70** A3
Salobreña **75** D3
Salon-de-Provence **43** D3
Salorino **67** E1
Salorno **38** C2
Salou **58** C4
Salouël **16** A2
Salsadella **65** E3
Salses-le-Château **42** A4
Salsomaggiore Terme **38** A4
Salt **59** E3
Saltara **47** D3
Salteras **73** E2
Salto **60** C1
Saltum **1** E2
Saludecio **47** D2
Saluggia **36** C4
Salussola **36** C3
Saluzzo **44** B1
Salvacañete **64** B4
Salvagnac **41** E2
Salvaleón **67** E3
Salvaterra de Magos **66** B2
Salvaterra do Extremo **67** E1
Salvatierra **56** C2
Salvatierra de los Barros **67** E3
Salvatierra de Santiago **67** F2
Salve **51** F4
Salviac **41** E1
Salzburg **30** A2
Salzgitter **11** F1
Salzhausen **6** A3
Salzhemmendorf **11** E1
Salzkotten **11** D2
Salzmünde **12** C2
Salzwedel **6** B4
Salzweg **30** B1
Samadet **40** B3
Samarate **37** D3
Samatan **41** D3
Sambade **61** E1
Sambiase **52** B2
Samboal **62** C2
Sambuca Pistoiese **46** B2
Sambuco **44** A1
Samedan **38** A1
Sameiro **61** D3
Samer **16** A1
Sames **55** D2
Samil **61** E1
Samir de los Caños **61** F1
Sammichele di Bari **51** D3
Samnaun **29** D4
Samoëns **36** A2
Samões **61** D2
Samolaco **37** E2
Samora Correia **66** B2
Samos **54** A3
Samper de Calanda **65** D2
Sampeyre **44** A1
Sampierdarena **45** D1
Samswegen **12** B1
Samtens **7** E1
San Adrián **56** C3
San Agustín de Guadalix **63** D3
San Amaro **53** F3
San Andrés del Rabanedo **54** C3
San Antolín de Ibias **54** A2
San Antoniño **53** E3
San Antonio **70** C1
Sanary-sur-Mer **43** E4
San Asensio **56** B3
San Bartolomé de las Abiertas **62** B4
San Bartolomé de la Torre **73** D2
San Bartolomé de Pinares **62** C3
San Bartolomeo al Mare **44** B2
San Bartolomeo in Galdo **50** A2
San Benedetto dei Marsi **49** D2
San Benedetto del Tronto **47** F4
San Benedetto Po **38** B4
San Benito **68** C3
San Benito de la Contienda **67** E3
San Biagio di Callalta **39** D3
San Bonifacio **38** C3
San Buono **49** F2
San Candido **39** D1
San Carlos del Valle **69** E3
San Casciano dei Bagni **46** C4
San Casciano in Val di Pesa **46** B3
San Cataldo **51** F3
San Cebrián de Castro **62** A1
Sancergues **25** E4
Sancerre **25** E3
San Cesario sul Panaro **46** B1
Sancey-le-Grand **27** E3
Sanchidrián **62** C2
San Chirico Nuovo **50** C3
San Chirico Raparo **50** C4
San Cibrão das Viñas **53** F3
San Cipriano d'Aversa **49** E4
San Clemente **70** A2
San Clodio **54** A3
Sancoins **25** E4
San Colombano al Lambro **37** E4
San Cosme **54** A1
San Costantino Albanese **50** C4
San Costanzo **47** D3
San Cristóbal de Entreviñas **54** C4
San Cristóbal de la Vega **62** C2
Sancti-Spiritus **68** B3
Sancti-Spíritus **61** F3
Sand (Bad Emstal) **11** E3
Sandager **2** C3
San Damiano d'Asti **44** B1
San Damiano Macra **44** A1
San Daniele del Friuli **39** E2
San Daniele Po **38** A4
Sandau **6** C4
Sandberg **19** F1
Sandby **3** D4
Sande *Ger.* **5** D3
Sande *Port.* **60** C2
San Demetrio Corone **52** B1
San Demetrio ne Vestini **49** D1
Sandersdorf **12** C2
Sandershausen (Niestetal) **11** E3
Sandersleben **12** B2
Sandiás **53** F4
Sandillon **25** D2
Sandkrug **7** F4
Sandl **31** D1
Sando **61** F2
San Donaci **51** E3
San Donà di Piave **39** E3
San Donato di Lecce **51** F4
San Donato di Ninea **52** A1
San Donato Milanese **37** E3
San Donato Val di Comino **49** E2
Sandstedt **5** E3
Sandved **3** D3
Sanem **17** F3
San Emiliano **54** C2
San Esteban de Gormaz **63** E1
San Esteban de la Sierra **62** A3
San Esteban de Litera **58** A3
San Esteban del Molar **54** C4
San Esteban del Valle **62** B4
San Fele **50** B3
San Felice a Cancello **49** F4
San Felice Circeo **49** D3
San Felices de los Gallegos **61** E2
San Felice sul Panaro **38** C4
San Ferdinando **52** A3
San Ferdinando di Puglia **50** C2
San Fernando **73** E4
San Fernando de Henares **63** D3
San Fili **52** B2
Sanfins do Douro **61** D2
Sanfront **44** A1
Sangarcía **62** C2
Sangatte **8** A3
San Gemini **48** C1
Sangerhausen **12** B3
San Germano Chisone **36** B4
San Gimignano **46** B3
San Ginesio **47** E4
San Giorgio a Liri **49** E3
San Giorgio della Richinvelda **39** E2
San Giorgio del Sannio **50** A2
San Giorgio di Lomellina **37** D4
San Giorgio di Nogaro **39** E2
San Giorgio di Piano **46** B1
San Giorgio Ionico **51** E3
San Giorgio la Molara **50** A2
San Giorgio Lucano **50** C4
San Giovanni a Piro **50** B4
San Giovanni Bianco **38** A2
San Giovanni d'Asso **46** B4
San Giovanni Incarico **49** D3
San Giovanni in Croce **38** B4
San Giovanni in Fiore **52** B2
San Giovanni in Persiceto **46** B1
San Giovanni Lupatoto **38** C3
San Giovanni Rotondo **50** B1
San Giovanni Teatino **49** E1
San Giovanni Valdarno **46** B3
San Giuliano Terme **46** A3
San Giuseppe Vesuviano **49** F4
San Giustino **46** C3
San Godenzo **46** B2
San Gregorio **52** A4
San Gregorio Magno **50** B3
San Gregorio Matese **49** F3
Sangüesa **57** D3
San Guiliano Milanese **37** E3
San Guim de Freixenet **58** C3
Sanguinet **40** A1
Sanguinetto **38** C4
San Ildefonso **63** D2
Sanitz **7** D1
San Javier **76** C2
San Jorge **65** E3
San Jorge de Alor **67** E3
San José **76** A4
San José de Malcocinado **73** F4
San Juan de Alicante **71** D4
San Juan de Aznalfarache **73** E2
San Juan de la Nava **62** C3
San Juan del Puerto **73** D2
San Justo de la Vega **54** C3
Sankt Andreasberg **11** F2
Sankt Gallen *Austria* **30** C3
Sankt Gallen *Switz.* **28** B3
Sankt Martin *Austria* **31** D1
Sankt Martin *Austria* **30** B3
Sankt Peter **27** F2
San Lazzaro di Savena **46** B1
San Leo **47** D2
San Leonardo de Yagüe **56** B4
San Leonardo in Passiria **38** C1
San Lorenzo **52** A4
San Lorenzo al Mare **44** B2
San Lorenzo Bellizzi **50** C4
San Lorenzo de Calatrava **69** D3
San Lorenzo de El Escorial **62** C3
San Lorenzo de la Parrilla **63** F4
San Lorenzo di Sebato **39** D1
San Lorenzo in Campo **47** D3
San Lorenzo Nuovo **48** B1
San Luca **52** A4
Sanlúcar de Barrameda **73** E3
Sanlúcar de Guadiana **72** C2
Sanlúcar la Mayor **73** E2
San Lucido **52** A2
San Maddalena Vallalta **39** D1
San Mamés de Campos **55** E3
San Marcello **47** E3
San Marcello Pistoiese **46** A2
San Marco Argentano **52** B1
San Marco dei Cavoti **50** A2
San Marco in Lamis **50** B1
San Marcos **53** E2
San Marino **47** D2
San Martín *Spain* **55** F2
San Martín *Spain* **56** C2
San Martín de la Vega **63** D4
San Martín de la Vega del Alberche **62** B3
San Martin del Pimpollar **62** B3
San Martín de Montalbán **68** C1
San Martín de Pusa **68** C1
San Martin de Unx **57** D3
San Martín de Valdeiglesias **62** C3
San Martino Buon Albergo **38** C3
San Martino di Castrozza **39** D2
San Martino di Lupari **39** D3
San Martino di Venezze **39** D4
San Martino in Badia **39** D1
San Martino in Passiria **38** C1
San Martino in Pensilis **50** A1
San Mateo de Gállego **57** E4
San Mauro Forte **50** C3
San Mauro Marchesato **52** C2
San Mauro Pascoli **47** D2
San Mauro Torinese **36** C4
San Menaio **50** B1
San Michele al Tagliamento **39** E3
San Michele Mondovì **44** B1
San Michele Salentino **51** E3

San Miguel de Arroyo **62** C1
San Miguel de Bernuy **63** D1
San Miguel de Salinas **76** C1
San Millán de la Cogolla **56** B3
San Miniato **46** A3
Sannazzaro de'Burgondi **37** D4
Sannicandro di Bari **51** D2
Sannicandro Garganico **50** B1
Sannicola **51** F4
San Nicola dell'Alto **52** C2
San Nicolás del Puerto **68** A4
San Nicolò **46** C1
San Pablo de los Montes **69** D1
San Pancrazio **38** C1
San Pancrazio Salentino **51** E3
San Paolo di Civitate **50** A1
San Pedro **70** B3
San Pedro de Alcántara **74** B4
San Pedro de Ceque **54** C4
San Pedro del Arroyo **62** B3
San Pedro de Latarce **55** D4
San Pedro del Pinatar **76** C2
San Pedro del Romeral **55** F2
San Pedro de Rozados **62** A3
San Pedro Manrique **56** C4
San Pedro Palmiches **63** F3
San Pellegrino Terme **38** A2
San Piero a Sieve **46** B2
San Pietro di Cadore **39** E1
San Pietro in Cariano **38** B3
San Pietro in Casale **46** B1
San Pietro in Guarano **52** B2
San Pietro Vernotico **51** E3
San Polo d'Enza **46** A1
San Prospero **38** B4
San Quirico d'Orcia **46** B4
San Rafael del Río **65** E3
San Remo **44** B2
San Román **54** A2
San Román de Cameros **56** B4
San Román de la Cuba **55** D4
San Román de los Montes **62** B4
San Roque *Spain* **74** A4
San Roque *Spain* **53** E2
San Roque *Spain* **53** F4
San Rufo **50** B3
San Salvador de Cantamunda **55** E2
San Salvatore Monferrato **37** D4
San Salvatore Telesino **49** F3
San Salvo **49** F2
San Sebastián de los Ballesteros **74** B1
San Sebastián de los Reyes **63** D3
San Secondo Parmense **38** A4
Sansepolcro **46** C3
San Severa **48** B2
San Severino Lucano **50** C4
San Severino Marche **47** E4
San Severo **50** B1
San Silvestre de Guzmán **72** C2
Sansol **56** C3
San Sosti **52** A1
San Spirito **51** D2
Santa Amalia **67** F2
Santa Ana **70** B3
Santa Ana de Pusa **68** C1
Santa Ana la Real **73** D1
Santa Bárbara **65** E3
Santa Bárbara de Casa **72** C1
Santacara **57** D3
Santa Catalina de Armada **53** E2
Santa Catarina **66** C4
Santa Catarina da Fonte do Bispo **72** B2
Santa Caterina dello Ionio **52** B3
Santa Cesarea Terme **51** F4
Santa Cilia de Jaca **57** E3
Santa Clara-a-Nova **72** B2
Santa Clara-a-Velha **72** A2
Santa Clara de Louredo **66** C4
Santa Coloma de Farners **59** E3
Santa Coloma de Queralt **58** C4
Santa Colomba de Somoza **54** B3
Santa Columba de Curueño **55** D3
Santa Comba Dão **60** C3
Santa Comba de Rossas **61** E1
Santa Cristina de la Polvorosa **54** C4
Santa Croce del Sannio **50** A2
Santa Croce di Magliano **50** A1
Santa Croce sull'Arno **46** A3
Santa Cruz **66** B4
Santa Cruz da Tapa **60** C3
Santa Cruz de Bezana **55** F1
Santa Cruz de Campezo **56** C3
Santa Cruz de la Serós **57** E3
Santa Cruz de la Sierra **68** A2
Santa Cruz de la Zarza **63** E4
Santa Cruz de los Cáñamos **69** F3
Santa Cruz del Retamar **62** C4
Santa Cruz de Moya **64** B4
Santa Cruz de Mudela **69** E3
Santa Domenica Talao **52** A1
Santa Elena **69** E4
Santa Elena de Jamuz **54** C4
Santaella **74** B2
Santa Engracia **56** C3
Santa Eufemia **68** C3
Santa Eugenia **53** D3
Santa Eulália **67** D2
Santa Eulalia *Spain* **64** B3
Santa Eulalia *Spain* **54** C2
Santa Eulalia *Spain* **55** D1
Santa Eulalia de Oscos **54** A2
Santa Eulàlia de Riuprimer **59** D3
Santa Fe **75** D2
Santa Fiora **46** B4
Sant'Agata di Puglia **50** B2
Sant'Agata Feltria **46** C2
Santa Giustina **39** D2
Sant'Agostino **38** C4
Sant Agustí de Lluçanès **59** D3
Santa Iria **67** D4
Santa Justa **66** C2
Sant'Alberto **46** C1
Santalha **54** A4
Santa Liestra y San Quílez **58** A2
Santa Luce **46** A3
Santa Lucía **53** E3
Santa Luzia **72** B1
Santa Magdalena de Pulpís **65** E3
Santa Margarida da Serra **66** B4
Santa Margarida de Montbui **58** C4
Santa Margarida do Sádão **66** C4
Santa Margherita Ligure **45** D2
Santa María **57** E3
Santa Maria **38** B1
Santa Maria Capua Vetere **49** E3
Santa Maria da Feira **60** B2
Santa María de Cayón **55** F2
Santa María de Corcó **59** D3
Santa María de Huertas **63** F2
Santa Maria del Berrocal **62** A3
Santa María del Campo **55** F4
Santa María del Campo Rus **70** A1
Santa Maria del Cedro **52** A1
Santa Maria della Versa **37** E4
Santa María de los Llanos **70** A1
Santa María del Páramo **54** C3
Santa María del Val **64** A3
Santa María de Nieva **76** A2
Santa Maria di Castellabate **50** A4
Santa Maria di Sala **39** D3
Santa María la Real de Nieva **62** C2
Santa Maria Maggiore **37** D2
Santa Maria Nuova **47** E3
Santa Maria Rezzonico **37** E2
Santa Marina **50** B4
Santa Marina del Rey **54** C3
Santa Marinella **48** B2
Santa Marta *Spain* **70** A2
Santa Marta *Spain* **67** E3
Santa Marta de Penaguião **60** C2
Santa Marta de Tormes **62** A2
Santana *Port.* **60** B4
Santana *Port.* **66** B3
Santana da Serra **72** B2
Santana de Cambas **72** C1
Santana do Mato **66** C3
Sant'Anastasia **49** F4
Sant'Anatolia di Narco **47** D4
Santander **55** F1
Sant'Angelo **52** B3
Sant'Angelo in Lizzola **47** D2
Sant'Angelo in Vado **47** D3
Sant'Angelo Lodigiano **37** E4
Sant'Antonio Abate **49** F4
Santa Olalla **62** C4
Santa Oliva **58** C4
Santa Ollala del Cala **67** F4
Santa Pau **59** E2
Santa Pola **71** D4
Santar **60** C3
Santarcangelo di Romagna **47** D2
Santarém **66** B2
Santa Severina **52** C2
Santas Martas **55** D3
Santa Sofia *Italy* **46** C2
Santa Sofia *Port.* **66** C3
Santa Sofia d'Epiro **52** B1
Santa Susana *Port.* **67** D3
Santa Susana *Port.* **66** C3
Santa Vitória **66** C4
Santa Vitória do Ameixial **67** D3
Sant Boix de Llobregat **59** D4
Sant Carles de la Ràpita **65** E3
Sant Celoni **59** E3
Sant Cugat del Vallès **59** D4
Sant'Egidio alla Vibrata **47** E4
Sant'Elia a Pianisi **50** A1
Sant Elia Fiumerapido **49** E3
San Telmo **73** D1
Sant'Elpidio a Mare **47** E4
Santeramo in Colle **51** D3
Santervás de la Vega **55** D3
Santes Creus **58** C4
Santesteban **57** D2
Sant Feliu de Guíxols **59** E3
Sant Feliu de Palterols **59** E3
Sant Feliu Sasserra **59** D3
Santhià **36** C3
Sant Hilari Sacalm **59** E3
Sant Hipòlit de Voltregà **59** D3
Santiago de Alcántara **67** D1
Santiago de Calatrava **74** C1
Santiago de Compostela **53** E2
Santiago de la Espada **70** A4
Santiago de la Ribera **76** C2
Santiago del Campo **67** F1
Santiago do Cacém **66** B4
Santiago do Escoural **66** C3
Santiagomillas **54** C3
Santibáñez de Béjar **62** A3
Santibáñez de la Peña **55** E2
Santibáñez de la Sierra **62** A3
Santibáñez de Tera **54** C4
Santibáñez de Vidriales **54** C4
Santibáñez el Bajo **61** F4
Santibáñez Zarzaguda **55** F3
Sant'Ilario d'Enza **38** B4
Santillana **55** E1
Santiponce **73** E2
Santisteban del Puerto **69** E4
Santiuste de San Juan Bautista **62** C2
Santiz **62** A2
Sant Jaume d'Enveja **65** E3
Sant Joan de les Abadesses **59** D2
Sant Joan de Vilatorrada **59** D3
Sant Joan les Fonts **59** E2
Sant Julià de Lòria **58** C2
Sant Llorenç de Morunys **58** C2
Sant Martí de Tous **58** C3
Sant Martí Sarroca **58** C4
Sant Mateu **65** E3
Santo Aleixo **67** D2
Santo Aleixo da Restauração **67** E4
Santo Amador **67** D4
Santo André **66** B4
Santo António dos Cavaleiros **66** A3
Santo Domingo de la Calzada **56** B3
Santo Domingo de Silos **56** A4
Santo Estêvão *Port.* **72** C2
Santo Estêvão *Port.* **66** B3
Santo Isidro de Pegões **66** B3
Santomera **76** C1
Sant Omero **47** F4
Santoña **55** F1
Santo Stefano al Mare **44** B2
Santo Stefano Belbo **44** C1
Santo Stefano d'Aveto **45** D1
Santo Stefano di Cadore **39** E1
Santo Stefano di Magra **45** E2
Santo Stino di Livenza **39** E3
Santo Tirso **60** B2
Santo Tomé **69** E4
Santovenia **54** C4
Santpedor **59** D3
Sant Pere de Ribes **58** C4
Sant Pere de Torelló **59** D3
Sant Pere Pescador **59** E2
Sant Pol de Mar **59** E3
Sant Privat d'en Bas **59** D2
Sant Quintí de Mediona **58** C4
Sant Quirze de Besora **59** D2
Santullano de las Regueras **54** C1
Santurtzi **56** B1
Sant Vicenç del Horts **59** D4
Sant Vincenç de Castellet **59** D3
San Venanzo **46** C4
San Vendemiano **39** D2

San Vicente **53** E2
San Vicente de Alcántara **67** E2
San Vicente de Arana **56** C3
San Vicente de la Barquera **55** E1
San Vicente de la Sonsierra **56** B3
San Vicente del Raspeig **71** D4
San Vicente de Palacio **62** B2
San Vicente de Toranzo **55** F2
San Vincenzo **46** A4
San Vincenzo Valle Roveto **49** D2
San Vitero **54** B4
San Vito al Tagliamento **39** E2
San Vito Chietino **49** F1
San Vito dei Normanni **51** E3
San Vito di Cadore **39** D1
San Vito Romano **48** C2
San Vito sullo Ionio **52** B3
San Vittoria in Matenano **47** E4
Sanxenxo **53** E3
Sanza **50** B4
Sanzoles **62** A1
São Barnabé **72** B2
São Bartolomeu **66** C2
São Bartolomeu da Serra **66** B4
São Bartolomeu de Messines **72** B2
São Bento do Cortiço **67** D2
São Brás **67** D4
São Brás de Alportel **72** B2
São Brás do Regedouro **66** C3
São Brissos **66** C4
São Cosmado **61** D2
São Domingos **66** B4
São Facundo **66** C2
São Francisco da Serra **66** B4
São Geraldo **66** C3
São Gregório **66** C3
São Jacinto **60** B3
São João da Madeira **60** B2
São João da Pesqueira **61** D2
São João da Venda **72** B2
São João do Campo **60** B4
São João dos Caldeireiros **72** B1
São José da Lamarosa **66** C2
São Lourenço de Mamporcão **67** D3
São Luís **72** A1
São Manços **67** D3
São Marcos da Ataboeira **72** B1
São Marcos da Serra **72** B2
São Marcos do Campo **67** D4
São Martinho da Cortiça **60** C4
São Martinho das Amoreiras **72** A1
São Martinho de Angueira **61** F1
São Martinho do Porto **66** B1
São Matias **66** C4
São Miguel de Acha **61** D4
São Miguel de Machede **67** D3
São Miguel de Rio Torto **66** C2
São Miguel do Outeiro **60** C3
São Miguel do Pinheiro **72** B2
Saône **27** D3
São Pedro da Cadeira **66** A2
São Pedro de Muel **66** B1
São Pedro de Solis **72** B2
São Pedro do Sul **60** C3
Saorge **44** B2
São Romão **67** D3
São Romão do Sado **66** C4
São Sebastião dos Carros **72** C2
São Teotónio **72** A2
São Vicente **61** D1
São Vicente da Beira **61** D4
Sappada **39** E1
Sapri **50** B4
Saracena **52** B1
Saramon **41** D3
Saran **25** D2
Sarcelles **16** A4
Sarconi **50** B4
Sardoal **66** C1
Sare **40** A3
Sarentino **38** C1
Sarezzo **38** A3
Sargans **28** B4
Sariegos **54** C3
Sariñena **58** A3
Sarlat-la-Canéda **33** E4
Sarnadas do Ródão **67** D1
Sarnano **47** E4
Sarnen **28** A4
Sarnico **38** A3
Sarno **49** F4
Saronno **37** D3
Sarow **7** E2
Sarracín **55** F3
Sarral **58** C4
Sarralbe **18** B4
Sarraquinhos **61** D1
Sarras **35** D4
Sarre **36** B3
Sarreaus **53** F4
Sarrebourg **27** E1
Sarreguemines **18** B3
Sarre-Union **18** B4
Sarria **54** A2
Sarrià de Ter **59** E3
Sarrians **43** D2
Sarrión **64** C4
Sarroca de Segre **58** B4
Sarry **17** D4
Sarsina **46** C2
Sarstedt **11** E1
Sartaguda **56** C3
Sarteano **46** C4
Sartilly **23** E1
Sarvisé **58** A2
Sarzana **45** E2
Sarzeau **23** D3
Sarzedas **67** D1
Sarzedo **61** D2
Sasamón **55** F3
Sasbach *Ger.* **28** A1
Sasbach *Ger.* **27** F2
Sassano **50** B4
Sassello **44** C1
Sassen **7** E2
Sassenage **35** F4
Sassenberg **10** C2
Sassenheim **9** D1
Sassetta **46** A4
Sassnitz **7** E1
Sassocorvaro **47** D3
Sassoferrato **47** D3
Sasso Marconi **46** B1
Sassuolo **46** A1
Sástago **65** D2
Sas Van Gent **8** C3
Satão **61** D3
Satillieu **35** D4
Satow **6** C2
Satriano di Lucania **50** B3
Satrup **2** B4
Satteins **28** C3
Satteldorf **19** F3
Sattledt **30** C2
Saúca **63** F2
Saucats **40** B1
Sauerlach **29** E2
Saugues **34** C4
Saujon **32** B3
Saulce-sur-Rhône **43** D1
Sauldorf **28** B2
Saulgau **28** B2
Saulgrub **29** D3
Saulieu **26** A3
Sault **43** E2
Sault-lès-Rethel **17** D3
Saulx **27** D3
Saulzais-le-Potier **34** A1
Saumur **24** A4
Sauris **39** E1
Sausset-les-Pins **43** D3
Sautens **29** D3
Sautron **23** E4
Sauvagnon **40** B3
Sauve **42** B2
Sauveterre-de-Béarn **40** A3
Sauveterre-de-Guyenne **40** C1
Sauviat-sur-Vige **33** E2
Sauxillanges **34** C3
Sauzé-Vaussais **32** C2
Sava **51** E4
Savelli **52** C2
Savenay **23** E3
Saverdun **41** E4
Saverne **27** F1
Savigliano **44** B1
Savignac-les-Églises **33** D4
Savignano Irpino **50** A2
Savignano sul Rubicone **47** D2
Savigné-l'Évêque **24** B2
Savigneux **35** D3
Savigny-sur-Braye **24** C2
Savines-le-Lac **43** F1
Savognin **38** A1
Savona **44** C2
Sax **71** D3
Saxen **31** D2
Saxon **36** B2
Sayalonga **74** C3
Sayatón **63** E3
Sayda **13** D4
Scaër **22** B2
Scafa **49** E1
Scalea **52** A1
Scandale **52** C2
Scandiano **46** A1
Scandicci **46** B3
Scandriglia **48** C2
Scanno **49** E2
Scansano **48** A1
Scanzano Jonico **51** D4
Scardovari **39** D4
Scario **50** B4
Scarlino **46** A4
Scarperia **46** B2
Scerni **49** F2
Scey-sur-Saône-et-St-Albin **27** D3
Schaan **28** B4
Schaerbeek **9** D4
Schaesberg **10** A4
Schaffhausen **28** A3
Schafflund **2** B4
Schafstädt **12** B3
Schafstedt **5** F1
Schäftlarn **29** E2
Schagen **4** A4
Schalchen **30** B2
Schalkau **20** A1
Schalksmühle **10** B3
Schänis **28** B4
Schapen **10** C1
Schaprode **7** E1
Scharbeutz **6** B2
Schardenberg **30** B1
Schärding **30** B1
Scharendijke **8** C2
Scharnebeck **6** B3
Scharnitz **29** E3
Scharnstein **30** C2
Scharrel (Oldenburg) **5** D3
Scharwoude **4** A4
Schashagen **6** B1
Schattendorf **31** F2
Schebheim **19** F2
Scheemda **4** C3
Scheer **28** B2
Scheeßel **5** F3
Schefflenz **19** E3
Scheggia e Pascelupo **47** D3
Scheggino **47** D4
Scheibbs **31** D2
Scheiblingkirchen **31** E3
Scheidegg **28** C3
Scheifling **30** C4
Scheinfeld **20** A2
Schelklingen **28** C1
Schellerten **11** F1
Schemmerhofen **28** C2
Schenefeld *Ger.* **6** A1
Schenefeld *Ger.* **6** A2
Schenkenfelden **30** C1
Schenklengsfeld **11** E4
Schermbeck **10** B2
Schermen **12** C1
Schermerhorn **4** A4
Scherpenheuvel **9** E3
Scherpenzeel **9** E1
Scherwiller **27** F1
Scherzingen **28** B3
Scheßlitz **20** A2
Schiavi di Abruzzo **49** F2
Schiedam **9** D2
Schieder-Schwalenberg **11** D2
Schieren **17** F2
Schierling **20** C4
Schiermonnikoog **4** B3
Schiers **28** C4
Schiffdorf **5** E2
Schifferstadt **19** D3
Schifflange **17** F3
Schiffweiler **18** B3
Schijndel **9** E2
Schilde **9** D3
Schillings-fürst **19** F3
Schilpario **38** A2
Schiltach **28** A1
Schiltigheim **27** F1
Schinveld **10** A3
Schio **38** C3
Schipkau **13** E2
Schirmeck **27** E1
Schirmitz **20** C2
Schkeuditz **12** C3
Schkölen **12** C3
Schköna **12** C2
Schkopau **12** C3
Schlabendorf **13** E2
Schladen **11** F2
Schlangen **11** D2
Schlangenbad **18** C2
Schleching **30** A2
Schleiden **10** A4
Schleife **13** F2
Schleinbach **31** F1
Schleitheim **28** A2
Schleiz **12** B4
Schlema **13** D4
Schlepzig **13** E2
Schleswig **6** A1
Schleusingen **11** F4
Schlieben **13** D2
Schlier **28** C2
Schlierbach **30** C2
Schlieren **28** A3
Schliersee **29** F2
Schlitters **29** F3
Schlitz **11** E4
Schloßberg **31** E4
Schloß Holte-Stukenbrock **11** D2
Schloßvippach **12** B3
Schlosswil **27** F4
Schlotheim **11** F3
Schluchsee **28** A2
Schlüchtern **19** E1
Schlüsselfeld **20** A2
Schmallenberg **10** C3
Schmelz **18** B3
Schmidgaden **20** C3
Schmidmühlen **20** C3
Schmiedeberg **13** E4
Schmölln *Ger.* **7** F3
Schmölln *Ger.* **12** C4
Schnabelwaid **20** B2
Schnackenburg **6** C3
Schnaittach **20** B3
Schneeberg **13** D4
Schneidlingen **12** B2
Schneizlreuth **30** A3
Schnellmannshausen **11** F3
Schneverdingen **6** A3
Schobüll **5** F1
Scholen **5** E4
Schollene **7** D4
Schöllnach **30** B1
Schömberg **28** A2
Schönau *Ger.* **19** D3
Schönau *Germany* **30** A1
Schönbach **31** D1
Schönberg *Ger.* **7** E4
Schönberg *Ger.* **6** B2
Schönberg (Holstein) **6** B1
Schönberg am Kamp **31** E1
Schönberg im Stubaital **29** E3
Schönborn **13** E2
Schondra **19** E1
Schönebeck **7** D3
Schönebeck (Elbe) **12** B2
Schöneck **20** C1
Schönecken **17** F1
Schönermark **7** E3
Schönewalde **13** D2
Schönewörde **6** B4
Schongau **29** D2
Schönhausen **6** C4
Schöningen **12** A1
Schönkirchen **6** A1
Schönow **7** E4
Schönsee **20** C3
Schöntal **19** E3
Schönthal **20** C3
Schönwalde **13** E2
Schönwalde am Bungsberg **6** B1
Schönwies **29** D3
Schoondijke **8** C3
Schoonebeek **4** C4
Schoonhoven **9** E2

Schopfheim 27 F3
Schopfloch 19 F3
Schöppenstedt 11 F1
Schoppernau 28 C3
Schöppingen 10 B1
Schörfling am Attersee 30 B2
Schorndorf *Ger.* 19 E4
Schorndorf *Ger.* 20 C3
Schortens 5 D3
Schoten 9 D3
Schotten 11 D4
Schramberg 28 A2
Schrecksbach 11 E4
Schrepkow 7 D4
Schriesheim 19 D3
Schrobenhausen 29 E1
Schröder 30 C3
Schrozberg 19 F3
Schruns 28 C4
Schübelbach 28 B4
Schuby 6 A1
Schulenberg im Oberharz 11 F2
Schulzendorf 7 F4
Schüpfheim 27 F4
Schutterwald 27 F1
Schüttorf 10 B1
Schwaan 7 D2
Schwabach 20 A3
Schwäbisch Gmünd 19 E4
Schwäbisch Hall 19 E3
Schwabmünchen 29 D2
Schwabstedt 5 F1
Schwaförden 5 E4
Schwaigern 19 D3
Schwalbach 18 B3
Schwalmstadt-Treysa 11 E4
Schwalmstadt-Ziegenhain 11 E4
Schwanberg 31 D4
Schwanden 28 B4
Schwandorf 20 C3
Schwanebeck 12 B2
Schwanenstadt 30 B2
Schwanewede 5 E3
Schwangau 29 D3
Schwan-stetten 20 B3
Schwarme 5 F4
Schwarmstedt 6 A4
Schwarz 7 D3
Schwarza 11 F4
Schwarzach 21 D4
Schwarzau im Gebirge 31 E2
Schwarzenau 31 D1
Schwarzenbach 31 F3
Schwarzen-bach am Wald 20 B1
Schwarzenbek 6 B3
Schwarzenberg 13 D4
Schwarzenborn 11 E4
Schwarzenburg 27 F4
Schwarzenfeld 20 C3
Schwarzheide 13 E3
Schwaz 29 E3
Schwechat 31 F2
Schwedeneck 6 A1
Schwedt an der Oder 7 F3
Schwegenheim 19 D3
Schwei (Stadland) 5 E3
Schweiburg 5 E3
Schweich 18 B2
Schweigen-Rechtenbach 18 C4
Schweinfurt 19 F2
Schweinitz 13 D2
Schweinrich 7 D3
Schwelm 10 B3
Schwendau 29 F3
Schwendi 28 C2
Schwenningen 28 A2
Schwepnitz 13 E3
Schwerin 6 C2
Schweringen 5 F4
Schwerte 10 C3
Schwetzingen 19 D3
Schwichtenberg 7 E2
Schwieberdingen 19 E4
Schwiesau 6 C4
Schwindegg 29 F1
Schwinkendorf 7 D2
Schwoich 29 F3
Schwyz 28 A4
Sciez 36 A2
Scigliano 52 B2
Scilla 52 A4
Scionzier 36 A2
Scopello 36 C3
Scoppito 49 D1
Scorbé-Clairvaux 33 D1
Scorrano 51 F4
Scorzè 39 D3
Scuol 38 B1
Scurcola Marsicana 49 D2
Seara 60 B1
Sebal 60 B4
Sébazac-Concourès 41 F1
Sebbersund 1 E2
Sebnitz 13 F3
Seckach 19 E3
Seckau 31 D3
Seclin 16 B1
Secondigny 32 C1
Sedan 17 E2
Sedano 55 F3
Seden 2 C3
Séderon 43 E2
Sedico 39 D2
Sedrina 38 A2
See *Austria* 30 B4
See *Austria* 29 D4
Seebach 11 F4
Seebad Ahlbeck 7 F2
Seebad Bansin 7 F2
Seebad Heringsdorf 7 F2
Seeboden 30 B4
Seebruck 30 A2
Seeburg 11 F2
Seedorf 6 B2
Seefeld *Ger.* 29 E2
Seefeld *Ger.* 7 E4
Seefeld (Stadland) 5 E3
Seefeld in Tirol 29 E3
Seeg 29 D3
Seehausen *Ger.* 7 F3
Seehausen *Ger.* 12 B1
Seehausen (Altmark) 6 C4
Seeheim-Jugenheim 19 D2
Seekirchen am Wallersee 30 A2
Seelow 13 F1
Seelze 11 E1
Seeon 29 F2
Sées 24 B1
Seesen 11 F2
Seeshaupt 29 E2
Seethal 30 C4
Seevetal 6 A3
Seewiesen 31 D3
Séez 36 A3
Segeletz 7 D4
Seggiano 46 B4
Segni 49 D2
Segonzac 32 C3
Segorbe 65 D4
Segovia 62 C2
Segré 23 F3
Segura 67 E1
Segura de la Sierra 70 A4
Segura de León 67 F4
Segura de los Baños 64 C2
Segurilla 62 B4
Sehlde 11 F1
Sehma 13 D4
Sehnde 11 E1
Seia 61 D3
Seiches-sur-le-Loir 24 A3
Seiersberg 31 D4
Seifhennersdorf 13 F4
Seignelay 25 F2
Seignelégier 27 E3
Seilhac 33 F3
Seillans 43 F3
Seinsheim 19 F2
Seissan 41 D3
Seixal 66 B3
Sejerby 3 D2
Sejerslev 1 E2
Sejet 2 C2
Selaya 55 F2
Selb 20 C1
Selbitz 20 B1
Selde 1 E2
Selent 6 B1
Sélestat 27 F2
Seligenstadt 19 D2
Sella 71 E3
Sellano 47 D4
Selles-St-Denis 25 D3
Selles-sur-Cher 25 D4
Sellia Marina 52 B3
Sellières 26 C4
Selling 2 C1
Sellingen 4 C4
Sellrain 29 E3
Selm 10 B2
Selmes 67 D4
Selmsdorf 6 B2
Selommes 24 C3
Seloncourt 27 E3
Selongey 26 C3
Selow 6 C2
Selsingen 5 F3
Selters (Westerwald) 10 C4
Seltz 18 C4
Selva 51 D3
Selva dei Molini 29 F4
Selva di Progno 38 C3
Selva di Val Gardena 38 C1
Selvazzano Dentro 39 D3
Selvino 38 A2
Selzthal 30 C3
Sembrancher 36 B2
Séméac 40 C4
Semide 60 C4
Seminara 52 A4
Semlow 7 D1
Semmenstedt 11 F1
Semoutiers-Montsaon 26 C2
Sempach 28 A4
Semproniano 46 B4
Semriach 31 E3
Semur-en-Auxois 26 B3
Semur-en-Brionnais 35 D2
Semussac 32 B3
Sena 58 A3
Senales 38 B1
Sénas 43 D3
Senden *Ger.* 28 C1
Senden *Ger.* 10 B2
Sendenhorst 10 C2
Sendim *Port.* 60 C1
Sendim *Portugal* 61 E1
Seneffe 17 D1
Senes 76 A3
Senftenberg *Austria* 31 E1
Senftenberg *Ger.* 13 E2
Senhora do Rosário 67 D2
Senigallia 47 E3
Senise 50 C4
Senlis 16 B3
Sennels 1 D2
Sennwald 28 B3
Senonches 24 C1
Senones 27 E1
Sens 25 F2
Sens-de-Bretagne 23 E2
Senterada 58 B2
Seon 28 A3
Sepino 49 F3
Septèmes-les-Vallons 43 E3
Septeuil 15 F4
Septfonds 41 E2
Sepulcro-Hilario 61 F3
Sepúlveda 63 D2
Sequàls 39 E2
Sequeros 62 A3
Seraing 17 E1
Seravezza 45 E2
Seregno 37 E3
Séreilhac 33 E3
Sérent 23 D3
Serfaus 29 D4
Sergines 25 F1
Sergnano 38 A3
Seriate 38 A3
Sérifontaine 16 A3
Sérignan 42 A4
Sérignan-du-Comtat 43 D2
Serina 38 A2
Serino 50 A3
Serinyà 59 E2
Sermaises 25 D2
Sermaize-les-Bains 17 E4
Sermide 38 C4
Sermoneta 48 C3
Sernancelhe 61 D2
Serno 12 C2
Serón 75 F2
Serón de Nájima 63 F1
Seròs 58 A4
Serpa 67 D4
Serpins 60 C4
Serquigny 15 E3
Serra 71 D1
Serracapriola 50 A1
Serrada 62 B1
Serra de'Conti 47 D3
Serra de Outes 53 D2
Serradilla 67 F1
Serradilla del Arroyo 61 F3
Serramazzoni 46 A1
Serranillos 62 B4
Serra Riccò 45 D1
Serra San Bruno 52 B3
Serrastretta 52 B2
Serravalle 47 D2
Serravalle di Chienti 47 D4
Serravalle Scrivia 44 C1
Serre 50 A3
Serrejón 62 A4
Serres 43 E1
Serrières 35 D4
Serrig 18 A3
Serritslev 1 F1
Serrungarina 47 D3
Sersale 52 B2
Sertã 66 C1
Servance 27 E2
Servian 42 B3
Servigliano 47 E4
Servon-sur-Vilaine 23 E2
Servoz 36 A2
Serzedo 60 B2
Sesa 58 A3
Seseña 63 D4
Sesma 56 C3
Sessa Aurunca 49 E3
Sessa Cilento 50 A4
Seßlach 20 A1
Sesta Godano 45 E2
Sestao 56 B2
Sestino 46 C3
Sesto 39 D1
Sesto al Reghena 39 E2
Sesto Calende 37 D3
Sesto Campano 49 E3
Sesto Fiorentino 46 B2
Sestola 46 A2
Sesto San Giovanni 37 E3
Sestriere 36 A4
Sestri Levante 45 D2
Sète 42 B3
Setenil 74 B3
Setiles 64 B3
Settimo Torinese 36 C4
Settimo Vittone 36 C3
Setúbal 66 B3
Seubersdorf in der Oberpfalz 20 B3
Seuil-d'Argonne 17 E4
Seurre 26 C4
Seva 59 D3
Sevel 2 A1
Sevenum 10 A3
Sévérac-le-Château 42 A2
Sever do Vouga 60 C3
Seveso 37 D3
Sevilla 73 E2
Sevilla la Nueva 63 D3
Sevilleja de la Jara 68 C1
Sévrier 35 F2
Sexau 27 F2
Seyches 40 C1
Seyda 13 D2
Seyne 43 F1
Seynod 35 F2
Seyssel 35 F2
Seysses 41 E3
Sézanne 16 C4
Sezze 49 D3
's-Gravendeel 9 D2
's-Gravenhage 9 D1
's-Gravenpolder 8 C2
's-Gravenzande 9 D1
Sgurgola 49 D2
's-Heerenberg 10 A2
's-Hertogenbosch 9 E2
Sibari 52 B1
Sickte 11 F1
Siddeburen 4 C3
Siderno 52 B4
Siebenlehn 13 D3
Siegburg 10 B4
Siegen 10 C4
Siegenburg 29 E1
Sieggraben 31 F3
Sieghartskirchen 31 E1
Siegsdorf 30 A2
Siek 6 A2
Siena 46 B3
Sierck-les-Bains 17 F3
Sierentz 27 F3
Sierksdorf 6 B1
Sierndorf 31 E1
Sierning 30 C2
Sierra de Fuentes 67 F2
Sierra de Luna 57 E4
Sierra de Yeguas 74 B2
Sierra Engarcerán 65 D4
Sierre 36 B2
Sierro 75 F2
Siershahn 10 C4
Siersleben 12 B2
Siete Iglesias de Trabancos 62 B1
Sietow 7 D3
Sieversdorf 7 D4
Sieverstedt 2 B4
Sig 2 A2
Sigean 42 A4
Siggelkow 6 C3
Sigillo 47 D3
Sigmaringen 28 B2
Sigmaringendorf 28 B2
Sigmundsherberg 31 E1

Signa **46** B2
Signes **43** E3
Signy-l'Abbaye **17** D2
Signy-le-Petit **17** D2
Sigoulès **40** C1
Sigüeiro **53** E2
Sigüenza **63** F2
Sigües **57** E3
Silandro **38** B1
Silenen **28** A4
Siles **70** A4
Silkeborg **2** B1
Silla **71** D2
Sillano **46** A2
Silleda **53** E3
Sillé-le-Guillaume **24** A2
Sillian **39** D1
Sils *Spain* **59** E3
Sils *Switz.* **38** A1
Silvaplana **38** A1
Silvares **61** D4
Silveiras **66** C3
Silvi **49** E1
Silz **29** D3
Simancas **62** B1
Simandre **35** E1
Simat de la Valdigna **71** D2
Simbach **30** A1
Simbach am Inn **30** A1
Simbario **52** B3
Simeri-Crichi **52** B2
Simested **1** E3
Simmelsdorf **20** B3
Simmerath **10** A4
Simmerberg **28** C3
Simmern (Hunsrück) **18** C2
Simonsberg **5** E1
Simpelveld **10** A4
Simplon **36** C2
Sinabelkirchen **31** E4
Sinalunga **46** C4
Sinarcas **70** C1
Sindal **1** F1
Sindelfingen **28** B1
Sines **66** B4
Singen (Hohentwiel) **28** B2
Sinlabajos **62** B2
Sin-le-Noble **16** B1
Sinn **10** C4
Sinopoli **52** A4
Sins **28** A4
Sinsheim **19** D3
Sintra **66** A3
Sinzheim **28** A1
Sinzig **10** B4
Sion **36** B2
Sipplingen **28** B2
Sirmione **38** B3
Sirnach **28** B3
Sirnitz **30** C4
Sirolo **47** E3
Siròr **39** D2
Siruela **68** B2
Sisante **70** B2
Sissa **38** A4
Sissach **27** F3
Sissonne **16** C3
Sisteron **43** E2
Sistrans **29** E3
Sitges **59** D4
Sittard **9** F3
Sittensen **6** A3
Sitzendorf an der Schmida **31** E1
Sitzenroda **13** D3
Sivry **17** D2
Sixt-Fer-à-Cheval **36** A2
Sizun **22** B2
Sjølund **2** B3
Sjørring **1** D2
Sjørslev **2** B1
Sjørup **2** B1
Skælsør **3** D3
Skærbæk **2** A3
Skævinge **3** E2
Skagen **1** F1
Skals **2** B1
Skanderborg **2** C2
Skarp Salling **1** E2
Skarrild **2** A2
Skårup **2** C3
Skave **2** A1
Skelby **3** E3
Skelde **2** B4
Skelhøje **2** B1
Skelund **1** F3
Skibbild **2** A1
Skibby **3** E2
Skibinge **3** E3
Skive **2** B1
Skjern **2** A2
Skjød **2** C1
Skodborg **2** B3
Skørping **1** F2
Skovby **2** C1
Skovlund **2** A2
Skovsgård **1** E2
Skuldelev **3** E2
Slagelse **3** D3
Slangerup **3** E2
Sleen **4** C4
Sliedrecht **9** E2
Slimminge **3** E3
Slochteren **4** C3
Slootdorp **4** A4
Słubice **13** F1
Sluderno **38** B1
Sluis **8** C3
Sluiskil **8** C3
Smarves **33** D1
Smidstrup *Denmark* **3** E1
Smidstrup *Denmark* **2** B2
Smilde **4** C4
Snaptun **2** C2
Snedsted **1** D2
Sneek **4** B3
Snejbjerg **2** A1
Snertinge **3** D2
Snøde **3** D3
Snoghøj **2** B3
Snoldelev **3** E2
Soajo **53** E4
Soave **38** C3
Sobernheim **18** C2
Soboth **31** D4
Sobradelo **54** A3
Sobradiel **57** E4
Sobrado *Spain* **53** F2
Sobrado *Spain* **53** F4
Sobral da Adiça **67** D4
Sobral de Monte Agraço **66** A2
Sobreira Formosa **66** C1
Søby **2** C4
Socchieve **39** E1
Sochaux **27** E3
Socovos **76** A1
Socuéllamos **70** A2
Soerendonk **9** E3
Soest *Ger.* **10** C2
Soest *Neth.* **9** E1
Søften **2** C1
Sögel **5** D4
Sohland **13** F3
Sohren **18** B2
Soignies **16** C1
Soings-en-Sologne **25** D3
Soire-le-Château **17** D1
Soissons **16** C3
Solana de los Barros **67** F3
Solana del Pino **69** D3
Solana de Rioalmar **62** B3
Solbjerg **2** C2
Solda **38** B1
Sölden **29** D4
Soldeu **58** C2
Solesino **38** C4
Solesmes *France* **16** C1
Solesmes *France* **24** A2
Soleto **51** F4
Solferino **38** B3
Soliera **38** B4
Solignano **45** E1
Solingen **10** B3
Solivella **58** C4
Söll **29** F3
Sollenau **31** F2
Søllested **3** D4
Söllichau **13** D2
Solliès-Pont **43** E4
Solliès-Toucas **43** E4
Söllingen **12** A1
Sollstedt **11** F3
Solms **11** D4
Solofra **50** A3
Solopaca **49** F3
Solórzano **55** F1
Solosancho **62** B3
Solothurn **27** F3
Solsona **58** C3
Soltau **6** A4
Soltendieck **6** B4
Somain **16** B1
Sombernon **26** B3
Sombreffe **17** D1
Someren **9** F3
Sommacampagna **38** B3
Somma Lombardo **37** D3
Sommariva del Bosco **44** B1
Somme-Leuze **17** E1
Sömmerda **12** B3
Sommerfeld **7** E4
Sommersted **2** B3
Sommières **42** C3
Somontín **75** F2
Son **9** E2
Sona **38** B3
Sonadell **58** B4
Sonceboz **27** E4
Soncillo **55** F2
Soncino **38** A3
Sondalo **38** B1
Sønder Balling **1** E3
Sønder Bjerre **2** C2
Sønder Bjert **2** B3
Sønderborg **2** B4
Sønderby **3** E2
Sønder Dråby **1** E2
Sønder Felding **2** A2
Sønderho **2** A3
Sønderholm **1** E2
Sønder Hygum **2** B3
Sønder Nissum **2** A1
Sønder Omme **2** A2
Sønder Onsild **2** B1
Sønder Rubjerg **1** F1
Sondershausen **12** A3
Søndersø **2** C3
Sønder Stenderup **2** B3
Sønder Vilstrup **2** B3
Sønder Vissing **2** B2
Sønder Vium **2** A2
Sondrio **38** A2
Soneja **65** D4
Songeons **16** A3
Sonim **61** D1
Sonneberg **20** B1
Sonneborn **11** F3
Sonnefeld **20** B1
Sonnewalde **13** E2
Sonnino **49** D3
Sonntag **28** C3
Sonntagberg **31** D2
Sonseca **69** D1
Sontheim an der Brenz **28** C1
Sonthofen **29** D3
Sontra **11** E3
Sopeira **58** B2
Sopelana **56** B1
Sopronkövesd **31** F3
Sopuerta **56** A2
Sora **49** D2
Soraga **38** C1
Soragna **38** A4
Sorano **48** B1
Sorbas **76** A3
Sorbolo **38** B4
Sørbymagle **3** D3
Sorcy-St-Martin **17** F4
Sore **40** B2
Soresina **38** A3
Sorèze **41** F3
Sorge **11** F2
Sorges **33** D4
Sorgues **43** D2
Soria **56** C4
Soriano Calabro **52** B3
Soriano nel Cimino **48** B1
Sorihuela **62** A3
Sorihuela del Gaudalimar **69** F4
Sornac **33** F3
Sorø **3** D3
Sorrento **49** F4
Sorring **2** B1
Sort **58** C2
Sortelha **61** D3
Sörup **2** B4
Sørvad **2** A1
Sorvilán **75** E3
Sos del Rey Católico **57** D3
Soses **58** B4
Sospel **44** B2
Sotés **56** B3
Sotiel Coronada **73** D1
Sotillo de la Adrada **62** C4
Sotillo del Rincón **56** B4
Soto **54** C1
Soto de la Vega **54** C3
Soto del Real **63** D3
Soto de Ribera **54** C1
Soto en Cameros **56** C3
Sotopalacios **55** F3
Sotos **63** F4
Sotoserrano **62** A3
Soto y Amio **54** C3
Sotres **55** E2
Sotresgudo **55** E3
Sotrondio **54** C2
Sotteville-lès-Rouen **15** E3
Sottomarina **39** D4
Sottrum **5** F3
Sotuélamos **70** A2
Soual **41** F3
Soucy **25** F2
Soudan **23** F3
Souesmes **25** D3
Soufflenheim **18** C4
Souillac **33** E4
Souilly **17** E4
Soulac-sur-Mer **32** B3
Soulaines-Dhuys **26** B1
Soullans **32** A1
Soultz-Haut-Rhin **27** E2
Soultz-sous-Forêts **18** C4
Soumagne **17** F1
Soumoulou **40** B4
Souppes-sur-Loing **25** E2
Souprosse **40** B3
Sourdeval **23** F1
Soure **60** B4
Sournia **59** D1
Souro Pires **61** D3
Sours **25** D1
Sourzac **33** D4
Sousceyrac **33** F4
Sousel **67** D2
Soustons **40** A3
Souto *Port.* **61** E3
Souto *Port.* **66** C1
Souto *Port.* **60** B1
Souto *Spain* **53** F2
Souto da Casa **61** D4
Souvigny **34** B1
Soverato **52** B3
Soveria Mannelli **52** B2
Sovicille **46** B3
Søvind **2** C2
Soyaux **33** D3
Spa **17** F1
Spaichingen **28** A2
Spalt **20** A3
Spangenberg **11** E3
Spantekow **7** E2
Sparanise **49** E3
Spartà **52** A4
Spay **18** C1
Specchia **51** F4
Speicher **18** A2
Speichersdorf **20** B2
Spello **47** D4
Spenge **11** D1
Spentrup **2** C1
Sperlonga **49** D3
Speyer **19** D3
Spezzano Albanese **52** B1
Spielberg bei Knittelfeld **31** D3
Spiez **27** F4
Spigno Monferrato **44** C1
Spigno Saturnia **49** E3
Spijk **4** C3
Spijkenisse **9** D2
Spilamberto **46** B1
Spilimbergo **39** E2
Spilinga **52** A3
Spinazzola **50** C2
Spincourt **17** F3
Spinea **39** D3
Spinetoli **47** F4
Spiss **29** D4
Spital am Pyhrn **30** C3
Spital am Semmering **31** E3
Spittal an der Drau **30** B4
Spitz **31** D1
Spjald **2** A1
Splügen **37** E1
Spodsbjerg **3** D4
Spoleto **47** D4
Spoltore **49** E1
Spondigna **38** B1
Spornitz **6** C3
Spotorno **44** C2
Spraitbach **19** E4
Sprakensehl **6** B4
Spreenhagen **13** E1
Spremberg **13** F2
Sprendlingen **18** C2
Spresiano **39** D3
Spriana **38** A2
Sprimont **17** E1
Springe **11** E1
Sprockhövel **10** B3
Squillace **52** B3
Squinzano **51** F3
Staatz **31** F1
Stabroek **9** D3
Staby **2** A1
Stade **5** F2
Staden **8** B3
Stadl-Paura **30** B2
Stadskanaal **4** C4
Stadtallendorf **11** D4
Stadtbergen **29** D1
Stadthagen **11** E1
Stadtilm **12** B4
Stadtkyll **18** A1
Stadtlauringen **20** A1
Stadtlohn **10** B2

Stadtroda **12** B4
Stadtschlaining **31** F3
Stadum **2** B4
Stäfa **28** A3
Staffelstein **20** A2
Staffolo **47** E3
Staig **28** C1
Stainach **30** C3
Stainz **31** D4
Staìti **52** A4
Stakroge **2** A2
Stalden **36** C2
Stall **30** A4
Stallwang **20** C4
Stammham **20** B4
Stams **29** D3
St'Angelo a Fasanella **50** A3
St'Angelo dei Lombardi **50** A3
Stans **28** A4
St'Antimo **49** E4
Stanzach **29** D3
Stanz im Mürztal **31** E3
Stapel **6** B3
Stapelburg **11** F2
Stapelfeld **6** A2
Staphorst **4** B4
Stara Rudnica **7** F4
Starkenberg **12** C3
Starnberg **29** E2
Starosiedle **13** F2
St'Arsenio **50** B3
Starup **2** B3
Staßfurt **12** B2
Stauchitz **13** D3
Staufenberg **11** D4
Staufen im Breisgau **27** F2
Staupitz **13** E2
Stavelot **17** F1
Stavenisse **9** D2
Stavning **2** A2
Stavoren **4** A4
Stavtrup **2** C1
Steccato **52** C2
Stechow **7** D4
Steckborn **28** B3
Stedesdorf **5** D2
Stedten **12** B3
Steeg **28** C3
Steenbergen **9** D2
Steenvoorde **8** B4
Steenwijk **4** B4
Stefanaconi **52** B3
Steffisburg **27** F4
Stegaurath **20** A2
Stege **3** E4
Stegelitz **12** C1
Stegersbach **31** F4
Steigra **12** B3
Steimbke **5** F4
Stein *Ger.* **20** A3
Stein *Neth.* **9** F3
Stein *Switz.* **27** F3
Steinach *Ger.* **27** F1
Steinach *Ger.* **20** C4
Steinach *Ger.* **12** B4
Steinach am Brenner **29** E4
Stein am Rhein **28** B3
Steinau **5** E2
Steinau an der Straße **19** E1
Steinbach *Ger.* **11** D4
Steinbach *Ger.* **13** D4
Steinbach am Attersee **30** B2
Steinbach am Wald **20** B1
Steinberg *Ger.* **20** C3
Steinberg *Ger.* **2** B4
Steinen **27** F3
Steinfeld *Austria* **30** B4
Steinfeld *Ger.* **18** C4
Steinfeld (Oldenburg) **5** E4
Steinfort **17** F2
Steinfurt **10** B1
Steingaden **29** D3
Steinheim **11** D2
Steinhöring **29** F2
Steinhorst **6** B4
Steinigtwolmsdorf **13** F3
Steinkirchen **6** A2
Steinsdorf **13** F2
Steinsfeld **19** F3
Steinwiesen **20** B1
Stekene **9** D3
Stelle **6** A3
Stellendam **9** D2
Stemmen **6** A3
Stemshorn **11** D1
Stenay **17** E3
Stenbjerg **1** D2
Stendal **6** C4
Stenderup **2** A2
Stenico **38** B2
Stenlille **3** D3
Stenløse **3** E2
Stenstrup **2** C3
Stensved **3** E4
Stenum **1** F1
Stenvad **2** C1
Stepping **2** B3
Sternberg **6** C2
Stes-Maries-de-la-Mer **42** C3
Stetten am kalten Markt **28** B2
Steuerberg **30** C4
Steutz **12** C2
Stevnstrup **2** C1
Steyr **30** C2
Steyregg **30** C1
Stia **46** C2
Stiege **12** A2
Stiens **4** B3
Stienta **38** C4
Stigliano **50** C4
Stignano **52** B3
Stilling **2** C2
Stilo **52** B3
Stimpfach **19** F3
Stio **50** A4
Stiring-Wendel **18** B3
Stjær **2** C1
Stockach **28** B2
Stockelsdorf **6** B2
Stockenboi **30** B4
Stockerau **31** E1
Stockheim **20** B1
Stockstadt am Rhein **19** D2
Stoholm **2** B1
Stokkemarke **3** D4
Stolberg (Harz) Kurort **12** A2
Stolberg (Rheinland) **10** A4
Stollberg **13** D4
Stolpe *Ger.* **7** F4
Stolpe *Ger.* **6** A1
Stolpen **13** E3
Stolzenau **11** D1
Stoob **31** F3
Store Damme **3** E4
Store Darum **2** A3
Store Heddinge **3** E3
Store Merløse **3** E3
Store Rise **2** C4
Store Rørbæk **1** E3
Storkow **13** E1
Stornara **50** B2
Stornarella **50** B2
Storo **38** B2
Storvorde **1** F2
Stößen **12** C3
Stössing **31** E2
Stötten am Auerberg **29** D2
Stotternheim **12** B3
Stouby **2** B2
Stoumont **17** F1
Støvring **1** F2
Stra **39** D3
Straach **12** C2
Strackholt (Großefehn) **5** D3
Stradella **37** E4
Straelen **10** A3
Strallegg **31** E3
Stralsund **7** E1
Strambino **36** C3
Stramproy **9** F3
Strandby *Denmark* **1** E2
Strandby *Denmark* **1** F1
Strande **6** A1
Strangolagalli **49** D3
Strasbourg **27** F1
Strasburg **7** E3
Straßberg *Ger.* **28** B2
Straßberg *Ger.* **12** B2
Straßburg **30** C4
Strassen **17** F2
Straßengel **31** D4
Strasshof an der Norbahn **31** F1
Straßkirchen **21** D4
Straßwalchen **30** B2
Straubing **20** C4
Straupitz **13** E2
Strausberg **7** F4
Straußfurt **12** A3
Streek **5** E3
Strehla **13** D3
Strem **31** F4
Strembo **38** B2
Strengberg **30** C2
Strengen **29** D4
Stresa **37** D2
Streufdorf **20** A1
Strib **2** B3
Strigno **38** C2
Ströbeck **12** A2
Strobl **30** B2
Strøby **3** E3
Strøby Egede **3** E3
Ströhen **11** D1
Stromberg **18** C2
Stroncone **48** C1
Strongoli **52** C2
Stronsdorf **31** F1
Stroppiana **37** D4
Stroppo **44** A1
Strücklingen (Saterland) **5** D3
Struer **2** A1
Strullendorf **20** A2
Struth **11** F3
Stubbæk **2** B4
Stubbekøbing **3** E4
Stubben **5** E3
Stubenberg **31** E3
Stüdenitz **7** D4
Stühlingen **28** A2
Stuhr **5** E3
Stülpe **13** D1
Stumm **29** F3
Sturzelbronn **18** C4
Stuttgart **28** B1
Stützerbach **12** A4
Suances **55** F1
Subbiano **46** C3
Suben **30** B1
Subiaco **49** D2
Sucina **76** C1
Suckow **6** C3
Süden **5** E1
Süderbrarup **2** B4
Süderhastedt **5** F1
Süderlügum **2** A4
Süderstapel **5** F1
Südlohn **10** B2
Sudwalde **5** E4
Sueca **71** D2
Suèvres **25** D3
Suhl **11** F4
Suhlendorf **6** B4
Suippes **17** D3
Sukow **6** C3
Suldrup **1** E2
Sulęcin **13** F1
Sulingen **5** E4
Sully-sur-Loire **25** E2
Sulmona **49** E2
Sulniac **23** D3
Sulsted **1** F2
Sulz **28** C3
Sulz am Neckar **28** A1
Sulzbach am Main **19** E2
Sulzbach an der Murr **19** E4
Sulzbach-Laufen **19** F4
Sulzbach-Rosenberg **20** B3
Sulzbach/Saar **18** B3
Sulzdorf an der Lederhecke **20** A1
Sulzemoos **29** E1
Sulzfeld **20** A1
Sulzheim **20** A2
Sulzthal **19** F1
Sumbilla **57** D2
Sumène **42** B2
Sumiswald **27** F4
Sumvitg **28** B4
Sundby *Denmark* **1** D2
Sundby *Denmark* **1** D2
Sundern (Sauerland) **10** C3
Sunds **2** B1
Sünna **11** F4
Supersano **51** F4
Supino **49** D3
Surbo **51** F3
Surgères **32** B2
Surhuisterveen **4** B3
Súria **58** C3
Surier **36** B3
Sursee **28** A4
Surwold **5** D4
Surzur **23** D3
Susa **36** B4
Susch **28** C4
Susegana **39** D2
Süsel **6** B1
Susteren **9** F3
Sustinente **38** B4
Sutri **48** B1
Suvereto **46** A4
Suzzara **38** B4
Svallerup **3** D2
Svebølle **3** D2
Svejbæk **2** B1
Svendborg **2** C3
Svenstrup *Denmark* **1** F2
Svenstrup *Denmark* **2** B3
Svenstrup *Denmark* **3** D3
Svindinge **2** C3
Svinninge *Denmark* **3** D2
Svinninge *Denmark* **3** D2
Svogerslev **3** E2
Swalmen **10** A3
Swifterbant **4** B4
Świnoujście **7** F2
Syke **5** E4
Syrau **12** C4
Syrgenstein **28** C1
Syvsten **1** F2
Szczecin **7** F3
Szentpéterfa **31** F4

T

Tabanera de Cerrato **55** E4
Tábara **54** C4
Tabarz **11** F4
Tabernas **75** F3
Taberno **76** A2
Taboada **53** F3
Taboadela **53** F4
Tábua **60** C3
Tabuaço **61** D2
Tabuenca **57** D4
Tacherting **30** A2
Tafalla **57** D3
Tafers **27** E4
Taggia **44** B2
Tagliacozzo **49** D2
Taglio di Po **39** D4
Tahal **76** A3
Taibòn Agordino **39** D1
Taíde **60** C1
Tain-l'Hermitage **35** E4
Taintrux **27** E2
Taio **38** C1
Talamantes **57** D4
Talamona **38** A2
Talamone **48** A1
Talant **26** B3
Talarrubias **68** B2
Taaván **67** F1
Talavera de la Reina **62** B4
Talavera la Real **67** E3
Talayuela **62** A4
Talayuelas **64** B4
Talence **32** B4
Talensac **23** E2
Tales **65** D4
Talhadas **60** C3
Taliard **43** E1
Táliga **67** E3
Talla **46** C3
Talloires **35** F2
Tallós **53** E3
Talmont-St-Hilaire **32** A1
Talsano **51** D3
Tama **55** E2
Tamajón **63** E2
Tamames **61** F3
Tamarite de Litera **58** A3
Tambach-Dietharz **11** F4
Tamins **28** B4
Tamm **19** E4
Tammensiel **5** E1
Tamsweg **30** B4
Tamurejo **68** C2
Tancarville **15** E3
Tange **2** B1
Tangerhütte **12** C1
Tangermünde **12** C1
Tangstedt **6** A2
Taninges **36** A2
Tanlay **26** A2
Tann **30** A1
Tann (Rhon) **11** F4
Tanna **12** C4
Tannay **25** F3
Tanne **11** F2
Tannenbergsthal **12** C4
Tännesberg **20** C3
Tannheim **29** D3
Tannroda **12** B4
Tanowo **7** F2
Tapfheim **29** D1
Tapia de Casariego **54** A1
Tappenbeck **11** F1
Tappernøje **3** E3
Taps **2** B3
Taracena **63** E3
Taradeau **43** F3
Taradell **59** D3
Taramundi **54** A1
Tarancón **63** E4
Tarano **48** C1
Taranto **51** D3
Tarare **35** D2
Tarascon **42** C3

Tarascon-sur-Ariège **41** E4
Tarazona **57** D4
Tarazona de la Mancha **70** B2
Tárbena **71** E3
Tarbes **40** C4
Tarcento **39** E2
Tardajos **55** F3
Tardelcuende **63** F1
Tardets-Sorholus **40** B4
Tardienta **57** E4
Targon **40** B1
Tarm **2** A2
Tarmstedt **5** F3
Tarnos **40** A3
Tarnow **6** C2
Tarouca **60** C2
Tarp *Denmark* **2** A2
Tarp *Ger.* **2** B4
Tarquinia **48** B1
Tarquinia Lido **48** B1
Tarragona **58** C4
Tàrrega **58** C3
Tarrenz **29** D3
Tarrio **53** E2
Tarroja de Segarra **58** C3
Tårs *Denmark* **1** F1
Tårs *Denmark* **3** D4
Tarsia **52** B1
Tartas **40** B3
Tårup **3** D3
Tarvisio **39** F1
Täsch **36** C2
Tassin-la-Demi-Lune **35** D3
Tåstrup **3** E2
Tating **5** E1
Tauberbischofsheim **19** E2
Taucha **12** C3
Tauche **13** E1
Tauer **13** F2
Taufkirchen *Ger.* **30** A2
Taufkirchen *Ger.* **29** E2
Taufkirchen (Vils) **29** F1
Taulé **22** B1
Taulignan **43** D1
Tauplitz **30** C3
Taurasi **50** A2
Taurianova **52** A4
Taurisano **51** F4
Tauste **57** D4
Tauves **34** A3
Tavagnacco **39** E2
Tavannes **27** E3
Tavarnelle Val di Pesa **46** B3
Tavaux **26** C4
Taveiro **60** B4
Tavel **42** C2
Taverna **52** B2
Tavernelle **46** C4
Tavernes **43** E3
Tavernes de la Valldigna **71** E2
Taverny **16** A4
Tavertet **59** D3
Taviano **51** F4
Tavira **72** C2
Tavullia **47** D2
Taxenbach **30** A3
Tazones **55** D1
Teano **49** E3
Teba **74** B3
Tebar **70** B1
Tebstrup **2** C2
Techendorf **30** B4
Tegelen **10** A3
Teggiano **50** B4
Teglio **38** A2
Teichwolf-ramsdorf **12** C4
Teisendorf **30** A2
Teisnach **21** D4
Teistungen **11** F3
Teixeiro **53** F2
Teixoso **61** D3
Tejadillos **64** B4
Tejado **63** F1
Tejeda de Tiétar **62** A4
Teldau **6** B3
Telese **49** F3
Telfs **29** E3
Telgte **10** C2
Telhado **61** D4
Tellin **17** E2
Tellingstedt **5** F1
Telões **61** D1
Teltow **13** D1
Tembleque **69** E1
Templin **7** E3
Temse **9** D3
Temù **38** B2
Tenay **35** E2
Ten Boer **4** C3
Tence **35** D4
Tende **44** B2
Tendilla **63** E3
Tengen **28** A2
Teningen **27** F2
Tennenbronn **28** A2
Tenneville **17** E2
Tentúgal **60** B4
Teora **50** A3
Teramo **49** D1
Ter Apel **4** C4
Terborg-Silvolde **10** A2
Terena **67** D3
Teresa **64** C4
Teresa de Cofrentes **70** C2
Tergnier **16** B2
Terlano **38** C1
Terlizzi **50** C2
Terme Luigiane **52** A1
Térmens **58** B3
Termignon **36** A4
Termoli **49** F2
Ternaard **4** B3
Ternberg **30** C2
Terndrup **1** F2
Terneuzen **8** C3
Terni **48** C1
Ternitz **31** E2
Terracina **49** D3
Terrades **59** E2
Terranova da Sibari **52** B1
Terranova di Pollino **50** C4
Terranuova Bracciolini **46** B3
Terrassa **59** D4
Terrasson-la-Villedieu **33** E4
Terravecchia **52** C2
Terricciola **46** A3
Terriente **64** B4
Terrinches **70** A3
Terrugem *Port.* **66** A3
Terrugem *Port.* **67** D3
Terslev **3** E3
Teruel **64** C3
Terves **32** C1
Tervuren **9** D4
Tesero **38** C2
Tesimo **38** C1
Tespe **6** B3
Tessenderlo **9** E3
Tessin **7** D2
Tessy-sur-Vire **14** C4
Testa del Gargano **50** C1
Teterow **7** D2
Tettens **5** D2
Tettnang **28** C3
Teublitz **20** C3
Teuchern **12** C3
Teufen **28** B3
Teufenbach **30** C4
Teulada **71** E3
Teunz **20** C3
Teupitz **13** E1
Teuschnitz **20** B1
Teutschenthal **12** B3
Thal **11** F4
Thale (Harz) **12** B2
Thalfang **18** B2
Thalheim **12** C2
Thalheim bei Wels **30** C2
Thalmässing **20** B3
Thalwil **28** A3
Thann **27** E2
Thannhausen **29** D1
Thaon-les-Vosges **27** D2
Tharandt **13** E4
't Harde **10** A1
Tharsis **73** D1
Thayngen **28** A2
Thedinghausen **5** F4
Theillay **25** D3
Theißen **12** C3
Theix **23** D3
Them **2** B1
Themar **11** F4
Thénezay **32** C1
Thenon **33** E4
Théoule-sur-Mer **44** A3
Theux **17** F1
Thèze **40** B3
Thiaucourt-Regniéville **17** F4
Thiberville **15** E3
Thiéblemont-Farémont **17** D4
Thiendorf **13** E3
Thiene **38** C3
Thierhaupten **29** D1
Thierrens **27** E4
Thiers **34** C3
Thiersee **29** F3
Thiersheim **20** C2
Thießow **7** E1
Thionville **17** F3
Thiron Gardais **24** C2
Thise **27** D3
Thisted **1** D2
Thiviers **33** D3
Thizy **35** D2
Thoissey **35** D2
Tholen **9** D2
Tholey **18** B3
Thommen **17** F1
Thônes **36** A2
Thonon-les-Bains **36** A1
Thorigny-sur-Oreuse **25** F1
Thörl **31** D3
Thorn **9** F3
Thorning **2** B1
Thorsager **2** C1
Thorshøj **1** F1
Thorsø **2** C1
Thouarcé **24** A4
Thouaré-sur-Loire **23** E4
Thouars **24** A4
Thourotte **16** B3
Thuès-entre-Valls **59** D2
Thueyts **42** C1
Thuin **17** D1
Thuine **10** C1
Thuir **59** E1
Thum **13** D4
Thun **27** F4
Thüngen **19** E2
Thüngersheim **19** E2
Thuré **33** D1
Thüringen **28** C3
Thurins **35** D3
Thürkow **7** D2
Thurnau **20** B2
Thury-Harcourt **14** C4
Thusis **28** B4
Thyborøn **1** D3
Thyez **36** A2
Thyregod **2** B2
Thyrnau **30** B1
Tibi **71** D3
Tiddische **11** F1
Tiebas **57** D3
Tiedra **62** B1
Tiefenbach *Ger.* **30** B1
Tiefenbach *Ger.* **20** C3
Tiefenbronn **19** D4
Tiefencastel **38** A1
Tiefensee **7** F4
Tiel **9** E2
Tielt **8** C3
Tienen **9** E4
Tiengen **28** A3
Tiercé **24** A3
Tierga **64** B1
Tierzo **64** A3
Tignale **38** B3
Tignes **36** A3
Tigy **25** D3
Tijnje **4** B3
Tíjola **75** F2
Tikob **3** E2
Tilburg **9** E2
Tillières-sur-Avre **24** C1
Tilly-sur-Seulles **14** C3
Tim **2** A1
Timau **39** E1
Timelkam **30** B2
Timmendorfer Strand **6** B2
Timring **2** A1
Tinajas **63** F3
Tinalhas **67** D1
Tinchebray **23** F1
Tineo **54** B1
Tinglev **2** B4
Tiñosillos **62** C2
Tinqueux **16** C3
Tinténiac **23** E2
Tintigny **17** E2
Tione di Trento **38** B2
Tirano **38** A2
Tirgo **56** B3
Tiriez **70** A3
Tirig **65** D3
Tiriolo **52** B3
Tirrenia **46** A3
Tirschenreuth **20** C2
Tirstrup **2** C1
Tirteafuera **69** D3
Tistrup Stationsby **2** A2
Tisvilde **3** E2
Titaguas **64** C4
Tito **50** B3
Titting **20** B4
Tittmoning **30** A2
Titulcia **63** D4
Tivenis **65** E2
Tivissa **58** B4
Tivoli **48** C2
Tjæreborg **2** A3
Toano **46** A1
Tobarra **70** B3
Tocane-St-Apre **33** D4
Tocco da Casauria **49** E1
Tocha **60** B3
Tocón **75** D2
Todi **47** D4
Todolella **65** D3
Todtmoos **27** F2
Todtnau **27** F2
Toén **53** F3
Tofterup **2** A2
Toftlund **2** B3
Toirano **44** C2
Tolbaños **62** C3
Toledo **63** D4
Tolentino **47** E4
Tolfa **48** B2
Tolk **2** B4
Tollo **49** E1
Tølløse **3** E2
Tolmezzo **39** E1
Tolne **1** F1
Tolosa *Port.* **67** D2
Tolosa *Spain* **56** C2
Tolox **74** B3
Tolva **58** B2
Tolve **50** B3
Tomar **66** C1
Tomares **73** E2
Tomelloso **69** F2
Tommerup **2** C3
Tona **59** D3
Tondela **60** C3
Tønder **2** A4
Tonezza del Cimone **38** C2
Tongeren **9** E4
Tonnay-Boutonne **32** B2
Tonnay-Charente **32** B2
Tonneins **40** C1
Tonnerre **26** A2
Tönning **5** E1
Topares **76** A1
Töpchin **13** E1
Töpen **20** C1
Töplitz **13** D1
Toppenstedt **6** A3
Torá de Riubreós **58** C3
Toral de los Guzmanes **54** C4
Toral de los Vados **54** B3
Torano Castello **52** B1
Torchiara **50** A4
Torchiarolo **51** F3
Torcy **26** B4
Tordehumos **55** D4
Tordera **59** E3
Tordesillas **62** B1
Tordesilos **64** B3
Toreby **3** E4
Torellano **71** D4
Torelló **59** D3
Toreno **54** B3
Torgau **13** D2
Torgelow **7** F2
Torgiano **47** D4
Torhout **8** B3
Torigni-sur-Vire **14** C4
Torija **63** E3
Torino **36** B4
Toritto **50** C2
Torla **58** A1
Tormón **64** B4
Tornadizos de Ávila **62** C3
Tornavacas **62** A4
Tornby **1** F1
Tornemark **3** D3
Tornesch **6** A2
Torno **37** D2
Tornos **64** B2
Tornow **7** E3
Toro **62** B1
Torquemada **55** E4
Torralba de Calatrava **69** D2
Torralba **63** F3
Torralba de Aragón **57** E4
Torralba de El Burgo **63** E1
Torralba de Oropesa **62** B4
Torralba de Sisones **64** B2
Torrão **66** C4
Torre-Alháquime **74** B3
Torre Annunziata **49** F4
Torrebaja **64** B4
Torreblanca **65** E4
Torreblascopedro **69** E4
Torrebruna **49** F2
Torrecaballeros **63** D2
Torrecampo **68** C3
Torre Canne **51** E3
Torre-Cardela **75** D2
Torrecilla de Alcañiz **65** D2
Torrecilla de la Jara **68** C1
Torrecilla de la Orden **62** B2

Torrecilla del Rebollar **64** C2
Torrecillas de la Tiesa **68** A1
Torrecuso **49** F3
Torre da Gadanha **66** C3
Torre das Vargens **66** C2
Torre de Coelheiros **66** C3
Torre de Dona Chama **61** E1
Torre de Embesora **65** D3
Torredeita **60** C3
Torre de Juan Abad **69** E3
Torre de la Higuera **73** D3
Torre del Bierzo **54** B3
Torre del Burgo **63** E3
Torre del Campo **75** D1
Torre del Greco **49** F4
Torre del Mar **74** C3
Torredembarra **58** C4
Torre de Miguel Sesmero **67** E3
Torre de Moncorvo **61** E2
Torre de'Passeri **49** E1
Torre de Santa María **67** F2
Torredonjimeno **75** D1
Torre do Terrenho **61** D2
Torrefarrera **58** B3
Torregamones **61** F1
Torregrossa **58** B3
Torreiglesias **63** D2
Torreira **60** B3
Torrejoncillo **67** F1
Torrejoncillo del Rey **63** F4
Torrejón de Ardoz **63** D3
Torrejón del Rey **63** E3
Torrejón el Rubio **67** F1
Torrelacarcel **64** B3
Torrelaguna **63** D3
Torrelapaja **64** A1
Torrelavega **55** F1
Torrellas **57** D4
Torrelles de Foix **58** C4
Torrelobatón **62** B1
Torrelodones **63** D3
Torremaggiore **50** A1
Torremanzanas- La Torre de les Macanes **71** D3
Torremayor **67** F3
Torremegía **67** F3
Torre Mileto **50** B1
Torremocha **67** F2
Torremocha de Jiloca **64** B3
Torremolinos **74** C3
Torrenostra **65** E4
Torrent **71** D2
Torrente de Cinca **58** A4
Torrenueva **69** E3
Torre Nuovo Scalo **45** E3
Torreorgaz **67** F2
Torre Orsaia **50** B4
Torre-Pacheco **76** C2
Torreperogil **69** E4
Torres **75** D1
Torresandino **55** F4
Torre San Giovanni **51** F4
Torres de Albánchez **70** A3
Torres de Berrellén **57** E4
Torres de la Alameda **63** E3
Torres del Carrizal **62** A1
Torresmenudas **62** A2
Torres Novas **66** B1
Torre Sta Susanna **51** E3
Torres Vedras **66** A2
Torrevelilla **65** D2
Torrevieja **71** D4
Torrice **49** D2
Torricella **51** E4
Torricella in Sabina **48** C1
Torricella Peligna **49** E2
Torricella Sicura **49** D1
Torricella Taverne **37** D2
Torrico **62** B4
Torri del Benaco **38** B3
Torriglia **45** D1
Torrijas **64** C4
Torrijo **64** A1
Torrijo del Campo **64** B2
Torrijos **62** C4
Tørring **2** B2
Torrita di Siena **46** C4
Torroal **66** B4
Torroella de Montgrí **59** F3
Torrox **75** D3
Torrubia del Campo **63** E4
Tørsbøl **2** B4
Torsminde **2** A1
Tortellà **59** E2
Tórtola de Henares **63** E3
Tórtoles de Esgueva **55** F4
Tortona **37** D4
Tortora **52** A1
Tortoreto **47** F4
Tortosa **65** E3
Tortozendo **61** D4
Tortuera **64** B2
Tor Vaianica **48** C3
Torvizcón **75** E3
Torzym **13** F1
Toscolano-Maderno **38** B3
Tossa **59** E3
Tosse **40** A3
Tossicia **49** D1
Tostedt **6** A3
Totana **76** B2
Tôtes **15** E2
Touça **61** D2
Toucy **25** F3
Toul **17** F4
Toulon **43** E4
Toulon-sur-Allier **34** C1
Toulon-sur-Arroux **26** A4
Toulouges **59** E1
Toulouse **41** E3
Touques **15** D3
Toural **53** E3
Tourcoing **8** C4
Tourlaville **14** B2
Tournai **16** C1
Tournan-en-Brie **16** B4
Tournay **40** C4
Tournon-d'Agenais **41** D1
Tournon-St-Martin **33** E1
Tournon-sur-Rhône **35** E4
Tournus **35** E1
Tourouvre **24** B1
Tours **24** B3
Tourteron **17** D3
Tourves **43** E3
Toury **25** D2
Tous **71** D2
Touvois **23** E4
Trabada **54** A1
Trabanca **61** F2
Trabazos **54** B4
Traben **18** B2
Traboch **31** D3
Tradate **37** D3
Tragacete **64** A3
Tragwein **30** C1
Traid **64** B3
Traiguera **65** E3
Train **29** E1
Traînou **25** D2
Traisen **31** E2
Traiskirchen **31** F2
Traismauer **31** E1
Traitsching **20** C3
Tramacastilla **64** B3
Tramagal **66** C1
Tramayes **35** D2
Tramelan **27** E3
Tramonti di Sopra **39** E1
Tramonti di Sotto **39** E2
Tramutola **50** B4
Tranbjerg **2** C1
Trancoso **61** D3
Tranebjerg **2** C2
Trani **50** C2
Trans-en-Provence **43** F3
Tranum **1** E2
Trappes **16** A4
Trarbach **18** B2
Trasacco **49** D2
Trasmiras **53** F4
Trasobares **64** B1
Traun **30** C2
Traunreut **30** A2
Traunstein *Austria* **31** D1
Traunstein *Ger.* **30** A2
Travagliato **38** A3
Travanca do Mondego **60** C3
Travassô **60** B3
Travenbrück **6** A2
Travers **27** E4
Traversetolo **46** A1
Travo **45** D1
Trebaseleghe **39** D3
Trebatsch **13** E1
Trebbin **13** D1
Trebel **6** C4
Treben **12** C3
Trebenow **7** F3
Trèbes **41** F4
Trébeurden **22** C1
Trebisacce **52** B1
Trebolle **54** A2
Trebsen **13** D3
Trebujena **73** E3
Trebur **19** D2
Trecate **37** D3
Trecchina **50** B4
Trecenta **38** C4
Tredozio **46** C2
Treffen **30** B4
Treffurt **11** F3
Trégastel **22** C1
Tregnago **38** C3
Trégueux **23** D1
Tréguier **22** C1
Trégunc **22** B3
Treia *Ger.* **5** F1
Treia *Italy* **47** E3
Treignac **33** F3
Treis **18** B1
Trélazé **24** A3
Trélissac **33** D4
Trélon **17** D2
Tremblay-les-Villages **24** C1
Tremedal de Tormes **61** F2
Tremelo **9** D3
Trémentines **23** F4
Tremês **66** B2
Tréméven **22** C2
Tremezzo **37** E2
Tremp **58** B2
Trendelburg **11** E2
Trent **7** E1
Trento **38** C2
Tréon **24** C1
Treppeln **13** F1
Trept **35** E3
Trepuzzi **51** F3
Trequanda **46** C4
Trescore Balneario **38** A3
Tresenda **38** A2
Tresigallo **39** D4
Tresjuncos **70** A1
Trets **43** E3
Treuchtlingen **20** A4
Treuenbrietzen **13** D1
Trévé **23** D2
Trevélez **75** E3
Trèves **42** B2
Trevi **47** D4
Treviana **56** B3
Trévières **14** C3
Treviglio **37** E3
Trevignano Romano **48** B2
Treviño **56** B3
Treviso **39** D3
Trevões **61** D2
Trévoux **35** D2
Trezzo sull'Adda **37** E3
Triacastela **54** A2
Triaize **32** B1
Tribsees **7** D1
Tricarico **50** C3
Tricase **51** F4
Tricesimo **39** E2
Trichiana **39** D2
Tricot **16** B3
Trieben **30** C3
Triebes **12** C4
Trie-Château **16** A3
Trier **18** A2
Trieste **39** F3
Trie-sur-Baïse **40** C3
Trieux **17** F3
Triftern **30** A1
Trigaches **66** C4
Triggiano **51** D2
Triglitz **7** D3
Trignac **23** D4
Triguères **25** E2
Trigueros **73** D2
Trigueros del Valle **55** E4
Trillo **63** F3
Trilport **16** B4
Trimmis **28** C4
Trindade *Port.* **66** C4
Trindade *Port.* **61** E1
Trinitapoli **50** C2
Trino **36** C4
Trins **29** E4
Trinta **61** D3
Trinwillershagen **7** D1
Triollo **55** E2
Triora **44** B2
Tripkau **6** B3
Triptis **12** C4
Trittau **6** B2
Trittenheim **18** B2
Trivento **49** F2
Trivero **36** C3
Trivigno **50** B3
Troarn **15** D3
Tröbitz **13** D2
Trochtelfingen **28** B1
Troense **2** C4
Trofa **60** B1
Trofaiach **31** D3
Troia **50** A2
Tróia **66** B3
Troisdorf **10** B4
Trois-Ponts **17** F1
Troissereux **16** A3
Troisvierges **17** F2
Troldhede **2** A2
Tromello **37** D4
Tronco **61** D1
Trontano **36** C2
Tronzano Vercellese **36** C3
Tropea **52** A3
Trossin **13** D2
Trossingen **28** A2
Tröstau **20** C2
Trostberg **30** A2
Trouville-sur-Mer **15** D3
Trouy **25** E4
Troviscal **66** C1
Troyes **26** A1
Trubia **54** C1
Truchas **54** B3
Truchtersheim **27** F1
Trujillanos **67** F2
Trujillo **68** A1
Trulben **18** C3
Trun *France* **24** B1
Trun *Switz.* **28** B4
Trusetal **11** F4
Trustrup **3** D1
Tryggelev **2** C4
Trzebiel **13** F2
Trzebież **7** F2
Trzrcińsko-Zdrój **7** F4
Tschagguns **28** C4
Tschernitz **13** F2
Tubilla del Agua **55** F3
Tübingen **28** B1
Tubize **17** D1
Tubre **38** B1
Tuchan **42** A4
Tüchen **7** D3
Tuchheim **12** C1
Tudela **57** D4
Tudela de Duero **62** C1
Tuejar **70** C1
Tuenno **38** B1
Tuffé **24** B2
Tui **53** E4
Tulette **43** D2
Tulle **33** F4
Tullebølle **3** D4
Tullins **35** E4
Tulln **31** E1
Tulstrup **3** E2
Tuntenhausen **29** F2
Tuoro sul Trasimeno **46** C4
Tuplice **13** F2
Turbenthal **28** B3
Turcia **54** C3
Turcifal **66** A2
Turégano **63** D2
Turi **51** D3
Turís **71** D2
Türkheim **29** D2
Turleque **69** E1
Turnau **31** D3
Turnhout **9** E3
Türnitz **31** E2
Turquel **66** B1
Turrach **30** B4
Turre **76** A3
Tursi **50** C4
Turup **2** C3
Tuscania **48** B1
Tuse **3** E2
Tussenhausen **29** D2
Tüßling **30** A2
Tutow **7** E2
Tuttlingen **28** B2
Tutzing **29** E2
Tützpatz **7** E2
Tvede **2** C1
Tversted **1** F1
Tvis **2** A1
Twello **10** A1
Twist **4** C4
Twiste (Twistetal) **11** D3
Twistringen **5** E4
Tylstrup **1** F2
Tzummarum **4** B3

U

Ubby **3** D2
Úbeda **69** E4
Überherrn **18** A3
Überlingen **28** B2
Übersee **30** A2
Ubidea **56** B2
Ubrique **74** A3
Ubstadt-Weiher **19** D3
Uccle **9** D4
Uceda **63** D2
Ucel **42** C1
Ucero **56** B4
Ucha **60** B1

Uchte **11** D1
Üchtelhausen **20** A2
Uchtspringe **6** C4
Ückeritz **7** F2
Uckro **13** E2
Uclés **63** E4
Udby **3** E2
Uden **9** F2
Udenhout **9** E2
Uderns **29** F3
Udine **39** F2
Uebigau **13** D2
Ueckermünde **7** F2
Uehlfeld **20** A2
Uelsen **10** B1
Uelzen **6** B4
Uetendorf **27** F4
Uetersen **6** A2
Uettingen **19** E2
Uetze **11** F1
Uffenheim **19** F3
Uffing am Staffelsee **29** E2
Uftrungen **12** A2
Ugarana **56** B2
Uge **2** B4
Ugelbølle **2** C1
Ugento **51** F4
Ugerløse **3** E2
Uggelhuse **2** C1
Uggerby **1** F1
Uggerslev **2** C3
Uggiano la Chiesa **51** F4
Ugíjar **75** E3
Ugine **36** A3
Uglev **1** D3
Uhingen **28** C1
Uhldingen **28** B3
Uhlstädt **12** B4
Uhyst **13** F3
Uitgeest **9** D1
Uithoorn **9** E1
Uithuizen **4** C3
Uithuizermeeden **4** C3
Ulbjerg **1** E3
Uldum **2** B2
Uleila del Campo **76** A3
Ulfborg **2** A1
Ulldecona **65** E3
Ulldemolins **58** B4
Ullerslev **2** C3
Ullits **1** E3
Ulm **28** C1
Ulmbach **19** E1
Ulme **66** C2
Ulmen **18** B1
Ulrichsberg **30** C1
Ulrichstein **11** E4
Ulsted **1** F2
Ulstrup *Denmark* **3** D2
Ulstrup *Denmark* **2** C1
Ulvenhout **9** E2
Umbertide **47** D3
Umbriatico **52** C2
Umhausen **29** D4
Ummern **6** B4
Uña **64** A4
Uña de Quintana **54** C4
Uncastillo **57** D3
Undingen **28** B1
Undløse **3** D2
Ungerhausen **28** C2
Unhais da Serra **61** D4
Unhais-o-Velho **60** C4
Unieux **35** D3
Unken **30** A3
Unlingen **28** B2
Unna **10** C2
Unterägeri **28** A4
Unterammergau **29** D3
Unterdießen **29** D2
Untergriesbach **30** B1
Unterhaching **29** E2
Unterkulm **28** A3
Unterlüß **6** A4
Untermaßfeld **11** F4
Untermerzbach **20** A1
Untermünkheim **19** E3
Unterneukirchen **30** A2
Unterpleichfeld **19** F2
Unterreit **29** F2
Unterschächen **28** A4
Unterschleißheim **29** E1
Untersiemau **20** A1
Untersteinach **20** B2
Unterweißenbach **31** D1
Unterwössen **30** A2
Unverre **24** C2
Upgant-Schott **5** D3
Urago d'Oglio **38** A3
Urbania **47** D3
Urbe **44** C1
Urberach **19** D2
Urbino **47** D3
Urbisaglia **47** E4
Urcuit **40** A3
Urda **69** E2
Urdax **57** D2
Urdorf **28** A3
Urdos **40** B4
Ureterp **4** B3
Urk **4** B4
Urnäsch **28** B3
Urnieta **56** C2
Urrea de Gaén **65** D2
Urrea de Jalón **64** B1
Urretxu **56** C2
Urriés **57** D3
Urros **61** E2
Urroz **57** D2
Urrugne **57** D1
Ursberg **29** D2
Ursensollen **20** B3
Urt **40** A3
Urtenen **27** F4
Urueña **55** D4
Ururi **50** A1
Urville Nacqueville **14** B2
Urzy **25** F4
Usagre **67** F4
Uschlag (Staufenberg) **11** E3
Uscio **45** D1
Usedom **7** F2
Usingen **19** D1
Uslar **11** E2
Usseglio **36** B4
Ussel **33** F3
Usson-du-Poitou **33** D2
Usson-en-Forez **34** C3
Ustaritz **40** A3
Uster **28** A3
Usurbil **56** C2
Utarp **5** D2
Utebo **57** E4
Utelle **44** A2
Utersum **2** A4
Uthleben **12** A3
Uthlede **5** E3
Utiel **70** C1
Utrecht **9** E1
Utrera **74** A2
Utrillas **64** C3
Uttendorf *Austria* **30** A2
Uttendorf *Austria* **30** A3
Uttenweiler **28** C2
Utterslev **3** D4
Utting am Ammersee **29** E2
Utzedel **7** E2
Üxheim **18** B1
Uzel **23** D2
Uzerche **33** E3
Uzès **42** C2

V

Vaale **5** F2
Vaals **10** A4
Vaas **24** B3
Vaassen **10** A1
Vabre **41** F3
Vabres-l'Abbaye **42** A2
Vaccarizzo Albanese **52** B1
Vacheresse **36** A2
Vadocondes **63** D1
Vado Ligure **44** C2
Vadum **1** F2
Vaduz **28** C4
Væggerløse **3** E4
Vaglia **46** B2
Vaglio Basilicata **50** B3
Vagli Sotto **46** A2
Vagney **27** E2
Vagos **60** B3
Vaiamonte **67** D2
Vaiano **46** B2
Vaiges **24** A2
Vailly-sur-Aisne **16** C3
Vailly-sur-Sauldre **25** E3
Vairano Patenora **49** E3
Vairano Scalo **49** E3
Vaison-la-Romaine **43** D2
Vaivre-et-Montoille **27** D3
Valada **66** B2
Valadares **53** E4
Valanjou **24** A4
Valareña **57** D4
Valbom **60** B2
Valbona **64** C4
Valbondione **38** A2
Valbonnais **35** F4
Valbonne **44** A3
Valbuena de Duero **62** C1
Valdagno **38** C3
Valdahon **27** D4
Valdaora **39** D1
Valdealgorfa **65** D2
Valdeblore **44** A2
Valdecaballeros **68** B2
Valdecañas de Tajo **68** B1
Valdecarros **62** A3
Valdecilla **55** F1
Valdecuenca **64** B3
Valdefuentes **67** F2
Valdeganga **70** B2
Valdelacasa **62** A3
Valdelacasa de Tajo **68** B1
Valdelamusa **73** D1
Valdelinares **64** C3
Valdemanco del Esteras **68** C2
Valdemeca **64** B4
Val-de-Meuse **26** C2
Valdemorillo **62** C3
Valdemoro **63** D4
Valdemoro-Sierra **64** B4
Valdenoches **63** E3
Valdeobispo **61** F4
Valdeolivas **63** F3
Valdepeñas **69** E3
Valdepeñas de Jaén **75** D1
Valderas **55** D4
Val-de-Reuil **15** E3
Valderiès **41** F2
Valderrobres **65** E2
Val de Santo Domingo **62** C4
Valdestillas **62** B1
Valdetormo **65** D2
Valdetorres **67** F2
Valdeverdeja **62** B4
Valdevimbre **54** C3
Valdidentro **38** B1
Valdilecha **63** E4
Val-d'Isère **36** B3
Valdisotto **38** B1
Valdivienne **33** D1
Val-d'Izé **23** F2
Valdobbiadene **39** D2
Valdoie **27** E3
Valdunquillo **55** D4
Vale da Rosa **72** B2
Vale das Mós **66** C2
Vale de Açor *Port.* **72** B1
Vale de Açor *Port.* **66** C2
Vale de Cambra **60** C2
Vale de Cavalos **66** B2
Vale de Espinho **61** E4
Vale de Estrela **61** D3
Vale de Figueira **66** B2
Vale de Lobo **72** B3
Vale de Prazeres **61** D4
Vale de Reis **66** B3
Vale de Salgueiro **61** D1
Vale de Santarém **66** B2
Vale do Peso **67** D2
Válega **60** B2
Valeggio sul Mincio **38** B3
Valença **53** E4
Valença do Douro **61** D2
Valençay **25** D4
Valence *France* **41** D2
Valence *France* **35** E4
Valence-d'Albigeois **41** F2
Valence-sur-Baïse **40** C2
Valencia **71** D2
Valencia de Alcántara **67** D2
Valencia de Don Juan **54** C3
Valencia de las Torres **67** F3
Valencia del Mombuey **67** E4
Valencia del Ventoso **67** F4
Valenciennes **16** C1
Valensole **43** E2
Valentano **48** B1
Valentigney **27** E3
Valenza **37** D4
Valenzano **51** D2
Valenzuela **74** C1
Valenzuela de Calatrava **69** D3
Valera de Arriba **63** F4
Vales Mortos **72** C1
Valfabbrica **47** D4
Valfarta **58** A4
Valfurva **38** B1
Valgrisenche **36** B3
Valhelhas **61** D3
Valhermoso **64** A3
Valjunquera **65** D2
Valkenburg **9** F4
Valkenswaard **9** E3
Vallabrègues **42** C2
Valladolid **62** B1
Valladolises **76** C2
Vallata **50** A2
Vallauris **44** A3
Vallbona d'Anoia **58** C4
Vall d'Alba **65** D4
Vall de Uxó **65** D4
Valle **55** E2
Valle Castellana **47** E4
Vallecorsa **49** D3
Valle de Abdalajís **74** B3
Valle de la Serena **68** A3
Valle de Matamoros **67** E3
Valle de Santa Ana **67** E4
Valle di Cadore **39** D1
Valleiry **35** F2
Valle Mosso **36** C3
Vallenca **64** B4
Vallendar **18** C1
Valleraugue **42** B2
Vallerotonda **49** E3
Vallet **23** F4
Valley **29** E2
Vallfogona de Riucorb **58** C4
Vallmoll **58** C4
Valløby **3** E3
Vallo della Lucania **50** A4
Vallo di Nera **47** D4
Valloire **36** A4
Vallombrosa **46** B3
Vallon-en-Sully **34** B1
Vallon-Pont-d'Arc **42** C1
Vallorbe **27** D4
Vallorcine **36** A2
Vallouise **36** A4
Valls **58** C4
Valmadrera **37** E2
Valmadrid **64** C1
Valmojado **62** C4
Valmont **15** E2
Valmontone **48** C2
Valmorel **36** A3
Valognes **14** B3
Valongo *Port.* **66** C2
Valongo *Port.* **60** B2
Válor **75** E3
Valoria la Buena **55** E4
Valpaços **61** D1
Valpalmas **57** E4
Valpelline **36** B2
Valperga **36** B3
Valras-Plage **42** A4
Valréas **43** D1
Valros **42** B3
Vals **37** E1
Valsavarenche **36** B3
Vålse **3** E4
Valseca **62** C2
Valsequillo **68** B3
Valsgård **1** F3
Valsinni **50** C4
Vals-les-Bains **42** C1
Valstagna **38** C2
Valtablado del Río **63** F3
Valtiendas **63** D1
Valtierra **57** D4
Valtopina **47** D4
Valtournenche **36** B2
Valverde de Burguillos **67** F4
Valverde de Júcar **70** B1
Valverde de la Virgen **54** C3
Valverde del Camino **73** D2
Valverde de Leganés **67** E3
Valverde del Fresno **61** E4
Valverde de Llerena **68** A4
Valverde del Majano **62** C2
Valverde de Mérida **67** F3
Vamdrup **2** B3
Vammen **2** B1
Vandel **2** B2
Vandellós **65** F2
Vandœvre-lès-Nancy **17** F4
Vandoies **38** C1
Vañes **55** E2
Vannes **23** D3
Vanzone **36** C2
Vaour **41** E2
Vaqueiros **72** C2
Vara del Rey **70** A2
Varades **23** F3
Varallo **36** C2
Varano de'Melegari **38** A4
Varapodio **52** A4
Varazze **44** C1
Varces **35** F4
Varde **2** A2
Varel **5** E3
Varengeville-sur-Mer **15** E2
Varenna **37** E2

Varennes-en-Argonne 17 E3
Varennes-St-Sauveur 35 E1
Varennes-sur-Allier 34 C2
Varennes-Vauzelles 25 F4
Varese 37 D2
Varese Ligure 45 E1
Varetz 33 E4
Varilhes 41 E4
Varlosen (Niemetal) 11 E2
Varna 38 C1
Varrel 5 E4
Vars 32 C3
Varsi 45 E1
Varsseveld 10 A2
Vårst 1 F2
Varzi 45 D1
Varzo 36 C2
Varzy 25 F3
Vasanello 48 C1
Vassy 23 F1
Vasto 49 F1
Vastorf 6 B3
Vatan 25 D4
Vaterstetten 29 E2
Vaubecourt 17 E4
Vauclaix 26 A3
Vaucouleurs 17 F4
Vauvert 42 C3
Vauvillers 27 D2
Vaux-le-Pénil 25 E1
Vaux-sur-Mer 32 B3
Vaux-sur-Sûre 17 E2
Vayrac 33 F4
Veauche 35 D3
Vebbestrup 1 F3
Vecchiano 46 A2
Vechelde 11 F1
Vechta 5 E4
Vecinos 62 A3
Veckerhagen (Reinhardshagen) 11 E2
Vedde 3 D3
Veddelev 3 E2
Veddum 1 F3
Vedelago 39 D3
Vedène 43 D2
Vedra 53 E2
Vedsted 2 B3
Veendam 4 C3
Veenendaal 9 E1
Veenhusen 5 D3
Veflinge 2 C3
Vegacervera 54 C2
Vega de Espinareda 54 B3
Vegadeo 54 A1
Vega de Pas 55 F2
Vega de Tirados 62 A2
Vega de Valcarce 54 A3
Vega de Valdetronco 62 B1
Veganzones 63 D2
Vegaquemada 55 D2
Vegarienza 54 C2
Vegas del Condado 55 D3
Vegas de Matute 62 C3
Vegger 1 E2
Veghel 9 E2
Veglie 51 E4
Vehlow 7 D3
Veiros 67 D2
Veitsbronn 20 A3
Veitsch 31 E3
Vejano 48 B1
Vejby 3 E2
Vejen 2 B3
Vejer de la Frontera 73 E4
Vejle *Denmark* 2 C3
Vejle *Denmark* 2 B2
Vejrum 2 B1
Vejstrup 2 C3
Velamazán 63 F1
Velaux 43 D3
Velbert 10 B3
Velburg 20 B3
Velden 29 F1
Veldhoven 9 E3
Velefique 75 F2
Velen 10 B2
Vélez-Blanco 76 A2
Vélez de Benaudalla 75 D3
Vélez-Málaga 74 C3
Vélez-Rubio 76 A2
Velgast 7 D1
Velilla de Cinca 58 A3
Velilla del Río Carrión 55 D2
Vélines 32 C4
Vellahn 6 B3
Vellberg 19 F3
Velletri 48 C2
Velling 2 A1
Vellisca 63 E4
Vellmar 11 E3
Velpke 12 A1
Velten 7 E4
Velturno 38 C1
Vemb 2 A1
Venafro 49 E3
Venansault 32 A1
Venarey-les-Laumes 26 B3
Venaria 36 B4
Venarotta 47 E4
Venasca 44 A1
Vence 44 A3
Venda Nova 60 C1
Vendargues 42 B3
Vendas Novas 66 B3
Vendays-Montalivet 32 B3
Vendeuvre-du-Poitou 33 D1
Vendeuvre-sur-Barse 26 B2
Vendinha 67 D3
Vendœuvres 33 E1
Vendôme 24 C3
Venelles 43 E3
Venezia 39 D3
Venhuizen 4 A4
Venialbo 62 A1
Venizel 16 C3
Venlo 10 A3
Venosa 50 B2
Venoy 25 F2
Venray 10 A2
Venta de Baños 55 E4
Venta de las Ranas 54 C1
Venta del Charco 69 D4
Venta del Moro 70 C1
Venta de los Santos 69 E4
Venta Nueva 54 B2
Ventas de Huelma 75 D2
Ventas de Zafarraya 74 C3
Ventimiglia 44 B2
Ventschow 6 C2
Venzone 39 E1
Vera 76 A3
Vera Cruz 67 D4
Vera de Bidasoa 57 D2
Verbania 37 D2
Verberie 16 B3
Verbicaro 52 A1
Verbier 36 B2
Verceia 37 E2
Vercelli 37 D3
Verchen 7 D2
Verden (Aller) 5 F4
Verdun 17 E3
Verdun-sur-Garonne 41 E2
Verdun-sur-le-Doubs 26 B4
Verfeil 41 E3
Vergato 46 B2
Vergaville 18 B4
Vergel 71 E3
Verges 59 E3
Vergèze 42 C3
Verghereto 46 C3
Vergigny 25 F2
Vergongheon 34 B3
Vergt 33 D4
Verín 54 A4
Veringenstadt 28 B2
Verl 11 D2
Verlaine 17 E1
Vermand 16 B2
Vermenton 26 A3
Vermiglio 38 B2
Vermiosa 61 E2
Vermoil 66 B1
Vernante 44 B2
Vernantes 24 B3
Vernayaz 36 B2
Vern-d'Anjou 23 F3
Vernet 41 E3
Vernet-les-Bains 59 D2
Verneuil-sur-Avre 24 C1
Verneuil-sur-Vienne 33 E3
Vernier 35 F2
Vernio 46 B2
Verniolle 41 E4
Vernole 51 F4
Vernon 15 F3
Vernouillet 24 C1
Vernoux-en-Vivarais 35 D4
Vern-sur-Seiche 23 E2
Verny 17 F4
Verolanuova 38 A3
Veroli 49 D2
Verona 38 B3
Verres 36 C3
Versailles 16 A4
Versmold 10 C1
Versoix 35 F2
Verson 14 C3
Verteillac 33 D3
Vertheuil 32 B4
Verton 15 F1
Vertou 23 E4
Vertus 16 C4
Verucchio 47 D2
Verviers 17 F1
Vervins 16 C2
Verzino 52 C2
Verzuolo 44 B1
Verzy 17 D3
Vescovato 38 A4
Vesime 44 C1
Vesløs 1 E2
Vesoul 27 D3
Vespolate 37 D3
Vessem 9 E3
Vestbjerg 1 F2
Vester Åby 2 C3
Vesterby 3 D4
Vester Hæsinge 2 C3
Vester Hassing 1 F2
Vester Herborg 2 A1
Vester Hjermitslev 1 F2
Vester Hornum 1 E2
Vester Nebel 2 B2
Vester Torup 1 E2
Vester Vedsted 2 A3
Vestervig 1 D2
Vestone 38 B3
Vetralla 48 B1
Vetschau 13 E2
Vetterslev 3 E3
Vetto 46 A1
Veulettes-sur-Mer 15 E2
Veurne 8 B3
Vevey 36 A1
Vex 36 B2
Veynes 43 E1
Veyre-Monton 34 B3
Veyres 33 D3
Veyrier-du-Lac 35 F2
Vezdemarbán 62 B1
Vézelise 27 D1
Vézénobres 42 C2
Vézins-de-Lévézou 42 A2
Vezza d'Oglio 38 B2
Vezzano 38 B2
Viadana 38 B4
Viana 56 C3
Viana de Cega 62 C1
Viana do Alentejo 66 C4
Viana do Bolo 54 A4
Viana do Castelo 60 B1
Vianden 17 F2
Vianen 9 E1
Viaño Pequeno 53 E2
Vianos 70 A3
Viareggio 45 E2
Viarmes 16 A3
Vias 42 B3
Viatodos 60 B1
Viator 75 F3
Vibonati 50 B4
Viborg 2 B1
Vibo Valentia 52 A3
Vibraye 24 C2
Viby 3 E3
Vic 59 D3
Vícar 75 F3
Vicchio 46 B2
Vicdessos 58 C1
Vicedo 53 F1
Vic-en-Bigorre 40 C3
Vicenza 38 C3
Vic-Fezensac 40 C3
Vichy 34 C2
Vic-le-Comte 34 B3
Vico del Gargano 50 B1
Vico Equense 49 F4
Vicoforte 44 B1
Vico nel Lazio 49 D2
Vicovaro 48 C2
Vic-sur-Cère 34 A4
Vic-sur-Seille 27 D1
Vidago 61 D1
Vidais 66 B2
Vidángoz 57 E2
Vidauban 43 F3
Videbæk 2 A1
Videmonte 61 D3
Vidigueira 67 D4
Vidrieres 59 E3
Vidstrup 1 F1
Viechtach 21 D4
Vieira de Leiria 66 B1
Vieira do Minho 60 C1
Vielank 6 B3
Vielha 58 B1
Vielle-Aure 40 C4
Vielle-Brioude 34 C4
Vielmur-sur-Agout 41 F3
Vielsalm 17 F1
Vienenburg 11 F2
Vienne 35 E3
Viereck 7 F2
Viereth-Trunstadt 20 A2
Vierlingsbeek 10 A2
Viernau 11 F4
Vierraden 7 F3
Viersen 10 A3
Vierville-sur-Mer 14 C3
Vierzon 25 D4
Viesecke 6 C4
Vieste 50 C1
Vietri di Potenza 50 B3
Vietri sul Mare 50 A3
Vieux-Boucau-les-Bains 40 A3
Vieux-Condé 16 C1
Vif 35 F4
Vig 3 D2
Vigarano Mainarda 38 C4
Vigasio 38 B3
Vigaun 30 A3
Vigeois 33 E3
Vigevano 37 D3
Viggianello 50 C4
Viggiano 50 B4
Vigliano Biellese 36 C3
Vignacourt 16 A2
Vignale Monferrato 37 D4
Vignanello 48 B1
Vigneulles-les-Hattonchâtel 17 F4
Vignola 46 B1
Vignory 26 C1
Vigny 16 A4
Vigo 53 E3
Vigodarzere 39 D3
Vigo di Cadore 39 D1
Vigo di Fassa 38 C1
Vigone 36 B4
Vigonza 39 D3
Vigo Rendena 38 B2
Viguzzolo 37 D4
Vigy 17 F3
Vihiers 24 A4
Vila 53 F4
Vila Boa 61 E3
Vila Boa do Bispo 60 C2
Vila Caiz 60 C2
Vila Chã de Sá 60 C3
Vila Cova da Lixa 60 C2
Vilada 59 D2
Vila da Igrexa 53 F1
Viladamat 59 E2
Vila da Ponte 60 C1
Viladecans 59 D4
Vila de Cruces 53 F2
Vila de Frades 67 D4
Vila de Rei 66 C1
Vila do Bispo 72 A2
Vila do Conde 60 B1
Viladrau 59 D3
Vila Fernando 67 D2
Vila Flor 61 D2
Vila Franca das Naves 61 D3
Vilafranca del Penedès 58 C4
Vila Franca de Xira 66 B2
Vilagarcía de Arousa 53 E3
Vilajüiga 59 E2
Vilalba 53 F1
Vilallonga 59 D2
Vilamartín de Valdeorras 54 A3
Vilamarxant 71 D1
Vilamoura 72 B2
Vilanant 59 E2
Vila Nogueira de Azeitão 66 B3
Vila Nova da Baronia 66 C4
Vilanova d'Alcolea 65 D4
Vilanova de Arousa 53 E3
Vila Nova de Cacela 72 C2
Vila Nova de Foz Coa 61 D2
Vila Nova de Gaia 60 B2
Vilanova de la Barca 58 B3
Vilanova de l'Aguda 58 C3
Vilanova de Lourenzá 54 A1
Vilanova de Meià 58 B3
Vila Nova de Ourém 66 B1
Vila Nova de Paiva 61 D2
Vila Nova de Poiares 60 C4
Vilanova de Prades 58 B4
Vila Nova de São Bento 67 D4
Vilanova de Sau 59 D3
Vilanova i la Geltrú 58 C4

Vila Pouca da Beira **60** C3
Vila Pouca de Aguiar **61** D1
Vila Praia de Âncora **60** B1
Vilar *Port.* **60** C1
Vilar *Portugal* **66** A2
Vilarandelo **61** D1
Vilarchao **53** F3
Vilar da Veiga **60** C1
Vilar de Andorinho **60** B2
Vilar de Barrio **53** F4
Vilar de Santos **53** F4
Vilardevós **54** A4
Vila Real **61** D2
Vila-real de los Infantes **65** D4
Vila Real de Santo António **72** C2
Vilarelho da Raia **61** D1
Vilar Formoso **61** E3
Vilarinho da Castanheira **61** D2
Vilarinho do Bairro **60** B3
Vilariño de Conso **54** A4
Vila-rodona **58** C4
Vila Ruiva **66** C4
Vila Seca **60** B1
Vilaseca de Solcina **58** C4
Vilassar de Mar **59** D4
Vila Velha de Ródão **67** D1
Vila Verde *Port.* **60** C1
Vila Verde *Port.* **60** B4
Vila Verde *Port.* **61** D1
Vila Verde da Raia **61** D1
Vila Verde de Ficalho **67** D4
Vila Viçosa **67** D3
Vilches **69** E4
Vildbjerg **2** A1
Villa Bartolomea **38** C4
Villablanca **72** C2
Villablino **54** B2
Villabona **56** C2
Villabrágima **55** D4
Villabuena del Puente **62** A1
Villacañas **69** E1
Villa Carcina **38** A3
Villacarriedo **55** F2
Villacarrillo **69** E4
Villa Castelli **51** E3
Villacastín **62** C3
Villach **39** F1
Villaciervos **56** B4
Villaconejos **63** D4
Villaconejos de Trabaque **63** F3
Villada **55** D3
Villa d'Almè **38** A3
Villa del Prado **62** C4
Villa del Río **69** D4
Villadepera **61** F1
Villa de Ves **70** C2
Villadiego **55** F3
Villadose **39** D4
Villadossola **36** C2
Villaeles de Valdavia **55** E3
Villaescusa de Haro **70** A1
Villafáfila **54** C4
Villafamés **65** D4
Villafeliche **64** B2
Villaflores **62** B2
Villafranca d'Asti **36** C4
Villafranca de Córdoba **68** C4
Villafranca de Ebro **64** C1
Villafranca del Bierzo **54** B3
Villafranca del Campo **64** B3
Villafranca del Cid **65** D3
Villafranca de los Barros **67** F3
Villafranca de los Caballeros **69** E2
Villafranca di Verona **38** B3
Villafranca in Lunigiana **45** E2
Villafranca-Montes de Oca **56** A3
Villafranco del Guadalquivir **73** E2
Villafrechos **55** D4
Villafruela **55** F4
Villafuerte **55** E4
Villagarcía de Campos **55** D4
Villagarcía de la Torre **67** F4
Villagarcía del Llano **70** B2
Villagio Mancuso **52** B2
Villagonzalo **67** F3
Villaharta **68** C4
Villahermosa **69** F3
Villahermosa del Campo **64** B2
Villahermosa del Río **65** D4
Villaherreros **55** E3
Villahizán **55** F4
Villahoz **55** F4
Villaines-la-Juhel **24** A1
Villajoyosa-La Vila Joíosa **71** E3
Villa Lagarina **38** C2
Villalago **49** E2
Villalar de los Comuneros **62** B1
Villa Latina **49** E3
Villalba de Duero **63** D1
Villalba de Guardo **55** D3
Villalba del Alcor **73** E2
Villalba de la Sierra **64** A4
Villalba de los Alcores **55** D4
Villalba de los Barros **67** F3
Villalba del Rey **63** F3
Villalba dels Arcs **58** A4
Villalba de Rioja **56** B3
Villalcampo **62** A1
Villalcázar de Sirga **55** E3
Villalengua **64** B1
Villalgordo del Júcar **70** B2
Villa Literno **49** E4
Villalobos **54** C4
Villalón de Campos **55** D4
Villalonga **71** E3
Villalpando **55** D4
Villalpardo **70** B2
Villaluenga de la Sagra **63** D4
Villalumbroso **55** E4
Villamalea **70** C2
Villamañán **54** C3
Villamandos **54** C4
Villamanrique **69** F3
Villamanrique de la Condesa **73** E2
Villamanta **62** C4
Villamartín **74** A3
Villamartín de Campos **55** E4
Villamayor **62** A2
Villamayor de Calatrava **69** D3
Villamayor de Campos **55** D4
Villamayor de Santiago **69** F1
Villamayor de Treviño **55** E3
Villamblard **33** D4
Villamediana **55** E4
Villamediana de Iregua **56** C3
Villamejil **54** C3
Villamesías **68** A2
Villamiel **61** E4
Villa Minozzo **46** A1
Villamor de los Escuderos **62** A2
Villamuelas **63** D4
Villamuriel de Cerrato **55** E4
Villandraut **40** B1
Villanova **51** E3
Villanova d'Albenga **44** C2
Villanova d'Asti **36** C4
Villanova del Battista **50** A2
Villanova Monferrato **37** D4
Villanterio **37** E4
Villanúa **57** E3
Villanueva de Alcardete **69** F1
Villanueva de Alcorón **63** F3
Villanueva de Algaidas **74** C2
Villanueva de Argaño **55** F3
Villanueva de Bogas **69** E1
Villanueva de Cameros **56** B4
Villanueva de Castellón **71** D2
Villanueva de Córdoba **68** C4
Villanueva de Gállego **57** E4
Villanueva de Gómez **62** C2
Villanueva de la Cañada **63** D3
Villanueva de la Concepción **74** C3
Villanueva de la Fuente **70** A3
Villanueva de la Jara **70** B2
Villanueva de la Reina **69** D4
Villanueva del Arzobispo **69** F4
Villanueva de las Cruces **73** D1
Villanueva de la Serena **68** A2
Villanueva de la Sierra **61** F4
Villanueva de las Torres **75** E2
Villanueva de la Vera **62** A4
Villanueva del Campo **55** D4
Villanueva del Duque **68** B4
Villanueva del Fresno **67** E4
Villanueva de los Castillejos **72** C2
Villanueva de los Infantes **69** F3
Villanueva del Rey **68** B4
Villanueva del Río Segura **76** B1
Villanueva del Río y Minas **74** A1
Villanueva del Rosario **74** C3
Villanueva del Trabuco **74** C3
Villanueva de Mesía **74** C2
Villanueva de San Carlos **69** D3
Villanueva de San Juan **74** B2
Villanueva de Tapia **74** C2
Villanueva de Valdegovia **56** B2
Villanuño de Valdavia **55** E3
Villa Opicina **39** F3
Villapalacios **70** A3
Villapiana **52** B1
Villapiana Lido **52** B1
Villa Poma **38** C4
Villaquejida **54** C4
Villaquilambre **54** C3
Villaralbo **62** A1
Villaralto **68** B3
Villarcayo **55** F2
Villard-Bonnot **35** F4
Villard-de-Lans **35** F4
Villar de Cañas **70** A1
Villar de Chinchilla **70** C3
Villar de Ciervo **61** E3
Villardeciervos **54** B4
Villardefrades **62** B1
Villar del Arzobispo **71** D1
Villar de la Yegua **61** E3
Villar del Buey **61** F1
Villar del Cobo **64** B3
Villar del Humo **64** B4
Villar de los Barrios **54** B3
Villar de los Navarros **64** C2
Villar del Pedroso **68** B1
Villar del Rey **67** E2
Villar del Salz **64** B3
Villar de Olalla **63** F4
Villar de Peralonso **61** F2
Villar de Rena **68** A2
Villar de Torre **56** B3
Villardompardo **74** C1
Villarejo de Fuentes **70** A1
Villarejo de Montalbán **68** C1
Villarejo de Orbigo **54** C3
Villarejo de Salvanés **63** E4
Villa Rendena **38** B2
Villarente **54** C3
Villares de la Reina **62** A2
Villargordo **69** D4
Villargordo del Cabriel **70** C1
Villarino de los Aires **61** F2
Villarluengo **64** C3
Villarquemado **64** B3
Villarramiel **55** D4
Villarrasa **73** D2
Villarreal de Huerva **64** B2
Villarrín de Campos **54** C4
Villarrobledo **70** A2
Villarrodrigo **70** A3
Villarroya de la Sierra **64** B1
Villarroya de los Pinares **64** C3
Villarrubia de los Ojos **69** E2
Villarrubia de Santiago **63** D4
Villarrubio **63** E4
Villars **35** D3
Villars del Saz **63** F4
Villars-les-Dombes **35** E2
Villars-sur-Var **44** A2
Villar-St-Pancrace **36** A4
Villarta **70** B2
Villarta de los Montes **68** C2
Villarta de San Juan **69** E2
Villasana de Mena **56** A2
Villasandino **55** E3
Villa San Giovanni **52** A4
Villa Santa Maria **49** E2
Villasante de Montija **55** F2
Villa Santina **39** E1
Villasarracino **55** E3
Villasayas **63** F1
Villasbuenas **61** E2
Villasdardo **61** F2
Villaseca de Laciana **54** B2
Villaseca de la Sagra **63** D4
Villaseco de los Gamitos **61** F2
Villaseco de los Reyes **61** F2
Villaseco del Pan **62** A1
Villasequilla de Yepes **63** D4
Villasrubias **61** E3
Villastar **64** C4
Villatobas **63** E4
Villatoro **62** B3
Villatoya **70** C2
Villatuerta **56** C3
Villaturiel **54** C3
Villaumbrales **55** E4
Villava **57** D2
Villavallelonga **49** D2
Villavelayo **56** B4
Villaverde de Guadalimar **70** A3
Villaverde del Río **73** F1
Villaverde y Pasaconsol **63** F4
Villavernia **45** D1
Villaviciosa de Asturias **55** D1
Villaviciosa de Córdoba **68** B4
Villaviciosa de Odón **63** D3
Villavieja **65** D4
Villavieja de Yeltes **61** E2
Villaviudas **55** E4
Villayón **54** B1
Villazanzo de Valderaduey **55** D3
Villé **27** E1
Villebois-Lavalette **33** D3
Villebrumier **41** E2
Villecroze **43** F3
Villedieu-la-Blouère **23** F4
Villedieu-les-Poêles **23** F1
Villedieu-sur-Indre **33** E1
Ville-en-Tardenois **16** C3
Villefagnan **32** C2
Villefontaine **35** E3
Villefort **42** B1
Villefranche-d'Albigeois **41** F2
Villefranche-d'Allier **34** B1
Villefranche-de-Lauragais **41** E3
Villefranche-de-Lonchat **32** C4
Villefranche-de-Rouergue **41** F2
Villefranche-du-Périgord **41** D1
Villefranche-sur-Cher **25** D3
Villefranche-sur-Mer **44** A3
Villefranche-sur-Saône **35** D2
Villegas **55** F3
Villel **64** B4
Ville-la-Grand **35** F2
Villelaure **43** E3
Villemandeur **25** E2
Villemoustaussou **41** F4

Villemur-sur-Tarn **41** E2
Villena **71** D3
Villenauxe-la-Grande **16** C4
Villeneuve *France* **41** F1
Villeneuve *France* **43** E2
Villeneuve *Switz.* **36** A1
Villeneuve-d'Ascq **16** B1
Villeneuve-de-Berg **42** C1
Villeneuve-de-Marsan **40** B2
Villeneuve-la-Guyard **25** F1
Villeneuve-l'Archevêque **25** F2
Villeneuve-lès-Avignon **43** D2
Villeneuve-Loubet **44** A3
Villeneuve-sur-Lot **41** D1
Villeneuve-sur-Yonne **25** F2
Villepinte **41** F4
Villeréal **41** D1
Villerías **55** D4
Villers-Bocage *France* **14** C4
Villers-Bocage *France* **16** A2
Villers-Bretonneux **16** B2
Villers-Cotterêts **16** B3
Villers-Écalles **15** E3
Villersexel **27** D3
Villers-Farlay **26** C4
Villers-lès-Nancy **17** F4
Villers-Outréaux **16** C2
Villers-Semeuse **17** D2
Villers-sur-Mer **15** D3
Ville-sur-Tourbe **17** D3
Villetta Barrea **49** E2
Villeveyrac **42** B3
Villevocance **35** D4
Villiers-en-Lieu **17** E4
Villiers-en-Plaine **32** B1
Villiers-St-Georges **16** C4
Villingen **28** A2
Villoldo **55** E3
Villora **70** C1
Villorba **39** D3
Villoria **62** B2
Villoruela **62** A2
Viloví d'Onyar **59** E3
Vils *Austria* **29** D3
Vils *Denmark* **1** D2
Vilsbiburg **30** A1
Vilseck **20** B3
Vilshofen **30** B1
Vilslev **2** A3
Vilsted **1** E2
Vilsund Vest **1** D2
Vilvestre **61** E2
Vilvoorde **9** D3
Vimbodi **58** B4
Vimeiro **66** A2
Vimercate **37** E3
Vimianzo **53** D2
Vimieiro **66** C3
Vimioso **61** E1
Vimory **25** E2
Vimoutiers **15** D4
Vimy **16** B1
Vinadio **44** A1
Vinaixa **58** B4
Vinaròs **65** E3
Vinay **35** E4
Vinça **59** E1
Vincey **27** D1
Vinchiaturo **49** F3
Vinci **46** A2
Vind **2** A1
Vindblæs **1** E2
Vindeballe **2** C4
Vindeby **2** C3
Vinderslev **2** B1
Vinderup **2** A1
Vindinge *Denmark* **2** C3
Vindinge *Denmark* **3** E2
Vinebre **58** B4
Vineuil *France* **24** C3
Vineuil *France* **25** D4
Vinhais **61** E1
Vinhas **61** E1
Viniegra de Arriba **56** B4
Vinningen **18** C3
Vinon-sur-Verdon **43** E3
Viñuelas **63** E3
Vinuesa **56** B4
Vinzelberg **6** C4
Viöl **2** B4
Violay **35** D3
Violès **43** D2
Vipiteno **29** E4
Vipperød **3** E2
Vipperow **7** D3
Virazeil **40** C1
Vire **23** F1
Vireux-Wallerand **17** D2
Virgen **30** A4
Viriat **35** E2
Virieu-le-Grand **35** F2
Virklund **2** B1
Virton **17** E3
Viry **35** F2
Visan **43** D2
Visbek **5** E4
Visborg **1** F3
Visby **2** A3
Visé **9** F4
Viserba **47** D2
Viseu **60** C3
Visiedo **64** C3
Viso del Marqués **69** E3
Visone **44** C1
Visp **36** C2
Visselhövede **6** A3
Vissenbjerg **2** C3
Visso **47** E4
Vissoie **36** B2
Vistabella del Maestrazgo **65** D4
Viterbo **48** B1
Vitigudino **61** E2
Vitorchiano **48** B1
Vitoria-Gasteiz **56** B2
Vitré **23** F2
Vitrey-sur-Mance **26** C2
Vitrolles **43** D3
Vitry-en-Artois **16** B1
Vitry-le-François **17** D4
Vitteaux **26** B3
Vittel **27** D2
Vittorio Veneto **39** D2
Vitulano **49** F3
Vitulazio **49** E3
Vitzenburg **12** B3
Viveiro **53** F1
Vivel del Río Martín **64** C2
Viver **64** C4
Viverols **34** C3
Viveros **70** A3
Vivier-au-Court **17** D2
Viviers **42** C1
Viviez **41** F1
Vivild **2** C1
Vivonne **33** D1
Vix **32** B2
Vizille **35** F4
Vlaardingen **9** D2
Vledder **4** B4
Vleuten **9** E1
Vlijmen **9** E2
Vlissingen **8** C2
Vlotho **11** D1
Vöcklabruck **30** B2
Vöcklamarkt **30** B2
Vodskov **1** F2
Vodstrup **1** D2
Voel **2** B1
Voerde (Niederrhein) **10** A2
Voerladegård **2** B2
Voerså **1** F2
Vogelsang **7** E3
Vogelsdorf **13** E1
Vogelweh **18** C3
Voghera **37** D4
Voghiera **39** D4
Vognsild **1** E3
Vogt **28** C2
Vogtareuth **29** F2
Vohburg an der Donau **20** B4
Vohenstrauß **20** C2
Vöhl **11** D3
Vöhringen *Ger.* **28** A1
Vöhringen *Ger.* **28** C1
Void-Vacon **17** F4
Voiron **35** F3
Voiteur **26** C4
Voitsberg **31** D4
Vojens **2** B3
Voldby *Denmark* **2** C1
Voldby *Denmark* **3** D1
Voldum **2** C1
Volendam **4** A4
Volkach **19** F2
Völkermarkt **30** C4
Volketswil **28** A3
Völklingen **18** B3
Volkmarsen **11** D3
Völlen **5** D3
Vollenhove **4** B4
Vollersode **5** E3
Volmunster **18** B3
Volonne **43** E2
Volpago del Mòntello **39** D2
Volpedo **37** D4
Volpiano **36** C4
Völs **29** E3
Völschow **7** E2
Voltaggio **45** D1
Volta Mantovana **38** B3
Volterra **46** A3
Voltlage **10** C1
Voltri **44** C1
Volturara Appula **50** A1
Volturara Irpina **50** A3
Volturino **50** A2
Volvic **34** B2
Volx **43** E2
Vomp **29** E3
Vonge **2** B2
Voorburg **9** D1
Voorschoten **9** D1
Voorst **10** A1
Vorbasse **2** B2
Vorchdorf **30** C2
Vorden **10** A1
Vordernberg **31** D3
Vordingborg **3** E4
Vordorf **11** F1
Voreppe **35** F3
Vorey **34** C4
Vorgod **2** A1
Vorra **20** B3
Vorsau **31** E3
Vorst **9** E3
Vorwerk **5** F3
Vosselaar **9** E3
Vouillé *France* **32** C1
Vouillé *France* **32** C2
Voulx **25** E2
Vouneuil-sous-Biard **33** D1
Voutezac **33** E4
Vouvray **24** C3
Vouvry **36** A2
Vouzela **60** C3
Vouziers **17** D3
Vouzon **25** D3
Voves **25** D2
Vozmediano **56** C4
Vrå **1** F1
Vreden **10** B1
Vrees **5** D4
Vrensted **1** F1
Vresse **17** E2
Vridsted **2** B1
Vries **4** C3
Vriezenveen **10** A1
Vrinners **2** C1
Vroomshoop **10** A1
Vrouwenpolder **8** C2
Vught **9** E2
Vulpellac **59** E3

W

Waabs **6** A1
Waal **29** D2
Waalre **9** E3
Waalwijk **9** E2
Waarschoot **8** C3
Wabern **11** E3
Wachow **13** D1
Wachtebeke **8** C3
Wächtersbach **19** E1
Wacken **5** F2
Wackersdorf **20** C3
Waddeweitz **6** B3
Waddinxveen **9** D1
Wädenswil **28** A3
Wadern **18** B3
Wadersloh **10** C2
Wadgassen **18** B3
Wagenborgen **4** C3
Wagenfeld **5** E4
Wagenhoff **6** B4
Wageningen **9** F1
Waghäusel **19** D3
Waging am See **30** A2
Wagna **31** E4
Wagrain **30** B3
Wahlhausen **11** E3
Wahlsdorf **13** D2
Wahlstedt **6** A2
Wahrenholz **6** B4
Waiblingen **19** E4
Waibstadt **19** D3
Waidhofen an der Ybbs **31** D2
Waigolshausen **19** F2
Waimes **17** F1
Wain **28** C2
Waischenfeld **20** B2
Waizenkirchen **30** B1
Wakendorf II **6** A2
Walburg **11** E3
Walchum **5** D4
Walcourt **17** D1
Wald *Ger.* **28** B2
Wald *Ger.* **20** C3
Wald *Switz.* **28** B3
Waldachtal **28** A1
Waldböckelheim **18** C2
Waldbreitbach **10** B4
Waldbröl **10** C4
Waldburg **28** C2
Waldbüttelbrunn **19** E2
Walddrehna **13** E2
Waldegg **31** E2
Waldenbuch **28** B1
Waldenburg *Ger.* **19** E3
Waldenburg *Switz.* **27** F3
Walderbach **20** C3
Waldershof **20** C2
Waldfischbach-Burgalben **18** C3
Waldhausen **31** D1
Waldhausen im Strudengau **31** D1
Waldheim **13** D3
Walding **30** C1
Waldkappel **11** E3
Waldkirch **27** F2
Waldkirchen **30** B1
Waldkraiburg **30** A2
Wald-Michelbach **19** D3
Waldmünchen **21** D3
Waldrach **18** B2
Waldsassen **20** C2
Waldshut **28** A3
Waldstatt **28** B3
Waldstetten **28** C1
Walenstadt **28** B4
Walferdange **17** F2
Walkendorf **7** D2
Walldorf *Ger.* **19** D3
Walldorf *Ger.* **19** D2
Walldorf *Ger.* **11** F4
Walldürn **19** E3
Wallenfels **20** B1
Wallerfing **30** A1
Wallersdorf **30** A1
Wallerstein **20** A4
Wallgau **29** E3
Wallhausen *Ger.* **19** F3
Wallhausen *Ger.* **18** C2
Wallisellen **28** A3
Wallsbüll **2** B4
Wallstawe **6** B4
Wałowice **13** F2
Wals **30** A2
Walschleben **12** A3
Walsleben **7** D4
Walsrode **6** A4
Waltenhofen **29** D3
Waltershausen **11** F4
Wamba **62** B1
Wanderup **2** B4
Wandlitz **7** E4
Wang **31** D2
Wangen **27** F3
Wangen im Allgäu **28** C3
Wängi **28** B3
Wankendorf **6** A1
Wanna **5** E2
Wanze **17** E1
Wanzleben **12** B1
Wapenveld **10** A1
Warberg **12** A1
Warburg **11** D3
Wardenburg **5** E3
Waregem **8** C4
Waremme **9** E4
Waren **7** D3
Warendorf **10** C2
Warffum **4** C3
Warin **6** C2
Warmeriville **17** D3
Warmsen **11** D1
Warnemünde **7** D1
Warngau **29** E2
Warnow **6** C2
Warnsveld **10** A1
Warsingsfehn **5** D3
Warstein **10** C3
Wartberg an der Krems **30** C2
Wartenberg **29** F1
Wartenberg-Angersbach **11** E4
Warth **28** C3
Wartin **7** F3
Wartmannsroth **19** E1
Wasbek **6** A1
Wäschenbeuren **28** C1
Waspik **9** E2
Wasselonne **27** F1
Wassen **28** A4
Wassenaar **9** D1
Wassenberg **10** A3
Wasseralfingen **19** F4
Wasserburg am Inn **29** F2
Wasserlosen **19** F2
Wassertrüdingen **20** A4

Wassigny **16** C2
Wassy **26** B1
Wasungen **11** F4
Waterloo **9** D4
Wathlingen **6** A4
Watten **8** A4
Wattenbek **6** A1
Wattens **29** E3
Wattenwil **27** F4
Wattwil **28** B3
Wavre **9** D4
Wavrin **16** B1
Waxweiler **17** F2
Wechmar **12** A4
Wechselburg **13** D3
Wedde **4** C3
Weddingstedt **5** F1
Wedel (Holstein) **6** A2
Weede **6** B2
Weener **5** D3
Weerberg **29** E3
Weert **9** F3
Weesen **28** B4
Weesp **9** E1
Weeze **10** A2
Weferlingen **12** B1
Wegberg **10** A3
Wegenstedt **12** B1
Weggis **28** A4
Wegscheid *Austria* **31** D3
Wegscheid *Ger.* **30** B1
Wehdel **5** E3
Wehl **10** A2
Wehr **27** F3
Wehringen **29** D2
Weibern **18** B1
Weibersbrunn **19** E2
Weichering **29** E1
Weichs **29** E1
Weida **12** C4
Weidenberg **20** B2
Weiden in der Oberpfalz **20** C2
Weiding **21** D3
Weigersdorf **13** F3
Weihmichl **29** F1
Weikersheim **19** F3
Weil **29** D2
Weil am Rhein **27** F3
Weilbach **19** E2
Weilburg **10** C4
Weil der Stadt **28** B1
Weilerbach **18** C3
Weilerswist **10** B4
Weilheim an der Teck **28** B1
Weilheim in Oberbayern **29** E2
Weilmünster **11** D4
Weimar **12** B3
Weinbach **10** C4
Weinböhla **13** E3
Weinfelden **28** B3
Weingarten **28** C2
Weingarten (Baden) **19** D4
Weinheim **19** D3
Weinsberg **19** E3
Weinsheim **18** C2
Weinstadt **19** E4
Weischlitz **12** C4
Weisen **6** C3
Weiskirchen **18** B3
Weismain **20** B2
Weissach **19** D4
Weißbriach **30** B4
Weißenbach am Lech **29** D3
Weißenberg **13** F3
Weißenbrunn **20** B1
Weißenburg in Bayern **20** A4
Weißenfels **12** C3
Weißenhorn **28** C1
Weißensee **12** B3
Weißenstadt **20** C2
Weißenstein **30** B4
Weißig **13** E3
Weißkeißel **13** F3
Weißkirchen in Steiermark **31** D4
Weißkollm **13** F3
Weißwasser **13** F2
Weistrach **30** C2
Weisweil **27** F2
Weitefeld **10** C4
Weiten **31** D1
Weiten-hagen **7** E2
Weitensfeld **30** C4
Weitersfeld **31** E1
Weiterstadt **19** D2
Weitra **31** D1
Weixdorf **13** E3
Weiz **31** E3
Wekerom **9** F1
Welkenraedt **10** A4
Well **10** A2
Wellaune **12** C2
Welle **6** A3
Wellheim **20** A4
Wellin **17** E2
Welling **18** B1
Wels **30** C2
Welschbillig **18** A2
Welsickendorf **13** D2
Welsleben **12** B2
Welzheim **19** E4
Welzow **13** E2
Wemding **20** A4
Wendeburg **11** F1
Wendelsheim **18** C2
Wendelstein **20** B3
Wenden **10** C3
Wendisch Priborn **7** D3
Wendisch Rietz **13** E1
Wendlingen am Neckar **28** B1
Wengen **36** C1
Wengsel (Isterberg) **10** B1
Wennigsen (Deister) **11** E1
Wenningstedt **2** A4
Wenns **29** D4
Wentorf **6** B2
Wentorf bei Hamburg **6** A3
Wenzenbach **20** C4
Wenzlow **12** C1
Werbach **19** E2
Werbellin **7** E4
Werben **13** E2
Werben (Elbe) **6** C4
Werbig **13** D2
Werdau **12** C4
Werder *Ger.* **13** D1
Werder *Ger.* **7** E2
Werdohl **10** C3
Werfen **30** B3
Werl **10** C2
Werlte **5** D4
Wermsdorf **13** D3
Wernau **28** B1
Wernberg-Köblitz **20** C3
Werndorf **31** E4
Werne **10** C2
Werneck **19** F2
Werneuchen **7** E4
Wernigerode **11** F2
Wernshausen **11** F4
Werpeloh **5** D4
Wertach **29** D3
Wertheim **19** E2
Werther **11** F3
Werther (Westfalen) **11** D1
Wertingen **29** D1
Wervershoof **4** A4
Wervik **8** B4
Wesel **10** A2
Wesenberg **7** E3
Wesendorf **6** B4
Wesselburen **5** E1
Wesseling **10** B4
Wesseln **5** F1
Weßling **29** E2
Wessobrunn **29** D2
Westendorf **29** F3
Westensee **6** A1
Westerbeck (Sassenburg) **11** F1
Westerbork **4** C4
Westerburg **10** C4
Westeregeln **12** B2
Westerende-Kirchloog (Ihlow) **5** D3
Westergellersen **6** A3
Westerholt **5** D2
Westerhorn **6** A2
Westerland **2** A4
Westerlo **9** E3
Westerrönfeld **6** A1
Westerstede **5** D3
Westerstetten **28** C1
Westervoort **10** A2
Westhausen **19** F4
Westkapelle **8** C2
Westmalle **9** D3
West-Terschelling **4** A3
Wethau **12** C3
Wetschen **5** E4
Wetter (Hessen) **11** D4
Wetteren **8** C3
Wetterzeube **12** C3
Wettin **12** B2
Wettingen **28** A3
Wettrup **5** D4
Wetzikon **28** B3
Wetzlar **11** D4
Wevelgem **8** C4
Wewelsfleth **5** F2
Weyarn **29** E2
Weyerbusch **10** B4
Weyer Markt **31** D2
Weyhausen **11** F1
Weyhe **5** E4
Wichelen **9** D3
Wickenrode (Helsa) **11** E3
Widnau **28** C3
Widuchowa **7** F3
Wieck am Darß **7** D1
Wieda **11** F2
Wiedensahl **11** D1
Wiederau **13** D3
Wiednitz **13** E3
Wiefelstede **5** E3
Wiehe **12** B3
Wiehl **10** B4
Wiek **7** E1
Wielenbach **29** E2
Wiemersdorf **6** A2
Wien **31** F2
Wienerbruck **31** D2
Wiener Neustadt **31** F2
Wienrode **12** A2
Wiepke **6** C4
Wierden **10** A1
Wieren **6** B4
Wieringerwerf **4** A4
Wies **31** D4
Wiesa **13** D4
Wiesau **20** C2
Wiesbaden **18** C2
Wieselburg **31** D2
Wiesen *Austria* **31** F2
Wiesen *Ger.* **19** E2
Wiesen *Switz.* **28** C4
Wiesenau **13** F1
Wiesenburg **12** C1
Wiesenfelden **20** C4
Wiesent **20** C4
Wiesenthau **20** B2
Wiesentheid **20** A2
Wiesloch **19** D3
Wiesmath **31** F3
Wiesmoor **5** D3
Wietmarschen **10** B1
Wietze **6** A4
Wietzen **5** F4
Wietzendorf **6** A4
Wiggensbach **28** C2
Wijchen **9** F2
Wijk aan Zee **9** D1
Wijk bij Duurstede **9** E1
Wil **28** B3
Wildalpen **31** D3
Wildau **13** E1
Wildberg *Ger.* **28** A1
Wildberg *Ger.* **7** D4
Wildberg *Ger.* **7** E2
Wildeck-Richelsdorf **11** F3
Wildenfels **12** C4
Wildeshausen **5** E4
Wildflecken **19** E1
Wildon **31** E4
Wildpoldsried **29** D2
Wildshut **30** A2
Wilhelmsburg *Austria* **31** E2
Wilhelmsburg *Ger.* **7** F2
Wilhelmsdorf **28** B2
Wilhelmshaven **5** E3
Wilkau-Haßlau **12** C4
Willebadessen **11** D2
Willebroek **9** D3
Willemstad **9** D2
Willich **10** A3
Willingen (Upland) **11** D3
Willingshausen **11** E4
Willisau **27** F4
Wilmersdorf **7** F3
Wilnsdorf **10** C4
Wilsdruff **13** E3
Wilsickow **7** F3
Wilster **5** F2
Wilsum **4** C4
Wiltersdorf **31** F1
Wiltingen **18** A2
Wiltz **17** F2
Wimereux **8** A4
Wimmelburg **12** B2
Wimmis **36** B1
Wimpassing **31** E3
Wincrange **17** F2
Windach **29** E2
Windeby **6** A1
Windigsteig **31** D1
Windischeschenbach **20** C2
Windischgarsten **30** C2
Windorf **30** B1
Windsbach **20** A3
Wingene **8** C3
Wingen-sur-Moder **18** B4
Winklarn **20** C3
Winklern **30** A4
Winklern bei Oberwölz **30** C3
Winnenden **19** E4
Winnert **5** F1
Winningen **12** B2
Winschoten **4** C3
Winsen (Aller) **6** A4
Winsen (Luhe) **6** A3
Winsum *Neth.* **4** B3
Winsum *Neth.* **4** C3
Winterberg **11** D3
Winterfeld **6** C4
Winterswijk **10** B2
Winterthur **28** A3
Wintzenheim **27** E2
Winzenburg **11** E2
Winzer **30** A1
Wipperdorf **11** F3
Wipperfürth **10** B3
Wippra Kurort **12** B2
Wirdumer (Wirdum) **4** C3
Wirsberg **20** B2
Wischhafen **5** F2
Wismar **6** C2
Wissant **8** A3
Wissembourg **18** C4
Wissen **10** C4
Wissenkerke **8** C2
Wistedt **6** A3
Witmarsum **4** A3
Witnica **7** F4
Witry-lès-Reims **17** D3
Wittdün **2** A4
Wittelsheim **27** E2
Witten **10** B3
Wittenbach **28** B3
Wittenberge **6** C4
Wittenburg **6** B3
Wittenförden **6** C2
Wittenhagen **7** E1
Wittenheim **27** F2
Wittibreut **30** A1
Wittichenau **13** E3
Wittighausen **19** E2
Wittingen **6** B4
Wittlich **18** B2
Wittmar **11** F1
Wittmund **5** D2
Wittstock **7** D3
Witzenhausen **11** E3
Witzin **6** C2
Witzwort **5** E1
Wizernes **8** A4
Wöbbelin **6** C3
Woerden **9** E1
Wœrth **18** C4
Wohlen **28** A3
Wohlmirstedt **12** B3
Wohltorf **6** A3
Wöhrden **5** F1
Woippy **17** F3
Woldegk **7** E3
Woldendorp **4** C3
Wolfach **28** A1
Wolfegg **28** C2
Wolfen **12** C2
Wolfenbüttel **11** F1
Wolfenschiessen **28** A4
Wölfersheim **19** D1
Wolfhagen **11** D3
Wölfis **12** A4
Wolfpassing **31** D2
Wolfratshausen **29** E2
Wolfsberg **31** D4
Wolfsburg **11** F1
Wolfstein **18** C3
Wolfurt **28** C3
Wolgast **7** E2
Wolin **7** F2
Wolkersdorf **31** F1
Wollbach **19** F1
Wollerau **28** A4
Wolmirstedt **12** B1
Wolnzach **29** E1
Wolpertshausen **19** F3
Wolpertswende **28** C2
Wölpinghausen **11** E1
Woltersdorf *Ger.* **13** D1
Woltersdorf *Ger.* **6** C4
Wolvega **4** B4
Wommelgem **9** D3
Wommels **4** B3
Wonfurt **20** A2
Wonsees **20** B2
Worb **27** F4
Worbis **11** F3
Wörgl **29** F3
Workum **4** A4
Wörlitz **12** C2
Wormeldange **17** F2
Wormerveer **4** A4
Wormhout **8** B4

Worms **19** D2
Worpswede **5** F3
Wörrstadt **18** C2
Wörschach **30** C3
Wörth **30** A3
Wörth am Rhein **19** D4
Woudrichem **9** E2
Woudsend **4** B4
Woustviller **18** B4
Wouw **9** D2
Wredenhagen **7** D3
Wremen **5** E2
Wrestedt **6** B4
Wriedel **6** A3
Wriezen **7** F4
Wrist **6** A2
Wrohm **5** F1
Wulfen **12** C2
Wulfersdorf **7** D3
Wülfershausen an der Saale **20** A1
Wulfsen **6** A3
Wulften **11** F2
Wulkau **6** C4
Wullersdorf **31** E1
Wundschuh **31** E4
Wünnenberg **11** D2
Wünsdorf **13** E1
Wunsiedel **20** C2
Wunstorf **11** E1
Wuppertal **10** B3
Wurmlingen **28** B2
Würselen **10** A4
Wurzbach **12** B4
Würzburg **19** F2
Wurzen **13** D3
Wüstenrot **19** E3
Wusterhausen **7** D4
Wusterhusen **7** E1
Wustermark **13** D1
Wusterwitz **12** C1
Wustrau-Altfriesack **7** D4
Wustrow *Ger.* **7** E3
Wustrow *Ger.* **6** B4
Wutha **11** F4
Wutöschingen **28** A3
Wuustwezel **9** D3
Wyhl **27** F2
Wyk auf Föhr **2** A4

X

Xanceda **53** E2
Xanten **10** A2
Xátiva **71** D2
Xeraco **71** E2
Xeresa **71** E2
Xermade **53** F1
Xerta **65** E2
Xertigny **27** D2
Xinzo de Limia **53** F4
Xirivella **71** D2
Xonrupt-Longemer **27** E2
Xove **54** A1
Xunqueira de Ambía **53** F4

Y

Yanguas **56** C4
Yatova **71** D2
Ybbs an der Donau **31** D2
Ybbsitz **31** D2
Ychoux **40** A2
Ydby **1** D3
Ydes **34** A3
Yebra **63** E3
Yebra de Basa **58** A2
Yecla **70** C3
Yecla de Yeltes **61** E2
Yémeda **70** B1
Yenne **35** F3
Yepes **63** D4
Yerseke **9** D2
Yerville **15** E2
Yesa **57** D3
Yeste **70** A4
Yport **15** D2
Yssingeaux **35** D4
Yuncler **63** D4
Yuncos **63** D4
Yunquera **74** B3
Yunquera de Henares **63** E3
Yutz **17** F3
Yverdon **27** E4
Yvetot **15** E3
Yvignac **23** D2
Yvoire **36** A1
Yvonand **27** E4
Yzeure **34** C1
Yzeures-sur-Creuse **33** D1

Z

Zaandam **9** E1
Zabeltitz-Treugeböhla **13** E3
Zafarraya **74** C3
Zafra **67** F3
Zafra de Záncara **63** F4
Zafrilla **64** B4
Zagarise **52** B2
Zagra **74** C2
Zahara **74** A3
Zahara de los Atunes **73** F4
Zahinos **67** E4
Zahna **13** D2
Zaidín **58** A3
Zalamea de la Serena **68** A3
Zalamea la Real **73** D1
Zaldívar **56** B2
Zalla **56** A2
Zaltbommel **9** E2
Zambrana **56** B3
Zambujal de Cima **66** A3
Zambujeira do Mar **72** A2
Zamora **62** A1
Zams **29** D4
Zandhoven **9** D3
Zandvliet **9** D3
Zandvoort **9** D1
Zaorejas **63** F3
Zapponeta **50** B1
Zaragoza **64** C1
Zaratamo **56** B2
Zaratán **62** B1
Zarautz **56** C2
Zarcilla de Ramos **76** A1
Żarki Wielkie **13** F2
Zarpen **6** B2
Zarra **70** C2
Zarrentin **6** B2
Zarza Capilla **68** B3
Zarza de Alange **67** F3
Zarza de Granadilla **62** A4
Zarza de Tajo **63** E4
Zarzadilla de Totana **76** B1
Zarza la Mayor **67** E1
Zarzuela del Monte **62** C3
Zarzuela del Pinar **62** C2
Zas **53** D2
Zavattarello **37** E4
Zaventem **9** D4
Zebreira **67** E1
Zechlin Dorf **7** D3
Zechlinerhütte **7** D3
Zedelgem **8** C3
Zederhaus **30** B4
Zeebrugge **8** C3
Zeeland **9** F2
Zegama **56** C2
Zehdenick **7** E4
Zehna **7** D2
Zehren **13** D3
Zeilarn **30** A1
Zeiselmauer **31** E1
Zeiskam **18** C3
Zeist **9** E1
Zeithain **13** D3
Zeitlofs **19** E1
Zeitz **12** C3
Zele **9** D3
Zelhem **10** A1
Zell **20** B2
Zell (Mosel) **18** B2
Zella-Mehlis **11** F4
Zell am Harmersbach **28** A1
Zell am See **30** A3
Zell am Ziller **29** F3
Zell im Wiesental **27** F3
Zellingen **19** E2
Zeltweg **31** D3
Zelzate **8** C3
Zemitz **7** E2
Zemmer **18** A2
Zemst **9** D3
Zerbst **12** C2
Zerf **18** A3
Zerlach **31** E4
Zermatt **36** C2
Zernez **38** A1
Zernien **6** B3
Zernitz **7** D4
Zero Branco **39** D3
Zerpenschleuse **7** E4
Zerrenthin **7** F3
Zestoa **56** C2
Zetel **5** D3
Zeulenroda **12** C4
Zeven **5** F3
Zevenaar **10** A2
Zevenbergen **9** D2
Zevio **38** C3
Zgorzelec **13** F3
Zibello **38** A4
Zibreira **66** B1
Zickhusen **6** C2
Ziegelroda **12** B3
Ziegendorf **6** C3
Ziegenrück **12** B4
Ziegra **13** D3
Zielitz **12** B1
Zierenberg **11** E3
Zierikzee **8** C2
Ziersdorf **31** E1
Zierzow **6** C3
Ziesar **12** C1
Zillis **37** E1
Ziltendorf **13** F1
Zimmersrode (Neuental) **11** E3
Zinnowitz **7** F1
Zirchow **7** F2
Zirndorf **20** A3
Zistersdorf **31** F1
Zittau **13** F4
Zitz **12** C1
Zizers **28** C4
Zoagli **45** D1
Zöblitz **13** D4
Zoersel **9** D3
Zoetermeer **9** D1
Zofingen **27** F3
Zogno **38** A2
Zola Predosa **46** B1
Zolder **9** E3
Zoldo Alto **39** D1
Zölkow **6** C2
Zollikofen **27** F4
Zollikon **28** A3
Zomergem **8** C3
Zonhoven **9** E3
Zonnebeke **8** B4
Zörbig **12** C2
Zorita **68** A2
Zorita del Maestrazgo **65** D3
Zorneding **29** E2
Zornheim **18** C2
Zörnigal **13** D2
Zossen **13** E1
Zottegem **8** C4
Zoutkamp **4** B3
Zschaitz **13** D3
Zscherben **12** C3
Zschopau **13** D4
Zschortau **12** C3
Zuazo de Cuartango **56** B2
Zubia **75** D2
Zubiaur **56** B2
Zubiena **36** C3
Zubieta **56** C2
Zubiri **57** D2
Zucaina **65** D4
Zuchwil **27** F3
Zudaire **56** C2
Zudar **7** E1
Zuera **57** E4
Zufre **73** E1
Zug **28** A4
Zuheros **74** C2
Zuidhorn **4** C3
Zuidlaren **4** C3
Zuidwolde **4** C4
Zújar **75** E2
Zülpich **10** A4
Zulte **8** C3
Zumaia **56** C1
Zumarraga **56** C2
Zundert **9** D2
Zungri **52** A3
Zunzarren **57** D2
Zuoz **38** A1
Zúrgena **76** A2
Zürich **28** A3
Zurow **6** C2
Zurzach **28** A3
Zusmarshausen **29** D1
Züsow **6** C2
Züssow **7** E2
Zutendaal **9** F3
Zutphen **10** A1
Zuzurkil **56** C2
Zwartsluis **4** B4
Zweibrücken **18** B3
Zweisimmen **36** B1
Zwenkau **12** C3
Zwethau **13** D2
Zwettl **31** D1
Zwevegem **8** C4
Zwickau **12** C4
Zwiefalten **28** B2
Zwiesel **21** D4
Zwijndrecht *Belgium* **9** D3
Zwijndrecht *Neth.* **9** D2
Zwinge **11** F2
Zwingen **27** F3
Zwingenberg **19** D2
Zwochau **12** C3
Zwolle **4** B4
Zwönitz **13** D4
Zwota **20** C1